Lecture Notes in Computer Science   12504

More information about this subseries at http://www.springer.com/series/7409

Emi Ishita · Natalie Lee San Pang ·
Lihong Zhou (Eds.)

Digital Libraries at Times of Massive Societal Transition

22nd International Conference
on Asia-Pacific Digital Libraries, ICADL 2020
Kyoto, Japan, November 30 – December 1, 2020
Proceedings

Springer

Editors
Emi Ishita (iD)
Kyushu University
Fukuoka, Japan

Natalie Lee San Pang (iD)
National University of Singapore
Singapore, Singapore

Lihong Zhou (iD)
Wuhan University
Wuhan, China

ISSN 0302-9743 ISSN 1611-3349 (electronic)
Lecture Notes in Computer Science
ISBN 978-3-030-64451-2 ISBN 978-3-030-64452-9 (eBook)
https://doi.org/10.1007/978-3-030-64452-9

LNCS Sublibrary: SL3 – Information Systems and Applications, incl. Internet/Web, and HCI

This Springer imprint is published by the registered company Springer Nature Switzerland AG
The registered company address is: Gewerbestrasse 11, 6330 Cham, Switzerland

Preface

This volume contains papers accepted at the 22nd International Conference on Asia-Pacific Digital Libraries (ICADL 2020; https://icadl.net/icadl2020/). Due to the COVID-19 pandemic, the conference was organized as a virtual meeting which took place during November 30 – December 1, 2020. The ICADL conference series brings together researchers and practitioners in various aspects of research and practice in digital libraries. This year, the conference ran under the theme "Digital Libraries at Times of Massive Societal Transition – Collaborating and Connecting Community during Global Change."

ICADL 2020 was organized in collaboration with the Asia-Pacific Chapter of iSchools (AP-iSchools), as both groups share common research interests and goals. Other than the focus in broad applications of digital libraries and the development of library and information science communities, there are emerging research areas that would benefit from intra-disciplinary and inter-disciplinary exchanges between scholars and practitioners. For instance, research areas such as digital humanities, open science, and social informatics which originated from digital library research continued to evolve and develop through the conference. ICADL 2020 being held during the COVID-19 pandemic also holds special meaning as societies experience upheavals in work, culture, health services, politics, education, and economy. These circumstances require even more innovations in our digital information environments, and the conference functioned as a forum for the exchange and development of important ideas to address these needs.

A plenary panel titled "New Mode of Academic Environment and Activities Enhanced by Knowledge, Information and Data in the Digital Sphere" was organized, which saw the participation of the Program Committee (PC) chairs (Emi Ishita, Natalie Pang, and Lihong Zhou), Chern Li Liew (Victoria University of Wellington, New Zealand), and Min Song (Yonsei University, South Korea) – all active and younger members of the digital libraries and iSchools communities representing five different institutions. Moderated by conference chair Adam Jatowt (Kyoto University, Japan), the panelists discussed the developments of emerging research areas such as digital humanities and data science, as well as COVID-19 experiences at their respective institutions.

Other than the plenary panel, a doctoral consortium was also organized in collaboration with the Asia-Pacific Chapter of iSchools (AP-iSchools) and the Asia Library Information Research Group (ALIRG). Co-chaired by Songphan Choemprayon (Chulalongkorn University, Thailand), Youngseek Kim (Sungkyunkwan University, South Korea), and Chei-Sian Lee (Nanyang Technological University, Singapore), the consortium brought together doctoral students to provide opportunities for them to connect with each other as well as to seek advice from experienced scholars on their research.

In response to the conference call, 79 papers were submitted to the conference and each paper was reviewed by at least three PC members. Based on the reviews and recommendations from the PC, 10 long papers, 15 short papers, 4 practitioners' papers, and 10 work-in-progress papers were selected and included in the proceedings. Collectively, the submissions came from 20 countries – contributing to the diversity of ICADL 2020.

The success of ICADL 2020 was the result of teamwork from many individuals. We would like to thank the PC members for their effort and time spent on reviewing submitted contributions, Adam Jatowt and Atsuyuki Morishima (conference chairs), Shigeo Sugimoto (panel chair), Songphan Choemprayon, Youngseek Kim, and Chei-Sian Lee (doctoral consortium chairs), Ricardo Campos, Songphan Choemprayong, Chei-Sian Lee, Jiang Li, Akira Maeda, Hao-Ren Ke, Min Song, and Sueyeon Syn (publicity chairs), and Shun-Hong Sie, Thalhath Rehumath Nishad, Karuna Yampray, Di Wang, and Nadeesha Wijerathna (web and media chairs).

Finally, we would like to thank all authors, presenters, and participants of the conference. We hope that you enjoyed the conference proceedings.

November 2020

Emi Ishita
Natalie Lee San Pang
Lihong Zhou

Organization

Organizing Committee

Conference Co-chairs

Adam Jatowt   Kyoto University, Japan
Atsuyuki Morishima   University of Tsukuba, Japan

Program Committee Co-chairs

Emi Ishita   Kyushu University, Japan
Natalie Pang   National University of Singapore, Singapore
Lihong Zhou   Wuhan University, China

Panel Chair

Shigeo Sugimoto   University of Tsukuba, Japan

Doctoral Consortium Committee

Songphan Choemprayon   Chulalongkorn University, Thailand
  (Co-chair)
Youngseek Kim (Co-chair)   Sungkyunkwan University, South Korea
Chei-Sian Lee (Co-chair)   Nanyang Technological University, Singapore
Gaohui Cao   Central China Normal University, China
Wirapon Chansanam   Khon Kaen University, Thailand
Norhayati Hussin   Universiti Teknologi Mara, Malaysia
Chunqiu Li   Beijing Normal University, China
Rahmi   Universitas Indonesia, Indonesia
Masao Takaku   University of Tsukuba, Japan
Yuen-Hsien Tseng   National Taiwan Normal University, Taiwan
Kulthida Tuamsuk   Khon Kaen University, Thailand
Qinghua Zhu   Nanjing University, China

Publicity Co-chairs

Ricardo Campos   Polytechnic Institute of Tomar, Portugal
Songphan Choemprayon   Chulalongkorn University, Thailand
Chei-Sian Lee   Nanyang Technological University, Singapore

Jiang Li	Nanjing University, China
Hao-Ren Ke	National Taiwan Normal University, Taiwan
Akira Maeda	Ritsumeikan University, Japan
Min Song	Yonsei University, South Korea
Sueyeon Syn	Catholic University of America, USA

Web Media Co-chairs

Shun-Hong Sie	National Taiwan Normal University, Taiwan
Thalhath Rehumath Nishad	University of Tsukuba, Japan
Karuna Yampray	Dhurakij Bundit University, Thailand
Di Wang	Wuhan University, China
Nadeesha Wijerathna	University of Tsukuba, Japan

Program Committee

Trond Aalberg	Norwegian University of Science and Technology, Norway
Jae-Eun Baek	Daegu University, South Korea
Biligsaikhan Batjargal	Ritsumeikan University, Japan
Si Chen	Nanjing University, China
Songphan Choemprayong	Chulalongkorn University, Thailand
Gobinda Chowdhury	University of Strathclyde, UK
Chiawei Chu	City University of Macau, Macau
Mickaël Coustaty	University of La Rochelle, France
Fabio Crestani	Università della Svizzera italiana, Switzerland
Milena Dobreva	UCL Qatar, Qatar
Yijun Duan	Kyoto University, Japan
Edward Fox	Virginia Tech, USA
Dion Goh	Nanyang Technological University, Singapore
Simon Hengchen	University of Gothenburg, Sweden
Norhayati Hussin	Universiti Teknologi Mara, Malaysia
Jon Jablonski	University of California, Santa Barbara, USA
Makoto P. Kato	University of Tsukuba, Japan
Marie Katsurai	Doshisha University, Japan
Yukiko Kawai	Kyoto Sangyo University, Japan
Hao-Ren Ke	National Taiwan Normal University, Taiwan
Christopher S. G. Khoo	Nanyang Technological University, Singapore
Yunhyong Kim	The University of Glasgow, UK
Gaël Lejeune	Sorbonne Université, France
Chunqiu Li	Beijing Normal University, China
Xuguang Li	Nankai University, China
Shaobo Liang	Wuhan University, China
Chern Li Liew	Victoria University of Wellington, New Zealand
Fernando Loizides	Cardiff University, UK
Akira Maeda	Ritsumeikan University, Japan

Bill Mischo	University of Illinois at Urbana-Champaign, USA
Muhammad Syafiq Mohd Pozi	Universiti Utara Malaysia, Malaysia
Thi Tuyet Hai Nguyen	University of La Rochelle, France
David Nichols	University of Waikato, New Zealand
Chifumi Nishioka	Kyoto University, Japan
Hiroaki Ohshima	University of Hyogo, Japan
Gillian Oliver	Monash University, Australia
Georgios Papaioannou	UCL Qatar, Qatar
Christos Papatheodorou	Ionian University, Greece
Minhui Peng	Wuhan University, China
Congjing Ran	Wuhan University, China
Edie Rasmussen	The University of British Columbia, Canada
Andreas Rauber	Vienna University of Technology, Austria
Ali Shiri	University of Alberta, Canada
Panote Siriaraya	Kyoto Sangyo University, Japan
Shigeo Sugimoto	University of Tsukuba, Japan
Kazunari Sugiyama	Kyoto University, Japan
Sue Yeon Syn	The Catholic University of America, USA
Masao Takaku	University of Tsukuba, Japan
Giannis Tsakonas	University of Patras, Greece
Nicholas Vanderschantz	University of Waikato, New Zealand
Diane Velasquez	University of South Australia, Australia
Di Wang	Wuhan University, China
Chiranthi Wijesundara	University of Colombo, Sri Lanka
Dan Wu	Wuhan University, China
Gang Wu	Wuhan University, China
Zhiqiang Wu	Wuhan University, China
Sohaimi Zakaria	Universiti Teknologi Mara, Malaysia
Yuxiang Zhao	Nanjing University of Science and Technology, China
Tim Zijlstra	University of Derby, UK
Maja Žumer	University of Ljubljana, Slovenia

Additional Reviewers

Hiroyoshi Ito
Ola Karajeh
Monica Landoni
Masaki Matsubara
Muhammad Syafiq Mohd Pozi
Shinya Oyama
Leonidas Papachristopoulos
Florina Piroi
Panote Siriaraya
Yuanyuan Wang

Contents

Scholarly Data Mining

Natural Language Processing

Improving Scholarly Knowledge Representation: Evaluating BERT-Based Models for Scientific Relation Classification

Ming Jiang[1]([✉]), Jennifer D'Souza[2][iD], Sören Auer[2][iD],
and J. Stephen Downie[1][iD]

[1] University of Illinois at Urbana-Champaign, Champaign, USA
{mjiang17,jdownie}@illinois.edu
[2] TIB Leibniz Information Centre for Science and Technology and L3S Research
Center at Leibniz University of Hannover, Hannover, Germany
{jennifer.dsouza,auer}@tib.eu

Abstract. With the rapid growth of research publications, there is a vast amount of scholarly knowledge that needs to be organized in digital libraries. To deal with this challenge, techniques relying on knowledge-graph structures are being advocated. Within such graph-based pipelines, inferring relation types between related scientific concepts is a crucial step. Recently, advanced techniques relying on language models pre-trained on large corpora have been popularly explored for automatic relation classification. Despite the remarkable contributions that have been made, many of these methods were evaluated under different scenarios, which limits their comparability. To address this shortcoming, we present a thorough empirical evaluation of eight BERT-based classification models by focusing on two key factors: 1) BERT model variants, and 2) classification strategies. Experiments on three corpora show that domain-specific pre-training corpus benefits the BERT-based classification model to identify the type of scientific relations. Although the strategy of predicting a single relation each time achieves a higher classification accuracy than the strategy of identifying multiple relation types simultaneously in general, the latter strategy demonstrates a more consistent performance in the corpus with either a large or small number of annotations. Our study aims to offer recommendations to the stakeholders of digital libraries for selecting the appropriate technique to build knowledge-graph-based systems for enhanced scholarly information organization.

Keywords: Digital library · Information extraction · Scholarly text mining · Semantic relation classification · Knowledge graphs · Neural machine learning

E. Ishita et al. (Eds.): ICADL 2020, LNCS 12504, pp. 3–19, 2020.
https://doi.org/10.1007/978-3-030-64452-9_1

1   Introduction

Today scientific endeavors are facing an increasing publication deluge, which results in the rapid growth of document-based scholarly publications in digital libraries. While abundant resources of scholarly information have been provided in digital libraries, it is still challenging for researchers to obtain comprehensive, fine-grained and context-sensitive scholarly knowledge for their research—a problem that is more acute in multi-disciplinary research [12]. According to [3,4], current keyword-based methods for indexing scholarly articles may not be able to cover all aspects of knowledge involved in each article. Further, single keyword searches on scholarly articles fail to consider the semantic associations among the units of scholarly information. Thus, for better scholarly knowledge organization in digital libraries, some initiatives [12,24] advocate for building an interlinked and semantically rich knowledge graph structure combining human curation with machine learning.

The key to building a knowledge graph from a scholarly article is the identification of relations between scientific terms in the article. In the natural language processing (NLP) community, within the context of human annotations on the abstracts of scholarly articles [5,9], seven relation types between scientific terms have been studied. They are HYPONYM-OF, PART-OF, USAGE, COMPARE, CONJUNCTION, FEATURE-OF, and RESULT. The annotations are in the form of generalized relation triples: ⟨experiment⟩ COMPARE ⟨another experiment⟩; ⟨method⟩ USAGE ⟨data⟩; ⟨method⟩ USAGE ⟨research task⟩. Since human language exhibits the paraphrasing phenomenon, identifying each specific relationship between scientific concepts is impractical. In the framework of an automated pipeline for generating knowledge graphs over massive volumes of scholarly records, the task of classifying scientific relations (i.e., identify the appropriate relation type for each related concept pair from a set of predefined relations) is therefore indispensable.

In this age of the "deep learning tsunami", many studies have developed neural network models to improve the construction of automated scientific relation (SR) classification systems [17]. With the recent introduction of language pre-training techniques such as the BERT [8] models, the opportunity to obtain boosted machine learning systems is further accentuated. While prior work [6,23] has demonstrated high classifier performances, the evaluation of these studies were mainly conducted under a single scenario, e.g. the testing data is from a single resource. This leads to difficulty in obtaining comparable results and conclusive insights about the robustness of the classifiers in real-world practice. For example, in the context of academic digital libraries, it is very difficult to select the appropriate technique to improve their knowledge organization services using the findings of the prior evaluations as their underlying data differ in content, scale and diversity.

To help to fill in the aforementioned gap, we conducted an set of empirical evaluations of selected pre-trained BERT-based models for SR classification. In particular, we implemented and analyzed eight BERT-based classification models by exploring the impact of two key factors: 1) classification strategies (i.e., predicting either a single relation or multiple relations at one time); and 2) BERT model variants with respect to the domain and vocabulary case of the pre-training corpus. To further explore the potential influence of data settings, we assess the performance of each model on three corpora including: 1) a single-domain corpus with sparse relation annotations on scholarly publication abstracts in the NLP area [9]; 2) a multiple-domain corpus covering more abundant relations annotated on the publication abstracts from various artificial intelligence (AI) conference proceedings [15]; and 3) the combination of previous two corpora where the distribution of data domains are unbalanced and annotations are provided by two different groups of annotators. The motivation in building this corpus is to simulate the real data settings in digital libraries. Our ultimate goal is to help the stakeholders in digital libraries select the optimal tool to implement knowledge-based scientific information flows.

In summary, we address the following research questions in this paper:

RQ1: What is the impact of the eight classifiers on scientific relation classification?

RQ2: Which of the seven relation types studied are easy or challenging for classification?

RQ3: What is the practical relevance of the seven relation types in a scholarly knowledge graph?

2 Related Work

Relations Mined from Scientific Publications. Overall, knowledge is organized in digital libraries based on the following three aspects of the digital collections: 1) metadata, 2) free-form content, and 3) ontologized content [11,21]. In this context, the main categories of relations explored in scholarly publications can be divided into two groups. One group includes metadata relations such as authorship, co-authorship, and citations [20,22]. Research in this group mainly focuses on examining the social dimension of scholarly communication, such as co-author prediction [20] and scholarly community analysis [22]. The second group includes semantic relations, either as free-form semantic content classes [13,14] or as ontologized classes [18,19]. In the framework of automatic systems, content relations have been examined in terms of: 1) relation identification (i.e., recognize related scientific term pairs) [9,13], and 2) relation classification (i.e., determine the relation type of each term pair, where the relation types are typically pre-defined) [6,15,23]. With respect to ontologized relation classes, prior work primarily considers the conceptual hierarchy based on formal concept analysis [18,19].

We attempt the task of classifying semantic relations that were created from free-form text. Given that digital libraries are interested in the creation of linked data [10], our attempted task directly facilitates the creation of scholarly knowledge graphs and offers structured data to support librarians in generating linked data.

Techniques Developed for Relation Classification. Both rule-based [1] and learning-based [7,25] methods have been developed for relation classification. Traditionally, learning-based systems relied on hand-crafted semantic and/or syntactic features [1,7]. In recent years, deep learning techniques have been popularly studied because they can more effectively learn latent feature representations for discriminating between relations. An attention-based bidirectional long short-term memory network (BiLSTM) [25] was one of the first top-performing systems that leveraged neural attention mechanisms to capture important information per sentence for relation classification. Another advanced system [16] leveraged a dynamic span graph framework based on BiLSTMs to simultaneously extract terms and infer their pairwise relations. Aside from these neural methods considering the word sequence order, transformer-based models such as BERT [8] that use self-attention mechanisms to quantify the semantic association of each word to its context have become the current state-of-the-art in relation classification. In addition to the generic BERT models trained on books and Wikipedia, recently, Beltagy et al. [6] have developed SciBERT, which are BERT models trained on scholarly publications.

Table 1. Overview of corpus statistics (also is accessible at https://www.orkg.org/orkg/comparison/R38012). 'Total' and '%' columns show the number and percentage of instances annotated with the corresponding relation over all abstracts, respectively.

Id	Relation	SemEval18		SciERC		Combined	
		Total	%	Total	%	Total	%
1	USAGE: a scientific entity that is used for/by/on another scientific entity. E.g. *MT system* is applied to *Japanese*	658	42.13%	2,437	52.43%	3,095	49.84%
2	FEATURE-OF: An entity is a characteristic or abstract model of another entity. E.g. *computational complexity* of *unification*	392	25.10%	264	5.68%	656	10.56%
3	CONJUNCTION: Entities that are related in a lexical conjunction i.e., with 'and' 'or'. E.g. videos from *Google Video* and a *NatGeo documentary*	–	–	582	12.52%	582	9.37%
4	PART-OF: scientific entities that are in a part-whole relationship. E.g. describing the processing of *utterances* in a *discourse*	304	19.46%	269	5.79%	573	9.23%
5	RESULT: An entity affects or yields a result. E.g. With only 12 *training speakers* for SI recognition, we achieved a 7.5% *word error rate*	92	5.89%	454	9.77%	546	8.79%
6	HYPONYM-OF: An entity whose semantic field is included within that of another entity. E.g. *Image matching* is a problem in *Computer Vision*	–	–	409	8.80%	409	6.59%
7	COMPARE: An entity is compared to another entity. E.g. *conversation transcripts* have features that differ significantly from *neat texts*	116	7.43%	233	5.01%	349	5.62%
	Overall	1,562	100%	4,648	100%	6,210	100%

With respect to the classification strategy, the single-relation-at-a-time classification (SRC) that identifies the relation type for an entity pair each time are regularly adopted in prior work [6,16,25]. To improve the classification efficiency, Want et al. [23] designed a BERT-based classifier that could recognize multiple pairwise relationships at one time, which can be regarded as a multiple-relations-at-a-time classification (MRC). Differing from prior work that emphasizes classification improvement, we focus on providing a fine-grained analysis of existing resources for selecting the proper tool to extract and organize scientific information in digital libraries.

3 Corpus

In this study, we select two publicly available datasets [9,15] that contain scholarly abstracts with manual annotation of scientific terms and their semantic relations. Additionally, we combine these two datasets as a third new dataset, which offers a more realistic evaluation setting since it provides a larger, more diverse task representation. Table 1 shows the overall corpus statistics. The details of each corpus is provided as follows:

C1: The SemEval18 Corpus. This corpus was created for the seventh Shared Task organized at SemEval-2018 [9]. It comprised 500 abstracts of scholarly publications that are available in the ACL Anthology. Of these abstracts, 350 were partitioned as training data and the remaining 150 as testing data. Originally, annotations in this corpus contained six discrete semantic relations that were defined to capture the predominant information content. Since the relation TOPIC has far fewer annotations than other type of relations, for our evaluation, we omit this relation type and consider the following five relation types: USAGE, RESULT, MODEL, PART_WHOLE, and COMPARISON.

C2: The SciERC Corpus. Our second evaluation corpus [15] also contains 500 manually annotated abstracts of scholarly articles with their scientific terms and their pairwise relations. Unlike the SemEval18 corpus, the SciERC corpus represents diverse underlying data domains where the abstracts were taken from 12 artificial intelligence (AI) conference/workshop proceedings in five research areas: artificial intelligence, natural language processing, speech, machine learning, and computer vision. These abstracts were annotated for the following seven relations: COMPARE, PART-OF, CONJUNCTION, EVALUATE-FOR, FEATURE-OF, USED-FOR, and HYPONYM-OF. Similar to *C1*, this corpus was pre-partitioned by the corpus creators. They adopted a 350/50/100 train/development/testing dataset split. Comparing *C2* with *C1*, we found that there are five relations, excepting CONJUNCTION and HYPONYM-OF, in *C2* that are semantically identical to the relations annotated in *C1*.

C3: The Combined Corpus. Finally, this evaluation corpus was created by merging *C1* and *C2*. In the merging process, we renamed some relations that are semantically identical but have different labels. First, USED-FOR in *C2* and USAGE in *C1* were unified as USAGE. Further, by observing relation annotations in *C1* and *C2*, we found that RESULT in *C1* and EVALUATE-FOR in *C2* essentially express a similar meaning but the arguments of these two relations were in reverse order. For example, "[accuracy] for [semantic classification]" is labeled as "accuracy" → EVALUATE-FOR → "semantic classification" in *C2*, which can be regarded as "semantic classification" → RESULT → "accuracy". Therefore, we renamed all instances annotated with relation EVALUATE-FOR in corpus *C2* into RESULT by flipping their argument order. By combining 1000 abstracts with human annotations from two resources, our third evaluation corpus presents a comparatively more realistic evaluation scenario of large and heterogeneous data.

4   Bert-Based Scientific Relation Classifiers

BERT (i.e., Bidirectional Encoder Representations from Transformers) [8], as a pre-trained language representation built on cutting-edge neural technology, provides NLP practitioners with high-quality language features from text data simply out-of-the-box that improves performance on many NLP tasks. These models return *contextualized* word embeddings that can be directly employed as features for downstream tasks. Further, with minimal task-specific extensions over the core BERT architecture, the embeddings can be relatively inexpensively fine-tuned to the task at hand, in turn facilitating even greater boosts in task performance.

In this study, we employ BERT embeddings and fine-tune them with two classification strategies: 1) single-relation-at-a-time classification (SRC); and 2) multiple-relation-at-a-time classification (MRC). In the remainder of the section, we first describe the BERT models that we employ and then introduce our fine-tuned SRC and MRC classifiers, respectively.

4.1   Pre-trained Bert Variants

BERT models as pre-trained language representations are available in several variants depending on model configuration parameters and on the underlying training data. While there are over 16 types, in this work we select the following four core variants.

BERT$_{BASE}$[1] The first two models we use are in the category of the pre-trained BERT$_{BASE}$. They were pre-trained on billions of words from text data comprising the BooksCorpus (800M words) [26] and English Wikipedia (2,500M words). Our selected two models are: 1) a cased model (where the case of the underlying words were preserved when training BERT$_{BASE}$), and 2) an uncased model (where the underlying words were all lowercased when training BERT$_{BASE}$).

SCIBERT[2] The next two models adopted in this study are in the category of the pre-trained scientific BERT called SCIBERT. They are language models based on BERT but trained on a large corpus of scientific text. In particular, the pre-training corpus is a random sample of 1.14M papers from Semantic Scholar [2] consisting of full text of 18% papers from the computer science domain and 82% from the broad biomedical domain. Like BERT$_{BASE}$, for SCIBERT, we use both of its cased and uncased variants.

---

[1] https://github.com/google-research/bert.
[2] https://github.com/allenai/scibert.

4.2 Fine-Tuned Bert-Based Classifiers

We implement the aforementioned BERT models within two neural system extensions that respectively adopt different classification strategies.

Single-Telation-at-a-Time Classification (SRC). Classification models built for SRC generally extend the core BERT architecture with one additional linear classification layer that has $K \times H$ dimensions, where K is the number of labels (i.e., relation types) and H denotes the dimension of the word embedding space. The label probabilities are further normalized by using a softmax function and the classifier assigns the label with the maximum probability to each related concept pair.

Multiple-Relations-at-a-Time Classification (MRC). This strategy is a more recent innovation on the classification problem in which the classifier can be trained with all the relation instances in a sentence at a time or predicts all the instances in one pass, as opposed to separately for each instance. In this case, however, the core BERT architecture's self-attention mechanism is modified to efficiently consider the representations of the relative positions of scientific terms [23]. While this modification enables encoding of the novel multiple-relations-at-a-time problem, for obtaining the classification probabilities, the MRC is also extended with a linear classification layer, though not identical to the SRC since it has to model the modified architecture.

5 Evaluation

5.1 Experimental Setup

Experimental Datasets, BERT Word Embeddings, and Classification Strategies. Our comprehensive evaluation set-up involved three different corpora, four BERT embedding variants, and two classification strategies. In total, we trained *eight* different classifiers on each of the three corpora and finally resulted in 24 trained models. Each corpus has been split into training/dev/testing set by the original dataset creators. To obtain the optimal classifiers on each corpus, we tuned the learning rate parameter η for values $\{2e-5, 3e-5, 5e-5\}$. For other parameters such as the number of epochs, we used default values in SciBERT and BERT models.

Evaluation Metrics. We employ standard machine learning classification evaluation indicators including: Precision (P), Recall (R), F1-score ($F1$), and Accuracy (Acc).

5.2 Results and Analysis

In this section, we present results from our comprehensive evaluations with respect to the three main research questions.

10   M. Jiang et al.

RQ1: What Is the Impact of the Eight Classifiers on Scientific Relation Classification? The eight classifiers are obtained from two classification strategies built over four BERT model variants. We examine their classification results (see Table 2) in terms of the following three key characteristics of the classifiers.

The Classification Strategy, i.e., SRC vs. MRC. From the *Acc* and *F1* shown in Table 2, we see that SRC outperforms MRC on two corpora except the SemEval18 corpus. One characteristic of the SemEval18 corpus is that it has a significantly lower number of annotations than the other two copora. Thus, we infer that the novel MRC strategy is more robust than SRC because its performance level is unaffected by a drop in the number of annotations.

Table 2. Scientific relation classification results over three datasets (SemEval18, SciERC, & Combined), four BERT model variants (BERT cased & uncased; SciBERT cased & uncased), and two classification strategies (SRC & MRC). *Acc.* is accuracy and *F1* is the macro F1-score; Top scores are in bold.

	SRC						MRC						Avg ± Std	
	SemEval18		SciERC		Combined		SemEval18		SciERC		Combined		Acc	F1
	Acc	F1	Acc	F1	Acc	F1	Acc	F1	Acc	F1	Acc	F1		
Bert-base uncased	76.42	71.74	84.6	77.25	81.75	77.38	80.4	79.98	83.42	74.84	80.84	76.29	81.24 ± 2.84	76.25 ± 2.78
Bert-base cased	73.58	71.14	85.32	77.92	78.73	74.38	79.55	78.44	83.72	75.07	79.42	74.8	80.05 ± 4.14	75.29 ± 2.65
Scibert cased	73.58	69.72	**86.86**	**79.65**	**84.46**	**81.60**	80.11	78.32	83.42	74.35	**81.80**	**77.68**	81.71 ± 4.60	76.89 ± 4.25
Scibert uncased	**80.97**	**79.42**	86.14	79.49	83.11	80.27	**81.82**	**80.54**	**84.33**	**77.44**	81.06	76.76	**82.91 ± 2.04**	**78.99 ± 1.54**
Avg. Scores	Acc. 84.10 F1 80.22						Acc. 82.35 F1 77.52							

Word Embedding Features, i.e., BERT vs. SciBERT. Regarding the word embedding features encoded by different BERT-based models, SciBERT outperformed BERT on all three corpora with higher accuracy and F1 scores. Since our experimental corpora are all scholarly data, as an expected result, word embeddings encoded by domain-specific BERT models can better capture the token-level semantic associations to support relation classification in the in-domain corpus than the embedding features encoded by the generic BERT models.

Vocabulary Case in BERT Models, i.e., Cased vs. Uncased. We observe that the uncased BERT models (SciBERT: 82.91, BERT: 81.24) show a higher classification accuracy than their cased counterparts (SciBERT: 81.71, BERT: 80.05) on average. Further, the uncased models have an overall lower standard deviation in accuracy (SciBERT: 2.04, BERT: 2.84) than the cased models (SciBERT: 4.60, BERT: 4.14); comparisons on *F1* are along similar lines. Hence, our results suggest that uncased BERT models can achieve more stable performances than the cased variants.

In conclusion, with respect to the classification strategy, we observe that SRC outperforms MRC (see averaged scores in the last row in Table 2). Nevertheless, the advanced MRC strategy demonstrates consistently robust performance that remains relatively unaffected by smaller dataset sizes compared to the SRC (e.g. SRC vs. MRC results on the SemEval18 corpus). On the other hand, with respect to BERT word embedding variants, from the averaged scores in the last column in Table 2, the SCIBERT uncased model posits as the optimal word embedding features model on scholarly articles.

RQ2: Which of the Seven Relation Types Are Easy/challenging to Be Classified? Examining the fine-grained per-relation classification results in Tables 3 to 5 across all our evaluation corpora for both SRC and MRC, we note the classification ranked order. Of all relations, USAGE (USED-FOR) is the easiest classification target. One explanation for this result is that USAGE is the most predominant type in all corpora and hence classifiers can better identify the latent linguistic patterns of this relation type in the training process than other relation types.

For the challenging relations, we examine the results of each corpus. Starting with Table 3 for the SemEval18 corpus, we observe that PART-WHOLE is more difficult to be identified than other relations. We surmise that this relation displays a high diversity in terms of language expressions and hence the classifier is unable to generalize a consistent set of patterns for it. By observing classification performance ranks, we observe that the SRC classifier and MRC classifier obtained the same classification rank order for USAGE, MODEL-FEATURE and

Table 3. Per-relation classification scores of SRC and MRC best systems on SemEval18.

Relationship type SemEval18	SRC			MRC		
	P	R	F1	P	R	F1
USAGE	**87.22**	89.71	**88.45**	90.53	**87.43**	**88.95**
RESULT	78.26	**90.00**	83.72	**100.00**	75.00	85.71
COMPARE	85.71	85.71	85.71	75.00	85.71	80.00
MODEL-FEATURE	66.67	75.76	70.92	70.83	77.27	73.91
PART-WHOLE	79.25	60.00	68.29	70.83	72.86	71.83

Table 4. Per-relation classification results of SRC and MRC best systems on SciERC.

Relationship type SciERC	SRC			MRC		
	P	R	F1	P	R	F1
USED-FOR	**93.30**	91.37	**92.32**	**88.75**	90.24	**89.49**
CONJUNCTION	87.97	**95.12**	91.41	80.69	**95.12**	87.31
HYPONYM-OF	92.31	89.55	90.91	80.00	82.93	81.44
EVALUATE-FOR	82.29	86.81	84.49	84.44	83.52	83.98
COMPARE	72.73	84.21	78.05	83.87	68.42	75.36
PART-OF	66.04	55.56	60.34	65.52	60.32	62.81
FEATURE-OF	59.02	61.02	60.00	73.68	47.46	57.73

Table 5. Per-relation classification results of the best SRC and MRC systems on the Combined corpus.

Relationship type combined	SRC			MRC		
	P	R	F1	P	R	F1
CONJUNCTION	**92.56**	**91.06**	**91.80**	85.07	**92.68**	**88.72**
USAGE	91.30	88.98	90.13	**87.96**	87.71	87.84
HYPONYM-OF	89.39	88.06	88.72	83.12	78.05	80.50
COMPARE	86.89	89.83	88.33	73.85	81.36	77.41
RESULT	76.36	75.68	76.02	84.69	74.77	79.43
PART-OF	75.86	66.17	70.68	68.33	61.65	64.82
FEATURE-OF	58.02	75.20	65.51	60.28	68.00	63.91

PART-WHOLE. While for RESULT and COMPARE, the order is opposite and the SRC classifier has a higher ability to identify RESULT than the MRC classifier.

In Table 4 results for SciERC, both classifiers perform significantly low on two relations, viz. FEATURE-OF and PART-OF. Since these two relations are not the most underrepresented in the corpus, we theorize that their low classification performance is owed to the natural language text diversity from which they are deduced. In this case, obtaining more annotated instances is one way to boost classifier performance. In terms of the ranked order of performances on the relations, SRC and MRC perform identically on SciERC data.

And lastly in Table 5 results on the Combined corpus, for the challenging relations, both SRC and MRC have the same result as they did on SciERC—i.e., FEATURE-OF followed by PART-OF are the most challenging. And we theorize the same reason for the low scores on these relations, since Combined contains SciERC data. Given the two corpora in the Combined dataset, SciERC additionally introduced CONJUNCTION which SemEval18 did not have. CONJUNCTION is among the top two easiest relations to classify, with USAGE as the other, for the classifiers trained on SciERC and on the Combined corpus. Further, its classification is better in the Combined corpus than in SciERC. This lends an understanding to the realistic evaluation settings that the Combined corpus presents. To elaborate, for USAGE, instances from SemEval18 and SciERC (i.e. USED-FOR) are combined, resulting in an insignificant dip in performance (on the Combined corpus, USAGE ranks second easiest compared with SemEval18 and SciERC) since they are now non-uniform annotation signals. As opposed to the case of CONJUNCTION, the Combined corpus obtains a uniform annotation signal from just the SciERC corpus and ranks a minor degree higher at classifying it.

Finally, a list summarizing the top-scoring per-relation performances for scientific relation classification across all three tables, includes the following: USAGE (SRC in SciERC), CONJUNCTION (SRC in Combined), HYPONYM-OF (SRC in SciERC), RESULT (MRC in SemEval18), PART-OF (MRC in SemEval18 for

PART-WHOLE), and FEATURE-OF (MRC in SemEval18 for MODEL-FEATURE). Since the SemEval18 corpus appears the most times in the top-ranked results, we conclude that its annotations obtain a relatively better trained classifier. However, the SemEval18 corpus only includes scholarly abstracts from one AI domain i.e. NLP (in the ACL Anthology), whereas SciERC is more comprehensively inclusive across various AI domains. Thus, an additional factor that classifiers trained on SciERC handle is domain diversity.

Error Analysis. A closer look at the misclassifications is portrayed in the confusion matrices in Fig. 1 for SRC classification and Fig. 2 for MRC classification on the Combined corpus. Four of the seven relations, i.e. HYPONYM-OF, RESULT, PART-OF, and FEATURE-OF, are highly likely to be misclassified as USAGE. This shows that our classifiers are biased by the predominant USAGE relation. In general, unbalanced distribution of training samples (see the details in the corpus section) is, more often than not, one of the main factors for confusion learned in machine learning systems. For the most challenging relations FEATURE-OF and PART-OF, after USAGE, are highly likely to be confused with each other (FEATURE-OF as PART-OF ($\sim$10% confusion), and vice-versa ($\sim$9.4% confusion)). For the relations HYPONYM-OF and FEATURE-OF that loosely demonstrate a relation hierarchy such that HYPONYM-OF subsumes FEATURE-OF, but not the other way around, we find the classification confusion demonstrates a consistent pattern to this data. From the matrices, we see that HYPONYM-OF has $\sim$6% likelihood to be predicted as FEATURE-OF, but none of the FEATURE-OF (0%) instances were confused with HYPONYM-OF.

To offer another pertinent angle on the classifier error analysis, we compute the distribution of word distances between related scientific term pairs in the Combined corpus. The result is depicted in Fig. 3. In general, the majority of box plots shown in Fig. 3 are skewed with a long upper whisker and a short lower whisker. This pattern indicates that the distance between paired scientific terms is typically closed in the text. Differ from other relations, the word distance of CONJUNCTION is much shorter, which makes sense because term pairs with this relationship are typically connected by a single connection term such as "and" and "or". This consistent pattern could be another reason why CONJUNCTION is comparatively easier than other relations to be classified. Further, the average word distance of FEATURE-OF, PART-OF, HYPONYM-OF, and COMPARE is closer to the lower quartile than the other relations. Such varied distribution may bring challenges for a classifier to identify these relations. Notably, the similar median value and spread range between FEATURE-OF and PART-OF could account for why they are challenging to be identified by the classification models.

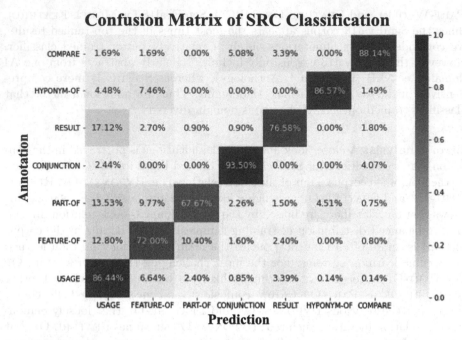

Fig. 1. The confusion matrix of SRC classification on the Combined corpus.

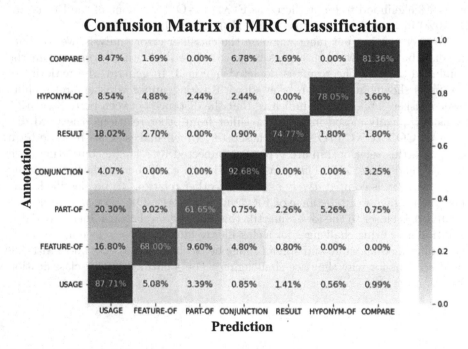

Fig. 2. The confusion matrix of MRC classification on the Combined corpus.

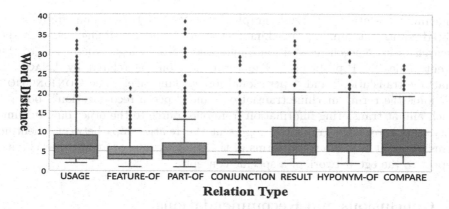

Fig. 3. Distributions of word distances in the combined corpus text between scientific term pairs.

RQ3: What Is the Practical Relevance of the Seven Relations Studied in this Paper in a Scholarly Knowledge Graph?

As a practical illustration of the relation triples studied in this work, we build a knowledge graph from the annotations in the Combined corpus. This is depicted in Fig. 4. Looking at the corpus-level graph (the right graph), we observe that generic scientific terms such as "method," "approach," and "system" are the most densely connected nodes, as expected since generic terms are found across research areas. In the zoomed-in ego-network of the term

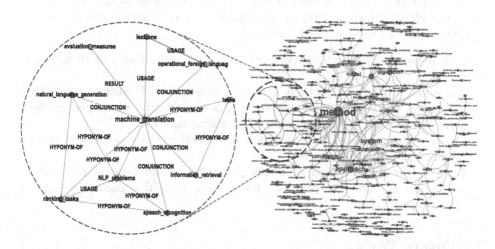

Fig. 4. A knowledge graph constructed from the relation triples in the Combined corpus. The graph on the left is the "ego-network" of the scientific term "machine_translation". The node size is determined by node weighted degree. Colors denote the modularity classes based on the graph structure. The graph was generated using Gephi (https://gephi.org/)

"machine_translation" (the left graph), HYPONYM-OF is meaningfully high-lighted by its role linking "machine_translation" and its sibling nodes as the research tasks "speech_recognition," and "natural_language_generation" to the parent node "NLP_problems." The term "lexicon" is related by USAGE to "machine_translation" and "operational_foreign_language." The CONJUNCTION link joins the term "machine_translation" and "speech_recognization", both of which aim at translating information from one source to the other one. In sum-mary, this knowledge graph can represent the relationships between scientific terms either at macro-level in terms of the whole corpus or at micro-level with respect to the ego-network of a specific concept.

6   Conclusions and Recommendations

We have investigated the scientific relation classification task for improving schol-arly knowledge representations in digital libraries. Our surveyed systems offer a comprehensive view of eight BERT-based classification models. Our observa-tions indicate that the performance of classifiers are mainly associated with two aspects. First, from the perspective of training algorithms, three main factors including classification strategies, the pre-training corpus domain and vocabu-lary case determine the optimal model to apply in practice. Second, with respect to the annotation of scientific relations for training, there are two key factors that influence the ability of a BERT-based classification model to identify each relation type: 1) the number of annotations of each relation type, and 2) the regularity of each relation's syntactic context.

In summary, we provide the following recommendations to the stakeholders of digital libraries for applying the optimal technique to automatically classify scientific relations from scholarly articles:

- Domain-specific pre-training corpus benefits the performance of BERT-based classifiers.
- According to the classification strategy, although SRC outperforms MRC in general, the latter strategy demonstrates consistently robust performance regardless of the size of the underlying training corpus.
- Overall, the uncased BERT models achieve better and more stable perfor-mances than the cased models.
- For each pre-defined relation, the large number of annotations and/or fixed syntactic structure in expressions results in a more discriminative relation classifier.

7   Future Work

To assist those digital library designers who want to build structural semantic representations over scholarly articles using scientific relation classifiers, there are three main avenues that are worthy of future exploration. First, as we have seen in the process of examining our **RQ2**, there exist annotation biases in the corpora such as the unbalanced distribution of relation labels, which can lead to the preference of classifiers to recognize some well-represented relations (e.g., USAGE). Given that, human annotations in the corpora need to be further curated by experts to improve recognizability of each relation type. Second, digital libraries generally deal with various domains in science, while our evaluations in this study mainly focus on the corpora covering AI-related research areas. The assessment of classifiers for identifying scientific relations in other domains need to be further studied. Finally, beyond examining classifiers to identify pre-defined relations, techniques that are developed under the paradigm of open information extraction to identify more diverse relational tuples will be explored in future.

References

1. Agichtein, E., Gravano, L.: Snowball: extracting relations from large plain-text collections. In: Proceedings of the 5th ACM Conference on Digital Libraries, pp. 85–94 (2000)
2. Ammar, W., et al.: Construction of the literature graph in semantic scholar. In: Proceedings of the 2018 Conference of the North American Chapter of the Association for Computational Linguistics: Human Language Technologies, Volume 3 (Industry Papers), pp. 84–91 (2018)
3. Auer, S., Kovtun, V., Prinz, M., Kasprzik, A., Stocker, M., Vidal, M.E.: Towards a knowledge graph for science. In: Proceedings of the 8th International Conference on Web Intelligence, Mining and Semantics, pp. 1–6 (2018)
4. Auer, S., Mann, S.: Toward an open knowledge research graph. Ser. Libr. **76** (2019)
5. Augenstein, I., Das, M., Riedel, S., Vikraman, L., McCallum, A.: SemEval 2017 task 10: scienceie-extracting keyphrases and relations from scientific publications. In: Proceedings of the 11th International Workshop on Semantic Evaluation (SemEval-2017), pp. 546–555 (2017)
6. Beltagy, I., Lo, K., Cohan, A.: SciBERT: a pretrained language model for scientific text. In: Proceedings of the 2019 Conference on Empirical Methods in Natural Language Processing and the 9th International Joint Conference on Natural Language Processing (EMNLP-IJCNLP), Hong Kong, China pp. 3615–3620. ACL, November 2019
7. Culotta, A., Sorensen, J.: Dependency tree kernels for relation extraction. In: Proceedings of the 42nd Annual Meeting of the Association for Computational Linguistics (ACL-04), pp. 423–429. ACL (2004)
8. Devlin, J., Chang, M.W., Lee, K., Toutanova, K.: BERT: Pre-training of deep bidirectional transformers for language understanding. In: Proceedings of the 2019 Conference of the North American Chapter of the Association for Computational Linguistics: Human Language Technologies, Volume 1 (Long and Short Papers), Minneapolis, Minnesota, pp. 4171–4186. ACL, June 2019
9. Gábor, K., Buscaldi, D., Schumann, A.K., QasemiZadeh, B., Zargayouna, H., Charnois, T.: Semeval-2018 task 7: semantic relation extraction and classification in scientific papers. In: Proceedings of The 12th International Workshop on Semantic Evaluation, pp. 679–688 (2018)
10. Hallo, M., Luján-Mora, S., Maté, A., Trujillo, J.: Current state of linked data in digital libraries. J. Inf. Sci. **42**(2), 117–127 (2016)

11. Haslhofer, B., Isaac, A., Simon, R.: Knowledge graphs in the libraries and digital humanities domain. In: Sakr, S., Zomaya, A. (eds.) Encyclopedia of Big Data Technologies (2018)
12. Jaradeh, M.Y., et al.: Open research knowledge graph: next generation infrastructure for semantic scholarly knowledge. In: Proceedings of the 10th International Conference on Knowledge Capture, New York, NY, USA, pp. 243–246. ACM (2019)
13. Jiang, M., Diesner, J.: A constituency parsing tree based method for relation extraction from abstracts of scholarly publications. In: Proceedings of the Thirteenth Workshop on Graph-Based Methods for Natural Language Processing (TextGraphs-13), pp. 186–191 (2019)
14. Klampfl, S., Kern, R.: An unsupervised machine learning approach to body text and table of contents extraction from digital scientific articles. In: Aalberg, T., Papatheodorou, C., Dobreva, M., Tsakonas, G., Farrugia, C.J. (eds.) TPDL 2013. LNCS, vol. 8092, pp. 144–155. Springer, Heidelberg (2013). https://doi.org/10.1007/978-3-642-40501-3_15
15. Luan, Y., He, L., Ostendorf, M., Hajishirzi, H.: Multi-task identification of entities, relations, and coreference for scientific knowledge graph construction. In: Proceedings of the 2018 Conference on Empirical Methods in Natural Language Processing, pp. 3219–3232 (2018)
16. Luan, Y., Wadden, D., He, L., Shah, A., Ostendorf, M., Hajishirzi, H.: A general framework for information extraction using dynamic span graphs. In: Proceedings of the 2019 Conference of the North American Chapter of the Association for Computational Linguistics: Human Language Technologies, Volume 1 (Long and Short Papers), pp. 3036–3046, June 2019
17. Manning, C.D.: Computational linguistics and deep learning. Comput. Linguist. **41**(4), 701–707 (2015)
18. Quan, T.T., Hui, S.C., Fong, A.C.M., Cao, T.H.: Automatic generation of ontology for scholarly semantic web. In: McIlraith, S.A., Plexousakis, D., van Harmelen, F. (eds.) ISWC 2004. LNCS, vol. 3298, pp. 726–740. Springer, Heidelberg (2004). https://doi.org/10.1007/978-3-540-30475-3_50
19. Silvescu, A., Reinoso-Castillo, J., Honavar, V.: Ontology-driven information extraction and knowledge acquisition from heterogeneous, distributed, autonomous biological data sources. In: Proceedings of the IJCAI-2001 Workshop on Knowledge Discovery from Heterogeneous, Distributed, Autonomous, Dynamic Data and Knowledge Sources (2001)
20. Sivasubramaniam, A., et al.: Learning metadata from the evidence in an on-line citation matching scheme. In: Proceedings of the 6th ACM/IEEE-CS Joint Conference on Digital Libraries, pp. 276–285. IEEE (2006)
21. Soergel, D.: Digital libraries and knowledge organization. In: Kruk, S.R., McDaniel, B. (eds.) Semantic Digital Libraries, pp. 9–39. Springer, Heidelberg (2009). https://doi.org/10.1007/978-3-540-85434-0_2
22. Vahdati, S., Palma, G., Nath, R.J., Lange, C., Auer, S., Vidal, M.-E.: Unveiling scholarly communities over knowledge graphs. In: Méndez, E., Crestani, F., Ribeiro, C., David, G., Lopes, J.C. (eds.) TPDL 2018. LNCS, vol. 11057, pp. 103–115. Springer, Cham (2018). https://doi.org/10.1007/978-3-030-00066-0_9
23. Wang, H., et al.: Extracting multiple-relations in one-pass with pre-trained transformers. In: Proceedings of the 57th Annual Meeting of the Association for Computational Linguistics, Florence, Italy, pp. 1371–1377. ACL, July 2019
24. Weigl, D.M., Kudeki, D.E., Cole, T.W., Downie, J.S., Jett, J., Page, K.R.: Combine or connect: practical experiences querying library linked data. Proc. Assoc. Inf. Sci. Technol. **56**(1), 296–305 (2019)

25. Zhou, P., et al.: Attention-based bidirectional long short-term memory networks for relation classification. In: Proceedings of the 54th Annual Meeting of the ACL (volume 2: Short Papers), pp. 207–212 (2016)
26. Zhu, Y., et al.: Aligning books and movies: towards story-like visual explanations by watching movies and reading books. In: Proceedings of the IEEE International Conference on Computer Vision, pp. 19–27 (2015)

A Framework for Classifying Temporal Relations with Question Encoder

Yohei Seki[1(✉)], Kangkang Zhao[1], Masaki Oguni[1], and Kazunari Sugiyama[2]

[1] University of Tsukuba, Kasuga, Tsukuba 305-8550, Japan
yohei@slis.tsukuba.ac.jp
[2] Kyoto University, Kyoto 606-8501, Japan

Abstract. Temporal-relation classification plays an important role in the field of natural language processing. Various deep learning-based classifiers, which can generate better models using sentence embedding, have been proposed to address this challenging task. These approaches, however, do not work well because of the lack of task-related information. To overcome this problem, we propose a novel framework that incorporates prior information by employing awareness of events and time expressions (time–event entities) as a filter. We name this module "question encoder." In our approach, this kind of prior information can extract task-related information from sentence embedding. Our experimental results on a publicly available *Timebank-Dense* corpus demonstrate that our approach outperforms some state-of-the-art techniques.

Keywords: Temporal-relation classification · Neural networks · Event and time expressions · Timebank

1 Introduction

With the rapid development of information technology, the number of distributed news services on the Internet is growing exponentially. Thus, quickly searching for news relevant to user interests is becoming more difficult. To address this problem, temporal-relation classification is a promising approach to constructing timelines with which a search engine can provide much more relevant results and tips for users [7]. In addition, as COVID-19 spreads worldwide, a vast number of clinical papers are being published online [21]. To extract and collect the most informative parts from clinical papers, effective information extraction [19] is an essential technique. Improving the accuracy of temporal-relation classification for the extracted time and event entities is also important to observe disease progression and some longitudinal effects of medications [11].

Temporal-relation classification aims to identify the relations (e.g., "BEFORE," "OVERLAP," and "AFTER,") between event and time expressions (i.e., time–event entities). For example, the following sentence is an example of the "BEFORE" relation between events **"established"** and **"believed"**:

E. Ishita et al. (Eds.): ICADL 2020, LNCS 12504, pp. 20–32, 2020.
https://doi.org/10.1007/978-3-030-64452-9_2

Example 1: He said he **believed** the *"conditions for a meeting" between Mr. Trump and Mr. Rouhani "in the next few weeks"* had been **established**.

In recent years, several feature-based methods have been proposed to address temporal-relation classification [9,15,16]. However, most of them rely on the manual annotation of features and rules, which is very time-consuming and labor-intensive. Following the recent success of neural networks (NNs), various NN-based models, including convolutional NN (CNN) [4,5,12] and recurrent NN (RNN) [2,18,20], have been proposed to achieve higher performance with less manual work in temporal-relation classification.

In many NN-based models proposed thus far, the classification module generates labels from sentence embedding without any prior information. However, lacking prior information causes some problems. For example, the decoder generates irrelevant labels even with well-trained sentence embedding as classifiers cannot choose a necessary feature among dense features for specific tasks.

Researchers have encoded input sentences into high-dimensional vectors that contain the semantic information required for classification. For example, as a variant of RNN, long short-term memory (LSTM) can automatically choose what to remember or forget when modeling long sequences by using four specially designed "gate" structures (input modulation gate, input gate, forget gate, and output gate) [6]. In contrast, CNNs manipulate word tokens sequentially by using sliding windows, resulting in a loss of long dependency information, but extract local semantic features from pretrained word embeddings with convolutional filters. For temporal-relation classification tasks, we assume that we do not need to capture semantic information completely because the clues of temporal-relation classification tend to appear locally around the time–event entities.

In this paper, we propose a novel framework to classify temporal relations with a "question encoder" by using the context of time–event entities as prior information. Our contributions are summarized as follows.

(1) We present an extractor module named "question encoder" to extract required information from sentence embeddings for classification by using expressions for time and event.
(2) We conduct experiments on the *Timebank-Dense* corpus [1]. Experimental results show that our proposed model can significantly improve performance.
(3) To solve the problem of the lack of training data, we expand some of the *Timebank-Dense* dataset by including the reversed examples, and this significantly improves the performance.

2 Related Work

In earlier work, traditional feature-based machine learning approaches have achieved acceptable performance in temporal-relation classification. For example, Mirza and Tonelli [15] employed L2-regularized logistic regression to classify temporal relations by incorporating word-embedding features, demonstrating its effectiveness.

However, to make machine learning algorithms work much better, the unstructured texts need to be converted into numeric representations that can be understood by machine learning algorithms. Traditional machine learning algorithms require laborious feature engineering.

In addition, challenges remain and human-annotated features do not guarantee satisfactory performance because of the impact of errors from the subjective judgment in the process. In temporal-relation classification, these shortcomings indicate that the traditional approaches do not work well, motivating researchers to employ NNs. Instead of complicated feature engineering, NNs can automatically extract effective features.

At the same time, NN-based models can not only learn the rules automatically but can also achieve higher performance by simply giving more input data. For example, Cheng and Miyao [2] employed LSTM in a bidirectional form (Bi-LSTM) by taking dependency paths as the input, resulting in better temporal-relation classification. To improve on their work, Zhang et al. [20] proposed using deep Bi-LSTM, indicating that the deep neural approach can learn representations more semantically.

In contrast, several researchers have proposed temporal-relation classification methods using CNNs [4,5]. Do and Jeong [5] proposed CNN architecture for temporal-relation classification. They used lexical features for window processing and contextual features for convolution and max-pooling operations, but they did not outperform state-of-the-art methods. Dligach et al. [4] found that CNN models outperformed LSTM models for temporal-relation extraction tasks, although their dataset differs from ours introduced in Sect. 4.1.

Building on previous work, we take the CNN model as our base system with the question encoder and compare it with the RNN model in Sect. 5.1.

3   Our Proposed Model

In this section, we propose a framework for temporal-relation classification. As shown in Fig. 1, our CNN-based framework consists of four main components: sentence encoder, question encoder, extractor, and classifier, which we explain in the following sections.

3.1   Sentence Encoder

The sentence encoder module encodes input sentences into high-dimensional embeddings. As shown in Fig. 2, we employ a variant of CNN [8] to encode input sentences, demonstrating its ability to encode semantic features of sentences.

Given a sentence $S = \{x_1, x_2, ..., x_T\}$, where T denotes the length of the sentence, the objective of the word-embedding layer is to map each word x_t into a high-dimensional vector e_t.

The vector e_t can be looked up via an embedding matrix. In the convolutional layer, filter c_i calculates a window size of l words to extract features from them, using the following formula:

$$c_i = f(we_{i:i+l-1} + b). \tag{1}$$

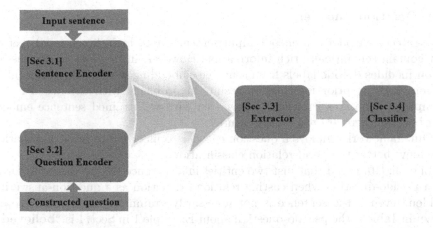

Fig. 1. Architecture of our proposed framework.

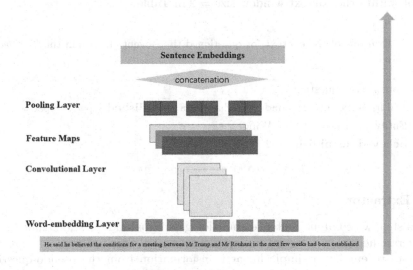

Fig. 2. Architecture of our sentence encoder.

In Eq. (1), f is a nonlinear function and w and b are weights and bias, respectively. The feature map for the given sentence is formulated as follows.

$$g = [c_1, c_2, ..., c_{T-l+1}] \tag{2}$$

After feature mapping generation, we apply a max-pooling algorithm to identify the most important feature in the feature map by taking the maximum value as the feature for filters.

3.2   Question Encoder

The sentence encoder can encode input sentences into high-dimensional vectors that contain semantically rich information. However, in previous work, classification modules decode labels from sentence embedding without any prior information. Lacking prior information results in problems with the decoder. For example, it generates irrelevant labels even with well-trained sentence embedding because there are too many features.

Our framework employs a question encoder to incorporate prior information to achieve better temporal-relation classification.

Li et al. [10] noted that just two entities in a sentence can be viewed as forming a pseudo-question when casting relation extraction as a question-answering problem, even if the sentence is not necessarily grammatical. For example, as shown in Table 1, the pseudo-question about Example 1 in Sect. 1 is "**believed**," "**established**," and their contexts. Note that "<pad> " is used as the padding symbol, within the context window size = 2 in Table 1.

Table 1. Example of the context for questioned time–event entities in the *Timebank-Dense* corpus.

Constructed question		
said he **believed** the conditions; had been **established** <pad> <pad>		
Entity 1	Entity 2	Window size
believed	**established**	2

3.3   Extractor

In this step, we combine sentence embeddings and pseudo-question embeddings to generate necessary information representation for classification.

First, we employ a simple linear transformation from the pseudo-question embedding space to a question space. Then, we put the question space through the *tanh* activation function and multiply it by the sentence embeddings, with which we can only extract the information necessary for the task.

3.4   Classifier

The classifier allows the model to output temporal relations for input examples. We simply employ a *Softmax* classifier to classify input sentences into the predefined five classes described in Sect. 4.1.

3.5   GloVe Word Vectors

Global vectors for word representation capture sublinear relationships of words in the vector space [17]. GloVe word vectors are commonly used as pretrained word representations trained by the unsupervised learning algorithm. Generally, GloVe outperforms the word2vec [14] algorithm in the word analogy tasks. Hence, in this work, we initialize the word embeddings with the publicly available 300-dimensional GloVe word vectors.

4 Experiments

The experiments were set up to investigate whether our proposed models could effectively improve the performance for temporal-relation classification. First, we introduce the dataset and baseline systems used in the experiments. Next, we compare the performance of our model with some baselines. To further evaluate the effects of our proposed model, we also replace the CNN part with Bi-LSTM and present our experimental results with different divisions of training data in Sect. 5.

4.1 Dataset

We conduct our experiments on the *Timebank-Dense* corpus [1], which contains 36 documents, including 12,715 examples. We divide the 36 documents into 27 and 9 documents for training and testing, respectively. Following previous work [2], we adopt sentence-level cross-fold validation for our experiments.

The *Timebank-Dense* corpus is constructed to identify temporal relations between events and times in terms of the following four combinations: event and event (E-E), time and time (T-T), event and time (E-T), and event and document creation time (E-D). This dataset contains the following six temporal relation types: "AFTER," "BEFORE," "SIMULTANEOUS," "INCLUDES," "IS_INCLUDED," and "VAGUE."

As in previous work, we skip the "SIMULTANEOUS" relation type as it has only a small number of instances.

4.2 Baseline Systems

To investigate the effectiveness of our model, we compare our model with the following three representative state-of-the-art models:

MIRZA [15]. This system comprises four classifiers: a rule set for T-T pairs and three L2-regularized logistic regression classifiers for E-D, E-T, and E-E pairs.

CHENG [2]. This system comprises two dependency path-based Bi-LSTM classifiers: one for E-E and E-T pairs and one for E-D pairs.

ZHANG [20]. This is a multilayer neural Bi-LSTM model. This model classifies temporal relations for E-E pairs only.

4.3 Overall Results

We now report our experimental results on the *Timebank-Dense* corpus.

Table 2 compares the results obtained by our model with two state-of-the-art models, MIRZA [15] and CHENG [2]. We observe that the NN-based models outperform the feature-based model, MIRZA [15]. In addition, our proposed model significantly improves the other state-of-the-art model [2] by an F1 score of 0.111 (21.3%), indicating the effectiveness of our model.

Table 2. Overall comparison between our proposed framework and two state-of-the-art models.

Systems	Proposed	MIRZA [15]	CHENG [2]
Micro F1	**0.631**	0.512	0.520

Because ZHANG classifies temporal relations between E-E pairs only, we compare the results for E-E pairs in Table 3. Note that our proposed model outperforms the other three models for all types of relations with statistical significance (using a two-tailed t-test, at a significance level of 5% for MIRZA, CHENG, and ZHANG in Macro F1), particularly the "INCLUDES" and "BEFORE" types. Because of limited data for the "INCLUDES" type (5% of all data), it is always the most difficult type to find temporal relations. However, note that the proposed model improves the F1 score by 0.287 (270.8%) for this type compared with the best state-of-the-art model, ZHANG [20].

Table 3. Comparison for E-E relations. "*" denotes the difference between our proposed approach (bold scores) and the other three models in Macro F1 is statistically significant for $p < 0.05$.

Relation	Proposed	MIRZA [15]	CHENG [2]	ZHANG [20]
AFTER	0.702	0.430	0.440	0.526
BEFORE	0.722	0.471	0.460	0.503
INCLUDES	0.393	0.049	0.025	0.106
IS_INCLUDED	0.369	0.250	0.170	0.325
VAGUE	0.654	0.613	0.624	0.626
Macro F1	**0.568***	0.363	0.344	0.417
Micro F1	**0.627**	0.519	0.529	0.548

5   Discussion

In our proposed framework, the sentence encoder part plays an important role because the sentence embeddings affect the final classification accuracy. In this section, we demonstrate the impact of applying Bi-LSTM to encoding sentences. In addition, we employ a self-attention-based Bi-LSTM model to evaluate further the effectiveness of our proposed framework. Because the performance of NN-based models is always limited by small training datasets in supervised learning, to address this issue, we expand some of the *Timebank-Dense* dataset by including the reversed examples and report experimental results conducted on the expanded *Timebank-Dense* dataset.

5.1   Comparison with Other NN-Based Models

RNN is the most widely used network in the NLP field for its power in modeling sequences. Hence, in this part, we change the CNN to Bi-LSTM in our proposed framework. That is, we apply Bi-LSTM to encode sentence embeddings in the sentence encoder part (in Fig. 2), while the other parts (question encoder, extractor, and classifier in Fig. 1) remain unchanged. At the same time, as self-attention [13] has been proposed and has achieved great success in many NLP-related tasks, we also compare our proposed method with the self-attention-based Bi-LSTM model.

To perform this comparison, we first feed the embedded sequence $E = \{e_1, e_2, ..., e_T\}$ to a forward LSTM from the beginning to the end and then to a backward LSTM from the end to the beginning. Then, the forward $\overrightarrow{h_t}$ and backward $\overleftarrow{h_t}$ results of each word x_t are combined as $[\overrightarrow{h_t} \oplus \overleftarrow{h_t}]$ by a concatenation operation. Then, we use the same operations (see Sect. 3.3) to construct pseudo-questions and extract required information representation for classification. Finally, the model generates labels with the same classifier (see Sect. 3.4). For the Bi-LSTM layer, we set each hidden layer as 256-dimensional and trained our model for up to 50 epochs with a learning rate of 0.01.

Table 4 shows that our CNN-based method outperforms the Bi-LSTM-based model in our proposed framework for "BEFORE," "AFTER," "INCLUDES," and "ISJNCLUDED" types, indicating that CNN is effective in our proposed framework. As discussed in Sect. 1, we assume that we do not need to capture semantic information completely using Bi-LSTMs because the clues of temporal-relation classification tend to appear locally around the time–event entities. These results demonstrate that our hypothesis was correct because CNN has the advantage of utilizing convolutional filters to extract local semantic features from pretrained word embeddings.

The proposed CNN-based and Bi-LSTM-based methods also outperform the self-attention-based Bi-LSTM model with statistical significance (using a two-tailed t-test at a significance level of 5% for self-attention in Macro F1). These results demonstrate that our question encoder module is quite effective, not only with CNNs but also with Bi-LSTMs.

Table 4. Comparison with other NN-based models. "*" denotes the difference between our proposed approach (bold and italic scores) and self-attention-based Bi-LSTM model in Macro F1 is statistically significant for $p < 0.05$.

Relation	Proposed method		Self-attention [13]
	CNN-based	Bi-LSTM-based	
AFTER	0.731	0.659	0.423
BEFORE	0.729	0.641	0.308
INCLUDES	0.405	0.270	0.071
IS_INCLUDED	0.369	0.258	0.116
VAGUE	0.638	0.670	0.599
Macro F1	**0.574***	*0.500**	0.303
Micro F1	**0.631**	*0.608*	0.474

In addition, the most notable difference between the proposed model and the self-attention-based model is that the proposed model artificially filters the sentence by employing a linear transformation of the question as the query part. This technique enables our model to more accurately find important information relevant to the task.

LSTM can automatically choose what to remember or forget when modeling long sequences by using four gates (input modulation gate, input gate, forget gate, and output gate). Inevitably, it still keeps or forgets the wrong information required for identifying temporal relations because of the small training dataset.

However, the extractor in our proposed framework can select the necessary information to decide the relevant temporal relation based on a generated question.

Figure 3 compares our experimental results obtained by varying the ratio of training data by 30%, 50%, and 70% in the CNN-based and Bi-LSTM-based models. We observe that, in either case, the CNN-based model gives better results. Furthermore, by employing our proposed framework, the two models achieve satisfactory results with limited data, and the CNN-based model is comparable with some of the state-of-the-art models with only 30% training samples.

Table 5 also compares our experimental results of each relation type obtained by varying the ratio of training data. We note that the relation types "INCLUDES" and "IS_INCLUDED" do not improve the F1 score according to the increase in training data size. In Sect. 5.2, we discuss how to improve the accuracy of these types with a smaller number of training samples.

5.2   Effect of Data Expansion

Due to limited data, classifying the temporal relation for the "INCLUDES" and "IS_INCLUDED" types can be more difficult. In our proposed model, thanks to the question encoder, we can differentiate two event entities in the temporal relation. We found that the training data could be expanded by reversing the

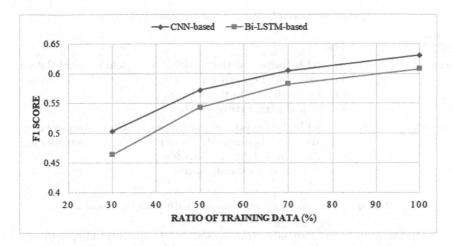

Fig. 3. Comparison between the CNN-based model and the Bi-LSTM-based model by varying the ratio of training data.

Table 5. Comparison of relation types in the CNN-based and the Bi-LSTM-based models with varying the ratio of training data.

Relation	CNN-based			Bi-LSTM-based		
	30%	50%	70%	30%	50%	70%
AFTER	0.542	0.632	0.629	0.437	0.547	0.625
BEFORE	0.587	0.622	0.645	0.463	0.586	0.622
INCLUDES	0.272	0.107	0.363	0.171	0.327	0.360
IS_INCLUDED	0.237	0.284	0.151	0.250	0.301	0.326
VAGUE	0.537	0.620	0.657	0.558	0.604	0.624
Macro F1	0.435	0.453	0.489	0.376	0.473	0.511
Micro F1	0.503	0.572	0.605	0.464	0.543	0.582

temporal relation between entity A and entity B from "AFTER" ("INCLUDES") and "BEFORE" ("IS_INCLUDED"), and *vice versa*.

Based on this observation, we can expand the *Timebank-Dense* dataset by including the reversed training examples for "AFTER," "BEFORE," "INCLUDES," and "IS_INCLUDED." This framework enables us to double the training data available for relations other than the "VAGUE" type.

Tables 6 and 7 show examples of our data expansion method and its statistics in each temporal relation, respectively. For the original data, there is a BEFORE relation between the event **"established"** and the event **"believed,"** while the relation between the event **"believed"** and the event **"established"** is AFTER.

Because of limited data in Table 7, classifying temporal relations for the "INCLUDES" and "IS_INCLUDED" types is more difficult. As shown in Table 8, the F1 score is improved with statistical significance (using a two-tailed *t*-test at

Table 6. Example of an expanded data instance.

	Text	Label	Relation
Original instance	He said he **believed** the "conditions for a meeting" between Mr. Trump and Mr. Rouhani "in the next few weeks" had been **established**.	Before	**established** ⇒ **believed**
Expanded instance	He said he **believed** the "conditions for a meeting" between Mr. Trump and Mr. Rouhani "in the next few weeks" had been **established**	After	**believed** ⇒ **established**

Table 7. Training data size changes with data expansion.

Relation	# Expanded training data	# Original training data
AFTER	4,316	1,889
BEFORE	4,316	2,427
INCLUDES	1,733	695
IS_INCLUDED	1,733	1,038
VAGUE	442	442

Table 8. Experimental results conducted on expanded data. "*" denotes the difference between our proposed approach using expanded training data (bold score) and our proposed approach using original training data in Macro F1 is statistically significant for $p < 0.05$.

Relation	Expanded training data	Original training data
AFTER	0.687	0.731
BEFORE	0.875	0.729
INCLUDES	0.712	0.405
IS_INCLUDED	0.650	0.369
VAGUE	0.850	0.638
Macro F1	**0.755***	0.574
Micro F1	**0.780**	0.631

a significance level of 5% in Macro F1) as the amount of available training data increases, particularly for "INCLUDES" and "IS_INCLUDED."

6   Conclusions and Future Work

In this paper, we designed a framework for temporal-relation classification with a question encoder. We assumed that task-related information can be extracted by introducing pseudo-questions as prior information and then by classifying labels through a classifier. Our proposed model was more interpretable and robust through the constructed questions.

Experimental results on the *Timebank-Dense* corpus demonstrated the effectiveness of our model, especially with a CNN-based model compared with a Bi-LSTM-based model. Our proposed model outperformed state-of-the-art systems and the self-attention-based Bi-LSTM model. It could classify comparably with those baselines even with a small training dataset (30%). In addition, we demonstrated that expanding the training data by reversing the temporal relation improved the accuracy effectively for the relation types with a limited number of training datasets.

Learning sentence representation, however, remains a core issue for temporal-relation classification. In future work, we plan to enhance the word-embedding and sentence-encoding approach based on contextualized word representations such as BERT [3] to further improve the classification accuracy.

Acknowledgments. This work was partially supported by a JSPS Grant-in-Aid for Scientific Research (B) (#19H04420).

References

1. Chambers, N., Cassidy, T., McDowell, B., Bethard, S.: Dense event ordering with a multi-pass architecture. Trans. Assoc. Comput. Linguist. **2**, 273–284 (2014)
2. Cheng, F., Miyao, Y.: Classifying temporal relations by bidirectional LSTM over dependency paths. In: Proceedings of the 55th Annual Meeting of the Association for Computational Linguistics (ACL 2017), pp. 1–6, July 2017
3. Devlin, J., Chang, M.W., Lee, K., Toutanova, K.: BERT: pre-training of deep bidirectional transformers for language understanding. In: Proceedings of the 2019 Conference of the North American Chapter of the Association for Computational Linguistics, Minneapolis, MN, USA, pp. 4171–4186, June 2019
4. Dligach, D., Miller, T., Lin, C., Bethard, S., Savova, G.: Neural temporal relation extraction. In: Proceedings of the 15th Conference of the European Chapter of the Association for Computational Linguistics, Valencia, Spain, vol. 2, pp. 746–751, April 2017
5. Do, H.W., Jeong, Y.S.: Temporal relation classification with deep neural network. In: Proceedings of the 2016 International Conference on Big Data and Smart Computing (BigComp), Hong Kong, China, pp. 454–457, January 2016
6. Hochreiter, S., Schmidhuber, J.: Long short-term memory. Neural Comput. **9**(8), 1735–1780 (1997)
7. Jin, P., Lian, J., Zhao, X., Wan, S.: TISE: a temporal search engine for web contents. Intell. Inf. Technol. Appl. (2008). https://doi.org/10.1109/IITA.2008.132. 2007 Workshop on 3, 220–224
8. Kim, Y.: Convolutional neural networks for sentence classification. In: Proceedings of the 2014 Conference on Empirical Methods in Natural Language Processing (EMNLP 2014), pp. 1746–1751 (2014)
9. Laokulrat, N., Miwa, M., Tsuruoka, Y., Chikayama, T.: UTTime: temporal relation classification using deep syntactic features. Second Joint Conference on Lexical and Computational Semantics. Volume 2: Proceedings of the Seventh International Workshop on Semantic Evaluation, Atlanta, Georgia, USA, pp. 88–92, June 2013

10. Li, X., Yin, F., Sun, Z., Li, X., Yuan, A., Chai, D., Zhou, M., Li, J.: Entity-relation extraction as multi-turn question answering. In: Proceedings of the 57th Annual Meeting of the Association for Computational Linguistics (ACL 2019), pp. 1340–1350, July 2019
11. Lin, C., Dligach, D., Miller, T., Bethard, S., Savova, G.: Multilayered temporal modeling for the clinical domain. J. Am. Med. Inform. Assoc. **23**, 387–395 (2016)
12. Lin, C., Miller, T., Dligach, D., Bethard, S., Savova, G.: Representations of time expressions for temporal relation extraction with convolutional neural networks. In: Proceedings of the 2017 Biomedical Natural Language Processing Workshop, pp. 322–327, August 2017. https://doi.org/10.18653/v1/W17-2341
13. Lin, Z., Feng, M., dos Santos, C.N., Yu, M., Xiang, B., Zhou, B., Bengio, Y.: A structured self-attentive sentence embedding. In: Proceedings of the 5th International Conference on Learning Representations (ICLR 2017) (2017)
14. Mikolov, T., Chen, K., Corrado, G., Dean, J.: Efficient estimation of word representations in vector space. CoRR abs/1301.3781 (2013)
15. Mirza, P., Tonelli, S.: Classifying temporal relations with simple features. In: Proceedings of the 2014 Conference of the European Chapter of the Association for Computational Linguistics (EACL 2014), pp. 308–317, April 2014
16. Mirza, P., Tonelli, S.: On the contribution of word embeddings to temporal relation classification. In: Proceedings of COLING 2016, the 26th International Conference on Computational Linguistics: Technical Papers, Osaka, Japan, pp. 2818–2828. The COLING 2016 Organizing Committee, December 2016
17. Pennington, J., Socher, R., Manning, C.: Glove: global vectors for word representation. In: Proceedings of the 2014 Conference on Empirical Methods in Natural Language Processing (EMNLP 2014), pp. 1532–1543, October 2014
18. Tourille, J., Ferret, O., Névéol, A., Tannier, X.: Neural architecture for temporal relation extraction: a bi-LSTM approach for detecting narrative containers. In: Proceedings of the 55th Annual Meeting of the Association for Computational Linguistics (Volume 2: Short Papers), pp. 224–230, July 2017. https://doi.org/10.18653/v1/P17-2035
19. Wang, Y., et al.: Clinical information extraction applications: a literature review. J. Biomed. Inform. **77**, 34–49 (2018)
20. Zhang, Y., Li, P., Zhou, G.: Classifying temporal relations between events by deep BiLSTM. In: Proceedings of the 2018 International Conference on Asian Language Processing (IALP 2018), pp. 267–272, November 2018
21. Zheng, N., et al.: Predicting COVID-19 in China using hybrid AI model. IEEE Trans. Cybern. **50**(7), 2891–2904 (2020)

When to Use OCR Post-correction for Named Entity Recognition?

Vinh-Nam Huynh[1], Ahmed Hamdi[2](✉) ⓘ, and Antoine Doucet[2] ⓘ

[1] ICT Lab, University of Science and Technology of Hanoi, Hanoi, Vietnam
namhv.ictlab@gmail.com
[2] University of La Rochelle, La Rochelle, France
{ahmed.hamdi,antoine.doucet}@univ-lr.fr

Abstract. In the last decades, a huge number of documents has been digitised, before undergoing optical character recognition (OCR) to extract their textual content. This step is crucial for indexing the documents and to make the resulting collections accessible. However, the fact that documents are indexed through their OCRed content is posing a number of problems, due to the varying performance of OCR methods over time. Indeed, OCR quality has a considerable impact on the indexing and therefore the accessibility of digital documents. Named entities are among the most adequate information to index documents, in particular in the case of digital libraries, for which log analysis studies have shown that around 80% of user queries include a named entity. Taking full advantage of the computational power of modern natural language processing (NLP) systems, named entity recognition (NER) can be operated over enormous OCR corpora efficiently. Despite progress in OCR, resulting text files still have misrecognised words (or noise for short) which are harming NER performance. In this paper, to handle this challenge, we apply a spelling correction method to noisy versions of a corpus with variable OCR error rates in order to quantitatively estimate the contribution of post-OCR correction to NER. Our main finding is that we can indeed consistently improve the performance of NER when the OCR quality is reasonable (error rates respectively between 2% and 10% for characters (CER) and between 10% and 25% for words (WER)). The noise correction algorithm we propose is both language-independent and with low complexity.

Keywords: Named entity recognition · Optical character recognition · Character degradation · Spelling correction

1 Introduction

Large quantities of valuable documents have been scanned as images for digital archives. In order to extract text information from those images, OCR techniques are widely used. The OCR process usually begins with loading text images as

E. Ishita et al. (Eds.): ICADL 2020, LNCS 12504, pp. 33–42, 2020.
https://doi.org/10.1007/978-3-030-64452-9_3

input and improving the input quality, a step that may involve multiple techniques, such as deskewing, noise removal, etc. In the next steps, OCR systems binarize images and detect text zones. Then, the core part of OCR systems will take place by mapping each character image to the most proper character code. Finally, the OCR system generates a text file corresponding to the input image. However, due to storage conditions or poor quality of printing materials, the image quality may be low, in which case the OCR may generate very noisy texts, strongly diverging from the original text, known as the Ground Truth (GT). Often, these noisy texts are nonetheless readable by humans in digital libraries, which lessens the motivation to re-digitize and/or re-OCR them, which is a costly process. The key problem is that this noisy text is used for building the indexes used for instance by search engines. This implies that a keyword query will return documents containing the adequate keyword only if it was properly recognized by the OCR system. Many relevant documents may thus be missed, in proportions that are very hard to quantify.

A study has shown that named entities are the first point of entry for users in a search system [4]. For instance, on the Gallica digital library[1], 80% of user queries contain at least one named entity [1]. For this reason, named entities can be given a higher semantic value than other words to index digitised documents. In order to improve the quality of user searches in a system, it is thus necessary to ensure the quality of these particular terms. In the presence of OCR errors, NER systems are not able to override the degradation caused by the OCR in the extracted text. For this reason, post-OCR task should be helpful in order to improve the effectiveness of NER systems over noisy textual data.

This work extends a previous work studying the performance of an effective neural network-based NER system over several noisy versions of a NER corpus with variable rates of OCR errors [5]. We aim to use a post-OCR correction to this variety of OCRed texts in order to quantitatively estimate its contribution on NER performance. The underlying idea of this work is to evaluate the impact of post-OCR correction on the performance of NER over noisy text, a task strongly related to information access in digital libraries.

The remainder of this paper is organized as follows: Sect. 2 surveys related works on misspellings, OCR errors and post-OCR approaches. Then, we introduce the dataset in Sect. 3. In Sect. 4, we analyze OCR errors and give many useful statistics, before summarizing our major findings in Sect. 5.

2   Related Work

Many studies focused on the impact of OCR errors on NLP [9] and Information Retrieval (IR) [20]. Miller *et al.* [13], for instance studied the NER performances under a variety of spoken and OCRed data. They showed that over noisy texts, NER F-score may lose about 8 points with a word error rate of only 15%. Recently, Hamdi et al. [6] simulated many noisy versions of NER resources with different types of noise in order to study the correlation between OCR error

---

[1] Gallica is the digital portal of the National Library of France.

rates and NER accuracy. In a similar setting, Van Strien *et al.* [18] studied the impact of OCR errors on different NLP tasks. They concluded that NER is less affected by OCR errors than sentence segmentation or dependency parsing.

A few amount of works studied the contribution of post-OCR correction on NLP and IR tasks. Magdy and Darwish [12], for instance, examined the effect of OCR error correction on document retrieval. On named entity recognition, Rodriquez *et al.* [17], reported that manual correction of OCR output have not a very observable improvement on NER results.

Our work is similar to Rodriquez *et al.* [17], we study the impact of post-OCR correction on NER performance. However, unlike them, we automatically rectify erroneous tokens over a variety of noisy texts using a low-complexity algorithm. We perform NER using three accurate neural network NER systems.

3   Dataset Overview

The dataset used in this work is the English corpus given by the Conference on Natural Language Learning in 2003 (CoNLL-2003) [19]. The dataset defines four classes of named entities: **Persons** (PER) including individuals and groups. **Locations** (LOC) includes countries, regions, addresses as well as states and provinces. **Organisations** (ORG) concerns commercial, educational, government as well as medical-science, religious, sports. **Miscellaneous** (MISC) annotates all other named entities such as nationalities and events. The dataset defines more than 40,000 named entities.

As we mentioned in the introduction, this work extends a previous study on the impact of OCR errors on named entity recognition [5]. Authors simulated several OCRed versions[2] of the test data adapted to this real-life problem. This simulation of document degradation is required because while there exist datasets with OCRed text and corrected text, as well as text with NER markup, there are no datasets contain both, and even less so with different levels and types of OCR noise. First of all, raw texts in the test set have been extracted and then converted into images. With the help of the DocCreator tool [7], common OCR degradation have been added to these images by putting noise texture to their backgrounds. Degradation include bleeding effect, blurring, character degradation, and phantom character. For each type of noise, two levels of degradation were applied: level 1 corresponds to noises that are sparsely applied on the original document and level 2 corresponds to noises that appear more often. Thus, level 1 of each degradation means that the simulated text contains less noise than level 2. These degradations define typical OCR noises when storing documents in digital libraries or using a document scanner [3]. The open source OCR engine Tesseract v-3.04.01 has been used to extract noisy texts from the degraded images. In order to quantify OCR error rates in the obtained versions of the test set, two common metrics have been used: the character error rate (CER) and the word error rate (WER) which correspond respectively to the rate of erroneous output characters (resp. words) out of the total number of

---

[2] https://zenodo.org/record/3877554.

characters (resp. words) in the corpus [10]. In the end, many OCRed versions of the test set are obtained with a CER and WER rates respectively varying from 1% to 20% and from 8% to 50%.

4   Named Entity Recognition on Noisy Texts

For NER, we utilized the DeLFT[3] (Deep Learning Framework for Text) framework. This library re-implements standard state-of-the-art deep learning architectures relevant to named entity recognition. Among the existing architectures, we chose to use BiLSTM ones due to their ability to overcome some of the OCR errors [16]. We built three models based on BiLSTM-CRF [8], BiLSTM-CNN [2] and BiLSTM-CNN-CRF [11]. We also used the Stanford Global Vectors (GloVe) as our word embedding in order to represent document vocabulary and word features. GloVe is an unsupervised learning algorithm that produces a word vector space based on global word co-occurrence statistics [15].

Results show comparable NER performances of the three systems. However, they are harmfully impacted by the OCR quality especially when the OCR error rates are relatively high. Figure 1 shows the correlation between the NER performances and the character error rate. We show also the evolution of the word error rate (dotted line). Regardless of the system used NER results may fall by about 30% points due to OCR noise when the OCR error rates are respectively 20% and 50% at the character and the word levels. Unsurprisingly, the higher the OCR error rates, the greater the degradation of NER F1-score. For all systems, the NER F1-score achieves less than 80% when the CER reaches around 3% and the WER is about 20%.

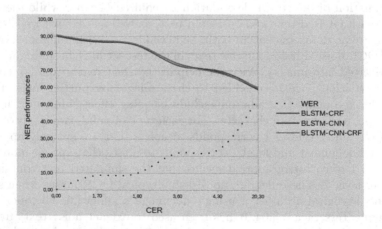

Fig. 1. NER F1-score degradation according character error rates

---

[3] https://github.com/kermitt2/delft.

As proof, noisy texts contain many out-of-vocabulary words, which NER models cannot identify as named entities. Following our analysis of the output predictions, we made several observations:

1. Contaminated named entities were well recognised by NER system in both clean and noisy versions: for instance, the named entity *Mittermayer*, which corresponds to a person name is correctly associated to *Minermayer*. However, it is well extracted and labeled by the NER system.
2. Contaminated named entities were detected and well classified in the clean text version, but their alternative in noisy version were wrongly recognized by the NER system: the location *Japan* for example is associated to *Japgfl* which is not recognized by any NER system.
3. Named Entities that were not corrupted after the OCR process still failed to be recognized by NER systems, because of noisy context surrounding them.

```
{
    "text": "charlton",
    "class": "ORG",
    "score": 0.6170039176940918,
    "beginOffset": 86,
    "endOffset": 93
}
```

Fig. 2. Correctly-OCRed named entity were wrongly classified by NER system due to noisy paragraph surround

The example in Fig. 2 shows that even if the named entity is not contaminated by the OCR system, it can be impacted by noisy surrounding words and therefore associated to a wrong class.

- GT: "Prime Minister Dick Spring who said the honour had been made in recognition of **Charlton** 's achievements as the national soccer manager."
- OCR: "Prime Minister Dick Spring who said the homur had been made in recognimm on **Charlton** s ac icvcmcnts as thc national soccer manager."

Since these noisy words had the same problem, the existing NER systems wrongly classified or did not recognize them. Hence, noisy texts dramatically reduced NER performance. In order to solve this problem, we proposed to use an edit distance based algorithm as a spell-checker including a dictionary in order to carefully examine each word and compare it with every dictionary entry.

5 Experiments

To reduce the impact of OCR on the NER results, we pre-processed the noisy texts before parsing them using the NER models with an efficient and low-complexity text correction method named SymSpell[4]. In our work, the algorithm is based on Levenshtein distance which calculates the minimum steps (insertion, deletion or substitution) to transform a string into another string.

---

[4] https://github.com/mammothb/symspellpy.

5.1   Noisy Text Correction

SymSpell consists of two steps: pre-calculation and searching. At first, SymSpell generates all possible terms within the pre-set edit distance by deletion only. In this work, the max edit distance is set to 2. According to a recent study, OCR post-processing approaches are recommended to focus on correcting erroneous words with edit distances 1 and 2 [14]. For example, with (italy, 2) meaning the word "italy" and a max edit distance of 2, we have:

- delete (italy, 0) == italy
- delete (italy, 1) == ital or itay or taly or ... (for a total of $\binom{5}{1}$ possible strings)
- delete (italy, 2) == ita or itl or aly or ... (for a total of $\binom{5}{2}$ possible strings)
- Many different entries may share the same result string: delete (italy, 1) == delete (vital, 1) == ital

Second, upon receiving input, SymSpell starts to erase each single character within an edit distance from that term. By doing so, both imprecise dictionary generated strings and imprecise input-generated string might match and meet in the middle. Thus, SymSpell will choose possible candidates and give suggestions to correct the misspelled input. Setting an edit distance threshold allows SymSpell to remove many irrelevant candidates. SymSpell automatically chooses the one with the highest frequency when it encounters multiple candidates that satisfy the max edit distance threshold.

5.2   Results and Discussion

Figure 3 presents the output of SymSpell text pre-processing. Well corrected named entities are colored in red.

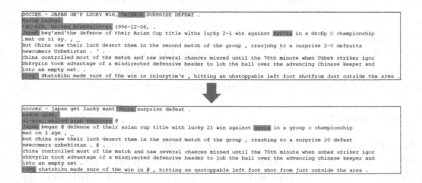

Fig. 3. SymSpell correction output (Color figure online)

In order to evaluate the contribution of SymSpell on NER results, we calculated NER F1-scores of different models before and after the post-OCR correction. Table 1 compares the F1-scores given on the original noisy data and the ones that applied the SymSpell method.

Table 1. F1-score comparison between original noise and SymSpell correction

OCR error rate		BidLSTM-CRF		BidLSTM-CNN		BidLSTM-CRF-CNN	
CER	WER	Original	SymSpell	Original	SymSpell	Original	SymSpell
1.7	8.5	**86.8**	79.8	**86.9**	78.9	**87.6**	80.0
1.7	8.8	**85.6**	79.6	**85.7**	78.9	**87.0**	80.0
1.8	8.0	**84.6**	79.4	**85.0**	78.8	**85.2**	79.8
1.8	8.5	**85.2**	79.7	**85.0**	78.9	**86.1**	80.0
1.8	8.6	**84.6**	79.8	**84.7**	78.8	**84.0**	80.0
3.6	20.0	73.1	**78.6**	74.2	**77.6**	74.1	**78.2**
4.3	21.8	70.9	**78.7**	69.4	**77.6**	68.8	**78.7**
6.3	23.7	71.0	**78.0**	71.0	**77.6**	71.0	**77.2**
20.3	54.0	59.8	**68.4**	59.0	**68.3**	60.3	**68.0**

Table 1 shows that the BiLSTM-CNN-CRF model globally outperforms the two other NER models in both OCRed and post-OCR corrected texts. The post-OCR correction improves NER results when the OCR error rates are relatively high. Very satisfactory results (up to 77%) are reached when the word error rate is less than 25%. However, post-OCR correction may also degrade NER F1-scores especially when the OCR error rate is very low (less than 2% at the character level and less than 10% at the word level). The SymSpell method did not take care of surrounding context and relied only on pure edit-distance, then chose the most suitable word by frequency index, the algorithm sometimes changed original words into ones that were not related to the context (e.g., substituted "Al-ain" - a location NE - with the word "Again"). This mechanism would reduce the performance of existing NER systems mentioned above.

In order to stress the impact of the OCR noise and the contribution of the post-OCR correction on NER F1-scores, we calculated two δ measures:

- δ_{noisy} which gives the decrease rate between the F1-score given in clean data and the F1-score given in noisy data using BiLSTM-CNN-CRF.
- $\delta_{symSpell}$ which indicates the decrease rate between the F1-score given in clean data and the F1-score given in post-OCR corrected data using BiLSTM-CNN-CRF.

Figure 4 shows the evolution of the δ measures according to the character error rate. The WER curve (dotted) is also given to ease comparison. The curves show that NER F1-scores are considerably impacted by OCR errors when the

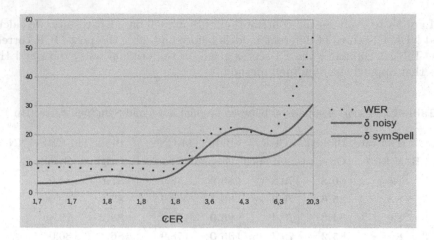

Fig. 4. F1-score decrease on noisy and corrected text

OCR error rate is more than 20% at the character level and exceeds 50% at the word level.

The decrease rate δ_{noisy} jumps from 20% to 30%. The post-OCR correction allowed us to overcome this issue. $\delta_{symSpell}$ is almost constant ~10% which means that SymSpell allowed us to overcome OCR issues and propose a NER F1-score exceeding 80%. However, Fig. 4 also showed that for low error rates (less than 2% and 10% at the character level and the word level respectively), a post-OCR correction is not a suitable solution to recover the NER degradation and it is better to simply run NER systems on the original noisy text, as if they contained no noise.

6   Conclusion

The main aim of this research was to propose methods that help to increase the performances of NER over noisy texts, by applying post-OCR correction. The result has shown that the SymSpell algorithm (with max edit distance set to 2) can consistently increase NER results over noisy texts when the CER and the WER respectively exceed 2% and 10%, while standard techniques are otherwise preferable. In future work, we plan to further study this phenomenon, using different max edit distances and exploiting other post-OCR correction techniques.

Acknowledgments. This work has been supported by the European Union Horizon 2020 research and innovation programme under grant 770299 (NewsEye).

References

1. Chiron, G., Doucet, A., Coustaty, M., Visani, M., Moreux, J.P.: Impact of OCR errors on the use of digital libraries: towards a better access to information. In: Proceedings of the 17th ACM/IEEE Joint Conference on Digital Libraries, pp. 249–252. IEEE Press (2017)
2. Chiu, J.P., Nichols, E.: Named entity recognition with bidirectional LSTM-CNNs. arXiv preprint arXiv:1511.08308 (2015)
3. Farahmand, A., Sarrafzadeh, H., Shanbehzadeh, J.: Document image noises and removal methods (2013)
4. Gefen, A.: Les enjeux épistémologiques des humanités numériques. Socio-La nouvelle revue des sciences sociales (4), 61–74 (2014)
5. Hamdi, A., Jean-Caurant, A., Sidere, N., Coustaty, M., Doucet, A.: An analysis of the performance of named entity recognition over OCRed documents. In: 2019 ACM/IEEE Joint Conference on Digital Libraries (JCDL), pp. 333–334. IEEE (2019)
6. Hamdi, A., Jean-Caurant, A., Sidère, N., Coustaty, M., Doucet, A.: Assessing and minimizing the impact of OCR quality on named entity recognition. In: Hall, M., Merčun, T., Risse, T., Duchateau, F. (eds.) TPDL 2020. LNCS, vol. 12246, pp. 87–101. Springer, Cham (2020). https://doi.org/10.1007/978-3-030-54956-5_7
7. Journet, N., Visani, M., Mansencal, B., Van-Cuong, K., Billy, A.: DocCreator: a new software for creating synthetic ground-truthed document images. J. Imaging 3(4), 62 (2017)
8. Lample, G., Ballesteros, M., Subramanian, S., Kawakami, K., Dyer, C.: Neural architectures for named entity recognition. arXiv preprint arXiv:1603.01360 (2016)
9. Lopresti, D.: Optical character recognition errors and their effects on natural language processing. Int. J. Doc. Anal. Recognit. (IJDAR) 12(3), 141–151 (2009)
10. Lund, W.B., Kennard, D.J., Ringger, E.K.: Combining multiple thresholding binarization values to improve OCR output. In: Document Recognition and Retrieval XX, vol. 8658, p. 86580R. International Society for Optics and Photonics (2013)
11. Ma, X., Hovy, E.: End-to-end sequence labeling via Bi-directional LSTM-CNNs-CRF. arXiv preprint arXiv:1603.01354 (2016)
12. Magdy, W., Darwish, K.: Effect of OCR error correction on Arabic retrieval. Inf. Retr. 11(5), 405–425 (2008)
13. Miller, D., Boisen, S., Schwartz, R., Stone, R., Weischedel, R.: Named entity extraction from noisy input: speech and OCR. In: Proceedings of the Sixth Conference on Applied Natural Language Processing, pp. 316–324. Association for Computational Linguistics (2000)
14. Nguyen, T.T.H., Jatowt, A., Coustaty, M., Nguyen, N.V., Doucet, A.: Deep statistical analysis of OCR errors for effective post-OCR processing. In: 2019 ACM/IEEE Joint Conference on Digital Libraries (JCDL), pp. 29–38. IEEE (2019)
15. Pennington, J., Socher, R., Manning, C.: Glove: global vectors for word representation. In: Proceedings of the 2014 Conference on Empirical Methods in Natural Language Processing (EMNLP), pp. 1532–1543 (2014)
16. Riedl, M., Padó, S.: A named entity recognition shootout for German. In: Proceedings of ACL, Melbourne, Australia, pp. 120–125 (2018). http://aclweb.org/anthology/P18-2020.pdf
17. Rodriquez, K.J., Bryant, M., Blanke, T., Luszczynska, M.: Comparison of named entity recognition tools for raw OCR text. In: KONVENS, pp. 410–414 (2012)

18. van Strien, D., Beelen, K., Ardanuy, M., Hosseini, K., McGillivray, B., Colavizza, G.: Assessing the impact of OCR quality on downstream NLP tasks. In: Proceedings of the 12th International Conference on Agents and Artificial Intelligence, Valletta, Malta, pp. 484–496. SCITEPRESS - Science and Technology Publications (2020). https://doi.org/10.5220/0009169004840496. http://www.scitepress.org/DigitalLibrary/Link.aspx?doi=10.5220/0009169004840496

19. Tjong Kim Sang, E.F., De Meulder, F.: Introduction to the CoNLL-2003 shared task: language-independent named entity recognition. In: Proceedings of the Seventh Conference on Natural Language Learning at HLT-NAACL 2003-Volume 4, pp. 142–147. Association for Computational Linguistics (2003)

20. Zuccon, G., Nguyen, A.N., Bergheim, A., Wickman, S., Grayson, N.: The impact of OCR accuracy on automated cancer classification of pathology reports. In: HIC, pp. 250–256 (2012)

Semi-supervised Named-Entity Recognition for Product Attribute Extraction in Book Domain

Hadi Syah Putra, Faisal Satrio Priatmadji, and Rahmad Mahendra[✉]

Faculty of Computer Science, Universitas Indonesia, Kampus UI Depok,
Depok, West Java, Indonesia
rahmad.mahendra@cs.ui.ac.id

Abstract. Products sold in today's marketplace are very numerous and varied. One of them is the book product. Detail information about the book, such as the title of the book, author, and publisher, is often presented in unstructured format in the product title. In order to be useful for the commercial applications, for example catalogs, search functions, and recommendation systems, the attributes need to be extracted from the product title. In this study, we apply Named-Entity Recognition model in semi-supervised style to extract the attributes of e-commerce products in book domain. We experiment with the number of features extraction, i.e. lexical, position, word shape, and embedding features. We extract the book attributes from near to 30K product title data with F-1 measure 65%.

Keywords: Book · Named-Entity Recognition · Attribute extraction · Product title · E-commerce

1 Background

Nowadays, almost all aspects of human activity take place online and one of them is shopping. A huge number of categories of products have been offered through the marketplace platform as the result of e-commerce companies try to fulfill their customers' needs. To manage products effectively and provide the best user experience, the e-commerce companies need to arrange their inventory data into descriptive name-value pairs (called properties) and ensure the products with the same type are described using unique property collections. One way to manage inventory data is to automate the creation of product catalogs.

The information about product is mostly presented in unstructured text format, e.g. product title and description. While the structured fields are sometimes provided as product features, the sellers, mostly in C2C marketplaces, does not fill the data in the proper manner.

A product title is a series of words that describe the product with a limited number of words [8] and can be written by the seller or the product owner. It is used to generate search result pages for the users of the website.

© Springer Nature Switzerland AG 2020
E. Ishita et al. (Eds.): ICADL 2020, LNCS 12504, pp. 43–51, 2020.
https://doi.org/10.1007/978-3-030-64452-9_4

Product titles actually contain attribute information that is needed for building the product catalog. For example, the product title of book category provide information about the book title, author, or publisher (sometimes one or two of them are missing). However, those information is not ready to be processed by machine as it is written as single free text [2]. If the attributes can be extracted from the product title, they will be useful for several applications, such as demand forecasting and recommendation systems. Besides, they can also be useful to create search and filter functions in the marketplace platform corresponding to the existing attributes.

The Named-Entity Recognition (NER) is a classic task in Natural Language Processing, which is the task of recognising and assigning a class to mentions of proper names (named entities like Person, Location, Organization, etc.) in the text [7]. This task has been explored into domain-specific text, for example biomedical and e-commerce. In domain of e-commerce, NER task is applied to extract the value of product attribute from free-text product title.

A number of works has been conducted to perform attribute extraction from the product titles in marketplace data. Ghani et al. [2] experimented to extract product attributes in the fashion category. Putthividhya and Hu [8] extracted attributes of clothing and shoe products. Meanwhile, Joshi et al. [3] focused on the extraction of attributes in five product categories: cell phones, cell phone accessories, male shoes, watches, and women clothes. Rif'at et al. [9] studied the fine-grained attributes extraction of marketplace products in 15 diverse categories. Those works apply the Conditional Random Fields (CRF) models [4]. To our knowledge, the only work on e-commerce text in book domain is identifying ambiguous authors from book product category [1].

Our work is a novel study in extracting attributes from the product titles of book, the category that has not been much explored in e-commerce domain. We then bootstrap the model in semi-supervised style to expand the data that can be extracted.

The rest of this paper is outlined as followings. We describe the dataset and annotation process in Sect. 2. In Sect. 3, we explain and report the result and analysis of our method in building a supervised NER model. Then, we discuss the adoption of a semi-supervised style to expand the data in Sect. 4. Finally, Sect. 5 concludes the paper.

2   Data and Annotation

In our work, we utilize data from two different sources. The first dataset contains 925,528 product titles of book category, crawled from one of the marketplace platform in Indonesia[1]. 1000 product titles are sampled and annotated with the book attributes. We use 7 attribute labels in our annotation scheme, as followings:

1. **Title.** Words listed on the title page of a work that distinguishes it from other works. Moreover, it may include additional title, alternative title, or

---

[1] https://www.bukalapak.com.

other relevant descriptions, but does not include the name of authors, editors, translators, and so on.

2. **Author**. Person or corporation that is responsible for the intellectual or artistic content, such as artist, composer, painter, photographer, composer of bibliography, etc.

3. **Publisher**. Person, company, or corporation that has a responsibility to publish the work as distinguished from the printer.

4. **Date of publication**. Publication year of work and can be referred to as an imprint date.

5. **Edition**. Number of copies printed at once with changes, both in the text or the rearrangement of the printing plates.

6. **Volume**. Publication that is distinguished from other parts of work because it has its title page in the bibliography. This kind of bibliography unit is sometimes called a part or volume by the publisher. Some volumes can be published in one book with their respective title pages.

7. **Series**. Books that are published sequentially. Each of them includes a collective title as a sign of the relationship of others. They are usually issued by the same corporation in a uniform style and numbered sequentially.

The annotation process starts with tokenizing the product title into a sequence of tokens. The whitespace character is used as a token boundary. Every single non-alphanumeric character (e.g. punctuation) is examined as an individual token.

BIO encoding is used to label the sequence of tokens. For each sequence of tokens corresponding to a particular attribute X, the first token in that sequence is labeled with B-X, while any other tokens are labeled with I-X. Tokens with label O are not part of any attributes in a certain product title.

Table 1 shows the example of the annotated product title. Those 1000 product titles are annotated by three human annotators. The Fleiss Kappa score [5] of attribute annotation is 0.859. Distribution of attributes frequency in our annotated product titles is shown in Fig. 1. The most frequent attribute label is Title (992), while the least one is Year (13).

Table 1. Example of annotated product titles

Deluxe	.	Sleeping	Beauty	Age	3
B-Publisher	O	B-Title	I-Title	I-Title	B-Volume
Eyewitness	Travel	Top	10	Los	Angeles
B-Series	I-Series	B-Title	I-Title	I-Title	I-Title
FARMAKOPE	INDONESIA	edisi	ketiga	1979	termurah
B-Title	I-Title	B-Edition	I-Edition	B-Year	O
Mengelola	zakat	indonesia	-	Yusuf	wibisono
B-Title	I-Title	I-Title	O	B-Author	I-Author
Robinson	Crusoe	(	Daniel	Defoe	)
B-Title	I-Title	O	B-Author	I-Author	O

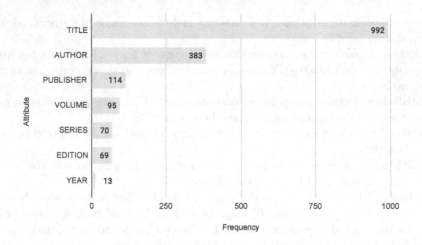

Fig. 1. Distribution of attributes frequency in annotated product titles

The second dataset is tabular data, scrapped from one of the Indonesian book e-commerce, Gramedia[2]. The data consists of 51,651 instances, which is composed by a number of book attributes, i.e. the title, author, publisher, imprint date, dimension (length, width, height, and weight), language, ISBN, number of pages, producer, and category.

We utilize the second dataset to create a silver standard by automatically tagging unlabeled data from the first set. The silver labeled data is constructed by pairing the product title with tabular data. We compute cosine similarity among pairs and filter out the pairs with similarity score less than 0.587[3]. If one product title is still paired with more than two tabular data, we only consider the pair with the highest similarity.

We apply regular expression to tag the mention of book attributes in the product title based on tabular data. In total, our silver standard consists of 82,698 product titles which are annotated with 3 attributes: `title`, `author`, and `publisher`.

3   Supervised Named-Entity Recognition

In this section, we explain the method to build a Named-Entity Recognition model to solve the attribute extraction task. We formulate it as a sequence labeling problem. Given a product title containing N tokens $W = (w_1, w_2, \ldots, w_N)$, we want to find the best sequence of labels $Y = (y_1, y_2, \ldots, y_N)$. Each label is determined using probability $P(y_i | w_{i-1}, \ldots, w_{i+1}, y_{i-1}, \ldots, y_{i+1})$.

---

[2] https://www.gramedia.com/.
[3] This number is obtained after conducting empirical observation.

3.1   Experiment

In the experiment, we use the number of features extraction, namely lexical, position, word shape, dictionary, and embedding features. The information about them is described in Table 2.

Table 2. Features used in the experiment

Feature	Description
Lexical	5-gram bag of words (current token and two tokens before/after the current token)
Position	Relative position of token in product title
Word shape	Orthographic feature of current token and two tokens before/after the current token (e.g. *contain digit*)
Dictionary	The occurrence of current token and two tokens before/after the current token in English and Indonesian dictionaries
Embedding	Skip-gram model of word2vec pretrained by in-domain dataset, i.e. the dataset of product titles. We use the word vector representation of the current token and two tokens before/after the current token

The experiment is carried out with 4-fold cross-validation, in which for each fold, 75% data is used as training data and other as testing data.

We evaluate the results of the experiment of attribute extraction in entity-level with full match methods. Full match examines the prediction for multi-token attributes is true if all of the tokens are correctly predicted and no other token is included in the predicted label. The metrics measured for evaluation are precision, recall, and F1-measure.

3.2   Result and Analysis

According to the precision metric, our model performs the best on `publisher` attribute which occurs in 114 product titles. It gives 90.42% precision, 48.10% recall, and 62.47% F1-measure. We find that the limited range of token values in `publisher` attribute facilitates it to achieve the highest precision value. However, the recall score for this attribute is not satisfying enough as, in most cases, it is predicted as author.

Meanwhile, prediction on `author` attribute achieves the highest score of F1-measure (66.30%) and recall (61.25%) among all product attributes. In our data, 383 product titles contain this attribute. The predictor works well because of the recurring patterns, e.g. `<Title> - <Author>` or `<Title> (<Author>)`.

Some of the product titles contain more than one author. We find that our model still predicts the multiple authors as a single entity.

Edition is the third-best extracted attributes. We observed that prediction on **Edition** attribute has a convincing precision score because, most of the time, it is indicated with specific word (e.g. *edisi*, *edition*) and ordinal number. Nevertheless, its recall is not good as the precision because on occasion it is indistinguishable from imprint date and volume. Also, the model is less able to capture when it involves abbreviation, such as "ed.".

Finally, **series** and **year** are predicted the worst. Our model is not able to capture the **series** well since they are almost similar to the **title** attributes, which consist of a collection of words that do not indicate a person or institution name. **Year** attribute is completely cannot be predicted due to its very small occurrence in the dataset. The evaluation of each attribute is shown in Table 3a.

We also explore the performance of the model if the predefined attributes are reduced into 3 attributes: **title**, **author**, and **publisher**. In this case, tokens of other attributes are labeled **O**. The evaluation of attribute extraction for model with 7 and 3 defined attributes is described in Table 3b. Overall, there is a slight increase in F1-measure for **title** and **publisher** attributes if the model is trained to only 3 predefined attributes.

Table 3. Evaluation of attribute extraction

(a)

Attribute	Precision	Recall	F1-Measure
Title	56.29	56.13	56.18
Author	72.32	61.25	66.30
Publisher	90.42	48.10	62.47
Series	29.17	7.81	11.92
Edition	69.02	52.58	59.43
Volume	52.08	46.51	48.80
Year	0.00	0.00	0.00

(b)

Attribute	Model	Precision	Recall	F1-Measure
Title	7 attr	56.29	56.13	56.18
	3 attr	57.17	55.75	56.41
Author	7 attr	72.32	61.25	66.30
	3 attr	72.04	61.50	66.30
Publisher	7 attr	90.42	48.10	62.47
	3 attr	88.26	49.13	62.74

4   Semi-supervised Named-Entity Recognition

In this section, we describe the idea to expand the number of product title data that can be extracted into attribute information. We apply NER model in semi-supervised way. We use bootstrapping method to generate more labeled data from unlabeled data. In our experiment, the unlabeled data is a collection of product titles in silver standard. The semi-supervised model is trained to extract only 3 attributes (**title**, **author**, and **publisher**).

4.1   Experiment

In this experiment, we change a little of the features setting to reduce the complexity of our algorithm to extract the attributes since the silver standard contains a great number of rows. We restrict the dictionary and embedding features only to cover the current token and one token before/after the current token.

We randomly split the silver standard into a hundred chunks, hence each chunk incorporates 827 product titles with their corresponding label (last chunk: 825 rows). Then, we split the first dataset into 75% training data and 25% testing data. Iteratively, for each chunk, we execute the following actions:

1. Leverage the training data to build a supervised CRF NER model;
2. Model is evaluated using the testing data and subsequently predicts the label of product titles in the chunk;
3. Predicted label is matched with the label in the chunk; and
4. Product titles with matching label are added to the training data;

The bootstrapping algorithm is illustrated in Algorithm 1.

Algorithm 1. Bootstrapping Algorithm

Data: L for labeled data, S for silver standard,
Randomize S and split it into a hundred chunks;
Split L into random train L_{train} and test L_{test} subsets;
for each chunk C (product titles P, labels P_{label}) **do**
    Train CRF classifier M using L_{train};
    Evaluate the performance of M using L_{test};
    Classify P with M obtaining their predicted label $C_{predicted}$;
    Match $C_{predicted}$ with P_{label} obtaining product titles with matching label L';
    Add L' to L_{train};

4.2   Result and Analysis

Initially, the value of the evaluation metrics is 65.69%, 59.79%, and 62.47% for precision, recall, and F1-measure respectively. After 20 iterations, we get the highest value of recall (66.14) and F1-measure (67.04%) due to a significant increase in recall for `title` attribute (from 58.90% to 65.85%). The highest value of precision is 68.96% and it is reached after 48 iterations. At this point, the precision of `publisher` attribute is up to 95.00%. In the end, we get 66.40%, 64.02%, and 64.91% for precision, recall, and F1-measure respectively or, in other words, the bootstrapping algorithm using silver standard can increase the performance of the model. As we can see from Fig. 2, the F1-measure score for all attributes increases. `Publisher` attribute has a significant increase of precision (from 79.17% to 95.00%). In contrast to publishers, `title` and `author` have increased quite dramatically in recall score (`title`: 59.79% to 64.02% and `author`: 62.00% to 70.00%).

Using bootstrapping method, we automatically label 29,647 product titles (35.85% of silver standard), which consists of 29,647 `title`, 9,709 `author`, and 578 `publisher` attribute labels.

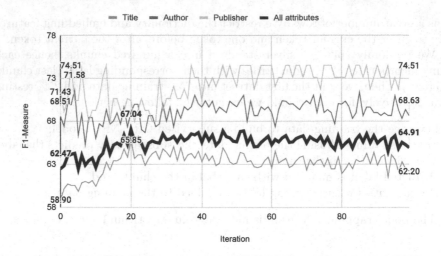

Fig. 2. F1-measure on each iteration of semi-supervised model

5   Conclusion

In this paper, we have demonstrated the attribute extraction from the product titles of book category products using named-entity recognition approach. We implemented Conditional Random Fields (CRF) to tackle the task that is modeled as sequence labeling problem. We carried out two sub-tasks. The first subtask is model building using 1,000 annotated product titles. The features used are lexical, position, word shape, dictionary, and embedding features. The second one is data expansion using the bootstrapping method. Our semi-supervised model achieved precision of 66.40%, recall of 64.02%, and F1 of 64.91% when extracting book attributes from 29,647 product titles.

For future work, we are going to experiment with deep neural network algorithm as attribute extraction model. Another direction is to propose more robust model to detect infrequent attributes.

Acknowledgments. This research was supported by the research grant from Universitas Indonesia, namely Publikasi Terindeks Internasional (PUTI) Prosiding year 2020 no NKB-854/UN2.RST/HKP.05.00/2020.

References

1. Dumont, B., Maggio, S., Sidi Said, G., Au, Q.-T.: Who wrote this book? A challenge for e-commerce. In: Proceedings of the 5th Workshop on Noisy User-generated Text (W-NUT 2019), pp. 121–125 (2019)
2. Ghani, R., et al.: Text mining for product attribute extraction. ACM SIGKDD Explor. Newsl. **8**(1), 41–48 (2006)

3. Joshi, M., et al.: Distributed word representations improve NER for e-commerce. In: Proceedings of the 1st Workshop on Vector Space Modeling for Natural Language Processing, pp. 160–167 (2015)
4. Lafferty, J., McCallum, A., Pereira, F.: Conditional random fields: probabilistic models for segmenting and labeling sequence data. In: Proceedings of the Eighteenth International Conference on Machine Learning, ICML, vol. 1, pp. 282–289 (2001)
5. Landis, J.R., Koch, G.: The measurement of observer agreement for categorical data. Biometrics, 159–174 (1977)
6. More, A.: Attribute extraction from product titles in ecommerce. arXiv preprint arXiv:1608.04670 (2016)
7. Nadeau, D., Sekine, S.: A Survey of named entity recognition and classification. J. Linguist. Investig. **30**(1), 1–20 (2007)
8. Putthividhya, D., Hu, J.: Bootstrapped named entity recognition for product attribute extraction. In: Proceedings of the 2011 Conference on Empirical Methods in Natural Language Processing, pp. 1557–1567 (2011)
9. Rif'at, M., Mahendra, R., Budi, I.: Towards product attributes extraction in Indonesian e-commerce platform. Computación y Sistemas **22**(4) (2018)

Knowledge Structures

Semantic Segmentation of MOOC Lecture Videos by Analyzing Concept Change in Domain Knowledge Graph

Ananda Das[(✉)] and Partha Pratim Das[(✉)]

Indian Institute of Technology, Kharagpur, Kharagpur, India
anandadas2005@gmail.com, ppd@cse.iitkgp.ac.in

Abstract. Long lecture video metadata needs to have topic wise annotation information for quick topic searching and video browsing. In this work we perform topical segmentation of long MOOC lecture videos to obtain start-time and end-time of different topics taught by the instructor. During teaching instructor uses different concepts to explain a topic. So instructor has his own way of selecting and binding these concepts to represent a topic. Additionally knowledge graph of a subject domain contains inherent domain knowledge. In this work we analyze how the instructor changes concepts during topic change, the inherent knowledge available in a domain knowledge graph, semantic similarity and contextual relationship between different concepts to perform topical segmentation of long lecture videos. As output, we get semantically coherent topics taught by the instructor along with their interval (start-time and end-time). We tested our approach on 61 long NPTEL[1] videos delivered on *software engineering* domain. Experimentally we find that the topic intervals generated by our system has ~83% similarity with the intervals present in the ground truth. Holistic evaluation shows that our approach performs better than the other approaches in the literature.

Keywords: Concept mapping · E-learning · Knowledge graph analysis · MOOC lecture video · Multimedia processing · Semantic segmentation · Video segmentation

1 Introduction

Massive open online courses (MOOC) is a great initiative aimed at open online access of educational contents. Renowned universities are also encouraging and contributing in this initiative. In India, National Program on Technology enhanced Learning (NPTEL) is taking this initiative by hosting lecture series of different subjects. In NPTEL, each course comes into series form, containing ~40 lecture videos. Each video is ~1 h long and consists of multiple topics taught sequentially by the instructor. As the video metadata lacks topical annotation, it requires to watch the whole video to locate a desired topic inside it. Automatically creating topical segmentation and annotation of lecture videos will reduce

© Springer Nature Switzerland AG 2020
E. Ishita et al. (Eds.): ICADL 2020, LNCS 12504, pp. 55–70, 2020.
https://doi.org/10.1007/978-3-030-64452-9_5

user effort of topic searching, locating and browsing inside a particular lecture video as well as in the whole lecture series.

Several research efforts have been put on topical segmentation of long lecture videos. In [6,17–19] topical segmentation is performed by analyzing transcript file associated with the lecture video. Later [8,10] applied deep learning based framework to perform topical and semantic segmentation of long lecture videos. Also [5,13,16,19] analyzed lecture videos synchronized with lecture slides to perform this task. The shortcomings of these approaches include 1) unavailability of large volume of labeled data to train deep learning based framework 2) noise present in the synchronized lecture slides displayed in the video 3) unavailability of auxiliary teaching material like power-point/beamer presentation. Also no work in the literature used domain knowledge at the time of performing topical segmentation. Usually knowledge of a subject domain can be represented in graphical form where each node denotes a concept and an edge represents the relationship between two concepts it connects. This graph is called domain knowledge graph that provides an overview of a subject and how different concepts are related to each other.

In this work we perform topical segmentation of long lecture videos by leveraging the inherent knowledge available in a domain knowledge graph ($\mathcal{KG}$). Also, at the time of teaching, instructor has his own way of selecting different concepts, connecting and combining them together to explain a topic. We combine these two information to perform topical segmentation of long MOOC lecture videos. We take NPTEL lecture videos, each of them is synchronized with lecture slides and associated with speech-to-text transcript. We identify unique slides shown in the video, their time interval and associated textual information from the transcript file. Using these information we construct graphlets, each represents a unique lecture slide shown in the lecture video. In each graphlet, the nodes are the concepts used by the instructor, an edge indicates presence of a direct connection between two concepts in the $\mathcal{KG}$ and edge weight represents the contextual semantic similarity between two adjacent concepts of that edge. Here 'contextual semantic similarity' means semantic similarity between two concepts in the context of the way instructor combines them together during teaching. The basis of our work is to analyze all these graphlets and find how concept change occurs between two adjacent graphlets. Finally, measuring the amount of concept change and contextual semantic similarity among concepts, our system provides boundaries (starting-time and ending-time) of different topics taught in a lecture video. The idea is schematically shown in Fig. 1 where we take a lecture video on 'Overview of waterfall model'. The diagram represents different concepts used by the instructor which are distributed into five different topics. Connectivities between these concepts are taken from the $\mathcal{KG}$ and edge weight represents contextual semantic similarity among concepts. After analyzing all the graphlets created from the unique slides, we can perform topical segmentation and mark the topic boundaries.

This paper is organized as follows. In Sect. 2 we discuss the literature. We describe the dataset and methodology in Sect. 3 and Sect. 4 respectively.

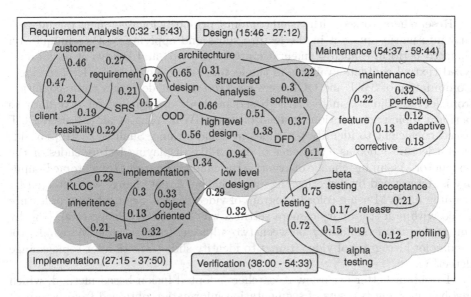

Fig. 1. Illustration of knowledge graph based topical segmentation of lecture videos. All the concepts covered in a lecture video are shown. Edge weight represents contextual semantic similarity among the concepts. Each topic, represented as a cloudy shape, consists of multiple concepts. Text in each rectangular box represents corresponding topic name and its interval.

Section 5 will show experimental results and related discussion. Finally we conclude our work in Sect. 6.

2   Literature Review

In literature, topical segmentation of lecture video is performed using either textual information or visual information or both. Textual information is available in the form of transcript or subtitle file. Visual information is obtained from the lecture slides shown in the video itself or from the auxiliary teaching material like power-point/beamer presentation.

Text based segmentation approach usually divides the text data into fixed size block with some overlapping. Then semantic similarity is measured between two adjacent text block and using a threshold value topic boundaries are determined. To obtain similarity, Lin et al. [15] used noun phrases, verb classes, pronouns and cue phrases as feature vectors. Modifying the above approach Shah et al. [19] represented the cue phrases by N-gram based model while Galanopoulos et al. [10] used word2Vec [17] based word embedding. In an another work Shah et al. [20] modified the above approach with the help of wikipedia text. They computed similarity between a wikipedia topic and each fixed size text block obtained from sub-title file. Based on all the similarity scores and a threshold value segment boundaries were determined.

Researchers worked with visual contents, primarily focused on extracting textual information present in the lecture slides and applying NLP techniques on them to perform topical segmentation. Che et al. [7] and Baidya et al. [5] analyzed textual contents available in the lecture slides shown in the lecture video. Combination of SWT and OCR were used to text line detection and recognition from lecture slides. Finally, NLP based methods are applied on text data to perform topic segmentation. Instead of using SWT, Yang et al. [23] used DCT based coefficient to identify text lines in a slide frame. Shah et al. [19] considered a lecture video as a sequence of events like displaying lecture slides or the instructor. Assuming change of event as the change of current topic, topic boundary is determined by detecting the event change. Event change was detected by training an SVM using color histogram of video frames. Segmentation of lecture video with non stationary camera settings was handled by Jeong et al. [13], by computing frame similarity between two adjacent frames, while Ma et al. [16] used color histogram of video frames to identify slide transition for topic change detection.

To obtain better accuracy, researchers adopted fusion based method, which involves merging two sets of segmentation information obtained from heterogeneous sources like speech transcripts, video content, subtitle file or OCRed text. Shah et al. [19,20] used both subtitle file and video frames and wikipedia text to get final segmentation. While, Yang et al. [22] proposed keyword extraction from slide text line and analyzing OCR and ASR transcripts of the video.

3   Data Acquisition and Preprocessing

3.1   Data Acquisition

In this work we use NPTEL lecture videos on *software engineering* domain. Each video is one hour long and associated with Transcript file. Details of the dataset is given in Sect. 5.1. We also create a knowledge graph in *software engineering* domain using the approach described by Zhao et al. [24]. This knowledge graph contains 44765 concepts taken from Stack Overflow [3] tagWiki and 35279 relationship triplets. We compute contextual semantic similarity (described in Sect. 3.3) between all pair of concepts and use them as edge weight. In our work we only use these concepts, their interconnections and edge weights while ignoring the concept properties and relationship names among different concepts.

3.2   Data Preprocessing

Text Data Preprocessing. In this step we perform preprocessing of the transcript file, available in pdf form. We parse the pdf file using third party open source library pdfminer [2]. We remove some information related to the lecture, like course name, instructor name, host institute name etc. which are located on top of the transcript file. Finally, We clean the file by removing junk characters.

Video Data Preprocessing. Video file displays lecture slides used by the instructor. We extract unique lecture slides and construct a graphlet from each of them. First we extract frames from the video file sampled at 3 s interval. There are three different type of frames are shown in the video and they are, presentation slide, instructor face and board work. In this work we are only interested in slide frames as instructor face do not contain any semantic information and we ignore board work as handwritten character recognition is out of scope of this work. To classify the slide frames, we apply transfer learning using inception-V3 [21] pre-trained model. Retraining is done using ∼4000 frames from each category and we obtain ∼96% accuracy ($F1$ score). Finally, we apply frame differencing technique [11] to remove duplicate frames and obtain unique slide frames. Time interval of a unique slide is considered as its first display in the video up to the first display of the next unique slide. We mark the boundary (first and last display time) of each unique slide frame and find its associated text data from the transcribed text. These boundary information and textual part are used in the later stages of our system.

3.3   Edge Weight Computation

In this step, we compute the edge weight between different concepts present in the $\mathcal{KG}$. Essentially, edge weight represents how two concepts are semantically similar with each other in the context of transcript file. We find semantic similarity between them considering the context of their co-occurrence. To determine the context we use FLAIR [4] api that runs on top of the BERT [9] model. Unlike static word embedding, BERT can produce dynamic word embedding considering the sentences in which a word has occurred. Here in our work, we capture the contextual semantic similarity between two concepts, so that we can analyze how instructor correlates and connects different concepts during teaching. We observe, a concept might occur multiple times in the transcript file. So, during similarity score computation, we consider all pairwise co-occurrences between two given concepts. We take the text chunk that contains first such co-occurrence and send it to the FLAIR api to find 2048 dimensional word embedding of each concept and calculate cosine similarity between them. We take all the co-occurrences between any two concepts, find multiple similarity scores between them and take the average to find final contextual similarity between them. After similarity computation is done, we use it as the edge weight in the $\mathcal{KG}$ if there exist a link between these two concepts. We maintain a dictionary which holds the contextual semantic similarity score between all pair of concepts present in the transcript file.

4   Methodology

In this step we create multiple graphlets, each of them is an induced subgraph of the $\mathcal{KG}$ and represents a unique slide in the lecture video. Time intervals associated with these graphlets are mutually exclusive and collectively they cover the whole lecture video. For finding topic boundaries, we analyze these graphlets to determine the concept change occurs in different time interval and how concepts are closely connected inside a topic. During our analysis we perform several operations on these graphlets like merging of two consecutive graphlets or finding centroid etc. We denote these resultant graphs as $G_t^z = (V_t^z, E_t^z)$ where, $t = \{0, 1, ...N \mid N \in \mathbb{N}^+\}$ represents the tth time interval and z will indicate the name of the graph generated by different operations. Following sub sections describe the detail segmentation steps.

4.1   Slide Graph Construction

First we construct an undirected weighted graph representing each unique slide frame and we call it *slide_graph*. To construct n^{th} *slide_graph* (G_n^s) we use transcribed text (say, TXT_n) associated with n^{th} unique slide, the $\mathcal{KG}$ and the edge weight dictionary created in Sect. 3.3. Construction steps are given below.

1. A vertex is created for each concept word in TXT_n, set vertex name as the concept and vertex weight as the term frequency of that concept in TXT_n.
2. We draw an edge between two vertices if there is a corresponding edge present in the $\mathcal{KG}$. Edge weight is assigned using the dictionary created in Sect. 3.3.
3. We remove direction information from the generated graph because during graph analysis in the next phase, a node may not be reachable from the other nodes, though there exists a strong connection amongst them.
4. If the generated graph is not connected, we draw an edge between two connected components whose weight is the maximum among all the possible edges between these two components.

4.2   Finding Potential Topic Boundary

In this step, we determine potential topic boundaries by analyzing all the *slide_graph*. During lecture, instructor changes current slide at the time of going to a different topic, but vice versa is not necessarily true. In fact usually multiple slides are used for explaining a particular topic and few consecutive slides are closely related. Here closely related means, these consecutive slides represent almost same concepts. In this step we identify closely related consecutive slides and merge them together. Also, we mark the slides which are not close and those slide changes might be the topic boundaries. We measure how much concept changes have been occurred between two consecutive lecture slides. We define *concept_change_score*, $CCS(j, j+1)$ between two consecutive *slide_graph*, $G_j^s = (V_j^s, E_j^s)$ and $G_{j+1}^s = (V_{j+1}^s, E_{j+1}^s)$ as follows.

$$CCS(j, j+1) = \begin{cases} 0 & : \{V_j^s \cap V_{j+1}^s\} = \phi \\ \dfrac{\sum\limits_{k=0}^{N} min(tf(v_k|v_k \in V_j^s), tf(v_k|v_k \in V_{j+1}^s))}{\sum\limits_{k=0}^{M} max(tf(v_k|v_k \in V_j^s), tf(v_k|v_k \in V_{j+1}^s))} & : Else \end{cases}$$

where, $N = |\{V_j^s \cap V_{j+1}^s\}|$ and $M = |\{V_j^s \cup V_{j+1}^s\}|$ and $tf(v_k|v_k \in V_j^s)$ indicates term frequency of vertex v_k when $v_k \in V_j^s$. Here consideration of term frequency is important. We observe that, instructor puts more emphasis on few concepts while other concepts are used for giving example or reference purpose. Throughout this paper we call them as primary and auxiliary concepts respectively. Usually, primary concepts have higher term frequency than the auxiliary concepts. Also, Concepts with higher term frequency indicates that instructor has spent more time on them than the concepts with lower term frequency. Leveraging this fact we consider term frequency in *concept_change_score* computation. Clearly *concept_change_score* is in range between $[0, 1]$ and its value is 1 if two consecutive *slide_graph* are exactly similar and 0 if their vertices are disjoint. An illustrative example of *concept_change_score* is shown in Fig. 2.

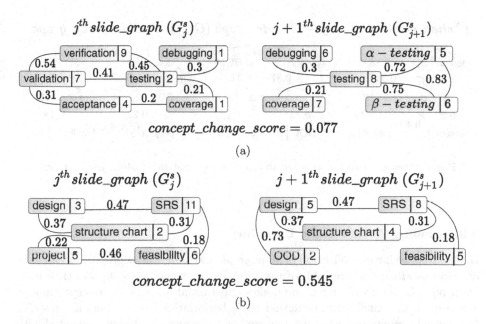

Fig. 2. An example of *concept_change_score* between two consecutive *slide_graph*. Each node represents a concept and its term frequency, edge weights indicate contextual semantic similarity among concepts. Slide changes shown in (a) is a potential candidate of being a topic boundary as most of the concepts are different and $CCS(j, j + 1)$ is low (0.077). While, (b) shows G^s_j and G^s_{j+1} are closely related as most of the concepts present in these two slides are same and $CCS(j, j + 1)$ is large (0.545) compared to the other.

We use this *concept_change_score* to identify consecutive *slide_graph* where significant amount of concept change happens and mark those slide transitions as potential topic boundaries. We also identify closely related consecutive *slide_graph* and merge them together as those corresponding slides represent almost same concepts. Steps to perform these operations are,

1. We compute *concept_change_score* between all pair of consecutive *slide_graph* and select those changes where the *concept_change_score* is less than the average value. We mark these changes as potential topic boundaries.

2. We merge those pair of consecutive *slide_graph* where *concept_change_score* is higher than the average value. We call this merged graph as *slide_group_graph*. A sample illustration of constructing *slide_group_graph* is shown in Fig. 3.

3. *slide_graph* merging policy is as follows. Consider two consecutive *slide_graph*, $G_j^s = (V_j^s, E_j^s)$ and $G_{j+1}^s = (V_{j+1}^s, E_{j+1}^s)$ which are merged to get *slide_group_graph*, denoted as, $G^g = (V^g, E^g)$. where, $V^g = V_j^s \cup V_{j+1}^s$ and $E^g = E_j^s \cup E_{j+1}^s$. Vertex weight is modified as the summation of its weight in G_j^s and G_{j+1}^s.

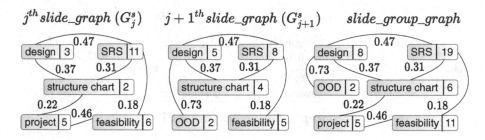

Fig. 3. Merging two consecutive *slide_graph* to construct a *slide_group_graph*.

4.3   Finding Actual Topic Boundary

In this step we have a collection of *slide_graph* and *slide_group_graph*. We call each of them as *cluster* where each of them represents some concepts and transition from one *cluster* to the next one makes substantial amount of concept change. Some of these transitions are actual topic boundaries while others are not. To find actual topic boundaries, we analyze how concepts are closely connected with each other within a topic than the concepts belonging in two different topics.

Primary and Auxiliary Concepts. In our dataset we observe, in each *cluster*, instructor primarily focuses on some concepts and rest are used for explanation or reference purpose. We call them as primary concepts and auxiliary concepts respectively. For example, to explain a topic, say "Agile Methods", instructor primarily focuses on concepts like, "sprint", "scrum", "eXtreme Programming", "face-to-face conversation" etc. But sometimes he also mentions "waterfall", "spiral" for reference purpose or "Zoho Sprints", "Kanbanize" to mention the tools used for agile. We also find that term frequency of primary concepts are higher than the auxiliary concepts. Leveraging this fact, we take only the primary concepts and their interconnection for finding actual topic boundaries. we create *cluster_centroid* from each *cluster* which represents the primary concepts and the interconnections among them. In this computation we consider top 70% concepts as primary concepts. We discuss the selection of this value in Sect. 5.3. Steps to construct a *cluster_centroid* are given below.

1. Sort the concepts in non increasing order according to their term frequency.
2. In case of tie in term frequency, we consider total weight of the incident edges to a concept. Here higher weight signifies a concept is semantically closer to other concepts than that of the concept with lower weight in incident edges.
3. Consider top 70% concepts and their interconnecting edges during formation of the *cluster_centroid*.

To detect actual topic boundaries, we consider three consecutive (say, i^{th}, $i+1^{th}$, and $i+2^{th}$) *cluster_centroid* denoted as $G_i^c = (V_i^c, E_i^c)$, $G_{i+1}^c = (V_{i+1}^c, E_{i+1}^c)$ and $G_{i+2}^c = (V_{i+2}^c, E_{i+2}^c)$ respectively. We represent the transition from G_i^c to G_{i+1}^c as $\tau(i, i+1)$ and from G_{i+1}^c to G_{i+2}^c as $\tau(i+1, i+2)$. We may encounter three different cases as described below.

1. **Case A:** If we find both $\{V_i^c \cap V_{i+1}^c\} = \phi$ and $\{V_{i+1}^c \cap V_{i+2}^c\} = \phi$, we mark $\tau(i, i+1)$ as a topic boundary. Otherwise there may arise two more cases with different situations.
2. **Case B:** G_i^c and G_{i+2}^c are in two different topics (say, *topic_x* and *topic_y* in chronological order). Instructor gradually changes from *topic_x* to *topic_y* through G_{i+1}^c. Different situations may occur like,
   (a) <u>Situation-1</u> Most of the concepts covered in G_{i+1}^c are part of *topic_x*, hence $\tau(i+1, i+2)$ is a topic boundary as shown in Fig. 4(a).
   (b) <u>Situation-2</u> Most of the concepts covered in G_{i+1}^c are part of *topic_y*, hence $\tau(i, i+1)$ is a topic boundary as shown in Fig. 4(b).
3. **Case C:** G_i^c, G_{i+1}^c and G_{i+2}^c all falls under same topic.
   (a) <u>Situation-1</u> There are some changes in concepts between G_i^c and G_{i+1}^c, but in G_{i+2}^c instructor again back to the concepts present in G_i^c as shown in Fig. 4(c).
   (b) <u>Situation-2</u> Most of the concepts covered in a particular topic are present in G_i^c and very few additional concepts are taught in G_{i+1}^c and G_{i+2}^c as shown in Fig. 4(d).
   (c) <u>Situation-3</u> Similar to the Case C: Situation-2, while most of the concepts are covered in G_{i+1}^c as shown in Fig. 4(e).
   (d) <u>Situation-4</u> Similar to the Case C: Situation-2, while most of the concepts are covered in G_{i+2}^c as shown in Fig. 4(f).

To handle these situations, we measure how different concepts are densely connected to each other within a topic. For a graph G, we define graph density metric $\delta(G)$ as, $\delta(G) = \frac{\sum_{k=1}^{N} w(e_k)}{N(N-1)}$, while, $w(e_k)$ is the weight of edge e_k and N is the total number of vertices in G. We take different combinations of *cluster_centroid*, compute their density and compare these density values with each other to find the actual topic boundaries. Here the idea is, concepts belong in same topic have more contextual semantic similarity than they are in different topics. Combined graph, denoted as, $\mathcal{C}(G_i^c, G_{i+1}^c) = (V', E')$ is formed by combining $G_i^c = (V_i^c, E_i^c)$ and $G_{i+1}^c = (V_{i+1}^c, E_{i+1}^c)$ where, $V' = \{V_i^c \cup V_{i+1}^c\}$ and $E' = \{E_i^c \cup E_{i+1}^c \cup \mathcal{E}\}$. Here, $\mathcal{E}$ represents set of additional edges present in the $\mathcal{KG}$ between any pair of concepts that belongs in G_i^c or G_{i+1}^c. Using these

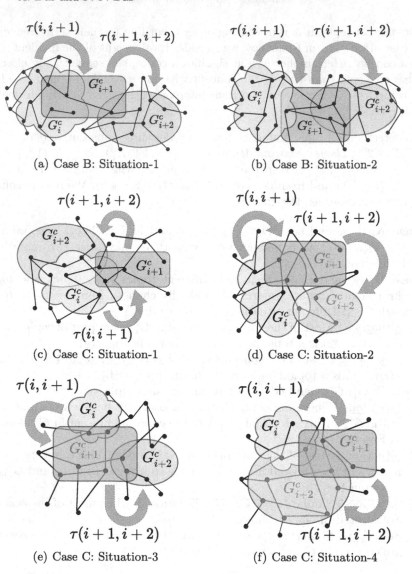

Fig. 4. Illustration of different situations occur during teaching. Small dots represent different concepts and lines connecting them are the edges. Cloudy, rectangular and oval shapes represent three consecutive *cluster_centroid* G_i^c, G_{i+1}^c and G_{i+2}^c respectively. Thick gray arrows represent the transition from one *cluster_centroid* to the next one.

density measure we compute actual topic boundaries using the algorithm shown in Algorithm 1.

Lines 5–10 handle *Case A* by computing vertex intersection between three consecutive *cluster_centroid* and mark $\tau(i, i+1)$ as topic boundary. *Case B* and *Case C* are determined by comparing density of different combined graph formed

---

Algorithm 1. Compute Topic Boundary List

1:   $tpBoundaries \leftarrow [\ ], start\_time \leftarrow centroidList[0].startTime, end\_time \leftarrow 0, i \leftarrow 0$
2:   $len \leftarrow centroidList.length$
3:   **while** $i < len - 2$ **do**
4:       $c0 \leftarrow centroidList[i],\ \ c1 \leftarrow centroidList[i + 1],\ \ c2 \leftarrow centroidList[i + 2]$
5:       **if** $c0.vertices \cap c1.vertices = \phi$ & $c1.vertices \cap c2.vertices = \phi$ **then**   ▷ Case A
6:          $end\_time \leftarrow c0.endTime$
7:          $tpBoundaries \leftarrow tpBoundaries \cup (start\_time, end\_time)$ ▷ $\tau(i, i + 1)$ is topic boundary
8:          $start\_time \leftarrow c1.startTime$ ▷ set start_time value for the next topic
9:          $i \leftarrow i + 1$
10:         $continue$
                                           ▷ compute density of different combination of *cluster_centroid* as described
11:       $m01 \leftarrow combine(c0, c1),\ \ delta01 = density(m01)$
12:       $m02 \leftarrow combine(c0, c2),\ \ delta02 = density(m02)$
13:       $m12 \leftarrow combine(c1, c2),\ \ delta12 = density(m12)$
14:       $m123 \leftarrow combine(c1, c2, c3),\ \ delta123 = density(m123)$
15:       **if** $delta02 > delta01$ & $delta02 > delta12$ **then**   ▷ Case C: Situation-1
16:          $i \leftarrow i + 2$
17:          $continue$
18:       **else if** $delta123 > delta01$ **or** $delta123 > delta12$ **or** $delta123 > delta02$ **then**   ▷ Case C:
      Situation-2,3,4
19:          $i \leftarrow i + 2$
20:          $continue$
21:       **else if** $delta01 > delta12$ **then**   ▷ Case B: Situation-1
22:          $end\_time \leftarrow c1.endTime$
23:          $tpBoundaries \leftarrow tpBoundaries \cup (start\_time, end\_time)$ ▷ $\tau(i + 1, i + 2)$ is topic
      boundary
24:          $start\_time = c2.startTime$ ▷ set start_time value for the next topic
25:          $i \leftarrow i + 2$
26:          $continue$
27:       **else if** $delta12 > delta01$ **then**   ▷ Case B: Situation-2
28:          $end\_time \leftarrow c0.endTime$
29:          $tpBoundaries \leftarrow tpBoundaries \cup (start\_time, end\_time)$ ▷ $\tau(i, i + 1)$ is topic boundary
30:          $start\_time \leftarrow c1.startTime$ ▷ set start_time value for the next topic
31:          $i \leftarrow i + 1$
32:          $continue$
33:   $end\_time \leftarrow centroidList[len - 1].endTime$ ▷ taking end-time of last cluster
34:   $tpBoundaries \leftarrow tpBoundaries \cup (start\_time, end\_time)$
35:   **return** $tpBoundaries$

---

by G_i^c, G_{i+1}^c and G_{i+2}^c. For *Case B:Situation-1*, graph density of $\mathcal{C}(G_i^c, G_{i+1}^c)$ is more than density of $\mathcal{C}(G_{i+1}^c, G_{i+2}^c)$ as G_i^c and G_{i+1}^c both belong in same topic and G_{i+1}^c and G_{i+2}^c belong in two different topics. Hence $\tau(i + 1, i + 2)$ is a topic boundary. These are handled in lines 21–26. In similar manner *Case B:Situation-2* is handled in lines 27–32. In *Case C:Situation-1*, concepts covered in G_i^c and G_{i+2}^c are almost similar but there is some concept change in G_{i+1}^c. So $\mathcal{C}(G_i^c, G_{i+2}^c)$ will have higher density value than that of $\mathcal{C}(G_{i+1}^c, G_{i+2}^c)$ and $\mathcal{C}(G_i^c, G_{i+1}^c)$ which is handled in lines 15–17. For *Case C:Situation-2,3,4* all G_i^c, G_{i+1}^c and G_{i+2}^c are in same topic, so density of $\mathcal{C}(G_i^c, G_{i+1}^c, G_{i+2}^c)$ is higher than the individual density of $\mathcal{C}(G_i^c, G_{i+1}^c)$ or $\mathcal{C}(G_i^c, G_{i+2}^c)$ or $\mathcal{C}(G_{i+1}^c, G_{i+2}^c)$. These kind of situations are handled in lines 18–20.

5 Experiments

5.1 Dataset and Ground Truth

In this work we use NPTEL lecture videos. NPTEL offers different courses, each contains ∼40 one hour long lecture videos. Each video is synchronized with lecture slides, *i.e.* at the time of lecture, instructor uses power-point/beamer presentation which is displayed in the video. Each video is associated with speech-to-text transcript file. NPTEL also maintains course syllabus containing different topics taught in the whole course. Usually each video consists of multiple topics taught sequentially and each topic constitutes of multiple concepts as chosen by the instructor. We collect lecture videos, transcript file and course syllabus of three lecture series related to *software engineering* for the experiment.

Ground truth are prepared by the course instructor and/or teaching assistants of the corresponding courses. From three courses on software engineering we get 61 annotated lecture videos. Ground truth is prepared by consulting the lecture videos and the course syllabus available in NPTEL website. Ground truth of a lecture video consists of several topics along with their start-time and end-time. An overview of the ground truth is shown in Table 1.

Table 1. Sample ground truth

Topic name	Start time (mm:ss)	End time (mm:ss)
Requirement Analysis	00:32	15:43
Design	15:46	27:12
Implementation	15:46	37:50
Verification	38:00	54:33
Maintenance	54:37	59:43

5.2   Evaluation and Comparison

We determine the topic name of a video segment by matching the textual similarities between slide titles and topic list present in course syllabus. Slide titles are extracted using standard methods described by Yang et al. [22]. Then, we measure cumulative similarity score between these titles and all topic names present in course syllabus. Topic name that have highest similarity score is assigned to the video segment under consideration. Once a topic name is assigned, we remove that name from the topic name list so that same name is not assigned to multiple video segments. We use Word Mover's Distance [14] for the similarity measure.

For evaluation, we measure the similarity between topic intervals generated from our system and intervals present in the ground truth. To find interval similarity of a topic, we measure the overlapping time ratio (*otr*) between ground truth and system generated interval information for a given topic. Conceptually *otr* is similar as Jaccard Similarity [12] and we define it as,

$$otr = \frac{\min(eTime_{gr}, eTime_{sys}) - \max(sTime_{gr}, sTime_{sys})}{\max(eTime_{gr}, eTime_{sys}) - \min(sTime_{gr}, sTime_{sys})}$$

Where, $(sTime_{gr}, eTime_{gr})$ is the time interval of a topic in ground truth and $(sTime_{sys}, eTime_{sys})$ is the time interval generated by the system. For multiple topics, we take arithmetic mean of *otr* for all the topics. We perform holistic evaluation of all the lecture videos in our dataset and measure similarity score of them. Table 2 shows similarity score of different lecture series.

Table 2. Interval similarity measure and comparison

Course name (no. of videos)	No. of topics	Interval similarity				
		Ours	Comparison with other methods			
			MTT	D&V	ATLAS	LectureKhoj
Software Testing (29)	123	**0.82**	0.72	0.69	0.75	0.65
Software Engineering (17)	75	**0.81**	0.74	0.72	0.65	0.70
Software Project Management (15)	68	**0.84**	0.77	0.78	0.73	0.77
ALL (61)	266	**0.83**	0.74	0.73	0.71	0.71

We also compare our approach with four different approaches present in the literature. They are, Modified Text Tiling (MTT) [15], D&V [10], ATLAS [19] and LectureKhoj [5]. MTT and D&V used transcribed text for segmentation, LectureKhoj considered only lecture videos with synchronized lecture slides and ATLAS used both textual and visual information to perform topical segmentation. Brief description of these approaches are given in Sect. 2. Due to the unavailability of their dataset we have applied their approach on our dataset. Holistic evaluation shows that our method performs better than other approaches. A detail comparison report is shown in Table 2.

5.3 Discussion

1. In Sect. 4.3, during *cluster_centroid* construction we used top 70% concepts of a *cluster* as primary concepts. Here we perform some experiments to find the optimal value for the primary concept percentage. This value is important because, for high value, we will take auxiliary concepts in *cluster_centroid* construction. These auxiliary concepts will create irrelevant connections between two consecutive topics hence, the system will discard some actual topic boundaries. While taking low value, we ignore some primary concepts resulting the *cluster_centroid* will be trimmed, resulting in introducing some topic boundaries which actually do not exist. In this experiment, we take different values of primary concept percentage and measure corresponding interval similarity. Fig. 5 shows the similarity score of different lecture videos under different settings. We observe, similarity is highest in the range [60%, 80%] for primary concept and it varies from instructor to instructor. Throughout the experiment we use this value as 70%.
2. We find, during teaching instructor changes topic in two different ways. One is to abrupt topic change, other is to changing a topic gradually. Handling of

these situations are explained in Sect. 4.3 and denoted as *Case A* and *Case B*. We find ∼26% topic change falls under *Case A* while rest are of type *Case B*. Our system achieves ∼94% interval similarity for *Case A* while, it drops to ∼79% for *Case B*. The reason is, for *Case B* topic boundaries in the ground truth usually reside in the transition part from one topic to the next one. While our system combines the transition part with the topic that is semantically closer to it, hence the system will never create topic boundary in the transition part. So for *Case B* topic boundary detection is not as exact as it is in the ground truth.

3. Sometimes instructor spends initial few minutes of a lecture video for introduction, which gives a bird's-eye view of all the topics to be covered. So, term frequency of the concepts in introduction part is not that relevant and the concepts may not be directly related to each other in the $\mathcal{KG}$. As our system leverages the term frequency and concept interconnections present in the $\mathcal{KG}$, it is not always able to successfully mark the introductory topic boundary. Our system marks introduction part successfully if next topic transition falls under *Case A*. Otherwise it merges the introduction part with the next topic taught, hence reducing interval similarity score.

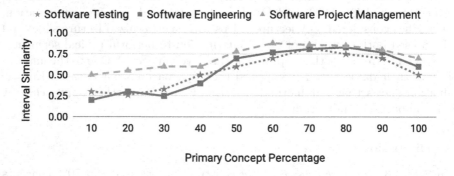

Fig. 5. Interval similarity vs primary concept percentage

6   Conclusion and Future Work

In this work we have performed semantic segmentation of long MOOC videos into different topics that helps in easy video searching and topic browsing. To do this we have utilized both domain knowledge and concept correlation created by the instructor during teaching. Domain knowledge is extracted from a knowledge graph in "software engineering" domain and concept correlation is obtained by computing contextual concept similarity using BERT model. In future we have a plan to improve our work by utilizing other information available in the knowledge graph such as relationship information between concepts, semantic properties of the concepts and hierarchical relationship between them.

References

1. National program on technology enhanced learning (2019). https://nptel.ac.in/
2. Python pdf parser (2019). https://github.com/euske/pdfminer
3. Stack overflow (2019). https://stackoverflow.com/
4. Akbik, A., Bergmann, T., Blythe, D., Rasul, K., Schweter, S., Vollgraf, R.: FLAIR: an easy-to-use framework for state-of-the-art NLP. In: Proceedings of the 2019 Conference of the North American Chapter of the Association for Computational Linguistics (Demonstrations), pp. 54–59 (2019)
5. Baidya, E., Goel, S.: LectureKhoj: automatic tagging and semantic segmentation of online lecture videos. In: 2014 Seventh International Conference on Contemporary Computing (IC3), pp. 37–43. IEEE (2014)
6. Basu, S., Yu, Y., Singh, V.K., Zimmermann, R.: Videopedia: lecture video recommendation for educational blogs using topic modeling. In: Tian, Q., Sebe, N., Qi, G.-J., Huet, B., Hong, R., Liu, X. (eds.) MMM 2016. LNCS, vol. 9516, pp. 238–250. Springer, Cham (2016). https://doi.org/10.1007/978-3-319-27671-7_20
7. Che, X., Yang, H., Meinel, C.: Lecture video segmentation by automatically analyzing the synchronized slides. In: Proceedings of the 21st ACM International Conference on Multimedia, pp. 345–348. ACM (2013)
8. Das, A., Das, P.P.: Automatic semantic segmentation and annotation of MOOC lecture videos. In: Jatowt, A., Maeda, A., Syn, S.Y. (eds.) ICADL 2019. LNCS, vol. 11853, pp. 181–188. Springer, Cham (2019). https://doi.org/10.1007/978-3-030-34058-2_17
9. Devlin, J., Chang, M.W., Lee, K., Toutanova, K.: BERT: pre-training of deep bidirectional transformers for language understanding. arXiv preprint arXiv:1810.04805 (2018)
10. Galanopoulos, D., Mezaris, V.: Temporal lecture video fragmentation using word embeddings. In: Kompatsiaris, I., Huet, B., Mezaris, V., Gurrin, C., Cheng, W.-H., Vrochidis, S. (eds.) MMM 2019. LNCS, vol. 11296, pp. 254–265. Springer, Cham (2019). https://doi.org/10.1007/978-3-030-05716-9_21
11. Gonzalez, R.C., Woods, R.E.: Digital Image Processing, 3rd edn. Prentice-Hall, Inc., USA (2006)
12. Jaccard, P.: Nouvelles recherches sur la distribution florale. Bull. Soc. Vaud. Sci. Nat. **44**, 223–270 (1908)
13. Jeong, H.J., Kim, T.E., Kim, M.H.: An accurate lecture video segmentation method by using sift and adaptive threshold. In: Proceedings of the 10th International Conference on Advances in Mobile Computing & Multimedia. pp. 285–288. ACM (2012)
14. Kusner, M., Sun, Y., Kolkin, N., Weinberger, K.: From word embeddings to document distances. In: International Conference on Machine Learning, pp. 957–966 (2015)
15. Lin, M., Nunamaker Jr, J.F., Chau, M., Chen, H.: Segmentation of lecture videos based on text: a method combining multiple linguistic features. In: Null, p. 10003c. IEEE (2004)
16. Ma, D., Agam, G.: Lecture video segmentation and indexing. In: Document Recognition and Retrieval XIX, vol. 8297, p. 82970V. International Society for Optics and Photonics (2012)
17. Mikolov, T., Chen, K., Corrado, G., Dean, J.: Efficient estimation of word representations in vector space. arXiv preprint arXiv:1301.3781 (2013)

18. Repp, S., Grob, A., Meinel, C.: Browsing within lecture videos based on the chain index of speech transcription. IEEE Trans. Learn. Technol. **1**(3), 145–156 (2008)
19. Shah, R.R., Yu, Y., Shaikh, A.D., Tang, S., Zimmermann, R.: ATLAS: automatic temporal segmentation and annotation of lecture videos based on modelling transition time. In: Proceedings of the 22nd ACM International Conference on Multimedia, pp. 209–212. ACM (2014)
20. Shah, R.R., Yu, Y., Shaikh, A.D., Zimmermann, R.: TRACE: linguistic-based approach for automatic lecture video segmentation leveraging Wikipedia texts. In: 2015 IEEE International Symposium on Multimedia (ISM), pp. 217–220. IEEE (2015)
21. Szegedy, C., Vanhoucke, V., Ioffe, S., Shlens, J., Wojna, Z.: Rethinking the inception architecture for computer vision. In: Proceedings of the IEEE Conference on Computer Vision and Pattern Recognition, pp. 2818–2826 (2016)
22. Yang, H., Meinel, C.: Content based lecture video retrieval using speech and video text information. IEEE Trans. Learn. Technol. **1**(2), 142–154 (2014)
23. Yang, H., Siebert, M., Luhne, P., Sack, H., Meinel, C.: Automatic lecture video indexing using video OCR technology. In: 2011 IEEE International Symposium on Multimedia (ISM), pp. 111–116. IEEE (2011)
24. Zhao, X., Xing, Z., Kabir, M.A., Sawada, N., Li, J., Lin, S.W.: HDSKG: harvesting domain specific knowledge graph from content of webpages. In: 2017 IEEE 24th International Conference on Software Analysis, Evolution and Reengineering (SANER), pp. 56–67. IEEE (2017)

Towards Customizable Chart Visualizations of Tabular Data Using Knowledge Graphs

Vitalis Wiens[1,2(✉)], Markus Stocker[1], and Sören Auer[1,2]

[1] TIB Leibniz Information Centre for Science and Technology, Hanover, Germany
markus.stocker@tib.eu
[2] L3S Research Center, Leibniz University of Hannover, Hanover, Germany
{wiens,auer}@l3s.de

Abstract. Scientific articles are typically published as PDF documents, thus rendering the extraction and analysis of results a cumbersome, error-prone, and often manual effort. New initiatives, such as ORKG, focus on transforming the content and results of scientific articles into structured, machine-readable representations using Semantic Web technologies. In this article, we focus on tabular data of scientific articles, which provide an organized and compressed representation of information. However, chart visualizations can additionally facilitate their comprehension. We present an approach that employs a human-in-the-loop paradigm during the data acquisition phase to define additional semantics for tabular data. The additional semantics guide the creation of chart visualizations for meaningful representations of tabular data. Our approach organizes tabular data into different information groups which are analyzed for the selection of suitable visualizations. The set of suitable visualizations serves as a user-driven selection of visual representations. Additionally, customization for visual representations provides the means for facilitating the understanding and sense-making of information.

Keywords: Scholarly communication · Knowledge graphs · Customizable visualizations · Information visualization

1 Introduction

Scholarly communication has not changed in its core during the last centuries. Research articles are typically distributed as PDF documents, and the amount of publications increases continuously every year [8]. As a consequence, searching, understanding, and organizing information becomes a burden. Finding and reviewing the literature is tying up cognitive capacity [1], and consumes time which consequently reduces the time available for original research.

The purpose of scientific articles is to inform and share findings. As a means for scholarly communication, the information is presented in documents using text, figures, and tables. While the descriptive text provides detailed insights,

© Springer Nature Switzerland AG 2020
E. Ishita et al. (Eds.): ICADL 2020, LNCS 12504, pp. 71–80, 2020.
https://doi.org/10.1007/978-3-030-64452-9_6

figures and tables serve as a visual, structured, and compressed representation of information. However, this information is buried in PDF representations [10].

The current developments in scholarly communication exploit Semantic Web technologies. These advancements transform the scholarly communication from document-based to knowledge-based information systems employing structured, interlinked, and semantically rich knowledge graphs [1]. In contrast to other Digital Library applications that organize primarily bibliographic metadata, the Open Research Knowledge Graph [7] (ORKG)[1] captures the content of research articles (e.g., research problem, materials, methods, and results).

Generally, the view on the information in scientific articles becomes static and frozen following publication. Thus, further analysis of presented information continues to be a manual effort for readers. Knowledge-based representations provide machine-readable access to information, which serves as input for various applications, including those addressing its presentation to humans. Therefore, it is beneficial to extract and transform the information of scientific articles into structured and machine-readable representations. However, due to its design for machine-interoperatbility and processing of information, the cognitive load for humans increases with growing size and complexity of such data structures. Visualizations serve a purpose of addressing specific information needs for the data at hand and human's ability to understand complex data through visual representations, "*a picture is worth a thousand words*" [13]. Following the information seeking mantra (overview, zooming/filtering, and details on demand) [15], we argue that user-driven approach for the generation of visualizations and their customization can further facilitate the sense-making of information.

In this article, we focus on the results of scientific articles in the form of tables. Tables provide an *organized* and compressed depiction of information. Various works, such as the recent work of Vu et al. [16], address the transformation of tabular data into knowledge-based representations. In contrast, the objective of our approach is to extract such information and provide customizable and meaningful chart visualizations of tabular data from knowledge graphs. In particular, we address the following challenges:

i) What minimal information structure is required in a knowledge graph to obtain visual representations of tabular data.
ii) How to analyze this structured information for visualization generation.

Our approach employs a human-in-the-loop technique to transform tabular data into knowledge graph representations with additional semantics. These additional semantics serve as the foundation for obtaining views of the knowledge graph that feed into various data visualization. Using the additional semantics, our approach recreates tables from knowledge graphs and enables the analysis of their content for the creation of customizable chart visualizations.

The remainder of this article is structured as follows. Section 2 summarizes related work, and Sect. 3 describes the proposed approach. Section 4 discusses the

---

[1] https://orkg.org.

limitations and implications for additional use cases. Finally, Sect. 5 concludes with an outlook on future work.

2   Related Work

The related work can be categorised into two groups: a) transformation of tables into knowledge graph representations; b) visualization of knowledge graphs. Addressing the former, the recent work of Vu et al. [16] represents the transformation process in the form of a mapping language (D-REPR). Heterogeneous datasets, such as tables in CSV or JSON formats, with different layouts are described in a model that defines components for the transformation into RDF. These components describe the dataset resource, its attributes and how data alignment is realized. A semantic model component describes how the data is transformed into RDF. Other approaches, such as XLWrap [9], focus on the transformation of spreadsheets into RDF. R2RML [3] is a W3C recommendation that addresses the mapping of relational databases to RDF. However, relational databases can be seen as tables, and therefore, R2RML techniques are also applied to transform tabular data into Semantic Web representations such as RDF. Due to the flexible nature of tables, the challenge of transforming tables into Semantic Web representations typically results in transformation models that are specifically tailored for individual datasets. Similarly, our approach is currently tailored for the representation of row-based-entries for one dimensional values.

Several definitions of knowledge graphs and its features exist; however, we lack a unified definition [5]. Ehrlinger and Wöß [5] argue additionally that "an ontology does not differ from a knowledge base", meaning that visualization methods for ontologies are also applicable for the visualization of the structure of knowledge graphs. According to a recent survey [4], most methods and tools visualize the content of ontologies using two-dimensional graph-based representations in the form of node-link diagrams.

Approaches, such as RelFinder [6] or the Neo4j graph visualization [11] address the visualization of knowledge graphs based on their structure (i.e., nodes and links). While node-link diagrams are well suited to represent the data structure of knowledge graphs, in some contexts, such as the visualization of tables, the structural representation will not facilitate the comprehension of information. Knowledge graphs have different structures and also contain additional information that does not serve the purpose for information interpretation (e.g., URIs or class assertions). Therefore, in order to generate suitable visualizations, the context and the semantics of the retrieved entries from a knowledge graph need to be incorporated and processed properly for the reconstruction of a table.

The Wikidata Query Service[2] is an application that is closely related to our approach. The system leverages SPARQL and presents results using different visualization methods. It provides a selection of visual representations (e.g.,

---

[2] https://query.wikidata.org/.

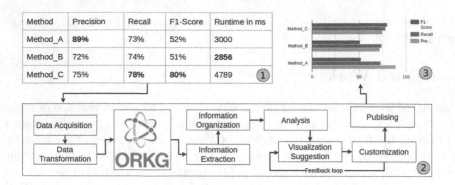

Fig. 1. Overview: (1) A table for artificial results of Precision, Recall, F1-Score, and Runtime. (2) Processing pipeline. (3) Resulting visual representation.

Table, Tree, and Timeline) for the resulting data. While the Wikidata Query Service provides a generic solution for the customizable visualization of knowledge graphs, we present an approach that incorporates additional semantics and guides the visualization generation process that is designed for the visual representation of tabular data in the form of customizable charts.

3   Approach

Our approach is motivated and aligned with the objectives of the Open Research Knowledge Graph (ORKG) [7], i.e., the structured representation of contributions in scientific articles and the facilitation of information perception and its sense-making. However, our approach addresses the customizable visualization for tabular data that originates from knowledge graphs. As a running example, we use an imaginary table summarizing the performance of different methods, which is common in Computer Science articles (see Fig. 1).

3.1   Data Acquisition and Transformation

At first, the data acquisition phase transforms the table into a knowledge graph representation and ensures the correct assignment of additional semantics using a human-in-the-loop approach. Knowledge graph structures typically reflect a triple-based representation $<s\ p\ o>$, where the subject s and the object o are interlinked by the predicate p. Our approach augments tabular data with additional semantics during the data acquisition phase, preserving the *context* which allows more efficiently to create further analysis and visualizations from this structured data. Our transformation model builds upon the following heuristics:

i) The cell entries of the first column provide the subjects; in our example, these are the methods. Thus, cell values of a row are bound to the method. Related to this, our transformation model is also row-based.

Build	Cancel	Add Row	Add Col			
Map to : Method ▾	Map to : Metric ▾	Map to : Metric ▾	Map to : Metric ▾	Map to : Metric ▾	Column Mappers
Method	Precision	Recall	F1-Score	Runtime	Headers
Method_A	89	73	52	3000	
Method_B	72	74	51	2856	
Method_C	75	78	80	4789	
	Unit : Percentage ▾	Unit : Percentage ▾	Unit : Percentage ▾	Unit : Mili second ▾	Unit Selection

Fig. 2. Widget for the tabular data transformation process eases the data input process and appends additional semantics to cell values.

ii) Other columns provide values for measurements of a metric. Thus, our transformation model adds to the cell value two additional attributes, namely the metric and the unit of the cell value. The header values of the columns determine the metric, while a human-in-the-loop approach assigns the units for the corresponding columns.

As illustrated in Fig. 2, a simple tabular input widget eases the process for the user to enter the data and also ensures the correct assignment of additional semantics for the table.

While, in general, the particular value is of interest, it is also necessary to incorporate the *context*. The numerical value "89" is just a data point lacking any meaning. Adding metric and unit to this value captures more *context*. This context enables to describe the cell value as: The value "89" describes *Precision*, it has the unit percentage, and it refers to a method (Method_A).

3.2 Information Extraction and Organization

The reconstruction of a table requires the information about the transformation model and its structural representation. This information is obtained from the data acquisition phase. However, due to the unknown order of returned triples, the ordering of rows and columns can change. Nevertheless, we obtain a reconstructed table with sufficient *context* for our example. Furthermore, the reconstructed table becomes interactive through corresponding implementations, e.g., sorting the columns ascending or descending based on their values. As illustrated in Fig. 3, this straight forth and back transformations provide already interactions with tabular data and another view on the information.

Method	Precision	Recall	F1-Score	Runtime in ms
Method_A	89%	73%	52%	3000
Method_B	72%	74%	51%	2856
Method_C	75%	78%	80%	4789

	Table View			
Method	Runtime ▾	F1-Score	Recall	Precision
1 Method_C	4,789	80	78	75
2 Method_A	3,000	52	73	89
3 Method_B	2,856	51	74	72

Fig. 3. Illustration of the original table and the reconstructed table from a knowledge graph. *Note*: The ordering of the columns is not preserved.

The reconstructed table serves as input data for chart visualizations. However, we argue that the *context* is viable for the creation of suitable chart visualizations. In this article, we define the context of a cell value as follows:

Definition 1. *Context(value(i, j)) = (RowLabel(0, j), Unit(i), Metric(i)) Where i >= 1, is the column index and j the row index.*

The *RowLabel* refers to the entries from the first column that are used as subject anchors in the knowledge graph representation. The *Unit* is provided by the user, and the *Metric* is obtained from the header values of the corresponding column. Data units are a crucial factor in creating meaningful chart visualizations. We argue that metrics with the same units provide *reasonable* candidates for grouping information and avoid false interpretations when visualized in the same chart, i.e., significant differences in data ranges shift the attention focus to the visual elements that have a higher presence in the chart, see Fig. 4.

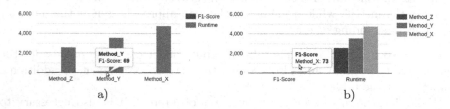

Fig. 4. Column chart visualization indicating the possible false first impression through unrelated units and large differences in the data ranges.

The semantics of *Units* provide the means to create information groups by clustering columns, i.e., the extraction of sub-tables through the matching of compatible units. These groups reflect information that relates (or co-relates) to a certain extend. The semantics of *Metrics* provide the means to guide the selection of suitable chart visualization types. In particular, it is the definition of compatible chart types for individual metrics.

Units: The additional semantics of *Units* provide means to align the cell values to a uniform representation for a particular unit. These semantics serve as alignment definitions between them. For example, percentage and per-mil are easily brought into correspondence using an alignment factor of 10, or milliseconds are transformed to seconds using an alignment factor of 1000. The semantics for unit alignment enable the approach to detect compatible units and bring them into correspondence for clustering related (or co-related) information.

Metrics: The semantics of metrics provide additional criteria for building information groups (i.e., the subdivision of sub-tables). As mentioned before, units provide *reasonable* candidates for clustering related (or co-related) information into groups. However, identical units are used in different metrics. For example, percentage can refer to performance measurements in information retrieval tasks or statistical distributions. The definition of compatible metrics refines the grouping of related information and determines which columns serve as input.

Metrics provide additional value validation mechanisms. In particular, they define a data range. For example, the metric *Precision* has a range of $[0, ..., 100]$, or *Runtime* cannot be expressed as negative values. This value range restrictions define a validation mechanism for transformation models that populate knowledge graphs with tabular data. However, the value range restrictions for the myriad of measurement factors need to be defined individually for each metric.

3.3   Customizable Visualization Generation

The analysis of the additional semantics performs the most of the heavy lifting. However, the dimensions of the table also pose restrictions on the selection of suitable chart visualizations. For example, spider-charts require at least 3 dimensions in order to span an area for a value. While this criteria is met when the number of rows is adequate (e.g., visualizing *Precision* with the corresponding methods as axial dimension), this representation becomes invalid if the axis mapping is flipped and the dimensional criteria is not met (e.g., only *Precision* serves as the axial dimension). This simple example indicates that the selection for axis mapping is also crucial for the visualization suggestion. As illustrated in Fig. 1, this refers to the feedback loop for the visualization suggestion.

4   Discussion

Our approach builds upon the semantics and the structure of the tabular data representation in a knowledge graph. Thus, it is currently limited to the chosen transformation model. Furthermore, the approach addresses the one dimensional representation of columns and rows. In our approach, the first column of the table refers to unsorted entries. However, when dealing with order dependent entries, such as time series or physical distances, the position on the axis (sorting) is significant for the information comprehension. Currently, our approach does not address order dependent entries in the first column.

The approach has been described in the context of tabular data visualizations within a single paper. However, tables are frequently used in scientific articles of various type. Incorporating additional semantics enables new opportunities for analysis of information across papers, too. In particular, through the additional semantics of units and metrics the information distributed across several tables (in different articles) can be organized for further analysis. Figure 5 show-cases the visualization generation of tables across different articles.

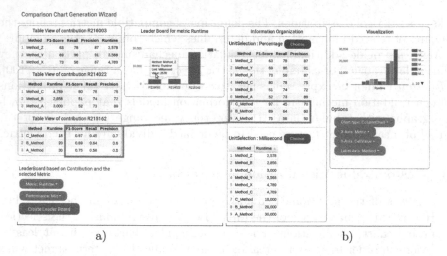

Fig. 5. Prototype for chart visualization using the comparison feature of ORKG: a) The individual tables, selection options for leader-board generation and a leader-board visualization; b) Information organization for merged tables and the resulting column chart. The value representation transformation is indicated in red. (Color figure online)

5   Conclusion

In this article, we have presented an approach for customizable chart visualizations of tabular data using knowledge graphs. The approach builds on additional semantics that are added during the data acquisition process. Using these semantics, tables are reconstructed and organized in information groups, i.e., sub-tables based on metrics and units. The semantics of *Metrics* select suitable visualization from a large space of all chart types. Customizations are enabled through chart type selection and axis mappings. Using the paper comparison feature of ORKG [12], the approach realizes advanced use cases, such as the visualization of information distributed among tables in multiple articles and leader-boards.

The *context* plays an important role in extracting tabular data from knowledge graphs and the creation of visual representations. Our approach creates the context using the a-priory known data structure and its additional semantics. Future work will address the extension for the definition of additional semantics related to order dependent entries for the first column. The semantics of *Metrics* define the interplay among them and which chart visualizations are suitable. Thus, future work will address the many definitions of metrics. Additionally, we plan to investigate the alignment to existing vocabularies related to units [14] and the RDF Data Cube Vocabulary [2] in order to increase the flexibility and robustness of the approach. Furthermore, we argue that pattern matching and sub-graph identification will enable the realization of semi-automated generation for context items that guide the information organization and the analysis, enabling the chart visualization of non-tabular data from knowledge graphs.

In conclusion, we argue that the approach introducing additional semantics and further rules will foster the creation of suitable and custom visual representations for tabular data using knowledge graphs and that it facilitates comprehension through different perspectives on the information in tables.

Acknowledgments. This work is co-funded by the European Research Council project ScienceGRAPH (Grant agreement #819536). Additionally, we would like to thank our colleagues Mohamad Yaser Jaradeh and Kheir Eddine for valuable discussions and suggestions.

References

1. Auer, S., Kovtun, V., Prinz, M., Kasprzik, A., Stocker, M., Vidal, M.E.: Towards a knowledge graph for science. In: Proceedings of the 8th International Conference on Web Intelligence, Mining and Semantics, pp. 1–6 (2018)
2. Cyganiak, R., Reynolds, D.: The RDF data cube vocabulary (2014). https://www.w3.org/TR/vocab-data-cube/
3. Das, S., Sundara, S., Cyganiak, R.: R2RML: RDB to RDF mapping language (2012). https://www.w3.org/TR/r2rml/
4. Dudáš, M., Lohmann, S., Svátek, V., Pavlov, D.: Ontology visualization methods and tools: a survey of the state of the art. Knowl. Eng. Rev. **33** (2018)
5. Ehrlinger, L., Wöß, W.: Towards a definition of knowledge graphs. SEMANTiCS (Posters Demos SuCCESS) **48**, 1–4 (2016)
6. Heim, P., Hellmann, S., Lehmann, J., Lohmann, S., Stegemann, T.: RelFinder: revealing relationships in RDF knowledge bases. In: Chua, T.-S., Kompatsiaris, Y., Mérialdo, B., Haas, W., Thallinger, G., Bailer, W. (eds.) SAMT 2009. LNCS, vol. 5887, pp. 182–187. Springer, Heidelberg (2009). https://doi.org/10.1007/978-3-642-10543-2_21
7. Jaradeh, M.Y., et al.: Open research knowledge graph: next generation infrastructure for semantic scholarly knowledge. In: Proceedings of the 10th International Conference on Knowledge Capture, K-CAP 2019, New York, NY, USA, pp. 243–246. Association for Computing Machinery (2019)
8. Johnson, R., Watkinson, A., Mabe, M.: The STM Report. An Overview of Scientific and Scholarly Publishing, 5th edn. (2018)
9. Langegger, A., Wöß, W.: XLWrap – querying and integrating arbitrary spreadsheets with SPARQL. In: Bernstein, A., Karger, D.R., Heath, T., Feigenbaum, L., Maynard, D., Motta, E., Thirunarayan, K. (eds.) ISWC 2009. LNCS, vol. 5823, pp. 359–374. Springer, Heidelberg (2009). https://doi.org/10.1007/978-3-642-04930-9_23
10. Mons, B.: Which gene did you mean? BMC Bioinform. **6**, 142 (2005)
11. Neo4j. Neo4j graph visualization. https://neo4j.com/developer/graph-visualization/. Accessed Mar 2020
12. Oelen, A., Jaradeh, M.Y., Farfar, K.E., Stocker, M., Auer, S.: Comparing research contributions in a scholarly knowledge graph. In: Proceedings of the Third International Workshop on Capturing Scientific Knowledge Co-located with the 10th International Conference on Knowledge Capture (K-CAP 2019), Marina del Rey, California, 19 November 2019, vol. 2526. CEUR Workshop Proceedings, pp. 21–26. CEUR-WS.org (2019)

13. Peña, O., Aguilera, U., López-de Ipiña, D.: Linked open data visualization revisited: a survey. Semant. Web J. (2014)
14. Rijgersberg, H., van Assem, M., Top, J.: Ontology of units of measure and related concepts. Semant. Web **4**(1), 3–13 (2013)
15. Shneiderman, B.: The eyes have it: a task by data type taxonomy for information visualizations. In: Proceedings of the 1996 IEEE Symposium on Visual Languages, Boulder, Colorado, USA, 3–6 September 1996, pp. 336–343 (1996)
16. Vu, B., Pujara, J., Knoblock, C.A.: D-REPR: a language for describing and mapping diversely-structured data sources to RDF. In: Proceedings of the 10th International Conference on Knowledge Capture, pp. 189–196 (2019)

Wikipedia-Based Entity Linking for the Digital Library of Polish and Poland-Related News Pamphlets

Maciej Ogrodniczuk[1]([✉]) [ID] and Włodzimierz Gruszczyński[2] [ID]

[1] Institute of Computer Science, Polish Academy of Sciences,
Jana Kazimierza 5, 01-248 Warszawa, Poland
maciej.ogrodniczuk@ipipan.waw.pl
[2] Institute of Polish Language, Polish Academy of Sciences,
al. Mickiewicza 31, 31-120 Kraków, Poland
wlodzimierz.gruszczynski@ijp.pan.pl

Abstract. The paper presents a series of experiments related to enhancing the content of digital library items with links to relevant Wikipedia entries that could offer the reader additional background information. Two methods of gathering such links are investigated: a Wikifier-based solution and search in Wikipedia using its integrated engine. The results are additionally filtered using frequency information from a large corpus and additional rules.

Keywords: Digital library · Entity linking · Middle Polish

1 Introduction

Creators of digital libraries storing older prints, such as The Digital Library of Polish and Poland-related Ephemeral Prints from the 16th, 17th and 18th Centuries [9] (Polish: *Cyfrowa Biblioteka Druków Ulotnych Polskich i Polski Dotyczących z XVI, XVII i XVIII Wieku*, hence CBDU), may have difficulties with providing users with background information about the items on a large scale. Adding manual explanations is costly: the attempt of augmenting CBDU with such information [10] resulted in historical commentaries added to only 65 prints, as compared to nearly 2000 objects present in the digital library.

In this paper we present the preliminary results of experiments of an enhancement based on automated linking of prints to relevant Polish Wikipedia entries. This task may seem straightforward taking into account the multitude of existing wikifiers, search engines and language models based on Wikipedia. Still, it presents several difficulties. The quality of the tools is not always high, also

---

The work was financed by a research grant from the Polish Ministry of Science and Higher Education under the National Programme for the Development of Humanities for the years 2019–2023 (grant 11H 18 0413 86, grant funds received: 1,797,741 PLN).

E. Ishita et al. (Eds.): ICADL 2020, LNCS 12504, pp. 81–88, 2020.
https://doi.org/10.1007/978-3-030-64452-9_7

because they may offer excessive hints, e.g. pointing to terms obvious to contemporary library user, hiding the valuable among the trivial ones. Thirdly, a simple search for named entities may not offer deep enough insight into the context, e.g. showing the user links to pages describing places but not events relevant to the item just because the event was not directly referenced in the text.

Wikipedia was used as the target resource for the linking process due to its universal character. Even though there exist several other resources useful for interpreting named entities (such as The Geographical Dictionary of the Kingdom of Poland and other Slavic Countries[1] [1] or Polish Biographical Dictionary[2] [5]), they are hardly as broad as encyclopaedic resources. The most accessible one, Wikipedia, contains not just references to people and places but also e.g. to important events such as battles or conventions which may be very relevant to interpretation of the contents of library items. What is more, for historical material the exhaustiveness of Wikipedia redirections covering e.g. multiple historical names of a place can be also very useful and not necessarily straightforward (such as redirection from Kircholm, a site of the battle in which forces of the Polish–Lithuanian Commonwealth defeated a much more numerous army of Sweden, to its present name Salaspils, currently a town in Latvia).

The paper follows the subsequent steps of the linking procedure. Sect. 2 presents resources used in the process, Sect. 3 comments on data preparation, Sect. 4 details the phases of the experiment and Sect. 5 comments on its results and attempts at analysing its errors.

2   Related Work and Resources Used

Entity linking is the task of associating name mentions in a text with their referent entities in some knowledge base. Wikipedia has long been used for this purpose [3,4,6] with several productive-level systems available. The two most popular ones are Babelfy[3] [7], a joint word sense disambiguation and entity linking system, and Wikifier[4] [2], the Wikipedia-linking system making use of the rich internal structure of hyperlinks between Wikipedia pages.

It must also be noted that the size of Wikipedia in particular language is of grave importance for the whole task since the linking process may be successful only when relevant articles are present in the resource. Luckily, Polish Wikipedia is one of the world's largest and most actively updated[5] and it provides a solid background to such experiments.

---

[1] See also https://en.wikipedia.org/wiki/Geographical_Dictionary_of_the_Kingdom_of_Poland.

[2] See also https://en.wikipedia.org/wiki/Polish_Biographical_Dictionary.

[3] http://babelfy.org/.

[4] http://wikifier.org/.

[5] Tenth place both in terms of the number of articles (over 1.4 million) and edits (over 60 million) according to https://en.wikipedia.org/wiki/List_of_Wikipedias#Detailed_list, as of September 2020.

Apart from wikization-based solutions, i.e. linking fragments of the texts being analyzed with corresponding Wikipedia articles (e.g. mentions of a city name with its Wikipedia page), another method worth investigating is topic discovery-based linking, i.e. identifying Wikipedia articles relevant to the text of the item as a whole. By combining the results of both methods the process may offer much broader context information and hint articles on issues not directly referenced in the article title or in article text alone.

The most straightforward mechanism to be used in the search and linking process is Wikipedia search engine itself, i.e. CirrusSearch extension of the default MediaWiki Elasticsearch[6]. CirrusSearch features e.g. faster updates of the index and template expansion capabilities to always include the full content in the results.

The last resource used in our experiments is the list of lemmatized unigram frequency counts extracted from a 300-million token balanced subcorpus of the National Corpus of Polish [12], serving for the frequency-based filtering of the results.

3   Data Preparation

The list of prints included in CBDU was based on an existing bibliography by Zawadzki [14] containing extensive metadata of objects such as full and abbreviated title, information about the author, publisher, place of publication, etc. These data was transcribed directly from the source item and as such they were in different languages (not just Polish but also German, Italian, French or Swedish since CBDU contains Poland-related prints coming from a variety of sources, also foreign ones). Since our experiment was intended to cover Polish, we decided to limit the current processing to one metadata field offering the longest textual content: Zawadzki's short descriptions of items attached to most records.

Since CBDU contains groups of related prints (e.g. referring to the same event such as victory of Polish troops over some foreign army, or being variants of the same account), print descriptions are often very similar. Therefore it seemed reasonable to pre-process the data to gather descriptions as much distant from one another as possible. To achieve that, one seed print was randomly selected and then prints the least similar to all items in the partially constructed result set were added until the target number of prints was reached.

Perl String::Similarity module[7] [8,13] was used to calculate the similarity between strings, expressed as a value between 0 (the strings are entirely different) and 1 (they are identical) with respect to the number of edits needed to change one string into the other. The value of 0.5 was used as similarity threshold and 100-character limit was arbitrarily chosen to eliminate shorter, less meaningful descriptions (such as 'Description of a big battle').

---

[6] See https://www.mediawiki.org/wiki/Help:CirrusSearch.
[7] See https://metacpan.org/pod/String::Similarity.

4 The Linking Process

The first part of the process was Wikipedia-based entity linking using existing solutions. Initial experiments with Babelfy and Wikifier showed that the first system offers very poor quality of lemmatization and disambiguation of Polish named entities (contrary to Wikifier) so the latter one was used for further experiments. The Wikifier returns a set of Wikipedia pages indicated as relevant to the given text (with respect to a certain pagerank threshold) with detailed information about which mentions support each annotation and alternative candidate annotations. The experiment in this study used the default threshold of 0.025.

It quickly became clear that pure wikification-based approach seemed unsatisfactory for providing context information since in many cases Wikipedia articles offered extensive information on a particular detail in one of their subsections even though the whole article title was too general to be present in the text being wikified. This is why search-based approach was investigated to supplement the inline results with a set of links. Among the many available approaches to searching full-text, the default Wikipedia search engine seemed sufficient with threshold set to three highest-ranked entries.

The relevance of results was then improved with a series of filters eliminating excessive entries. Firstly, dates frequently identified as relevant by Wikifier were removed as too general and non-informative. Secondly, frequency information from the National Corpus of Polish was used to keep only entries with a rank exceeding 10 000 on the list of lemmatized unigrams. This helped e.g. eliminate names of countries or larger cities such as Vilnius, familiar to the modern library user, and preserve the less-known places, such as Orsha[8] which might be worth linking in the interface. Thirdly, whenever lemmatized titles of Wikipedia articles overlapped, the less-specific entry was discarded (e.g. when both *Orsha* and *battle of Orsha* were indicated, only the article describing the battle was preserved by the algorithm).

5 Initial Notes on the Results

No formal evaluation of the process was yet performed but over 100 sample prints were automatically linked as part of the development phase in the process described above to provide data for future experiments. To preliminarily assess the linking quality they were at the same time manually annotated with links to Wikipedia by a linguist (not directly familiar with the content of the library to simulate the expectations of a non-expert user).

Table 1 presents the results for two sample prints: number 1: *List nuncjusza papieskiego w Polsce, Jakuba Piso, dat. w Wilnie 26 IX 1514 r., zawierający wiadomości o zwycięstwie wojsk polsko-litewskich pod Orszą 8 IX 1514. (En. Letter from the Papal Nuncio in Poland, Jakub Piso, dated in Vilnius 26 September 1514, containing news of the victory of the Polish-Lithuanian army*

---

[8] https://en.wikipedia.org/wiki/Orsha.

*in the battle of Orsha on 8 September 1514.) and 276: Relacja o wyprawie
króla Zygmunta III we wrześniu 1598 do Szwecji oraz o walkach prowadzonych
z ks. Karolem Sudermańskim, m.in. o bitwach pod Stegeborg i Linköping. (En.
An account of King Sigismund III's expedition to Sweden in September 1598
and the battles with Prince Charles of Södermanland, including the battles of
Stegeborg and Linköping.).*

The diagram shows how various stages of automated analysis intervened in
the results. For print 1, the notion of *Muscovite–Lithuanian War* (having a
separate Wikipedia article in Polish Wikipedia and a section *Fourth war (1512–
1522)* of an article on *Muscovite–Lithuanian Wars*) provides a valid context
not identified by the user while *Lithuanian–Polish–Ukrainian Brigade* is a clear
miss, present in the results because the brigade, formed in 2009, was named after
Konstanty Ostrogski, the commanded in the Battle of Orsha.

For print 276, the results were similar to user's choices. The only notion
excessively captured by the Wikipedia full-text search is the *Polish–Swedish
union* reference which seems too general to be included (while it still provides a
valid context).

At the same time it must be noted that surprisingly good ('semantically-
aware') results of wikification in several cases (such as with linking *the victory of
Polish-Lithuanian army at Orsha on 8 September 1514* (Pol. *zwycięstwo wojsk
polsko-litewskich pod Orszą 8 IX 1514*) with Wikipedia article *Battle of Orsha*
(Pol. *Bitwa pod Orszą (1514)*) may be caused by lucky co-incidence of the prepo-
sitional phrase *pod Orszą* in both the processed text and article header, without
any deeper understanding of the connection between the notion of a battle and
corresponding army triumph. Still, Polish battle naming convention (*'bitwa pod'*
(e.g. Waterloo) for 'battle of') is so fixed that it occurs it may be safely used for
discovery of relevant Wikipedia articles.

6 Conclusions and Future Inquiries

The presented experiments were intended to be the next step of linking digital library data, including CBDU, with external sources, following the process
described e.g. in [11]. Similarly to hyperlinking library item metadata, dictionary
annotations can also be created directly in the textual content of items, using
not just short abstracts but also its full content as the source for the linking
process.

Another path not investigated here is using different language versions of
Wikipedia. Since CBDU contains texts in a number of languages, its users might
be interested in a setting adjusted to their cultural context. At the same time
linking to foreign language Wikipedia also poses new problems related to differences between these resources both in size and in coverage (e.g. descriptions
of events in France relevant for the Polish reader may not even be present in
French Wikipedia).

A more careful analysis of the examples showed that sources other than
Wikipedia can in certain cases provide more useful information about the entities

Table 1. Annotation of two sample prints

Entity in Polish	Entity in English	Identified by a linguist	Identified with Wikifier	Identified with Wiki search	After date filter	After frequency filter	After overlap removal
Wilno	Vilnius		✓		✓		
1514	1514		✓		✓	✓	
Rzeczpospolita Obojga Narodów	Polish–Lithuanian Commonwealth		✓		✓	✓	✓
Polska	Poland		✓		✓	✓	
Orsza	Orsha		✓		✓	✓	✓
Nuncjusz apostolski	Papal nuncio		✓		✓	✓	✓
Bitwa pod Orszą (1514)	Battle of Orsha	✓	✓	✓	✓	✓	✓
Wojna litewsko-moskiewska	Muscovite–Lithuanian War			✓	✓	✓	✓
Brygada litewsko-polsko-ukraińska	Lithuanian–Polish–Ukrainian Brigade			✓	✓	✓	
Linköping	Linköping		✓		✓	✓	
Szwecja	Sweden		✓		✓	✓	✓
Karol IX Waza	Charles IX of Sweden	✓	✓		✓	✓	✓
1598	1598		✓		✓	✓	✓
Zygmunt III Waza	Sigismund III Vasa	✓			✓	✓	✓
Bitwa pod Linköping	Battle of Stångebro	✓		✓	✓	✓	✓
Unia polsko-szwedzka	Polish–Swedish union			✓	✓	✓	
Bitwa pod Stegeborgiem	Battle of Stegeborg			✓	✓	✓	✓

identified in the text. For instance, Jakub Piso, a person referenced in print 1 analysed in the previous section, is not present in Wikipedia but has an entry in the online Encyclopaedia of Cracow[9]. Such discoveries can be non-trivial but may hint that the wikization process can serve as an initial step to further manual annotation of items.

The proposed workflow can be applied both to the entire collections of prints in digital libraries as well as individual items enhanced with links to data. In the context of CDBU, processing of the whole collection would also help create a new, 'wikified' edition of Zawadzki's bibliography with links from electronic text directly to Wikipedia or other sources.

Acknowledgments. The authors would like to thank Grzegorz Kulesza for his diligent proofreading of this paper.

References

1. Słownik geograficzny Królestwa Polskiego i innych krajów słowiańskich (Geographical Dictionary of the Kingdom of Poland), Warszawa (1880). (in Polish)
2. Brank, J., Leban, G., Grobelnik, M.: Semantic annotation of documents based on Wikipedia concepts. Informatica **42**(1), 23–31 (2018). http://www.informatica.si/index.php/informatica/article/view/2228
3. Bunescu, R., Paşca, M.: Using encyclopedic knowledge for named entity disambiguation. In: 11th Conference of the European Chapter of the Association for Computational Linguistics, Trento, Italy. Association for Computational Linguistics (2006). https://www.aclweb.org/anthology/E06-1002
4. Cucerzan, S.: Large-scale named entity disambiguation based on Wikipedia data. In: Proceedings of the 2007 Joint Conference on Empirical Methods in Natural Language Processing and Computational Natural Language Learning (EMNLP-CoNLL), Prague, Czech Republic, pp. 708–716. Association for Computational Linguistics (2007). https://www.aclweb.org/anthology/D07-1074
5. Konopczyński, W.: Polski słownik biograficzny (Polish Biographical Dictionary). Polska Akademia Umiejętności (1935). (in Polish)
6. Milne, D., Witten, I.H.: Learning to link with Wikipedia. In: Proceedings of the 17th ACM Conference on Information and Knowledge Management, CIKM 2008, New York, NY, USA, pp. 509–518. Association for Computing Machinery (2008). https://doi.org/10.1145/1458082.1458150
7. Moro, A., Raganato, A., Navigli, R.: Entity linking meets word sense disambiguation: a unified approach. Trans. Assoc. Comput. Linguist. (TACL) **2**, 231–244 (2014)
8. Myers, E.W.: An O(ND) difference algorithm and its variations. Algorithmica **1**(1), 251–266 (1986). https://doi.org/10.1007/BF01840446
9. Ogrodniczuk, M., Gruszczyński, W.: Digital library of Poland-related old ephemeral prints: preserving multilingual cultural heritage. In: Proceedings of the Workshop on Language Technologies for Digital Humanities and Cultural Heritage, Hissar, Bulgaria, pp. 27–33 (2011). http://www.aclweb.org/anthology/W11-4105

---

[9] https://encyklopediakrakowa.pl/slawni-i-zapomniani/103-p/958-piso-jakub.html.

10. Ogrodniczuk, M., Gruszczyński, W.: Digital library 2.0 — source of knowledge and research collaboration platform. In: Calzolari, N., et al. (eds.) Proceedings of the Ninth International Conference on Language Resources and Evaluation (LREC 2014), Reykjavík, Iceland, pp. 1649–1653. European Language Resources Association (2014). http://www.lrec-conf.org/proceedings/lrec2014/pdf/14_Paper.pdf
11. Ogrodniczuk, M., Gruszczyński, W.: Connecting data for digital libraries: the library, the dictionary and the corpus. In: Jatowt, A., Maeda, A., Syn, S.Y. (eds.) ICADL 2019. LNCS, vol. 11853, pp. 125–138. Springer, Cham (2019). https://doi.org/10.1007/978-3-030-34058-2_13
12. Przepiórkowski, A., Bańko, M., Górski, R.L., Lewandowska-Tomaszczyk, B. (eds.): Narodowy Korpus Języka Polskiego (National Corpus of Polish). Wydawnictwo Naukowe PWN, Warsaw (2012). (in Polish)
13. Ukkonen, E.: Algorithms for approximate string matching. Inf. Control **64**(1–3), 100–118 (1985). https://doi.org/10.1016/S0019-9958(85)80046-2
14. Zawadzki, K.: Gazety ulotne polskie i Polski dotyczące z XVI, XVII i XVIII wieku (Polish and Poland-related Ephemeral Prints from the 16th-18th Centuries). National Ossoliński Institute, Polish Academy of Sciences, Wrocław (1990). (in Polish)

Representing Semantified Biological Assays in the Open Research Knowledge Graph

Marco Anteghini[1,2(✉)] (ID), Jennifer D'Souza[3] (ID),
Vitor A. P. Martins dos Santos[1,2] (ID), and Sören Auer[3] (ID)

[1] Lifeglimmer GmbH, Markelstr. 38, 12163 Berlin, Germany
{anteghini,vds}@lifeglimmer.com
[2] Laboratory of Systems and Synthetic Biology, Wageningen University & Research,
Stippeneng 4, 6708 WE Wageningen, The Netherlands
[3] TIB Leibniz Information Centre for Science and Technology, Hanover, Germany
{jennifer.dsouza,soeren.auer}@tib.eu

Abstract. In the biotechnology and biomedical domains, recent text mining efforts advocate for machine-interpretable, and preferably, semantified, documentation formats of laboratory processes. This includes wet-lab protocols, (in)organic materials synthesis reactions, genetic manipulations and procedures for faster computer-mediated analysis and predictions. Herein, we present our work on *the representation of semantified bioassays in the Open Research Knowledge Graph (ORKG)*. In particular, we describe a semantification system work-in-progress to generate, automatically and quickly, the critical semantified bioassay data mass needed to foster a consistent user audience to adopt the ORKG for recording their bioassays and facilitate the organisation of research, according to FAIR principles.

Keywords: Bioassays · Open Research Knowledge Graph · Open science graphs

1 Introduction

More and more scholarly digital library initiatives aim at fostering the digitalization of traditional document-based scholarly articles [1–3,6,10,11,18,26]. This means structuring and organizing, in a fine-grained manner, knowledge elements from previously unstructured scholarly articles in a Knowledge Graph. These efforts are analogous to the digital transformation seen in recent years in other information-rich publishing and communication services, e.g., e-commerce product catalogs instead of mailorder catalogs, or online map services instead of

Supported by TIB Leibniz Information Centre for Science and Technology, the EU H2020 ERC project ScienceGRaph (GA ID: 819536) and the ITN PERICO (GA ID: 812968).

E. Ishita et al. (Eds.): ICADL 2020, LNCS 12504, pp. 89–98, 2020.
https://doi.org/10.1007/978-3-030-64452-9_8

printed street maps. For these services, the traditional document-based publication was not just digitized (by making digitized PDFs of the analog artifacts available) but has seen a comprehensively transformative digitalization.

Of available scholarly knowledge digitalization avenues [1–3,6,10,11,18], we highlight the Open Research Knowledge Graph (ORKG) [12]. It is a next-generation digital library (DL) that focuses on ingesting information in scholarly articles as machine-actionable knowledge graphs (KG). In it, an article is represented with both (bibliographic) metadata and semantic descriptions (as subject-predicate-object triples) of its *contributions*. ORKG has a number of advantages as: 1) it enables flexible semantic content modeling (i.e., ontologized or not, depending on the user or domain); 2) it semantifies *contributions* at various levels of granularity from shallow to fine-grained; and 3) it publishes persistent KG links per article contribution that it contains. For further technical details about the platform, we refer the reader to the introductory paper [12].

The ORKG DL aims to integrate and interlink contributions' KGs for Science at large, i.e. multidisciplinarily. Thus far, ongoing efforts are in place for integrating scholarly contributions from at least two disciplines, viz. Math [21] (e.g., https://www.orkg.org/orkg/paper/R12192) and the Natural Language Processing subdomain in AI [9] (e.g., https://www.orkg.org/orkg/paper/R44253). Moreover, the ORKG also has a separate feature to automatically import individual articles' contributions data found tabulated in survey articles [20]. E.g., an ORKG object for Earth Science articles' contributions surveyed: https://www.orkg.org/orkg/comparison/R38484. Since surveys are written in most disciplines, this latter feature directly targets the ORKG aim; however, its sole limitation is that it is restricted only to those papers that have been surveyed. On the other hand, with the per-domain semantification models, articles not surveyed can be also modeled in the ORKG.

In this paper, we describe our ongoing work in extending the ORKG to integrate biological assays from the Biochemistry discipline. For bioassays, a semantification model already exists as the BioAssay Ontology (BAO) [25]. However, we need to design a pragmatic workflow for integrating bioassays semantified by the BAO in the ORKG DL. To this end, we discuss the manual and automatic process of integrating such semantified data in the ORKG DL. Furthermore, we show how these semantified data integrated in the ORKG is amenable to advanced computational processing support for the researcher.

With the volume of research burgeoning [14], adopting a finer-grained semantification as KG for scholarly content representation is compelling. Better semantification means better machine actionability, which in turn means innumerable possibilities of advanced computational functions on scholarly content. One function especially poignant in this era of the publications deluge [13], is computational support to alleviate the manual information ingestion cognitive burden. This is precisely the computational support showcase we depict from the ORKG DL over our integrated bioassay KGs, consequently highlighting the benefits of digitalizing bioassays and of the ORKG DL platform.

2   Our Work-In-Progress Aims and Motivations

Allowing practitioners to easily search for similar bioassays as well as compare these semantically structured bioassays on their key properties.

Why Integrate Bioassays in a Knowledge Graph? Until their recent semantification in an expert-annotated dataset of 983 bioassays [7,22,24] based on the BAO [25], bioassays were published in the form of plain text. Integrating their semantified counterpart in a KG facilitates their advanced computational processing. Consider that key assay concepts related to biological screening, including Perturbagen, Participants, Meta Target and Detection Technology, will be machine-actionable. This widens the potential for relational enrichment and interlinking when integrated with machine-interpretable formats of wet lab protocols and inorganic materials synthesis reactions and procedures [15–17,19]. Furthermore, in this era of neural-based ML technologies, KG-based word embeddings foster new inferential discovery mechanisms given that they encode high-dimensional semantic spaces [5] with bioassay KGs so far untested for.

Why the ORKG DL [2]? The core of the setup of knowledge-based digitalized information flows is the distributed, decentralized, collaborative creation and evolution of information models. Moreover, vocabularies, ontologies, and knowledge graphs to establish a common understanding of the data between the various stakeholders. And, importantly, the integration of these technologies into the infrastructure and processes of search and knowledge exchange toward a research library of the future. The ORKG DL is such a solution. Implemented within TIB, as a central library and information centre for science and technology, it also promises development longevity: the Leibniz Association institutional networks presents a critical mass of application domains and users to enhance the infrastructure and continuously integrate new knowledge disciplines.

With these considerations in place, the work described in the subsequent sections is being carried forth. Next, we describe our approach in the context of two main research questions.

3   Approach: Digitalization of Biological Assays

RQ1: *What are steps for manually digitalizing a Bioassay in the ORKG?* The digitalization is based on the prior requirement that text-based bioassays are semantified based on the BioAssay Ontology (BAO) [25]. This is the manual aspect of the digitalization process involving domain experts or the assay authors themselves. In Fig. 1, we show an example of a manually pre-semantified bioassay integrated in ORKG. This bioassay was semantified on eight properties based on the BAO. It was drawn from an expert-annotated set of 983 bioassays [22,24]. In terms of salient features, the bioassays in this dataset have 53 triple semantic statements on average with a minimum of 5 and a maximum of 92 statements; there are 42 different types of bioassays (e.g., luciferase reporter gene assay,

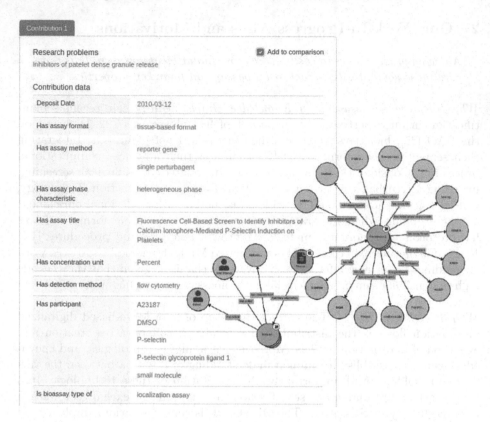

Fig. 1. An ORKG representation of a semantified Bioassay with an overlayed graph view of the assay. Accessible at: https://www.orkg.org/orkg/paper/R48178

protein-protein interaction assay—see in appendix the full list); and there are 11 assay formats (e.g., cell-based, biochemical). Thus, the manual semantification task complexity can be viewed as 53 modeling decisions.

In gist, the manual digitalizaton of a bioassay in the ORKG includes: 1) *a BAO-based semantification step*: forming subject-predicate-object triples of the bioassay text content based on the BAO. E.g., for the assay in Fig. 1, a few of its semantic triples are: (Contribution, Has assay format, tissue-based format), (Contribution, Has assay method, reporter gene), among others. And as a recommended step, 2) associating each ontologized resource (i.e., a subject, a predicate, an object) with a URI as its defining class in the original ontology, which for bioassays is the BAO.

Having just described the manual digitalization workflow, we next present our hybrid workflow that is currently in development. In this, we decide to incorporate automated semantification which levies pragmatic considerations in the digitalization of bioassays in the ORKG. Relatedly, there is an existing hybrid system [7] for semantifying bioassays involving machine learning and expert interaction which inspires our work. Nonetheless, we differ. While their learning-based component relies heavily on explicitly encoded syntactic features of the text, ours relies on neural networks based on the current state-of-the-art transformer models [23] trained on millions of scientific articles [4]. Such systems by encoding high-dimensional semantic spaces of the underlying text, obviate the need to make explicit considerations for features of the text. Moreover, they significantly outperform systems designed based on explicit features [8]—with due credit to the system by Clark et al. [7] designed prior to the onset of this revolutionary technology. Next, our hybrid workflow is designed toward a practical end—to be integrated in the ORKG DL which has a predominant focus on the digitalization of scholarly knowledge content multidisciplinarily, thus setting it apart from any existing DL.

RQ2: *What are the modules needed in the hybrid digitalization of Bioassays in the ORKG?* Essentially, given a new bioassay text input, we are implementing two modules in a two-step workflow as follows: 1) an automated semantifier; and 2) a human-in-the-loop curation of the predicted labels either by the assay author or a dedicated curator. Unlike the manual workflow, this presents a much easier and less time-intensive task for the human. They would be merely selecting the correctly predicted triples, deleting the incorrect ones, or defining new ones as needed. Assuming a well-trained machine learning module, the latter two steps may be entirely omitted. Toward this hybrid workflow, as work in progress, the automated semantifier is in development, and we are also implementing extensions in the ORKG infrastructure to include additional front-end views as assay curation interfaces.

4   Solving the Cognitive Information Ingestion Hurdle: Comparison Surveys Across KG-Based Bioassays

Premise: We need an information processing tool that can be used by biomedical practitioners to quickly comprehend bioassays' key properties.

The ORKG DL has a computational feature to generate and publish surveys in the form of a tabulated comparisons of the KG nodes [20]. To demonstrate this feature, we manually entered the data of three semantified bioassays in the ORKG DL. Applying then the ORKG survey feature on the three assays aggregates their semantified graph nodes in tabulated comparisons across the assays. This is depicted in Fig. 2. With such structured computations enabled, we have a novel approach to uncovering and presenting information relying on aggregated scholarly knowledge. The computation shown in Fig. 2 aligns closely with the notion of the traditional survey articles, except it is fully automated and operates on machine-actionable knowledge elements. The BAO-semantified assays are compared side-by-side on their graph nodes. Thus, tracking the progress on bioassays, can be eased from a task of several days to a few minutes.

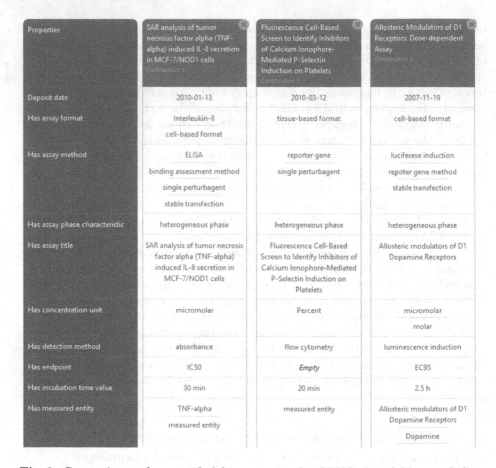

Fig. 2. Comparisons of semantified bioassays in the ORKG digital library. Online https://www.orkg.org/orkg/comparison?contributions=R48195,R48179,R48147

5   Conclusion

Thus in this paper, we outlined a vision in two separate workflows for integrating bioassay knowledge in the ORKG DL and our ongoing work to this end. The implications of bioassay structured and machine-actionable knowledge are broad.

To mention just one in the particular context of the current Covid-19 pandemic: The discovery of cures for diseases can be greatly expedited if scientists are given intelligent information access tools, and our work toward automatically semantifying bioassays are a step in this direction.

To this end, the workflows prescribed in this work offer the possibilities to chose between a manual or a semi-automatic strategy for bioassays' semantification within a real-world digital library.

We would like to invite interested researchers to collaborate with us on the following topics: 1) generating a large dataset of semantically structured bioassays;

2) user evaluation of our semi-automated system for semantically structuring bioassay data.

We deem this as a starting point for a discussion in the community ultimately leading to more clearly defined technical requirements, and a roadmap for fulfilling the potential of the ORKG as a next-generation digital library for fine-grained semantified access to scholarly content.

A Bioassay types

See Table 1.

Table 1. List of the different bioassay types present in our dataset

Bioassay types	
Protein-protein interaction	Hydrolase activity
Kinase activity	Protein-small molecule interaction
Viability	Beta lactamase reporter gene
Cytochrome P450 enzyme activity	Luciferase enzyme activity
Luciferase reporter gene	Oxidoreductase activity
Protein unfolding	Chaperone activity
Lyase activity	Transporter
Plasma membrane potential	Dye redistribution
Calcium redistribution	Apoptosis
Beta lactamase reporter gene	Beta galactosidase reporter gene
Phosphatase activity	cAMP redistribution
IP1 redistribution	Cell morphology
Phosphorylation	Transferase activity
Isomerase activity	Protein redistribution
Radioligand binding	Signal transduction
Ion channel	Platelet activation
Fluorescent protein reporter gene	Protein-DNA interaction
Protease activity	Cell permeability
Protein stability	Protein-turnover
Localization	Organism behavior
Cytotoxicity	Cell growth

B Preliminary Results of Automated Semantification: SciBERT-based Bioassay Semantifier

The semantic statements depicted in Fig. 3 were automatically generated from SciBERT-based [4] neural semantification system. These predictions were made

Labels:
has percent response -> efficacy
has role -> culture medium
has signal direction -> signal increase corresponding to inhibition
has manufacturer -> IntelliCyt Corporation
has assay method -> single perturbagen
has organism -> Homo sapiens
involves biological process -> platelet activation
has concentration throughput -> multiple concentration
has participant # has role -> membrane protein # target
has assay method -> binding assessment method
has role -> instrumentation manufacturer
has assay control -> negative control
has participant # has role -> small molecule # perturbagen
has assay medium -> FACS buffer, BD Biosciences
has manufacturer -> Perkin Elmer
has repetition throughput -> single repetition
has role -> biologics and screening manufacturer
has assay readout content -> single readout
has assay format -> tissue-based format
has target -> blood plasma
has percent response -> percent inhibition
has signal direction -> signal decrease corresponding to inhibition
is bioassay type of -> platelet activation assay
has assay format -> cell membrane format
has primary assay -> primary assay
has concentration throughput -> single concentration
has assay readout content parametricity -> single parameter
has repetition throughput -> multiple repetition
antibody -> Red-fluorescent labeled anti-P-selectin antibody CD62P, BD Biosciences
has participant # has role -> G protein coupled receptor # target
has bioassay type -> functional
has preparation method -> recombinant expression
is bioassay type of -> localization assay
has assay medium -> assay medium
has role -> inducer
has role -> assay provider
has participant -> P-selectin glycoprotein ligand 1
assay measurement type -> endpoint assay
has assay kit -> assay Kit
has participant -> DMSO
has assay control -> positive control
has participant # has role -> A23187 # substrate
has confirmatory assay -> confirmatory assay
compound library -> MLSMR library
has assay method -> stable transfection
has assay method -> reporter gene method
has measured entity -> measured entity
has function -> binding
has assay phase characteristic -> heterogeneous phase
has role -> culture serum
has assay format -> cell-based format
has alternate target assay -> alternate target assay
has percent response -> percent activation
has participant -> P-selectin
has detection method -> flow cytometry
has role -> potentiator
has manufacturer -> BD Biosciences

Fig. 3. Automatically semantified bioassay (human-annotated reference in Fig. 1)

for the same bioassay text depicted in Fig. 1. Comparing the automatically generated one against the reference, we see that almost all the manually curated labels are correctly predicted. Among 16 manually curated labels, excluding those we omit in our training procedure (e.g., has title, PubChem AID, Deposit Date, has incubation time value, has concentration unit), the model accurately predicts 12 statements, while the remaining were deemed by a domain-specialist as valid additional candidates to incorporate in the reference set (e.g., has significant direction, has concentration throughput).

References

1. Aryani, A., et al.: A research graph dataset for connecting research data repositories using RD-switchboard. Sci. Data **5**, 180099 (2018)
2. Auer, S.: Towards an open research knowledge graph, January 2018. https://doi.org/10.5281/zenodo.1157185
3. Baas, J., Schotten, M., Plume, A., Côté, G., Karimi, R.: Scopus as a curated, high-quality bibliometric data source for academic research in quantitative science studies. Quant. Sci. Stud. **1**(1), 377–386 (2020)
4. Beltagy, I., Lo, K., Cohan, A.: SciBERT: a pretrained language model for scientific text. In: Proceedings of the 2019 Conference on Empirical Methods in Natural Language Processing and the 9th International Joint Conference on Natural Language Processing (EMNLP-IJCNLP), pp. 3606–3611 (2019)
5. Bianchi, F., Rossiello, G., Costabello, L., Palmonari, M., Minervini, P.: Knowledge graph embeddings and explainable AI. arXiv preprint arXiv:2004.14843 (2020)
6. Birkle, C., Pendlebury, D.A., Schnell, J., Adams, J.: Web of science as a data source for research on scientific and scholarly activity. Quant. Sci. Stud. **1**(1), 363–376 (2020)
7. Clark, A.M., Bunin, B.A., Litterman, N.K., Schürer, S.C., Visser, U.: Fast and accurate semantic annotation of bioassays exploiting a hybrid of machine learning and user confirmation. PeerJ **2**, e524 (2014)
8. Devlin, J., Chang, M.W., Lee, K., Toutanova, K.: BERT: pre-training of deep bidirectional transformers for language understanding. In: Proceedings of the 2019 Conference of the North American Chapter of the Association for Computational Linguistics: Human Language Technologies, Volume 1 (Long and Short Papers), pp. 4171–4186 (2019)
9. D'Souza, J., Auer, S.: NLPcontributions: an annotation scheme for machine reading of scholarly contributions in natural language processing literature (2020)
10. Fricke, S.: Semantic scholar. J. Med. Libr. Assoc. JMLA **106**(1), 145 (2018)
11. Hendricks, G., Tkaczyk, D., Lin, J., Feeney, P.: Crossref: the sustainable source of community-owned scholarly metadata. Quant. Sci. Stud. **1**(1), 414–427 (2020)
12. Jaradeh, M.Y., et al.: Open research knowledge graph: next generation infrastructure for semantic scholarly knowledge. In: Proceedings of the 10th International Conference on Knowledge Capture, pp. 243–246 (2019)
13. Jinha, A.E.: Article 50 million: an estimate of the number of scholarly articles in existence. Learn. Publ. **23**(3), 258–263 (2010)
14. Johnson, R., Watkinson, A., Mabe, M.: The STM Report. An Overview of Scientific and Scholarly Publishing, 5th edn. (2018)
15. Kononova, O., et al.: Text-mined dataset of inorganic materials synthesis recipes. Sci. Data **6**(1), 1–11 (2019)

16. Kulkarni, C., Xu, W., Ritter, A., Machiraju, R.: An annotated corpus for machine reading of instructions in wet lab protocols. In: NAACL: HLT, Volume 2 (Short Papers), New Orleans, Louisiana, pp. 97–106, June 2018. https://doi.org/10.18653/v1/N18-2016

17. Kuniyoshi, F., Makino, K., Ozawa, J., Miwa, M.: Annotating and extracting synthesis process of all-solid-state batteries from scientific literature. In: LREC, pp. 1941–1950 (2020)

18. Manghi, P., et al.: OpenAIRE research graph dump, December 2019. https://doi.org/10.5281/zenodo.3516918

19. Mysore, S., et al.: The materials science procedural text corpus: annotating materials synthesis procedures with shallow semantic structures. In: Proceedings of the 13th Linguistic Annotation Workshop, pp. 56–64 (2019)

20. Oelen, A., Jaradeh, M.Y., Stocker, M., Auer, S.: Generate fair literature surveys with scholarly knowledge graphs. In: Proceedings of the ACM/IEEE Joint Conference on Digital Libraries in 2020, JCDL 2020, New York, NY, USA, pp. 97–106. Association for Computing Machinery (2020). https://doi.org/10.1145/3383583.3398520

21. Runnwerth, M., Stocker, M., Auer, S.: Operational research literature as a use case for the open research knowledge graph. In: Bigatti, A.M., Carette, J., Davenport, J.H., Joswig, M., de Wolff, T. (eds.) ICMS 2020. LNCS, vol. 12097, pp. 327–334. Springer, Cham (2020). https://doi.org/10.1007/978-3-030-52200-1_32

22. Schürer, S.C., Vempati, U., Smith, R., Southern, M., Lemmon, V.: Bioassay ontology annotations facilitate cross-analysis of diverse high-throughput screening data sets. J. Biomol. Screen. 16(4), 415–426 (2011)

23. Vaswani, A., et al.: Attention is all you need. In: Advances in Neural Information Processing Systems, pp. 5998–6008 (2017)

24. Vempati, U.D., et al.: Formalization, annotation and analysis of diverse drug and probe screening assay datasets using the bioassay ontology (BAO). PLoS ONE 7(11), e49198 (2012)

25. Visser, U., Abeyruwan, S., Vempati, U., Smith, R.P., Lemmon, V., Schürer, S.C.: Bioassay ontology (BAO): a semantic description of bioassays and high-throughput screening results. BMC Bioinform. 12(1), 257 (2011)

26. Wang, K., Shen, Z., Huang, C., Wu, C.H., Dong, Y., Kanakia, A.: Microsoft academic graph: when experts are not enough. Quant. Sci. Stud. 1(1), 396–413 (2020)

Construction of Dunhuang Cultural Heritage Knowledge Base: Take Cave 220 as an Example

Xiaofei Sun, Ting Zhang, Lei Chen, Xiaoyang Wang(✉) ⓘ, and Jiakeng Tang

Library, Zhejiang University, Hangzhou 310058, People's Republic of China
libwxy@zju.edu.cn

Abstract. Based on the research of Dunhuang resources and the Silk Road culture and history, this paper discusses applying digital culture to humanities research. With advanced computing technology and network technology, this paper aims to create an open collaboration environment for academic resources, and it finally proposes a new knowledge organization and management paradigm which is helpful for "Belt and Road Initiative" studies and Dunhuang studies.

Keywords: Dunhuang culture heritage · Knowledge base · Digital humanities · Belt and Road Initiative · Academic resource

1 Introduction

For the construction of Dunhuang Cave 220 cultural heritage knowledge base, we analyze the relationship between digital images and literature resources and other resources, taking the cave as the unit, based on the mural image, superimposing the meta-knowledge to form a multidimensional knowledge group composed of images, words, audio-visuals, providing comprehensive knowledge discovery and knowledge services for academic research and knowledge dissemination, and forming all-media features Knowledge base of advanced digital representations. For the construction of knowledge base, digital culture is applied to the traditional humanities research, using advanced computing technology and network technology to create an open-cooperative and multi-innovation academic resource environment for Dunhuang studies to meet the diverse needs of Dunhuang studies and the Silk Road civilization research, and to establish a new knowledge organization and management paradigm. In the review and prospect of digital humanities research, this paper discusses the academic and practical value of the construction of Dunhuang cultural heritage knowledge base.

2 Practice of Digital Humanistic Application in the Dunhuang Cultural Heritage Knowledge Base

The construction of Dunhuang cultural heritage knowledge base is a huge system with vast literature resources, multiple types of data and complex data structure. It deals with various types of media resources which include non-removable cultural relics, movable

E. Ishita et al. (Eds.): ICADL 2020, LNCS 12504, pp. 99–104, 2020.
https://doi.org/10.1007/978-3-030-64452-9_9

cultural relics and intangible cultural heritage digital resources. It is obvious that they have different data structure and expression mode. Exploring the academic background of Dunhuang studies cannot ignore the understanding of the humanistic environment of the ancient Dunhuang area [1]. In the era of big data, cross-epoch, cross-region, cross-media, interdisciplinary digital objects and data sources are the characteristics of Dunhuang cultural heritage knowledge base, and the goal of the knowledge base include discovery and utilization of various resources, knowledge exploration and innovation.

2.1 Digital Object and Data Association Analysis of Dunhuang Cultural Heritage Knowledge Base

The digital objects of Dunhuang cultural heritage knowledge base mainly include grotto resources and literature resources. Literature resources include about 50,000 volumes of historical documents found in the research of Dunhuang Grottoes, as well as hundreds of thousands of research documents of modern Dunhuang academic resources, such as books, periodicals, conference records, local chronicles, maps and so on. The cultural heritage of Dunhuang Grottoes contains 492 Caves (numbered) and many of the murals and statues.

The diversity of digital objects illustrates the complexity of data sources and determines the multiplicity of data associations. The data association of Dunhuang cultural heritage knowledge base is divided into macro and micro categories, and the macro association of the data is divided into four layers, which are divided into grotto data and all kinds of data related to grotto according to the coverage range. In order to express the association between the data, this paper takes Dunhuang Cave 220 as an example to reveal the multiple associations of the massive data contained in Dunhuang cultural heritage knowledge base (see Fig. 1).

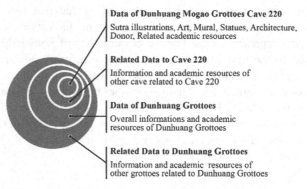

Data of Dunhuang Mogao Grottoes Cave 220
Sutra illustrations, Art, Mural, Statues, Architecture, Donor, Related academic resources

Related Data to Cave 220
Information and academic resources of other cave related to Cave 220

Data of Dunhuang Grottoes
Overall informations and academic resources of Dunhuang Grottoes

Related Data to Dunhuang Grottoes
Information and academic resources of other grottoes related to Dunhuang Grottoes

Fig. 1. Macro-relevance map of Dunhuang Cave 220 data

Cave 220 is 220th cave at Dunhuang Mogao Grottoes. Cave 220 was built in the early Tang Dynasty and was rebuilt in the middle Tang Dynasty, late Tang Dynasty, Five Dynasties, Song Dynasty and Qing Dynasty. In the Cave 220, Vimalakirti is an extraordinary figure painting, and illustration of the Emperor and ministers seeing a doctor can be comparable to Yan Liben's "Portraits of the Emperors"; the dance and the band in Medicine Buddha Sutra illustration are not only the representative works in Zhen-guan's heyday, but also provide valuable information for the study of the music and dance in Tang Dynasty. As its long history and excellent murals, Cave 220 plays an exemplary role in the study of Dunhuang Grottoes and grotto art. And it is the reason why this paper selects Cave 220 to study on.

The macro and micro associations of data can be divided into two types according to the content: explicit and implicit. The explicit data associations can be directly related by digital visual images, related information and controlled lexical tables. Implicit data associations can be found through the literature content. For example, we can use the migration information of the donors to analyze the influence of the Central Plains culture on ancient Chinese architecture.

Taking Cave 220 as an example, the explicit data include: the age of the construction, the description of the caves, the description of murals and so on. According to the explicit data we can directly discover the associations between the data.

- Construction Period: Early Tang Dynasty (Mid-Tang, Late Tang, Five Dynasties, Song Dynasty and Qing Dynasty)
- Grotto-shaped: covered with bucket-shaped roof, dig a niche on the wall.
- Mural content: murals in Cave 220 which are all masterpieces. The representative works are: illustration of Prince and officials seeing a Doctor, Amitabha Sutra illustration, illustration of Emperors and ministers seeing a Doctor, illustration of Vimalakirti, Double Flying Apsaras, orchestra image, etc. [2] (see Fig. 2).

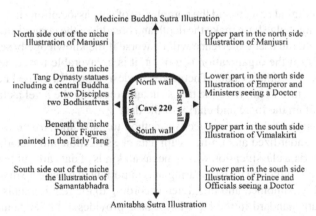

Fig. 2. Examples of caves and murals in Dunhuang Cave 220

The implicit data of the Cave 220 include: cultural value, historical information, character information and so on. And the implicit data needs to be related to other caves so that we can obtain more valuable information after comparative analysis. "Medicine Buddha Sutra illustration" (many scholars as "hu xuan dance") and its band, not only for the study of the history of music and dance, but also it is the masterpiece of the art of painting [3]. Through the collection of mural architectural images, it can be found that the influence of the Central Plains culture on the ancient north and south culture and the developed traffic between the ancient north and south area [4].

The digital object of the Cave 220 covers almost all resources, and the research content involves the interdisciplinary fields of Buddhism, architecture, art (music, dance), folk culture and so on. The results of the content exploration of the Cave 220 shows that the diversity of digital objects and the multiplicity of data association can link the cave of different times through the content of murals, cultural value and character information, thus depicting a complete history of Chinese culture and cultural exchanges with foreign countries. This also shows that the diversity of digital objects not only increases the difficulty of content management, but also provides great possibilities for content exploration and knowledge innovation.

2.2 System Framework and Function Design of the Knowledge Base

In the Internet era, the construction of Dunhuang cultural heritage knowledge base will tend to be decentralized and flat. It will also have modular open cooperation and multi-innovation model. Decentralization means any digital object and any data can become central and can be effectively organized and managed; flat means the relationship between digital objects and data is no longer a traditional multilevel system, but uses modular design to set fewer levels to improve data processing and utilization efficiency.

1. Flat organization structure and modular data design.

The diversity of digital objects and the complexity of data associations in Dunhuang cultural heritage knowledge base make the depth and breadth of the content structure. In this data environment, the user experience will be worse if the knowledge base organization is tree-based. But if the organization is too flat, it is unfavorable for content disclosure and management of complex data. Therefore, the designing idea of the knowledge base is to use flat structure to improve the tree structure, reducing the level as far as possible in order to maintain the logic and clarity of the data.

Modular design of data is an effective method to make the structure flat. Modular design can be standardized and unified with data classification and metadata standards. The first thing is data classification which means all kinds of data are cut to the minimum unit. Secondly, pay attention to data sharing. It is important to make sure that each module data can be freely combined and integrated according to the requirements.

The metadata standard in the knowledge base provides a unified standard for data management, communication, sharing and utilization. Meanwhile flat and modular design also put forward higher requirements for standardized management of data. In fact, the different types of metadata standards which are designed according to the minimum unit of digital objects are the quality assurance of data management. The integrity of the standard system is the key of the construction of the knowledge base. These standards include: the standards and norms of descriptive metadata, the standards and norms of management and preservation of metadata, the standards and norms of technical and service, intellectual property protection and information security mechanisms.

2. System Framework and Function Design

Dunhuang cultural heritage knowledge base classifies the needs of users and management into three aspects: resources, management and service. The knowledge base designs six basic functions: data entry, data storage, data management, system management, long-term preservation and data access. This also constitutes the institutional framework of the knowledge base (see Fig. 3).

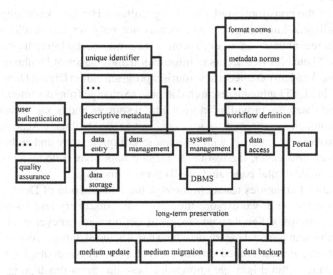

Fig. 3. Framework of Dunhuang cultural heritage knowledge base

The knowledge base is also built around resources, services and management, as follows:

- First, the construction of all kinds of database. The contents include: digital resource base (document base and index base), meta-database (resource description base and portal management metadata base), knowledge consulting base (forum community database, commentary, etc.), user information and authority database, user behavior and interest database, portal information base, etc.
- Second, the construction of service system composed of various service components. The contents include: text retrieval, multimedia retrieval, personalized retrieval, information services, personal use of environmental services, navigation services, forum community services and so on.
- Third, the establishment of various technologies and mechanisms. The contents include: user authentication and authorization mechanism, user behavior analysis, interoperability technology (distributed object technology, metadata and XML technology, middleware technology, etc.), information security and protection mechanism of intellectual property, etc.

3   Conclusion

For the knowledge base, all resources exist as data in digital form, and all requirements can be expressed by data. Facing massive data resources, how to organize and manage content is the key of the knowledge base. From the development of the Internet, decentralization, flattening, modularization are all feasible ideas and methods to solve the complexity and diversity of data for the construction of Dunhuang cultural heritage knowledge base.

The goal of the construction of Dunhuang Cultural Heritage knowledge base is to create an intelligent knowledge base, which is not only for the public, but also for researchers. In recent years, in order to protect the grottoes, the International Dunhuang Project (IDP) [5] enables free access to information and images of Dunhuang resources. And Dunhuang Academy created a new tourism program called Digital Dunhuang which makes it possible for Dunhuang research database to change from document database to comprehensive database, providing more digital resources and more convenient digital research environment for the study of grottoes. Just as the Dunhuang Academic resource database, it provides researchers with systematic, comprehensive and authoritative academic resources. Moreover, the resources include paper-based documents and digital murals, and provide digital panorama of 30 caves online [6].

In the field of humanities research, through the construction of Dunhuang cultural heritage knowledge base, we explore the knowledge discovery and knowledge innovation mode of complex digital resources, constructing a new encyclopedic knowledge organization and management paradigm which has advanced data processing and content analysis functions, and can embed various media forms. It is no doubt that the construction of Dunhuang cultural heritage knowledge base has great practical significance to meet the different needs of the public and researchers.

References

1. Chai, J.: Paying attention to the academic background and connection of Dunhuang Studies. Study Explor. **03**, 201–203 (2008)
2. Gallery of Mogao Caves. http://gallery.dha.ac.cn/exhibit/item/150/. Accessed 10 May 2020
3. Ji, X.: A dictionary of Dunhuang Studies, 1st edn. Shanghai Lexicographic Publishing House, Shang Hai (1998)
4. Dunhuang Mural and Hakka Round House. http://public.dha.ac.cn/Content.aspx?id=477396 911191&Page=6&types=1. Accessed 10 May 2020
5. IDP. http://idp.bl.uk. Accessed 10 My 2020
6. Dunhuang Academic Resources Database. http://dh.dha.ac.cn/AllResource/. Accessed 10 May 2020

Citation Data Analysis

ReViz: A Tool for Automatically Generating Citation Graphs and Variants

Sven Groppe[(✉)] [iD] and Lina Hartung

Institute of Information Systems (IFIS), University of Lübeck, Lübeck, Germany
groppe@ifis.uni-luebeck.de, lina.hartung@protonmail.com

Abstract. A systematic literature review provides an overview of multiple scientific publications in an area of research and visualizations of the data of the systematic review enable further in-depth analyses. The creation of such a review and its visualizations is a very time- and labor-intensive process. For this reason, we propose a tool for automatically generating visualizations for systematic reviews. Using this tool, the citations between the included articles can be depicted in a citation graph. However, because the clearness of the information contained in the citation graph is highly dependent on the number of included publications, several strategies are implemented in order to reduce the complexity of the graph without loosing (much) information. The generated graphs and developed strategies are evaluated using different instruments, including an user survey, in which they are rated positively.

Keywords: Citation graph · Visualizations · Systematic review

1 Motivation

The number of scientific publications increases steadily every year. More and more research results are published, so that there is an exponential increase in publications [6]. Consequently, it is more and more time-consuming to inform oneself in detail about the current state of research of a subject area, such that the importance of systematic reviews grows.

A *systematic review* is prepared on the basis of already published research work and presents a current and detailed summary and evaluation of several research results of a certain scientific topic. In this respect, the review offers the reader a suitable opportunity to obtain further information in his or her field of work and to bring it up to date [22]. For the authors of a review, on the other hand, the already enormous amount of time and effort required for its preparation increases due to the large number of available scientific papers. Taking several further barriers for the creation process of a systematic review into account, the support of a tool especially designed for systematic reviews is very useful in this step [1]. For this purpose, some tools are already available. However, since different steps are required to create a review and the overall work is very extensive, it is difficult to

© Springer Nature Switzerland AG 2020
E. Ishita et al. (Eds.): ICADL 2020, LNCS 12504, pp. 107–121, 2020.
https://doi.org/10.1007/978-3-030-64452-9_10

support the entire creation process, such that existing tools have gaps and do not address all the requirements of a review [1].

Furthermore, deep insights might become evident by visualizing the data of systematic reviews in a proper way, but existing tools provide only basic and very limited support for automatically generating visualizations for systematic reviews. For example, the following two types of visualizations are not generated by existing tools at all: 1) a flow chart of the publication selection process presenting the flow of information during the different phases of the review and 2) the citation graph illustrating the relationships between the included publications of a review, thus giving the user a new perspective on the work used.

Our contributions are:

- A tool for automatically generating flow charts of and citation graphs for systematic reviews.
- Our developed software for the creation of the visualizations (i.e., flow chart as well as citation graph) can be downloaded at https://github.com/l-hartung/reviz and is freely available to users worldwide by using docker containers.[1]
- Different variants of citation graphs for simplifying the presentation by summarizing nodes and edges, and introducing factors like direct and indirect citations as well as coloring publications with common authors for further analysis.
- An extensive evaluation of the different variants of the citation graphs.

In the following Sect. 2, we introduce the basics of systematic reviews. In addition, previous work on the support of reviews as well as various visualizations and their selection for our work are presented. Subsequently, Sect. 3 details the methods and strategies for the flow chart and the citation graphs with its various variants for simplification and adding information for the purpose of in-depth analysis. Afterwards in Sect. 4, we evaluate the created visualizations and Sect. 5 provides a summary and the future work.

2   Basics

In this section, some basic principles are presented in order to shed more light on systematic reviews and their preparation. In addition, some already existing tools supporting systematic reviews are considered in order to select one of these tools for the present work. Furthermore, different types of visualizations in reviews are introduced, including the flow chart of the publication selection process and the citation graph.

---

[1] In addition to the use of Parsifal and the export of data from it, it is also possible to generate a citation graph without creating a systematic review, using a Bibtex file and the referenced publications as PDF documents (local files or remotely accessible via urls) as input. However, the generation of a flow chart is only possible using Parsifal. Since this requires the use of a fork, the modified code of Parsifal is also available in the form of a docker container at https://github.com/l-hartung/parsifal/.

2.1 Systematic Reviews

Systematic reviews provide an overview of selected scientific papers on a research topic. Firstly, all available publications relevant to the research area are identified, evaluated and interpreted [16]. A central advantage of a systematic review over other scientific papers is its high informative value. While individual research papers are often based on the expectations of the scientists and results that do not correspond to the desired results can also be omitted from the publication, a systematic review is fundamentally more objective and very comprehensive. By summarizing a large number of existing research results on a topic, gaps, contradictions, relationships, or inconsistencies in the research can be identified, thus providing clues and directions for future research [16].

There are guidelines for the development of a systematic review in order to create uniform and comparable results. In the medical field these are for example the *Cochrane Reviewer's Handbook* [27] and the *CRD Guidelines for those Carrying out or Commissioning Reviews* [14]. In [16], these guides have been adapted for the research area of software engineering. In principle, however, the procedure of a review is mostly identical in every area.

2.2 Related Work for Supporting Systematic Reviews

As in other publications, the quality of a systematic review can vary greatly and depends to a large extent on the approach and thoroughness of the authors and the scope and quality of the publications included. In order to ensure uniform standards, the PRISMA (*Preferred Reporting Items for Systematic reviews and Meta-Analyses*) statement was specified as a guideline for the report of systematic reviews [22]. Although the statement is designed for medical reviews, it can also serve as a basis for reviews from other areas. The PRISMA statement consists of a checklist of 27 points that should be included in the review report and a 4-phase flow chart (see Fig. 1).

The extremely high effort required for the preparation of systematic reviews leads to an increased need for automatic support during this process. Many software tools are already available to help authors in this context. These range from basic word processing programs, *Reference Management Tools* and statistical programs to specially designed tools, which are intended to support the entire systematic review process - or large parts of it - [21]. *Reference Management Tools*, such as RefWorks and EndNote, are widely used by review authors [21]. Such tools are available in large numbers, but only take up a very small portion of the work in a review. The Cochrane Collaboration also offers several tools to support the management and analysis of systematic reviews, including Covidence [9], EPPI-Reviewer [29] and RevMan [28]. These tools are designed specifically for Cochrane medical reviews. However, Eppi-Reviewer and RevMan can also be used for other types of reviews, although in this case some features cannot be used, and provide good support in some areas of the systematic review process [21].

In [1] six other widely-used tools are compared and evaluated from different perspectives. These provide support throughout the systematic review process and are not limited to a specific application area, although Al-Zubidy et al. refer to the software engineering area. The authors identify various barriers during the review process and requirements for supporting tools, and examine the six selected tools in relation to these. From these tools, only Parsifal [23] is free and open source software, and is additionally among the three tools with the best overall results in [1], such that our proposed tool extends it for generating the flow chart of the publication selection process and the citation graph.

There are other works that deal with the comparison of tools with respect to the requirements during the systematic review process, such as [20]. However, most of the tools either overlap with those already mentioned or support far less of the overall systematic review process. Accordingly, there are promising approaches to support systematic reviews; nevertheless, there are gaps in the existing tools, and optimal support cannot be provided.

2.3   Visualizations in Systematic Reviews

Visualizations in scientific works enable a better understanding of data sets, provide deeper insights or facilitate the analysis and presentation of large amounts of data [11]. Furthermore, in systematic reviews, different types of visualizations are used, for example to present information about the included publications in a clear way. Table 1 presents some types of visualizations frequently used in reviews and some sample reviews that include these visualizations.

Table 1. Various systematic literature reviews (SLR) and their applied visualizations. The first four reviews are from the medical area, the following four from the software engineering area and the last two from other areas.

SLR	Flow chart: selection of publications	Table study properties	Other tables	Distribution of publ. years	Other distributions	Forest Plot	Funnel chart	Other
[13]	✓		✓			✓	✓	Risk of bias diagram classifications of relevant publications
[32]	✓		✓			✓		
[25]	✓					✓	✓	
[18]	✓	✓				✓		
[33]	✓			✓	✓			
[3]			✓	✓				
[4]	✓	✓	✓	✓				
[26]	✓		✓	✓	✓			
[10]	✓		✓					
[8]	✓	✓	✓					

Flow charts for the selection of the included publications during the entire review process are included in almost all of the reviews examined. It is part of the PRISMA statement and is displayed in all systematic reviews in the form specified there or in a very similar manner. Some of the systematic reviews display tables with the most important characteristics of the included publications to provide an overview of them. In most cases, different tables are also shown to illustrate the different properties and characteristics of the respective systematic review. Diagrams showing the distribution of the publication years of the included publications are only used in the reviews examined in the area of software engineering. Other distribution diagrams like the publications sources or their geographical distribution, are also frequently found in this area. In medical reviews, on the other hand, forest plots are always presented to summarize and support their clues of the respective studies (e.g. relative risk or odds ratio). Funnel charts are also used here, for example, which can provide information on publication bias.

The most commonly used presentation is the flow chart of the publication selection process, which obviously forms a fundamental part of a review. Therefore it is implemented as one of the visualizations in this work to allow a quick and easy representation of the diagram in all systematic reviews.

Citation Graphs: None of the examined systematic reviews includes a citation graph. A citation graph is a directed graph in which publications are the nodes and citations are the edges. Thus, the relationships between the publications are represented by the citations themselves [24]. With the analysis of citations and citation graphs, knowledge flows and the spread of ideas and perceptions as well as the relevance of information sources can be examined [34]. This can be of importance during the preparation of a systematic review. By illustrating the relationships of included publications in a graph, for example, the spread of different methods, ideas or conceptions among the works can be made visible. Furthermore, knowledge can be gained about the relevance of individual works and about which works serve as a basis for further work. The fact that a citation graph does not appear in any of the examined systematic reviews is therefore not necessarily an indication of its insignificance for systematic reviews, but could rather be an expression of the complexity and efforts behind the creation of a citation graph. Therefore, a semi-automatic creation of citation graphs is a useful addition to the tool support of systematic reviews.

Visualization Tools for Scholarly Datasets: Please see Table 2 for tools for visualizing scholarly datasets. Existing tools are not primarily designed for systematic reviews and offer many types of visualizations not necessarily including citation graphs suitable for systematic reviews. Hence our proposed tool ReViz offers some important unique features: Integrated in the tool Parsifal for conducting systematic reviews, the citation graphs of ReViz are automatically constructed (with possibility of manual correction) from a set of paper documents. ReViz further supports various simplification approaches for citation graphs.

Table 2. Various visualization tools for scholarly datasets.

Visualization tool	Visualizations[a]	Citation graph from set of paper documents	Support of systematic reviews	Comments
CitNetExplorer [31]	C	–	–	Clustering of very large citation networks
VOSViewer [30]	B	–	–	Visualized bibliometric networks constructed based on citation, bibliographic coupling, co-citation, or co-authorship relations may include journals, researchers, or individual publications
Sci^{2}Tool [5]	B	–	–	Temporal, geospatial, topical, and network analysis and visualization of scholarly datasets at the micro (individual), meso (local), and macro (global) levels
CiteSpace [7]	B	–	–	Structural and temporal analyses including collaboration networks, author co-citation networks, and document co-citation networks with support of hybrid node types such as terms, institutions, and countries, and hybrid link types such as co-citation, co-occurrence, and directed citing links
CiteWiz [12]	C	–	–	Visualization of citation networks using causality visualization techniques, interactive timelines, and concept maps
Proposed tool ReViz	C	✓	✓	Tool especially designed for systematic reviews, and running stand-alone or integrated in Parsifal for visualizing citation graphs constructed from a set of paper documents. Support of various approaches for simplifying citation graphs

[a]C: Focus on Citation Networks, B: General Bibliometric Network Visualizations

3   Flow Chart of the Publication Selection Process, Citation Graphs and Variants

We introduce our tool to generate the proposed visualizations (i.e., flow chart of the publication selection process and citation graphs in different variants) in this section.

3.1   Flow Chart of the Publication Selection Process

Our proposed visualization generator (integrated into Parsifal) generates a flow chart for the publication selection process (see Fig. 1), which is based on the structure of the template contained in the PRISMA statement [22]. In our study of several reviews on different topics, we observed

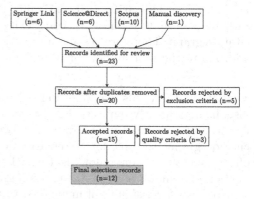

Fig. 1. Example flow chart of the publication selection process of systematic reviews as generated by our proposed tool

differences in the presentation of the flow charts, but the content is always based on the PRISMA statement. In these flow charts, nodes present publications found in various digital libraries or other sources. Furthermore, nodes for the number of publications after duplicate elimination, as well as after removal of publications by inclusion and exclusion criteria and quality criteria should be included. Thus, each step in the publication selection process of the review is shown in a summarized form.

3.2 Structure of the Citation Graphs

Citation graphs in the context of systematic reviews should provide an insight into the relationships between the publications included in the review. The aim is to create a meaningful graph for the reader that provides as much information as possible. In order to achieve this goal, a further component is included here in our graphs: the arrangement of the publications should be based on their respective year of publication. This means that all publications which appeared in the same year are arranged next to each other, making additional information visible. For illustration purposes, a timeline is printed below the graph itself, so that it is possible to see exactly which publication appeared in which year. In addition, it can be quickly determined in which period of time the included research work is conducted and from which years more or less work originates.

The basis for the citation graph is therefore primarily the timeline. It covers the period of all publication years of the included works. Based on the timeline, the works are then drawn as nodes at the respective position on the timeline and the works linked by quotations are connected to each other with edges. Furthermore, different components within the graph should be visibly separated from each other. From a graph-theoretical point of view, it is possible that the citation graph is not only represented by a single directed graph, but consists of several independent subgraphs. In the context of this work, however, it is useful to consider the citation graph always as a single unit and thus as a graph with several *components*. Here, a component is defined as a subset of nodes and edges in which each node has at least one incoming or outgoing edge to another node of this subset. In addition, each node that has no edges is also its own component. To make the independence of the components visible, they should be drawn one below the other.

3.3 Node Summaries

Although various methods are used here to obtain an illustrative result, the large number of nodes and edges in a citation graph can still lead to very confusing results. An example is shown in Fig. 2a. In order to reduce this complexity, further methods to simplify the graph are necessary.

One way to reduce overlaps of many edges and the resulting confusion is to reduce the number of nodes. A smaller number of nodes results in fewer edges and a less dense overall graph. If many publications are included in a review, the only way to reduce the number of nodes is to merge several individual nodes.

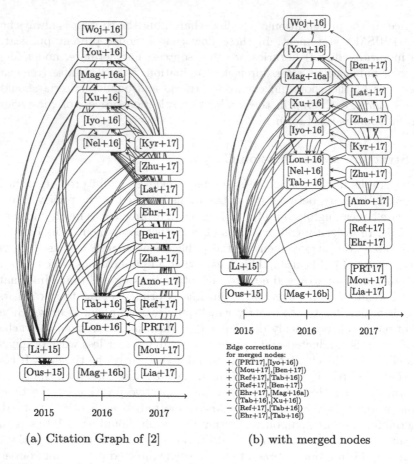

(a) Citation Graph of [2]   (b) with merged nodes

Fig. 2. Example of a) a citation graph (for the systematic review presented in [2]), and b) the same graph after merging several nodes with respective corrections of the edges

In this respect, a summary of the original graph is generated. The difficulty in creating small graph summaries is the minimization of the resulting errors [19], so that no information is missing from the original graph and no wrong information is added.

There are various approaches to summarizing graphs, but they are not necessarily applicable to such relatively small graphs like our citation graphs. A merging of several nodes to a *supernode* with *superedges* is a well realizable possibility. Several nodes with the same or very similar incoming and outgoing edges are merged into one large node. In order to minimize errors and to reconstruct the original graph exactly, the merge consists not only of the graph itself, but also of a list of corrections of the edges.

This method can quickly become very inefficient for large graphs, since numerous comparisons of the nodes with each other must be processed to find those with similar edges. In [15] such an algorithm is presented, where first similar nodes are searched for to avoid unnecessary comparisons between all nodes. Then a summary of the graph is iteratively generated by merging original nodes or already existing *supernodes*.

In case of the citation graphs, only merges of nodes in the same level, i.e. publications with the same publication year, are reasonable. Because of this, *supernodes* with a large number of merges are extremely unlikely, so it makes more sense to focus on good merges of two or three nodes each. For this purpose, all possible candidates for the merging of two nodes are found first. Using a weight based on common and different edges for each pair of candidates, the best possible candidates are then selected. Based on these results, the calculation of connection components with three nodes from the candidate pairs is performed to determine good merges of three nodes.

We present the above described example in Fig. 2b as a summary after merging nodes: A total of 5 nodes and 37 edges are removed.

3.4   Summarizing Transitive Edges

If the publications in the graph are scattered over a longer period of time, there are inevitably fewer ways to merge nodes, since there are far fewer nodes in a plane. We present an example in Fig. 3.

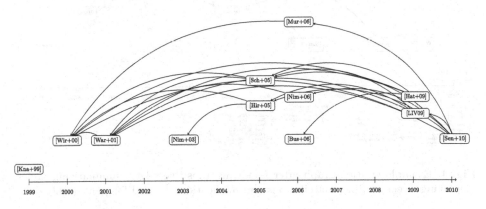

Fig. 3. Example of a citation graph covering a longer time period (for the systematic review presented in [17])

In this case, the clarity is impaired by many very long edges. To avoid this, more edges would have to be reduced, regardless of the number of nodes. Transitivities are suitable for this purpose. After the summary of transitive edges, some information is lost in the graph. For example, the number of incoming edges is no longer a clear indication of the number of citations of this node. In order to keep this information, we propose to increase the width of the remaining incoming edges of a node for omitted transitive edges (see Fig. 4). Thus, depending on the size of the incoming edges, the actual number of citations can be better inferred.

As a further variant and in order to have a metric for the influence of single publications to other research contributions, we propose to display exact numbers in the nodes of the citation graphs for (direct) citations as well as for indirect ones. Indirect citations represent a path of direct citations (see Fig. 4), i.e., A indirectly cites B if A cites B, or A cites C and C indirectly cites B, where A, B and C are publications. This allows a direct comparison between the citations of the individual nodes, despite the omitted edges. In order not to enlarge the nodes too much by the two additional numbers in the label, they must be displayed relatively small. In order to enable a quick comparison of the quotations of the individual nodes at first glance, these numbers are additionally highlighted in color. By means of a color scale, nodes with many citations can be quickly distinguished from those with fewer citations.

Additionally, it should be possible to identify publications with many common authors, for example to recognize follow-up publications and related approaches more easily. We hence propose to draw these publications in the same color (see Fig. 4).

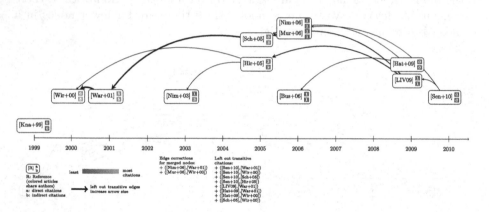

Fig. 4. Example citation graph after removing transitive edges, summarizing nodes, displaying direct and indirect citations and publications colored for joint authors

4   Evaluation

The evaluation of the visualizations introduced in this work mainly focuses on different aspects of the citation graph. The developed flow chart, which is largely based on the 4-phase flow chart of the PRISMA statement, offers little scope for variation and therefore takes up only a small part of the evaluation.

For the citation graph, on the other hand, several decisions are made regarding the layout and the used elements. However, the evaluation of the results is complex and can only partly be calculated mathematically.

Since the evaluation of the visualizations is partly subject to the subjective perceptions of the reader, part of the evaluation consists of a user survey. Thus, different aspects of the created variants of the citation graph as well as the flow chart can be evaluated. In addition to the survey, some calculations regarding the number of nodes and edges in the citation graph are carried out for evaluation.

4.1   Reduction of the Complexity of Citation Graphs

The number of nodes and edges can vary greatly in the introduced variants of citation graphs. Fewer nodes and edges reduce the complexity in the graph. We present in Table 3 the results for different calculations regarding nodes and edges for two graphs in different variants.

The upper part of the table contains the number of nodes, edges, and edges per node. Overall, there is a very strong reduction of the evaluated values. In the first graph, only about half of the edges of the original graph are drawn using both the node summary and the summary of transitive edges, while in the second example, there is even a reduction of 73% in total edges and 67% in edges per node.

In the lower part of the table, three additional parameters are considered that make it difficult to track edges: the number of nodes hiding one or more edges, the number of edges hidden by nodes, and the number of edge overlaps. Since these parameters are sometimes difficult to measure visually and could only be examined manually, some of the values are approximate values. Here, too, the results with node summary and summary of transitive edges are to a large extent highly reduced. In the case of edge overlaps, even 90% and 95% lower values can be achieved in both graphs when using both functionalities (i.e., node summary and removing transitive edges).

Long edges, which run over a longer span on the timeline and thus across several layers, add to the confusion, as they are more likely to cross more other edges and nodes, making it more difficult to quickly capture the course of all edges. Therefore, in Fig. 5, we present the lengths of edges occurring in the two graphs considered earlier, so that a comparison of the edge lengths in the graph variants is possible. In addition to the general reduction in the number of edges, which is already shown in Table 3, it is also apparent that many of the longer edges are eliminated by removing transitive edges.

Overall, very high reductions for the evaluated values occur in the calculations presented here, whenever node summaries and summaries of transitive edges are performed in the graphs. Thus, a lower complexity of the graphs can be concluded. In order to determine whether better final results for the graphs can be achieved as a consequence, the results of the user survey follow in the next section.

Table 3. Results for the number of nodes, edges and edges per node, as well as the number of nodes hiding edges, edges hidden by nodes and edge overlaps for two graphs (Graph 1 contains the publications of [17], Graph 2 contains the publications of [2]). In the first line the original – normal – graph is taken as starting point. This is followed by the graph with a summary of similar nodes, where an edge deviation of two has been allowed for nodes to be combined, and the graph with a summary of transitive edges. In the last line, both functionalities are combined.

		Nodes	Edges	Edges per Node
Graph 1 [17]	Normal Graph	12	21	3,5
	1. Node summary	11 (−8%)	18 (−14%)	3,27 (−7%)
	2. Transitivity	12 (0%)	13 (−38%)	2,17 (−38%)
	1. & 2.	11 (−8%)	10 (−52%)	1,81 (−48%)
Graph 2 [2]	Normal graph	22	92	8,36
	1. Node summary	18 (−18%)	60 (−35%)	6,67 (−20%)
	2. Transitivity	22 (0%)	40 (−57%)	3,64 (−56%)
	1. & 2.	18 (−18%)	25 (−73%)	2,78 (−67%)
		Hiding nodes	Hidden edges	Overlaps
Graph 1 [17]	Normal graph	4	8	∼42
	1. Node summary	4 (0%)	10 (+25%)	33 (−21%)
	2. Transitivity	3 (−25%)	2 (−75%)	7 (−83%)
	1. & 2.	3 (−25%)	2 (−75%)	4 (−90%)
Graph 2 [2]	Normal graph	18	∼77	∼220
	1. Node summary	14 (−22%)	∼47 (−39%)	∼90 (−59%)
	2. Transitivity	18 (0%)	∼32 (−58%)	∼44 (−80%)
	1. & 2	13 (−28%)	∼19 (−75%)	10 (−95%)

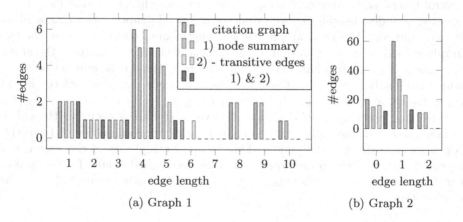

(a) Graph 1   (b) Graph 2

Fig. 5. Comparison of the edge lengths without any reduction, using node summary, removing transitive edges and both functionalities. The edge length on the x-axis indicates how many layers (i.e., years) an edge passes over.

4.2 User Survey

In a user survey created for the evaluation of the visualizations, the different implemented variants of the citation graphs as well as the flow chart are assessed by external persons. This allows to determine how well the results are understandable and appealing to outsiders and whether the desired goals for the visualizations have been achieved. The graphs are primarily examined with regard to the points "clarity" (*Are all information quickly and easily grasped at a glance?*), "comprehensibility" (*Are all necessary information available to understand the overall picture?*) and "layout" (*Is the result visually appealing?*). Due to space limits, we only discuss the results of the user survey here without going into detail[2].

With 22 participants, the sample is relatively small and the answers of the participants varied from one another. Nevertheless, a clear tendency in the answers can already be determined.

In general, the clarity of the citation graphs, which contain more edges and/or nodes, is rated as relatively poor. As confirmed by the evaluation, the clarity is improved by the different functionalities. However, even after the improvement, a "good" result cannot necessarily be assumed. In order to be able to combine many nodes and thus save many nodes and edges, a high number of nodes within one year is necessary. In this case, however, the graph is likely to be very confusing, so that the result is likely to be complex even after the summary is performed. If, on the other hand, fewer nodes are within a year, but are scattered over a longer period of time, there are fewer possibilities to summarize, so that the clarity of the result will also not change much. However, if you use the summary of transitive edges, you often save a lot of edges, which certainly has a positive effect on the clarity of the graphs. Nevertheless, much of the information is obscured and the presentation of the omitted edges in the legend enables to trace the citations of a publication without gaps, but it is very time-consuming. Nevertheless, both functions are considered useful and are in any case capable of creating a new, clearer, presentation method for many citation graphs. The use of the flow chart created by our tool is also a useful addition to the creation of a systematic review.

5   Summary and Conclusions

We introduce a tool for the creation of visualizations for systematic reviews. In particular, we integrated the generation of a flow chart for the publication selection process of the systematic review and different variants of citation graphs (with and without merging nodes, removing transitive edges, adding numbers for direct and indirect citations and coloring publications with common authors) for the analysis of the citations of the publications among each other. The basis for these visualizations is the data from the tool *Parsifal*, which supports the creation process of a systematic review. We verify good results in an extensive

---

[2] We will provide the details in a forthcoming extended paper.

evaluation by determining and comparing the number of hidden edges and hiding nodes in the citation graph variants and by a user survey for assessing subjective opinions of users.

References

1. Al-Zubidy, A., Carver, J.C., Hale, D.P., Hassler, E.E.: Vision for SLR tooling infrastructure: prioritizing value-added requirements. Inf. Softw. Technol. **91**, 72–81 (2017)
2. Babačić, H., Mehta, A., Merkel, O., Schoser, B.: CRISPR-cas gene-editing as plausible treatment of neuromuscular and nucleotide-repeat-expansion diseases: a systematic review. PLoS ONE **14**(2), e0212198 (2019)
3. Badawi, H.F., Laamarti, F., El Saddik, A.: ISO/IEEE 11073 personal health device (X73-PHD) standards compliant systems: a systematic literature review. IEEE Access **7**, 3062–3073 (2019)
4. Bonidia, R., Rodrigues, L.A.L., Avila-Santos, A.P., Sanches, D., Brancher, J.: Computational intelligence in sports: a systematic literature review. Adv. Hum. Comput. Interact. **2018**, 3 426 178:1–3 426 178:13 (2018)
5. Börner, K., Polley, D.E.: Visual Insights: A Practical Guide to Making Sense of Data. MIT Press, Cambridge (2014)
6. Bornmann, L., Mutz, R.: Growth rates of modern science: a bibliometric analysis based on the number of publications and cited references. J. Assoc. Inf. Sci. Technol. **66**(11), 2215–2222 (2015)
7. Chen, C.: CiteSpace II: detecting and visualizing emerging trends and transient patterns in scientific literature. J. Assoc. Inf. Sci. Technol. **57**(3), 359–377 (2006)
8. Chen, F., Lui, A.M., Martinelli, S.M.: A systematic review of the effectiveness of flipped classrooms in medical education. Med. Educ. **51**(6), 585–597 (2017)
9. Covidence Team: Covidence. https://www.covidence.org
10. De Vries, H., Bekkers, V., Tummers, L.: Innovation in the public sector: a systematic review and future research agenda. Public Adm. **94**(1), 146–166 (2016)
11. DiBiase, D., MacEachren, A., Krygier, J., Reeves, C.: Animation and the role of map design in scientific visualization. Cartogr. Geogr. Inf. Sci. **19**, 201–214 (1992)
12. Elmqvist, N., Tsigas, P.: CiteWiz: a tool for the visualization of scientific citation networks. Inf. Vis. **6**(3), 215–232 (2007)
13. Finnerup, N.B., et al.: Pharmacotherapy for neuropathic pain in adults: a systematic review and meta-analysis. Lancet Neurol. **14**(2), 162–173 (2015)
14. Khan, K.S., Ter Riet, G., Glanville, J., Sowden, A.J., Kleijnen, J. et al.: Undertaking systematic reviews of research on effectiveness: CRD's guidance for carrying out or commissioning reviews. NHS Centre for Reviews and Dissemination, no. CRD Report 4, 2nd edn. (2001)
15. Khan, K.U., Nawaz, W., Lee, Y.-K.: Set-based approximate approach for lossless graph summarization. Computing **97**(12), 1185–1207 (2015)
16. Kitchenham, B.: Procedures for performing systematic reviews. Keele UK Keele Univ. **33**(2004), 1–26 (2004)
17. Kubben, P.L., ter Meulen, K.J., Schijns, O.E., ter Laak-Poort, M.P., van Overbeeke, J.J., van Santbrink, H.: Intraoperative MRI-guided resection of glioblastoma multiforme: a systematic review. Lancet Oncol. **12**(11), 1062–1070 (2011)
18. Liu, J., Hua, C., Pan, J., Han, B., Tang, X.: Piezosurgery vs conventional rotary instrument in the third molar surgery: a systematic review and meta-analysis of randomized controlled trials. J. Dent. Sci. **13**(4), 342–349 (2018)

19. Liu, X., Tian, Y., He, Q., Lee, W.-C., McPherson, J.: Distributed graph summarization. In: CIKM, Shanghai, China (2014)
20. Marshall, C., Brereton, P.: Tools to support systematic literature reviews in software engineering: a mapping study. In: International Symposium on Empirical Software Engineering and Measurement, pp. 296–299, October 2013
21. Marshall, C., Brereton, P., Kitchenham, B.: Tools to support systematic reviews in software engineering: a cross-domain survey using semi-structured interviews. In: EASE (2015)
22. Moher, D., Liberati, A., Tetzlaff, J., Altman, D.G., The PRISMA Group: Preferred reporting items for systematic reviews and meta-analyses: the PRISMA statement. Ann. Intern. Med. **151**(4), 264–269 (2009)
23. Parsifal Ltd.: Parsifal. https://parsif.al/
24. Rosenthal, F., Groppe, S.: Purposeful searching for citations of scholarly publications. Open J. Inf. Syst. (OJIS) **4**(1), 27–48 (2017)
25. Shalaby, M., Emile, S., Elfeki, H., Sakr, A., Wexner, S.D., Sileri, P.: Systematic review of endoluminal vacuum-assisted therapy as salvage treatment for rectal anastomotic leakage. BJS Open **3**(2), 153–160 (2018)
26. Soheilirad, S., Govindan, K., Mardani, A., Zavadskas, E.K., Nilashi, M., Zakuan, N.: Application of data envelopment analysis models in supply chain management: a systematic review and meta-analysis. Ann. Oper. Res. **271**(2), 915–969 (2018)
27. The Cochrane Collaboration: Cochrane handbook for systematic reviews of interventions (2011). http://handbook.cochrane.org
28. The Cochrane Collaboration: Review Manager (RevMan) [Computer Program], version 5.3 ed. The Nordic Cochrane Centre, Copenhagen (2014)
29. Thomas, J., Graziosi, S., Brunton, J.: Eppi-reviewer. http://eppi.ioe.ac.uk/cms/Default.aspx?tabid=2914
30. van Eck, N.J., Waltman, L.: Software survey: vosviewer, a computer program for bibliometric mapping. Scientometrics **84**(2), 523–538 (2010)
31. van Eck, N.J., Waltman, L.: CitNetExplorer: a new software tool for analyzing and visualizing citation networks. J. Inf. **8**(4), 802–823 (2014)
32. Whiting, P.F., et al.: Cannabinoids for medical use: a systematic review and meta-analysis. JAMA **313**(24), 2456–2473 (2015)
33. Yli-Huumo, J., Ko, D., Choi, S., Park, S., Smolander, K.: Where is current research on blockchain technology? — a systematic review. PLoS ONE **11**(10), e0163477 (2016)
34. Zhao, D., Strotmann, A.: Analysis and visualization of citation networks. Synth. Lect. Inf. Concepts Retr. Serv. **7**(1), 1–207 (2015)

A Large-Scale Analysis of Cross-lingual Citations in English Papers

Tarek Saier(✉)[iD] and Michael Färber[iD]

Institute AIFB, Karlsruhe Institute of Technology (KIT), Karlsruhe, Germany
{tarek.saier,michael.faerber}@kit.edu

Abstract. Citation data is an important source of insight into the scholarly discourse and the reception of publications. Outcomes of citation analyses and the applicability of citation based machine learning approaches heavily depend on the completeness of citation data. One particular shortcoming of scholarly data nowadays is language coverage. That is, non-English publications are often not included in data sets, or language metadata is not available. While national citation indices exist, these are often not interconnected to other data sets. Because of this, citations between publications of differing languages (cross-lingual citations) have only been studied to a very limited degree. In this paper, we present an analysis of cross-lingual citations based on one million English papers, covering three scientific disciplines and a time span of 27 years. Our results unveil differences between languages and disciplines, show developments over time, and give insight into the impact of cross-lingual citations on scholarly data mining as well as the publications that contain them. To facilitate further analyses, we make our collected data and code for analysis publicly available.

Keywords: Scholarly data · Citations · Cross-lingual · Citation analysis

1 Introduction

Citations are an essential tool for scientific practice. By allowing authors to refer to existing publications, citations make it possible to position one's work within the context of others', critique, compare, and point readers to supplementary reading material. In other words, citations enable scientific discourse. Because of this, citations are a valuable indicator for the academic community's reception of and interaction with published works. Their analysis is used, for example, to quantify research output [12], qualify references [1], and detect trends [2]. Furthermore, citations can be utilized to aid researchers through, for example, summarization [6] or recommendation [7,25] of papers, and through applications driven by document embeddings in general [3].

Because such analyses and applications require data to be based on, the availability of citation data or lack thereof is decisive with regard to the areas,

© Springer Nature Switzerland AG 2020
E. Ishita et al. (Eds.): ICADL 2020, LNCS 12504, pp. 122–138, 2020.
https://doi.org/10.1007/978-3-030-64452-9_11

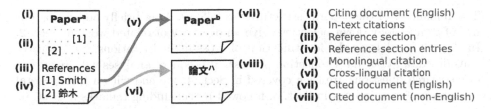

Fig. 1. Schematic explanation of terminology.

in which respective insights can be gained and approaches developed. Here, the literature points in two mayor directions with much potential for improvement—namely the humanities [4,18] and non-English publications [22,26,27,32]. Due to citation data's lack of language coverage and lack of language metadata, a particular practice not well researched so far is cross-lingual citation. That is, references where the citing and cited documents are written in different languages (see *(vi)* in Fig. 1). Because English is currently the de facto academic lingua franca, citations from non-English languages to English can be assumed to generally be significantly more prevalent than the other way around. This dichotomy is reflected in existing literature, where usually either citations from English [18,21], or to English [15,16,29,31] are analyzed. As both directions involve a non-English document on one side of the citation, the analysis of either is challenging with today's Anglocentric state of citation data.

To add to the body of work studying cross-lingual citations *from English*, we perform a large-scale analysis on one million documents and address the following research questions.[1]

1. How prevalent are English to non-English references? We consider prevalence in general, in different disciplines, across time, and within publications that use them.
2. Is self-citation a driving factor for citing non-English work?
3. Are non-English works deemed "citable" in the context of English papers?
4. Do cross-lingual citations pose a particular challenge for data mining?
5. Does citing other languages impact the success of a publication?

Through our analysis, we make the following contributions.

1. We give insight into cross-lingual citations in English papers at a scale, that is considerably larger than analyses in existing literature.
2. We highlight key challenges concerning cross-lingual citations that can inform future developments.
3. To facilitate further analyses, we make our collected data, the code used for analysis, and full results publicly available.[2]

---

[1] The selection of RQs is motivated by existing literature [18,21] (1–3) as well as the intent to inform future endeavors in handling multilingual scholarly data (4–5).
[2] See https://github.com/IllDepence/icadl2020.

The remainder of the paper is structured as follows. After briefly addressing our use of terminology down below, we give an overview of related work in Sect. 2. In Sect. 3 we discuss the identification of cross-lingual citations, data sources considered, and our data collection process. Subsequent analyses with regard to our research questions are then covered in Sect. 4. We end with a brief general discussion of our findings in Sect. 5, followed by concluding remarks in Sect. 6.

Terminology

Because *citation*, *reference* and related terms are not used consistently in literature, we shortly address their use in this paper. As shown in Fig. 1, a cit*ing* document creates a bibliographical link to a cit*ed* document. We use the terms *citation* and *reference* interchangeably for this type of link (e.g., "*(vi)*" in Fig. 1 marks a cross-lingual reference," or "Paper[a] makes two citations"). The textual manifestation of a bibliographic reference, often found at the end of a paper (e.g., "[1] Smith" in Fig. 1), is referred to as *reference section entry*, or sometimes *reference* for short. We call the combined set of these entries *reference section*. Lastly, parts within the text of a paper, which contain a marker connected to one of the reference section entries, are called *in-text citations*.

2   Related Work

2.1   Cross-lingual Citations in Academic Publications

Literature concerning cross-lingual citations in academic publications can be found in the form of analyses and applications. In [18] Kellsey and Knievel conduct an analysis of 468 articles containing 16,138 citations. The analysis spans 4 English language journals in the humanities (disciplines: history, classics, linguistics, and philosophy) over 5 particular years (1962, 1972, 1982, 1992, and 2002). The authors find that 21.3% of the citations in their corpus are cross-lingual, but note strong differences between the covered disciplines. Over time, they observe a steady total, but declining relative number of cross-lingual citations per article. The authors furthermore find, that the ratio of publications that contain at least one cross-lingual citation is increasing.

Lillis et al. [21] investigate if the global status of English is impacting the "citability" of non-English works in English publications. They base their analysis on 240 articles from 2000 to 2007 in psychology journals, and furthermore use the Social Sciences Citation Index and ethnographic records. Their corpus contains 10,688 references, of which 8.5% are cross-lingual. Analyzing the prevalence of references in various contexts, they find that authors are more likely to cite a "local language" in English-medium national journals than in international journals. Further conducting analyses of e.g. in-text citation surface forms, they come to the conclusion that there are strong indicators for a pressure to cite English rather than non-English publications.

Similar observations are made by Kirchik et al. [20] concerning citations to Russian. Analyzing 498,221 papers in Thomson Reuters' Web of Science between

1993 and 2010, they find that Russian scholars are more than twice as likely to cite Russian publications when publishing in Russian language journals (21% of citations) than when they publish in English (10% of citations).

In [29] Schrader analyzes citations from non-English documents to English articles in open access and "traditional" journals. The corpus used comprises 403 cited articles published between 2011 and 2012 in the discipline of library and information science. The articles were cited 5,183 times (13.8% by non-English documents). In their analysis the author observes that being open access makes no statistically significant difference for the ratio of incoming cross-lingual citations of an article, or the language composition of citations a journal receives.

Apart from analyses, there are also approaches to prediction tasks based on cross-lingual citations [15,16,25,31]. Tang et al. [31] propose a bilingual context-citation embedding algorithm for the task of predicting suitable citations to English publications in Chinese sentences. To train and evaluate their approach, they use 2,061 articles from 2002 to 2012 in the Chinese Journal of Computers, which contain citations to 17,693 English publications. Comparing to several baseline methods, they observe the best performance for their novel system. Similarly, in [15] and [16] Jiang et al. propose two novel document embedding methods jointly learned on publication content and citation relations. The corpus used in both cases consists of 14,631 Chinese computer science papers from the Wanfang digital library. The papers contain 11,252 references to Chinese publications and 27,101 references to English publications. For the task of predicting a list of suitable English language references for a Chinese query document, both approaches are reported to outperform a range of baseline methods.

In Table 1 we show a comparison of corpora between related work and our analysis.

Table 1. Comparison of corpora

Work	Type[a]	#Docs[b]	#Refs[b]	#Years	#Disciplines
Kellsey and Knievel [18]	en→*	468	16k	5[c]	4
Lillis et al. [21]	en→*	240	10k	7	1
Schrader [29]	*→en	403	5k	2	1
Tang et al. [31]	zh → en	2k	17k	10	1
Jiang et al. [15,16]	zh → {en,zh}	14k	38k	n/a	1
Kirchik et al. [20]	{en,ru} → ru	497k	n/a	17	(unrestricted)
Ours	en → *	1.1 M	39 M	27	3

[a] type=focus reference type (en=English, ru=Russian, zh=Chinese, *=any)
[b] docs=documents, refs=references
[c] over a span of 40 years

2.2 Cross-lingual Interconnections in Other Types of Media

Apart from academic publications, cross-lingual connections are also described in other types of media. Hale [11] analyzes cross-lingual hyperlinks between online blogs centered around a news event in 2010. In a corpus of 113,117 blog pages in English, Spanish, and Japanese, 12,527 hyperlinks (5.6% of them cross-lingual) are identified. Analysis finds that less than 2% of links in English blogs are cross-lingual, while the number in Spanish and Japanese blogs is slightly above 10%. Hyperlinks between Spanish and Japanese are almost inexistent (7 in total). Further investigating the development of links over time, the author observes a gradual decrease of language group insularity driven by individual translations of blog content—a phenomenon described as "bridgeblogging" by Zuckerman [34].

Similar structural features are reported by Eleta et al. [5] and Hale [10] for Twitter, where multilingual users are bridging language communities. As with academic publications, there also exists literature on link prediction tasks. In [17] Jin et al. analyze cross-lingual information cascades and develop a machine learning approach based on language and content features to predict the size and language distribution of such cascades.

3 Data Collection

3.1 Identification of Cross-lingual Citations

Identifying cross-lingual citations requires information about the language of the citing and cited document, but this is often missing in scholarly data sets (cf. Table 2). Identifying the involved documents' language on the fly, however, is also challenging, because (a) full text (especially of cited documents) is not always available, and (b) language identification on short strings (e.g., titles in references) is unreliable [14]. To nevertheless be able to conduct an analysis of cross-lingual citations on a large scale, we utilize the practice of authors appending an explicit marker in the form of *"(in <Language>)"* to such references. This shifts the requirements from language metadata to the existence of (ideally unfiltered) reference section entries in the data.[3]

The question then remains, how common the practice of using such explicit markers is, compared to the use of untranslated non-English reference titles (without a marker). Conducting a comparison of both variants[4] on a random sample of one million reference section entries from the data set unarXive [28], we get a reliable estimate for non-Latin script languages (e.g., Chinese, Japanese, Russian), but inconclusive results for Latin script languages (e.g., German).[5]

---

[3] Language information is given for the cited document by the *"<Language>"* part of the marker, and for the citing document by the fact, that the marker is in English.

[4] Identification of marked entries is detailed in Sect. 3.3. For the identification of non-English titles we used the reference string parser module of GROBID [24] and the Python module langdetect (see https://github.com/Mimino666/langdetect).

[5] This is because the detection of untranslated non-English reference titles requires language identification on reference titles, which turned out to be unreliable for Latin script languages (e.g., many English titles were falsely identified as German).

Where we get reliable results, explicit marking appears to be the norm. In case of Russian, we observe 567 explicit markers and 3 untranslated titles without a marker. For Chinese, Japanese, and Greek, the number of explicit markers is 60, 57, and 7, respectively, compared to zero untranslated titles. Manual inspection of the noisy results for Latin script languages suggests a significant tendency toward using untranslated titles. These observations mean two things. First, a direct comparison between our numbers on non-Latin and Latin script languages is only valid for *explicitly marked* cross-lingual citations. Second, the number of undetected cross-lingual citations for non-Latin script languages such as Chinese, Japanese, and Russian, is negligible. Accordingly, concerning these languages, our results are valid for cross-lingual citations *in general.*

3.2   Data Source Selection

As our data source we considered five large scholarly data sets commonly used for citation related tasks [7,19]. Table 2 gives an overview of their key properties. The Microsoft Academic Graph (MAG) and CORE are both very large data sets with some form of language metadata present. In the MAG the language is given not for documents themselves, but for URLs associated with papers. CORE contains a language label for 1.79% of its documents. S2ORC, the PubMed Central Open Access Subset (PMC OAS), and unarXive do not offer language metadata, but all contain some form of reference sections (GROBID [24] parse output, JATS [13] XML, and raw strings extracted from LaTeX source files respectively).

From these five, we decided to use unarXive and the MAG. This decision was motivated by two key reasons: (1) metadata of cited documents, and (2) evaluation of the "citability" of non-English works in English papers. As for (1), both S2ORC and the PMC OAS link references in their papers to document IDs within the data set itself (only partly in the PMC OAS, where also MEDLINE IDs and DOIs are found [9]). This is problematic in our case, because S2ORC is restricted to English papers, and the PMC OAS is constrained to Latin script contents,[6] which means metadata on non-English cited documents is inexistent (S2ORC) or very limited (PMC OAS). In unarXive, on the other hand, references are linked to the MAG, which contains metadata on publications regardless of language. Concerning reason (2), the fact that unarXive is built from papers on the preprint server arxiv.org, and the MAG contains metadata on paper's preprint *and* published versions, allows us to analyze whether or not cross-lingual citations are affected by the peer review process.

With these two data sources selected, the extent of our analysis is one million documents, across 3 disciplines (physics, mathematics, computer science), over a span of 27 years (1992–2019).

3.3   Data Collection

To identify references with *"(in <Language>)"* markers, we iterate through the total of 39.7M reference section entries in unarXive and first filter for the

---

[6] See https://www.ncbi.nlm.nih.gov/pmc/about/faq/#q16.

Table 2. Overview of data sets

Data set	#D.[a]	Lang.meta.[b]	R.r.t.[c]	Reference sections	Used
MAG[d] [30,33]	230M	(48%[e])	MAG	–	✓
CORE[f]	123M	1.79%	CORE	–	
S2ORC [23]	81M	–	S2ORC	34% (in GROBID parse)	
PubMed Central OAS[g]	2M	–	Mixed	100% (in JATS XML)	
unarXive [28]	1M	–	MAG	100% (dedicated entity)	✓

[a] Number of documents
[b] Language metadata
[c] References resolved to
[d] Using version 2019-12-26
[e] Language given for source URLs (not always matching paper language)
[f] See https://core.ac.uk/. Using version 2018-03-01
[g] See https://www.ncbi.nlm.nih.gov/pmc/tools/openftlist/

regular expression \(\s*in\s+[a-zA-Z][a-z]+\s*\). This yields 51,380 matches with 207 unique tokens following *"in"* within the parentheses. Within these 207 tokens we manually identify non-languages (e.g., "press" or "preparation") and misspellings (e.g., "japanease" or "russain"), resulting in 44 unique language tokens. These are (presented in ISO 639-1 codes) be, bg, ca, cs, da, de, el, en, eo, es, et, fa, fi, fr, he, hi, hr, hu, hy, id, is, it, ja, ka, ko, la, lv, mk, mr, nl, no, pl, pt, ro, ru, sa, sk, sl, sr, sv, tr, uk, vi, and zh. These 44 languages cover 43 of the 78 languages, in which journals indexed in the Directory of Open Access Journals[7] (DOAJ) are published as of July 2020. The one language found in our data, but with no journal in the DOAJ, is Marathi. In terms of journal count by language, above 44 languages cover 97.54% of the DOAJ. In total, our data contains 33,290 reference section entries in 18,171 unique citing documents. We refer to this set of documents as the *cross-lingual set*.

To analyze differences between papers containing cross-lingual citations in unarXive and a comparable random set, we also generate a second set of papers. To ensure comparability we go through each year of the cross-lingual set, note the number of documents per discipline and then randomly sample the same number of documents from all of unarXive within this year and discipline. This means the *cross-lingual set* and the *random set* have the same document distribution across years and disciplines. Table 3 gives an overview of the resulting data used.

4   Results

In this section we describe the results of our analyses with regard to the research questions laid out in the introduction. We begin with general numbers indicating the prevalence of cross-lingual citations (based on unarXive alone) and follow with more in depth observations (utilizing the MAG metadata).

---

[7] See https://doaj.org/.

Table 3. Overview of data used

	Cross-lingual set	Random set	unarXive
#Docs	18,171	18,171	1,192,097
#Docs (MAG)	16,300	16,464	1,087,765
#Refs	635,154	536,672	39,694,083
#Refs (MAG)	290,421	242,090	15,954,664
#Cross-lingual refs	33,290	642	33,290

*docs = documents, refs = reference section entries, (MAG) = with a MAG ID.

4.1 Prevalence of Cross-lingual Citations in English Papers

We find *"(in <Language>)"* markers in 33,290 out of 39,694,083 reference section entries (0.08%). These appear in 18,171 out of 1,192,097 documents (1.5%)—in other words in every 66th document. Of these 18k documents, 17,223 cite one language other than English, 864 cite two, 76 three, 7 documents four, and a single document cites works in English and five further languages (Russian, French, Polish, Italian, and German). The five most common language pairs within a single document are Russian-Ukrainian (277 documents), German-Russian (166), French-Russian (135), French-German (68), and Chinese-Russian (59).

Table 4 shows the absolute number of reference section entries and unique citing documents for the five most prevalent languages, which combined make up over 90% in terms of both references and documents. As we can see, Russian is by far the most common, making up about two thirds of the cross-lingual set. When breaking down these numbers by year or

Table 4. Most prevalent languages

Language	#References	#Documents
Russian	23,922	12,304
Chinese	2,351	1,582
Japanese	1,843	1,397
German	1,244	965
French	931	719

discipline, it is important to also factor in the distribution of documents along these dimensions in the whole data set. Doing so, we show in Fig. 2 the relative number of documents with cross-lingual citations over time for each of the aforementioned five languages. While the numbers in earlier years can be a bit unstable due to low numbers of total documents, we can observe a downwards trend of citations to Russian, an upwards trend of citations to Chinese, and a somewhat stable proportion in documents citing Japanese works. Looking at the numbers per discipline in Fig. 3, we can see that cross-lingual citations occur most often in mathematics papers, and are about half as common in physics and computer science.

Lastly, within the reference section of a document that has at least one cross-lingual citation, the mean value of "cross-linguality" (i.e., what portion of the reference section is cross-lingual) is 0.083 with a standard deviation of 0.099. Breaking these numbers down by discipline, we can see in Fig. 4 that there is

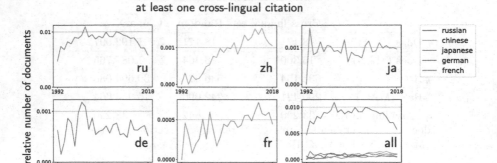

Fig. 2. Relative number of documents citing Russian, Chinese, Japanese, German, and French works. Showing all aforementioned in the bottom right.

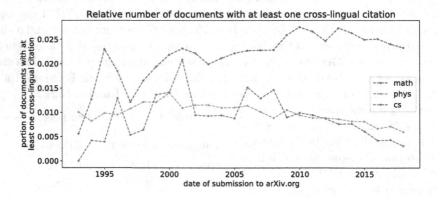

Fig. 3. Relative number of mathematics, physics, and computer science documents citing non-English works.

no large difference, although mathematics papers tend to have a slightly higher portion of cross-lingual citations. The mean values for mathematics, physics and computer science are 0.090, 0.078, and 0.080 respectively.

In terms of the prevalence of cross-lingual citations in English papers, we note that (in the disciplines of physics, mathematics and computer science) about 1 in 66 papers contains citations to non-English documents. About two thirds of these citations are to Russian documents, although in the last years there is a downwards trend with regard to Russian and an upwards trend in citations to Chinese. Citations to documents in Russian, Chinese, Japanese, German, and French make up 90% of the total of cross-lingual citations.

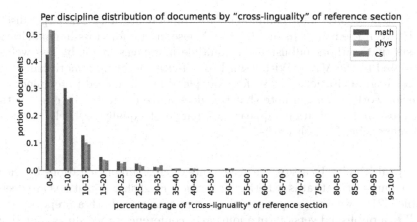

Fig. 4. "Cross-linguality" of reference sections by discipline.

4.2 Impact of Cross-lingual Citations in English Papers

As outlined in our research questions, apart from the prevalence of cross-lingual citations (RQ1), we also want to address whether or not self-citation is a driving factor (RQ2), if they are seen as an "acceptable" practice (RQ3), whether or not they pose a particular challenge for citation data mining (RQ4), and their potential impact on the success of the paper they're part of (RQ5). Our results concerning these aspects are described in the following sections.

Self-citation. To assess the relative degree of self-citation when referring to publications in other languages, we compare the ratio of self-citations in (a) the *cross-lingual citations* within the documents of the cross-lingual set, and (b) the *monolingual citations* within the documents of the cross-lingual set. Comparing two sets of citations from identical documents

Table 5. Self-citations

References to	Self-citations	
	loose	strict
non-English	19%	5%
English	17.9%	11.3%

allows us to control for e.g. author specific self-citation bias. To determine self-citation, we rely on the author metadata in the MAG and therefore require both the citing and cited document of a reference to have a MAG ID. Within the cross-lingual set, this is the case for 3,370 cross-lingual references and 264,341 monolingual references. While at first, we strictly determined a self-citation by a match of MAG IDs, manual inspection of matches and non-matches revealed, that author disambiguation within the MAG is somewhat lacking—that is, in a non-trivial amount of cases there are several IDs for a single author. We therefore measure self-citation by two metrics. A strict metric which only counts a match of MAG IDs, and a loose metric which counts an overlap of the sets of author names on both ends of the reference as a self-citation.

Table 5 shows that going by the strict metric, self-citation is twice as common in monolingual citations. Applying the loose metric, however, self-citation appears to be slightly more common in cross-lingual citations. The larger discrepancy between the results of the strict and loose metric for cross-lingual citations suggests that authors publishing in multiple languages might be less well disambiguated in the MAG. With regard to self-citation being a motivating factor for cross-lingual citations—be it, for example, due to the need to reference one's own prior work—, we can note that this does not seem to be the case. Authors using cross-lingual citations appear to be at least equally as likely to self-cite when referencing English works.

"Acceptability". To assess the acceptance of cross-lingual citations by the scientific community—that is, whether or not non-English publications are deemed "citable" [21]—we analyze papers in our data that have both a preprint version as well as a published version (in a journal or conference proceedings) dated later than the preprint. This is the case for 2,982 papers. For each preprint-published paper pair, we check if there is a difference in cross-lingual citations. This gives an indication of how the process of peer review affects cross-lingual citations. We perform a manual as well as an automated analysis.[8]

For the manual evaluation, we take a random sample of 100 paper pairs. We then retrieve a PDF file of both the preprint and the published version, and manually compare their reference sections. For the automated evaluation, we find that 599 of the 2.9k paper pairs have PDF source URLs given in the MAG. After automatically downloading these and parsing them with GROBID, we are left with 498 valid sets of references. For these, we identify explicitly marked cross-lingual references as described in Sect. 3 and calculate their differences.

Table 6 shows the results of our evaluations. In both, cross-lingual citations are more often removed than added, but in the majority of cases left intact. The larger volatility in the automated evaluation is likely due to parsing inconsistencies of GROBID. Our findings complement those of Lillis et al. [21], who, analyzing psychology journals, observe *"some evidence that gatekeepers [...] are explicitly challenging citations in other languages."* For the fields of physics, mathematics, and computer science, we find no clear indication of a consistent in- or decreasing effect of the peer review process on cross-lingual citations.

Table 6. Changes in cross-ling. cit. between preprints and published papers

Evaluation	#Pairs	#Increased	#Deceased	Mean[a]	SD[a]
Manual	100	4	7	−0.02	0.529
Automated	498	33	70	−0.12	0.821

[a]of the differences in the amount of cross-lingual citations

---

[8] Full evaluation details can be found at https://github.com/IllDepence/icadl2020.

Impact on Citation Data Mining. To assess if cross-lingual citations pose a particular challenge for scholarly data mining—and are therefore likely to be underrepresented in scholarly data—, we compare the ratio of references that could be resolved to MAG metadata records for the cross-lingual set and the whole unarXive data set. Of the 39M references in unarXive 42.6% are resolved to a MAG ID. For the complete reference sections of the papers in the cross-lingual set (i.e., references to both non-English and English documents) the number is 45.7% (290,421 of 635,154 references). Looking only at the cross-lingual citations, the success rate of reference resolution drops to 11.2% (3,734 of 33,290 references). We interpret this as a clear indication that resolving cross-lingual references is a challenge. Possible reasons for this are, for example:

1. A lack of language coverage in the target data set.
   For example, if the target data set only contains records of English papers, references to non-English publications cannot be found within and resolved to that target data set.
2. Missing metadata in the target data set.
   For example, when there is a primary non-English as well as an alternative English title of a publication, only the former is in the target data set's metadata, but the latter is used in the cross-lingual reference.
3. The use of a title translated "on the fly."
   If a non-English publication has no alternative English title, a self translated title in a reference cannot be found in any metadata. To give an example, reference [14] in `arXiv:1309.1264` titled *"Hierarchy of reversible logic elements with memory"* is only found in metadata[9] as 記憶付き可逆論理素子の能力の階層構造について.
4. The use of a title transliterated "on the fly." Similar to an unofficial translated title, if a title is transliterated and this transliteration is not existent in metadata, the provided title is not resolvable. A concrete example of this is the third reference in `arXiv:cs/9912004` titled *"Daimeishi-ga Sasumono Sono Sashi-kata"* which is only found in metadata[9] as 代名詞が指すもの, その指し方.

Cases 4 and especially 3 additionally impose a challenge on human readers, as the referred documents can only be found by trying to translate or transliterate back to the original. References to non-English documents which do not have an alternative English title should therefore ideally include enough information to (a) identify the referenced document (i.e., at least the original title), and (b) a way for readers not familiar with the cited document's language to get an idea of what is being cited (e.g., by adding a freely translated English title).[10] There are, however, situations where an original title cannot be used. Documents in PubMed Central, for example, cannot contain non-Latin scripts,[11] meaning that

---

[9] See http://hdl.handle.net/2433/172983, https://ci.nii.ac.jp/naid/10008827159/.

[10] As, for example, in reference [15] in `arXiv:1503.05573`: "Шафаревич И. Р. Основы алгебраической геометрии// МЦНМО, Москва, 2007. (English translation: Shafarevich I.R. Foundations of Algebraic Geometry MCCME, Moscow. 2007)."

[11] See https://www.ncbi.nlm.nih.gov/pmc/about/faq/#q16.

references to documents in Russian, Chinese, Japanese, etc. which do not have alternative English titles are inevitably a challenge for both human readers as well as data mining approaches, unless there is a DOI, URL, or similar identifier that can be referred to.

In light of this, taking a closer look at the 88.8% of unmatched references in the cross-lingual set broken down by languages, we note the following matching failure rates for the five most prevalent languages: Russian: 88.6%, Chinese: 87.0%, Japanese: 91.0%, German: 85.4%, and French: 83.2%. While all of these are high, the numbers for the three non-Latin script languages are noticeably higher than those of German and French. As can be seen with the task of resolving references—and as also indicated through our self-citation data shown in Table 5—cross-lingual citations do pose a particular challenge for scholarly data mining.

Impact on Paper Success. To get an indication of whether or not an English paper's success is influenced by the fact that it contains citations to non-English documents, we compare our cross-lingual set with the random set (cf. Table 2). For both sets we first determine the number of papers that in the MAG metadata have a published version (journal or conference proceedings) in addition to the preprint on arxiv.org. That is, we assume that papers which only have a preprint version did not make it through the peer review process. Using this measure, we observe 9,390 of 16,224 (57.88%) successful papers in the cross-lingual set, and 10,966 of 16,378 (66.96%) successful papers in the random set. Unsurprisingly, due to the higher ratio of published versions, the papers in the random set are also cited more. Table 7 shows a comparison of the average number of citations that documents in both sets received. Due to the high standard deviation in the complete sets, we also look at papers which received between 1 and 100 citations, which are comparably frequent in both sets. As we can see, in the unfiltered as well as the filtered case, documents with cross-lingual citations tend to be cited a little less. Because here we can only control for the distribution of papers across years and disciplines, and not for individual authors (as we did in the "Self-citation" section), there might be various confounding factors involved.

Table 7. Comparison of citations received

Filter criterion		Cross-lingual set	Random set
–	#Docs	16,300	16,464
	Mean #cit	13.7	18.2
	SD	75.0	51.7
$1 \leq \#cit \leq 100$	#Docs	12,074	12,852
	Mean #cit	12.0	15.1
	SD	15.8	18.4

5   Discussion

Even though citations in English publications are typically to other English documents, we have seen that in preprints as well as conference proceedings and journal articles cross-lingual citations are used to refer to documents in a wide range of languages. Their prevalence is probably not high enough to greatly impact performance scores of general citation data driven approaches in e.g. information retrieval and recommendation—i.e., the evaluation of a system would not drastically change by introducing capabilities to handle references to other languages. However, as we could observe clear differences in prevalence across different disciplines and different cited languages, it might be advisable for specific approaches to evaluate the situation on a case by case basis. For example, a citation driven analysis of research trends in mathematics might benefit from being able to track "citation trails" into the realm of Russian publications.

We furthermore observed clear indicators that cross-lingual citations pose a challenge for citation data mining. As citation based performance evaluation is still a relevant steering mechanism in science, a lack in capabilities to automatically trace citations from e.g. international to national venues creates an imbalance between "supported" and "unsupported" publication languages. Furthermore, because some countries have sophisticated national systems and resources with regard to citation data—like Japan's CiNii[12] which has been used for research trend analysis [8]—, successful handling of cross-lingual citations would not just be a few additional data points on a subset of publications, but rather enable the detection of bridges between what are currently data silos that are not well interconnected.

6   Conclusion

Utilizing two large data sets, unarXive and the MAG, we performed a large-scale analysis of citations from English documents to non-English language works (cross-lingual citations). The data analyzed spans one million citing publications, 3 disciplines, and 27 years. We gain insights into cross-lingual citations' prevalence and impact, which we hope can inform further developments tackling the challenges of handling scholarly data.

Regarding English to non-English citations, we want to expand our investigation to further disciplines in the future. As our present analysis is based on papers in mathematics, physics, and computer science, insights into the humanities would be of particular interest. As for cross-lingual citations in general, analyses of non-English to English citations are likely to be more challenging to perform on a large scale, but might also yield insights with a larger impact, as citing English language publications is rather common in other languages, and has already given rise to approaches like cross-lingual citation recommendation.

---

[12] See https://support.nii.ac.jp/cia/cinii_db.

References

1. Abu-Jbara, A., Ezra, J., Radev, D.: Purpose and polarity of citation: to- wards NLP-based bibliometrics. In: Proceedings of the 2013 Conference of the North American Chapter of the Association for Computational Linguistics: Human Language Technologies, pp. 596–606. Association for Computational Linguistics, Atlanta (2013)
2. Chen, C.: CiteSpace II: detecting and visualizing emerging trends and transient patterns in scientific literature. J. Am. Soc. Inf. Sci. Tech. **57**(3), 359–377 (2006). https://doi.org/10.1002/asi.20317
3. Cohan, A., Feldman, S., Beltagy, I., Downey, D., Weld, D.: SPECTER: document-level representation learning using citation-informed transformers. In: Proceedings of the 58th Annual Meeting of the Association for Computational Linguistics, pp. 2270–2282. Association for Computational Linguistics (2020)
4. Colavizza, G., Romanello, M.: Citation mining of humanities journals: the progress to date and the challenges ahead. J. Eur. Period. Stud. **4**(1), 36–53 (2019)
5. Eleta, I., Golbeck, J.: Bridging languages in social networks: how multilingual users of Twitter connect language communities? In: Proceedings of the American Society for Information Science and Technology, vol. 49, no. 1, pp. 1–4 (2012). https://doi.org/10.1002/meet.14504901327
6. Elkiss, A., Shen, S., Fader, A., Erkan, G., States, D., Radev, D.: Blind men and elephants: what do citation summaries tell us about a research article? J. Am. Soc. Inf. Sci. Technol. **59**(1), 51–62 (2008)
7. Färber, M., Jatowt, A.: Citation recommendation: approaches and datasets. Int. J. Digit. Libraries (to appear)
8. Fukuda, S., et al.: Construction of a CiNii データベースを用いた研究動向分析システムの構築 database driven research trend analysis system. In: 言語処理学会第 18 回年次大会発表論文, pp. 539–542 (2012). (in Japanese)
9. Gipp, B., Meuschke, N., Lipinski, M.: CITREC : an evaluation framework for citation-based similarity measures based on TREC genomics and PubMed central. In: iConference 2015 Proceedings. iSchools (2015)
10. Hale, S.A.: Global connectivity and multilinguals in the Twitter network. In: Proceedings of the SIGCHI Conference on Human Factors in Computing Systems, CHI 2014, pp. 833–842. Association for Computing Machinery, Toronto (2014). https://doi.org/10.1145/2556288.2557203
11. Hale, S.A.: Net increase? Cross-lingual linking in the blogosphere. J. Comput. Mediated Commun. **17**(2), 135–151 (2012). https://doi.org/10.1111/j.1083-6101.2011.01568.x
12. Hirsch, J.E.: An index to quantify an individual's scientific research output. Proc. Nat. Acad. Sci. **102**(46), 16569–16572 (2005)
13. Huh, S.: Journal article tag suite 1.0: national information standards organization standard of journal extensible markup language. Sci. Edit. **1**(2), 99–104 (2014). https://doi.org/10.6087/kcse.2014.1.99
14. Jauhiainen, T.S., Lui, M., Zampieri, M., Baldwin, T., Lindén, K.: Automatic language identification in texts: a survey. J. Artif. Intell. Res. **65**, 675–782 (2019)
15. Jiang, Z., Lu, Y., Liu, X.: Cross-language citation recommendation via publication content and citation representation fusion. In: Proceedings of the 18th ACM/IEEE on Joint Conference on Digital Libraries, JCDL 2018, pp. 347–348. Association for Computing Machinery, Fort Worth (2018). https://doi.org/10.1145/3197026.3203898

16. Jiang, Z., Yin, Y., Gao, L., Lu, Y., Liu, X.: Cross-language citation recommendation via hierarchical representation learning on heterogeneous graph. In: The 41st International ACM SIGIR Conference on Research & Development in Information Retrieval, SIGIR 2018, pp. 635–644. Association for Computing Machinery, New York (2018). https://doi.org/10.1145/3209978.3210032

17. Jin, H., Toyoda, M., Yoshinaga, N.: Can cross-lingual information cascades be predicted on Twitter? In: Ciampaglia, G.L., Mashhadi, A., Yasseri, T. (eds.) SocInfo 2017. LNCS, vol. 10539, pp. 457–472. Springer, Cham (2017). https://doi.org/10.1007/978-3-319-67217-5_28

18. Kellsey, C., Knievel, J.E.: Global English in the humanities? A longitudinal citation study of foreign-language use by humanities scholars. Coll. Res. Libr. **65**(3), 194–204 (2004)

19. Khan, S., Liu, X., Shakil, K.A., Alam, M.: A survey on scholarly data: from big data perspective. Inf. Process. Manage. **53**(4), 923–944 (2017). https://doi.org/10.1016/j.ipm.2017.03.006

20. Kirchik, O., Gingras, Y., Larivière, V.: Changes in publication languages and citation practices and their effect on the scientific impact of Russian science (1993–2010). J. Am. Soc. Inf. Sci. Technol. **63**(7), 1411–1419 (2012). https://doi.org/10.1002/asi.22642

21. Lillis, T., Hewings, A., Vladimirou, D., Curry, M.J.: The geolinguistics of English as an academic lingua franca: citation practices across English-medium national and English-medium international journals. Int. J. Appl. Linguist. **20**(1), 111–135 (2010). https://doi.org/10.1111/j.1473-4192.2009.00233.x

22. Liu, X., Chen, X.: CJK languages or English: languages used by academic journals in China, Japan, and Korea. J. Sch. Publish. **50**(3), 201–214 (2019)

23. Lo, K., Wang, L.L., Neumann, M., Kinney, R., Weld, D.: S2ORC: the semantic scholar open research corpus. In: Proceedings of the 58th Annual Meeting of the Association for Computational Linguistics, pp. 4969–4983. Association for Computational Linguistics (2020)

24. Lopez, P.: GROBID: combining automatic bibliographic data recognition and term extraction for scholarship publications. In: Agosti, M., Borbinha, J., Kapidakis, S., Papatheodorou, C., Tsakonas, G. (eds.) ECDL 2009. LNCS, vol. 5714, pp. 473–474. Springer, Heidelberg (2009). https://doi.org/10.1007/978-3-642-04346-8_62

25. Ma, S., Zhang, C., Liu, X.: A review of citation recommendation: from textual content to enriched context. Scientometrics **122**(3), 1445–1472 (2020). https://doi.org/10.1007/s11192-019-03336-0

26. Moed, H.F., Markusova, V., Akoev, M.: Trends in Russian research output indexed in Scopus and Web of science. Scientometrics **116**(2), 1153–1180 (2018). https://doi.org/10.1007/s11192-018-2769-8

27. Moskaleva, O., Akoev, M.: Non-English language publications in Citation In- dexes - quantity and quality. In: Proceedings 17th International Conference on Scientometrics & Informetrics, pp. 35–46. Edizioni Efesto, Italy (2019)

28. Saier, T., Färber, M.: *unarXive*: a large scholarly data set with publications' full-text, annotated in-text citations, and links to metadata. Scientometrics (2), 1–24 (2020). https://doi.org/10.1007/s11192-020-03382-z

29. Schrader, B.: Cross-language Citation Analysis of Traditional and Open Access Journals (2019). https://doi.org/10.17615/djpr-1k06

30. Sinha, A., et al.: An overview of microsoft academic service (MAS) and applications. In: Proceedings of the 24th International Conference on World Wide Web, WWW 2015 Companion, pp. 243–246. ACM (2015). https://doi.org/10.1145/2740908.2742839

31. Tang, X., Wan, X., Zhang, X.: Cross-language context-aware citation recommendation in scientific articles. In: Proceedings of the 37th International ACM SIGIR Conference on Research & Development in Information Retrieval, SIGIR 2014, pp. 817–826. Association for Computing Machinery, New York (2014). https://doi.org/10.1145/2600428.2609564

32. Vera-Baceta, M.-A., Thelwall, M., Kousha, K.: Web of science and scopus language coverage. Scientometrics **121**(3), 1803–1813 (2019). https://doi.org/10.1007/s11192-019-03264-z

33. Wang, K., et al.: A review of Microsoft academic services for science of science studies. Front. Big Data **2**, 45 (2019). https://doi.org/10.3389/fdata.2019

34. Zuckerman, E.: Meet the bridgebloggers. Public Choice **134**(1), 47–65 (2008). https://doi.org/10.1007/s11127-007-9200-y

How Do Retractions Influence the Citations of Retracted Articles?

Siluo Yang and Fan Qi[✉]

Wuhan University, Wuhan, China
909591921@qq.com

Abstract. Scientific retraction helps purge the continued use of flawed research. However, the practical influence of it needs to be identified and quantified. In this study, we analyzed the citations of 106 psychological articles from Web of Science to explore the influence of retraction using quantitative methods. Our results show that 1) retraction caused a significant decline (1.6–1.8 times) in the post-retraction citations; 2) retractions from open accessed or high-quality journals are effective; 3) retraction is incapable to eliminate the dissemination of flawed results thoroughly. Our findings may provide useful insights for scholars and practitioners to understand and integrate the retraction system.

Keywords: Retractions · Scientific misconduct · PSM · Difference-in-differences · Non-parametric test

1 Introduction

Retraction offers an objective manner to flag problematic publications. Since 2001, the rate of retracted articles has been increasing rapidly in all academic fields. Most of them were retracted for scientific misconduct (i.e., falsification, plagiarism) (Steen, Casadevall and Fang 2013). Thus, it is important that whether retraction can help scholars identify erroneous papers and to avoid developing incorrect results or not (COPE 2009). The influence of retractions needs to be measured and assessed. In the context of disciplines, retractions also show differences. Existing studies focus on retractions from Hard Sciences, especially medical fields. While retractions from Social Sciences remain to be explored.

Due to the collective and cumulative nature of knowledge production, citations to previous literature are recognitions and validations of research quality. However, it can be harmful if retracted articles were still cited as valid works after they were retracted (Bar-Ilan and Halevi 2017; Redman et al. 2008). Retractions should prevent flawed results from spreading via citations, which can be observed from the influence of retraction on citations. Enhancing the understanding of retraction influence is also helpful to integrate scientific processes and to improve the quality of academic outputs.

This study explored how do retractions influence the citations of retracted articles. Our contributions are as follows. 1) we quantified the influence of retractions on citations and managed to conduct the causal analysis on it; 2) we investigated the situation of

E. Ishita et al. (Eds.): ICADL 2020, LNCS 12504, pp. 139–148, 2020.
https://doi.org/10.1007/978-3-030-64452-9_12

retracted articles in psychology, which is often ignored among numerous studies on retraction. We expect to make the process of citation and retraction standardized to minimize problems and errors by exploring the actual influence of retraction.

2 Related Studies

2.1 Bibliometric Analysis on Retraction

Retraction plays an important role in the scientific system by removing flawed or erroneous publications, although retracted articles represented only 0.02% of total publications (Bik et al. 2016). However, the scientific community paid insufficient attention to it given that the number and citations of retracted articles are still on the rise (Cokol et al. 2008; Pfeifer and Snodgrass 1990). At present, most of studies on retraction are the investigation of the whole situation from a macroscopic scale in the form of review or survey. He (2013) analyzed retraction of global scientific publications from Science Citation Index Expanded quantitatively and found that different patterns of retraction existed in each field. Therefore, some studies focused on retraction from a certain discipline, mostly related to medical fields. Chauvin et al. (2017) characterized retracted publications in emergency medicine. Also, national phenomena of retraction attracted some attention to scholars, such as retraction from Malaysia (Aspura et al. 2018), China (Lei and Zhang, 2018), and India (Elango et al. 2019).

2.2 Interactions Between Citation and Retraction

The citations of retracted articles contributed to the spread of retraction, which calls for a closer examination. Existing research studies have made attempts on it but are still on a preliminary stage. In 1998, Budd et al. found that the continued positive citations to retracted articles indicated potential problems for biomedical science. Then, several pieces of research exploring the nature of post retraction citation qualitatively arose. It turns out that positive citations to retracted literature abound (Hamilton 2019; Bar-Ilan and Halevi 2017). With regard to the quantitative analysis of retraction citation, Shuai et al. (2017) investigated the effects of retraction on scholarly impact, stating that the spread of retraction is limited and localized. Additionally, research studies on citations of retracted articles are mostly case studies concerning medical fields. Suelzer et al. (2019) took a retracted article from clinical fields published in 1998 as an example to examine the characteristics of its citations.

Previous studies demonstrate that problems still exist in the process of retraction and the research integrity has yet to be improved. Most of them focused on medical related fields. The analysis and discussion unfolded with the correlation between retraction and citation. The causal link remains to be explored and the influence of retraction needs to be quantified. In this study, we expect to further analyze the influence of retraction on citation, which is significant to the dissemination of erroneous results, with causal inferences to clarify the deficiency and problem in the system of retraction. Meanwhile, we selected psychology as a case to explore the phenomena of retraction in social sciences, which is often underrated.

3 Data and Methods

3.1 Data Collection

Web of Science is the world's largest publisher-neutral citation index and research intelligence platform (Web of Science Confident Research Begins Here, 2019), from which we obtained biographic data and citing articles of retracted articles. On 3rd June 2020, we accessed WoS and identified all retractions from Psychology Science using the string "DT = (retracted publication) AND WC = (PSYCHOLOGY*)". 106 retracted articles were downloaded as the raw dataset.

To conduct the comparable experiment, we defined the retraction dataset as treatment group and the similar dataset we selected as control group. On 3rd June 2020, we collected 12364 articles from the same source journals and publication years with retracted articles in treatment group. We matched control group using Propensity Score Matching (PSM) and obtained 65 articles as control group. Citations of each year from publication to retraction were the control variables.

3.2 Indicators and Methods

A post-retraction citation was defined as any publication which cited a retracted article. A pre-retraction citation was calculated by subtracting post-retraction citation from the total citation counts.

Wilcoxon signed-rank was conducted to test the difference between treatment and control groups. We used a difference-in-differences specification to assess the influence of retraction on post retraction citation of retracted articles.

$$\ln Citation_{it} = \beta_0 + \beta_1 retract + \beta_2 year + \beta_3 D_{it} + \beta_4 control\_variables + \varepsilon \qquad (1)$$

$Citation_{it}$ is a measure of citation of retracted article i in year t. Retract is a dummy variable that equals one in the treatment group and equals zero otherwise. Year is a dummy variable that equals one in the years after retraction year and equals zero otherwise. D_{it} is a dummy variable that equals one in the years after article i was retracted and equals zero otherwise. ε_{it} is the error term. Control variables included the number of authors, the number of references, the length of title, and the length of paper. The coefficient, β_3, therefore indicates the influence of retraction on citation of retracted articles. A positive and significant β_3 suggests that retraction exerts a positive effect on citation, while a negative and significant β_3 indicates that retraction pushed citation lower. In total, we have data for 90 retracted articles and 2148 article-year observations serve as the basis for much of our analysis.

$$\ln Citation_{it} = \alpha_0 + \alpha_1 D_{it} + \alpha_2 P_{OA} + \alpha_3 D_{it} \times P_{OA} + \alpha_4 control\_variables + \varepsilon \qquad (2)$$

To examine whether the influence of retraction on citation is affected by the way journals were accessed, we built model above (2). $Citation_{it}$, D_{it}, and control_variables are the same as model (1). P_{OA} equals one when the retracted articles are from open accessed journals and equals zero otherwise.

$$\ln Citation_{it} = \gamma_0 + \gamma_1 D_{it} + \gamma_2 IF + \gamma_3 D_{it} \times IF + \gamma_4 control\_variables + \varepsilon \qquad (3)$$

To examine whether the influence of retraction on citation is affected by the impact factors of journals, we built model above (3). $Citation_{it}$, D_{it}, and control_variables are the same as model (1). IF is the impact factors of journals in recent five years, which is obtained from WoS.

4 Results

4.1 General Situation

Table 1 presents the descriptive statistics of main variables. The citation counts of retracted articles are relatively high and imbalanced. The oldest retracted article was published in 1996, while the first article was retracted in 2002 in psychology science. It showed that the awareness of retraction arose comparatively late in this field. The mean retraction gap was 3.71 years, which was longer than results in previous studies.

Table 1. The descriptive statistics of retracted articles in psychology science.

	Citation	Publication year	Retraction year	Retraction gap
N	65	65	65	65
Mean	16.44	2008	2012	3.71
Std. Dev	15.939	4.636	3.496	3.494
Mini.	0	1996	2002	0
Q1	4	2006	2010	1
Median	12	2008	2012	3
Q3	21	2011	2013	5
Max.	70	2018	2018	16

Figure 1 presented top reasons of retractions in psychology science. Falsification/fabrication of data and error in data accounted for 18% of total retractions. Likewise, quite a few articles were connected to misconduct by authors (10%). Due to improper research methods and inaccurate dataset, 7% retracted articles were questioned about results. 13% of retracted articles were investigated by research management departments, such as company and institution.

4.2 Test on the Result of Propensity Score Matching

In Fig. 2, we conducted four pairs of Wilcoxon tests to verify the effect of PSM. We found that the difference of citation before retraction between treatment and control groups was not significant (NS), which indicates that articles in treatment and control groups have the parallel trend in citation counts before retraction. While the differences of post retraction citations between treatment and control group were significant. It

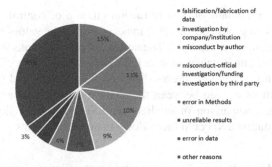

Fig. 1. The distribution of retraction reasons in psychology science.

demonstrated the influence of retraction to some extent imprecisely. We also found that the citation counts before and after retraction were different in both treatment and control group, which can be explained by the cumulative effect of citation. Usually, citation counts decreased with time. It caused the endogenous problem when we assess the influence of retraction on citation. Thus, it needs to be further analyzed in next part.

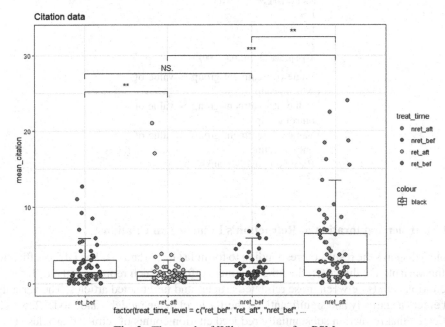

Fig. 2. The result of Wilcoxon test after PSM.

4.3 Preliminary Exploration of Retraction's Influence on Citation

We first conducted a Wilcoxon signed ranks test between treatment group and control group to examine the influence of retraction on citation counts. The results are shown in Table 2. First, the medians of post retraction citation of control group were larger than those of treatment group. Second, the ranks of difference values between treatment group and control group were reported. The number of positive ranks was less than that of negative ranks. Third, the Z values of four indicators were negative. The P values were all <0.05, indicating that the difference between the medians and 0 was statistically significant. Differences existed between the citation of treatment and control groups. Combined with the comparison of median, we found that retraction might have an adverse effect on citation and could bring down the citation counts.

Table 2. Wilcoxon rank-sum test of post retraction citation.

Reports	Post retraction citation
Median	
Treatment group	6
Control group	21
Difference	−15
Ranks	
Negative ranks[a]	48
Positive ranks[b]	13
Ties[c]	4
Test statistics	
Z[d]	−5.128
Asymp. Sig. (2-tailed)	0.000

[a]Value of treatment group < value of control group
[b]Value of treatment group > value of control group
[c]Value of treatment group = value of control group
[d]Based on positive ranks.

4.4   Further Exploration of Retraction's Influence on Citation

Table 3 displays the results corresponding to formula (1), (2) and (3). The DID coefficient of the variable D_{it} directly reflect the treatment effects, which represents the difference in citation counts between those retracted articles and unretracted articles. The variable Dit enters negatively and significantly at the 1% level in the model 1 and model 2, which indicated that retraction substantially reduced citation counts of retracted articles. That said, retraction induced around 1.6 to 1.8 times of citations reduction. In model 3, the coefficient for variable Dit and interaction Dit*IF are negative. This indicates that the influence of retractions from journals with high impact factors on citation is significant. High-quality journals tend to publish effective retractions. In model 4, the coefficient for variable Dit and interaction Dit*OA are negative. This indicates that retractions from open accessed journals have advantages on dissemination, so that they can purge the impact of erroneous results.

Table 3. Differences of citation counts before and after retraction between treatment and control groups.

Variables	Model 1	Model 2	Model 3	Model 4
Dit	−0.496***	−0.598***	−0.27***	−0.381***
no_author		0.064**	0.035**	0.033**
no_reference		0.009***	0.008***	0.008***
len_title		−0.023**	−0.014***	−0.014***
len_paper		0.017**	0.009**	0.009**
IF		0.102***	0.084***	0.071***
OA		−0.084	−0.098*	−0.031
Dit*IF			−0.033*	
Dit*OA				−0.183*
Cons	−0.757***	−1.594***	0.178**	0.233***
Pseudo R2	0.029	0.095	0.24	0.239
Observations	2148	2148	2148	2148
Model description	Standard DID	Model 1 + control	Model 1 + interaction 1	Model 1 + interaction 2

Figure 3 presents the dynamic influence of retraction on citation. Before retraction the coefficient has no significant difference with zero, indicating that the DID model satisfied the hypothesis of parallel trend. The curve was below x-axis and decreased intensively after retraction, revealing that retraction cause a long-term and negative influence on citation. Also, the influence enhanced with time.

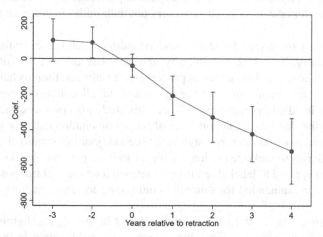

Fig. 3. The dynamic influence of retraction on citation of retracted articles.

5 Discussion and Conclusions

Some research studies related to retractions have been investigated and discussed in this section. Most of the characteristics of retraction in psychology were in line with those in other fields. Slightly different from the past research, the mean time from publication to retraction was fairly long in our study (3.71 years). While Redman et al. (2008) and Budd et al. (1999) measured this period as 20.75 and 28 months respectively. As a critical signal to scientific community, retraction has a statistically significant influence on citation. Our findings that the post retraction citation received by retracted articles was less than that of controlled articles was in line with existing research studies from various fields (Lu et al. 2013; Furman et al. 2012; Hamilton 2019). In the long run, the substantial decline in citation caused by retraction also leads to a drop in the impact of literature and authors. In radiant oncology, the majority of citations occurred in the second year after retraction (Hamilton 2019). However, our results indicated that the retraction induced a continuous drop of citation so the majority of citations appeared before retraction.

This study sought to explore the nature of retractions' influence on citation and quantify it. Retracted articles in psychology were selected as the research subject. We expect to integrate the self-correcting system and improve the institutional monitoring by learning about the phenomena of retraction. Our main findings are summarized as follows.

To conclude, the influence of retraction on citations can be observed clearly. However, the role retractions play in the self-correcting system and governance of knowledge need to be improved. First, retraction reduced 1.6–1.8 times of citation of retracted articles on average. Second, the influence of retractions from journals with high impact factors on citation is significant. Retractions from open accessed journals have advantages on dissemination. Third, although retraction have clear and negative influence on citation, post retraction citation still exists. Retraction is incapable to eliminate the dissemination of flawed results thoroughly. The undesirable performance of retraction urged the authors, editors, and database vendors to carry out their duties to integrate the retraction system.

This study is expected to deepen the understanding of retraction's influence for scientific community. To ensure the integrity and authority of academic literature, it is necessary to make researchers aware of problematic results and limit its harmful effects. It is helpful for the quality of future research and the allocation of research funding if retraction is handled appropriately. Hence, this study also provided practical implications. First, the disordered phenomenon of retraction citation calls for guidelines on citing retractions, such as reference style, etc. Second, journals should closely collaborate with databases to make retraction visible as soon as possible. Marks, stamps, and tags need to be applied to label all editions of retracted articles. Third, post-publication peer review is recommended for scientific community to self-correcting (Cokol et al. 2007).

Several limitations to the present study should be noted, highlighting important directions for future research. First, the sample size of this study is limited. Future research would include more articles from different fields to verify the influence of retraction. Second, to obtain a more precise result and further explore the causality, more control variables should be taken into account. Also, we would like to explore the influence of retraction on the network of citation diffusion and the whole scientific ecosystem.

Acknowledgements. This research is funded by the National Social Science Fund Key Project of People's Republic of China (17ATQ009). Thanks Pai Li for the analysis of data and insightful comments on this study.

References

Aspura, M.K.Y.I., Noorhidawati, A., Abrizah, A.: An analysis of Malaysian retracted papers: misconduct or mistakes? Scientometrics **115**(3), 1315–1328 (2018). https://doi.org/10.1007/s11192-018-2720-z

Bar-Ilan, J., Halevi, G.: Post retraction citations in context: a case study. Scientometrics **113**(1), 547–565 (2017). https://doi.org/10.1007/s11192-017-2242-0

Bik, E.M., Casadevall, A., Fang, F.C.: The prevalence of inappropriate image duplication in biomedical research publications. MBio **7**, e00809–e00816 (2016)

Budd, J.M., Sievert, M., Schultz, T.R., Scoville, C.: Effects of article retraction on citation and practice in medicine. Bull. Med. Libr. Assoc. **87**(4), 437–443 (1999)

Chauvin, A., De Villelongue, C., Pateron, D., Yordanov, Y.: A systematic review of retracted publications in emergency medicine. Eur. J. Emergency Med. **26**(1), 19–23 (2017)

Cokol, M., Ozbay, F., Rodriguez-Esteban, R.: Retraction rates are on the rise. EMBO Rep. **9**(1), 2 (2007). https://doi.org/10.1038/sj.embor.7401143

Cokol, M., Ozbay, F., Rodriguezesteban, R.: Retraction rates are on the rise. EMBO Rep. **9**(1), 2 (2008)

COPE Council, COPE Guidelines: Retraction Guidelines, November 2019. https://doi.org/10.24318/cope.2019.1.4

Elango, B., Kozak, M., Rajendran, P.: Analysis of retractions in Indian science. Scientometrics **119**(2), 1081–1094 (2019). https://doi.org/10.1007/s11192-019-03079-y

Fang, F.C., Steen, R.G., Casadevall, A.: Misconduct accounts for the majority of retracted scientific publications. Proc. Natl. Acad. Sci. **109**(42), 17028–17033 (2013). https://doi.org/10.1073/pnas.1212247109

Furman, J.L., Jensen, K., Murray, F.: Governing knowledge in the scientific community: exploring the role of retractions in biomedicine. Res. Policy **41**(2), 276–290 (2012)

Hamilton, D.G.: Continued citation of retracted radiation oncology literature—do we have a problem? Int. J. Radiat. Oncol. Biol. Phys. **103**(5), 1036–1042 (2019)

He, T.: Retraction of global scientific publications from 2001 to 2010. Scientometrics **96**(2), 555–561 (2013)

Lei, L., Zhang, Y.: Lack of improvement in scientific integrity: an analysis of WoS retractions by Chinese Researchers (1997–2016). Sci. Eng. Ethics **24**(5), 1409–1420 (2018)

Lu, S.F., Jin, G.Z., Uzzi, B., Jones, B.: The retraction penalty: evidence from the Web of Science. Sci. Rep. **3**, 3146 (2013)

Pfeifer, M.P., Snodgrass, G.L.: The continued use of retracted, invalid scientific literature. JAMA **263**(10), 1420–1423 (1990)

Redman, B.K., Yarandi, H.N., Merz, J.F.: Empirical developments in retraction. J. Med. Ethics **34**(11), 807–809 (2008)

Shuai, X., Rollins, J., Moulinier, I., Custis, T., Edmunds, M., Schilder, F.: A multidimensional investigation of the effects of publication retraction on scholarly impact. J. Assoc. Inf. Sci. Tech. **68**(9), 2225–2236 (2017)

Suelzer, E.M., Jennifer, D., Hanus, K.L., Barbara, R., Rita, S., Elizabeth, W.: Assessment of citations of the retracted article by wakefield et al with fraudulent claims of an association between vaccination and autism. JAMA Network Open **2**(11), 20–29 (2019)

Web of Science Group: Web of Science Confident research begins here (2019). https://clarivate.com/webofsciencegroup/solutions/web-of-science/. Accessed 1 April 2020

Identification of Research Data
References Based on Citation Contexts

Tomoki Ikoma[1]([⊠])[iD] and Shigeki Matsubara[2][iD]

[1] Graduate School of Informatics, Nagoya University, Nagoya, Japan
ikoma.tomoki@h.mbox.nagoya-u.ac.jp
[2] Information and Communications, Nagoya University, Nagoya, Japan

Abstract. In this paper, a method for the automatic identification of research data references in publications is proposed for automatically generating research data repositories. The International Conference on Language Resources and Evaluation (LREC) requires authors to list research data references separately from other publication references. The goal of our research is to automate the discrimination process. We investigated the reference lists in LREC papers and the citation contexts to find characteristic features that are useful for identifying research data references. We confirmed that key phrases appeared in the citation contexts and the bibliographical elements in the reference lists. Our proposed method uses the presence or absence of key phrases to identify research data references. Experiments on LREC proceedings papers proved the effectiveness of using key phrases in the citation context.

Keywords: Research data · Text classification · Scholarly papers

1 Introduction

The demand for the share and reuse of research data has significantly increased with the spread of open science. In the field of natural language processing, organizations such as Linguistic Data Consortium (LDC) [3], International Standard Language Resource Numbe (ISLRN) [5,7], and Common Language Resources and Technology Infrastructure (CLARIN) [11] have created data repositories. However, these repositories do not thoroughly collect research data, because they are manually maintained.

To enhance the repositories, automatic construction and updates are mandatory. This may be achieved by utilizing the information of research data references in scholarly papers. However, since research data references and bibliographical references are usually mixed in publications, it is required to distinguish research data references from other types of references.

In this paper, a method is proposed for the automatic identification of research data references in publications. Although bibliographical elements in the reference lists contain several useful clues, they are not always available, for example, when the provided information is incomplete. Our proposed method

© Springer Nature Switzerland AG 2020
E. Ishita et al. (Eds.): ICADL 2020, LNCS 12504, pp. 149–156, 2020.
https://doi.org/10.1007/978-3-030-64452-9_13

uses key phrases extracted from citation contexts as well as bibliographical elements for classification even without sufficient clues in the bibliographical elements. Experiments on international conference proceedings proved the effectiveness of using clues derived from citation contexts.

This paper is organized as follows: in Sect. 2, we describe how authors list research data references; in Sect. 3, the characteristic features of research data references are investigated; in Sect. 4, a method is proposed for identifying research data references; finally, we describe the experiments for evaluating the proposed model in Sect. 5.

2   Research Data References in Reference Lists

While the format of the bibliography of cited publications is uniformly determined, authors often decide how to list research data references. As a result, different methods for listing research data in reference lists have been applied, such as listing publications that are related to the research data, the URL of the site where the data is available, or the user guide of the research data.

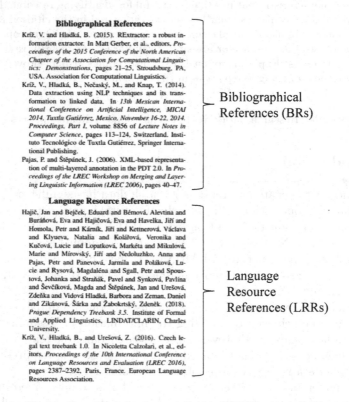

Fig. 1. Example of reference lists in LREC proceedings

Distinguishing research data references from other references is highly beneficial for readers that are interested in using the research data. Since 2016, the International Conference on Language Resources and Evaluation (LREC) has required authors to list references in two divisions, as shown in Fig. 1: Bibliographical References (BRs) for references to publications and Language Resource References (LRRs) for references to language resources (research data in the natural language processing field) [2]. This requirement contributes to the organization of information on research data cited in publications, and the spread of such rules can facilitate the utilization of research data. The goal of our work is to automate the discrimination process for the generation of research data repositories from academic papers [6,8,10].

3   Investigation of Research Data References

We investigated the characteristic features of research data references. In the proceedings of LREC 2016, 2018, and 2020 [4], 416 papers cited language resources. We collected these papers and randomly split them into 10 blocks (blocks 0–9) with equal size as the dataset for our research.

We investigated block 8 of the dataset (investigation data), and the subjects of our investigation were as follows:

Bibliographical elements: Information, such as the title, name of the journal, and where the cited item is available, that was listed in the citation list.

Citation context: The title of the section and the sentences in the text that contain the citation tag.

Table 1. Key phrases in bibliographic elements

Appears in	Key phrase	LRR ratio (%)	
Title	corpus, corpora, dictionary, lexicon, language resources	26.8	(37/138)
Title	data, set, bank	38.7	(36/93)
Title	annotate, construct, build	19.2	(14/73)
Title	name of languages (i.e. English, Chinese)	26.5	(31/117)
Bibliographical elements	University, institute, center	29.9	(20/67)
Bibliographical elements	proceedings, journal	8.0	(25/435)
Bibliographical elements	http(s)://, www	50.0	(29/58)
Bibliographical elements	LDC, CLARIN, ISLRN, LREC	42.7	(41/96)

The investigation data contain 963 references: 841 (87.3%) BRs and 122 (12.7%) LRRs. We extracted words and phrases that can serve as clues for distinguishing BRs and LRRs as key phrases and calculated the ratio of the LRRs to their appearances in the text (LRR ratio) for each of the key phrases.

The classification criteria for BRs and LRRs vary from author to author, as LREC's author guidelines do not define any specific rules. This investigation focuses on understanding the tendency of the classification criteria and citation methods adopted by authors.

Table 2. Key phrases in citation contexts

Appears in	Key phrase	LRR ratio (%)	
Section title	corpus, corpora	16.8	(28/167)
Section title	data, set, bank	45.3	(24/53)
Section title	method, algorithm	18.9	(7/37)
Section title	introduction, conclusion, related work	7.5	(29/387)
Section title	experiment, evaluation	6.1	(5/82)
Citation sentence	corpus, corpora, dictionary, lexicon, word embedding, word2vec, WordNet	18.9	(43/227)
Citation sentence	data, set, bank, collection	14.9	(28/188)
Citation sentence	tool, parser, library, code, repository, resource	8.3	(10/120)
Citation sentence	capitalized words	12.3	(73/594)
Citation sentence	We	11.2	(43/375)
Citation sentence	They	3.4	(2/59)
Citation sentence	(use, apply, utilize, etc.) and names of language resources	17.4	(32/184)
Citation sentence	reference tag at the top of the citation sentence	9.3	(49/528)
Citation sentence	reference tag at the end of the citation sentence	9.6	(60/626)

3.1 Key Phrases Related to Bibliographical Elements

Table 1 summarizes the key phrases extracted from bibliographical elements and the LRR ratio for each key phrase. Examples include:

Language names and language resource categories: Titles of publications on language resource construction often include language names and language resource categories, such as Corpus of Reading Comprehension Exercises in German (CREG).

URL: Bibliographical elements for language resources usually contain the URL of the language resource, whereas it mainly consists of the conference and journal name for publications.

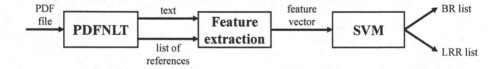

Fig. 2. Configuration of the proposed system

3.2 Key Phrases Related to Citation Contexts

Table 2 summarizes the key phrases extracted from citation contexts and the LRR ratio for each key phrase. Examples include:

Title of the section containing the citation context: The section of the experimental settings describes the language resources used in the experiment. In contrast, citations in the introduction and related work sections mainly describe the proposed ideas and preliminaries.

Citation text   List of references

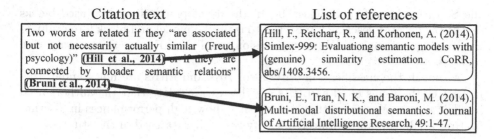

Fig. 3. Citation text to corresponding reference list entries

Language resource categories: The citation tags for language resources often
appear after the word that represents the language resource categories. For
instance, CREG is cited in the sentence "Second, we provide POS and normalization annotation on top of the CREG Corpus (Merrers et al., 2011).", in
which the citation tag (Merrers et al., 2011) appears after the word "Corpus".

Citation tag at the beginning of the sentence: Citation tags often serve
as the subject of the sentences that cite publications by appearing at the
beginning of the sentence. For instance, the sentence "Selinker (1972) coined
the term interlanguage for these language variants of individual learners."
describes the idea of interlanguage presented in the publication with the citation "Selinker (1972)".

Thus, the key phrases appear in the citation contexts and the bibliographical
elements.

4   Method

Our method identifies research data references based on the following steps (see
Fig. 2):

1. Extract the text and the reference list from the PDF file using PDFNLT [1].
2. Extract citation tags from the text and associate them with the corresponding
   item in the reference list (see Fig. 3).
3. Extract the features for identification from the bibliographical elements and
   the citation contexts for each item.
4. Classify each item as either research data or publication using support vector
   machine (SVM).

The method employs the presence or absence of each key phrase listed in
Tables 1 and 2.

5   Experiments

5.1   Experimental Setting

We conducted experiments to evaluate the effectiveness of citation contexts for
identifying research data references. We implemented the SVM classifier using

the SVM module of scikit-learn [9]. In the development stage, we used blocks 0–8 of the dataset described in Sect. 3 to train the model and block 9 to evaluate the model performance. We used precision, recall, and F-score as the evaluation metrics.

Although the classification criteria for BRs and LRRs are not standardized in LREC, the items cited as LRRs are the research data that the authors used in their works. We expect that models that show high performances in discriminating LRRs can appropriately identify research data used in the studies.

5.2   Negative Sampling

We compared the performances of models trained on different sample sizes. We set the sample size N based on the ratio of the BR samples to the LRR samples. For each N, we trained the model on N randomly sampled BRs and all 1,407 LRRs in blocks 0–8 and evaluated the performance on block 9.

We repeated the procedures for training and evaluating the model 100 times for each N and compared the averages of the corresponding F-scores. The best performance was observed for $N = 2,110$, which is 1.5 times the size of the LRRs.

5.3   Cross-validation Test

We assessed the proposed method by 10-fold cross-validation. At each step, we trained the model with nine blocks of the dataset and evaluated it with the other one block (i.e., blocks 1–9 for training and block 0 for evaluation and so on). To train the model, we used 2,110 randomly sampled BRs and all LRRs in the training blocks based on the result of the negative sampling experiment.

Blocks 0–7 were used for evaluation in the cross-validation test, and blocks 8 and 9 were used for key phrase investigation and model development, respectively. For each metric, we calculated the average of the values recorded in each of the eight steps.

We compared the proposed model performance to a baseline model that uses only bibliographical element-related features (listed in Table 1). We performed the cross-validation test 10 times and compared the average of each attempt as the final result, because the performance of the model fluctuates due to the random negative sampling.

5.4   Experimental Result

Table 3. Cross-validation result

	Precision (%)	Recall (%)	F1 score
Baseline (without citation context)	40.2	46.0	42.9
Proposed method (with citation context)	45.0	51.5	48.0

Table 3 summarizes the final result of the cross-validation test. Our proposed model outperforms the baseline model, proving the effectiveness of using citation context.

We describe an LRR instance that only the proposed model correctly classified as a language resource below:

Title of the cited item: Novel word-sense identification
Title of the section with the cited item: 3.1.2. Novel sense Dataset
Citation context: Here we use the dataset provided by (Cook et al., 2014).

The title of this instance does not include any key phrases. Meanwhile, the bibliographical elements include only the title, while lacking other information, such as the name of the journal or conference. With no clues in the bibliographical elements, the baseline model could not correctly classify this instance as a language resource.

On the contrary, the section title and citation context included the word dataset, which is a key phrase that enabled the proposed model to classify the instance as a language resource. Thus, our model is capable of identifying LRRs even without sufficient clues in the bibliographical elements.

6   Conclusion

In this paper, we proposed a method for the automatic identification of research data references in publications. Firstly, we described the reference list division rule in LREC and stated that the purpose of this work is to automate the discrimination process.

Furthermore, we investigated the reference lists in LREC papers and the citation contexts to find useful characteristic features for identifying research data references. We confirmed that key phrases appeared in the citation contexts and the bibliographical elements in the reference lists.

Our proposed method uses the presences or absences of key phrases to identify research data references. Experiments on LREC proceedings papers proved the effectiveness of using key phrases in the citation context.

In future work, we will evaluate the proposed method using datasets labeled based on the definite classification criteria for BRs and LRRs, which the author guidelines of LREC does not specify. Some authors still list research data used in their research in BRs, especially when they cite publications on constructing the research data. We investigated 36 randomly sampled papers without research data references and found that half of them included citations that the authors should have listed as LRRs. This result suggests that a more definite guideline is needed, which is easier for authors to follow.

Additionally, we will verify the effectiveness of citation contexts in other research fields and consider a method for automatic key phrase extraction.

References

1. PDFNLT. https://github.com/KMCS-NII/PDFNLT-1.0
2. LREC Author's kit (2016). https://www.lrec2016.lrec-conf.org/en/submission/authors-kit/
3. Ahtaridis, E., Cieri, C., DiPersio, D.: LDC language resource database: Building a bibliographic database. In: Proceedings of the Eighth International Conference on Language Resources and Evaluation (LREC 2012), pp. 1723–1728. European Language Resources Association (ELRA), Istanbul, May 2012
4. Calzolari, N. et al. (eds.): Proceedings of LREC 2016, 2018, and 2020. http://www.lrec-conf.org/proceedings/
5. Choukri, K., Arranz, V., Hamon, O., Park, J.: Using the international standard language resource number: practical and technical aspects. In: Proceedings of the Eighth International Conference on Language Resources and Evaluation (LREC 2012), pp. 50–54. European Language Resources Association (ELRA), Istanbul, May 2012
6. Kozawa, S., Tohyama, H., Uchimoto, K., Matsubara, S.: Collection of usage information for language resources from academic articles. In: Proceedings of the Seventh International Conference on Language Resources and Evaluation (LREC 2010). European Language Resources Association (ELRA), Valletta, May 2010
7. Mapelli, V., Popescu, V., Liu, L., Choukri, K.: Language resource citation: the ISLRN dissemination and further developments. In: Proceedings of the Tenth International Conference on Language Resources and Evaluation (LREC 2016), pp. 1610–1613. European Language Resources Association (ELRA), Portorož, May 2016
8. Namba, H.: Construction of an academic resource repository. In: Proceedings of Toward Effective Support for Academic Information Search Workshop, pp. 8–14 (2018)
9. Pedregosa, F., et al.: Scikit-learn: machine learning in Python. J. Mach. Learn. Res. **12**, 2825–2830 (2011)
10. Tohyama, H., Kozawa, S., Uchimoto, K., Matsubara, S., Isahara, H.: Construction of an infrastructure for providing users with suitable language resources. In: Coling 2008: Companion volume: Posters, pp. 119–122. Coling 2008 Organizing Committee, Manchester, August 2008
11. Zinn, C.: Squib: The language resource switchboard. Comput. Linguist. **44**(4), 631–639 (2018)

User Analytics

A Predictive Model for Citizens' Utilization of Open Government Data Portals

Di Wang[1,2]($\boxtimes$) (iD), Deborah Richards[2] (iD), Ayse Aysin Bilgin[2] (iD), and Chuanfu Chen[1]

[1] Wuhan University, Wuhan 430072, Hubei, China
{di.wang,cfchen}@whu.edu.cn
[2] Macquarie University, Sydney, NSW 2109, Australia
{deborah.richards,ayse.bilgin}@mq.edu.au

Abstract. Open government data (OGD) initiatives for building OGD portals have not yet delivered the expected benefits of OGD to the whole of society. Although citizens' reluctance to use OGD has become a key problem in the present OGD development, limited studies have been carried out to investigate citizens' actual usage of OGD and OGD portals. In order to fill this research gap, this study primarily focuses on predicting citizens' actual utilization of OGD portals. To find features influencing citizens' utilization of OGD portals and to predict their actual usage of OGD portals, an experiment was designed and carried out in China. A predictive model was built with C5.0 algorithm based on data collected through the experiment, with a predictive accuracy rate of 84.81%. Citizens' monthly income, the compatibility of OGD portals, and citizens' attentiveness regarding their interactions with OGD portals are found to be the most important factors influencing citizens' actual utilization of OGD portals. Positive effects of compatibility, attentiveness, and perceived usefulness on citizens' usage of OGD portals are noticed.

Keywords: Open government data portal · Open data utilization · Predictive model

1 Introduction

In different countries around the world, a great volume of official open government data (OGD) portals have been launched by the governments, providing data owned by public sectors to the whole society [1]. It is expected by the governments that when these data are publicly available, great social, political and economic benefits can be derived through its use, reuse, and distribution [2, 3]. However, data itself cannot automatically create value [4]. Researchers and organizations have criticized OGD initiatives, including launching OGD portals, for not yet delivering its promised positive impacts on the whole society, which circumstantially reflects possible problems in the present development of OGD [5, 6]. In fact, despite governments' expectation of public's participation, citizens are reluctant to use OGD and OGD portals [7], even if they are aware of its existence [8]. This phenomenon has already become a key problem in the present development

© Springer Nature Switzerland AG 2020
E. Ishita et al. (Eds.): ICADL 2020, LNCS 12504, pp. 159–175, 2020.
https://doi.org/10.1007/978-3-030-64452-9_14

of OGD [9, 10]. Therefore, scholars have recognized stimulating citizens' interests in effective OGD utilization as one of the most significant challenges for promoting OGD development [11, 12]. As a result, being the primary channel for publishing OGD [1], OGD portals are burdened with the responsibility of encouraging citizens' engagement with and utilization of the available data on the portal [13].

The utilization of OGD and OGD portals have not drawn enough attention in the present literature, especially from citizens' perspective [10, 14]. Limited methodical and comprehensive research has been carried out [15], which calls for more studies focusing on the utilization of OGD portals [16]. On the other hand, although scholars have tried to understand decisive factors of OGD utilization [17, 18], these studies focused more on understanding users' attitudes towards the adoption of e-government and OGD, as well as their intention to use the services [15], but seldom focused on the actual usage of OGD and OGD portals. Even though studies support that citizens' behavioral intention to use e-government services determines their actual system usage [19], limited studies have ever built models to predict and explain citizens' actual utilization of OGD and OGD portals. Existing technology acceptance models are also criticized for their questionable heuristic value and the lack of predictive power [20, 21].

Considering the limitations of present studies related to citizens' utilization of OGD, the current study aims at identifying features which influence citizens' actual usage of OGD portals and developing a predictive model to determine citizens' rate of effective OGD portal utilization. To build such a predictive model, an experiment including citizens' utilization of OGD and OGD portals to solve tasks has been carried out to collect training data. It is envisaged that besides contributing to the analysis of OGD adoption and utilization, such a model could benefit the future development of OGD and OGD portals to stimulate citizens' engagement in effective OGD utilization.

The structure of the remaining paper is as follows. Section 2 presents the theoretical foundation for the design of the initial model. Section 3 explains in detail the experiment for this study and data collection process. Results of the experiment are presented in Sect. 4. Details of building the predictive model together with the discussions of the final model are presented in Sect. 5. The paper ends with final conclusions in Sect. 6.

2   Theoretical Foundation and Initial Model

For OGD and areas closely related to OGD, such as the open data and e-government services, different theoretical approaches have been used by scholars to explain users' adoption of and intention to use the data. In this section, popular models and theories regarding the acceptance and intention to use OGD have been reviewed, followed by the explanations of the initial model for this study.

2.1   Citizens as OGD Users

In the study of OGD, users are treated as the main actors in the data utilization process. Scholars have divided OGD users into different types [22], including citizens [23, 24], business [25, 26], researchers [27, 28], developers [29], and journalists [30]. Citizens are commonly identified as the primary stakeholders who receive major benefits from the utilization of OGD [23]. Because the key motivation for releasing government data to the public is reducing the asymmetry of information between citizens and government bodies [31], therefore, this study chooses to focus on citizens for the investigation, which also increases the potential benefit of the proposed predictive model to a wider representation of the population and range of diverse characteristics.

The demographic characteristics of users are commonly treated as an important factor in understanding and predicting e-government adoption [32, 33]. Demographic characteristics, including gender, age, education, experience, have been found to influence users' acceptance of information technology [34]. Therefore, demographic characteristics of citizens are included in the initial model to analyze their impact on citizens' utilization of OGD and OGD portals.

2.2 Diffusion of Innovation

A diverse source of theoretical foundations could be applied in predicting and explaining human behaviors in different contexts [34], among which Diffusion of Innovation (DOI) is a popular one allowing for examining citizens' perceptions and identifying factors that influence their decisions about utilization of OGD [14]. The DOI model includes five main constructs, namely relative advantage, compatibility, complexity, observability and trialability, which can explain about half of the variance in users' technology acceptance rates [35]. Being adapted to a broad disciplinary background, DOI has been applied by scholars to the analysis of predictors affecting citizens' acceptance of OGD. Relative advantage, compatibility and observability have been validated as decisive factors for citizens' intention to use OGD [14]. Compatibility and complexity have also been confirmed for their impact on citizens' intention to use e-government services [36]. However, DOI has not yet been applied to the investigation of citizens' actual utilization of OGD and OGD portals, which leaves a gap in the present literature.

The strength of DOI is the ability to include system characteristics, organizational attributes, and environmental aspects in the analysis of the acceptance and adoption of a new technology. Thus, it can not only explain "the organizational, systemic and contextual effects" in the utilization process, but also "the push and pull effects of the innovators and the innovation adopters" [14] (p. 287). Since this study focuses on citizens' utilization of OGD portals, the advantages of DOI in considering different characteristics of OGD portals makes it a good fit for this study. Additionally, its ability to analyze users' perceptions of OGD utilization and the factors influencing their acceptance and usage of OGD makes DOI an appropriate choice for building the predictive model in this study. Therefore, all five DOI constructs are included in the initial model.

2.3 Technology Acceptance Model

Technology Acceptance model (TAM) is another widely used model [37] in the field of technology acceptance [38]. TAM states that users' attitude towards the utilization of a system is influenced by its perceived usefulness (PU) and perceived ease of use (PEOU) [39]. TAM has been tested and validated for various users and systems, including e-government services [36]. Many studies found support for PU and PEOU to explain a large portion of the variance for users' intention to use an information system [39]. For e-government services, a high level of PU was found to improve users' adoption of a e-government system [40].

Scholars have noticed overlaps and differences between TAM and DOI. Compared with other theories for explaining technology acceptance, DOI and TAM both focus more on the attitudes of users. DOI explains users' acceptance decision influenced by the characteristics of the technology. However, due to this concentration on innovation characteristics, DOI is less practical for predicting outcomes compared with other technology acceptance models like TAM [41]. The parsimonious nature of the TAM model leads to its high use frequency in the field of e-government services [15]. On the other hand, the ignorance of TAM for other external factors limits its applicability beyond the workplace [41]. Thus, scholars commonly choose to integrate it with other theories for better prediction of adoption intent [10]. In this study, PU and PEOU are included as supplements to the DOI model. These two constructs are used for analyzing specific functions instead of the whole OGD portal.

2.4 Trustworthiness

In the field of e-commerce, trustworthiness is treated as "the perception of confidence in the electronic marketer's reliability and integrity" [42] (p. 252). Scholars validated the impact of citizens' perception of trustworthiness on their intention to use e-government services [36, 43]. It is also important for reducing citizens' uncertainty in using e-government websites [44]. Therefore, including trustworthiness in the predictive model of citizens' utilization of OGD will help to consider the issue from the perspective of citizens' perceptions of risk and insecurity [36, 45].

2.5 Rapport

Rapport is originally a concept from psychology, referring to deepening interdependence over time as a result of instant responsiveness [46]. Tickle Degnen and Rosenthal specified three essential components of rapport [47]: mutual attentiveness, positivity and coordination. Mutual attentiveness refers to the focus of users directed to the interaction towards the information system, which may be negative. Positivity covers various positive feelings in rapport with the information system, such as friendliness and caring. Coordination conveys the equilibrium, regularity and predictability between the information system and the user. Although these three components are related, they are not equivalent [47].

Rapport is one of the important factors in a good interaction [48]. Users' sense of rapport is correlated with effective human-computer interaction, which consequently increases users' engagement in an information system and their intentions to use it [36]. Therefore, three constructs of rapport are included in the initial model of this study.

Combining the above theories and models from related literature, an integrated initial model has been built, as shown in Fig. 1.

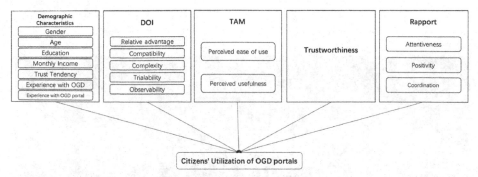

Fig. 1. An initial model for citizens' utilization of OGD portals

3 Methodology

To collect data for building the predictive model of this study, an experiment regarding citizens' utilization of OGD portals has been designed and carried out in China, the largest developing country. A predictive model is further built through machine learning. This section presents the methodology used in this study, starting with experiment design including materials, instruments, procedure, and recruitment, followed by the process of building the predictive model.

3.1 Experiment Materials

The whole experiment required two main materials: a simulated OGD portal and an online survey tool to direct participants to complete the experiment. A target was chosen to be imitated in order to build the simulated OGD portal. Because the experiment was carried out in China, Shanghai Portal, which is the best performing OGD portal in China according to the annual evaluation of DMG Lab, Fudan University [49], was selected as the imitation target. 100 datasets of 10 different data categories (local statistics, health, education, cultural activity, transportation, public safety, environment quality, registration, budget and spend, and credit records) were selected from the Shanghai portal and added to the simulated portal. The homepage of the portal for this experiment is shown in Fig. 2.

An online survey tool called Qualtrics was used to build the whole experiment environment, to guide participants to complete the experiment as well as to collect data from the experiment.

3.2 Experiment Instruments

Five instruments were included in this experiment according to the initial model proposed in Sect. 2. Instrument (1) is a demographic questionnaire for collecting background information including gender, age, education, monthly income, trust tendency, experience with OGD, and experience with OGD portal. Instrument (2) is a DOI questionnaire for the OGD portal developed from the study of Atkinson [50], covering five DOI constructs. Instrument (3) is a TAM questionnaire for 12 different functions provided by

Fig. 2. Home page of the simulated OGD portal

OGD portals, which are browsing, providing data formats to choose, downloading without registration, filtering search results, help functions, keyword search, metadata, open and machine-readable format, ranking, requesting new datasets, giving feedbacks and visualizing for quick viewing. All of these functions are recognized from related studies as important related to the usability of an OGD portal [51–54]. Instrument (4) is a trustworthiness questionnaire, which was developed from the study of Carter and Bélanger to fit the circumstance of OGD portals [36]. Instrument (5) is a rapport questionnaire developed from the study of Ranjbartabar, reflecting the three components of rapport [55]. Questions in Instrument (2), (4) and (5) use a 6-point Likert scale from "Strongly disagree" (1) to "Strongly agree" (6). Questions in Instrument (3) use a 5-point Likert scale from "Not at all useful/easy" (1) to "Extremely useful/easy" (5).

3.3 Experiment Procedure and Recruitment

Participants firstly read the participant information and consent form and decided to participate. Then they answered Instrument (1), followed by instructions about how to complete tasks given to them on the experiment OGD portal. After that, participants were guided to the simulated OGD portal. At the same time, five tasks were given to them to solve on the portal. Two of these five tasks were related to the regulations of using OGD, which could be found in the help functions provided by the portal. Another two were for the participants to search and find related datasets on the portal. A final task was set for which they could not find relevant datasets and, thus, participants needed to submit a data application. Details of these tasks are as follows:

- T1: Please find through "FAQ" in "Help" if the following statement is true or not: **Fees will be claimed for business use of the data on the portal.**
- T2: How many kindergartens are there in this area?
- T3: Please find through "FAQ" in "Help" if the following statement is true or not:

It is legal to resell the data downloaded from this portal.
- T4: What is the top first cause of death in 2016?
- T5: How many swimming pools are there in this area?

A timer of 5 min was set for the participants to complete these tasks, which means they needed to spend at least 5 min on the portal before moving to the next session. After the timer counted to zero and all five tasks were complete, Instruments (2) to (5) were shown to participants sequentially. Questions in Instrument (2) to (5) were presented to participants in an in-group random order, using the Qualtrics randomizer function.

Participants were recruited by putting advertisements on the main social media sites in China including WeChat and Weibo. A weblink to the experiment on Qualtrics was included in the advertisement. The recruitment lasted from 18 March 2019 to 2 July 2019.

3.4 Machine Learning

Machine learning algorithms are mainly designed for big data analysis. However, they are also used for small data sets in the literature. Since this study includes a categorical outcome variable and many predictor variables, the application of decision tree modeling would be suitable [56, 57]. IBM SPSS modeler was used for building the predictive decision tree model for citizens' utilization of OGD portals. Data collected through the experiment was imported to IBM SPSS modeler. 18 variables were selected as input (predictor) variables for the initial model, while the accuracy level of completing tasks on the portal was set as the target variable (outcome), which is further explained in Sect. 4.4.

An important prerequisite for choosing to use decision trees is assessing how good the method of decision tree is for the given data set. Since there are no goodness of fit measures for a single decision tree model, the best way to evaluate a decision tree is to compare it to other machine learning algorithms. Therefore, a range of popular machine learning algorithms for classification tasks were selected for this study, namely Chi-squared Automatic Interaction Detector (CHAID), Quick Unbiased Efficient Statistical Tree (Quest), Neural Network (NN), C5.0 Decision Tree (C5.0), Support Vector Machine (SVM), and CART.

A partition was added to set up a validation process in building the decision tree. 70% of the data were selected as training data, while 30% were selected as testing data. Ten-fold cross-validation was further used for C5.0 to increase the performance of the model. Analysis function was used to calculate the accuracy rate of each of the decision tree. All built models were compared and the best-performing model (based on accuracy) was selected as the final model for predicting citizens' proper utilization of OGD portals.

4   Experiment Results

In this section, results from the experiment are presented, including participants' demographics, reliability and adequacy test of Instruments (2) to (5), the distribution of Instruments (2) to (5), and the accuracy rate of completing tasks.

4.1   Participants and Demographics

In total, 160 participants volunteered to join the experiment, 79 (49.4%) completed the whole experiment. Many participants failed to complete the experiment because they did not click the link to the simulated portal, thus many stopped before completing required tasks. Detailed demographic characteristics of all participants are shown in Table 1. We excluded participants who did not complete the whole experiment in the following analysis. Fisher's exact tests showed no significant differences in the distribution of gender, age, education, income and experience with OGD and OGD portals between participants who were included and those who were excluded.

Table 1. Participants' socio-demographics

Topic	Dimension	Total	Percent	Included	Percent	Excluded	Percent
Gender	Male	71	44.4%	34	43.0%	37	45.7%
	Female	81	50.6%	44	55.7%	37	45.7%
	Other	1	0.6%	1	1.3%	0	0.0%
	Missing	7	4.4%	0	0.0%	7	8.6%
Age	18 - 25	22	13.8%	13	16.5%	9	11.1%
	26 - 30	41	25.6%	25	31.6%	16	19.8%
	31 - 40	37	23.1%	19	24.1%	18	22.2%
	41 - 50	25	15.6%	14	17.7%	11	13.6%
	51 - 60	28	17.5%	8	10.1%	20	24.7%
	Missing	7	4.4%	0	0.0%	7	8.6%
Education	Junior high	1	0.6%	0	0.0%	1	1.2%
	Senior high	10	6.3%	9	11.4%	4	4.9%
	Bachelor's degree	40	25.0%	46	58.2%	41	50.6%
	Master's degree	21	13.1%	20	25.3%	24	29.6%
	PhD.	4	2.5%	4	5.1%	4	4.9%
	Missing	7	4.4%	0	0.0%	7	8.6%
Montly Income	Below 2000RMB	17	10.6%	9	11.4%	8	9.9%
	2001-3000RMB	17	10.6%	8	10.1%	9	11.1%
	3001-5000RMB	33	20.6%	16	20.3%	17	21.0%
	5001-7000RMB	23	14.4%	12	15.2%	11	13.6%
	Above 7000RMB	63	39.4%	34	43.0%	29	35.8%
	Missing	7	4.4%	0	0.0%	7	8.6%
Total		160	100.0%	79	49.4%	81	50.6%
Ever use OGD before	Yes	58	37.9%	35	44.3%	23	31.1%
	No	95	62.1%	44	55.7%	51	68.9%
Total		153	100.0%	79	100%	74	100%
Ever use OGD Portal before	Yes	45	30.4%	25	31.6%	20	29.0%
	No	103	69.6%	54	68.4%	49	71.0%
Total		148	100.0%	79	100%	69	100%

Comparing participants' socio-demographics with that of Chinese netizens [58], we noticed a larger distribution of participants in higher educational backgrounds including bachelor's degree, master's degree and PhD, as well as in monthly income higher than 7000 RMB. This may indicate that although government data is opened for the whole society, citizens with better education and higher income may be the ones that have interests in its utilization or can make use of it [32, 33].

For participants' trust tendency, results show their neutral tendency to trust, with a mean of 4 in the 6-point Likert scale and a standard deviation of 1.04. The maximum and minimum values for participants' trust tendency were 6 and 1, meaning some of them build trust with others very easily (6) while others find this extremely hard (1).

4.2 Reliability and Adequacy

The reliability of Instruments (2) to (5) was examined with Cronbach's alpha [59], as shown in Table 2. The commonly accepted range for alpha is greater than 0.7 [60]. Thus, all instruments in the experiment showed high reliability. The sample adequacy of Instruments (2) to (5) was examined with the Kaiser-Meyer-Olkin measure of sampling adequacy [61]. All values were above 0.7, indicating the instruments to be suitable for factor analysis. The significance of Bartlett's test of sphericity was less than 0.05, which also indicates the high validity of all the instruments. These two tests showed the instruments in the experiment to be fit for data analysis because of high reliability and validity.

Table 2. Reliability and adequacy tests of experiment instruments

Instrument	Construct	Variable No.	Valid	%	Cronbach's Alpha
(2) DOI	Relative advantage	6	79	100%	0.866
	Compatibility	6	79	100%	0.893
	Complexity	8	79	100%	0.909
	Trialability	4	79	100%	0.852
	Observability	3	79	100%	0.908
(3) TAM	PU	12	79	100%	0.896
	PEOU	12	79	100%	0.890
(4) Trustworthiness		8	79	100%	0.928
(5) Rapport	Attentiveness	7	79	100%	0.917
	Positivity	8	79	100%	0.866
	Coordination	7	79	100%	0.884

		Bartlett's Test of Sphericity			Kaiser-Meyer-Olkin Measure of Sampling Adequacy.
		Approx. Chi-Square	df	Sig.	
(2) DOI	Relative advantage	232.203	15	0.000	0.000
	Compatibility	259.370	15	0.000	0.893
	Complexity	374.617	28	0.000	0.886
	Trialability	142.151	6	0.000	0.772
	Observability	155.682	3	0.000	0.743
(3) TAM	PU	439.048	66	0.000	0.810
	PEOU	459.981	66	0.000	0.821
(4) Trustworthiness		507.274	28	0.000	0.859
(5) Rapport	Attentiveness	384.473	21	0.000	0.895
	Positivity	383.834	28	0.000	0.843
	Coordination	356.496	21	0.000	0.896

4.3 Descriptive Analysis of Instruments

Results of Instrument (2) to (5) are shown in Table 3. Scores for each construct of the instruments were calculated by drawing the average scores of participants' answers belonging to that construct. Generally, participants show positive attitudes to all constructs. Among the five constructs of DOI, trialability receives the highest average score while complexity receives the lowest average score. Among the three constructs of rapport, attentiveness receives the lowest average score. The average score and median of trustworthiness also show participants' trust in the official portal provided by the government.

Table 3. Descriptive analysis of experiment instruments

| | DOI | | | | | Trustworthiness |
	Relative advantage	Compatibility	Complexity	Trialability	Observability	
No.	79	79	79	79	79	79
Average	4.70	4.83	4.41	4.87	4.62	4.79
Median	4.83	5.00	4.38	5.00	5.00	5.00
Std.	0.75	0.74	0.77	0.78	0.87	0.79
Min.	2.67	3.00	2.75	2.75	1.67	2.75
Max.	6.00	6.00	6.00	6.00	6.00	6.00

| | TAM | | Rapport | | | |
	PU	PEOU	Attentiveness	Positivity	Coordination	
No.	79	79	79	79	79	
Average	3.85	3.76	4.03	4.12	4.16	
Median	4.00	3.92	4.14	4.25	4.29	
Std.	0.63	0.63	1.08	0.87	0.87	
Min.	2.00	2.00	1.00	2.13	1.57	
Max.	5.00	5.00	6.00	6.00	6.00	

4.4 Accuracy of Completing Tasks

Table 4 shows the descriptive analysis of the accuracy rate for each of the tasks. The highest accuracy rate was achieved for Task 5, where participants could not find related datasets on the portal. The lowest accuracy rate was observed for Task 4, followed by Task 2, both of which are about searching datasets on the portal to find answers. The accuracy rates for Tasks 1 and 3 are relatively higher compared with Tasks 2 and 4, which related to the regulations of OGD utilization provided in the help functions.

Table 4. Descriptive analysis of the accuracy rate for tasks

	Accuracy-T1	Accuracy-T2	Accuracy-T3	Accuracy-T4	Accuracy-T5
Right No.	65	54	66	43	70
Right %	82.3%	68.4%	83.5%	54.4%	88.6%
Wrong No.	14	25	13	36	9
Wrong %	17.7%	31.6%	16.5%	45.6%	11.4%

To build the predictive model for citizens' utilization of OGD portals, a new classification variable was created as the dependent variable (target), relating to citizens' degree of proper utilization of OGD portals (DU). This variable was created according to the number of tasks completed correctly. If the participant completed 0 to 1 task correctly, DU will be "low"; 2–3 tasks correctly, DU will be "moderate"; 4–5 tasks correctly, DU will be "high". The description of DU is shown in Table 5.

Table 5. Description of citizens' degree of proper utilization of OGD portals

Classification	Task Accuracy	No.	%
Low	0	1	1.3%
	1	2	2.5%
Moderate	2	9	11.4%
	3	20	25.3%
High	4	17	21.5%
	5	30	38.0%
Total		79	100%

5 Predictive Model

The classification variable DU was set as the dependent variable (target) for building predictive models. 18 input (predictor) variables were selected as independent variables, including seven demographic characteristics (gender, age, education, income, trust tendency, experience with OGD, and experience with OGD portals), five DOI constructs (relative advantage, compatibility, complexity, trialability, and observability), two TAM constructs (PU and PEOU), trustworthiness, and three rapport constructs (attentiveness, positivity, and coordination). Six predictive models were built using different classification algorithms. The comparison of these models' prediction accuracy on training data and testing data are shown in Table 6.

Table 6. Comparison of models' predictive accuracy

	CHAID		Quest		NN		C5.0	
	Training	Testing	Training	Testing	Training	Testing	Training	Testing
Right No.	49	14	32	15	42	13	47	12
Right %	90.74%	56.00%	59.26%	60.00%	77.78%	52.00%	87.04%	48.00%
Wrong No.	5	11	22	10	12	12	7	13
Wrong %	9.26%	44.00%	40.74%	40.00%	22.22%	48.00%	12.96%	52.00%

	SVM		CART		C5.0		
	Training	Testing	Training	Testing	Ten-fold cross-validation		
Right No.	53	10	48	13	67		
Right %	98.15%	40.00%	88.89%	52.00%	84.81%		
Wrong No.	1	15	6	12	12		
Wrong %	1.85%	60.00%	11.11%	48.00%	15.19%		

The number of observations accurately predicted and proportion of accurately predicted observations for the training data and the testing data are presented in Table 6. The highest accuracy rate for predicting correct answers (right no. in Table 6) for training data is the SVM model, which also has the lowest accuracy rate for the testing data, that means it was overfitted to the training data. The highest accuracy rate for testing data is the Quest model, which also has the lowest accuracy rate for the training data. This may be related to the imbalance of different outcome classes. It can be noticed from Table 5 that the "high" class corresponds to 59.5% of all the data, while the "low" class has only 3.8%. Such an imbalance can have an impact on the classification algorithms [21]. To handle this imbalance as well as to increase the performance of the model, ten-fold cross-validation was used with the C5.0 algorithm. After the validation process, it can be noticed that the prediction accuracy rate has increased to 84.81% for the outcome category we are interested in (predicting correct answers). Therefore, the C5.0 model with cross validation has been selected as the best and final model for predicting citizens' proper utilization of OGD portals (Fig. 3).

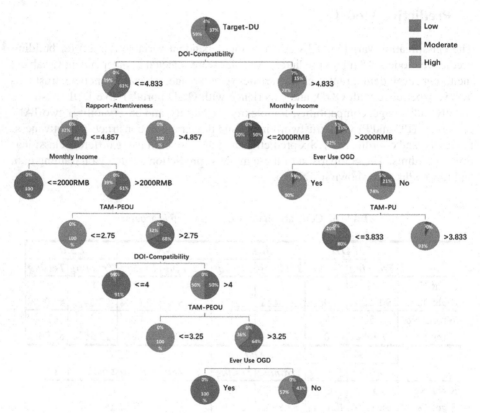

Fig. 3. Model for predicting citizens' utilization of OGD portals

Six out of 18 input variables have been identified as important variables by the predictive model. Monthly income (importance = 0.34), compatibility of DOI (importance = 0.3), and attentiveness of rapport (importance = 0.21) are the most important variables in this research model, followed by PU of TAM (importance = 0.08), experience with OGD (importance = 0.05), and PEOU of TAM (importance = 0.01). Citizens with monthly income lower than 2000 RMB per month are less likely to make proper use of OGD portals. It appears that the compatibility of OGD portals has a positive effect on citizens' utilization of OGD portals since higher percentage of the participants with higher compatibility (>4.833) obtained higher accuracy for the assigned tasks. If citizens feel the portal does not disturb their attentiveness, they are more likely to make proper use of the portal. PU of TAM also has a positive effect on citizens' utilization of OGD portals. While lower score in PEOU of TAM will lead to higher possibility of proper utilization of OGD portals.

Comparing the predictive model for citizens' utilization of OGD portals with related studies, both agreements and disagreements can be found. In the study of Weerakkody et al., which used DOI to explain citizens' intention to use OGD, the most important variable in their validated model was relative advantage, followed by compatibility [14]. While in our predictive model, compatibility of DOI has been recognized as the most important variable but relative advantage has not been included. This may be due to the target of the predictive model in this study being participants' actual utilization of OGD portals, instead of asking for their intention to use OGD portals. However, this result agrees with the findings of Carter and Bélanger [36] about compatibility having the greatest impact on citizens' intention to use e-government services. Our finding also agrees with Carter and Bélanger [36] for the positive effect of perceived ease of use on citizens' utilization of OGD portals. Whilst the predictive model does not support findings of Rana et al. for the high positive effect of perceived usefulness and trustworthiness on citizens' adoption of e-government [15]. This may be because their studies dealt with general e-government services, while this predictive model focuses specifically on the OGD portal built by governments. OGD portals have different characteristics from other e-government websites since they provide citizens with data resources and services relating to the utilization of data. Another possible reason is that our study and previous studies are based on different sizes and areas of samples. On the other hand, attentiveness of rapport, which is seldom considered in the analysis of citizens' adoption and intention to use of OGD or e-government services [15], has been validated as an important factor for predicting citizens' utilization of OGD portals.

6 Conclusion

Open government data is expected to bring various types of benefits to the whole of society through its utilization [11], and citizens are recognized as a main participant in the utilization process [62]. However, limited studies have been carried out to investigate citizens' actual utilization of OGD and OGD portals.

In order to fill the identified knowledge gap, this paper primarily focuses on predicting citizens' utilization of OGD portals, since citizens' reluctance to use OGD and OGD portals have become a key barrier for the further development of OGD. To find features influencing citizens' utilization of OGD portals and to predict their actual usage of OGD portals, an experiment was designed and carried out in a sample in China. A predictive model was built with C5.0 algorithm based on data collected through the experiment, with an accuracy rate of 84.81% for predicting correct answers by participants. Citizens' monthly income, the compatibility of OGD portals, and citizens' attentiveness when having interactions with OGD portals were found to be the most important factors influencing citizens' utilization of OGD portals. Positive effects of compatibility, attentiveness, and perceived usefulness on citizens' usage of OGD portals were noticed.

Several limitations could be pointed out with this study. Firstly, although the designed experiment tried to maintain strict controls over possible confounding variables, the lack of a realistic environment of citizens' utilization of OGD portals may limit the validity of the results. Secondly, the limited sample size of the experiment and self-selection bias representing a greater percentage of higher income and educated individuals, together with the geographic restrictions of participants also pose possible threats to the application of the proposed predictive model to other regions and populations. Thirdly, machine learning algorithms seek to make good predictions, but they could not fully explain the relationship between the predictors and the outcome. However, the decision tree model is capable of identifying the important predictor variables for classifying observations into outcome categories, which is exactly the purpose of this study.

Considering the limitation of the present experiment, future studies could be carried out on different real OGD portals, using the instruments of this experiment. Additional exploratory studies could also be conducted to test the accuracy of the proposed predictive model on other populations.

References

1. Attard, J., et al.: A systematic review of open government data initiatives. Gov. Inf. Q. **32**(4), 399–418 (2015)
2. Graves-Fuenzalida, A.: Improving the use of open government data using visualizations, Rensselaer Polytechnic Institute (2013)
3. Meijer, A., de Hoog, J., van Twist, M., van der Steen, M., Scherpenisse, J.: Understanding the dynamics of open data: from sweeping statements to complex contextual interactions. In: Gascó-Hernández, M. (ed.) Open Government. PAIT, vol. 4, pp. 101–114. Springer, New York (2014). https://doi.org/10.1007/978-1-4614-9563-5_7
4. Cranefield, J., Robertson, O., Oliver, G.: Value in the mash: Exploring the benefits, barriers and enablers of open data apps (2014)
5. Horrigan, J.B., Rainie, L., Page, D.: Americans' views on open government data. Pew Research Center (2015)
6. OpenDataBarometer: Open Data Barometer Leaders Edition: From Promise to Progress (2018)
7. Gauld, R., Goldfinch, S., Horsburgh, S.: Do they want it? Do they use it? The 'demand-side' of e-government in Australia and New Zealand. Gov. Inf. Q. **27**(2), 177–186 (2010)
8. Wang, D., Richards, D., Chen, C.: Connecting users, data and utilization: a demand-side analysis of open government data. In: Taylor, N.G., Christian-Lamb, C., Martin, M.H., Nardi, B. (eds.) iConference 2019. LNCS, vol. 11420, pp. 488–500. Springer, Cham (2019). https://doi.org/10.1007/978-3-030-15742-5_47
9. Ruijer, E., Grimmelikhuijsen, S., Meijer, A.: Open data for democracy: developing a theoretical framework for open data use. Gov. Inf. Q. **34**(1), 45–52 (2017)
10. Safarov, I., Meijer, A., Grimmelikhuijsen, S.: Utilization of open government data: a systematic literature review of types, conditions, effects and users. Inf. Polity **22**, 1–24 (2017)
11. Janssen, M., Charalabidis, Y., Zuiderwijk, A.: Benefits, adoption barriers and myths of open data and open government. Inf. Syst. Manage. **29**(4), 258–268 (2012)
12. Ubaldi, B.: Open government data: towards empirical analysis of open government data initiatives. OECD Working Papers on Public Governance, no. 22, p. 1 (2013)
13. Kassen, M.: A promising phenomenon of open data: a case study of the Chicago open data project. Gov. Inf. Q. **30**(4), 508–513 (2013)

14. Weerakkody, V., Irani, Z., Kapoor, K., Sivarajah, U., Dwivedi, Y.K.: Open data and its usability: an empirical view from the Citizen's perspective. Inf. Syst. Front. **19**(2), 285–300 (2016). https://doi.org/10.1007/s10796-016-9679-1
15. Rana, N.P., Dwivedi, Y.K., Williams, M.D.: A meta-analysis of existing research on citizen adoption of e-government. Inf. Syst. Front. **17**(3), 547–563 (2013). https://doi.org/10.1007/s10796-013-9431-z
16. Huang, Z., Benyoucef, M.: Usability and credibility of e-government websites. Gov. Inf. Q. **31**(4), 584–595 (2014)
17. Ruijer, E., et al.: Connecting societal issues, users and data scenario-based design of open data platforms. Gov. Inf. Q. **34**, 470–480 (2017)
18. Wang, H.-J., Lo, J.: Adoption of open government data among government agencies. Gov. Inf. Q. **33**(1), 80–88 (2016)
19. Carter, L., Belanger, F.: Citizen adoption of electronic government initiatives. In: Proceedings of the 37th Annual Hawaii International Conference on System Sciences (2004). IEEE
20. Chuttur, M.Y.: Overview of the technology acceptance model: Origins, developments and future directions. Working Papers Inf. Syst. **9**(37): 9–37 (2009)
21. Zhang, S., et al.: A predictive model for assistive technology adoption for people with dementia. IEEE J. Biomed. Health Inf. **18**(1), 375–383 (2013)
22. King, W.R., He, J.: A meta-analysis of the technology acceptance model. Inf. Manag. **43**(6), 740–755 (2006)
23. Parycek, P., Hochtl, J., Ginner, M.: Open government data implementation evaluation. J. Theoret. Appl. Electron. Commerce Res. **9**(2), 80–99 (2014)
24. Power, R., et al.: Scenario planning case studies using open government data. In: ISESS (2015)
25. Magalhaes, G., Roseira, C., Manley, L.: Business models for open government data. In: Proceedings of the 8th International Conference on Theory and Practice of Electronic Governance (2014). ACM
26. Susha, I., Grönlund, Å., Janssen, M.: Driving factors of service innovation using open government data: an exploratory study of entrepreneurs in two countries. Inf. Polity **20**(1), 19–34 (2015)
27. Gonzalez-Zapata, F., Heeks, R.: The multiple meanings of open government data: Understanding different stakeholders and their perspectives. Gov. Inf. Q. **32**(4), 441–452 (2015)
28. Whitmore, A.: Using open government data to predict war: a case study of data and systems challenges. Gov. Inf. Q. **31**(4), 622–630 (2014)
29. Veeckman, C., van der Graaf, S.: The city as living laboratory: empowering citizens with the citadel toolkit. Technol. Innovation Manage. Rev. **5**(3) (2015)
30. Heise, A., Naumann, F.: Integrating open government data with stratosphere for more transparency. Web Semant. Sci. Serv. Agents World Wide Web **14**, 45–56 (2012)
31. Murillo, M.J.: Evaluating the role of online data availability: the case of economic and institutional transparency in sixteen Latin American nations. Int. Polit. Sci. Rev. **36**(1), 42–59 (2015)
32. Dwivedi, Y.K., Williams, M.D.: Demographic influence on UK citizens' e-government adoption. Electron. Gov. Int. J. **5**(3), 261–274 (2008)
33. Venkatesh, V., Sykes, T.A., Venkatraman, S.: Understanding e-Government portal use in rural India: role of demographic and personality characteristics. Inf. Syst. J. **24**(3), 249–269 (2014)
34. Venkatesh, V., et al.: User acceptance of information technology: toward a unified view. MIS Q. **27**, 425–478 (2003)
35. Rogers, E.M.: Diffusion of innovations. Simon and Schuster, New York (2010)
36. Carter, L., Bélanger, F.: The utilization of e-government services: citizen trust, innovation and acceptance factors. Inf. Syst. J. **15**(1), 5–25 (2005)

37. Venkatesh, V., Davis, F.D.: A theoretical extension of the technology acceptance model: four longitudinal field studies. Manage. Sci. **46**(2), 186–204 (2000)
38. Wu, P.F.: User acceptance of emergency alert technology: a case study. In: Proceedings of the 6th International ISCRAM Conference (2009)
39. Davis, F.D.: Perceived usefulness, perceived ease of use, and user acceptance of information technology. MIS Q. **13**, 319–340 (1989)
40. Sang, S., Lee, J.-D., Lee, J.: E-government adoption in ASEAN: the case of Cambodia. Internet Research **19**(5), 517–534 (2009)
41. Taherdoost, H.: A review of technology acceptance and adoption models and theories. Procedia Manufact. **22**, 960–967 (2018)
42. Belanger, F., Hiller, J.S., Smith, W.J.: Trustworthiness in electronic commerce: the role of privacy, security, and site attributes. J. Strateg. Inf. Syst. **11**(3–4), 245–270 (2002)
43. Lim, E.T., et al.: Advancing public trust relationships in electronic government: the Singapore e-filing journey. Inf. Syst. Res. **23**(4), 1110–1130 (2012)
44. Venkatesh, V., et al.: Managing citizens' uncertainty in e-government services: the mediating and moderating roles of transparency and trust. Inf. Syst. Res. **27**(1), 87–111 (2016)
45. McKnight, D.H., Choudhury, V., Kacmar, C.: Developing and validating trust measures for e-commerce: an integrative typology. Inf. Syst. Res. **13**(3), 334–359 (2002)
46. Cassell, J.: Embodied Conversational Agents. MIT press, Cambridge (2000)
47. Tickle-Degnen, L., Rosenthal, R.: The nature of rapport and its nonverbal correlates. Psychol. Inq. **1**(4), 285–293 (1990)
48. Wei-Ern, J.W.: Establishing Rapport with Conversational Agents: Comparing the Effect of Envelope and Emotional Feedback (2012)
49. DMGLabFudanUniversity. China Open Data Index (2019). http://ifopendata.fudan.edu.cn/method
50. Atkinson, N.L.: Developing a questionnaire to measure perceived attributes of eHealth innovations. Am. J. Health Behav. **31**(6), 612–621 (2007)
51. Fajar Marta, R.: Open Government Data Portal Design Principles: Implementing Transparency, Privacy, and Information Quality Assurance by Design (2016)
52. SunlightFoundation: Ten Principles for Opening Up Government Information (2010)
53. Thorsby, J., et al.: Understanding the content and features of open data portals in American cities. Gov. Inf. Q. **34**(1), 53–61 (2017)
54. Bogdanović-Dinić, S., Veljković, N., Stoimenov, L.: How open are public government data? An assessment of seven open data portals. In: Rodríguez-Bolívar, M.P. (ed.) Measuring E-government Efficiency. PAIT, vol. 5, pp. 25–44. Springer, New York (2014). https://doi.org/10.1007/978-1-4614-9982-4_3
55. Ranjbartabar, H.: A virtual emotional freedom practitioner to deliver physical and emotional therapy (2016)
56. Hastie, T., Tibshirani, R., Friedman, J.: The Elements of Statistical Learning. SSS. Springer, New York (2009). https://doi.org/10.1007/978-0-387-84858-7
57. Jiawei Han, M., Pei, J.: Data Mining: Concepts and Techniques: Concepts and Techniques. Elsevier, Amsterdam (2011)
58. CNNIC: The 45th China Statistical Report on Internet Development (2020). CNNIC
59. Cronbach, L.J.: Coefficient alpha and the internal structure of tests. Psychometrika **16**(3), 297–334 (1951). https://doi.org/10.1007/BF02310555
60. Tavakol, M., Dennick, R.: Making sense of Cronbach's alpha. Int. J. Med. Educ. **2**, 53 (2011)

61. Bickmore, T., Cassell, J.: Social Dialongue with Embodied Conversational Agents. In: van Kuppevelt, J.C.J., Dybkjær, L., Bernsen, N.O. (eds.) Advances in Natural Multimodal Dialogue Systems Text, Speech and Language Technology, vol. 30, pp. 23–54. Springer, Dordrecht (2005). https://doi.org/10.1007/1-4020-3933-6_2
62. Zuiderwijk, A., Janssen, M.: A coordination theory perspective to improve the use of open data in policy-making. In: Wimmer, M.A., Janssen, M., Scholl, H.J. (eds.) EGOV 2013. LNCS, vol. 8074, pp. 38–49. Springer, Heidelberg (2013). https://doi.org/10.1007/978-3-642-403 58-3_4

Extracting User Interests from Operation Logs on Museum Devices for Post-Learning

Yuanyuan Wang[1]($\boxtimes$)(iD), Yukiko Kawai[2,3](iD), and Kazutoshi Sumiya[4](iD)

[1] Yamaguchi University, 2-16-1 Tokiwadai, Ube, Yamaguchi 755-8611, Japan
y.wang@yamaguchi-u.ac.jp
[2] Kyoto Sangyo University, Motoyama, Kamigamo, Kita-ku, Kyoto 603-8555, Japan
kawai@cc.kyoto-su.ac.jp
[3] Osaka University, 5-1 Mihogaoka, Ibaraki, Osaka 567-0047, Japan
[4] Kwansei Gakuin University, 2-1 Gakuen, Sanda, Hyogo 669-1337, Japan
sumiya@kwansei.ac.jp

Abstract. Nowadays, a variety of information on museum collections online has been stored as digital archives. With the increasing use of smartphones and tablets in daily life, visitors can obtain various knowledge of museum exhibits for pre-learning by using mobile devices and applications. Also, interactive learning systems in museums are very active in the field of information engineering, and interactive on-site learning is necessary for recent education. However, existing learning support systems mainly focused on support for pre-learning or on-site learning, and they are not enough to provide more advanced learning in per-learning or to deepen user interests in on-site learning. Therefore, it is necessary to support diverse knowledge levels of users on museum education for post-learning. In this paper, we aim to utilize video materials related to museums to support post-learning based on user interests by analyzing user interactions for exhibits on multimedia museum devices. For this, we propose a scoring method based on four features of user operation log data: keyword appearance frequency, keyword transition, media type, and media transition. Finally, we verified and discussed the effectiveness of our proposed scoring method through a user study.

Keywords: Museum education · User interaction · Post-learning

1 Introduction

With the rapid digitization of education, online museum collections have been stored as digital archives to provide various information on museum exhibits for visitors. Then, visitors can obtain various knowledge of museum exhibits for pre-learning by using mobile devices and applications. In recent education, interactive on-site learning is necessary and information on museum exhibits is commonly provided on the online learning platform. Wu [17] studied the use

© Springer Nature Switzerland AG 2020
E. Ishita et al. (Eds.): ICADL 2020, LNCS 12504, pp. 176–186, 2020.
https://doi.org/10.1007/978-3-030-64452-9_15

of "iPalace Channel"[1] that is an online learning platform of National Palace Museum of Taiwan. He confirmed the effectiveness of the online content of museum exhibits since most elementary and middle school teachers thought that video contents are quite effective in teaching museum exhibits. Also, several recent studies showed that they are quite effective in interactive learning using multimedia devices. For example, Li et al. [18] proposed a multimedia interactive system for children, and it could make children more creative.

In this work, we focused on multimedia museum devices in which users can obtain more information on museum exhibits than images or text. While users learn museum exhibits in class, there are three types of learning styles at the museum: pre-learning, on-site learning, and post-learning. However, existing learning support systems mainly focused on support for pre-learning and on-site learning. These learning support systems based on an approach of estimating user interests from their behavior in the museum, it could connect user interests and features of exhibits on-site. Spence et al. [14] proposed a mobile application that visitors can exchange their experiences at the museum. But it is not enough to provide more advanced learning in per-learning or to deepen user interests in on-site learning. Therefore, it is necessary to support diverse knowledge levels of users on museum education for post-learning.

In this paper, we aim to extract user interests on museum exhibits to recommend learning content to support post-learning. Some studies treat user interests in the museum as dynamic. For example, Hatala et al. [6] proposed a knowledge-based recommendation system support for museums called "ec(h)o", it connects the environment, interaction, objects, and users at an abstract semantic level instead of at the content level. Our work also treats user interests as dynamic, and extract the user interests at the museum from user operation log data on multimedia museum devices. In this paper, we extract user interests by analyzing user interactions for exhibits on museum devices. For this, we propose a scoring method based on four features of user operation log data: keyword appearance frequency, keyword transition, media type, and media transition. Also, we provide an interface to visualize user interests on museum exhibits.

2   Related Work

A large number of studies have been carried out on user interest extraction [9, 19]. Different strategies proposed in the literature for mining user interests from social networks [3, 15]. Information sources used for extracting user interests from social networks such as textual content (comments, #hashtags), social network structure, and images [2]. Many works in user interest mining from social networks extract users' explicit interests that are directly observable from user content [1, 10, 20]. However, these studies focused on extracting user interests from the social network, they do not consider user interactions with the content. Other techniques focus on passive users and extract their implicit interests by considering the interaction patterns between users and topics [12, 16]. They are

---

[1] iPalace Channel, National Palace Museum, https://ipalace.npm.edu.tw/#.

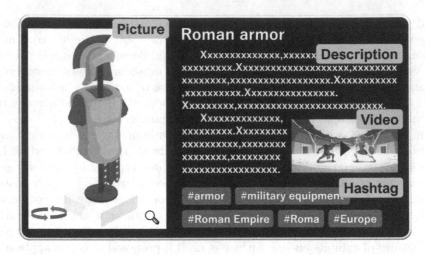

Fig. 1. An example of the multimedia museum device.

similar to our work to extract user interests by considering user interactions, and we aim to extract user interests on museum exhibits to support post-learning.

Recently, many applications and digital tools allow museums to gather statistics and useful data about physical and online visitors, such as analysis which focuses on the nature of exhibitions that attract the most interest, how long visitors interact with the exhibits, the ow of visitors through the exhibition, the multiple visits, determination of the most cost-effective way to engage with the visitors, evaluation of most effective communication channels [11]. Grammenos et al. [5] explored having a touch-enabled surface, where a digital catalog is presented to the visitors and they can browse through it for the objects in the exhibition. Hornecker [7] investigated the use of a multi-touch table for interaction in museums and further explored the gain of knowledge using an interactive installation. These studies only focused on personalizing and enriching the museum experience according to visitors' states, in this work, we aim to utilize multimedia museum devices to support post-learning.

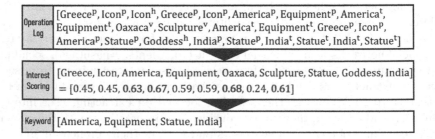

Fig. 2. An example of user interest extraction.

3 User Interest Extraction

3.1 Operation Log Analysis

In this work, we analyze users' operation logs on a multimedia museum device as their interests, which are tablet-type devices with direct access to hashtags (#), pictures, descriptions, and videos, as shown in Fig. 1. As an example of extracted keywords from operation log data are shown on the top part of Fig. 2. There are nouns extracted from titles, captions of pictures, descriptions, and hashtags in operation log data with a Japanese morphological analysis. Also, we extract four media types from operation log data: hashtag, picture, text, and video.

3.2 Keyword Scoring

To determine keywords as user interests on museum exhibits, we score nouns in operation log data by four scoring methods, (1) keyword appearance frequency (f), (2) keyword transitions on Wikipedia category structure (g), (3) media type (h), and (4) media type transitions (i). These scoring methods are set based on three conditions: nouns selected repeatedly by the user, nouns selected consecutively by the user, and nouns selected in multiple media by the user.

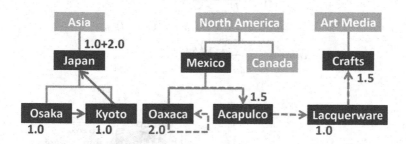

Fig. 3. An example of keyword scoring.

(1) f: **keyword appearance frequency.** The left part of Fig. 3 shows an example of keyword scoring based on keyword appearance frequency. When a user interacts with keywords, they may indicate the user's interests in the keywords that belong to a superordinate category. Therefore, the score is given to keywords in the superordinate category of the Wikipedia category structure when it appears in user operation log data.

(2) g: **keyword transition on Wikipedia structure.** The middle part of Fig. 3 shows an example of keyword scoring based on keyword transitions on the Wikipedia category structure. We count the number of transitions on the Wikipedia category structure and the score to the first keyword is 0. Since a user interacts with keywords that may indicate the user's interests in the keywords that belong to a superordinate category, three types of score: transitions to keywords without the superordinate category (1.0), keywords within the same superordinate category (1.5), and the same keywords (2.0).

(3) h: **media type.** The keyword scoring based on the media type is conducted by a specific score of each media type interacted by a user. This score is set as below based on the assumption of the amount of information that each media can provide to the user and the viewing time. The scores of the hashtag (m_h), picture (m_p), text (m_t), and video (m_v) are represented as follows: $m_h(1.0) < m_p(2.0) < m_t(3.0) < m_v(4.0)$.

(4) i: **media type transition.** In this scoring method, switching to different media is scored in binary. When a user interacts with the same media continuously, the score will be 0.

The interest score $Interest_k$ of a keyword k of all points of the user's operation log data is calculated by following equations. Firstly, the score of k is normalized at F_k by Eq. (1). Secondly, the scores of g, h and i of k at a point p of the user's operation log data are normalized at $G_{k,p}$, $H_{k,p}$, and $I_{k,p}$ by Eq. (1). Then, $X_{k,p}$ is a total value of the normalized values F_k, $G_{k,p}$, $H_{k,p}$, and $I_{k,p}$ by Eq. (2), and $X_{k,p}$ is normalized at $Y_{k,p}$ by Eq. (1). Thus, $Interest_k$ is an average value of all values of k at all points of the user's operation log data by Eq. (3). If $Interest_k$ of k is more than a threshold 0.50, k is extracted as an object of user interest.

$$W = \frac{U - U_{min}}{U_{max} - U_{min}} \tag{1}$$

$$X_{k,p} = F_k + G_{k,p} + H_{k,p} + I_{k,p} \tag{2}$$

$$Interest_k = \frac{\sum_{i=1}^{n} Y_{k,i}}{f_k} \tag{3}$$

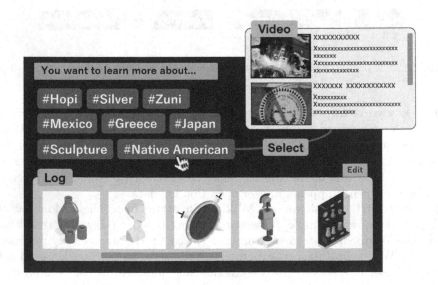

Fig. 4. User interface.

4 User Interface

The user interface of our proposed method is designed to visualize user interests on museum exhibits and recommend relevant video scenes for post-learning (see Fig. 4). It presents the user's operation log at the bottom and shows keywords as hashtags (#) that are extracted as user interests from the user's operation log data. Then, the video scene(s) related to the hashtag(s) is recommended by the user's selected hashtag(s). To make the post-learning more effective, it is necessary to extract video scenes related to user interests, and allow the user to select the extracted video scenes. Huh et al. [8] focused on hyperlinks in a system that recommends videos based on user interests. They extract targets of the video viewer's interests based on the ER model and create a smart video in the e-learning domain. It contains hyperlinks to other resources such as books, dictionaries, location information, people, and other videos, and these hyperlinks will be effective in deepening user interests and knowledge that the user has obtained in museum's on-site education. Therefore, our proposed method extracts user interests from user interactions with multimedia museum devices.

Our work is similar to the work of [8], it is possible to generate hyperlinks based on extracted user interests. Since post-learning requires more advanced learning, it is necessary to link user interests with topics that users need to learn. However, generating links based only on user interests is not enough to support post-learning. The topics that users need to learn could be detected based on their learning history, their tendency to test questions' answers, important topics in textbooks, and so on. They will correspond to the sequential-global continuum (how users prefer to organize and progress toward understanding information) among four dimensions in the learning style model of Felder and Silverman [4]. Sheeba et al. [13] proposed and evaluated an algorithm that determines the learning style of users based on the Felder and Silverman's proposed model in the e-learning domain. Their evaluation results showed that their proposed method is very effective in extracting and evaluating post-learning content.

5 Evaluation and Discussion

To evaluate the effectiveness of the proposed user interest extraction method, we compared the experimental results of the recall, precision, and F-measure of keywords extracted by the proposed method (A) with the experimental results based only on the keyword appearance frequency f (B). We first acquired evaluation data that is the operation log data of five subjects interacted with a multimedia museum device for three minutes. Then, we extracted keywords for user interests from the acquired log data. To investigate the relationships between subjects' intentions and the tendency of the subjects' operations, we asked the subjects to answer the intentions of their operations on the device.

- Q1: Please select keywords of your interests from a list.
- Q2: For what purpose did you interact with the app?

In Q1, nouns extracted from each subject's operation log as a keyword list. In Q2, each subject freely described the intentions of their operations.

Table 1. Results of extracted keywords for user interests

Subject	Method	Extracted keywords	Recall	Precision	F-measure
1	A	America, bangle, Zuni, statue, pincushion, Navajo, necklace, decoration, Venezuela, ornament, Solomon Islands	**0.67**	0.75	0.71
	B	America, bangle, decoration	0.33	1.00	0.50
	C	America, bangle, Zuni, statue, Navajo, necklace, decoration, Venezuela, Solomon Islands	—		
2	A	Morocco, candlestick, board, bow, basket, ritual, statue, Papua New Guinea, Oceania, Hawaiian Islands, jar, hook, living in the sea, Yap, Samoa, fishing basket, Caroline Islands	**0.67**	0.20	0.31
	B	Morocco, Oceania, Hawaiian Islands	0.67	0.67	0.67
	C	Papua New Guinea, Oceania, Hawaiian Islands	—		
3	A	Oaxaca, statue, Peru, calendar, North Korea, mask, ritual, South Korea, China, dynasty, Mali, clothes	**0.63**	0.42	0.50
	B	America, necklace, Zuni, Peru, calendar, North Korea, mask	0.38	0.43	0.40
	C	Necklace, statue, Peru, mask, ritual, Nigeria, sculpture, Mali	—		
4	A	America, tool, Oaxaca, statue, sculpture, goddess, India	**0.67**	0.33	0.44
	B	Greece, icon, America, tool, Oaxaca, statue, sculpture, goddess, India	1.00	0.50	0.67
	C	Greece, America, sculpture	—		
5	A	America, Colombia, Kazakhs, pipe, Peru, collapsing tool, Bolivia, Mexico, mask, Europe, USSR, dress, model	**0.40**	0.17	0.24
	B	America, Mexico, mask, Europe, USSR	0.20	0.20	0.20
	C	guitar, eating, Bolivia, Europe, dress	—		

5.1 Experimental Results

Table 1 shows the experimental results of the proposed method (A), the keyword appearance frequency f (B), and selected keywords in Q1 for each subject (C). The underlined keywords denote subjects' selected keywords in the methods (A) and (B). The recall scores of (A) for all subjects were higher than their precision and F-measure scores. We could confirm that our proposed method extracted keywords could indicate user interests. The recall scores of (A) for subjects 1, 3, and 5 were higher than those of (B) in Q1. In Q2, subjects 1, 3, and 5 answered that "I operated to learn more about topics I was interested in.", and "I operated to browse the information of related museum exhibits based on pictures that I was interested in.". According to these answers, we confirmed that our proposed interest extraction method is effective for users who want to know the details of museum exhibits or topics of their interests. It also shows the validity of the setting conditions of f, g, h, and i in the scoring method described in Sect. 3.2.

Subject 2 answered that "Firstly, I operated to browse interesting objects at random. After that, I operated to learn more about museum exhibits I was interested in." in Q2. The F-measure score of (A) for subject 2 was lower than that of (B). In this case, the keywords of user interests could not be accurately extracted by (A), because the random operation of subject 2 whose purpose of the operation was not specific. It was difficult to extract the interests of users who interact with the information of museum exhibits randomly based on (A). Subject 4 also answered that "I operated to browse the information on the exhibit I was interested in." But the F-measure score of (A) was low, it is probably because subject 4 spent a long time browsing the media containing each keyword, and the number of keywords extracted from log data was extremely small. Therefore, we considered that a more effective extraction of user interests can be achieved by extending the log acquisition time or incorporating the browsing time for each media in log data as an additional scoring method.

5.2 Discussion

Subjects who browsed a detail of a specific topic indicate their interests in various keywords, and subjects who browsed randomly in various topics mainly indicate their interests in location names. When targets are limited to spatial and temporal contents such as museum and art museum exhibits, post-learning based on locations may suitable for users whose interests are not clear. Regarding the media selection tendency, there were no differences in the types of media selected by subjects. They tend to select mainly pictures regardless of their intentions. Therefore, our proposed method can classify users into two types.

1. Users who want to learn more about specific topics. They tend to repeatedly or continuously select the same topics and are interested in various topics. By combining the keywords extracted by the proposed method, it can help users learn about the topics they want to know more deeply.
2. Users who are interested in topics at random. They tend to change topics frequently and are less likely to return to the same topics. They also tend to

be primarily interested in location names. By combining location names of keywords extracted by the proposed method, it can be utilized for extracting post-learning content for users.

As a result, we confirmed that our proposed method could extract user interests to reflect users' intentions, and it could help users to obtain detailed information on specific topics of museum exhibits. Therefore, it is possible to extract keywords of user interests suitable for post-learning to help users to deepen their interests in on-site learning. Also, we found that more effective interest extraction can be expected by incorporating the scoring method with media browsing time in the future.

6   Conclusion

In this paper, we proposed a method to extract and visualize user interests for supporting post-learning by analyzing user operation logs for exhibits on multimedia museum devices. Through the evaluation, we verified and discussed the effectiveness of our proposed scoring method for extracting user interests.

As future work, we plan to propose a video content generation method for post-learning support by analyzing users' learning styles based on classifications of important topics in textbooks and the tendency of the users' operations.

Acknowledgment. The authors would like to thank Ms. Honoka Kakimoto graduated from Kwansei Gakuin University for technical assistance with the experiments. The research was partially supported by ROIS NII Open Collaborative Research 2020-(20FC04).

References

1. Abel, F., Gao, Q., Houben, G.-J., Tao, K.: Semantic enrichment of Twitter posts for user profile construction on the social web. In: Antoniou, G., et al. (eds.) ESWC 2011. LNCS, vol. 6644, pp. 375–389. Springer, Heidelberg (2011). https://doi.org/10.1007/978-3-642-21064-8_26
2. Arabzadeh, N., Fani, H., Zarrinkalam, F., Navivala, A., Bagheri, E.: Causal dependencies for future interest prediction on Twitter. In: Proceedings of the 27th ACM International Conference on Information and Knowledge Management, CIKM 2018, pp. 1511–1514. Association for Computing Machinery, New York (2018). https://doi.org/10.1145/3269206.3269312
3. Fani, H., Bagheri, E., Zarrinkalam, F., Zhao, X., Du, W.: Finding diachronic like-minded users. Comput. Intell. **34**(1), 124–144 (2018)
4. Felder, R.M., Silverman, L.K., et al.: Learning and teaching styles in engineering education. Eng. Educ. **78**(7), 674–681 (1988)
5. Grammenos, D., et al.: A prototypical interactive exhibition for the archaeological museum of Thessaloniki. Int. J. Herit. Digit. Era **2**(1), 75–99 (2013). https://doi.org/10.1260/2047-4970.2.1.75

6. Hatala, M., Wakkary, R.: Ontology-based user modeling in an augmented audio reality system for museums. User Model. User Adapt. Interact. **15**(3–4), 339–380 (2005)
7. Hornecker, E.: "i don't understand it either, but it is cool" - visitor interactions with a multi-touch table in a museum. In: 3rd IEEE International Workshop on Horizontal Interactive Human Computer Systems, pp. 113–120 (2008)
8. Huh, S., Park, Y., Jang, J., Choi, W.: Making a video smart for smart e-learning. In: Proceedings of the 2015 International Conference on Information and Communication Technology Convergence, ICTC 2015, pp. 858–863. IEEE (2015)
9. Jay, P., Shah, P., Makvana, K., Shah, P.: An approach to identify user interest by reranking personalize web. In: Proceedings of the Second International Conference on Information and Communication Technology for Competitive Strategies, ICTCS 2016. Association for Computing Machinery, New York (2016). https://doi.org/10.1145/2905055.2905270
10. Liang, S., Ren, Z., Zhao, Y., Ma, J., Yilmaz, E., Rijke, M.D.: Inferring dynamic user interests in streams of short texts for user clustering. ACM Trans. Inf. Syst. **36**(1), (2017). https://doi.org/10.1145/3072606
11. Marshall, M.T.: Interacting with heritage: on the use and potential of IoT within the cultural heritage sector. In: Fifth International Conference on Internet of Things: Systems, Management and Security, pp. 15–22 (2018)
12. Piao, G., Breslin, J.G.: Inferring user interests for passive users on Twitter by leveraging followee biographies. In: Jose, J.M., et al. (eds.) ECIR 2017. LNCS, vol. 10193, pp. 122–133. Springer, Cham (2017). https://doi.org/10.1007/978-3-319-56608-5_10
13. Sheeba, T., Krishnan, R.: Prediction of student learning style using modified decision tree algorithm in e-learning system. In: Proceedings of the 2018 International Conference on Data Science and Information Technology, DSIT 2018, pp. 85–90. Association for Computing Machinery, New York (2018). https://doi.org/10.1145/3239283.3239319
14. Spence, J., et al.: Seeing with new eyes: designing for in-the-wild museum gifting. In: Proceedings of the 2019 CHI Conference on Human Factors in Computing Systems, CHI 2019, pp. 1–13. Association for Computing Machinery, New York (2019). https://doi.org/10.1145/3290605.3300235
15. Trikha, A.K., Zarrinkalam, F., Bagheri, E.: Topic-association mining for user interest detection. In: Pasi, G., Piwowarski, B., Azzopardi, L., Hanbury, A. (eds.) ECIR 2018. LNCS, vol. 10772, pp. 665–671. Springer, Cham (2018). https://doi.org/10.1007/978-3-319-76941-7_60
16. Wang, J., Zhao, W.X., He, Y., Li, X.: Infer user interests via link structure regularization. ACM Trans. Intell. Syst. Technol. 5(2) (2014). https://doi.org/10.1145/2499380
17. Wu, S.C.: Online learning and opinions of educator: a quantitative study of museum educational video platform's user. In: Proceedings of the 8th International Conference on Informatics, Environment, Energy and Applications, IEEA 2019, pp. 258–262. Association for Computing Machinery, New York (2019). https://doi.org/10.1145/3323716.3323756
18. Yan, L., Yan, M., Xu, F.: Multimedia interactive system and method based on preschool education (2017)

19. Zarrinkalam, F., Fani, H., Bagheri, E.: Social user interest mining: methods and applications. In: Proceedings of the 25th ACM SIGKDD International Conference on Knowledge Discovery & Data Mining, KDD 2019, pp. 3235–3236. Association for Computing Machinery, New York (2019). https://doi.org/10.1145/3292500.3332279

20. Zarrinkalam, F., Fani, H., Bagheri, E., Kahani, M., Du, W.: Semantics-enabled user interest detection from Twitter. In: IEEE/WIC/ACM International Conference on Web Intelligence and Intelligent Agent Technology (WI-IAT), vol. 1, pp. 469–476. IEEE (2015)

A Motivational Design Approach to Integrate MOOCs in Traditional Classrooms

Long Ma[1][✉] and Chei Sian Lee[2]

[1] International Business School, Zhejiang Gongshang University, Hangzhou, China
malong@zjgsu.edu.cn
[2] Wee Kim Wee School of Communication and Information, Nanyang Technological University, Singapore, Singapore
leecs@ntu.edu.sg

Abstract. Despite the promising benefits of blended Massive Open Online Courses (MOOCs) over traditional face-to-face class, it is still unclear how MOOCs should be integrated in the classroom. The findings regarding the effectiveness of such blended learning approach is mixed and inconclusive. The present study aims to address this gap by investigating how MOOCs can be embedded in traditional classrooms. An embedded MOOC learning approach is proposed, in which students use MOOCs together with their classmates during class under the guidance of their class instructors. Drawing from a motivational design perspective, we adopted the ARCS model (i.e. Attention, Relevance, Confidence and Satisfaction) to evaluate the proposed learning approach and compare it with traditional classroom learning and blended learning approaches. The results showed that students in the embedded MOOC learning group had higher evaluations regarding attention, satisfaction and relevance perceptions than those in the traditional face-to-face learning group. In addition, the embedded MOOC learning approach received higher scores in terms of attention, relevance, confidence and satisfaction perceptions compared to traditional approach of blended MOOCs. The implications for research, educators and practitioners are discussed at the end of the paper.

Keywords: Blended MOOCs · Motivational design · ARCS model · Experiments

1 Introduction

Massive Open Online Courses (MOOCs) provide quality course content and promote equity in educational opportunities for worldwide learners [1, 2]. It is regarded a digital collection of quality course materials for higher education uses. Despite the promising benefits and wide spread of MOOCs, the adoption rate of MOOC learning is still low while the dropout rate remains high [3, 4]. The underlying reasons include inadequate digital infrastructure, lack of pressure and support, lack of self-regulation skills, no sense of community [5, 6]. Recognizing the weakness of standalone MOOCs, educators

© Springer Nature Switzerland AG 2020
E. Ishita et al. (Eds.): ICADL 2020, LNCS 12504, pp. 187–195, 2020.
https://doi.org/10.1007/978-3-030-64452-9_16

attempt to blend MOOCs with traditional face-to-face learning in order to take advantage of both in-class interactions and online quality course content [7].

Separately, the Covid-19 pandemic has signaled the urgency for different stakeholders (e.g. educators, governments, providers) to explore ways to blend digital online learning and classroom as new teaching and learning approaches are required in the new normal after the pandemic. The blended learning approach has shown to increase students' engagement and satisfaction, reduce dropout rates, and improve students' academic performance [8]. However, the findings concerning the effectiveness of blended MOOCs are mixed. Previous studies found that there were no significant differences regarding students' performance between blended learning approaches and traditional face-to-face teaching [9]. In addition, previous studies found that students were dissatisfied with the course design and interaction methods of blended learning [10]. Lack of evidence may lead educators to make poor choices in deciding how to blend online materials with traditional classroom [11]. Thus, it is necessary to reconsider how to incorporate online materials into traditional learning settings [12] by comparing the effects of the different learning approaches (i.e. face-to-face learning, traditional blended learning, etc.).

Indeed, little is known about how MOOCs should be effectively blended into traditional class. Specifically, it is unclear to which degree they can enhance in-class instructions, and how they affect students' motivation and satisfaction [9]. As such, it is necessary to understand how MOOCs and other online learning resources can be integrated with traditional face-to-face class without compromising quality and interactions [3] and ultimately achieving learning effectiveness and satisfaction. Our objective is then to evaluate and compare the effectiveness of three types of learning approaches: a) traditional face-to-face classroom learning- no integration with MOOCs, b) traditional blended MOOCs learning -students are to conduct self-learning using MOOCs outside classroom, and c) embedded MOOCs learning - students are assigned to use MOOCs together with their classmates during the class under the guidance of class instructor. For assessing the effectiveness of the different learning approaches, we use the Attention, Relevance, Confidence and Satisfaction (ARCS) model. This model seeks to investigate and compare the motivational appeal of the proposed three learning approaches to meet learning needs of students [13]. On a broader scale, the findings of the present study shed light on how to use digital collections of quality educational resources to support new teaching methodologies in the new normal after the pandemic.

2   Literature Review

2.1   Traditional Approaches to Blend MOOCs

Though there is no standard way to blend MOOCs, a widely used approach is to assign students to use MOOCs before/after the class to complement in-class lectures. Concerns with the effectiveness of blended learning have led to an increasing number of research on this topic [14]. However, the findings are mixed and inconclusive. For instance, Bruffet al. [15] conducted a focus-group discussion after integrating an online course into a traditional campus-based class, and found that students' response to blended learning was generally positive. They also reported that students preferred to interact in the traditional face-to-face classroom rather than with the online community of MOOCs. However, students were unsatisfied with the misalignment between the video content and the face-to-face lectures. Holotescu et al. [16] reported that the overall satisfaction of blended learning was positive, though students felt disappointed as they did not receive direct feedback from instructors in the online learning section.

Griffith et al. [9] conducted an experiment in seven universities that lasted for two years and found that students in the blended learning tend to have a higher perceived value of classroom time, but reported a lower level of satisfaction. Prior research has reported that there are several reasons why students feel unsatisfied with the blended learning approach. First, the lack of instant feedback and interactions is a major problem. Students are generally reluctant to participate in online discussion and prefer face-to-face interactions [10]. Second, the content in MOOCs is not suitable or irrelevant [11]. If students found what they learned in online courses were irrelevant to their face-to-face class, they might simply fast-forward the online video courses to save time [9]. Third, blended learning needs instructors to devote more time to integrate online courses into their current in-class content while students are required to spend more time preparing for the class as they need to watch the video and learn the content on their own, they may see this as extra workload [17].

While MOOCs are not originally designed for blended learning [15], it has potential to create positive impacts when embedding MOOCs in face-to-face learning. Indeed, it has been confirmed that blended learning works. However, the concern is that there is a lack of research to demonstrate the best way to embed MOOCs to motivate and engage students to achieve learning outcomes [9].

2.2   An Embedded MOOC Learning Approach

In order to overcome the problems of blended MOOCs and take advantage of the online quality course content, the present study proposed an embedded learning approach. Embedded MOOCs is defined as integrating selective MOOC contents into the formal lessons and allowing students to consume the content in class hours and synchronous discussion on the MOOC contents will be conducted in class under the guidance of the instructors. The online courses can be shortened and restructured by the instructors to fit the existing courses. Such personalization of MOOCs is deemed favorably as the quality online courses can be utilized while the social presence of instructor can be guaranteed [15]. Social presence and support from instructors and peer learners are strong predictors of students' performance and perceptions [18].

The embedded MOOC learning approach can overcome the weakness of blended MOOC learning in several ways. First, by ensuring that the MOOC content is integrated into the formal lesson plan would provide opportunities for students to interact with each other and with the instructor regarding the content they consumed [19]. Second, embedded MOOC learning is able to alleviate the problem of misalignment between the online course video and the in-class course content. Instructors can interact with the video content in class and explain the details and focusing on selected segments. This means that the resources in MOOCs are embedded in the course design more tightly and cohesively integrated with the entire course [15]. Especially for students who lack self-regulation skills, the embedded MOOC learning is able to help them to reap the benefits of MOOCs under the supervision and support of the instructors. Last but not least, the embedded MOOC learning approach may help to decrease the excessive workload introduced by MOOCs and avoid students' superficial learning strategies such as fast-forwarding or skipping online course videos [9].

However, it is unclear how the embedded way of MOOC learning compares to other learning approaches. Therefore, the present study attempts to compare the embedded MOOC learning with traditional blended MOOC learning approach and traditional face-to-face class learning.

2.3 The ARCS Model

The present study utilizes the ARCS model to test the effectiveness of the different learning approaches. The ARCS model is based on a synthesis of motivational concepts and the four dimensions (i.e. Attention, Relevance, Confidence and Satisfaction) denote the conditions that are necessary for a person to be fully motivated [13]. The ARCS model is developed on the basis of behavioral, cognitive, and affective learning theories, aims at assessing and further stimulating student [20]. Attention refers to the extent to which the class can capture students' interests and curiosity. Relevance measures the extent to which the class is related to students' learning needs and goals. Confidence measures how confident students feel to take this course. Finally, satisfaction captures to which degree students are satisfied with the course design and their achievements. By applying ARCS, this preliminary research therefore seeks to better understand the effectiveness of the learning approaches from a motivational design perspective.

3   Methodology

3.1   Experiment Design

A randomized experiment was conducted in a local university in China in order to test the effectiveness of different learning approaches. We chose China because educational resources are not equally distributed in China and quality course content is needed in many economically disadvantaged areas. By embedding MOOC sections in traditional face-to-face class, students in such areas would have more opportunities to access to quality course content under guidance. The experiment was conducted in a university located in the northwest of China which was considered as a less developed area in China. Three experiment groups were organized as follows:

- Group 1 (G1): the students were taught in traditional face-to-face class without the use of MOOCs. This group was treated as the control group in the experiment. This is considered the "traditional classroom" approach.
- Group 2 (G2): the students were assigned to watch a online video from MOOCs before attending the class; This is considered the "traditional blended learning" approach.
- Group 3 (G3): the students were requested to use MOOCs during the class by watching the video from MOOCs together with their classmates under the guidance of the class instructor. This is considered the "embedded learning approach"

The three groups had the same class duration (forty five minutes), the same course content, and were delivered by the same instructor. The same video from MOOCs was used in G1 and G3. One hundred and forty three undergraduates were recruited and randomly assigned into the three groups. There were one hundred females and forty three males in all. The students who participated in the experiment were given course credits as incentives.

3.2 Measurements

After participating in the experimental classes, the students of each group were asked to fill a questionnaire based on their perceptions and experiences about the learning approach they were assigned to participate in the class. The questionnaire was to measure the students' motivational perceptions based the ARCS model [13, 21].

Eighteen question items were adapted from previous studies utilizing the ARCS model to measure students' learning motivations [13, 22]. The question items were measured through five-Likert scale, ranging from 1 (strongly disagree) to 5 (strongly agree). The scores of five questions were reversed according to the design. Cronbach's alpha coefficients were calculated to test each construct's reliability and all the values were above the acceptable criteria (above 0.6).

4 Preliminary Findings

The one-way ANOVA analysis was applied to test the difference of students' evaluations across the three experimental groups, and the results were presented in Table 1. It was found that the three groups showed significant differences in terms of attention ($F = 8.915$, $p < 0.001$) and satisfaction perceptions ($F = 8.395$, $p < 0.001$). In addition, the relevance perceptions ($F = 2.900$, $p = 0.058$) were significantly different at the 0.1 significance level across the three groups. However, these three groups showed no significant difference regarding confidence perception.

The Tukey HSD test was further conducted to find out which pairs of groups were significantly different from one another (shown in Table 2). It was found that both G3 (mean difference $= 0.439$, $p < 0.001$) and G2 (mean difference $= 0.370$, $p = 0.004$) reported higher levels of attention perception than G1. In addition, both G3 (mean difference $= 0.428$, $p < 0.001$) and G2 (mean difference $= 0.323$, $p = 0.01$) were found to be more satisfied with their learning approaches compared to G1. Furthermore, G3 (mean difference $= 0.242$, $p = 0.053$) reported a higher level of relevance perception than G1 (the difference is significant at the 0.1 significance level). The results also indicated that G3 has higher scores in terms of attention, relevance, confidence, and satisfaction than G2 and G1 (as the mean differences are all positive).

Table 1. Results of one-way ANOVA test

Variable	Comparison	Sum of Squares	df	F
Attention	Between Groups	5.483	2	8.915***
	Within Groups	43.047	140	
Relevance	Between Groups	1.496	2	2.900†
	Within Groups	36.115	140	
Confidence	Between Groups	.499	2	.777
	Within Groups	44.938	140	
Satisfaction	Between Groups	4.873	2	8.395***
	Within Groups	40.636	140	

Note: $^\dagger p < 0.1$, $^* p < 0.05$, $^{**} p < 0.01$, $^{***} p < 0.001$

Table 2. Results of post hoc tests (Tukey HSD)

Variable	Group comparisons	Mean difference	Std. error
Attention	G2 vs. G1	.370**	.113
	G3 vs. G1	.439***	.113
	G3 vs. G2	.070	.116
Relevance	G2 vs. G1	.064	.103
	G3 vs. G1	.242†	.103
	G3 vs. G2	.178	.106
Confidence	G2 vs. G1	.084	.115
	G3 vs. G1	.142	.115
	G3 vs. G2	.058	.118
Satisfaction	G2 vs. G1	.323*	.110
	G3 vs. G1	.428***	.110
	G3 vs. G2	.104	.112

Note: 1) $^\dagger p < 0.1$, $^* p < 0.05$, $^{**} p < 0.01$, $^{***} p < 0.001$; 2) G1 indicates the traditional face-to-face classroom learning; G2 indicates the traditional blended learning where students accessed the video content before the class; G3 indicates the embedded learning approach where students accessed the video content during the class together with their classmates and watched the video together under the guidance of class instructor.

5 Conclusion

Generally, the preliminary findings revealed that both the embedded learning approach group (i.e. G3) and the traditional blended learning approach group (i.e. G2) performed better than the traditional face-to-face learning class in terms of enhancing students' attention and satisfaction perceptions. In addition, students who watched the course video in class had a higher level of relevance perception compared to the traditional face-to-face class. This could be explained from the perspective of personalized learning. Specifically, the content from MOOCs is to cater to the masses and so is not able to personalize to students globally. In the embedded learning approach, the class instructors was able to adjust the learning to suit the particular group of students by tailoring the course content in MOOCs to suit the students. Furthermore, considering that the embedded approach of learning can decrease the workload for both instructors and students, it seems that this approach of integrating MOOCs is more feasible to be applied to learning in higher educations.

The preliminary findings provide valuable insights into how MOOCs should be integrated to address the motivational needs of students in traditional class. For example, as satisfaction was identified as a critical motivator in blended learning, instructors should pay more attention on how to improve students' satisfaction when utilizing MOOCs in the class, such as incorporating the MOOC content with an existing module in a seamless manner, controlling the length of video, interacting more with the video content in the class, etc. In addition, as embedded MOOC learning approach was found to effectively stimulate students' attention, it is important to trigger students' curiosity and maintain their interests by integrating only MOOC content and aligning with the course learning objectives. For MOOC platforms, they should encourage course providers to provide short course videos that are suitable for fitting into in-class learning and interacting activities. This implies that MOOCs platform can function as a digital library allowing course providers to contribute online resources. In the long run, such digital libraries of global educational resources would enable access to quality educational resources.

Caution needs to be exercised when interpreting the findings of the present preliminary study. First, this study was conducted in an economically disadvantage region in China where quality course content was lacking and needed. Thus, replicating this study in other regions in China and other countries will be needed to develop better understandings of the implications the embedded learning approach. In addition, we did not examine the long-terms effects of the different learning approaches. Thus, immediate extension to this study is to investigate the effects of the different learning approaches over a semester. Future extension also includes controlling the demographic information (e.g., age, gender) and other relevant factors (e.g., self-regulation ability) when comparing the different learning approaches using the ARCS model. Ultimately, the findings from this study will provide insights from a motivational design perspective to practitioners and researchers in developing collaborative and participatory information environments that are able to integrate both physical face-to-face environment and online resources seamlessly.

References

1. Barclay, C., Logan, D.: Towards an understanding of the implementation & adoption of massive online open courses (MOOCs) in a developing economy context. In: Annual Workshop of the AIS Special Interest Group for ICT in Global Development, Milano, Italy (2013)
2. Kennedy, J.: Characteristics of massive open online courses (MOOCs): a research review, 2009–2012. J. Interact. Online Learn. **13**, 1–16 (2014)
3. Chingos, M.M., et al.: Interactive online learning on campus: Comparing students' outcomes in hybrid and traditional courses in the university system of Maryland. J. High. Educ. **88**(2), 210–233 (2017)
4. Jordan, K.: MOOC completion rates: The data.http://www.katyjordan.com/MOOCproject. html. Accessed 16 Apr 2020
5. Liyanagunawardena, T.R., Adams, A.A., Williams, S.A.: MOOCs: a systematic study of the published literature 2008–2012. Int. Rev. Res. Open Distance Learn. **14**(3), 202–227 (2013)
6. Ma, L., Lee, C.S.: Understanding the barriers to the use of MOOCs in a developing country: an innovation resistance perspective. J. Educ. Comput. Res. **57**(3), 571–590 (2019)
7. Yousef, A.M.F., et al.: A usability evaluation of a blended MOOC environment: an experimental case study. Int. Rev. Res. Open Distrib. Learn. **16**(2), 69–93 (2015)
8. López-Pérez, M.V., Pérez-López, M.C., Rodríguez-Ariza, L.: Blended learning in higher education: students' perceptions and their relation to outcomes. Comput. Educ. **56**(3), 818–826 (2011)
9. Griffiths, R., et al.: Adopting MOOCS on campus: a collaborative effort to test MOOCS on campuses of the university system of Maryland. Online Learn. **19**(2), 7–21 (2015)
10. Israel, M.J.: Effectiveness of integrating MOOCs in traditional classrooms for undergraduate students. Int. Rev. Res. Open Distrib. Learn. **16**(5), 102–118 (2015)
11. Means, B., et al.: The effectiveness of online and blended learning: a meta-analysis of the empirical literature. Teach. College Record **115**(3), 134–162 (2013)
12. Emanuel, J.P., Lamb, A.: Open, online, and blended: transactional interactions with MOOC Content by learners in three different course formats. Soc. Sci. Electron. Publish. **21**(2), 17–41 (2017)
13. Keller, J.M.: Using the ARCS motivational process in computer-based instruction and distance education. New Direct. Teach. Learn. **78**, 37–47 (1999)
14. Liu, Q., et al.: The effectiveness of blended learning in health professions: systematic review and meta-analysis. J. Med. Internet Res. **18**(1), 1–18 (2016)
15. Bruff, D.O., et al.: Wrapping a MOOC: student perceptions of an experiment in blended learning. J. Online Learn. Teach. **9**(2), 187–199 (2013)
16. Holotescu, C., et al.: Integrating MOOCs in blended courses. Elearn. Softw. Educ. **1**, 243–250 (2014)
17. Deng, R., Benckendorff, P., Gannaway, D.: Progress and new directions for teaching and learning in MOOCs. Comput. Educ. **129**, 48–60 (2019)
18. So, H.J., Brush, T.A.: Student perceptions of collaborative learning, social presence and satisfaction in a blended learning environment: relationships and critical factors. Comput. Educ. **51**(1), 318–336 (2008)
19. Cocquyt, C., et al.: Examining the role of learning support in blended learning for adults' social inclusion and social capital. Comput. Educ. **142**, 103610 (2019)
20. Keller, J.M.: How to integrate learner motivation planning into lesson planning: the ARCS model approach. VII Semanario. Santiago, Cuba (2000)

21. Gutiérrez-Santiuste, E., Gámiz-Sánchez, V.M., Gutiérrez-Pérez, J.: MOOC & B-learning: students' barriers and satisfaction in formal and non-formal learning environments. J. Interact. Online Learn. **13**(3), 88–111 (2015)
22. Huang, W., Huang, W., Diefes-Dux, H.A., Imbrie, P.K.: A preliminary validation of attention, relevance, confidence and satisfaction model-based instructional material motivational survey in a computer-based tutorial setting. Br. J. Edu. Technol. **37**(2), 243–259 (2006)

Analysis of Crowdsourced Multilingual Keywords in the Futaba Digital Archive: Lessons Learned for Better Metadata Collection

Mari Kawakami[1], Tetsuo Sakaguchi[1] (ID), Tetsuya Shirai[1]([✉]), Masaki Matsubara[1] (ID), Takamitsu Yoshino[2], and Atsuyuki Morishima[1]

[1] University of Tsukuba, 1-2, Kasuga, Tsukuba, Ibaraki, Japan
takahashi.mari.gm@u.tsukuba.ac.jp,
{saka,tetsushi,masaki,mori}@slis.tsukuba.ac.jp
[2] Futaba Town, 19-4, Azumadamachi 2, Iwaki, Fukushima, Japan

Abstract. Metadata reflecting user needs is necessary to facilitate multilingual access to a digital archive. This paper describes the lessons learned from our experience of crowdsourcing the addition of multilingual keywords to the contents of the Futaba Digital Archive Project. We analyzed keywords offered for pictures of materials collected from evacuation shelters. We found that (1) the type of keyword differs according to the language, and (2) the term used for the same item is not always the same between languages. We propose to provide categories in the input interface and to create a keyword correspondence table for automatic completion of keywords for multilingual access.

Keywords: Digital archive · Multilingual access · Metadata

1 Introduction

We report the lessons learned from our analysis of multilingual keywords, collected through crowdsourcing, of the contents of the Futaba Digital Archive Project. The purpose is to find a better method of collecting multilingual metadata by clarifying the characteristics of the collected keywords. Futaba is where nuclear plants were located when the 2011 Great East Japan Earthquake occurred; it was evacuated due to nuclear pollution [1]. The Futaba Digital Archive Project [2] was launched in June 2013 to preserve memories of Futaba, and to enable people around the world to know about it.

Among the contents of the Futaba Digital Archive is a set of 272 photographs. They are scenes of the disaster area, and of materials presented by people in Japan and overseas, taken in the evacuation shelters. As we would like people around the world to know about Futaba town, we decided in 2016 to crowdsource the applying of keywords to some of the pictures. We used an open microtask-type crowdsourcing platform, "Crowd4U" [3]. Since multilingual access is becoming increasingly important with the increase in digital collections [4–7], we asked people from all over the world to provide keywords in a variety of languages.

A total of 4,493 keywords in 24 languages were collected. This paper shows the result of analyzing 96 of the 272 photographs. The procedure was as follows. First,

E. Ishita et al. (Eds.): ICADL 2020, LNCS 12504, pp. 196–204, 2020.
https://doi.org/10.1007/978-3-030-64452-9_17

keywords were categorized by language. Second, representative pictures were selected, and keywords were classified specifically.

The following two points were clarified as a result of the analysis. These insights can be applied to future multilingual keyword collection. (1) The type of keyword differs according to the language. For example, keywords that are trivial to volunteer workers in countries who use the language are not necessarily provided by these workers. Some effort is therefore necessary, such as explicitly indicating categories. (2) The term used for the same content is not always the same between languages. Therefore, simple machine translation of words is insufficient. The preparation of a correspondence table of expressions may be effective.

Related Work. Peters, Braschler and Clough comprehensively reviewed system design and development technologies for multilingual access [4]. Reyes Ayala et al. recommended the application of machine translation to metadata [8]. Chen [5] explored machine translation performance of metadata records. Lu [7] proposed a method for cross-lingual information retrieval in digital libraries.

Compared to them, our approach is bottom-up. Our contribution is to share the experience of collecting multilingual metadata from workers all over the world in a real world digital archive project. We found some of the techniques proposed in the literature would be effective in practice. For example, we found that constructing (non-direct) mappings between terms in different language will be necessary, which can be addressed by techniques such as one proposed in [7].

2 Method and Analysis Result

2.1 Keyword Collection

We launched a web page to solicit volunteer workers to provide multilingual keywords to pictures to be stored in the Futaba Digital Archive. The keywords were collected with microtasks generated by Crowd4U [3], a non-profit microtask crowdsourcing platform for solving public and academic problems. Some workers learned of this project at academic events and lectures, but most found it through web search engines and became interested in the project.

The workflow was as follows. First, workers visit the Futaba project top page [2]. When they click on a banner, a task appears with a picture in the archive (Fig. 1(a)). Previously input keywords are also shown (Fig. 1(b)). They choose one of the 33 languages offered (Fig. 1(c)) and freely input keywords for the picture (Fig. 1(d)). They can choose to skip the picture shown and take another one (Fig. 1(e)).

2.2 Classification by Language

We analyzed keywords added between January 24, 2016 and May 20, 2020: a total of 4,493 keywords in 24 languages. Variations in spelling and typing errors in keywords were corrected. When the language indicated by the worker and the language of the keyword differed, the latter was used for classification of the keyword. The numbers of keywords by language are plotted in Table 1.

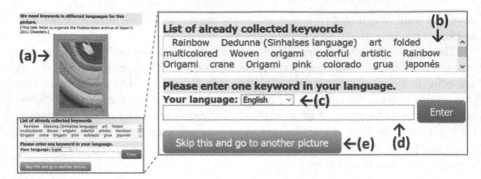

Fig. 1. Project page and task page

Table 1. Numbers of keywords in each language. Language codes: Arabic (ar), Bengali (bn), German (de), English (en), Spanish (es), Persian (fa), Finnish (fi), French (fr), Indian (hi), Indonesian (id), Italian (it), Japanese (ja), Korean (ko), Malaysian (ms), Dutch (nl), Portuguese (pt), Romanian (ro), Russian (ru), Sinhala (si), Thai (th), Tagalog (tl), Turkish (tr), Vietnamese (vi), Chinese (zh).

Lang.	ar	bn	de	en	es	fa	fi	fr	hi	id	it	ja
Num.	3	1	98	1,436	167	6	33	27	1	71	7	2,421
Lang.	ko	ms	nl	pt	ro	ru	si	th	tl	tr	vi	zh
Num.	103	3	6	20	1	2	15	1	2	1	1	67

From Table 1, 54% of the keywords were in Japanese, followed by English (32%), Spanish (4%), German and Korean (2% each), Indonesian and Chinese (1% each), and less than 1% in each of the other 17 languages. The maximum and minimum number of languages used for a picture were 13 and 2, respectively.

Table 2 shows the number of keywords and their language codes in descending order for six of the 96 pictures.

To observe the distribution of keywords by language, the keywords added to the six pictures in Table 2 were classified by appearance, name, and function. These categories were based on the standard of the International Council of Museums/The International Committee for Documentation (ICOM/CIDOC) [9]. (The three categories in [9] are Material and Technique, Title, and Original functions.) We added color as a subcategory of appearance. Europeana, the digital platform for cultural heritage in the European Union, proposes searching for objects by color as an information access method not dependent on metadata language [10]. The result is shown in Table 3. Words where elements from multiple categories are combined, such as "cardboard table", were classified in all relevant categories. Words that did not fit into any category ("fukushima" and "futaba", six times each, and "japonés", five times) were removed. Table 3 is limited to languages used for seven or more keywords.

Table 2. Number of languages, number of keywords, language codes in six pictures.

No. (Picture sign)	Number of languages	Number of keywords	Language codes
1 (Pic. A)	13	166	bn, de, en, es, fa, fi, fr, id, it, ja, ko, pt, zh
2	13	145	ar, de, en, es, fa, fi, fr, id, it, ja, ko, pt, ru,
3 (Pic. B)	11	144	ar, de, en, es, fr, id, ja, ko, ms, pt, zh
4	11	112	de, en, es, fa, fi, fr, it, ja, ko, pt, zh
5 (Pic. C)	10	119	de, en, es, fi, fr, ja, ko, nl, si, zh
6	10	115	de, en, es, fi, id, ja, ko, nl, pt, zh

Table 3. Three keyword categories. Multilingual keywords that were input depended on the language used by workers, and the distribution of categories was biased.

Lang.	de	en	es	fi	id	ja	ko	zh
Appearance	3	150	27	4	2	133	1	5
Name	7	51	15	11	5	380	9	3
Function	0	9	0	0	0	44	0	0

2.3 Analysis of Representative Pictures

We analyzed the keywords provided in Table 2. Here we show the results for Pics. A, B, and C (see Fig. 2) due to space limitations. We chose them for their dissimilarity to each other. Pic. A is a large box, plastic and portable, used as a changing room. Pic. B is a "senba-zuru", a decoration in which origami cranes are threaded together on strings and then hung. Pic. C is a work of art in which many small origami cranes are arranged at even intervals in a frame, to form an arc centered at the top corner of the frame. Japanese people can easily tell the difference. As a result, many keywords given in Japanese were correct, while in other languages, the common keywords for the pictures are "crane" but most of other keywords were wrong (such as paper "air plane" and "kusudama"). The result clearly shows that workers' cultures and languages affect the keywords given to pictures.

The classification of each picture is shown in Tables 4, 5 and 6. Subcategories were placed under main categories. The categories were as follows. (1) Appearance: (i) Impression; (ii) Shape, pattern, or state; (iii) Material or manufacturing procedure; (iv) Association. Words with multiple elements were classified in all categories. (2) Name: (i) Proper noun; (ii) Common noun. (3) Function (description of its unique function).

Pic. A. Portable
changing room

Pic. B.
A thousand cranes

Pic. C.
Crane drawing

Fig. 2. Pictures taken of materials in evacuation shelters.

The classification table shows the original text and its English translation (in brackets, and according to Google Translate).

Table 4. Classification of collected keywords of Picture A.

(1) Appearance

en	(i) brilliant, beautiful, White. (ii) 3-D, large, empty, square, rectangular, door, pricetag, boxy, opened, cube. (iii) cardboard, Hinge.
es	(i) blanco (white). (ii) abierto (open).
fi	(iii) Pahvi(cardboard).
ja	(i) 白(white), 貧相 (poor phase). (ii) 空席タグ (empty seat tags), 札 (tags), 扉付き (with door). (iii) 段ボール (cardboard).
zh	(ii) 空席 (empty seats), 开放 (open). (iii) 紙箱 (carton).

(2) Name

bn	(ii) baksho (box).
de	(i) Schrank (closet).
en	(i) cabinet, Cupboard, locker, safe, Storage, stove. (ii) white box, Cardboard box.
fa	(i) جعبه دیواری(wall box).
fi	(i) Kaappi (cabinet).
fr	(ii) boite (box).
id	(i) Lemari kecil (small cupboard), Kotak penyimpanan (storage box).
it	(ii) scatola (box).
ja	(i) akibeya (empty room), トイレ (toilet), プライベートスペース (private space), 移動式トイレ (mobile toilet), 仮設トイレ (temporary toilet), 仮設個室 (temporary private room), 仮設設備 (temporary equipment), 仮設部屋 (temporary room), 簡易トイレ (simple toilet), 簡易個室 (simple room), 簡易更衣室 (simple changing room), 金庫 (safe), 個室 (private room), 災害時プライベートスペース (private space at the time of disaster), 白い部屋 (white room), 非常時用個室 (emergency private room), 空室 (vacancy), 空席の個室 (vacant private room), 模型 (model). (ii) コンテナ (container), 段ボール箱 (cardboard box), 扉 (door), 箱 (box), 個別ボックス (individual box).
ko	(i) 탈의실 (fitting room).
pt	(i) Cacifo (locker).

(3) Function

en	stash.
ja	移動式トイレ (mobile toilet), 仮設トイレ (temporary toilet), 仮設個室 (temporary private room), 仮設設備 (temporary equipment), 仮設部屋 (temporary room), 仮設 (provisional), 簡易トイレ (simple toilet), 簡易個室 (simple room), 簡易更衣室 (simple changing room), 災害時プライベートスペース (private space at the time of disaster), 非常時用個室 (emergency private room).

Table 5. Classification of collected keywords of Picture B.

(1) Appearance

ar	(i) ملون (colored). (iii) origami.
en	(i) beautiful, bright, vibrant, colors, colourful, brilliant, bold. (ii) large, upside down, hanging, Bird shaped origami. (iii) folded, origami, paper, handmade. (iv) colourful hopes and dreams, veritable, Survivors, rainbow.
es	(i) colorado (synonym red), brillante (sparkly). (ii) Montaña de aviones de papel (mountain of paper planes).
fr	(ii) mélange (mixed).
id	(ii) Kreasi Kertas (paper creations).
ja	(i) 赤色 (red), カラフル (colorful), 色 (color), 色鮮やか (vivid). (ii) コメント (comment), メッセージ (message), メッセージ入り (with message), メッセージ付き折鶴 (paper crane with message), 折鶴とメッセージ (paper cranes and message), 千羽鶴に書かれたメッセージ (message written on Senbazuru). (iii) 折り紙 (origami), 正方形から折った何か (something folded from a square).
ms	(iii) origami.
pt	(iii) origami.

(2) Name

de	(i) Kranich (crane).
en	(i) festive crane, origami cranes, paper cranes, a thousand paper cranes, cranes. (ii) paper airplanes, Bird shaped origami.
es	(i) grua (crane), Grullas de papel (paper cranes). (ii) Montaña de aviones de papel (mountain of paper planes).
id	(ii) Kreasi Kertas (paper creations).
ja	(i) 折鶴 (paper crane), 折鶴とメッセージ (paper cranes and message), 千羽鶴 (thousand cranes), 千羽鶴に書かれたメッセージ (message written on Senbazuru), 千羽鶴に託した折り (prayers entrusted to Senbazuru), メッセージ付き折鶴 (paper crane with message). (ii) 七夕飾り (Tanabata decoration), 正方形から折った何か (something folded from a square).
ko	(i) 종이학 (paper crane).
zh	(i) 千纸鹤 (thousand paper cranes).

(3) Function   ja : 願い (wish), 祈り (prayer), 千羽鶴に託した折り (prayers entrusted to Senbazuru), 復興 (reconstruction).

In Pics. A–C we classified the collected keywords and obtained the following insights. Proper nouns were often provided in all languages. Pic. A had many types of descriptions, while B and C had few. The number of Japanese descriptions of functions was large, and similar descriptions were found in both English and Japanese.

The largest number of descriptions was in the appearance category. There were variations in trends in languages where many keywords described appearance. There were large shares in: (i) the impression subcategory in Spanish and English; (ii) the shape and pattern subcategory in Chinese, and; (iii) the material subcategory in English. The bias in descriptions in subcategories differed by language.

2.4 Noteworthy Subcategory Keywords of Appearance

In Pics. B and C, proper nouns were mostly entered, but associated keywords were also entered. The most common associated keyword was "Rainbow". Interestingly, the associated keyword was entered in some languages (en, fi, fr, ja, si), but not in others (de, es, ko, nl, zh). The keyword "LGBT", where the rainbow is regarded as a symbol of diversity and coexistence, was added to a similar picture.

Table 6. Classification of collected keywords of Picture C.

(1) Appearance

de	(i) Farbenfroh (colorful).
en	(i) pop of color, colorful, brilliant, beautiful, artistic, spectrum, decorative, pink, multicolored. (ii) large. (iii) knitting, folded, Woven, origami, Interwoven, crochet, rainbow origami art, rainbow woven rug, knit. (iv) Rainbow, Rainbow Origami.
es	(i) brillante (sparkly), colorado (synonym red), vibrante (vibrant), colorido (colorful).
fi	(iv) sateenkaari (rainbow).
fr	(iv) Arc-en-ciel (rainbow).
ja	(i) カラフル (colorful), きれい (beautiful), すごい (great), 迫力 (force), 多色と無色の対比 (contrast of multicolor and colorless). (iii) 折り紙 (origami). (iv) レインボー (rainbow), 太陽 (sun), 虹の折鶴 (rainbow crane).
nl	(iii) Wol (wool).
si	(iv) Dedunna (rainbow).
zh	(i) 彩色 (color).

(2) Name

de	(ii) Kunst (art).
en	(i) crane. (ii) art, framed picture, Kusudama.
es	(i) grúa (crane). (ii) arte (art), cuadro (picture).
fi	(ii) Taulu (board).
ja	(i) 折鶴 (paper crane), 折鶴絵 (Orizuru picture), 千羽鶴 (thousand cranes), 鶴 (crane), 鶴アート (crane art), 鶴の絵画 (crane painting), 鶴の絨毯 (crane carpet), 虹の折鶴 (rainbow crane). (ii) 額縁 (picture frame), 芸術 (art).
ko	(i) 종이학 (paper crane).
zh	(i) 紙鶴 (paper crane).

(3) Function   ja : 応援の証 (proof of support).

Descriptions in the (i) impression subcategory, especially color and light, were given in English and Spanish. The ratio of the appearance of keywords among all keywords was 30.7% in English and 69.2% in Spanish. Keywords are classified into hue and saturation or lightness, as shown in Table 7.

Table 7. Comparison between Spanish and English keywords in impression subcategory.

	es	en
Hue	blanco (white), colorado (synonym red)	white
Saturation, lightness	brillante (sparkly), vibrante (vibrant), colorido (colorful)	bright, brilliant, bold, vibrant, colors, colorful

There was less variation in Spanish, but the recognition of color was delicate, as can be indicated by the choice of a synonym of "red". On the other hand, there were more expressions for light in English.

Keywords did not equally reflect a presumed common recognition of the target. The number of expressions for color and saturation differed with the language.

3 Conclusion

3.1 Results

The following findings were obtained from the analysis.

(1) The collected multilingual keywords differed according to the language chosen by the worker. Keywords were focused on the categories of appearance, name, and function. The ratio of the numbers of keywords in the three categories varied with the language. Proper nouns were more frequently provided in the subcategories for "name" in all languages. Few keywords had the same meaning in two or more languages. Many keywords in the function category were in Japanese. Many keywords were provided in the appearance category, but its percentage was low in some languages. The trend in numbers of entries per subcategory varied with the language.

(2) Keywords collected by multilingual input cannot be handled entirely by simple machine translation because the breadth of expression depends on the language. The description that we translated literally was not necessarily provided even when there was a common recognition between languages. Moreover, the variation of expressions and the intent of the vocabulary differed.

3.2 Proposal

We propose to consider two issues when collecting metadata for multilingual access.

(1) To reduce bias in input keywords, stipulate "appearance" and "name" and "function" as main categories in the input interface. We propose three separated text fields for the three categories, to replace the text field for keywords (Fig. 1(d)). If possible, also provide subcategories (e.g., a proper noun and common noun for the "name" category, and impression, shape, material, and associated words for "appearance"). Explicit categories help workers without full knowledge of the objects shown to focus on categories where they can contribute (such as color).

(2) To reduce bias in expressions, use a keyword correspondence table for autocompletion in the input interface. For example, candidates for autocompletion should be taken from the correspondence table instead of machine-translated terms. When workers want to input keywords about saturation in English, autocompletion of brillante (es) should be brilliant (en), bright (en), and bold (en), instead of brilliant (en) only.

3.3 Future Work

We will verify whether the input form proposed in this paper can reduce inconsistencies between search keywords and collected data.

Acknowledgement. This work was partially supported by JSPS KAKENHI, Grant Number JP17H00772, JST CREST Grant Number JPMJCR16E3 including AIP challenge program and

JST Mirai Program Grant Number JPMJMI19G8, Japan. Most importantly, we are very grateful to contributors from all over the world. The contributors are partially listed at https://crowd4u. org/en/projects/ranking#group29.

References

1. Futaba, Fukushima. https://en.wikipedia.org/wiki/Futaba,_Fukushima. Accessed 10 July 2020
2. Preserving Futaba Town's Archive Materials of the Great East Japan Earthquake for Future Generations (2013). http://www.slis.tsukuba.ac.jp/futaba-archives/en/. Accessed 10 July 2020
3. Morishima, A., Shinagawa, N., Mitsuishi, T., Aoki, H., Fukusumi, S.: CyLog/Crowd4U: a declarative platform for complex data-centric crowdsourcing. Proc. VLDB Endowment **5**(12), 1918–1921 (2012)
4. Peters, C., Braschler, M., Clough, P.: Multilingual Information Retrieval From Research To Practice. Springer, Heidelberg (2012). https://doi.org/10.1007/978-3-642-23008-0
5. Chen, J., Azogu, O., Knudson, R: Enabling multilingual information access to digital collections: An investigation of metadata records translation. Proc. JCDL 467–468 (2014). https://doi.org/10.1109/JCDL.2014.6970228
6. Chen, J.: Multilingual Access and Services for Digital Collections, Libraries Unlimited Exeter (2016)
7. Lu, W.-H., Wang, J.-H., Chien, L.-F.: Towards web mining of query translations for cross-language information retrieval in digital libraries. In: Sembok, T.M.T., Zaman, H.B., Chen, H., Urs, Shalini R., Myaeng, S.-H. (eds.) ICADL 2003. LNCS, vol. 2911, pp. 86–99. Springer, Heidelberg (2003). https://doi.org/10.1007/978-3-540-24594-0_8
8. Ayala, B.R., Knudson, R., Chen, J., Cao, G., Wang, X.: Metadata records machine translation combining multi-engine outputs with limited parallel data. J. Assoc. Inf. Sci. Tech. **69**(1), 47–59 (2018)
9. http://old.cidoc-crm.org/docs/guidecat.htm (1995). Accessed 11 Sept 2020
10. https://pro.europeana.eu/post/best-practices-for-multilingual-access (2016). Accessed 04 Sept 2020

Aging Well with Health Information: Examining Health Literacy and Information Seeking Behavior Using a National Survey Dataset

Fang-Lin Kuo[1]([envelope]) [iD] and Tien-I Tsai[2]([envelope]) [iD]

[1] National Taipei University of Nursing and Health Sciences, Taipei City 11219, Taiwan
fanglin@ntunhs.edu.tw
[2] National Taiwan University, Taipei City 10617, Taiwan
titsai@ntu.edu.tw

Abstract. Health literacy is critical in disease prevention particularly in the older population. This secondary data analysis of a national survey is to determine the levels of health literacy, and to investigate how it links to health information seeking behavior, disease prevention behavior, and personal characteristics in adults aged 50 and above in Taiwan. Data were obtained from the Taiwan Longitudinal Study on Aging (TLSA) conducted in 2015 ($N = 8{,}300$). Cluster analysis and comparison analyses were used in this study. Health literacy was measured using self-rated questions about the barriers to communicate or learn health-related information in clinical and daily living scenarios. Health information seeking behavior was measured based on the engagement and frequency in using health information sources. Self-perceived health was measured based on self-rated health conditions. Disease prevention behavior was measured using self-reported activities regarding disease prevention. Two clusters of health literacy were identified: high (69.58%) and low (30.42%). The participants in the high health literacy cluster tended to have higher levels of education, younger age, and be male. In addition, high health literacy is associated with more frequent health information seeking behavior, better self-perceived health, and participation in more activities to prevent chronic diseases. Health professionals in geriatrics and librarians should pay more attention to those at risk with lower health literacy and facilitate the accessibility of health information sources. Social and regional characteristics of older adults' health literacy can be further explored for a better design of interventions to help people age well in the future.

Keywords: Information seeking · Health literacy · Older adults

1 Introduction

As the older population growing rapidly worldwide, Taiwan is no exception and is approaching a super-aged society by 2026 [1]. Taiwanese health policies highly emphasize on maintaining functional independence in older adults [2]. In Taiwan, the problem of health literacy among the older population has been noted. Wei and colleagues [3]

© Springer Nature Switzerland AG 2020
E. Ishita et al. (Eds.): ICADL 2020, LNCS 12504, pp. 205–211, 2020.
https://doi.org/10.1007/978-3-030-64452-9_18

investigated health literacy in Taiwanese adults and concluded that participants typically seek health information when having health challenges, providing healthcare services, and in need of emotional support. When attempting to obtain health information, they need to actively or passively communicate and interact with people or the environment; nevertheless, Taiwanese adults relied on subjective experiences and sources of health information to judge the quality of health information, then use the information on self-assessment [3]. The above health information behavior could be relevant to the barriers to health literacy, such as reading medical information and a lack of time in reading at medical visits [3].

Health literacy is conceptualized as functional health literacy, interactive health literacy and critical health literacy, which comprises the capacity to obtain, extract meaning, and critically analyze health-related information [4]. The risk factors of inadequate health literacy include old age and lower education [5]. Older adults with lower health literacy tended to have less income and education, being less satisfied with their health, have more hearing or visual problems, and need more assistance in dealing with reading or writing tasks [6]. In addition, health literacy is closely related to health information seeking behavior [7] and is critical in health care decision making in older adults [8]. Research showed that older adults are more likely to communicate with people to obtain health information than to manipulate searching tools like the internet [9]. This information-seeking preference makes health care providers, pharmacists, friends, and relatives more trusted health information sources than newspapers, internet, and radio [9]. Many of these information-seeking characteristics are associated with health literacy and health outcomes.

Therefore, health literacy has been considered an approach to overcome the barriers to patient education in health care systems [10]. Strategies used currently include the encouragement and empowerment of critical health literacy competencies, such as the appraisal of information and application to various contexts [11]. Inadequate health literacy could lead to poor health, patient safety concerns [12], and mortality [13]. Taiwanese adults reported that in medical visits, people had barriers to communicate with clinicians due to time constraints, physician's authoritarianism, and gaps in medical knowledge [3].

The purpose of this study is to examine the barriers to health literacy in Taiwanese aged 50 and above, and identify the general characteristics in the population regarding their demographics, health information seeking behavior, self-perceived health conditions, and disease prevention behavior. The ultimate goal is to help people age well with health information.

2   Methods

2.1   Data Collection

This secondary data analysis used a dataset collected from the Taiwan Longitudinal Study on Aging (TLSA), a national survey of health and living status of the middle-aged and older population in Taiwan. The TLSA collected information about the health of adults aged 50 and above. The participants were recruited from regular households, residents of old age homes, nursing homes, and long-term hospitals [14]. The TLSA is a longitudinal and cross-sectional dataset collected every 3–4 years. The survey was conducted by trained interviewers to approach eligible adults and had face-to-face interviews with them after obtaining their written consent. The samples were selected via random sampling design with proportional allocation for all regions in Taiwan.

The current study used the dataset of 2015 since it incorporated health literacy and health information seeking behavior questions. The sample of the dataset consists of 8300 participants. The use of data was approved by the National Taiwan University's Institutional Review Board (#202004EM008).

2.2 Data Analysis

The large dataset consists of 8300 participants. The inclusion criteria of this survey interview were adults who were 50 or older, who were d able to answer questions and make decisions for himself or herself. A total of 581 (7%) participants with missing data on health literacy were removed from the analyses. Descriptive statistics were used to examine the demographic characteristics of older adults' health literacy and their health information seeking behavior. Cluster analysis, t-tests, and chi-square tests were conducted.

3 Preliminary Findings

Preliminary findings show that distinctive groups of health literacy exist in the dataset, and the demographic characteristics reflected differences between the groups.

3.1 Health Literacy of Participants

Survey questions regarding health literacy focused on clinical and health activity scenarios including barriers to (1) describe health concerns when communicating with clinicians, (2) comprehend the feedback given by clinicians, (3) read and understand the dosing instructions of their own medicines, (4) follow the medication instructions given by their physicians, (5) read and understand the patient education materials related to disease management, (6) follow the disease management advice given by their healthcare providers, (7) learn to choose healthy food, (8) learn to achieve sufficient amounts of exercise (30 min 3 times a week), (9) learn ways to manage and reduce stress.

According to the concepts of health literacy [4], the items in the assessment could be categorized into three dimensions: (1) Functional health literacy can be assessed by Q3 and Q5, where the items demonstrate individuals' reading, writing and communication competence to obtain health information; (2) interactive health literacy can be assessed by Q1, Q2, Q4, Q6 and Q8, where the items involve individuals' competence in communication and reasoning of health information. (3) Critical health literacy can be assessed by Q6, Q7, Q8 and Q9, where items involve individuals' competence in judging, selecting, and then applying health information.

The instrument assessed barriers to health literacy using 8 five-point Likert scales (1 = Not a barrier, 2 = Somewhat of a barrier, 3 = Moderate barrier, 4 = High barrier,

5 = Extreme barrier), and a six-point Likert scale with an additional rating option, 6 = Illiterate.

The majority of participants reported a good capacity in clinical-related health literacy (Q1–Q6); however, they demonstrated a lower capacity in learning to choose healthy food, to achieve sufficient amounts of exercise, and to manage and reduce stress.

Clustering Performance. We used the health literacy question items to identify potential subgroups. Cluster analysis using the K-means method was conducted for 2- to 5-group solutions. The clustering showed that the 2-group solution presents the best fit and are proportionate in each group. The results demonstrate that cluster 1 consists of 5327 participants (69.58%) while cluster 2 consists of 2392 people (30.42%). The mean score of barriers to health literacy was 11.9 (out of 46) in cluster 1 and 22.49 in cluster 2. Therefore, the performance of health literacy is better in cluster 1 (high health literacy) than cluster 2 (low health literacy). Figure 1 shows the scatterplot of total scores of barriers to health literacy and frequencies of health information seeking behavior by clusters.

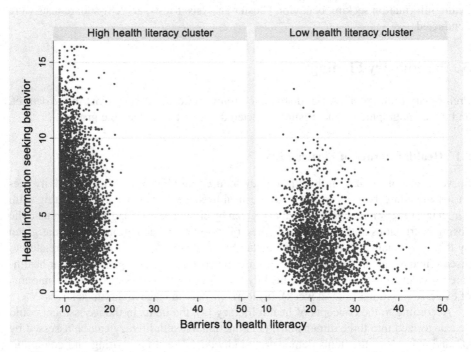

Fig. 1. Health information seeking behavior and health literacy scores in each group.

3.2 Demographic Characteristics of Participants by Health Literacy Cluster

The age categories of the dataset were 50–54 years old (12.7%), 55–59 years old (14.46%), 60–64 years old (20.43%), 65–69 years old (17.50%), 70–74 years old

(11.90%), 75–79 years old (10.11%), 80–84 years old (6.65%), and 85+ years old (6.26%). The age groups were dichotomized into a younger group aged from 50–64 (47.58%) and an older group aged 65 or above (52.42%) for data analysis.

Results of the association between barriers to health literacy and demographic characteristics showed a significant difference in age, education and gender that males are more likely to have lower barriers to health literacy than females. Participants with lower education had significantly higher barriers to health literacy. In addition, participants who were in the older group (65+) tended to have higher barriers to health literacy than those in the younger group (50–64 years old).

3.3 Health Information Seeking, Self-perceived Health and Disease Prevention Behavior by Health Literacy Cluster

Table 1 first shows the demographic characteristics of participants by health literacy clusters, and then presents variables related to health behaviors such as health information seeking behavior, disease prevention behavior, and self-perceived health. As to health information seeking behavior, the participants in high health literacy cluster have significantly higher frequencies in health information seeking ($p = 0.00$, $t = 40.93$). Participants also reported more disease prevention behavior ($p = 0.00$, $t = 10.21$) and better self-perceived health in high health literacy cluster ($p = 0.00$, $t = -22.02$).

Table 1. Demographic characteristics and health behaviors of participants by health literacy cluster ($n = 7719$).

Variable (*Significance)	High health literacy n = 5327 (69.58%)	Low health literacy n = 2392 (30.42%)
	n (%)	n (%)
*Sex***		
Male	2787 (52.32%)	939 (40.32%)
Female	2540 (47.68%)	1390 (59.68%)
*Age, n (%)***		
50–64	3,074 (57.7%)	569 (24.4%)
>=65	2,253 (42.3%)	1760 (75.6%)
*Education***		
Primary	1948 (36.58%)	1979 (85.0%)
Junior high school	978 (18.36%)	210 (9.02%)
Senior high school	1729 (32.46%)	118 (5.07%)
College and above	671 (12.6%)	22 (0.94%)
	Mean (SD)	*Mean (SD)*
Health Literacy score (barriers)***	11.90 (2.56)	22.49 (4.74)
Health information seeking behavior (frequencies)***	5.72 (2.93)	3.01 (1.90)
Self-perceived health (level of dissatisfaction) ***	2.51 (0.95)	3.02 (0.95)
Disease prevention behavior***	3.14 (1.84)	2.16 (1.74)

***$p < 0.001$

4 Conclusion

This secondary data analysis examined health literacy in the middle to older aged adults in Taiwan using a national dataset. The results are consistent with the existing literature associated with health literacy that education, gender and age could critically impact the levels of health literacy. The current study further investigates the comparison outcomes of health information seeking behavior, disease prevention behavior and self-perceived health, and suggested that the extent to which behavioral or social variables could mediate the relationships of health literacy and health outcomes. In order to help people age well with health information, examining how other behavioral and social variables, together with what the current study has explored, can mediate individuals' health literacy and health outcomes would be essential. Specifically, further investigation can focus on the mechanism of health literacy, roles of social demographic, social networks and regions, and health disparities. It is believed that the findings can be applied to develop a better design of interventions as the world population grows older and older. Although the data was collected in 2015, it represented the overall status of health literacy and health information seeking behaviors of adults over 50 in Taiwan. This study could serve as the starting point to identify what is known about information-related issues regarding the older population and for the trends of health information seeking behaviors in the future.

References

1. Taiwan National Development Council. Population Projections for Taiwan (2020). https://pop-proj.ndc.gov.tw/main_en/dataSearch.aspx?uid=78&pid=78
2. Taiwan Ministry of Health and Welfare: Health Promotion Administration Annual Report (2019)
3. Wei, M.-H., et al.: Development of mandarin multidimensional health literacy questionnaire (MMHLQ). Taiwan J. Public Health 36(6), 556–570 (2017)
4. Rudd, R.E.: Improving Americans' health literacy. N. Engl. J. Med. 363(24), 2283–2285 (2010)
5. Jeong, S.H., Kim, H.K.: Health literacy and barriers to health information seeking: a nationwide survey in South Korea. Patient Educ. Couns. 99(11), 1880–1887 (2016)
6. Cutilli, C.C., Simko, L.C., Colbert, A.M., Bennett, I.M.: Health literacy, health disparities, and sources of health information in US older adults. Orthop. Nurs. 37(1), 54–65 (2018)
7. Kim, S.H., Utz, S.: Association of health literacy with health information-seeking preference in older people: a correlational, descriptive study. Nurs. Health Sci. 20(3), 355–360 (2018)
8. Sak, G., Schulz, P.J.: Exploring health information-seeking preferences of older adults with hypertension: quasi-experimental design. JMIR cardio 2(1), e12 (2018)
9. Chaudhuri, S., Le, T., White, C., Thompson, H., Demiris, G.: Examining health information-seeking behaviors of older adults. Comput. Inform. Nurs. CIN 31(11), 547–553 (2013)
10. Wittink, H., Oosterhaven, J.: Patient education and health literacy. Musculoskelet Sci. Pract. 38, 120–127 (2018)
11. Sykes, S., Wills, J.: Challenges and opportunities in building critical health literacy. Global Health Promot. 25(4), 48–56 (2018)
12. Hersh, L., Salzman, B., Snyderman, D.: Health literacy in primary care practice. Am. Fam. Physician 92(2), 118–124 (2015)

13. Sudore, R.L., et al.: Limited literacy and mortality in the elderly. J. Gen. Intern. Med. **21**(8), 806–812 (2006)
14. Taiwan Provincial Institute of Family Planning, University of Michigan. Population Studies Center, and University of Michigan. Institute of Gerontology: 1989 Survey of Health and Living Status of the Elderly in Taiwan: Questionnaire and Survey Design. Population Studies Center, University of Michigan (1989)

Application of Cultural and Historical Data

Entity Linking for Historical Documents: Challenges and Solutions

Elvys Linhares Pontes[1(✉)], Luis Adrián Cabrera-Diego[1], Jose G. Moreno[2],
Emanuela Boros[1], Ahmed Hamdi[1], Nicolas Sidère[1], Mickaël Coustaty[1],
and Antoine Doucet[1]

[1] University of La Rochelle, L3i, 17000 La Rochelle, France
{elvys.linhares_pontes,luis.cabrera_diego,emanuela.boros,
ahmed.hamdi,nicolas.sidere,mickael.coustaty,antoine.doucet}@univ-lr.fr
[2] University of Toulouse, IRIT, UMR 5505 CNRS, 31000 Toulouse, France
jose.moreno@irit.fr

Abstract. Named entities (NEs) are among the most relevant type of information that can be used to efficiently index and retrieve digital documents. Furthermore, the use of Entity Linking (EL) to disambiguate and relate NEs to knowledge bases, provides supplementary information which can be useful to differentiate ambiguous elements such as geographical locations and peoples' names. In historical documents, the detection and disambiguation of NEs is a challenge. Most historical documents are converted into plain text using an optical character recognition (OCR) system at the expense of some noise. Documents in digital libraries will, therefore, be indexed with errors that may hinder their accessibility. OCR errors affect not only document indexing but the detection, disambiguation, and linking of NEs. This paper aims at analysing the performance of different EL approaches on two multilingual historical corpora, CLEF HIPE 2020 (English, French, German) and NewsEye (Finnish, French, German, Swedish), while proposes several techniques for alleviating the impact of historical data problems on the EL task. Our findings indicate that the proposed approaches not only outperform the baseline in both corpora but additionally they considerably reduce the impact of historical document issues on different subjects and languages.

Keywords: Entity linking · Deep learning · Historical data · Digital libraries.

1 Introduction

Historical documents are an essential resource in the understanding of our cultural heritage. The development of recent technologies, such as optical character recognition (OCR) systems, allows the digitisation of physical documents and the extraction of the textual content. Digitisation provides two major advantages in

E. Ishita et al. (Eds.): ICADL 2020, LNCS 12504, pp. 215–231, 2020.
https://doi.org/10.1007/978-3-030-64452-9_19

Digital Humanities: the exponential increase of target audiences, and the preservation of original documents from any damage when accessing them. The recent interest in massive digitisation raises multiple challenges to content providers including indexing, categorisation, searching, to mention a few. Although these challenges also exist when dealing with contemporary text documents, digitised version augments each challenge because of inherent problems associated with the source quality (natural degradation of the documents) and to the digitisation process itself (e.g., image quality and OCR bias).

While the number of works in natural language processing (NLP) and information retrieval (IR) domains concerning contemporary documents has known an important raise during the last decade, it has not been the case for historical documents. One of the main reasons is the additional difficulties that NLP and IR systems have to face regarding historical documents. For instance, tools need to know how to deal correctly with errors produced by OCR systems. Moreover, historical languages may contain a number of spelling variations with respect to modern languages, that might be difficult to recognise, as orthographic conventions can be reformed from time to time. Finally, some historic documents may also contain cases where the name of places is in a language different to the main text one. These particularities have then a significant impact on NLP and IR applications over historical documents.

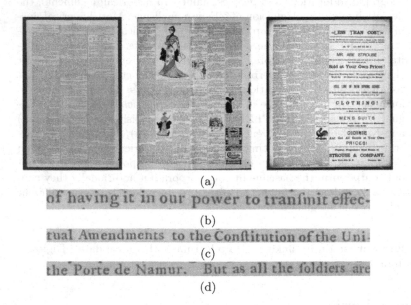

(a)

of having it in our power to tranfmit effec-

(b)

tual Amendments to the Conftitution of the Uni-

(c)

the Porte de Namur.   But as all the foldiers are

(d)

Fig. 1. Examples of historical documents from the Chronicling America newspapers used in CLEF HIPE 2020.

To illustrate some of the aforementioned problems, let us consider Fig. 1(a) which includes some English documents used in the evaluation campaign CLEF

HIPE 2020 [9]. Figure 1(b) and (c) are zoomed and cropped portions of most left document presented in Fig. 1(a). We can observe in these images a common characteristic found in multiple historical documents, the presence of a *Long S* ("*ſ*"), a character that is frequently confused by OCR systems for an "l" or "f" given its geometrical similarity. Figure 1(b) illustrates a case where the word "tran*ſ*mit" was recognised as "tranlinit" by a state-of-the-art OCR system.[1] Figure 1(c) illustrates a similar case where the word "Con*ſ*titution" was recognised as "Conftitution"[2] which makes harder for an automatic system to recognise that this document concerns the *Constitution of the Unites States of America*[3]. In Fig. 1(d), we observe a case where an article uses the French name "Porte de Namur" to make reference to "Namur Gate".[4]

Apart from digitising and recognising the text, the processing of historical documents consists as well on extracting metadata from these documents. This metadata is used to index the key information inside documents to ease the navigation and retrieval process. Among all the possible key information available, named entities are of major significance as they allow structuring the documents' content [12]. These entities can represent aspects such as people, places, organisations, and events. Nonetheless, historical documents may contain duplicated and ambiguous information about named entities due to the heterogeneity and the mix of temporal references [13,30]. A disambiguation process is thus essential to distinguish named entities to be further utilised by search systems in digital libraries.

Entity linking (EL) aims to recognise, disambiguate, and relate named entities to specific entries in a knowledge base. EL is a challenging task due to the fact that named entities may have multiple surface forms, for instance, in the case of a person an entity can be represented with their full or partial name, alias, honorifics, or alternate spellings [29]. Compared to contemporary data, few works in the state of the art have studied the EL task on historical documents [3,4,13,16,23,28,30] and OCR-processed documents [20].

In this paper, we present a deep learning EL approach to disambiguate entities on historical documents. We investigate the issues of historical documents and propose several techniques to overcome and reduce the impact of these issues in the EL task. Moreover, our EL approach decreases possible bias by not limiting or focusing the explored entities to a specific dataset. We evaluate our methods in two recent historical corpora, CLEF HIPE 2020 [9], and NewsEye datasets, that are composed of documents in English, Finnish, French, German, and Swedish. Our study shows that our techniques improve the performance of EL systems and partially solve the issues of historical data.

This paper is organised as follows: we describe and survey the EL task on historical data in Sect. 2. Next, the CLEF HIPE 2020 and NewsEye datasets are described in Sect. 3. We detail our multilingual approach in Sect. 4. Then the experiments and the results are discussed in Sects. 5 and 6. Lastly, we provide the conclusion and some final comments in Sect. 7.

---

[1] HIPE-data-v1.3-test-masked-bundle5-en.tsv#L45-L53.

[2] HIPE-data-v1.3-test-masked-bundle5-en.tsv#L56-L61.

[3] https://en.wikipedia.org/wiki/Constitution_of_the_United_States.

[4] HIPE-data-v1.3-test-en.tsv#L1663-L1665.

2   Entity Linking for Historical Data

Entity linking (EL) is an information extraction task that semantically enriches documents by identifying pieces of text that refer to entities, and by matching each piece to an entry in a knowledge base (KB). Frequently, the detection of entities is delegated to an external named entity recognition (NER) system. Thus, in the state of the art, EL tools are either *end-to-end systems*, i.e. tools that perform both tasks, or *disambiguation systems* [11,18], i.e. tools that perform only the matching of entities and consider the first task as an input.

End-to-end EL systems were initially defined for contemporary documents [5]. First systems were focused on monolingual corpora and then gradually moved to a multilingual context. Some recent configuration, named Cross-Lingual Named Entity Linking (XEL), consist in analysing documents and named entities in a language different from the one used in the knowledge base. Some recent works proposed different XEL approaches: zero-shot transfer learning method by using a pivot language [27], hybrid approach using language-agnostic features that combine existing lookup-based and neural candidate generation methods [31], and the use of multilingual word embeddings to disambiguate mentions across languages [21].

Regarding the application of end-to-end EL in Digital Humanities, some works have focused on using available EL approaches to analyse historical data [16,23,28]. Other works have concentrated on developing features and rules for improving EL in a specific domain [13] or entity types [3,4,30]. Furthermore, some researchers have investigated the effect of issues frequently found in historical documents on the task of EL [13,20].

Some NER and EL systems dedicated to historical documents have also been explored [16,23,24,28]. For instance, van Hooland *et al.* [16] evaluated three third-party entity extraction services through a comprehensive case study, based on the descriptive fields of the Smithsonian Cooper-Hewitt National Design Museum in New York. Ruiz and Poibeau [28] used DBpedia Spotlight tool to disambiguate named entities on Bentham's manuscripts. Finally, Munnelly and Lawless [24] investigated the accuracy and overall suitability of EL systems in 17th century depositions obtained during the 1641 Irish Rebellion.

Most of the developed end-to-end EL systems are monolingual like the work of Mosallam *et al.* [22]. The authors developed a monolingual unsupervised method to recognise person names, locations, and organisations in digitised French journals of the National Library of France (*Bibliothèque nationale de France*) from the 19th century. Then, they used a French entity knowledge base along with a statistical contextual disambiguation approach. Interestingly, their method outperformed supervised approaches when trained on small amounts of annotated data. Huet et al. [17] also analysed the French journal *Le Monde*'s archive, a collection of documents from 1944 until 1986 discussing different subjects (e.g., post-war period, end of colonialism, politics, sports, culture). The authors calculated a conditional distribution of the co-occurrence of mentions with their corresponding entities (Wikipedia article). Then, they linked these Wikipedia articles to YAGO [26] to recognise and disambiguate entities in the archive of *Le Monde*.

Monolingual disambiguation systems have also been studied by focusing on specific types of entities in historical documents, e.g., person and place names. Smith and Crane [30] investigated the identification and disambiguation of place names in the Perseus digital library. They concentrated on representing historical data in the humanities from Ancient Greece to 19th century America. In order to overcome with the heterogeneous data and the mix of temporal references (e.g., places that changed their name through time), they proposed a method based on honorifics, generic geographic labels, and linguistic environments to recognise entities, while they made use of gazetteers, biographical information, and general linguistic knowledge to disambiguate these entities. Another work [3,4] focused on authors' names in French literary criticism texts and scientific essays from the 19th and early 20th centuries. They proposed a graph-based method that leverages knowledge from different linked data sources to generate the list of candidates for each author mention. Then, it crawls data from other linked data sets using equivalence links and fuses graphs of homologous individuals into a non-redundant graph in order to select the best candidate.

Heino *et al.* [13] investigated EL in a particular domain, the Second World War in Finland, using the reference datasets of WarSampo. They proposed a ruled-based approach to disambiguate military units, places, and people in these datasets. Moreover, they investigated problems regarding the analysis and disambiguation of these entities in this kind of data while they proposed specific rules to overcome these issues.

The impact of OCR errors on EL systems, to our knowledge, has rarely been analysed or alleviated in previous research. Thus, the ability of EL to handle noisy inputs continuous to be an open question. Nevertheless, Linhares Pontes *et al.* [20], reported that EL systems for contemporary documents can see their performance decreased around 20% when OCR errors, at the character and word levels, reach rates of 5% and 15% respectively.

Differently from previous works, we propose a multilingual end-to-end approach to link entities mentioned in historical documents to a knowledge base. Our approach contains several techniques to reduce the impact of the problems generated by the historical data issues, e.g., multilingualism, grammatical errors generated by OCR engines, and linguistic variation over time.

3   Historical Datasets

Unlike contemporary data that have multiple EL resources and tools, historical documents face the problem of lacking annotated resources. Moreover, contemporary resources are not suitable to build accurate tools over historical data due to the variations in orthographic and grammatical rules, not to mention the fact that names of persons, organisations, and places could have significantly changed over time.

To the best of our knowledge, there are few publicly available corpora in the literature with manually annotated entities on historical documents. Most EL corpora are composed of contemporary documents. Unfortunately, they do not contain the distinctive features found in historical documents. In this work, we focus on two corpora that contain historical documents in English, Finnish, French, German, and Swedish.

The first corpus was produced for the CLEF HIPE 2020 challenge[5] [8]. This corpus is composed of articles published between 1738 and 2019 in Swiss, Luxembourgish, and American newspapers. It was manually annotated by native speakers according to HIPE annotation guidelines [8].

Table 1. Number of entities for the training, development, and test sets in CLEF HIPE 2020 and NewsEye corpora.

Split	CLEF HIPE 2020			NewsEye			
	German	English	French	German	Finnish	French	Swedish
Training	3,505	–	6,885	–	1,326	–	1,559
Development	1,390	967	1,723	–	284	–	335
Test	1,147	449	1,600	7,349	287	5,090	337

The second corpus was produced for the Horizon 2020 NewsEye project[6] and it is a collection of annotated historical newspapers in French, German, Finnish, and Swedish. These newspapers were collected by the national libraries of France[7] (BnF), with documents from 1814 to 1944, Austria[8] (ONB) with documents from 1845 to 1945, and Finland[9] (NLF), with Finnish and Swedish documents from 1771 to 1910 and 1920, respectively.

Both corpora contain named entities that are classified according to their type and, when possible, linked to their Wikidata ID. Non-existent entities in the Wikidata KB are linked to NIL entries. Table 1 shows the statistics of the datasets for the training, development, and test partitions.

4   Multilingual End-to-end Entity Linking

As aforementioned, historical documents present particular characteristics that make challenging the use of EL. In the following subsections, we describe the methods and techniques we developed for creating an EL system that addresses these challenges.

---

[5] https://impresso.github.io/CLEF-HIPE-2020/.
[6] https://www.newseye.eu.
[7] https://www.bnf.fr.
[8] https://www.onb.ac.at.
[9] https://www.kansalliskirjasto.fi.

4.1   Building Resources

By definition of the task, EL systems use knowledge bases (KB) as entry reference but their use is not limited to it. KBs are also used by EL systems for tasks such as extraction of supplementary contexts or surface names, disambiguation of cases, or linking of entities with a particular website entry. In the following paragraphs, we present the most representative KBs used in this domain.

Wikipedia[10], a multilingual encyclopedia available in 285 languages, is commonly used as KB in the state-of-the-art. For instance, [11,18] make use of the English Wikipedia to disambiguate entity mentions in newspapers. Agirre et al.[1] used Wikipedia not only to disambiguate mentions found in historical documents but also to explore the feasibility of matching mentions with articles on Wikipedia according to their cultural heritage.

Wikidata[11] is a KB created by the Wikimedia Foundation[12] to store, in a structured way, data generated and used by the different Wikimedia projects, e.g., Wikipedia and Wiktionary. For instance, it has been used to annotate historical corpora, such as those used on this paper, CLEF HIPE 2020 and NewsEye.

DBpedia [19] is a KB that structures and categorise information collected from different Wikimedia projects, including Wikipedia and Wikidata, while including links to other KBs such as YAGO [26] or GeoNames[13]. For instance, it was used by [6] for annotating mentions of locations in *Historische Kranten*, a historical newspaper corpus. While [23] used DBpedia for annotating historical legal documents. Other examples of EL and DBpedia can be found in the works of [10,16].

In this work, we decided to build our own KB consisting of information from Wikipedia. Nevertheless, rather than just focusing on the English Wikipedia, we make use as well of the versions found in the languages used in the datasets to evaluate: French, German, Finnish, and Swedish. The reasoning behind this is that despite the richness and coverage of the English Wikipedia, on occasion other versions of Wikipedia might contain information that is only found in a specific language. For instance, *Valentin Simond*, owner of the French newspaper *L'Écho de Paris*, has an entry only in the French Wikipedia[14].

4.2   Entity Embeddings

Based on the work of [11], we decided to create entity embeddings for each language by generating two conditional probability distributions. The first one, the "positive distribution", is a probability approximation based on word-entity co-occurrence counts, i.e. which words appear in the context of an entity. The counts were obtained, in the first place, from the entity Wikipedia page, and,

---

[10] https://www.wikipedia.org.
[11] https://www.wikidata.org.
[12] https://www.wikimedia.org.
[13] http://www.geonames.org.
[14] https://fr.wikipedia.org/wiki/Valentin_Simond.

in second place, from the context surrounding the entity in an annotated corpus using a fixed-length window. The second distribution, the "negative" one, was calculated by randomly sampling context windows that were unrelated to a specific entity. Both probability distributions were used to change the alignment of words embeddings with respect to an entity embedding. The positive probability distribution is expected to approach the embeddings of the co-occurring words with the embedding vector of the entity, while the negative probability distribution is used to distance the embeddings of words that are not related to an entity.

It should be noted that, unlike some works, where all the possible entities are known beforehand, in our work the creation of entity embeddings is not directed by a dataset. This is done to prevent bias and low generalisation. In case an entity does not have an entity embeddings, the EL system will propose a NIL.

4.3 Entity Disambiguation

The entity disambiguation model is based on the neural end-to-end entity linking architecture proposed by Kolitsas et al. [18]. The first advantage of this architecture is that it performs both entity linking and disambiguation. This method can then benefit from simplicity and from lack of error propagation. Furthermore, this architecture does not require complex feature engineering, which makes it easily adaptable to other languages.

For recognising all entity mentions in a document, Kolitsas *et al.* utilised an empirical probabilistic table entity−map, defined by $p(e|m)$. Where p is the probability of an entity e to be related to a mention m; $p(e|m)$ is calculated using the number of times that mention m refers e within Wikipedia. From this probabilistic table, it is possible to find which are the top entities that a mention span refers to.

The end-to-end EL model starts by encoding every token in the text input by concatenating word and character embeddings and fed into a Bidirectional Long Short Term Memory (BiLSTM) [14] network. This representation is used to project mentions of this document into a shared dimensional space with the same size as the entity embeddings. These embeddings are fixed continuous entity representations generated separately, namely in the same manner as presented in [11], and aforementioned in Subsect. 4.2. In order to analyse long context dependencies of mentions, the authors utilised the attention mechanism proposed by [11]. This mechanism provides one context embedding per mention based on surrounding context words that are related to at least one of the candidate entities.

The final local score for each mention is determined by the combination of the $\log p(e|m)$, the similarity between the analysed mention and the candidate entity, and the long-range context attention for this mention. Finally, a top layer in the neural network promotes the coherence among disambiguated entities inside the same document.

4.4 Match Corrections

Multiple EL approaches, including the one used in this work, rely on the matching of entities and candidates using a probability table. If an entity is not listed in the probability table, the EL system cannot disambiguate it and, therefore, it cannot propose candidates. In historic documents, not matching entities is a frequent problem, due to their inherent nature and processing, as explained in Sect. 1.

To increase the matching of entities in the probability table, we propose an analysis that consists of exploring several surface name variations using multiple heuristics. For instance, we evaluate variations by lower and uppercasing, capitalising words, concatenating surrounding words, removing stopwords, and transliterating special characters, like accentuated letters, to Latin characters. If after applying the previous heuristics, a match is still lacking, we use the Levenshtein distance to overcome more complex cases, such as spelling mistakes or transcription errors generated by the OCR systems.

4.5 Multilingualism

Historical and literary documents may contain words and phrases in a language different from that of the document under analysis. For instance, as shown in Fig. 1(d), an English article uses "Porte de Namur" instead of "Namur Gate". However, the former only exists in the French probability table while the latter is only found in the English one. To overcome this problem, we combined the probability tables of several languages in order to identify the surface names of entities in multiple languages.

4.6 Filtering

To improve the accuracy of the candidates provided by the EL systems, we use a post-processing filter based on heuristics and DBpedia. Specifically, we utilise DBpedia's SPARQL Endpoint Query Service[15]. This filter uses DBpedia's hierarchical structure for specifying categories that represent each named entity type. For instance, entities belonging to a location type were associated with categories such as "dbo:Location" and "dbo:Settlement". The categories associated with each entity type were manually defined. Specifically, after requesting to the EL system the top five candidates for each named entity, the filtering steps are the following:

1. Verify that each candidate is in DBpedia and is associated with the correct categories. Candidates not matching the categories are put at the bottom of the rankings after a NIL;
2. Request to DBpedia the name of the candidates in the language of analysis; if the named entity is of type person, request as well the year of birth;

---

[15] https://wiki.dbpedia.org/public-sparql-endpoint.

3. (Only if available) Remove those candidates that were born 10 years after the document publication;
4. Among the candidates with a retrieved name, find the most similar with respect to the named entity using Fuzzy Wuzzy Weighted Ratio[16];
5. The most similar candidate is ranked at the top;
6. If the ranking does not contain a NIL, add one as the last possible candidate.

Since DBpedia does not always contain the requested candidate or the candidate's name, we rely as well on DBpedia Chapters when available. For instance, "Turku" is categorised in DBpedia[17] but its name in Swedish, "Åbo" is not indexed; nevertheless, its Swedish name can be found in the Swedish DBpedia Chapter[18]. Another example is the case of "Luther-Werke", which does not exist in DBpedia, but it does exist in the German DBpedia Chapter[19].

5 Experimental Settings

In the context of multilingual historical newspapers, documents tend to contain local information that is often specific to a language and one or more related geographical areas. The use of KB in the historical newspaper's language is an obvious choice because it reduces problems of data consistency while decreases noise from entities in other languages. For instance, entities can represent different things according to each KB. For example, the English and the Finnish Wikipedia pages with the title "Paris" do not describe the same entity; in Finnish "Paris" make reference to Greek mythology while the French capital is known as "Pariisi". Therefore, we trained our EL model for the corresponding language of historical newspapers.

For the entity embeddings and the entity disambiguation model, we used the pre-trained multilingual MUSE[20] word embeddings with of size 300 for all the languages in the corpora. The character embeddings are of size 50. As no historical data is available for English, we used the AIDA dataset [15] and validated on the CLEF HIPE 2020 data. Based on the statistical analysis of the training data, we defined a Levenshtein distance ratio of 0.93 to search for other mentions in the probability table if this mention does not have a corresponding entry in the table[21].

For the evaluation, we compute precision (P), recall (R), and F-score (F1) measures calculated on the full corpus (micro-averaging). For the mentions without corresponding entries in the KB, EL systems provide a NIL entry to indicate that these mentions do not have a ground-truth entity in the KB.

---

[16] https://github.com/seatgeek/fuzzywuzzy.
[17] http://dbpedia.org/page/Turku.
[18] http://sv.dbpedia.org/page/%C3%85bo.
[19] http://de.dbpedia.org/page/Luther-Werke.
[20] https://github.com/facebookresearch/MUSE.
[21] The source code of our EL system is available at: https://github.com/NewsEye/Named-Entity-Linking/tree/master/multilingual_entity_linking.

6   Evaluation

As we previously stated, the semantic textual enrichment of historical documents depends on aspects such as the OCR quality or how a language has evolved. In order to analyse the EL performance on historical data and the impact of our techniques on the disambiguation of entities in historical data, we present in the Tables 2 and 3 a simple EL baseline $(p(e|m))$ and different combinations of our EL approach (henceforth MEL). For the filtering experiments (see Sect. 4.6), we predicted the five best candidate entities for a mention m based on the probability table $(p(e|m))$.

The configuration MEL+ML+MC+F[22] achieved the best results for French and German languages in CLEF HIPE 2020 corpora (Table 2).[23] Our model for English was trained on a contemporary dataset which degraded the performance of the MEL model and, consequently, all the variations. Despite the lack of historical training data, our model MEL+MC+F achieved the best results for the English data set (Table 2).

Table 2. Entity linking evaluation on the test CLEF HIPE 2020 data

Methods	English			French			German		
	P	R	F1	P	R	F1	P	R	F1
$p(e|m)$	0.595	0.593	0.594	0.586	0.583	0.585	0.532	0.530	0.531
MEL	0.549	0.546	0.547	0.535	0.532	0.533	0.484	0.482	0.483
MEL+F	0.608	0.607	0.607	0.591	0.588	0.590	0.528	0.528	0.528
MEL+ML	0.535	0.533	0.534	0.554	0.551	0.552	0.402	0.400	0.401
MEL+ML+F	0.595	0.593	0.594	0.602	0.600	0.601	0.538	0.537	0.538
MEL+MC	0.559	0.557	0.558	0.556	0.553	0.555	0.500	0.498	0.499
MEL+MC+F	**0.613**	**0.613**	**0.613**	0.621	0.619	0.620	0.538	0.537	0.538
MEL+ML+MC	0.547	0.546	0.547	0.577	0.574	0.576	0.507	0.505	0.506
MEL+ML+MC+F	0.589	0.589	0.589	**0.630**	**0.628**	**0.629**	**0.557**	**0.556**	**0.557**

ML: Multilingualism; MC: Match correction; F: Filter

For the NewsEye corpora, the MEL+MC+F version achieved the best results for all languages (Table 3). Similar to CLEF HIPE 2020, the MEL version generated the worst predictions. The filter increased the F-scores values of all EL versions. The combination of probability tables had almost no changes in the predictions.

Though we generated the embedding representation for the 1.5M most frequent entities in each Wikipedia language, several historical entities are not so

---

[22] The MEL+ML+MC+F model (team 10-run 1) [2] achieved the best performance for almost all metrics in English, French, and German on the CLEF HIPE 2020 shared task results.

[23] The filter used in CLEF HIPE 2020 was modified in this work to improve accuracy and support DBpedia Chapters.

Table 3. Entity linking evaluation on the test NewsEye data

Methods	Finnish			French			German			Swedish		
	P	R	F1	P	R	F1	P	R	F1	P	R	F1
$p(e|m)$	0.522	0.500	0.511	0.579	0.587	0.583	0.596	0.601	0.599	0.473	0.479	0.476
MEL	0.495	0.471	0.483	0.554	0.556	0.555	0.579	0.575	0.577	0.388	0.392	0.390
MEL+F	0.515	0.490	0.502	0.588	0.601	0.594	0.588	0.601	0.594	0.487	0.494	0.491
MEL+ML	0.505	0.481	0.493	0.555	0.558	0.557	0.575	0.573	0.574	0.392	0.397	0.394
MEL+ML+F	0.486	0.471	0.479	0.586	0.601	0.593	0.586	0.601	0.593	0.491	0.499	0.495
MEL+MC	0.501	0.481	0.491	0.562	0.568	0.565	0.582	0.580	0.581	0.386	0.390	0.388
MEL+MC+F	**0.527**	**0.502**	**0.515**	**0.597**	**0.611**	**0.604**	**0.597**	**0.611**	**0.604**	**0.513**	**0.521**	**0.517**
MEL+ML+MC	0.504	0.486	0.495	0.564	0.570	0.567	0.578	0.577	0.577	0.386	0.392	0.389
MEL+ML+MC+F	0.500	0.481	0.490	0.595	0.611	0.602	0.595	0.611	0.602	0.511	0.519	0.515

ML: Multilingualism; MC: Match correction; F: Filter

frequent on this KB. As our EL approach only disambiguates candidate entities that contain embedding representations, the MEL version achieved worse
results than the baseline $(p(e|m))$. The major impact of this limitation was on
the CLEF HIPE 2020 corpora where our approach had a drop of 0.05 in the
F-score values.

Multilingualism. The combination of probability tables of several languages
has slightly improved the results on both corpora. This combination provided
different surface names for an entity in different languages. In addition, this
combination of probability tables allowed our models to disambiguate entities
that are non-existent in some KBs. For example, the Russian politician "Nikolaï
Alexeïevitch Maklakov" who is mentioned in the Finnish data does not exist in
our Finnish KB, but he exists in our English and French KBs.

Despite providing additional surface variations, some surface names (e.g.,
acronyms) can have different meanings in different languages. Other potential
risks are mentions with some OCR mistakes that can make reference to another
entity in other languages and the combination of probability tables can increase
the number of candidate entities and the ambiguity of mentions.

Match Corrections. Our different analysis to normalise mentions and correct
small mistakes generated by the OCR engine improved the performance of our
approach. CLEF HIPE 2020 benefited sightly more from this technique than
NewsEye. This could be either due to differences in the images quality, type of
OCR used or manual correction.

On one hand, the combination of normalisation and Levenshtein distance
methods allowed our method to correct mentions like "Londires" and "Toujquet"
to "Londres" and "Touquet", respectively. On the other hand, our method could
not find the correct mentions for simple cases. In the example "Gazstte of the
Unites States", our approach did not find corresponding candidates for this
mention. The correct answer is "Gazette of the United States"; however, the
Levenshtein distance ratio is 0.928 and our threshold to correct a mention is

0.93. Another example of OCR errors is the mention "United Stares". In this case, the correct entity is "United States"; however, the candidate mention in the probability with the best Levenshtein distance ratio is "United Stars" which made our approach generated the wrong disambiguation. A lower Levenshtein distance ratio may find more degraded mention; however, this low ratio can generate too many mistakes for entities that not exist in KB. In the future, we will explore whether Fuzzy Wuzzy, an improved Levenshtein distance used in the filter (Sect. 4.6), could alleviate these issues.

Filtering. The use of a post-processing filter for refining the top five most probable candidates, allowed us to achieve the best results, as observed in Table 2 and Table 3. Specifically, with the filter, we prioritised the candidates that not only were the most similar to the named entity but also, those that agreed with the named entity type and publication year. For instance, in an English newspaper published in 1810 the named entity of type person "Mr. Vance"[24] had for candidates the following Wikidata IDS: "Q507981" (location), "Q19118257" (person born in 1885), "Q985481" (location), and "Q7914040" (person born in 1930). Thanks to the filter, we observed that most of the candidates belonged to locations, while the proposed people were born long after the journal publication; thus, the best candidate should be a NIL, which in fact was the correct prediction. Despite DBpedia does not support languages such as Finnish, the filter can still improve the results using only the information regarding named entity categories, as seen in Table 3. It should be noticed that the filter is not free of errors. In some cases, the best candidate was positioned at the end of the rankings because DBpedia's categories did not match the categories defined for the named entity type, e.g., the journal "Le Temps", a product-type named entity, is not classified as a human work in DBpedia[25].

As digital library frameworks tend to provide the top N most probable entities for a mention in a context, we analysed the performance of the best two EL approach versions when we provide the top three candidate entities for each mention. These results are presented in Table 4. The MEL+MC+F method achieved the best average F-score, which is remarkable considering that the issues encountered in multilingual historical data can increase the difficulty of

Table 4. F-scores values for the top three candidate entities on the test data sets.

Methods	CLEF HIPE 2020			NewsEye			
	English	French	German	Finnish	French	German	Swedish
MEL+MC+F	**0.726**	**0.691**	0.623	**0.598**	0.706	0.699	0.594
MEL+ML+MC+F	0.710	0.690	**0.645**	0.566	**0.710**	**0.700**	**0.605**

ML: Multilingualism; MC: Match correction; F: Filter

---

[24] HIPE-data-v1.3-test-en.tsv#L4232-L4234.
[25] http://dbpedia.org/page/Le_Temps_(Paris).

this task. Compared to Tables 2 and 3, the results are at least 14% better than the top one prediction.

Based on all the previous results, we can observe that our EL approach outperformed the baseline for both corpora in all languages. Thus, we can conclude that the proposed techniques partially attenuated the impact of historical data issues. As well, the proposition of the best candidates can accelerate the work of librarians and humanities professionals in the analysis of historical documents in several languages and on different subjects. Finally, despite the recent progress, the EL for historical data is still a challenging task due to the multiple constraints. Examples of these limitations are the lack of annotated training data and the existence of multiple missing historical entities in the KBs, which can limit the training of more robust models.

7   Conclusion

Historical documents are essential resources for cultural and historical heritage. Enriching semantically historical documents, with aspects such as named entity recognition and entity linking, can improve their analysis and exploitation within digital libraries. In this work, we investigated a multilingual end-to-end entity linking system created for processing historical documents and disambiguate entities in English, Finnish, French, German, and Swedish. Specifically, we make use of entities embeddings, built from Wikipedia in multiple languages, along with a neural attention mechanism that analyses context words and candidate entities embeddings to disambiguate mentions in historical documents.

Additionally, we proposed several techniques to minimise the impact of issues frequently found in historical data, such as multilingualism and errors related to OCR systems. As well, we presented a filtering process to improve the linking of entities. Our evaluation on two historical corpora (CLEF HIPE 2020 and News-Eye) showed that our methods outperform the baseline and considerably reduce the impact of historical document issues on different subjects and languages.

There are several potential avenues of research and application. Following the idea proposed by [7], entity linking in historical documents could be used to improve the coverage and relevance of historical entities within knowledge bases. Another perspective would be to adapt our entity linking approach to automatically generate ontologies for historical data. As well, it would be interesting to use diachronic embeddings to deal with named entities that have changed of name through the time, such as "Beijing" in English[26]. Finally, we would like to improve our post-processing filter by including information from knowledge bases such as Wikidata or BabelNet [25].

Acknowledgments. This work has been supported by the European Union's Horizon 2020 research and innovation program under grant 770299 (NewsEye) and 825153 (EMBEDDIA).

---

[26] Google N-grams in English for "Beijing", "Peking", and "Pekin" between 1700 and 2008: books.google.com/ngrams/.

References

1. Agirre, E., Barrena, A., de Lacalle, O.L., Soroa, A., Fernando, S., Stevenson, M.: Matching cultural heritage items to Wikipedia. In: Eight International Conference on Language Resources and Evaluation (LREC) (2012)
2. Boros, E., et al.: Robust named entity recognition and linking on historical multilingual documents. In: Cappellato, L., Eickhoff, C., Ferro, N., Névéol, A. (eds.) CLEF 2020 Working Notes. Working Notes of CLEF 2020 - Conference and Labs of the Evaluation Forum. CEUR-WS (2020)
3. Brando, C., Frontini, F., Ganascia, J.-G.: Disambiguation of named entities in cultural heritage texts using linked data sets. In: Morzy, T., Valduriez, P., Bellatreche, L. (eds.) ADBIS 2015. CCIS, vol. 539, pp. 505–514. Springer, Cham (2015). https://doi.org/10.1007/978-3-319-23201-0_51
4. Brando, C., Frontini, F., Ganascia, J.G.: REDEN: named entity linking in digital literary editions using linked data sets. Complex Syst. Inf. Model. Q. **7**, 60–80 (2016). https://doi.org/10.7250/csimq.2016-7.04. https://hal.sorbonne-universite.fr/hal-01396037
5. Cucerzan, S.: Large-scale named entity disambiguation based on Wikipedia data. In: Proceedings of the 2007 Joint Conference on mpirical Methods in Natural Language Processing and Computational Natural Language Learning (EMNLP-CoNLL), pp. 708–716. Association for Computational Linguistics, Prague, Czech Republic, Jun 2007. https://www.aclweb.org/anthology/D07-1074
6. Wilde, M.: Improving retrieval of historical content with entity linking. In: Morzy, T., Valduriez, P., Bellatreche, L. (eds.) ADBIS 2015. CCIS, vol. 539, pp. 498–504. Springer, Cham (2015). https://doi.org/10.1007/978-3-319-23201-0_50
7. Dredze, M., McNamee, P., Rao, D., Gerber, A., Finin, T.: Entity disambiguation for knowledge base population. In: Proceedings of the 23rd International Conference on Computational Linguistics (Coling 2010), pp. 277 285. Coling 2010 Organizing Committee, Beijing, China, August 2010. https://www.aclweb.org/anthology/C10-1032
8. Ehrmann, R., Clematide, F.: HIPE - Shared Task Participation Guidelines, January 2020. https://doi.org/10.5281/zenodo.3677171
9. Ehrmann, M., Romanello, M., Bircher, S., Clematide, S.: Introducing the CLEF 2020 HIPE shared task: named entity recognition and linking on historical newspapers. In: Jose, J.M., et al. (eds.) ECIR 2020, Part II. LNCS, vol. 12036, pp. 524–532. Springer, Cham (2020). https://doi.org/10.1007/978-3-030-45442-5_68
10. Frontini, F., Brando, C., Ganascia, J.G.: Semantic web based named entity linking for digital humanities and heritage texts. In: Proceedings of the First International Workshop Semantic Web for Scientific Heritage at the 12th ESWC 2015 Conference, vol. 1364, June 2015
11. Ganea, O.E., Hofmann, T.: Deep joint entity disambiguation with local neural attention. In: Proceedings of the 2017 Conference on Empirical Methods in Natural Language Processing. pp. 2619–2629. Association for Computational Linguistics (2017). https://doi.org/10.18653/v1/D17-1277
12. Gefen, A.: Les enjeux épistémologiques des humanités numériques. Socio (2015). https://doi.org/10.4000/socio.1296
13. Heino, E., et al.: Named entity linking in a complex domain: case second world war history. In: Gracia, J., Bond, F., McCrae, J.P., Buitelaar, P., Chiarcos, C., Hellmann, S. (eds.) LDK 2017. LNCS (LNAI), vol. 10318, pp. 120–133. Springer, Cham (2017). https://doi.org/10.1007/978-3-319-59888-8_10

14. Hochreiter, S., Schmidhuber, J.: Long short-term memory. Neural Comput. **9**(8), 1735–1780 (1997). https://doi.org/10.1162/neco.1997.9.8.1735
15. Hoffart, J., et al.: Robust disambiguation of named entities in text. In: Proceedings of the 2011 Conference on Empirical Methods in Natural Language Processing, pp. 782–792. Association for Computational Linguistics, Edinburgh, Scotland, UK, July 2011. https://www.aclweb.org/anthology/D11-1072
16. van Hooland, S., De Wilde, M., Verborgh, R., Steiner, T., Van de Walle, R.: Exploring entity recognition and disambiguation for cultural heritage collections. Digit. Sch. Humanit. **30**(2), 262–279 (2013). https://doi.org/10.1093/llc/fqt067
17. Huet, T., Biega, J., Suchanek, F.M.: Mining history with Le Monde. In: Proceedings of the 2013 Workshop on Automated Knowledge Base Construction, pp. 49–54. AKBC 2013. Association for Computing Machinery, New York, NY, USA (2013). https://doi.org/10.1145/2509558.2509567
18. Kolitsas, N., Ganea, O.E., Hofmann, T.: End-to-end neural entity linking. In: Proceedings of the 22nd Conference on Computational Natural Language Learning, pp. 519–529. Association for Computational Linguistics (2018). https://doi.org/10.18653/v1/K18-1050
19. Lehmann, J., et al.: DBpedia - a large-scale, multilingual knowledge base extracted from Wikipedia. Semant. Web J. **6**(2), 167–195 (2015). https://doi.org/10.3233/SW-140134
20. Linhares Pontes, E., Hamdi, A., Sidere, N., Doucet, A.: Impact of OCR quality on named entity linking. In: Jatowt, A., Maeda, A., Syn, S.Y. (eds.) ICADL 2019. LNCS, vol. 11853, pp. 102–115. Springer, Cham (2019). https://doi.org/10.1007/978-3-030-34058-2_11
21. Linhares Pontes, E., Moreno, J.G., Doucet, A.: Linking named entities across languages using multilingual word embeddings. In: Proceedings of the ACM/IEEE Joint Conference on Digital Libraries in 2020, JCDL 2020, pp. 329–332. Association for Computing Machinery, New York, NY, USA (2020). https://doi.org/10.1145/3383583.3398597
22. Mosallam, Y., Abi-Haidar, A., Ganascia, J.-G.: Unsupervised named entity recognition and disambiguation: an application to old French Journals. In: Perner, P. (ed.) ICDM 2014. LNCS (LNAI), vol. 8557, pp. 12–23. Springer, Cham (2014). https://doi.org/10.1007/978-3-319-08976-8_2
23. Munnelly, G., Lawless, S.: Investigating entity linking in early english legal documents. In: Proceedings of the 18th ACM/IEEE on Joint Conference on Digital Libraries, JCDL 2018, pp. 59–68. Association for Computing Machinery, New York, NY, USA (2018). https://doi.org/10.1145/3197026.3197055
24. Munnelly, G., Pandit, H.J., Lawless, S.: Exploring linked data for the automatic enrichment of historical archives. In: Gangem, A., et al. (eds.) ESWC 2018. LNCS, vol. 11155, pp. 423–433. Springer, Cham (2018). https://doi.org/10.1007/978-3-319-98192-5_57
25. Navigli, R., Ponzetto, S.P.: BabelNet: the automatic construction, evaluation and application of a wide-coverage multilingual semantic network. Artif. Intell. **193**, 217–250 (2012). https://doi.org/10.1016/j.artint.2012.07.001
26. Pellissier Tanon, T., Weikum, G., Suchanek, F.: YAGO 4: a reason-able knowledge base. In: Harth, A.A., et al. (eds.) ESWC 2020. LNCS, vol. 12123, pp. 583–596. Springer, Cham (2020). https://doi.org/10.1007/978-3-030-49461-2_34
27. Rijhwani, S., Xie, J., Neubig, G., Carbonell, J.: Zero-shot neural transfer for cross-lingual entity linking. In: Thirty-Third AAAI Conference on Artificial Intelligence (AAAI). Honolulu, Hawaii, January 2019. https://doi.org/10.1609/aaai.v33i01.33016924

28. Ruiz, P., Poibeau, T.: Mapping the Bentham Corpus: Concept-based Navigation. J. Data Min. Digit. Humanit. Special Issue: Digital Humanities between knowledge and know-how (Atelier Digit_Hum), March 2019. https://hal.archives-ouvertes.fr/hal-01915730

29. Shen, W., Wang, J., Han, J.: Entity linking with a knowledge base: Issues, techniques, and solutions. IEEE Trans. Knowl. Data Eng. **27**(2), 443–460 (2015). https://doi.org/10.1109/TKDE.2014.2327028

30. Smith, D.A., Crane, G.: Disambiguating geographic names in a historical digital library. In: Constantopoulos, P., Sølvberg, I.T. (eds.) ECDL 2001. LNCS, vol. 2163, pp. 127–136. Springer, Heidelberg (2001). https://doi.org/10.1007/3-540-44796-2_12

31. Zhou, S., Rijhwani, S., Neubig, G.: Towards zero-resource cross-lingual entity linking. In: Proceedings of the 2nd Workshop on Deep Learning Approaches for Low-Resource NLP (DeepLo 2019), pp. 243–252. ACL, China, November 2019. https://doi.org/10.18653/v1/D19-6127

Using Deep Learning to Recognize Handwritten Thai Noi Characters in Ancient Palm Leaf Manuscripts

Wichai Puarungroj[1]([⊠]), Narong Boonsirisumpun[1], Pongsakon Kulna[1],
Thanapong Soontarawirat[1], and Nattiya Puarungroj[2]

[1] Computer Science Department, Faculty of Science and Technology, Loei Rajabhat University,
Loei 42000, Thailand
{wichai,narong.boo,sb594028119,sb594028107}@lru.ac.th
[2] The Office of Arts and Culture, Loei Rajabhat University, Loei 42000, Thailand
nattiya.pua@lru.ac.th

Abstract. Extracting knowledge from ancient palm leaf manuscripts is essential for historians and other scholars who would like to access accumulated knowledge in the Thai Noi language manuscripts. In the absence of Thai Noi language readers, computer technologies play an important role in fulfilling this need. This research aims to apply deep learning approaches to recognize Thai Noi characters written in palm leaf manuscripts. The experiments were carried out by firstly collecting the page images of the manuscripts archived in the Museum of Art and Culture of Loei. Then the page images were preprocessed by converting to grayscale. To recognize Thai Noi characters, four convolutional neural network models based on inception and mobilenet networks namely Inception-v3, Inception-v4, MobileNetV1, and MobileNetV2 were evaluated. Handwritten Thai Noi characters were segmented from the grayscale images based on 26 Thai Noi characters. In this process, 100 images of each character were segmented and the whole dataset contained 2,600 images. Two image augmentation methods were applied to increase the amount of training data. Three experiments were carried out with three different datasets based on a 10-fold cross-validation design. The results indicate that MobileNetV1 outperformed other models in all experiments with an accuracy rate higher than 90%, while MobileNetV2 showed an interesting performance, which was almost equivalent to MobileNetV1 in the last experiment.

Keywords: Thai Noi characters · Palm leaf manuscript · Pattern recognition · Convolutional neural network · Deep learning

1 Introduction

One type of valuable old documents in Thailand is palm leaf manuscripts, which are mostly found in the Northern and Northeastern regions of the country. Instead of using papers, the manuscript pages are dry palm leaves, which are bound together to make a book. The knowledge is stored in the manuscripts by inscribing and blackening the

© Springer Nature Switzerland AG 2020
E. Ishita et al. (Eds.): ICADL 2020, LNCS 12504, pp. 232–239, 2020.
https://doi.org/10.1007/978-3-030-64452-9_20

characters. However, due to the condition of dry palm leaves, the manuscripts cannot be kept for a long time. Since palm leaves are easily cracked and broken, the old manuscripts are commonly protected or used with care. Various types of knowledge have been found in palm-leaf manuscripts such as Buddhism, medicine, customary law, culture, folklore, astrology, and folktale [11]. The knowledge written in the manuscripts was still important for learning and studied by different groups of people such as Buddhist monks, chemists, historians, librarians, and other researchers. One of the key problems of accessing the knowledge is that the Thai Noi language is an ancient language, which is no longer used and only a few scholars can read them.

Many studies have been carried out in prior literature attempting to automate the recognition of characters in palm leaf manuscripts. These studies are from Asian countries such as Thailand, India, Cambodia, and Indonesia [7, 8, 10, 11]. Several methods have been applied to suit the recognition of different languages. In India for example, the recognition of characters was based on a combination of 3D features of the characters using inscription [5]. This study detected the pressure used for inscribing the characters as Z coordinate and combined this feature with X and Y coordinates to improve character recognition. Another research focused on character recognition of the Balinese script in Indonesia [8]. This study applied feature extraction methods and proper classifiers such as SVM and kNN that could correctly classify Balinese characters (Fig. 1).

Fig. 1. Local palm leaf manuscripts written in Thai Noi collected from the Museum of Art and Culture of Loei, Loei Province, Thailand.

In our research, an experiment of Thai Noi character recognition was carried out based on the data collected from the Museum of Art and Culture of Loei. The images of palm leaf manuscripts were preprocessed and then the character images were segmented, which were used for training and testing with four Convolutional Neural Network (CNN) models namely Inception-v3, Inception-v4, MobileNetV1 and MobileNetV2 using a 10-fold cross-validation design. The data augmentation for training was applied to increase the amount of writing cases. The comparison of test accuracy results from the experiment among these four models is presented.

2 Related Work

2.1 Character Recognition of Handwritten Palm Leaf Manuscripts

Character recognition of handwritten palm leaf manuscripts has received high attention in prior research. Most research intended to read the scripts automatically by applying different methods to recognize ancient languages written in the manuscripts. A study of character recognition of Lanna Dharma language in Northern Thailand [6] employed kNN to classify the characters based on different feature extraction methods. The study shows satisfactory results with 1D, 2D wavelet transform and region properties feature extraction for all experimented wavelet functions. Another similar study was carried out by [8] to recognize Balinese scripts. This study conducted two main experiments; 1) applied kNN and SVM as classifiers together with 29 different schemes of feature extraction and 2) applied one convolutional neural network model to detect the characters. The results from these experiments suggested that a combination of NPW-Kirsch features, HoG features, and Zoning method could achieve 85% accuracy while a CNN method was slightly lower. However, as a CNN method has been largely improved in recent years, it has achieved high acceptance in an image recognition field and has been widely applied for palm leaf manuscripts' character recognition [7, 9].

2.2 Convolutional Neural Network Models

Deep learning is built on artificial neural networks. This research employed four CNN models called Inception-v3, Inception-v4, MobileNetV1, and MobileNetV2. The first version of an Inception model was created in 2014 [1] with the name "GoogleNet" or Inception-v1. This model is one of the pioneer models that employ a concept of "Inception block". The block combines several sizes of convolution filters in the same layer. By adding a 1×1 convolution before every 3×3 and 5×5 convolutions, the problems of location variation of information in the images and the overfitting problem caused by the very deep networks have been resolved. Inception v2–v4 was following year by year with different improvements. Begin with batch normalization (v2), factorization (v3) and addition of the whole block topping to v3 structure in the Inception-v4 model [2, 3]. MobileNets are another CNN models that are widely used for image recognition in different fields of applications [9]. MobileNetV1 was created by another Google team in 2017 [4] with the desire to add deep learning into mobile platforms by reducing the size of the model using a technique called "Depthwise separable". After that, MobileNetV2 was introduced in 2018 [12] as an improved version of MobileNetV1. It was built upon depthwise separable convolution as in version 1, and added a new layer module called inverted residuals with linear bottlenecks. MobileNetV2 was evaluated and found performing better than MobileNetV1 and other similar models such as ShuffleNet and NasNet [12].

3   Research Methodology

In this research, an experiment has been designed to compare the performance of four CNN models: Inception-v3, Inception-v4, MobileNetV1, and MobileNetV2. The experiment was carried out in the following steps. Firstly, the data collection was accomplished by scanning 140 page images of different local palm leaf manuscripts. The source manuscripts were from the Museum of Art and Culture of Loei. Secondly, the collected images were preprocessed by converting to grayscale. Figure 2 shows page image preprocessing results.

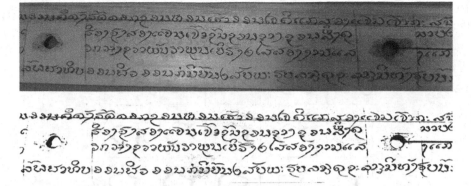

Fig. 2. An example of a grayscale image converted from the collected page image.

Thirdly, the grayscale images were segmented according to 26 Thai Noi characters. Figure 3 illustrates 26 characters of Thai Noi language comparing with characters of the current Thai language. In each row, each Thai Noi character is placed above the comparable current Thai character.

Fig. 3. A list of 26 characters of Thai Noi language [11].

In this step, 100 images for each character were segmented. For 26 characters, there were 2,600 images in the dataset. An example of the first Thai Noi character from the segmentation process is shown in Fig. 4. Fourthly, the augmentation of train data was prepared for the experiments. Two types of data augmentation, which were applied, included random 0–30 degree rotation and varied brightness. Therefore, the dataset of train data increased to double for each type of augmentation. Fifthly, the experiments based on

10-fold cross-validation were carried out with four CNN models namely Inception-v3, Inception-v4, MobileNetV1, and MobileNetV2.

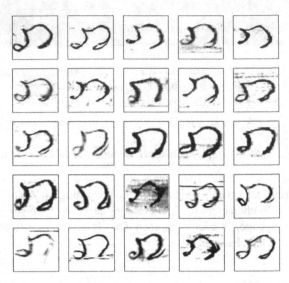

Fig. 4. Examples of the segmented images of the first character of the Thai Noi language.

4   Results

The research was carried out in three main experiments. Firstly, the dataset, which contained 2,600 images, was separated into distinctive folders based on a 10-fold cross-validation design. Each folder comprised 2,340 images for training and 260 images for testing with four convolutional neural network models. Table 1 shows the results of the first experiment, which indicates that MobileNetV1 outperformed other models with an accuracy rate of 91.88% while Inception-v3, Inception-v4, and MobileNetV2 achieved the accuracy rate of 76.50%, 73.11%, and 66.93% respectively. From the results of this experiment, two types of augmented data were generated to increase the samples of training data, which were expected to improve the performance of Inception-v3, Inception-v4, and MobileNetV2.

In the second experiment, 2,340 augmented images by making random 0-30 degree rotation were included in the training dataset. Therefore, there were 4,680 images in the training dataset. The results (Table 2) indicate that MobileNetV1 still outperformed others with slightly higher performance than the previous one with an accuracy rate of 92.26%. The performance of Inception-v3 and v4 was similar to the first experiment, while MobileNetV2 worked better with the new dataset. However, Inception-v3's accuracy was slightly lower than the prior experiment.

In the third experiment, two types of image augmentation including random 0-30 degree rotation and varied brightness were employed. Each augmentation produced

Table 1. Accuracy results from the first experiment.

Folder	Accuracy			
	Inception-v3 (%)	Inception-v4 (%)	MobileNetV1 (%)	MobileNetV2 (%)
Fold0	79.23	82.69	95.38	74.62
Fold1	81.92	78.46	94.61	63.46
Fold2	82.30	75.76	96.15	68.85
Fold3	76.53	73.46	94.23	71.54
Fold4	70.38	65.00	88.46	64.23
Fold5	71.53	64.23	88.07	71.92
Fold6	74.61	75.00	91.53	59.23
Fold7	75.00	71.15	86.92	59.62
Fold8	73.84	70.76	91.53	61.20
Fold9	79.61	74.61	91.92	74.62
Average	**76.50**	**73.11**	**91.88**	**66.93**

Table 2. Accuracy results from the second experiment.

Folder	Accuracy			
	Inception-v3 (%)	Inception-v4 (%)	MobileNetV1 (%)	MobileNetV2 (%)
Fold0	78.07	82.69	96.53	86.92
Fold1	80.76	78.46	95.38	80.00
Fold2	81.92	78.07	93.84	74.62
Fold3	75.38	75.38	95.76	88.07
Fold4	69.61	66.53	86.92	81.92
Fold5	73.46	63.48	87.69	73.07
Fold6	74.23	75.00	91.92	78.46
Fold7	75.76	71.92	90.00	71.92
Fold8	73.46	71.53	92.30	82.69
Fold9	80.76	74.61	92.30	81.54
Average	**76.34**	**73.77**	**92.26**	**79.92**

2,340 images, which were added to the training dataset. Therefore, the training dataset including the original images was increased to 7,020 images. The results from this experiment (Table 3) show that MobileNetV1 and V2 achieved high accuracy with 92.42% and 91.19%. This suggests that MobileNetV2 responded very well with a larger dataset. Inception-v4 was slightly higher than the prior experiment, while Inception-v3 achieved the lowest performance comparing to the prior two experiments.

Table 3. Accuracy results from the third experiment.

Folder	Accuracy			
	Inception-v3 (%)	Inception-v4 (%)	MobileNetV1 (%)	MobileNetV2 (%)
Fold0	76.92	81.53	96.15	96.54
Fold1	81.53	77.30	95.38	90.00
Fold2	81.53	78.07	93.07	84.23
Fold3	75.76	75.76	94.61	93.46
Fold4	70.38	65.38	88.84	85.38
Fold5	71.15	66.92	88.07	90.77
Fold6	75.38	73.46	91.92	95.00
Fold7	75.00	71.53	90.76	87.69
Fold8	71.92	72.69	92.30	96.15
Fold9	78.07	76.53	93.07	92.69
Average	**75.76**	**73.92**	**92.42**	**91.19**

5   Conclusion

The researchers conducted experiments of Thai Noi character recognition written on ancient palm leaf manuscripts found in the Northeastern part of Thailand. The experiments were carried out with four CNN models namely Inception-v3, Inception-v4, MobileNetV1, and MobileNetV2. The data were collected by scanning page images of Loei province's local palm leaf manuscripts from the Museum of Art and Culture of Loei. The collected page images were preprocessed by converting them to grayscale. To train and test the CNN models, the written Thai Noi characters were segmented from the grayscale images. There were 26 Thai Noi characters. The whole dataset contained 2,600 images (100 images for each character). The CNN models were evaluated in 3 experiments with the training datasets of 2,340 images, 4680 images (by adding augmented images using random 0-30 degree rotation), and 7020 images (by adding augmented images using random 0-30 degree rotation and varied brightness). The 10-fold cross-validation research design was applied to the experiments. The results show that MobileNetV1 outperformed Inception-v3, Inception-v4, and MobileNetV2 in all experiments with more than 90% of accuracy. However, MobileNetV2's performance was approximately equivalent to MobileNetV1 in the last experiment, which shows that MobileNetV2 model responded very well with a larger training dataset with both types of augmentation. MobileNetV1 achieves acceptable performance for future implementation of character detection and MobileNetV2 should be evaluated further to ensure its performance.

References

1. Szegedy, C., et al.: Going deeper with convolutions. aXiv preprntari:109442 7 (2014)

2. Szegedy, C., Vanhoucke, V., Ioffe, S., Shlens, J., Wojna, Z.: Rethinking the inception architecture for computer vision. In: Proceedings of the IEEE Conference on Computer Vision and Pattern Recognition, pp. 2818–2826 (2016)
3. Szegedy, C., Ioffe, S., Vanhoucke, V., Alemi, A.A.: Inception-v4, inception-resnet and the impact of residual connections on learning. In: Thirty-First AAAI Conference on Artificial Intelligence, pp. 4278–4284 (2017)
4. Howard, et al.: MobileNets: Efficient Convolutional Neural Networks for Mobile Vision Applications. arXiv preprint arXiv:1704.04861 (2017)
5. Vijaya Lakshmi, T.R., Sastry, P.N., Rajinikanth, T.V.: Feature selection to recognize text from palm leaf manuscripts. Signal, Image Video Process. **12**(2), 223–229 (2017). https://doi.org/10.1007/s11760-017-1149-9
6. Inkeaw, P., Chueaphun, C., Chaijaruwanich, J., Klomsae, A., Marukatat, S.: Lanna Dharma handwritten character recognition on palm leaves manuscript based on wavelet transform. In: 2015 IEEE International Conference on Signal and Image Processing Applications (ICSIPA), pp. 253–258. IEEE (2015)
7. Valy, D., Verleysen, M., Chhun, S., Burie, J.C.: Character and text recognition of Khmer historical palm leaf manuscripts. In: 16th International Conference on Frontiers in Handwriting Recognition (ICFHR), pp. 13–18. IEEE (2018)
8. Kesiman, M.W.A., Prum, S., Burie, J.C., Ogier, J.M.: Study on feature extraction methods for character recognition of Balinese script on palm leaf manuscript images. In: 23rd International Conference on Pattern Recognition (ICPR), pp. 4017–4022. IEEE (2016)
9. Puarungroj, W., Boonsirisumpun, N.: Recognizing hand-woven fabric pattern designs based on deep learning. In: Bhatia, S.K., Tiwari, S., Mishra, K.K., Trivedi, M.C. (eds.) Advances in Computer Communication and Computational Sciences. AISC, vol. 924, pp. 325–336. Springer, Singapore (2019). https://doi.org/10.1007/978-981-13-6861-5_28
10. Chueaphun, C., Klomsae, A., Marukatat, S., Chaijaruwanich, J.: Lanna Dharma printed character recognition using k-nearest neighbor and conditional random fields. In: Proceedings of the International Conference on Knowledge Discovery and Information Retrieval (KDIR) SCITEPRESS, pp. 169–174 (2012)
11. Puarungroj, W., Kulna, P., Soontarawirat, T., Boonsirisumpun, N.: Recognition of Thai Noi characters in palm leaf manuscripts using convolutional neural network. In: Asia-Pacific Conference on Library & Information Education and Practice (A-LIEP), pp. 408–415 (2019)
12. Sandler, M., Howard, A., Zhu, M., Zhmoginov, A., Chen, L.C.: MobilenetV2: inverted residuals and linear bottlenecks. In: Proceedings of the IEEE Conference on Computer Vision and Pattern Recognition, pp. 4510–4520 (2018)

Unchiku Generation Using Narrative Explanation Mechanism

Jumpei Ono[1] and Takashi Ogata[2(✉)]

[1] Faculty of Software and Information Technology, Aomori University, Tokyo, Japan
j.ono@aomori-u.ac.jp
[2] Faculty of Software and Information Science, Iwate Prefectural University, Takizawa, Japan
t-ogata@iwate-pu.ac.jp

Abstract. In this paper, the authors propose an *"unchiku* generation mechanism" they have developed to create deep rhetorical structures (narrative discourses) in a narrative. The system uses a mechanism that can generate *unchiku*, which refers to the detailed and excessive knowledge regarding a specific object, theme, or topic. In particular, the attribute information of each noun concept is automatically extracted from the Japanese Wikipedia and stored in the noun conceptual dictionary of an integrated narrative generation system. The proposed generation mechanism enables the generation of *unchiku* information related to various objects and topics by inserting parts of the extracted *unchiku* knowledge content into various points in the story created by the integrated narrative generation system. The attribute information related to Kabuki is derived from the Japanese Wikipedia and utilized by the formulated *unchiku* generation mechanism.

Keywords: *Unchiku* · Explanation · Narrative discourse · Narrative generation

1 Introduction

In this paper, *unchiku* generation is proposed as a rhetorical technique for studying narrative generation systems. The word *unchiku* is a Japanese term that refers to the deep knowledge and detailed description of any matter. As opposed to the formulation of simple explanations, the proposed method is an approach for developing knowledge presented in a narrative form [1, 2]. By processing the knowledge database into a narrative, it can be presented in a more comprehensible or impressive manner.

A deep accumulation of knowledge in a certain field is referred to as possession; however, it has been recently associated with interesting nuances. Moreover, various narratives have been presented—from full-fledged stories to humorous accounts.

For example, Victor Hugo [3] described an underpass in Paris in an entire chapter of his book, *Les Misérables. The Overcoat*, written by Gogol [4], is prefaced by a description of a tailor visited by the main character who says: "I will be forced to introduce Petrovich here." In Japan, Shiba's historical novels [5] are famous for explanations beginning with the word "aside." In Japanese, the phrase *"unchiku* wo katamukeru" originally means "deeply accumulated knowledge." Presently, however, it has a meaning like

© Springer Nature Switzerland AG 2020
E. Ishita et al. (Eds.): ICADL 2020, LNCS 12504, pp. 240–247, 2020.
https://doi.org/10.1007/978-3-030-64452-9_21

trivia. In human conversations, explaining word meanings naturally occurs because the information is necessary to shape the characters of a story.

Regardless of whether the discourse is treated seriously or otherwise in a story, it is an excess that is unnecessary for the eventual progression of the story. However, the story does not simply involve information required for the progression of the story line; the excess or deviation interfering with the rapid progression from the viewpoint of the story line also contains valuable details. In the classification of Genette's narrative discourse [6] (systematically organized by [7]), such a technique is employed for halting the time progress of a story and is termed an "explanation" or "description," which is afforded as a concrete example. The explanation is the development of events in the story, including the objects that appear in the story (e.g., characters, stage (place), concrete objects, abstract objects, and their relationship). That is, apart from itself, the story speaks through other descriptions (sometimes explanations and depictions are made through conversations during the development of events); hence, the statements made are a type of explanation.

In this study, we develop *unchiku* generation system using a narrative generation system [8] was developed based on the foundations of narrative theory, literary theory, and systematic thoughts and philosophies.

2 *Unchiku* Generation Mechanism

2.1 Input and Output

The input–output relationship of the story generation mechanism is shown in Fig. 1. This mechanism accepts a single-story tree as input, creates relationship using the relationship generation mechanism, and outputs the story tree in which the generated citation is inserted.

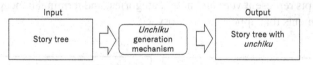

Fig. 1. Relationship between input and output

Here, a story tree refers to a tree structure that expresses the deep layout of a story; events are structured hierarchically. The partial data used in the generation example discussed in Sect. 3 are shown in Fig. 2. This story is generated using the integrated story generation system, and the names of the characters was replaced by the characters from Osamu Tezuka's "Black Jack" [9]. If only the events are extracted in this story tree and described in a fixed form sentence, the following will be obtained: "Hazama Kagemitsu goes out to Narita City; Hazama Kagemitsu picks tobacco (leaf) in Narita City; Pinoko bans Hazama Kuroo from going out (in Narita City); Pinoko asks Hazama Kuroo (in Narita City) to do an errand (get out of the temple)."

```
($Story
 ($問題[problem]
  ($予備部分[sub part]
   (event 出かける1[go out] (type action) (ID 1) (time (time1
   time2)) (agent age%間影充#1[Hazama Kagemitsu#1]) (location loc%
   成田市#1[Narita City#1]) (object obj%用事#1[task#1]))
   (event 摘む1[pick] (type action) (ID 2) (time (time2 time3))
   (agent age%間影充#1[Hazama Kagemitsu#1]) (location loc%成田市
   #1[Narita City#1]) (object obj%タバコ#1[tobacco#1]))
   (event 禁止する1[prohibit] (type action) (ID 3) (time (time3
   time4)) (agent age%ピノコ#1[Pinoko#1]) (counter-agent nil) (lo-
   cation loc%成田市#1[Narita City#1]) (object obj%外出#1[out-
   ing#1]) (to age%間黒男#1[Hazama Kuroo#1]))
   (event 頼む3[request] (type action) (ID 4) (time (time4 time5))
   (agent age%ピノコ#1[Pinoko#1]) (counter-agent age%間黒男#1[Hazama
   Kuroo#1]) (location loc%成田市#1[Narita City#1]))
   <Omitted> )
```

Fig. 2. Example of input

2.2 Conceptual Dictionary

In the integrated narrative generation system, the linguistic expression of the story is not directly created. The conceptual structure is first generated as a hierarchical framework of events having a case structure. This is the most important part that defines the structure and knowledge content of stories and discourses. A conceptual dictionary is a systematic dictionary that provides semantic information to individual elements in the events within these conceptual structures [10].

Conceptual dictionaries are illustrated in Fig. 3. The conceptual dictionary has a hierarchical structure that systematically stores noun concepts and verb concepts. Intermediate concepts represent verb and noun categories, and terminal concepts correspond to specific elements that appear in the story.

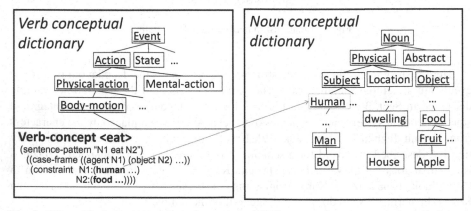

Fig. 3. Hierarchical structures of a verb conceptual dictionary and a noun conceptual dictionary

The noun concept dictionary is directly related to the generation mechanism. Elements created in a story generation are noun concepts, which is further classified into common and proper noun concepts (e.g., "volcano" and "Mt. Fuji," respectively). The information necessary for an explanation (accumulation) must be stored (or linked) in the general and proper noun concepts; in this study, this information is called attribute information.

2.3 Data for *Unchiku* Generation

The terminal concept in the noun concept dictionary must store concrete values related to the characteristics and properties. These values are called attributes or attribute information. The attribute information is described in a structured frame format; hence, it is occasionally referred to as an attribute frame. A specific person, object, place, and time appearing in the story are associated with a particular terminal concept in the noun concept dictionary; however, instances are generated from the class concept. For example, a character may correspond to the noun concept as a "male" class; however, the actual figure has information such as "the name of Taro, he is the male, he lives Japan." Therefore, the attribute is categorized into a class and an instance, each containing attribute information. The proper noun above corresponds to a part of the noun concept as an instance. For example, "(model and actress) Mizuki Yamamoto" in the class "woman" is an instance; however, in the concept dictionary, the attribute information must be stored in the (general) noun concept as a class and in the proper noun concept as an instance. As for the noun concept, the state that changes according to time must be recorded as the attribute information. In this study, the general noun concept and instance (proper noun) attribute information must be used for the explanation. As described in a later section, the material in this study includes the current Kabuki actor Ichikawa Ebizō XI and related information.

The survey that was implemented by the authors of this study indicated that the Wikipedia article on Kabuki was defective and insufficient to be the "starting point for systematically collecting, accumulating, and utilizing the knowledge of Kabuki." For example, about Tsuruya Nanboku IV in the Edo period, which is one of the greatest periods for Kabuki writers and has a significant value among Japanese story writers, the information in Wikipedia is insufficient. The amount and quality of information are deficient and hence elaborations cannot be made. Accordingly, the use of other Kabuki encyclopedias was considered; however, the authors of this study could not proceed because of copyright issues. A search in Wikipedia for other Kabuki items that have a certain amount of description reveals limited information other than that reported by Ichikawa Ebizō XI who is regarded as a contemporary Kabuki actor, entertainer, and TV star. The current Japanese Wikipedia writers have a considerable (nerd-like) interest in new entertainers and TV stars. Therefore, they wrote information about entertainers such as Ichikawa Ebizō XI.

This study focuses on Kabuki because it is linked to our previous studies [11–13]. Moreover, it is deemed essential to organize knowledge regarding Kabuki because it is a part of the Japanese cultural heritage.

3 Implementation and Result

For the noun that appears in the scene, the system inserts an *unchiku*; the scene referred to herein is the part of the story categorized based on location. For example, in the first scene, "Narita City" in the input example of Fig. 2 is the location, and in the second scene, "Hazama Kagemitsu picks tobacco (leaf) in Narita City" is the event.

The topic changes each time the mechanism generates an *unchiku*. The *unchiku* mechanism employs two steps. First, after inserting extensive knowledge of any element in the story, the co-occurring information is used to relate the Kabuki to the topic. Thereafter, according to the theory of Maynard [14], the topic transition is based on three types of theme development: the heterogeneous theme, the same theme, and the derivative theme. In this study, theme development is used. The methods are movements in the conceptual dictionary.

Here, the *unchiku* generation mechanism was implemented using Common LISP. The system interacts with the user based on the character user interface. Excluding data, the system is comprised of approximately 20 functions.

Figure 5 and Fig. 6 show the generation results, and the input is the story tree shown in Fig. 1. A pause in the legal rhetoric of description and explanation was previously tested in the integrated narrative generation system; the results of this study make it possible to extend such a pause. However, the profound knowledge generated does not seem to have any significant relevance to each topic. The generation of information was unintentional and broke the coherence of the sentence.

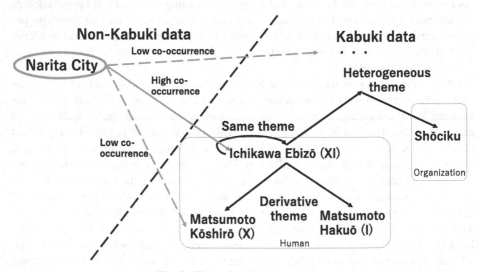

Fig. 4. Flow of *unchiku* generation

In this study, the experiment was first conducted using information from Ichikawa Ebizō XI. The information is considerably related to the keyword "Narita City" in the sample input story in this study.

間黒充がある用事で成田市に出かける。間黒充が成田市でタバコ(の)葉を摘む。ピノコが(成田市で)間黒男に外出(すること)を禁止する。間影充は「成田市と言えば、これらの地域郊外には農業地帯が広がる」と語る。間影充は「成田市と言えば、十一代目 市川海老蔵であり、屋号は成田屋。定紋は三升、替紋は杏葉牡丹」と語る。間影充は「十一代目 市川海老蔵と言えば鳴神であり、『鳴神』とは歌舞伎十八番のひとつ」と語る。ピノコが「うるさい」と言う。ピノコが(成田市で)間黒男に(ある用事を)頼む. <後略>[Hazama Kagemitsu goes out to Narita City for some business. Hazama Kagemitsu picks tobacco leaves in Narita. Pinoko prohibits Hazama Kuroo from going out (of Narita City). Hazama Kagemitsu says, "Speaking of Narita City, agricultural areas spread out in these suburbs." Hazama Kagemitsu says, "Speaking of Narita City, Ichikawa Ebizō XI is associated with it; the his Yagō is Naritaya. The Jōmon is Sanshō, and the Kaemon is Gyōyō Botan." Hazama Kagemitsu says, "Speaking of Ichikawa Ebizō XI, it's Narukami, and Narukami is one of the 18th Kabuki." Pinoko says "noisy." Pinoko asks (in Narita City) Hazama Kuroo (for an errand). <Omitted>]

Fig. 5. Example of generated story consisting of *unchikus* (Ichikawa Ebizō XI)

Examples of high co-occurrence relationships are shown in Fig. 5. The co-occurrence relationship between Narita City and Ichikawa Ebizō XI is rated 0.4.

Ichikawa Ebizō's "Yagō" is "Naritaya." Yagō means another name for each family of Kabuki, such as Ichikawa family and Onoe family. "Naritaya," which is Ichikawa family's Yagō, is related to Narita City.

Examples of low co-occurrence relationships are shown in Fig. 6. There is no co-occurrence between Narita City and Matsumoto Kōshirō X. However, there is a slight co-occurrence between Ichikawa Ebizō XI and Matsumoto Kōshirō X because of their blood relationship.

間黒充がある用事で成田市に出かける。間黒充が成田市でタバコ(の)葉を摘む。ピノコが(成田市で)間黒男に外出(すること)を禁止する。間影充は「成田市と言えば、これらの地域郊外には農業地帯が広がる」と語る。間影充は「成田市と言えば、歌舞伎役者の十一代目 市川海老蔵である。さらに十一代目 市川海老蔵と言えば、十代目 松本幸四郎である。十代目 松本幸四郎は、歌舞伎役者。歌舞伎名跡「松本幸四郎」の当代。」と語る。間影充は「屋号は高麗屋。定紋は四つ花菱、替紋は浮線蝶。」と語る。ピノコが「うるさい」と言う。ピノコが(成田市で)間黒男に(ある用事を)頼む. <後略>[Hazama Kagemitsu goes out to Narita City for some business. Hazama Kagemitsu picks tobacco leaves in Narita. Pinoko prohibits Hazama Kuroo from going out (in Narita City). Hazama Kagemitsu says, "Speaking of Narita City, agricultural areas spread out in these suburbs." Hazama Kagemitsu says, "The Narita City is home to the Kabuki actor Ichikawa Ebizō XI. Ichikawa Ebizō XI was also a Kabuki actor named Matsumoto Kōshirō X. Matsumoto Kōshirō X is a Kabuki actor. He is the current head of the famous Kabuki actor name 'Matsumoto Kōshirō X'." Hazama Kagemitsu says, "Yagō is Kōraiya. Jōmon is Yotsuhanabishi. Kaemon is Fusenchō." Pinoko asks (in Narita City) Hazama Kuroo (for an errand). <Omitted>]

Fig. 6. Example of generated story consisting of *unchikus* (Matsumoto Kōshirō X)

4 Conclusion

In this study, the proposed *unchiku* generation mechanism for an integrated narrative generation system was implemented. The *unchiku* generation of was initiated only by a direct stimulation; however, it was more efficient to use the associative method. Furthermore, the amount of information on Kabuki in the Japanese version of Wikipedia was not substantial. In the future, we will study and solve these problems and incorporate them into the integrated story generation system.

In the present study, the words that appeared in the story were used as stimuli to generate the conversation. However, in the future, the noun concept and attribute frame from direct relationships will not be referred to. The aim will be to generate an explanation that is not directly related to the story by using more indirect relationships (associations). Therefore, the articles collected at this time, the created attribute frames, and the Kabuki information that will be collected in the future will be stored in the concept dictionary of the integrated story generation system. Additionally, the co-occurrence relationships among the concepts and the relationships in the systematic structure of the dictionary are stored.

The Japanese version of Wikipedia was employed for the generation mechanism; however, specialized information in terms of the number of articles and content regarding Kabuki is limited. Furthermore, because of copyright issues, only the Japanese Wikipedia was used as reference material; solutions to problems with available reference materials will be required in the future.

Acknowledgements. The research for this chapter was supported by the Japan Society for the Promotion of Science (JSPS KAKENHI), Grant No. 18K18509.

References

1. Ono, J., Ito, T., Ogata, T.: Toward explanation generation in a narrative generation system. In: Proceedings of the 37th Annual Meeting of the Japanese Cognitive Society, pp. 746–754. Japanese Cognitive Society, Kanagawa (2020)
2. Ono, J., Kawai, M., Ogata, T.: Implementation of an explanation generation mechanism using attribute frames and a noun conceptual dictionary. In: 3rd International Conference on Computational Intelligence and Intelligent Systems (2020). (Abstract only)
3. Gogol, N.: The Overcoat (Trans.: Hirai, H.). Iwanami Shoten, Tokyo (1965)
4. Hugo. V.: Les misérables (Trans.: Toyoshima, Y.). Iwanami Shoten, Tokyo (1987)
5. Shiba, R.: Shiba Ryōtarō zenshū. Bungeishunjū, Tokyo (1984)
6. Genette, G.: Monogatari no discours (Trans.: Hanawa, H., Izumi, R.). Suiseisya, Tokyo (1985)
7. Ogata, T.: *Kabuki* as multiple narrative structures and narrative generation. In: Ogata, T., Akimoto, T. (eds.) Post-narratology Through Computational and Cognitive Approaches, pp. 192–275. Information Science Reference (IGI Global), Hershey (2019)
8. Fukuda, K., Ono, J., Ogata, T.: Introducing an extensive knowledge generation mechanism into a narrative generation system. In: Proceedings of the 34th Annual Conference of the Japanese Society for Artificial Intelligence, 3D1-OS-22a-03. Japanese Society of Artificial Intelligence, Tokyo (2020)
9. Tezuka, O.: Black Jack, vol. 1. Akita Shoten, Tokyo (1974)

10. Ogata, T.: Building conceptual dictionaries for an integrated narrative generation system. J. Robot. Network. Artif. Life **1**(4), 270–284 (2015)
11. Ogata, T.: A method of *naimaze* of narratives based on *kabuki* analyses and Propp's move techniques for an automated narrative generation system. J. Robot. Network. Artif. Life **6**(2), 71–78 (2019)
12. Ogata, T.: *Kabuki* as a synthetic narrative: synthesis and expansion. In: Ogata, T. (ed.) Internal and external narrative generation based on post-narratology: Emerging research and opportunities, pp. 109–254. Information Science Reference (IGI Global), Hershey (2020)
13. Kawai, M., Ono, J., Ogata, T.: Analyzing the stage performance structure of *kabuki*-dance "*Kyoganoko Musume Dojoji.*" In: Proceedings of the 34th Annual Conference of the Japanese Society of Artificial Intelligence, 3D1-OS-22a-04. Japanese Society of Artificial Intelligence, Tokyo (2020)
14. Maynard, S.K.: Kaiwa bunseki. Kuroshio Shuppan, Tokyo (1992)

Analyzing the Stage Performance Structure of a Kabuki-Dance, *Kyoganoko Musume Dojoji*, Using an Animation System

Miku Kawai[1], Jumpei Ono[2], and Takashi Ogata[1(✉)]

[1] Faculty of Software and Information Science, Iwate Prefectural University, Takizawa, Japan
g031p035@s.iwate-pu.ac.jp, t-ogata@iwate-pu.ac.jp
[2] Faculty of Software and Information Technology, Aomori University, Tokyo, Japan
j.ono@aomori-u.ac.jp

Abstract. Although Kabuki-dance *Kyōganoko Musume Dōjōji* is a type of sequel to the original Dōjōji legend, it has been performed by several excellent onnagata actors since the Edo era as a masterpiece that has original content beyond the original legends. Referring to the analysis of *Kyōganoko Musume Dōjōji* by Tamotsu Watanabe, this study aims to analyze in detail its "stage performance structures" that include characters, background (stage setting), music (instruments, musicians, and genres), poetry, prose, speech, and core conceptual themes of scenes as the main elements. Furthermore, using a system called KOSERUBE, that the authors have developed, as an animation tool for a narrative generation system, this study builds its stage performance structures as an easy visual image. The future goal of the application of the system as a representation method for narrative generation systems, computer games, and automatic generation content, among others.

Keywords: Kabuki · *Kyōganoko musume dōjōji* · Narrative generation · Stage performance structure

1 Introduction

Kabuki is a Japanese cultural heritage. We chose Kabuki because we thought it would lead to the maintenance and inheritance of cultural heritage.

Kabuki is a genre of performing arts that originated in Shijō-gawara, Kyōto, by a female entertainer called Izumo no Okuni around 1600 (the beginning of the Edo period). Although initially performed by all-female troupes (On'na Kabuki or women's Kabuki), because of the Edo shogunate's oppression it transformed to an all-male art or drama (Yarō Kabuki), and the tradition has continued to the present day. The vital characteristics of Kabuki are its synthesis and comprehensiveness. In other words, Kabuki is a kind of comprehensive art form that combines performing arts, drama, dance, and music (performance, song, and narration), and the stories performed in Kabuki are based on and incorporate several traditional Japanese stories, literature, history, and characters (this paragraph is a summary of Sect. 3 in [1]).

© Springer Nature Switzerland AG 2020
E. Ishita et al. (Eds.): ICADL 2020, LNCS 12504, pp. 248–254, 2020.
https://doi.org/10.1007/978-3-030-64452-9_22

In recent years, in Kabuki, there have been several stages using "Hatsune Miku" and computer graphics. "Hatsune Miku" is a vocal sound source compatible with the voice synthesis system, "Vocaloid." One can sing by entering the melody and lyrics. Therefore, there are several studies that introduced computer graphics in Kabuki. For example, Oda and Genda research characteristics motion in Kabuki using motion chaputer system [2]. Omoto et al. create a model of Minamiza in Kyōto (Minamiza is a traditional Kabuki theatre) [3].

In addition, there is a study comparing Western dance, the ballet *La sylphide*, and the Japanese dance of *Kyōganoko Musume Dōjōji* to approach creative dance [4]. That research focused below. This research focuses on "Furi" (swing), mainly analyzing small movements such as walking and hand expressions. However, our research is different. The purpose of this research is to understand the stage structure in detail and reproduce the entire stage. Further, we aim to incorporate Kabuki in automatic story generation. The purpose is to visualize the entire stage. Therefore, only the dance of *Kyōganoko Musume Dōjōji* was analyzed. Moreover, the dance part is simple. This system does not require the precise movements of the dance to be reproduced.

The authors of this paper have conducted a series of studies on Kabuki as a story generation system. Ogata [5, 6] investigated and analyzed several of the elements that comprise Kabuki and developed a system that simulates the interplay of stories. Initially, the authors proposed an approach to configure the stage performance structure of *Kyōganoko Musume Dōjōji* by adding elements to the analysis table presented by Watanabe [7]. This table focused on the performance aspects of the Kabuki-dance with the subject of *Kyōganoko Musume Dōjōji* as one key person. Hence, Kawai and Ogata [8] made certain corrections and additions. Specifically, in his table, Watanabe [7] presented "Kokoro" (core conceptual theme), "Furi" (performance), "Kashi" (music genre), "Ishō" (costumes), "Kodougu" (props), and "Nikutai no point" (focal point in the dance). Kawai added "Hito" (character), "Gakki" (musical instrument), and "Bamen" (scene) to Watanabe's table, and described the lyrics in "Kashi." This analysis was performed by observing the video material of *Kyōganoko Musume Dōjōji* by Tamasaburō Bandō [9]. Additionally, each part was subdivided to correspond with the change from one scene to the next. Furthermore, Kawai and Ogata [10] used a system called KOSERUBE [11] partially reproduced the visual image of the stage performance structure of *Kyōganoko Musume Dōjōji*.

In this study, based on the results by Kawai and Ogata [10], we attempted to visually reproduce the stage performance structure of *Kyōganoko Musume Dōjōji* using the KOSERUBE and added auditory elements.

2 Visualization of Stage Performance Structure of *Kyōganoko Musume Dōjōji*

2.1 Overview of the KOSERUBE

Figure 1 presents an overview of the KOSERUBE architecture. The system comprises two parts: a narrative generation module and a user interface. Each part is implemented using Common Lisp and HSP, respectively, and connected via input and output files.

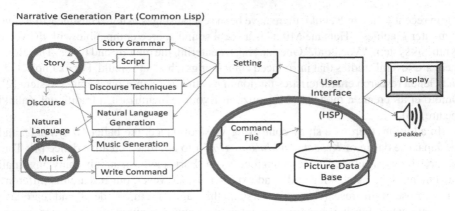

Fig. 1. The configuration of KOSERUBE

The narrative generation is executed as the structural operation in the story, discourse, and expression. Each process is performed by the three main functional components: conceptual dictionaries, story techniques, discourse techniques and control modules. The conceptual dictionaries provide semantic definitions for the components of an event, which is a fundamental element in narrative. The story techniques operate to build a story structure. The discourse techniques are generative rules to transform parts of a story structure. The control modules manage the entire generation process. Above conceptual dictionaries and above mechanisms are an integrated narrative generation [12–14]. The detailed description is illustrated by Ogata [12–14].

The KOSERUBE mainly uses above dictionaries and mechanisms. The difference is story techniques and a music mechanism. The central technique for the story generation phase is the Propp-based story grammar [15]. The music mechanism—although it adopts an original method—is fundamentally based on the music mechanism in the integrated narrative generation system [12–14].

The marked part (Fig. 1) is modified to reproduce the stage performance structure with people, background (stage equipment), music (instrument and performer), verse, and dance. In the command file, the chapters on the dance to be displayed, the reproduction timing of music, the switching of the background image enclosed with the picture database, and so on are described; animation control is described later.

2.2 Making a Stage Performance Structure

This study is based on a detailed analysis table of "stage performance structure," which is based on the analysis by Watanabe [7], a researcher and critic of modern Kabuki. Table 1 is part of the analysis table. This table has, as its main components, the characters, backgrounds (stage devices), music (instruments, performers, and genres), verses and lines, and the principal conceptual theme of each scene.

In the KOSERUBE, the words of the dance were entered in the text data and were displayed; the background and the person were displayed as images. At the back, Nagauta singers and instrumentalists lined up in the same manner as they would on the actual stage. The person singing and performing in each scene was indicated by an arrow, and

Table 1. An example of stage performance structure ("Dance of Chūkei" part)

Hito	白拍子花子 [Shirabyōshi Hanako]									
Kokoro (Core mental theme)	娘 [Musume (Young girl)]									
Furi (Performance)	白拍子 [Shirabyōshi]									
Kashi (Music genre)	能(鐘づくし) [Noh (Kane-zukushi)]									
(Lyrics)	鐘に恨みは数々ござる [Kane ni urami ha kazukazu gozaru]	初夜の鐘を撞く時は [Syoya no kane wo tsuku toki ha]	諸行無常と響くなり [Syogyō mujō to hibiku nari]	後夜の鐘を撞く時は [Goya no kane wo tsuku toki ha]	是生滅法と響くなり [Zeshoō meppō to hibiku nari]	晨朝の響き は 滅々 [Jinjō no hibiki ha shōmetsu metsui]	入相は寂滅為楽と響くなり [Iriai ha jakumetsu iraku to hibiku nari]	聞いて驚く人もなし [Kiite odoroku hito mo nashi]	われも五障の雲晴れて [Ware mo goshō no kumo harete]	真如の月を眺め明かさん [Shinnyo no tuki wo nagame akasan]
Gakki (Musical instrument)	三味線 [Shamisen (Japanese guitar)], 太鼓[Drum]	三味線 [Shamisen (Japanese guitar)]			三味線 [Shamisen (Japanese guitar)], 太鼓[Drum]	三味線 [Shamisen (Japanese guitar)]	三味線[Shamisen (Japanese guitar)], 太鼓 [Drum]		三味線 [Shamisen (Japanese guitar)]	三味線 [Shamisen (Japanese guitar)], 太鼓[Drum]
Bamen (Scene)	桜の木 (道成寺) [Sakura no ki (Cherry blossoms) (Dōjōji)]									
Ishō (Costumes)	赤 [Aka (Red)]									
Kodougu (Props)	中啓 [Chūkei]									
Nikutai no point (Focus point in the dance)	足 [Ashi (Foot)]									

a spotlight was applied to yield a visually recognizable expression. Additionally, the movement of the dance of Shirabyōshi Hanako was simply expressed.

Figure 2 depicts a screenshot of the dance of Chūkei (corresponding to Table 1). This illustrates the actual movement on the stage. In the actual stage, the actor moves his hand up and down on the spot. The objective of this research is not to pursue realistic human movements and to express them, but to visually reproduce the stage performance structure. Therefore, the dance is simplified in the KOSERBE.

In the KOSERUBE, the actual movement was simply expressed according to the code. In Fig. 2, the command "mov" is used. "mov, 11, v, -50, -25" represents move, character ID, vertical, movement distance, and speed, respectively from the left. In the first line of Fig. 2, the Shirabyōshi Hanako is moved vertically at a distance of 50 and a speed of 25 (The Shirabyōshi Hanako moves up from the current coordinates. Positive values move the Shirabyōshi Hanako downwards.). Overall, it implies bouncing Shirabyōshi Hanako three times.

Code	Animation
mov,11,v,-50,-25 mov,11,v,50,25 mov,11,v,-50,-25 mov,11,v,50,25 mov,11,v,-50,-25 mov,11,v,50,25	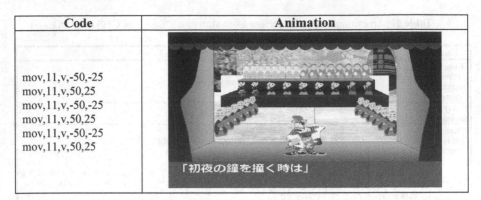

Fig. 2. An example of visualized stage performance structure

3 Expansion of Auditory Elements Introduction

In this paper, the KOSERUBE was expanded to include auditory elements, which were added from a music score titled *Music and Sound in Kabuki*. Haikawa [16] explains from debayashi (Nagauta) to sound effects in Kabuki.

This system used a music sequencer called "text music Sakura" (https://sakuramml.com/, last accessed on July 9, 2020). This tool can be used to compose and edit music by simply typing the notes (C, D, E, etc.) in text form. In the KOSERUBE, the auditory element is played along with an animation.

In addition, we created music using a free composer called "Wagakuhitosuji" by referring to the score in *Shamisen Bunkahu Nagauta Kyōganoko Musume Dōjōji* by Kineie [17]. Unlike several composer tools, "Wagakuhitosuji" corresponds to the scale of Japanese music, rather than Western music, and allows composition on shamisen notation.

4 Conclusion

On KOSERUBE, the stage, dancers, and performers of the actual *Kyōganoko Musume Dōjōji* were reproduced. In addition, a part of the scene was excerpted, and a simple dance was reproduced. Although we anticipate that this system could be applied to the automatic generation of content, the main goal is to generate the standard story of Chapter 1 in the integrated narrative generation system [12–14], under development.

The authors' study of Kabuki story generation is a concept that comprehensively examines the structure, methods, and techniques of the story in Kabuki. Chapter 2 in [13, 14] presents a comprehensive summary of the latest results. The "integrated approach to story generation" [13, 14] includes an integrated narrative generation system, an entertainment information system, post narratology as a theory, and a multiple story structure model, Kabuki. Its comprehensiveness (breadth) and thoroughness (depth) makes it the center of the story generation method, not simply one of several story genres [13].

Moreover, because this study is targeted at one genre of Kabuki called Kabuki-dance, multiple lines are not involved; it is stylistic, not realistic. Therefore, the analysis of the stage performance structure evaluated here is limited to the stage performance structure of the genre of Kabuki-dance. However, the structure is fundamentally the same as that of other genres in Kabuki, especially Kabuki Kyōgen plays that mainly use dialogue. Future work will focus on extending and developing this solution into a more comprehensive description format of the Kabuki stage performance structure, whilst retaining Watanabe's aim and intention to express the complex and multiple personality of the principal person. In addition, we anticipate that the proposed system will be used as the basis for the stage performance structure of Kabuki, and has the potential be adopted in other genres such as commercials and computer games.

Acknowledgment. The research for this chapter was supported by the Japan Society for the Promotion of Science (JSPS KAKENHI), Grant No. 18K18509.

References

1. Ogata, T.: Kabuki as multiple narrative structures. In: Ogata, T., Akimoto, T. (eds.) Computational and cognitive approaches to Narratology. pp. 391–422. Information Science Reference (IGI Global), Hershey (2016)
2. Oda, I., Genda, E.: Record of characteristic motion of the Kabuki using the motion capture system. JSSD **51**, 142–143 (2004)
3. Omoto, N., Hasegawa, K., Motojima, H., Nagata, S., Tanaka, S.: 3D model of Kyoto Minamiza theater and its application. In: IPSJ SIG-CH, pp. 109–112 (2005)
4. Kobayashi, S.: Approach to choreography "Kiyohime": a comparative study of Japanese traditional dance and western ballet for female. Doctoral dissertation. Osaka University of Arts (2018)
5. Ogata, T.: Kabuki as a synthetic narrative: synthesis and expansion. In: Ogata, T. (ed.) Internal and External Narrative Generation Based on Post-narratology: Emerging Research and Opportunities, pp. 109–254. Information Science Reference (IGI Global), Hershey (2020)
6. Ogata, T.: Kabuki as multiple narrative structures and narrative generation. In: Ogata, T., Akimoto, T. (eds.) Post-Narratology Through Computational and Cognitive Approaches, pp. 192–275. Information Science Reference (IGI Global), Hershey (2019)
7. Watanabe, T.: Musume Dōjōji. Shinshindo, Tokyo (1986)
8. Kawai, M., Ogata, T.: An analysis of Kyōganoko Musume Dōjōji for the generation of the staging structures of Kabuki from narrative plots. In: SIG-LSE Proceedings, vol. 63, pp. 25–61 (2019)
9. Kyōganoko Musume Dōjōji: Bandō Tamasaburō butō shū Vol.1 [DVD]. Shochiku home video, Japan, Tokyo (2003)
10. Kawai, M., Ogata, T.: Analyzing the stage performance structure of Kabuki-dance "Kyōganoko Musume Dōjōji". In: Proceedings of the 34th Annual Conference of the Japanese Society for Artificial Intelligence, 3D1-OS-22a-04. Japanese Society of Artificial Intelligence, Tokyo (2020)
11. Akimoto, T., et al.: Development of a generation/expression system of narratives in the style of a folk tale, KOSERUBE version 1. Trans. Jpn. Soc. Artif. Intell. **28**(5), 442–456 (2013)
12. Ogata, T.: A computational, cognitive, and narratological approach to narrative generation. In: Ogata, T., Akimoto, T. (eds.) Post-narratology Through Computational and Cognitive Approaches, pp. 1–84. Information Science Reference (IGI Global), Hershey (2019)

13. Ogata, T.: Toward an Integrated Approach to Narrative Generation: Emerging Research and Opportunities. Information Science Reference (IGI Global), Hershey (2020)
14. Ogata, T.: Internal and External Narrative Generation Based on Post-Narratology: Emerging Research and Opportunities. Information Science Reference (IGI Global), Hershey (2020)
15. Imabuchi, S., Ogata, T.: A story generation system based on Propp theory: as a mechanism in an integrated narrative generation system. In: Isahara, H., Kanzaki, K. (eds.) JapTAL 2012. LNCS (LNAI), vol. 7614, pp. 312–321. Springer, Heidelberg (2012). https://doi.org/10.1007/978-3-642-33983-7_31
16. Haikawa, M.: Music and Sound in Kabuki. Ongakunotomosha, Tokyo (2016)
17. Kineie, Y.: Syamisenbunkahu nagauta Kyōganoko Musume Dōjōji. Hogakusha, Tokyo (1952)

Artwork Information Embedding Framework for Multi-source Ukiyo-e Record Retrieval

Kangying Li[1]([✉]) [iD], Biligsaikhan Batjargal[2] [iD], Akira Maeda[3] [iD], and Ryo Akama[4]

[1] Graduate School of Information Science and Engineering, Ritsumeikan University,
Kusatsu, Japan
gr0319ss@ed.ritsumei.ac.jp
[2] Kinugasa Research Organization, Ritsumeikan University, Kyoto, Japan
[3] College of Information Science and Engineering, Ritsumeikan University, Kusatsu, Japan
[4] College of Letters, Ritsumeikan University, Kyoto, Japan

Abstract. Ukiyo-e culture has endured throughout Japanese art history to this day. With its high artistic value, ukiyo-e remains an important part of art history. Possibly more than one million ukiyo-e prints have been collected by institutions and individuals worldwide. Many public ukiyo-e databases of various scales have been created in different languages. The sharing of ukiyo-e culture could advance to a new stage if the information from all the databases could be shared without differences in information. However, understanding different languages in different databases, redundant data, missing data, uncertain data, and inconsistent data are all barriers to knowledge discovery in each database. Therefore, this paper uses Ukiyo-e Portal Database [1] prints that were released from the Art Research Center (ARC) of Ritsumeikan University as examples, explains the challenges that are currently solvable, and proposes a multi-source artwork information embedding framework for multimodal and multilingual retrieval.

Keywords: Cross-modal embedding · Multi-source data processing · Cross-lingual keyword retrieval

1 Introduction

The Ukiyo-e Portal Database includes information on ukiyo-e prints owned by Ritsumeikan University and provides portal services to retrieve ukiyo-e prints from other institutions or holders collaborating with the ARC. There are more than 177,113 ukiyo-e prints retrievable from the ARC Ukiyo-e Portal Database and 19,858 Ritsumeikan University ukiyo-e prints retrievable from ARC Japanese Woodblocks Prints [2]. Figure 1 shows the top five institutional databases in the ARC Ukiyo-e Portal Database with the highest number of records. Many of the records are from the databases of the Museum of Fine Arts, Boston and the Trustees of the British Museum. Many records do not have multilingual information; therefore, it is difficult to retrieve these records in multiple languages. Moreover, the Japanese titles of many records are represented by early modern Japanese that is difficult to split into words for semantic analysis.

© Springer Nature Switzerland AG 2020
E. Ishita et al. (Eds.): ICADL 2020, LNCS 12504, pp. 255–261, 2020.
https://doi.org/10.1007/978-3-030-64452-9_23

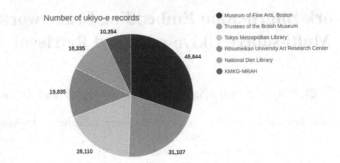

Fig. 1. Institutional databases with highest number of records.

Moreover, some records in the same database might have missing textual metadata or images, hindering information sharing and connection to the international community. In our previous research [3], we utilized a character segmentation method of extracting single characters from seals, and we proposed a method of retrieving ancient characters from seals extracted from ukiyo-e prints. If more information can be captured from an image, it will greatly improve retrieval results. Therefore, we propose an embedding framework that uses a combination of new technologies to implement cross-lingual, cross-modal retrieval in multi-source ukiyo-e records. This paper is organized as follows: 1) introducing the embedding framework of our cross-lingual and cross-modal ukiyo-e retrieval system, 2) introducing preliminary experimental results and demonstration at the present stage, 3) introducing a word2vec model for Japanese ukiyo-e retrieval, and 4) introducing our future plans.

2   Related Work

In the last few decades, there has been a growing interest in utilizing information technology to represent and preserve cultural heritage digitally [4–6]. Given the regional characteristics and historical backgrounds of art, digital resources need to be properly "linked" to bridge the gap between different languages. Nowadays, images are often embedded with additional features used for many different recommendation and retrieval tasks (e.g., embedding items in a low-dimensional space to calculate item similarities) [7]. Unlike movies or products, digital recommendations and retrievals for artwork is rare. A relative representation of a piece of art's record can provide a good base for identifying records, aligning records, giving recommendations, retrieving information and artwork, and so on.

3   Methodology

Figure 2 shows the structure of our framework.

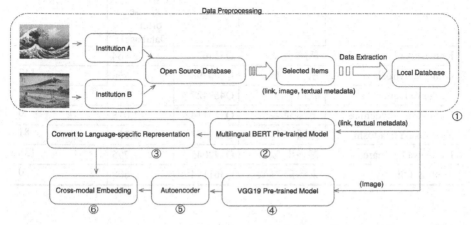

Fig. 2. Our proposed framework.

We describe our approach ①–⑥ in the following sections. In Sect. 3.1, we discuss data collection and processing ①. In Sect. 3.2, we discuss textual metadata processing ②③. In Sect. 3.3, we discuss image processing ④⑤ (see Fig. 2). In Sect. 3.4, we discuss cross-modal embedding ⑥ and methods of optimizing retrieval results.

3.1   Data Preprocessing

We used the works of five famous ukiyo-e artists who were introduced in a Google article[1] to demonstrate our framework. The data we collected was from the ARC Ukiyo-e Portal Database and WikiArt. Table 1 shows the English representation of the seven artists' names in the article and the common Japanese representations. Since the ukiyo-e artists' names can be expressed multiple ways, we also show the entity id of Wikidata (see "also known as") to check for other representations of their names. The table also shows the number of records that can be retrieved from both databases. From the ARC Ukiyo-e Portal Database, we extracted 1,375 public records cited by a famous ukiyo-e retrieval website, ukiyo-e.org. We also extracted all 1,998 related records (623 items from Wikidata in Table 1) as examples in this paper. To provide more complete information on both databases, the collected items include the work's title, the artist's name(s), the image, links, etc. The embedded textual metadata includes the artist's name(s) and the work's title.

---

[1] Google, The Ukiyo-e Artists You Need To Know, https://artsandculture.google.com/story/the-ukiyo-e-artists-you-need-to-know/BQKC6o0k2oBRLA.

Table 1. Artists and their work used in demonstrations.

Name (EN)	Name (JP)	Wikidata entity ID	Number of records (ARC Ukiyo-e Portal Database)	Number of records (WikiArt)
Katsushika Hokusai	葛飾 北斎	Q5586	2,864	293
Utagawa Hiroshige	歌川 広重	Q200798	2,566	112
Utagawa Kunisada	歌川 国貞	Q467427	761	97
Kobayashi Kiyochika	小林 清親	Q3121142	1,018	0
Tsukioka Yoshitoshi	月岡 芳年	Q467337	5,238	81
Kitagawa Utamaro	喜多川 歌麿	Q272045	1,795	138
Toshusai Sharaku	東洲斎 写楽	Q361174	608	0

3.2 Textual Metadata Embedding

Both the names of the artists and the titles of the ukiyo-e prints are very uniform in different databases. This also greatly affects retrieval results.

Figure 3 shows the representation of the artists' names in different languages. To project different representations into appropriate spaces, we extracted the features of the textual data using a multilingual Bidirectional Encoder Representations from Transformers (BERT) [8] pre-trained model and projected the English vectors into representations close to the Japanese representation space.

Fig. 3. Representation of names in different linguistic spaces.

The multilingual BERT pre-trained model released by Devlin et al. (2018) [9] uses a pre-trained single-language model of 104 languages and effectively performs a zero-shot cross-lingual model transfer. Figure 4 is a visualization of the vector representation of artists' names and ukiyo-e print titles in each language extracted by multilingual BERT in a Uniform Manifold Approximation and Projection space. Titles with the same semantic meaning exhibit a correspondence distribution in the space.

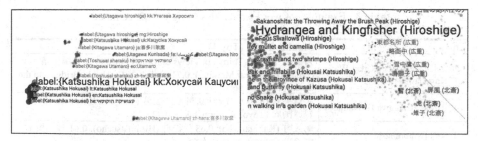

Fig. 4. Representation of textual metadata extracted using multilingual BERT.

However, we know that the vector distance between words in the same language is very close. To project words with similar semantics in different languages to the closest position, we used the method [10] by Liu et al. to find language-specific representations and shift the representation from English to Japanese.

3.3 Image Embedding

We utilized the VGG19 pre-trained model trained by ImageNet as an image feature extractor, and we resized all the images with RGB channels to 224×224. We used the autoencoder to compress the features to a size equal in length to the text vector. In future work, we will train an end-to-end embedding model with a new structure.

3.4 Improving Retrieval Performance

At this stage, we analyzed our collected data and connected the text vectors to image vectors. We used the PySparNN [11] by Facebook to retrieve the vectors. To expand textual queries, if they contained Japanese words, we used them for semantic expansion to recommend more extended results to users. Here, we used the word2vec model trained by all the Japanese Wikipedia articles. We used the Ukiyo-e Terminology Dictionary, the Dictionary of Japanese Personal Names, and the Dictionary of Ancient Japanese Geographical Names to create a user dictionary and optimize the tokenization of training data. Table 2 shows Japanese word similarities found when using our retrained word2vec model[2].

4 Evaluation

We developed a simple demonstration system for our method. The algorithm implementation is available on GitHub[3] as a reference. Table 3 shows some of the retrieval results. Since we included Chinese in our dataset, the results also show possible cross-language retrieval of Chinese using multilingual BERT. These few examples show that the extracted features performed well in multilingual and multimodal information matching, thereby achieving our aims and setting the foundations for future work.

---

[2] Github: https://github.com/timcanby/Japanese_word2vec_pretrain_model.

[3] Github: https://github.com/timcanby/simple_demoForMAWukiyoeSys.

Table 2. Examples of word similarities using word2vec model.

Input	Similar words (Top 3)
神奈川沖浪裏 (The Great Wave off Kanagawa)	富嶽三十六景 (Thirty-six Views of Mount Fuji): 0.72 凱風快晴 (Fine Wind, Clear Morning): 0.71 浪花百景 (Imabashi Bridge and the Tsukiji Area): 0.66
歌川広重 (Utagawa Hiroshige)	渓斎英泉 (Keisai Eisen): 0.74 歌川国芳 (Utagawa Kuniyoshi): 0.73 豊原国周 (Toyohara Kunichika): 0.72
日本橋 (Nihombashi)	蛎殻町 (Kakigaracho): 0.63 久松町 (Hisamatsucho): 0.61 日本橋本町 (Nihombashihoncho): 0.61

Table 3. Examples of retrieval results.

Input	Results
広重 (Utagawa Hiroshige) (Japanese)	[ARC Database] 井の頭の池弁財天天の社雪の景 by:広重——info.https://ukiyo-e.org/image/ritsumei/Z0173-081/n [ARC Database] 波上日の出に千羽鶴 by:広重——info.https://ukiyo-e.org/image/ritsumei/Z0173-116/n [ARC Database] 五月十七日水土性の人請ニ入 by:広重——info.https://ukiyo-e.org/image/ritsumei/arcUP6062/n
歌川廣重 (Utagawa Hiroshige) (Chinese)	[ARC Database] 井の頭の池弁財天天の社雪の景 by:広重———info.https://ukiyo-e.org/image/ritsumei/Z0173-081/n [ARC Database] 波上日の出に千羽鶴 by:広重———info.https://ukiyo-e.org/image/ritsumei/Z0173-116/n [ARC Database] 仮名手本忠臣蔵六段目 by:北斎———info.https://ukiyo-e.org/image/ritsumei/arcUP1720/n
Kitagawa (Utamaro Kitagawa) (English)	[WikiArt] you can check ID:233107:Kisegawa of Matsubaya, from the series 'Seven Komachis of Yoshiwara', c.1795 (woodblock print) by:Utamaro Kitagawain Wikiart, or search by using image from Wikiart or by using keywords:female-portraits, Forehead, Hairstyle, Geisha, Cheek, Black hair/n [ARC Database] 高名美人見立忠臣蔵三段目 by:歌麿———info.https://ukiyo-e.org/image/ritsumei/Z0168-118/n [ARC Database] 高名美人見立忠臣蔵二段目 by:歌麿———info.https://ukiyo-e.org/image/ritsumei/Z0168-117/n
	[WikiArt] ID:223618:The Great Wave off Kanagawa [WikiArt] ID:222207:Homoku view [WikiArt] ID:223604:The Big wave

5　Conclusion and Future Work

In this work, we analyzed ukiyo-e records from two different language databases and their multimodal representations using different embedding approaches. In future work, we will investigate how to map multilingual and multimodal information in a suitable space. We will also develop an end-to-end embedding model and consider using a knowledge graph to represent metadata.

References

1. ARC Ukiyo-e Portal Database. https://www.dh-jac.net/db/nishikie/search_portal.php?&lang=en. Accessed 25 June 2020
2. ARC Japanese Woodblocks Prints. https://www.dh-jac.net/db/nishikie/search.php?enter=default&lang=en. Accessed 25 June 2020
3. Li, K.Y., Batjargal, B., Maeda, A.: Character segmentation in collector's seal images: an attempt on retrieval based on ancient character typeface. In: Proceedings of the 5th International Workshop on Computational History (HistoInformatics 2019), pp. 40–49 (2019)
4. Messina, P., Dominguez, V., Parra, D., Trattner, C., Soto, A.: Content-based artwork recommendation: integrating painting metadata with neural and manually-engineered visual features. User Model. User-Adapt. Interact. **29**, 251–290 (2019)
5. Benouaret, I., Lenne, D.: Personalizing the museum experience through context-aware recommendations. In: Proceedings of the IEEE International Conference on Systems, Man, and Cybernetics (SMC), pp. 743–748 (2015)
6. He, R., Fang, C., Wang, Z., McAuley, J.: Vista: a visually, socially, and temporally-aware model for artistic recommendation. In: Proceedings of the 10th ACM Conference on Recommender Systems, RecSys 2016, pp. 309–316 (2016)
7. Barkan, O., Koenigstein, N.: Item2Vec: neural item embedding for collaborative filtering. In: IEEE 26th International Workshop on Machine Learning for Signal Processing (MLSP). IEEE (2016)
8. Pires, T., Schlinger, E., Garrette, D.: How multilingual is Multilingual BERT? arXiv preprint arXiv:1906.01502 (2019)
9. Devlin, J., Chang, M., Lee, M., Toutanova, K.: BERT: pre-training of deep bidirectional transformers for language understanding. In: Proceedings of NAACL (2019)
10. Liu, C.L., Hsu, T.Y., Chuang, Y.S., Lee, H.Y.: A study of cross-lingual ability and language-specific information in multilingual BERT. arXiv Preprint arXiv:2004.09205 (2020)
11. PySparNN. https://github.com/facebookresearch/pysparnn. Accessed 25 June 2020

A Preliminary Attempt to Evaluate Machine Translations of Ukiyo-e Metadata Records

Yuting Song[1]([✉]) [ID], Biligsaikhan Batjargal[2] [ID], and Akira Maeda[1] [ID]

[1] College of Information Science and Engineering, Ritsumeikan University, Kusatsu, Japan
songyt@fc.ritsumei.ac.jp, amaeda@is.ritsumei.ac.jp
[2] Kinugasa Research Organization, Ritsumeikan University, Kyoto, Japan
biligee@fc.ritsumei.ac.jp

Abstract. Providing multilingual metadata records for digital objects is a way expanding access to digital cultural collections. Recent advancements in deep learning techniques have made machine translation (MT) more accurate. Therefore, we evaluate the performance of three well-known MT systems (i.e., Google Translate, Microsoft Translator, and DeepL Translator) in translating metadata records of ukiyo-e images from Japanese to English. We evaluate the quality of their translations with an automatic evaluation metric BLEU. The evaluation results show that DeepL Translator is better at translating ukiyo-e metadata records than Google Translate or Microsoft Translator, with Microsoft Translator performing the worst.

Keywords: Machine translation evaluation · Metadata translation · Ukiyo-e · Japanese-English

1 Introduction

Metadata records are used to describe digital objects in museums, libraries, and archives; they consist of several descriptive metadata elements (e.g., title, artist, etc.). These metadata records provide information on digital objects and assist people in searching for and locating them. Most objects in digital cultural collections in particular are images or videos (e.g., images of paintings and old books) instead of textual materials, so they cannot be searched for through the content of digital objects.

One way of expanding access to digital cultural collections is to translate descriptions in metadata records into different languages. Bilingual or multilingual metadata records can help reduce the language barriers between digital objects and people who do not understand the objects' original languages.

Most translations of metadata records in digital libraries or museums are done by professional translators. However, manually translating metadata records is costly and time-consuming. As machine translation (MT) technologies have

© Springer Nature Switzerland AG 2020
E. Ishita et al. (Eds.): ICADL 2020, LNCS 12504, pp. 262–268, 2020.
https://doi.org/10.1007/978-3-030-64452-9_24

advanced, some research [1,13] has translated metadata records by combining translation outputs from multiple MT systems. However, MT-generated translations of metadata records should be used very carefully since the translation quality is critical. Thus, it is necessary to evaluate how MT performs with metadata records.

Ukiyo-e is known worldwide as a traditional Japanese art that flourished in the Edo period (1603–1868). Nowadays, many ukiyo-e prints have been digitized and exhibited on the internet with metadata descriptions (e.g., title, artist, production date, etc.). Thus, in this paper, we translated ukiyo-e metadata records from Japanese to English with Google Translate [5], Microsoft Translator [11], and DeepL Translator [3] to evaluate how these three well-known MT systems perform when translating the metadata records of ukiyo-e images. We evaluated the quality of these translations with bilingual evaluation understudy (BLEU) [12], a widely used automatic MT evaluation metric.

2   Related Work

MT evaluation is an important task in the field of natural language processing that has been studied extensively [6–8,12]. There are also some MT evaluation campaigns, such as WMT, IWSLT, and WAT. In these MT evaluation campaigns, the most common method of comparison is to compare the translation results of MT systems with human reference translations, then, calculate quality scores with an automatic evaluation metric such as BLEU [12], METEOR [8], or TER [14]. However, these evaluation metrics are mainly employed to evaluate how MT systems translate news texts, biomedical documents, or scientific papers.

The studies in closest relation to our work are presented in [1,2]. They investigated how MT systems perform in translating metadata records from English to Chinese and Spanish. They also employed manual human evaluation measures such as fluency and adequacy [9] to evaluate the quality of translated metadata records. However, we examine how MT systems perform in translating metadata records from Japanese to English and evaluate the translation quality with an automatic evaluation metric.

3   Evaluation Workflow

This section introduces our evaluation process, which consists of three steps: 1) preparing metadata records, 2) translating metadata records using three online MT systems, and 3) automatically evaluating the quality of the translation results.

3.1   Preparing Metadata Records

Our evaluation dataset contains 133 Japanese ukiyo-e titles and their English translation references.

Ukiyo-e Metadata Records in Japanese. We collected the Japanese metadata records of ukiyo-e images from the Edo-Tokyo Museum [4]. Each metadata record consists of 5 metadata elements (i.e., title, artist, series name, production date, and dimensions). We only selected the titles to evaluate the MT systems because titles summarize the contents of ukiyo-e images, which can better help people understand ukiyo-e than other elements. Moreover, using MT for ukiyo-e titles is challenging because the titles usually contain named entities (e.g., places, people, etc.) and the titles are in old Japanese, which is more difficult to translate than modern Japanese (see Table 1).

Translation References. To automatically evaluate MT results, we collected human reference translations of ukiyo-e titles. Many museums in western countries have the copies that were printed from the same ukiyo-e woodblocks and digitized them with metadata in their native languages (e.g., English), so identical ukiyo-e objects exist in different digital collections with metadata in different languages. For the Japanese metadata records collected from the Edo-Tokyo Museum, we obtained their corresponding English titles from the Metropolitan Museum of Art [10] by using an ukiyo-e search system based on image similarities [15], which finds identical ukiyo-e images across different digital collections. The English titles we obtained were used as reference translations. To ensure the quality of reference translations, we manually examined the English titles and removed titles of poor quality (e.g., inadequate translations). In the end, we gathered 133 Japanese ukiyo-e titles and their English reference translations as our evaluation dataset. Table 1 shows some examples of ukiyo-e titles and their translation references.

Table 1. Examples of ukiyo-e titles and their translation references.

Japanese title	Translation reference
甲州犬目峠	The Inume Pass in Kai Province
品川 日之出	Daybreak at Shinagawa
四世松本幸四郎の肴屋五郎兵衛	Matsumoto Koshiro IV as the Fish Peddler Gorobei
大星由良之助良雄	Portrait of Oboshi Yuranosuke Yoshio
高貴納涼ノ図	Nobility in the Evening Cool
女官洋服裁縫之図	Court Ladies Sewing Western Clothing

3.2 MT of Metadata Records

We translated metadata records by utilizing three well-known online MT systems: 1) Google Translate, 2) Microsoft Translator, and 3) DeepL Translator. These systems use state-of-the-art neural machine translation, which generates more accurate translations and closer to natural language. In our evaluations, we translated Japanese ukiyo-e titles into English with these MT systems on July 30, 2020.

3.3 Automatic Evaluation of MT Results

We evaluated the quality of the MT results using BLEU. When given a translation result and its reference translation, the BLEU metric automatically calculates their similarity and outputs a similarity score ranging from 0 to 1. The higher the score, the better the quality of the translation and the closer to human reference translations.

4 Evaluation Results

In this section, we show the evaluation results of how the three MT systems performed in translating ukiyo-e titles.

4.1 Performances of MT Systems

The Overall Performance. Table 2 shows the average BLEU scores for the translation results of the 133 ukiyo-e titles mentioned in Sect. 3.1. The average BLEU score of the DeepL Translator is higher than Google Translate or Microsoft Translator, indicating its translations of ukiyo-e titles are much closer to the human translation references. Microsoft Translator obtained the lowest average score, indicating that Microsoft Translator is the worst at translating ukiyo-e titles.

Table 2. Average BLEU scores for translations of ukiyo-e titles.

	BLEU
Google Translate	0.1628
Microsoft Translator	0.1428
DeepL Translator	0.1800

Distributions of BLEU Score. Figure 1 presents the distribution of the BLEU scores of the three MT systems for ukiyo-e titles. 44% of the translations from the DeepL Translator had a BLEU score equal to or higher than 0.2 (see Fig. 1c). On the other hand, only 30% of Microsoft Translator's translations received a BLEU score equal to or higher than 0.2 (see Fig. 1b).

4.2 Discussion

The average BLEU scores and the distribution of BLEU scores show that the DeepL Translator performed better than Google Translate or Microsoft Translator, indicating it is the best at translating ukiyo-e titles from Japanese to English. Table 3 shows examples of the MT results in which the DeepL Translator's translations are the best and the closest to the translation references.

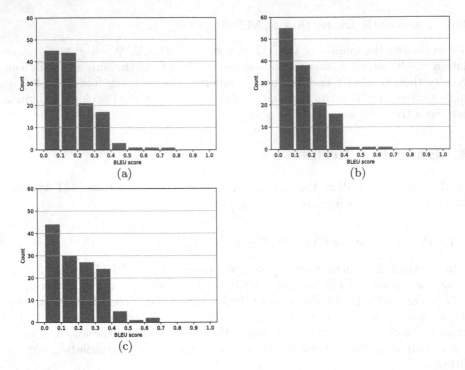

Fig. 1. Distribution of BLEU scores: (a) Google Translate, (b) Microsoft Translator, and (c) DeepL Translator.

Figure 1 shows that more than 50% of the translations have a BLEU score lower than 0.2 regardless of which MT system was used. This indicates that most of the translations from these three MT systems are dissimilar to the human translations.

4.3   Limitations of this Work

We used the BLEU evaluation metric to evaluate translation results. While this evaluation approach is faster, easier, and can reflect the degree of similarity between translation results and human translation references, it cannot recognize the specific errors such as inadequate or incorrect translations. Recognizing specific errors can help determine to what extent these MT systems can be applied to assist in translation of metadata records.

Table 3. Examples of MT translations of ukiyo-e titles.

Japanese title	大星由良之助良雄
Translation reference	Portrait of Oboshi Yuranosuke Yoshio
Google Translate	YOSHINOYOSHI Yoshio
Microsoft Translator	Yoshio Ōboshi
DeepL Translator	Yoshio Ohboshi-Yuranosuke Yoshio
Japanese title	亀戸龍眼寺の萩
Translation reference	Bush Clover at Ryuganji Temple, Kameido
Google Translate	Hagi of Kameido Ryugenji Temple
Microsoft Translator	Hagi at Kameido Ryuganji Temple
DeepL Translator	Hagiwara bush clover at Kameido Ryuganji Temple
Japanese title	世上各国写画帝王鏡
Translation reference	Mirror of Portraits of All Sovereigns in the World
Google Translate	Each country world picture royal mirror
Microsoft Translator	The Emperor's Mirror of the World's World
DeepL Translator	The mirror of the emperor's picture in every country in the world

5 Conclusion

We investigated the performance of three MT systems that translate ukiyo-e titles. We evaluated the translation results with the automatic evaluation metric BLEU. Our results showed that the DeepL Translator performed better than Google Translate or Microsoft Translator.

This work is our preliminary attempt to evaluate MT of ukiyo-e titles. In the future, we will evaluate a large dataset of metadata records for ukiyo-e and other digital collections. We will evaluate the performance of MT systems by utilizing other automatic evaluation metrics such as METEOR and TER. We will also employ manual human evaluation to examine the quality of MT regarding specific translation errors.

Acknowledgements. This work was supported in part by JSPS KAKENHI Grant Number 20K12567, 20K20135, and 19KK0256.

References

1. Chen, J., Azogu, O., Knudson, R.: Enabling multilingual information access to digital collections: an investigation of metadata records translation. In: Proceedings of the 2014 ACM/IEEE Joint Conference on Digital Libraries, pp. 467–468 (2014)
2. Chen, J., Ding, R., Jiang, S., Knudson, R.: A preliminary evaluation of metadata records machine translation. Electron. Libr. **30**(2), 264–277 (2012)
3. DeepL Translator. https://www.deepl.com/translator. Accessed 30 July 2020
4. Edo-Tokyo Museum. https://digitalmuseum.rekibun.or.jp/app/selected/edo-tokyo. Accessed 21 July 2020
5. Google Translate. https://translate.google.com/. Accessed 30 July 2020

6. Goto, S., Lin, D., Ishida, T.: Crowdsourcing for evaluating machine translation quality. In: Proceedings of the Ninth International Conference on Language Resources and Evaluation (LREC 2014), pp. 3456–3463 (2014)
7. Isabelle, P., Cherry, C., Foster, G.: A challenge set approach to evaluating machine translation. In: Proceedings of the 2017 Conference on Empirical Methods in Natural Language Processing, pp. 2486–2496 (2017)
8. Lavie, A., Agarwal, A.: METEOR: an automatic metric for MT evaluation with high levels of correlation with human judgments. In: Proceedings of the ACL Workshop on Intrinsic and Extrinsic Evaluation Measures for Machine Translation and/or Summarization, pp. 65–72 (2005)
9. Linguistic Data Consortium: Linguistic data annotation specification: assessment of fluency and adequacy in translations revision 1.5 (2005). http://web.archive.org/web/20100622130328/projects.ldc.upenn.edu/TIDES/Translation/TransAssess04.pdf. Accessed 4 Aug 2020
10. Metropolitan Museum of Art. http://www.metmuseum.org/. Accessed 21 July 2020
11. Microsoft Translator. https://www.bing.com/translator. Accessed 30 July 2020
12. Papineni, K., Roukos, S., Ward, T., Zhu, W.J.: BLEU: a method for automatic evaluation of machine translation. In: Proceedings of the 40th Annual Meeting of the Association for Computational Linguistics, pp. 311–318 (2002)
13. Reyes Ayala, B., Knudson, R., Chen, J., Cao, G., Wang, X.: Metadata records machine translation combining multi-engine outputs with limited parallel data. J. Assoc. Inf. Sci. Technol. **69**(1), 47–59 (2018)
14. Snover, M., Dorr, B., Schwartz, R., Micciulla, L., Makhoul, J.: A study of translation edit rate with targeted human annotation. In: Proceedings of the 7th Conference of the Association for Machine Translation of the Americas, pp. 223–231 (2006)
15. Ukiyo-e Search System. https://ukiyo-e.org/. Accessed 21 July 2020

Social Media

Collective Sensemaking and Location-Related Factors in the Context of a Brand-Related Online Rumor

Alton Yeow Kuan Chua(ID), Anjan Pal$^{(\boxtimes)}$ (ID), and Dion Hoe-Lian Goh(ID)

Wee Kim Wee School of Communication and Information, Nanyang Technological University, Singapore, Singapore
{altonchua,anjan001,ashlgoh}@ntu.edu.sg

Abstract. This paper examines collective sensemaking over the life cycle of an online rumor while considering two location-related factors: geographical proximity and cultural context. It has drawn data for a rumor case where a US-based customer claiming that Kentucky Fried Chicken (KFC) had served a fried rat. The rumor became viral on the Internet but was eventually debunked. The data included tweets across the three stages—parturition, diffusion, and control—of the rumor life cycle. Content analysis was employed followed by chi-square tests and binary logistic regression. Based on content analysis of 1,276 tweets, opinion-related posts were found to be prevalent at the onset of the rumor life cycle while information-related entries continued to swell through the stages. Tweets from both within as well as outside the US were evident in the early stages but they became localized before the rumor subsided. While there was a blurring of high and low cultural context in opinion-related tweets, information-related tweets reflected the communication of low-context culture as the process of collective sensemaking unfolded. The paper augments the rumor literature by exploring geographical proximity and cultural context in the process of collective sensemaking over the three stages of the rumor life cycle. It offers implications for practitioners to deal with online rumors.

Keywords: Rumor · Social media communication · Collective sensemaking · Geographical proximity · Cultural context

1 Introduction

Communication on the Internet has often been regarded as inherently transnational and transcultural. Specifically, social media enables people to easily communicate with the global audience, dissolving the barriers of space and time. Nonetheless, previous studies have shown that social media communication does not exist in a cultural void [1, 2].

This paper attempts to unpack social media communication in the context of online rumoring. Rumors are important to study because they have the potential to become viral on social media and trigger interactions that cross geographical and cultural boundaries [3, 4]. Moreover, as suggested by the seminal rumor theory [5], since personal

© Springer Nature Switzerland AG 2020
E. Ishita et al. (Eds.): ICADL 2020, LNCS 12504, pp. 271–286, 2020.
https://doi.org/10.1007/978-3-030-64452-9_25

involvement is intricately associated with rumoring, people often make sense of situation collectively across the globe while leaving traces of their culture.

On social media, the rise and fall of an online rumor can typically be depicted as a three-stage life cycle, comprising parturition, diffusion, and control [6]. With a dearth of verifiable information initially, speculations are rife. Users engage in what is known as collective sensemaking where they share personal opinions and whatever information they find within their online social networks. But as more facts emerge, the rumor loses traction and eventually dies out. While it is conceivable that the intensity and the flavor of collective sensemaking change with time, few studies empirically examine the process of collective sensemaking over the life cycle of a rumor on social media.

Meanwhile, rumor research has attracted substantial scholarly interest [7–9]. Among the factors that fuel rumors were found to include information ambiguity, a heightened state of anxiety and personal involvement [8, 10]. Yet, little attention has been paid to two important location-related factors, namely, users' geographical proximity to the origin of the rumor, and their cultural context [11–13]. Geographical proximity plays a major role in online rumors [14] because it is associated with perceived information credibility and personal involvement. Globalization notwithstanding, users' geographical location is often enmeshed with their cultural context which shapes users' information processing behavior [15], and hence how they express themselves in their online social networks [1]. This is why studying collective sensemaking through locational and cultural lenses represents a novelty and is especially suited for rumors that promulgate beyond the confines of the local community.

For these reasons, this paper examines collective sensemaking in the context of an online rumor. In addition, the roles of two location-related factors, which have been obscured hitherto, are also taken into consideration. Specifically, this paper seeks to address the following research questions:

RQ 1: How does collective sensemaking evolve over the life cycle of an online rumor?

RQ 2: How are geographical proximity and cultural context associated with collective sensemaking over the life cycle of an online rumor?

For the purpose of investigation, the Kentucky Fried Chicken (KFC) fried rat rumor was used. It initially sparked frenzied chatter on various social media platforms all over the world. The company stepped in to clarify with clinically-tested evidence and eventually quelled the myth. The lifespan of the rumor, which lasted for some two weeks, generated copious volume of messages from within and outside the US during the saga. This makes it a suitable case to study collective sensemaking and location-related factors in the spread of rumors.

This paper is significant to both theory and practice. On the theoretical front, it dovetails earlier studies [13] by taking into account each stage in the rumor life cycle more granularly and thus offering a finer analysis of the unfolding collective sensemaking process in online social networks. Additionally, it extends prior research with the inclusion of two location-related factors, namely, geographical proximity and cultural context which are hitherto unexplored.

The remainder of this paper is organized as follow: Sect. 2 provides an overview of the literature related to collective sensemaking, geographical proximity and cultural context. Section 3 describes the methods used in the research while Sect. 4 presents the results. The major findings are discussed in Sect. 5. In the sixth and final section, this paper concludes with theoretical and practical implications, as well as limitations and possible future research directions.

2 Literature Review

2.1 Sensemaking in Rumors

The theory of sensemaking was originally conceived to explain how people find ways to fill information gaps [16]. To cope with uncertainty, individuals muddle through together with others by sharing their thoughts to gain a better sense of reality [17]. The theory has been applied in a variety of settings that range from environmental communication [18] to social media communication [19]. Particularly in the context of online rumors where there is ambiguity over matters of shared concern, users are compelled to learn more about the situation from one another so as to manage risks, reduce uncertainty, and alleviate anxiety [8, 20–22].

Unlike individual sensemaking [23], collective sensemaking involves noisy and dynamic exchange of messages among users, many of whom would not remain individually engaged throughout the process. These messages are invariably opinion-related and information-related [12, 19]. While the former comprises views, criticisms or judgements from the members of the online community, the latter includes factual details, situation updates and questioning.

Depending on contextual and temporal factors, collective sensemaking unfolds as a negotiated process which mirrors the online rumor life cycle comprising three stages, namely, parturition, diffusion, and control [6, 12, 24]. Parturition refers to the time when a rumor is first conceived. During diffusion, the rumor gains traction and circulates freely in social networks. Finally, during control, the rumor is shown to be a hoax and dies out eventually. However, the ways in which collective sensemaking occur on social media in the wake of a rumor outbreak, from parturition till control, have not been studied hitherto.

2.2 Geographical Proximity

The first location-related factor that could have a bearing on collective sensemaking is users' geographical proximity. During crisis situations and mass emergencies such as natural calamities, complete information may not always be forthcoming in real-time. Moreover, information seeking and sharing behaviors invariably differ between those who were at the affected area and those from afar.

For instance, in the case of the Typhoon Haiyan, users residing in the Philippines tweeted more about relief coordination efforts and less about second-hand reporting and memorializing the victims when compared to users outside the Philippines [25]. This was because users at the site of calamity were knowledgeable about the ground situation and were poised to do something concrete with the information they had. Their overseas counterparts, on the other hand, could show solidarity only by passing on news they received and sharing words of comfort.

In the cases of the Red River flooding and Oklahoma fire in the United States, locals tweeted less on the topic than those located outside the areas. Moreover, locals retweeted messages that contained highly specific, emergency-related information relevant to other local users rather than trying to address the information needs of the broader audience [3].

Yet, extant literature has not pinpointed how geographical proximity to a location-based rumor shapes what users create and share online. Especially when such a rumor attracts both local and global attention, an investigation that incorporates geographical proximity would offer an interesting perspective on the collective sensemaking process across space and time.

2.3 Cultural Context

The second location-related factor that could have a bearing on collective sensemaking is users' cultural context. Culture is defined as a generally acceptable way of thinking, feeling and acting [26, 27]. Although amorphous, the culture of a community is manifested in symbols, heroes, rituals and values [15]. Furthermore, several dimensions have been identified to conceptualize culture. These include power distance, individualism, masculinity, uncertainty avoidance, context, and time [28].

When the focus is on human interaction, the dichotomy of high and low-context has often been relied to distinguish between cultures [1, 26, 29–32]. In high-context cultures such as those traditionally associated with the Japanese and South Koreans, individuals tend to maintain deep, long-term relationships and express themselves in implicit ways that can give rise to multiple interpretations [1, 33]. In low-context cultures which are typically associated with western nations including the United States and Canada, individuals are inclined to communicate in a factual and explicit manner [29]. Thus, communications in a low-context culture tend to be more directed, focused and analytic compared with communications in a high-context culture [26].

Although rumor-mongering can reflect cultural practice that conforms to standards of a community [34], little is known about the relationship between rumoring and the culture expressed through social media. The popularity and accessibility of Twitter provide the opportunity to use naturalistic data to analyze the role of cultural context in online rumors.

Informed by the literature which identifies textual dimensions differentiating between high- and low-context cultures [1, 29, 35], this paper conceptualizes cultural context in terms of emotiveness, tentativeness, and socialization. Emotiveness refers to the presence of emotions such as anger, sadness and contentment in a message [35–37]. Tentativeness in a message reflects a sense of uncertainty expressed through words such as "perhaps" and "probably" [1, 32, 38]. Socialization in a message is conveyed when a communicator directs it to a particular recipient [8, 39].

Given their communicative implicitness, communications in a high-context culture could be emotive, tentative in articulation, and less likely to communicate directly. In contrast, communications in a low-context culture could be less emotive, more definitive in expression, and show the tendency for socialization by explicitly addressing their social contacts [1, 35, 40, 41]. Together, emotiveness, tentativeness, and socialization offer a multifaceted representation of cultural context.

3 Methods

3.1 The Case of a Rumor Outbreak

On 11 June 2015, a Kentucky Fried Chicken (KFC) customer claimed on social media that a KFC branch in California had served him a deep-fried rat instead of chicken. To support his claim, he posted images of the piece of meat that resembled a rat. After 12 June, the post started to circulate on social media. On 14 June, KFC denied the allegations and sought to contact the customer for clarification. However, the original post continued to make rounds on social media and was even featured in mainstream media such as Cable News Network and The Telegraph from 16 June onwards. To get to the bottom of the matter, KFC requested the purported 'fried rat' from the customer and sent it to an independent laboratory for a DNA test on 19 June 2015. Three days later, KFC announced the test results which confirmed the meat was indeed chicken, and demanded an apology from the customer. The verdict went viral. The 'fried rat' saga eventually fizzled out on 27 June 2015, the day which saw a dramatic drop in the number of related messages. Table 1 shows the timeline of the key events of the rumor.

Table 1. Timeline of key events in the KFC "fried rat" rumor

Date	Key events
11 June	A KFC customer claimed on social media that he was served a deep-fried rat
14 June	KFC denied the allegation and sought to contact the customer
16 June	The case was featured in local and global media reports
19 June	KFC sent the "fried rat" for a DNA tes
22 June	The test results confirmed the meat was indeed chicken
27 June	The 'fried rat' saga fizzled out on social media

This case was chosen because of two reasons. First, since KFC is a global fast-food chain, the rumor outbreak quickly gained traction on social media all over the world. Second, although the rumor originated from the US, the copious volume of social media messages generated from within and outside the US during the saga makes this a suitable case to study collective sensemaking and location-related factors in the spread of the rumor.

3.2 Data Collection

Informed by prior research [9, 42, 43], Twitter was used to collect messages related to the rumor outbreak. The social media platform facilitated collecting related tweets that were publicly available. A common way to do so was by using Twitter search Application Programing Interface (API). The public search API was used to retrieve tweets based on event-specific keywords (e.g., #kfcrat, #friedrat, #kfcfriedrat, and kfcfriedrat) related to the rumor case.

A total of 1,934 tweets posted between 12 June and 27 June were collected. The data included content of tweets, time-stamp and other user-information such as the contributors' location, along with the geo-identifier of latitude and longitude if available. After eliminating 658 tweets that were non-relevant to the case (e.g., *"It plans to get Mexico to build a wall #kfc"*) and non-geotagged, the remaining 1,276 tweets were arranged chronologically using timestamp information and mapped to the three stages in the rumor life cycle. These tweets admitted for analysis were all geotagged.

The three stages in the rumor life cycle were determined on the basis of the events that took place. The parturition stage (Stage 1) started on 12 June when tweets appeared about the rumor case and lasted until 15 June, a day after KFC denied the allegations and sought to contact the customer for clarification. The diffusion stage (Stage 2) spanned from 16 June when the rumor turned viral and drew attention from both local and international media, until 21 June, a day before the verdict of the 'fried rat' was publicly announced. The control stage (Stage 3) lasted between 22 June and 27 June within which the rumor was debunked with clinical evidence and eventually died out.

Table 2 shows the distribution of tweets across the three stages of the rumor life cycle.

Table 2. Distribution of tweets across the three stages in the rumor life cycle

Stages	Date	#tweets
Parturition (Stage 1)	12 June–15 June	302
Diffusion (Stage 2)	16 June–21 June	633
Control (Stage 3)	22 June–27 June	341

3.3 Operationalization

Taking the cue from the prior works on rumoring phenomena [12, 19, 20, 44], collective sensemaking was operationalized by using two broad message-specific dimensions: opinion-related and information-related. The first dimension comprised views, criticisms or judgements from the members of the online community [11, 20, 44]. As a part of the iterative process of sensemaking, users are often involved in expressing their belief and disbelief through opinion-related messages. The second dimension included factual details, situation updates and questioning [12, 19]. Since communicating and interacting with others are key elements in the process of collective sensemaking on social media, users also engaged in activities such as sharing and seeking information among the members of the community. Therefore, all the tweets were coded along these two message-specific dimensions.

A tweet was coded as opinion-related when it expressed individuals' view, criticism or judgement about the rumor using phrases such as "I think" and "I don't believe".

Likewise, a tweet was treated as information-related tweet when it included factual details, situation updates, URLs, and questioning by using phrases such as "is it...?". Table 4 shows examples of such tweets. Furthermore, it is possible to have a tweet that contains both opinion as well as information. In that case, the tweet was coded as opinion-related as well as information-related tweet. For the purpose of coding, a randomly chosen pilot set of 200 tweets was assigned independently to two coders. The average inter-coder reliability in terms of Cohen's Kappa was greater than 0.70, and disagreements were resolved through discussion. The remaining tweets were divided equally among the coders for further coding.

With respect to geographical proximity, location was divided into within the US (coded as 1) and outside the US (coded as 0) since the rumor originated in US. To do this, geotag information of the tweets was used.

Cultural context of communications was operationalized using three variables, namely, emotiveness, tentativeness, and socialization. With respect to emotiveness, tweets were coded as 1 when they expressed emotions using phrases such as "wow" and "disgusting" (e.g., *Oh Rats! Disgusting!!! so now they are doing business with rat*"); and coded as 0 otherwise. With respect to tentativeness, tweets were coded as 1 when they contained uncertain words such as "perhaps" and "somewhat" (e.g., "...*perhaps some-one tried to sabotage kfc reputation... saying it rat meat*"); and coded as 0 otherwise. With respect to socialization, tweets were coded as 1 if they were directed to a specific user account using the symbol '@' followed by screen names (however, excluded for the cases of retweet); and coded as 0 otherwise.

Among the three variables of cultural context, emotiveness and tentativeness required human coding while the socialization can be extracted directly from the dataset. To established inter-coder reliability, the earlier approach was adopted for the coding, and the average inter-coder reliability in terms of Cohen's Kappa was greater than 0.70.

3.4 Data Analysis

To address RQ 1, we analyzed the trends of the collective sensemaking tweets throughout the rumor life cycle. In particular, Chi-square test of independence was used to compare the tweets across the three stages. This was because the variables involved in collective sensemaking and the stages of rumor life cycle were categorical in nature.

To address RQ 2, binary logistic regression was used to examine how geographical proximity and cultural context were associated with collective sensemaking. This statistical procedure was apt because the dependent variables involved in collective sensemaking were dichotomous. The analysis was repeated separately for predicting opinion-related tweets and information-related tweets.

4 Results

Among the 1,276 tweets, 167 tweets were exclusively opinion-related whereas 805 tweets were exclusively information-related. The remaining 304 tweets were both opinion-related and information-related.

For the purpose of analysis, tweets were divided into the opinion-related $(167 + 304 = 471)$ tweets, and the information-related $(805 + 304 = 1,109)$ tweets. The stage-wise descriptive statistics of the dataset are summarized in Table 3.

Table 3. Descriptive statistics of the dataset

	Stages	Geographical proximity	Emotiveness	Tentativeness	Socialization
Opinion-related tweets	Stage 1	0:124 (57.1%) 1:93 (42.9%)	0:106 (48.8%) 1:111 (51.2%)	0:174 (80.2%) 1:43 (19.8%)	0:118 (54.4%) 1:99 (45.6%)
	Stage 2	0:93 (48.9%) 1:97 (51.1%)	0:85 (44.7%) 1:105 (55.3%)	0:161 (84.7%) 1:29 (15.3%)	0:110 (57.9%) 1:80 (42.1%)
	Stage 3	0:28 (43.8%) 1:36 (56.3%)	0:45 (70.3%) 1:19 (29.7%)	0:53 (82.8%) 1:11 (17.2%)	0:49 (76.6%) 1:15 (23.4%)
Information-related tweets	Stage 1	0:129 (57.6%) 1:95 (42.4%)	0:121 (54%) 1:103 (46%)	0:185 (82.6%) 1:39 (17.4%)	0:96 (42.9%) 1:128 (57.1%)
	Stage 2	0:354 (62.8%) 1:210 (37.2%)	0:388 (68.8%) 1:176 (31.2%)	0:483 (85.6%) 1:81 (14.4%)	0:314 (55.7%) 1:250 (44.3%)
	Stage 3	0:186 (57.9%) 1:135 (42.1%)	0:290 (90.3%) 1:31 (9.7%)	0:293 (91.3%) 1:28 (8.7%)	0:252 (78.5%) 1:69 (21.5%)

RQ 1 focuses on how collective sensemaking evolved over the rumor life cycle. The chi-square analysis showed a significant relation between the presence of opinions in tweets and rumor life cycle, $[\chi^2 (df = 2, N = 1276) = 219.47, p < 0.001]$. As shown in Fig. 1, the proportion of opinion-related tweets saw a drastic drop from Stage 1 (71.85%) to Stage 2 (30.02%), and further decreased in Stage 3 (18.77%). Furthermore, the chi-square analysis showed a significant relation between the presence of information in tweets and rumor life cycle $[\chi^2 (df = 2, N = 1276) = 61.39, p < 0.001]$. The proportion of information-related tweets increased from Stage 1 (74.17%) to Stage 2 (89.10%), and then slightly increased in Stage 3 (94.13%) of the rumor life cycle. Examples of tweets over the three stages are given in Table 4.

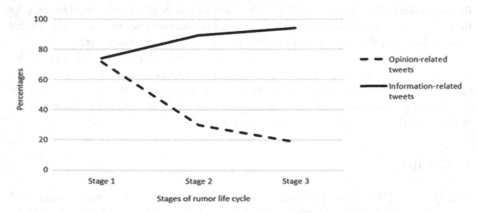

Fig. 1. Trends of tweets over the three stages of rumor life cycle

Table 4. Examples of tweets over the three stages of the rumor life cycle

Life cycle stages	Opinion-related tweets	Information-related tweets
Stage 1	"Someone playing a trick on KFC… that's defo not possible. It's so not possible fried rat wtf" [tid102]	"Did they really fry a rat? @xxx: KFC" [t99]
	"You know I actually thought that that KFC rat was just a thigh and a strip" [tid235]	"UPDATE: Kentucky fried rat #kfc #KFCRat @xxx pic.twitter.com/N2C1BvpSfg" [tid272]
Stage 2	"i think world is Heading 2wrds a #FoodSafetyCrisis its #KFCFriedRat after #Maggi in India! its time w think abt food" [tid426]	"KFC disputes fried rat claim: We currently have no evidence to support this allegation, KFC said" [tid540]
	"I don't believe KFC ever served a customer deep fried rat. No way would they serve something to their own customers." [tid517]	"Did KFC serve a customer a deep-fried rat? - Fox News" [tid619]
Stage 3	"looks like they jumped the gun on calling it a rat…." [tid960]	"…KFC asserts DNA test proves meat in this viral photo was not friedrat: pic.twitter.com/pon2czSzWo" [tid999]
	"I really hope that @kfc sues the guy for defamation, and brand reputation." [tid1151]	"KFC 'fried rat' was actually chicken, independent lab test confirms" [tid1181]

RQ2 examines the association of geographical proximity and cultural context with collective sensemaking across the three stages of the rumor life cycle. The results of the logistic regression models are summarized in Table 5.

With respect to geographical proximity, the non-significant results in Stage 1 and Stage 2 suggest that there were comparable proportions of tweets from both within as well as outside the US. However, in Stage 3, tweets posted from within the US were more likely to be opinion-related [$\exp(\beta) = 1.98$, $p < 0.05$] than information-related tweets [$\exp(\beta) = 0.19$, $p < 0.01$].

With respect to cultural context, emotiveness was positively associated with the likelihood for tweets to be opinion-related across the three stages [Stage 1: $\exp(\beta) = 3.26$, $p < 0.001$; Stage 2: $\exp(\beta) = 3.45$, $p < 0.001$; Stage 3: $\exp(\beta) = 5.62$, $p < 0.001$]. In contrast, it was negatively associated with the likelihood for tweets to be information-related in Stage 2 [$\exp(\beta) = 0.29$, $p < 0.001$] and Stage 3 [$\exp(\beta) = 0.15$, $p < 0.001$]. In other words, opinion-related tweets were consistently emotive whereas information-related tweets lacked emotiveness particularly in Stage 2 and Stage 3 of the rumor life cycle. It seems that users expressed their emotion through opinion-related tweets. Examples of opinion-related tweets expressing emotiveness included "Oh Rats!

Table 5. Logistic Regression Coefficients ($\exp(\beta)$)

	Stages	Stage 1	Stage 2	Stage 3
Opinion-related tweets	Geographical proximity (1)	0.73	1.26	1.98*
	Emotiveness (1)	3.26***	3.45***	5.62***
	Tentativeness (1)	1.65	1.36	3.59*
	Socialization (1)	0.63	1.00	0.66
Omnibus test χ^2		21.00***	54.69***	32.07***
Nagelkerke pseudo-R^2		0.10	0.12	0.15
Information-related tweets	Geographical proximity (1)	0.79	0.97	0.19**
	Emotiveness (1)	1.59	0.29***	0.15***
	Tentativeness (1)	0.85	0.55	0.31
	Socialization (1)	3.43***	1.20	0.81
Omnibus test χ^2		20.54**	23.10***	23.89***
Nagelkerke pseudo-R^2		0.10	0.08	0.19

Note. $\exp(\beta)$ = odds ratio; *$p < 0.05$; **$p < 0.01$; ***$p < 0.001$. For the four categorical variables, '0' was used as the baseline for comparison.

Disgusting!!! so now they are doing business with rat. No KFC meal" [tid83] and "I don't even eat chicken but thanks to this KFC rat story I will not be eating at fast food places EVER again *sick*" [tid201]. In contrast, information-related tweets such as "Man claims KFC served him a fried rat, company denies it" [tid579] and "This KFC customer is claiming he bit into a deep-fried rat" [tid646] lacked in emotion.

Tentativeness was positively associated with the likelihood for tweets to be opinion-related in Stage 3 [$\exp(\beta) = 3.59$, $p < 0.05$]. However, it was found to be non-significant for the information-related tweets. In other words, even at the tail end of the rumor life cycle, opinion-related tweets were still found to express tentativeness. Examples of such tweets included "So apparently @kfc came out and said ... perhaps making us fool" [tid1208] and "...perhaps someone tried to sabotage kfc reputation..." [tid1266].

Socialization was positively associated for the information-related tweets in Stage 1 [$\exp(\beta) = 3.43$, $p < 0.001$]. In other words, information-related tweets were used as socialization devices at the beginning of the rumor life cycle. Tweets such as "Did they really fry a rat? @screen_name" [tid99] and "#StopSnitching @screen_name ...Guy found a rat in his KFC order..." [tid167] were directed towards specific user account (@screen_name) within individuals' social contacts.

5   Discussions

Three major findings can be gleaned from this study. First, in terms of collective sense-making, opinion-related tweets were found to be prevalent at the onset of the rumor life cycle. As shown in Fig. 1, the proportion of opinion-related tweets saw a drastic drop from Stage 1 (71.85%) to Stage 2 (30.02%), and further decreased in Stage 3

(18.77%). This is likely a reflection of how the online rumor gained traction initially through the sharing of opinion-related tweets. In the absence of any authoritative voices at the beginning, users were caught up in a speculative frenzy on social media. They expressed views as a way to make sense of the situation collectively [8, 13]. However, as facts emerged with time, the level of ambiguity subsided. The official announcement of the DNA results quelled any lingering doubt about the meat that KFC actually served, and led to a drop in the volume of opinion-related tweets in the final stage of the rumor life cycle.

In contrast, the proportion of information-related tweets continued to swell through the rumor life cycle. As shown in Fig. 1, it increased from Stage 1 (74.17%) to Stage 2 (89.10%), and then slightly increased in Stage 3 (94.13%) of the life cycle. It seems that information-related tweets were prevalent over all the stages. At the onset where the rumor was fresh and sensational, users were perhaps eager to swap whatever details they had to reduce situational ambiguities. Later, when the rumor was quelled, users actively updated each other of the verdict. In this way, this paper augments the literature on information diffusion [45–47] by showing the process of collective sensemaking in terms of the distribution of the opinion-related and information-related tweets over the rumor life cycle.

Second, in terms of geographical proximity, the non-significant results in the earlier stages (Stage 1 and Stage 2) suggest that there were comparable proportions of tweets from both within as well as outside the US. This shows the transboundary nature of online rumors even in the early stage of the life cycle. In other words, any contentious issue about global brands has the potential to draw prompt interest on social media, which are unconstrained geographically.

However, at the tail end of the rumor life cycle, tweets posted from within the US were more likely to be opinion-related than information-related tweets. In the aftermath of the rumor, users who were in closer geographical proximity tend to be vocal in expressing their views. As the case had occurred in their own backyard, they must have keenly felt a strong sense of personal involvement. These findings extend the existing literature [14, 25, 48] by granularly teasing out the role of geographical proximity across the stages in the rumor life cycle.

Third, opinion-related tweets mirrored communications in a high-context culture, expressing emotions throughout all the three stages in this rumoring phenomenon. Although tentativeness was evident in opinion-related tweets only at the tail end of the rumor life cycle, the lack of tentativeness in the earlier stages corroborates with the unquestioning belief about the rumor initially. In other words, in the absence of any verification, users were definitive in expression, and simply embraced the rumor as improvised news [8, 49]. These findings suggest that communications during a rumor blur the lines between the traditional conceptualization of high and low cultural contexts.

On the other hand, information-related tweets mirrored communications in a low-context culture as the process of collective sensemaking unfolded. This was particularly so in terms of socialization at the early stage, and the lack of emotiveness in the subsequent stages. These results suggest that information-related tweets can be used as socialization devices at the onset of the rumor life cycle, and reflect how information sharing behavior is often sparked by users' sense of belongingness to the online community [50, 51]. Users are compelled to inform their social contacts promptly, and perhaps to gather additional information as part of their collective sensemaking efforts [52, 53]. Furthermore, the lack of emotiveness could be attributed to the inherently factual nature of information-related tweets in the process of sensemaking.

6 Conclusion

This paper examines the process of collective sensemaking in the context of an online rumor. Drawing data from Twitter, it specifically investigates the role geographical proximity and cultural context in the process of collective sensemaking over the life cycle of the rumor.

In response to RQ1, opinion-related tweets were found to be prevalent at the onset of the rumor life cycle while information-related entries continued to swell through the stages. On RQ2, geographical proximity-wise, tweets from both within as well as outside the US were evident in the early stages but they became localized before the rumor subsided. In terms of cultural context, while opinion-related tweets reflected high-context culture by being tentative, they also mirrored low-context culture by expressing emotiveness. On the other hand, information-related tweets echoed low-context culture in terms of socialization at the early stage, and mirrored high-context culture by showing a lack of emotiveness in the subsequent stages.

This paper has significant implications for both theory and practice. On the theoretical front, it augments the existing literature [19, 20, 45] by focusing on each of the three stages of the rumor life cycle granularly as the process of collective sensemaking unfolds. The results demonstrate how opinion-related and information-related tweets evolve, and provide a more holistic understanding of social media messages in a rumoring phenomenon. Furthermore, this paper extends online rumor literature [8, 11, 44] by including two location-related factors, namely, geographical proximity and cultural context in the process of collective sensemaking over the three stages of the rumor life cycle.

On the practical front, this paper offers implications for managers and social media administrators to deal with online rumors. For brands such as KFC, which have a global presence, efforts to contain a rumor may involve transboundary considerations. Apart from having a good grasp of users' sentiments and emotions associated with the rumor, relying on an independent, credible entity from the onset to fill any informational gap would also help douse the digital wildfire from spreading out of control.

These implications notwithstanding, three limitations need to be acknowledged. One, this paper examined the process of collective sensemaking in a single brand-related rumor case. Future research can expand the work to study multiple rumor cases including those that circulate during crises such as natural disasters and health epidemics. Two, this paper is constrained by the sampling bias inherent to research using the search API of Twitter. Admittedly, the set of all real-time tweets related to the case could not be captured in its entirety [54]. While the use of Twitter datasets is a common practice in rumor research [8, 44], future works could encompass user-generated content drawn across different social media platforms such as Facebook and Instagram to offer a richer understanding of the phenomenon. Non-English tweets may also be investigated. Third, another limitation resides in the geographic scope and the cultural context of the brand-related rumor case. For the purpose of analysis, only geotagged tweets were included in the dataset. And, this study has been conducted for a fast-food brand. Prior seminal works on cultural studies [26, 28] suggest that cultures differ on many other aspects such as communication (low context vs. high context) and group orientation (individualism vs. collectivism). Therefore, caution is advised when interpreting and generalizing the results. Future works need to be done by treating cultural context holistically with a large sample of geotagged data. In addition, further investigations are required to understand how online rumors can be controlled effectively using various response strategies such as attacking the attacker and refutation [55].

References

1. Pflug, J.: Contextuality and computer-mediated communication: a cross-cultural comparison. Comput. Hum. Behav. **27**(1), 131–137 (2011)
2. Tsai, W.H., Men, L.R.: Cultural values reflected in corporate pages on popular social network sites in China and the United States. J. Res. Interact. Market. **6**(1), 42–58 (2012)
3. Starbird, K., Palen, L.: Pass it on? Retweeting in mass emergency. In: Proceedings of the International Conference on Information Systems for Crisis Response and Management, pp. 1–10 (2010). https://www.researchgate.net/profile/Leysia_Palen2/publication/228512 367_Pass_It_On_Retweeting_in_Mass_Emergency/links/00b7d52bc84dca2d2f000000.pdf
4. Rojecki, A., Meraz, S.: Rumors and factitious informational blends: the role of the web in speculative politics. New Media Soc. **18**(1), 25–43 (2016)
5. Allport, G.W., Postman, L.: An analysis of rumor. Public Opin. Q. **10**, 501–517 (1946)
6. Rosnow, R.L.: Communications as cultural science. J. Commun. **24**(3), 26–38 (1974)
7. Chua, Alton Y.K., Banerjee, S.: Analyzing users' trust for online health rumors. In: Allen, Robert B., Hunter, J., Zeng, Marcia L. (eds.) ICADL 2015. LNCS, vol. 9469, pp. 33–38. Springer, Cham (2015). https://doi.org/10.1007/978-3-319-27974-9_4
8. Oh, O., Agrawal, M., Rao, H.R.: Community intelligence and social media services: a rumor theoretic analysis of tweets during social crises. MIS Q. **37**(2), 407–426 (2013)
9. Pal, A., Chua, A.Y.K., Goh, D.H.L.: Does KFC sell rat? Analysis of tweets in the wake of a rumor outbreak. Aslib J. Inf. Manage. **69**(6), 660–673 (2017)
10. Nadamoto, A., Miyabe, M., Aramaki, E.: Analysis of microblog rumors and correction texts for disaster situations. In: Proceedings of the International Conference on Information Integration and Web-based Applications and Services, pp. 44–52. ACM, New York (2013)
11. Oh, O., Kwon, K.H., Rao, H.R.: An exploration of social media in extreme events: Rumor theory and twitter during the Haiti earthquake 2010. In: Proceedings of the International Conference on Information Systems, vol. 231, AISeL (2010). http://aisel.aisnet.org/cgi/vie wcontent.cgi?article=1223&context=icis2010_submissions
12. Liao, Q., Shi, L.: She gets a sports car from our donation: rumor transmission in a Chinese microblogging community. In: Proceedings of the Conference on Computer Supported Cooperative Work and Social Computing, pp. 587–598. ACM, New York (2013)
13. Bordia, P., DiFonzo, N.: Problem solving in social interactions on the Internet: rumor as social cognition. Soc. Psychol. Q. **67**(1), 33–49 (2004)
14. Huang, Y.L., Starbird, K., Orand, M., Stanek, S.A., Pedersen, H.T.: Connected through crisis: emotional proximity and the spread of misinformation online. In: Proceedings of the Conference on Computer Supported Cooperative Work and Social Computing, pp. 969–980. ACM, New York (2015)

15. Steinwachs, K.: Information and culture - the impact of national culture on information processes. J. Inf. Sci. **25**(3), 193–204 (1999)
16. Dervin, B.: An overview of sensemaking research: concepts, methods and results to date. In: Presented at the International Communication Association Annual Meeting. ICA, Dallas (1983)
17. Dervin, B.: Chaos, order, and sense-making: a proposed theory for information design. In: Dervin, B., Foreman-Wernet, L., Lauterbach, E. (eds.) Sense-Making Methodology Reader: Selected Writings of Brenda Dervin, pp. 325–340. Hampton Press, Cresskill (2003)
18. Madden, K.M.: Making sense of environmental messages: an exploration of householders' information needs and uses. Electron. J. Commun. **9**(2), 3–4 (1999)
19. Heverin, T., Zach, L.: Use of microblogging for collective sensemaking during violent crises: a study of three campus shootings. J. Assoc. Inf. Sci. Technol. **63**(1), 34–47 (2012)
20. Andrews, C., Fichet, E., Ding, Y., Spiro, E.S., Starbird, K.: Keeping up with the tweet-dashians: the impact of 'official' accounts on online rumoring. In: Proceedings of the ACM Conference on Computer-Supported Cooperative Work and Social Computing, pp. 452–465. ACM, New York (2016)
21. DiFonzo, N., Bourgeois, M.J., Suls, J.M., Homan, C., Stupak, N., Brooks, B., Ross, D.S., Bordia, P.: Rumor clustering, consensus, and polarization: dynamic social impact and self-organization of hearsay. J. Exp. Soc. Psychol. **49**(3), 378–399 (2013)
22. Krafft, P., Zhou, K., Edwards, I., Starbird, K., Spiro, E. S.: Centralized, parallel, and distributed information processing during collective sensemaking. In: Proceedings of the CHI Conference on Human Factors in Computing Systems, pp. 2976–2987. ACM, New York (2017)
23. Zhang, P., Soergel, D.: Process patterns and conceptual changes in knowledge representations during information seeking and sensemaking: a qualitative user study. J. Inf. Sci. **42**(1), 59–78 (2016)
24. Chua, A. Y., Cheah, S. M., Goh, D. H. L., Lim, E. P.: Collective rumor correction on the death hoax of a political figure in social media. In: Proceedings of the Pacific Asia Conference on Information Systems, Chiayi, Taiwan (2016). http://aisel.aisnet.org/pacis2016/178
25. Takahashi, B., Tandoc Jr., E.C., Carmichael, C.: Communicating on Twitter during a disaster: an analysis of tweets during Typhoon Haiyan in the Philippines. Comput. Hum. Behav. **50**, 392–398 (2015)
26. Hall, E.T.: Beyond Culture. Anchor Press, New York (1976)
27. Marra, F.J.: Crisis communication plans: poor predictors of excellent crisis public relations. Public Relations Review **24**(4), 461–474 (1998)
28. Hofstede, G.: The business of international business is culture. Int. Bus. Rev. **3**(1), 1–14 (1994)
29. Kittler, M.G., Rygl, D., Mackinnon, A.: Special Review Article: Beyond culture or beyond control? Reviewing the use of Hall's high-/low-context concept. Int. J. Cross Cult. Manage. **11**(1), 63–82 (2011)
30. Lim, N.: Cultural differences in emotion: differences in emotional arousal level between the East and the West. Integr. Med. Res. **5**(2), 105–109 (2016)
31. Marcoccia, M.: The internet, intercultural communication and cultural variation. Lang. Intercult. Commun. **12**(4), 353–368 (2012)
32. Men, L.R., Tsai, W.H.S.: How companies cultivate relationships with publics on social network sites: evidence from China and the United States. Public Relat. Rev. **38**(5), 723–730 (2012)
33. Rösch, M., Segler, K.G.: Communication with Japanese. Manage. Int. Rev. **27**(4), 56–67 (1987). www.jstor.org/stable/40227860
34. Guille, A., Hacid, H., Favre, C., Zighed, D.A.: Information diffusion in online social networks: a survey. ACM Sigmod Rec. **42**(2), 17–28 (2013)

35. Cardon, P.W.: A critique of Hall's contexting model: a meta-analysis of literature on inter-cultural business and technical communication. J. Bus. Tech. Commun. **22**(4), 399–428 (2008)
36. Stieglitz, S., Dang-Xuan, L.: Emotions and information diffusion in social media—sentiment of microblogs and sharing behavior. J. Manage. Inf. Syst. **29**(4), 217–248 (2013)
37. Mazer, J.P., Thompson, B., Cherry, J., Russell, M., Payne, H.J., Kirby, E.G., Pfohl, W.: Communication in the face of a school crisis: examining the volume and content of social media mentions during active shooter incidents. Comput. Hum. Behav. **53**, 238–248 (2015)
38. Danescu-Niculescu-Mizil, C., Gamon, M., Dumais, S.: Mark my words! Linguistic style accommodation in social media. In: Proceedings of the International Conference on World Wide Web, pp. 745–754. ACM, New York (2011)
39. Hsu, M.H., Tien, S.W., Lin, H.C., Chang, C.M.: Understanding the roles of cultural differences and socio-economic status in social media continuance intention. Inf. Technol. People **28**(1), 224–241 (2015)
40. Merkin, R.S., Ramadan, R.: Communication practices in the US and Syria. SpringerPlus **5**(1), 1–12 (2016). https://doi.org/10.1186/s40064-016-2486-9
41. Park, H.S., Guan, X.: Culture, positive and negative face threats, and apology intentions. J. Lang. Soc. Psychol. **28**(3), 244–262 (2009)
42. Cheng, Y.C., Chen, P.L.: Global social media, local context: a case study of Chinese-language tweets about the 2012 presidential election in Taiwan. Aslib J. Inf. Manage. **66**(3), 342–356 (2014)
43. Zhao, Z., Resnick, P., Mei, Q.: Enquiring minds: early detection of rumors in social media from enquiry posts. In: Proceedings of the International Conference on World Wide Web, pp. 1395–1405. ACM, New York (2015)
44. Arif, A., Shanahan, K., Chou, F.J., Dosouto, Y., Starbird, K., Spiro, E.S.: How information snowballs: exploring the role of exposure in online rumor propagation. In: Proceedings of the Computer-Supported Cooperative Work and Social Computing, pp. 466–477. ACM, New York (2016)
45. Stieglitz, S., Bunker, D., Mirbabaie, M., Ehnis, C.: Sense-making in social media during extreme events. J. Contingencies Crisis Manag. **26**(1), 4–15 (2018)
46. Sung, M., Hwang, J.S.: Who drives a crisis? The diffusion of an issue through social networks. Comput. Hum. Behav. **36**, 246–257 (2014)
47. Yu, L., Li, L., Tang, L., Dai, W., Hanachi, C.: A multi-agent-based online opinion dissemination model for China's crisis information release policy during hazardous chemical leakage emergencies into rivers. Online Inf. Rev. **41**(4), 537–557 (2017)
48. Birdsey, L., Szabo, C., Teo, Y. M.: Twitter knows: understanding the emergence of topics in social networks. In: Proceedings of the Winter Simulation Conference, pp. 4009–4020. IEEE Press (2015)
49. Shibutani, T.: Improvised News: A Sociological Study of Rumor. The Bobbs-Merrill Company Inc., Indianapolis (1966)
50. Marett, K., Joshi, K.D.: The decision to share information and rumors: examining the role of motivation in an online discussion forum. Commun. Assoc. Inf. Syst. (2009). AISeL. http://aisel.aisnet.org/cais/vol24/iss1/4
51. Oh, S., Syn, S.Y.: Motivations for sharing information and social support in social media: a comparative analysis of Facebook, Twitter, Delicious, YouTube, and Flickr. J. Assoc. Inf. Sci. Technol. **66**(10), 2045–2060 (2015)
52. Lee, S.H., Workman, J.E.: Gossip, self-monitoring and fashion leadership: comparison of US and South Korean consumers. J. Consum. Market. **31**(6/7), 452–463 (2014)
53. Lewis, N., Martinez, L.S.: Does the number of cancer patients' close social ties affect cancer-related information seeking through communication efficacy? Testing a mediation model. J. Health Commun. **19**(9), 1076–1097 (2014)

54. Yu, Y., Wang, X.: World Cup 2014 in the Twitter World: a big data analysis of sentiments in US sports fans' tweets. Comput. Hum. Behav. **48**, 392–400 (2015)
55. Paek, H.J., Hove, T.: Effective strategies for responding to rumors about risks: the case of radiation-contaminated food in South Korea. Public Relat. Rev. **45**(3), 101762 (2019)

Identifying the Types of Digital Footprint Data Used to Predict Psychographic and Human Behaviour

Aliff Nawi[1]($\boxtimes$), Zalmizy Hussin[2], Chua Chy Ren[3], Nurfatin Syahirah Norsaidi[2],
and Muhammad Syafiq Mohd Pozi[4]

[1] School of Education, Universiti Utara Malaysia, 06010 Kedah, Malaysia
aliffnawi@yahoo.com
[2] School of Applied Psychology, Social Work and Policy, Universiti Utara Malaysia,
06010 Kedah, Malaysia
zalmizy@uum.edu.my, nfatins.norsaidi@gmail.com
[3] School of Business and Social Sciences, Albukhary International University,
05200 Kedah, Malaysia
safiyya.chua@aiu.edu.my
[4] School of Computing, Universiti Utara Malaysia, 06010 Kedah, Malaysia
syafiq.pozi@uum.edu.my

Abstract. Digital footprints can be defined any data related to any online activity. When engaging, the user leaves digital footprints that can be tracked across a range of digital activities, such as web explorer, checked-in location, YouTube, photo-tag and record purchase. Indeed, the use of all social media applications is also part of the digital footprint. This research was, therefore conducted to classify the types of digital footprint data used to predict psychographic and human behaviour. A systematic analysis of 48 studies was undertaken to examine which form of digital footprint was taken into account in ongoing research. The results show that there are different types of data from digital footprints, such as structured data, unstructured data, geographic data, time-series data, event data, network data, and linked data. In conclusion, the use of digital footprint data is a practically new way of completing research into predicting psychographic and human behaviour. The use of digital footprint data also provides a tremendous opportunity for enriching insights into human behaviour.

Keywords: Psychographic · Digital footprints · Human · Online behaviour

1 Introduction

What is a psychographic? According to the Merriam-Webster dictionary [1], the definition of psychography is market-related research or the classification of population group statistics by psychological variables such as attitudes, values or feelings. The functions of Psychographic are to concentrate on an individual's perception of cognitive, emotional, significance, interest and lifestyle [2]. Psychography is also closely related to the demographic history of the individual, such as gender, age, race and more.

© Springer Nature Switzerland AG 2020
E. Ishita et al. (Eds.): ICADL 2020, LNCS 12504, pp. 287–296, 2020.
https://doi.org/10.1007/978-3-030-64452-9_26

Although digital footprint can be described as the action and behaviour of online social networking users, including the words, photos, text, views and videos they post, the groups they join and like [3]. To many people, these data describing online consumer activities are less useful. However, one needs to realise that these data are highly valuable in aggregated form, which can be highly utilised for commercial values by third parties [4].

Digital footprints can also be used to research the trend that is taking place in the virtual world, particularly online social networking. Online social networking is a crucial medium used by all groups, especially young adults, to communicate with each other [5]. In reality, the usage of online social networks such as Instagram, Facebook, Snapchat and WeChat also contribute significantly to the happiness and motivation of teenagers [6]. Indirectly the Online social network has changed the landscape of social life and human life as a whole.

2 Problem Statement

Can we identify the personality or behaviour of a person based on their online behaviour and activities? As online social networks have become part of teen life activities around the world, they constitute a significant arena for socialisation today. Many teens use online social networks not only to connect with peers but also for self-presentation, frustration and emotional self-disclosure. [7]. Interacting with the online social network ensures that users leave a digital imprint in a digital world that can be traced and tracked from a variety of digital activities [4].

Digital behaviour refers to the traces of data left behind in the physical world that occur while using the internet [8]. The digital world creates an experience distinct from the reality of the person. Contrarily to the obvious, the digital environment provides the user with a different experience. Activities in the digital domain can put consumers at risk for a variety of risks and conflicts that could put themselves and their lives at risk.

Recent studies show that there are many instances of misconduct involving multiple layers of online users. Studies have reported that some users use aggressive online words [9], hateful speech [10], cyberbully [11], sexting [12] and cyber pornography [13]. These cases are very high among adolescents.

This abuse of online users also harms learning that is still in school [14]. Excessive use of social media can also lead to addiction [15] and health problems [16]. Without the control of many parties, teenagers' misbehaviour not only affects them but is also feared to affect other online users. The main objectives to conduct this research was to classify the types of digital footprint data used to predict human psychographic and online behaviour. The findings of the study will contribute to researchers in better understanding the functions of digital data footprints when examining a person's personality and behaviour.

3 Methodology

In this section, we will discuss the method used to retrieve articles related to digital footprints. The authors used the technique called PRISMA (Preferred Reporting Items

Systematic Reviews and Meta-Analysis). This method includes resources (Scopus) used to run the systematic review, eligibility and exclusion criteria, steps of the review process (identification, screening, eligibility) and data abstraction and analysis. PRISMA also used to be utilised to perform systematic article selection studies, to classify the eligibility requirements for an article and to remove the requirements for an article to be classified [17]. The primary resources of this review paper relied on the Scopus journal database.

All the articles used were among the steps in the review of the articles selected in this study (identifying, examining and qualifying). The review of this article included 105 papers reviewed extracted from the Scopus database with a search TITLE ("digital footprint" OR "digital traces"). Eligibility and exclusion criterion is determined. First, only articles journal are selected, which means review article, book series, book, chapter in book and conference proceeding are all excluded. Second, to avoid any confusion and difficulty in translating, the searching efforts excluded the non-English publication and focused only on articles published in English. Thirdly, about concerning timeline, it covers ten years (between 2010 and 2019), an adequate period to see the evolution of research and related publications.

This systematic review paper consists of four stages, started performed in January 2020. The first phase identified the keywords used in the search process. By referring the previous studies and using the thesaurus, it identifies the keywords similar and related to the digital footprint and digital traces. After careful screening, a total of 48 eligible articles to be reviewed and used for the qualitative analysis. At the same time, a total of 52 articles were excluded due to the reasons unrelated to digital footprint, book series, book chapter and conference proceeding and non-English articles.

The remaining articles (48 articles) were assessed and analysed. Efforts were concentrated on specific studies that responded to the formulated questions. The data were extracted by reading through the abstracts first, then the full articles (in-depth) to identify appropriate themes and sub-themes. Qualitative analysis was performed using content analysis to identify themes related to the types of digital footprint. The authors then organised sub-themes around the themes established by typology.

4 Finding

There are 48 articles identified using digital footprint data for various research purposes. Psychology, education, marketing, climate, health, safety, management, politics, tourism and entertainment are among the psychographic areas of research listed. All of these studies have used various types of comprehensive data to interpret the results of their study. Table 1 displays the 10 themes found by research conducted using data from digital footprints. Interestingly, the majority of studies conducted covering all research topics tend to use network data, such as social media data (Facebook, Twitter, Foursquare, YouTube, Flickr, Linkedin). This is followed by the use of unstructured image, audio, video and text data. The use of standardised (geographic) and geographical (address, house, road) data, time-series data, event data and related data is the most widely used data in all areas of this identification.

Besides the results have shown that digital footprints have been used in different fields. The areas described include behaviour, education, marketing, climate, health,

Table 1. Psychographic analysis trends & types of digital footprints data

| No. | Psychographic areas | Included codes | Types of digital footprints data | | | | | | | | No. of documents |
			Structured	Unstructured	Geographic	Time series	Event	Network	Linked	
1	Behaviour	Behaviour, psychology, emotion, attitude	✓	✓	✓	✓	✓	✓	✓	15/48
2	Education	Education, skills, information,		✓				✓		4/48
3	Marketing	Marketing, entrepreneurship, economy						✓		5/48
4	Environment	Environment, geo, location			✓	✓		✓		6/48
5	Health	Health, personal, mental,		✓			✓	✓		4/48
6	Safety	Safety, awareness, privacy	✓	✓				✓		5/48
7	Management	Management, research,	✓	✓				✓		4/48
8	Politics	Politics						✓		1/48
9	Tourism	Tourism, Vacation			✓			✓		3/48
10	Entertainment	Entertainment, games		✓						1/48

safety, management, politics, tourism and entertainment. Behavioural patterns are the higher frequently topics across digital footprint studies compare to other topics. Behaviour themes are the most widely used themes for various types of data, including structured, unstructured, geographical, time-series, event, network and linked data. The detailed findings may be described as follows:

4.1 Structured Data

Structured data is a number stored in rows and columns where each entity is specified as being accessible via a database management system. Such data are widely used by government agencies, real estate and enterprises, companies and transactions to produce organised data in every each operating phase. By referring to the Table 1, the structured data been used in this study involve the of online surveys, such as the online google form [18] and online polls [19].

4.2 Unstructured Data

Data Information other than table-shaped data identified by the data element belongs to the non-structured data group. Data in the form of images, audio, video and text, are known as unstructured data. Unstructured use of data in this study involves scholarly publications [20], Google calendar, contacts, [21], digital resources [22], online public access catalog [23], management systems [24], application [25], search tools [26], audio [27] and ticket games [28].

4.3 Geographic Data

Produced from geographical information systems such as addresses, places of work, buildings, transport routes and roads systems included in geographical data. The data of this element is easily accessed through sensors and geostatistics are used to monitor the environment. The use of geographic data in this study involved GPS data [29, 30], geo-tagged photos [31], public wifi probe [32], open street map [33].

4.4 Time Series

Measurements or observations of a particular index in chronological order are time series. In general, time-series data is observed at the same time interval. Time-series data were analysed to extract the hidden knowledge from the collected time data. Signal processing, statistics, earthquake forecasting systems, pattern recognition and many other areas use time-series data. The use of time-series data in this study involves data from cellular communication, including telephone number (calling volume pattern, daily pattern, weekly pattern, contact pattern, communication habit) [34].

4.5 Event Data

Event data is created by the relationship between external data and time-series data. The primary purpose of this type of event data is to differentiate important events from numerous events. Actions, intervals and conditions are the three components of event data. The combination of the three components generates event data. Event data reflects clustered, structured, and unscheduled functions. The use of event data in this study includes data from Rhythm applications in smartphones for the identification of specific patents and sleep patterns [35].

4.6 Network Data

Network data is a physical footprint data that is commonly used in many fields. Similarly, the use of network data is the highest finding in the results of this study relative to other forms of data. Big networks like Twitter, Youtube and Facebook are producing network data. Many knowledge networks, biological networks and development networks also serve as a source of network data. Network data can be a one-to-one or one-to-many relationship between network nodes. The use of network data in the findings of this study involves most data from social media networks such as Facebook [7, 21, 36], Twitter [21, 36–41], Foursquare [21, 33, 41, 42], YouTube [42], Flickr [33, 43], Sina Weibo [31, 44] and Linkedin [45].

4.7 Linked Data

Linked data forms include web technology URLs. Computers, built-in computers and other smartphones can exchange and retrieve information semantically. Users also can read and share this type of data using the linked data. The use of related data includes data from internet browsers such as Chrome and Safari [46].

5 Discussion

Based on previous research, data from digital footprints have been used in different studies to investigate the personality and behaviour of users. Initially, personality and behavioural assessment studies used conventional tools such as paper and pen question-naires [4, 20]. Nevertheless, the fast-paced world of information and communications technology has created a modern climate and improved digital data. This provides new gaps in the study of human personality and behaviour.

Different sources of digital footprints such as organised, unstructured, geographical, time-series, event, network and linked data also provide new opportunities in exploring human personality and actions. Such digital footprints are an accurate representation of the character or activities of an individual and can be monitored by researchers. The use of various data from these digital footprints provides different measurements as it precisely tests the user profile [46], predicts user' emotions [37], determines the level of user skills [22] and others.

Nonetheless, there are still concerns in the use of digital footprint data that may affect personality and behaviour study results. These are due to the use of bias data [47], data discrimination [48], privacy [49], data accuracy [50] and data misuse [51]. Digital footprint data have also been employe to train machines that used artificial intelligence technology to make more educated and reliable decisions or actions [52, 53]. Therefore, guidelines provided by the different parties to ensure the safety of human beings and the security of society around them. This attempt to ensure the quality of science results at the same time guarantees a stable and harmonious human life.

6 Conclusion and Suggestion

Many extraneous factors need to be considered while conducting research. In general, this paper had explored the variety of types of digital footprints that can be utilities to predict psychology and human behaviour. However, the primary condition is the reliabilities and accuracy of the data must be priorities. Hence, some of the scholars discourage to use the data of digital footprint to predict human behaviour [20]. At the other hand, the use of digital footprint data has also been able to accurately assess the emotional state of a person under strain or difficulty [21]. All of these viewpoints are important as digital signatures can be used as tools to expand more complex data, broader data, bias data, and so on.

As technology progresses exponentially, human interaction rates and the use of technology will naturally increase. The use of smartphones, computers, drones or vehicles would be connected to the internet to produce data online. Both these applications will change the landscape of human life now and in the future. All researchers have to continue to explore and learn different skills, and technology mainly related to data science such as phytonology, social network analysis, graph theory, modelling, and so on. The author hoped that this thesis would contribute a great deal of visibility for future researchers to explore possibilities, opportunities, threats and constraints in work involving digital data footprints.

Acknowledgement. This study was funded by Ministry of Higher Education Malaysia (MOHE) with a grant from Fundamental Research Grant Scheme for Research Acculturation of Early Career Researchers (FRGS-RACER) SO Code 14424 and FRGS-2019 SO Code 14396. Researchers would like to express special thanks to the Research & Innovation Management Centre Universiti Utara Malaysia (RIMC UUM) for the support and assistance provided throughout this research. Finally, we thank the three anonymous reviewers for their helpful comments.

References

1. Merriam-Webster Dictionary (1828). https://www.merriam-webster.com/dictionary/psycho graphics
2. Walker, B., Albertson, C., Freeberg, R.: Psychographic Segmentation and the Health Care Consumer. TPG, Philadelphia (2014)
3. Chen, Y.J., Chen, Y.M., Hsu, Y.J., Wu, J.H.: Predicting consumers' decision-making styles by analyzing digital footprints on Facebook. Int. J. Inf. Technol. Decis. Making **18**, 601–627 (2019)

4. Lambiotte, R., Kosinski, M.: Tracking the digital footprints of personality. Proc. IEEE **102**, 1934–1939 (2014)
5. Herring, S.C., Kapidzic, S.: Teens, gender, and self-presentation in social media. In: International Encyclopedia of the Social & Behavioral Sciences, pp. 146–152 (2015)
6. Kerešteš, G., Štulhofer, A.: Adolescents' online social network use and life satisfaction: a latent growth curve modeling approach. Comput. Hum. Behav. **104**, 106187 (2019)
7. Ophir, Y., Asterhan, C.S.C., Schwarz, B.B.: The digital footprints of adolescent depression, social rejection and victimization of bullying on Facebook. Comput. Hum. Behav. **91**, 62–71 (2018)
8. Martin, F., Gezer, T., Wang, C.: Educators' perception of student digital citizenship practices. Comput. Sch. **36**(4), 238–254 (2019)
9. Tommasel, A., Rodriguez, J.M., Godoy, D.: Textual aggression detection through deep learning. In: Proceedings of the First Workshop on Trolling, Aggression and Cyberbullying, pp. 177–187 (2018)
10. Vigna, F.D., Cimino, A., Dell'Orletta, F., Petrocchi, M., Tesconi, M.: Hate me, hate me not: hate speech detection on Facebook. In: Proceedings of the First Italian Conference on Cybersecurity, pp. 86–95 (2017)
11. Byrne, E., Vessey, J.A., Pfeifer, L.: Cyberbullying and social media: information and interventions for school nurses working with victims, students, and families. J. School Nurs. **34**(1), 38–50 (2017)
12. Van Ouytsel, J., Ponnet, K., Walrave, M., d'Haenens, L.: Adolescent sexting from a social learning perspective. Telematics Inform. **34**(1), 287–298 (2017)
13. Morelli, M., Bianchi, D., Baiocco, R., Pezzuti, L., Chirumbolo, A.: Sexting behaviors and cyber pornography addiction among adolescents: the moderating role of alcohol consumption. Sex. Res. Soc. Policy **14**(2), 113–121 (2016). https://doi.org/10.1007/s13178-016-0234-0
14. Gok, T.: The effects of social networking sites on students' studying and habits. Int. J. Res. Educ. Sci. (IJRES) **2**(1), 85–93 (2016)
15. Bányai, F., Zsila, Á., Király, O., Maraz, A., Elekes, Z., Griffiths, M.D., Demetrovics, Z.: Problematic social media use: results from a large-scale nationally representative adolescent sample. PLoS ONE **12**(1), e0169839 (2017)
16. Fardouly, J., Magson, N.R., Johnco, C.J., Oar, E.L., Rapee, R.M.: Parental control of the time preadolescents spend on social media: links with preadolescents' social media appearance comparisons and mental health. J. Youth Adolesc. **47**(7), 1456–1468 (2018). https://doi.org/10.1007/s10964-018-0870-1
17. Sierra-Correa, P.C., Cantera Kintz, J.R.: Ecosystem-based adaptation for improving coastal planning for sea-level rise: a systematic review for mangrove coasts. Mar. Policy, **51**, 385–393 (2015)
18. Wook, T.S.M., Mohamed, H., Noor, S.F.M., Muda, Z., Zairon, I.Y.: Awareness of digital footprints management in the new media amongst youth. Malays. J. Commun. **35**(3), 407–421 (2019)
19. Phillips, J.G., Sargeant, J., Ogeil, R.P., Chow, Y.-W., Blaszczynski, A.: Self-reported gambling problems and digital traces. Cyberpsychol. Behav. Soc. Network. **17**(12), 742–748 (2014)
20. Rafaeli, A., Ashtar, S., Altman, D. Digital traces: new data, resources, and tools for psychological-science research. Curr. Dir. Psychol. Sci. 096372141986141 (2019)
21. Vianna, D., Kalokyri, V., Borgida, A., Marian, A., Nguyen, T.: Searching heterogeneous personal digital traces. Proc. Assoc. Inf. Sci. Technol. **56**(1), 276–285 (2019)
22. Zhang, H.Z., Xie, C., Nourian, S.: Are their designs iterative or fixated? Investigating design patterns from student digital footprints in computer-aided design software. Int. J. Technol. Des. Educ. **28**(3), 819–841 (2017). https://doi.org/10.1007/s10798-017-9408-1
23. Ndumbaro, F.: Understanding user-system interactions: an analysis of OPAC users' digital footprints. Inf. Dev. **34**(3), 297–308 (2017)

24. Songsom, N., Nilsook, P., Wannapiroon, P.: The synthesis of the student relationship management system using the Internet of Things to collect the digital footprint for higher education institutions. Int. J. Online Biomed. Eng. (iJOE) **15**, 99 (2019)

25. Harjumaa, M., Saraniemi, S., Pekkarinen, S., Lappi, M., Similä, H., Isomursu, M.: Feasibility of digital footprint data for health analytics and services: an explorative pilot study. BMC Med. Inform. Decis. Making **16**(1) (2016)

26. Kim, C., Gupta, R., Shah, A., Madill, E., Prabhu, A.V., Agarwal, N.: Digital footprint of neurological surgeons. World Neurosurg. **113**, e172–e178 (2018)

27. Buchanan, R., Southgate, E., Smith, S.P., Murray, T., Noble, B.: Post no photos, leave no trace: children's digital footprint management strategies. E-Learn. Digit. Media **14**(5), 275–290 (2017)

28. Lee, M.-H., Cha, S., Nam, T.-J.: Impact of digital traces on the appreciation of movie contents. Digit. Creativity **26**(3–4), 287–303 (2015)

29. Liu, L., Andris, C., Ratti, C.: Uncovering cabdrivers' behavior patterns from their digital traces. Comput. Environ. Urban Syst. **34**(6), 541–548 (2010)

30. Chen, C., Zhang, D., Guo, B., Ma, X., Pan, G., Wu, Z.: TripPlanner: personalized trip planning leveraging heterogeneous crowdsourced digital footprints. IEEE Trans. Intell. Transp. Syst. **16**(3), 1259–1273 (2015)

31. Yi, J., Du, Y., Liang, F., Tu, W., Qi, W., Ge, Y.: Mapping human's digital footprints on the Tibetan Plateau from multi-source geospatial big data. Sci. Total Environ. **711**, 134540 (2019)

32. Traunmueller, M.W., Johnson, N., Malik, A., Kontokosta, C.E.: Digital footprints: using WiFi probe and locational data to analyze human mobility trajectories in cities. Computers, Environment and Urban Systems (2018)

33. Chen, C., et al.: MA-SSR: a memetic algorithm for skyline scenic routes planning leveraging heterogeneous user-generated digital footprints. IEEE Trans. Veh. Technol. **66**(7), 5723–5736 (2017)

34. Zinman, O., Lerner, B.: Utilizing digital traces of mobile phones for understanding social dynamics in urban areas. Pers. Ubiquit. Comput. **24**(4), 535–549 (2019). https://doi.org/10. 1007/s00779-019-01318-w

35. Lin, Y.H., Wong, B.Y., Pan, Y.C., Chiu, Y.C., Lee, Y.H.: Validation of the mobile app-recorded circadian rhythm by a digital footprint. JMIR Mhealth Uhealth **7**(5), e13421 (2019)

36. Garcia, D., Tessone, C.J., Mavrodiev, P., Perony, N.: The digital traces of bubbles: feedback cycles between socio-economic signals in the Bitcoin economy. J. R. Soc. Interface **11**(99), 20140623 (2014)

37. Garcia, D., Rimé, B.: Collective emotions and social resilience in the digital traces after a terrorist attack. Psychol. Sci. **30**, 617–628 (2019)

38. Obschonka, M., Fisch, C., Boyd, R.: Using digital footprints in entrepreneurship research: a twitter-based personality analysis of superstar entrepreneurs and managers. J. Bus. Ventur. Insights **8**, 13–23 (2017)

39. Liu, X., Huang, Q., Gao, S.: Exploring the uncertainty of activity zone detection using digital footprints with multi-scaled DBSCAN. Int. J. Geogr. Inf. Sci. **33**, 1196–1223 (2019)

40. Chen, B., Seo, D.-C., Lin, H.-C., Crandall, D.: Framework for estimating sleep timing from digital footprints. BMJ Innov. **4**(4), 172–177 (2018)

41. Salas-Olmedo, M.H., Moya-Gómez, B., García-Palomares, J.C., Gutiérrez, J.: Tourists' digital footprint in cities: comparing Big Data sources. Tour. Manag. **66**, 13–25 (2018)

42. Yang, D., Zhang, D., Yu, Z., Yu, Z., Zeghlache, D.: SESAME: mining user digital footprints for finegrained preference-aware social media search. ACM Trans. Internet Technol. **14**(4), 1–24 (2014)

43. Preis, T., Moat, H.S., Bishop, S.R., Treleaven, P., Stanley, H.E.: Quantifying the digital traces of Hurricane Sandy on Flickr. Sci. Rep. **3**(1), 1–3 (2013)

44. Luo, J., Pan, X., Zhu, X.: Identifying digital traces for business marketing through topic probabilistic model. Technol. Anal. Strateg. Manage. **27**(10), 1176–1192 (2015)
45. Arya, V., Sethi, D., Paul, J.: Does digital footprint act as a digital asset? – Enhancing brand experience through remarketing. Int. J. Inf. Manage. **4**, 142–156 (2019)
46. Bach, R.L., et al.: Predicting voting behavior using digital trace data. Soc. Sci. Comput. Rev. 1–22 (2019)
47. Marda, V.: Artificial intelligence policy in India: a framework for engaging the limits of data-driven decision-making. Philos. Trans. Roy. Soc. A Math. Phys. Eng. Sci. **376**(2133), 20180087 (2018)
48. Favaretto, M., De Clercq, E., Elger, B.S.: Big Data and discrimination: perils, promises and solutions. A systematic review. J. Big Data **6**, 12 (2019)
49. Veale, M., Kleek, M.V., Binns, R.: Fairness and accountability design needs for algorithmic support in high-stakes public sector decision-making. In: Proceedings of the 2018 CHI Conference on Human Factors in Computing Systems, Paper No 440 (2018)
50. Kroll, J.A.: The fallacy of inscrutability. Philos. Trans. Roy. Soc. A Math. Phys. Eng. Sci. **376**(2133), 1–14 (2018). https://doi.org/10.1098/rsta.2018.0084
51. Kesan, J.P., Hayes, C.M.: Liability for data injuries. Univ. Ill. Law Rev. **2019**(1), 295–363 (2018)
52. Helbing, D.: Societal, economic, ethical and legal challenges of the digital revolution: from big data to deep learning, artificial intelligence, and manipulative technologies. In: Helbing, D. (ed.) Towards Digital Enlightenment. Essays on the Dark and Light Sides of the Digital Revolution, pp. 47–72. Springer, Cham (2019)
53. Nawi, A.: Early exploration towards issues and impact the use of artificial intelligence technology towards human beings. Asian J. Civiliz. Stud. **1**(4), 24–33 (2019)

Profiling Bot Accounts Mentioning COVID-19 Publications on Twitter

Yingxin Estella Ye[(⊠)] and Jin-Cheon Na

Wee Kim Wee School of Communication and Information, Nanyang Technological University,
31 Nanyang Link, Singapore 637718, Singapore
yingxin001@e.ntu.edu.sg, tjcna@ntu.edu.sg

Abstract. This paper presents preliminary findings regarding automated bots mentioning scientific papers about COVID-19 publications on Twitter. A quantitative approach was adopted to characterize social and posting patterns of bots, in contrast to other users, in Twitter scholarly communication. Our findings indicate that bots play a prominent role in research dissemination and discussion on the social web. We observed 0.45% explicit bots in our sample, producing 2.9% of tweets. The results implicate that bots tweeted differently from non-bot accounts in terms of the volume and frequency of tweeting, the way handling the content of tweets, as well as preferences in article selection. In the meanwhile, their behavioral patterns may not be the same as Twitter bots in another context. This study contributes to the literature by enriching the understanding of automated accounts in the process of scholarly communication and demonstrating the potentials of bot-related studies in altmetrics research.

Keywords: Twitter · Bot · Network analysis · Altmetrics research

1 Introduction

The rapid development of technology has expanded the concept of scholarly communication beyond academic publishing to include informal and interactive research dissemination and discussion on the social web [1]. In the meanwhile, altmetrics, metrics that capture the attention a scholarly work received on online platforms, have emerged as a supplement to traditional bibliometrics in assessing the broader impact of research [2].

As one of the primary social media platforms used among scientists and researchers [3], Twitter is a major source of altmetrics. Researchers have recognized the potential for tracing fast-paced conversations about academic literature [4]. However, because of vulnerability of Twitter to bot activities, the validity of Twitter metric in accessing research impacts has been questioned by academic communities [5]. Even bots have been prevalently observed in current studies about Twitter metrics [7, 8, 10], bots in the context of scholarly communication are still understudied.

To examine the implications of bot accounts, it is critical to understand their behavioral patterns in the process of research dissemination or scholarly communication. Building upon existing scholarship, this paper serves as a preliminary study to profile

© Springer Nature Switzerland AG 2020
E. Ishita et al. (Eds.): ICADL 2020, LNCS 12504, pp. 297–306, 2020.
https://doi.org/10.1007/978-3-030-64452-9_27

bot accounts tweeting academic scientific publications on Twitter. Taking recent COVID-19 publications as a case study, it aims to observe how bots, as well as other users, react to the latest scientific literature of trending topics on Twitter. First, we present a review of related works, followed by an exploratory analysis of social and posting patterns of bots in contrast to non-bot accounts. Next, we make further comparisons between bots and non-bot accounts by characterizing articles that they tweeted. In the concluding section, we discuss directions for future research based on our preliminary findings.

2   Related Works

Bot activities are evident in scholarly communication on Twitter. Existing studies found that a considerable proportion of the most productive users tweeting scientific publications and generating a large volume of tweets are automated accounts [6]. For instance, Robinson-Garcia *et al.* reported that half of the top 25 Twitter users mentioning microbiology articles were bots, contributing to 4% of tweets in their sample [7]. While in Haustein's study, 15 out of the top 19 users citing academic articles across disciplines were self-identified bot accounts, each of which posted over 25,000 tweets on average [8]. Another study, examining a large scale of altimetric data, spotted that the discrepancy between the number of posts and the number of unique users can reach over 30,000, and the researcher attributed this to excessive bot activities [10].

It is commonly believed that bots and human accounts behave differently. It was observed in Haustein's study [8] that bots, specifically self-identified bots, are more engaged in tweeting scientific literature. It can be reflected by the higher volume and frequency of tweeting activities. Additionally, they may have a shorter tweet span, the number of days between the first and the last tweet. The researcher added that bots tweeting scholarly work may not share similar patterns as other Twitter bots, e.g., social bots in a generic context.

The issue of bots, specifically the extent of bots, have heavily caught attention from researchers. However, only a few studies have attempted to address the implications of bots on Twitter metrics and online academic communication. For instance, studying Twitter users with "arXiv" in their user names, handles, and Twitter bio, researchers found that over 80% accounts in their sample were automated platform feeds that push publication updates from arXiv, and topics feeds, i.e. automated feeds of publications relevant to a certain topic [9]. Due to the homogeneous nature of bot accounts, Haustein and her colleagues suggested that automated tweets, regardless of being good bots or bad bots, may not imply impact but rather reflect diffusion [11]. Adopting a network approach, Aljohani et al. [12] have demonstrated the significant role of bots in affecting the spread of the desired content in the altmetrics Twitter social network (ATSN). For example, bots were observed to be extensively used for research dissemination.

It was also identified that the degree distribution and community size distribution of an ATSN with a prevalent presence of bots tend to follow a power-law distribution [12].

There still lacks sufficient discussion on whether we should and how we can tackle the issue of bots to enhance the validity of Twitter metrics as alternative research impact indicators, such as identifying or eliminating bot accounts and bot-generated content. To fill this research gap and to facilitate the discussion, it is important to understand the role of bots in the process of scholarly communication on Twitter. To achieve this, a very first step could be characterizing the behavioral patterns of bot accounts in relevant activities.

3 Method

3.1 Data Collection

First, reusing the query string constructed by Kousha and Thelwall [13], COVID-19 publications were retrieved from Scopus. To trace Twitter users' reactions to the latest publications, we narrowed down the search results to English-written journal articles published in May 2020. To examine the characteristics of articles, articles without source title information were omitted. DOIs of articles were used to extract Twitter mentions from Altemtric.com. As our ultimate plan was to analyze the complete Twitter social networks at the article level, articles with less than 10 or over 100,000 Twitter mentions were excluded. We cross-checked Scopus, Altmetric.com, and Crossref API to retrieve the date when the article was first made available. 417 articles, from a variety of research areas (health Sciences: 69.96%, life sciences: 17.08%, social sciences & humanities: 5.14%, physical sciences: 4.94%, multidisciplinary: 2.88%), were retrieved. According to the statistics provided by Altmetric.com, these articles have been mentioned by 153,098 tweets and 100,620 unique users as of the date of data collection, June 22, 2020.

Utilizing Twitter API, we further collected information about tweets retrieved and Twitter users. As some tweets and user accounts are not active anymore, 89,258 user profiles and 139,298 unique tweets with user profiles available were retrieved from Twitter API. 131 tweets have mentioned multiple articles. Analysis in this paper was based on this matched set of data.

3.2 Identifying Explicit Bot Accounts

Twitter bots are software designed to autonomously perform Twitter activities, such as tweeting, retweeting, following, and replying via Twitter API without human judgment and selection [13, 14]. In this preliminary study, only explicit bots, including 1) self-identified bots and possible 2) spambots, were covered.

This section presents the method used to distinguish bot accounts from the collected data. First, the method introduced in Haustein's study [8] was adopted to identify self-identified bots by searching a pre-defined set of keywords from users' user names, handles, and bio on Twitter. We made minor changes to the original query string to include stricter criteria (see below).

("bot" | "robot" | "tweetbot" | "tweet bot" | "twitterbot" | "tweeter bot" | "a *robot")
& NOT ("bot hate" | "bot sniper" | "block *bot" | "not a *bot" | "nor a *bot" |
"neither a *bot"| "like a *bot" | "sometimes*bot" | "think i am a bot" | "roboti*"))
| ("automat*" & ("alert" | "update" | "feed" | "link" | "news" | "stream" | "script" |
"tweet") & NOT ("no* auto")) | (("article" | "literature" | "paper" | "peer-review*" |
"preprint" | "publications" | "pubmed" | "arxiv" | "biorxiv" | "medrxiv") & ("alert"
| "update" | "feed" | "links" | "stream")) & NOT ("editor" | "journalist" | "official"

| "feeding" | "links between")) | (("created by" | "developed by" | "programmed") & ("share" | "daily" | "latest" | "news" | "podcast")) | ("aggregator" | "news feed" | "datafeed" | "new submissions" | "latest publications" | "new publication" | "daily updates")

Second, extracting the value of the "source" field, the device or application from which a tweet was posted, of tweet objects from Twitter API, we identified accounts that employ bot clients using the query string below. We did not consider third-party social media marketing or management applications, such as Tweetdeck, IFTTT, and Hootsuite as bot clients as there might involve human selection of content.

("bot" & NOT "tweetbot for *" & NOT "roboti*") | ("paper" & NOT ("paper.li" | "instapaper")) | "retweet" | "update" | "alert" | "auto" | "curat*" | "aggregat*" | "combinator" | "feed" | "arxiv" | "biorxiv" | "medrxiv" | "journal" | "article" | "preprint" | "RT"

Next, we extracted a list of potential spambots by identifying accounts that have posted the same content more than three times and above.

Lastly, we did a manual check on profiles of identified bot accounts and removed selections that were explicitly wrong, e.g., "bot" as a part of the real name of the user or other word combinations not covered in the query string such as "bot killer", "blocked by bot", "not a creeper or a robot", etc.

As a result, 400 explicit bot accounts were identified, accounted for 0.45% of users in our dataset. It is worth highlighting that these accounts have contributed to around 2.9% of all selected tweets citing COVID-19 publications on Twitter. To facilitate the comparison of patterns of explicit between bot accounts (bots) and non-explicit bot accounts (non-bots), we randomly selected 400 accounts from the unclassified users. Similarly, we read through their user description to ensure that no explicit bot was included.

A major limitation of our method is that we were not able to measure the performance of the classification. The proportion of bot accounts was underestimated. On the one hand, only explicit bots were covered while those less explicit or more intelligent bots remain unclassified. On the other hand, as the set of predefined keywords are not exhaustive, the above-mentioned bot identification strategy may not be ideal regarding the rate of recall. It is also possible that cyborgs, bot-assisted humans or human-assisted bots, may fall under the category of bot accounts if they presented a high level of automation in the sample data. However, taking basic manual validation as a measure to enhance the precision, our study can still serve its purpose, as a preliminary study, to capture some patterns of bot accounts in Twitter scholarly communication.

3.3 Data Analysis

The data analysis can be divided into two parts. First, social and tweeting patterns of bots were studied in contrast to non-bots in our sample. Second, we characterized articles tweeted by both groups. Statistical analysis, such as Mann-Whitney U tests and chi-squared tests, was performed to compare the difference between bots and non-bots using SciPy in Python.

As suggested in existing scholarship, social patterns of a Twitter user can be generalized from information such as the number of followers and the number of friends, whereas tweeting patterns can be examined from aspects such as sources of contents, mediums of actions, patterns of contents (e.g., the use of hashtags and user mentions in tweets), as well as the timing (e.g., the frequency of tweets or retweets) [15–18]. Drawing upon these studies, we compiled a list of features commonly used in Twitter bot detection studies. Table 1 presents features that were tested in this study.

Table 1. Selected features for bots and non-bots comparison

Type	Features
User feature	Account age (days), Length of user bio (with URLs removed), Number of statuses, Favorites-statuses ratio, Followers-friends ratio, Number of listed
Tweet feature	Number of tweets, Average number of tweets per article, Average responding time to publications, Average number of tweets per day, Retweet-tweet ratio, Number of hashtags per tweet, Number of @mentions per tweet

To better understand bot accounts' tweeting patterns when mentioning scientific publications on Twitter, we also made efforts to characterize articles tweeted by bots and non-bots. Characteristics we analyzed include the open access status of the article, the impact of the source title, and their subject areas.

4   Results

As our sample data is not normally distributed, Mann-Whitney U tests were performed. Figure 1 shows the comparison between bots and non-bots regarding their user features. It is consistent with existing studies that bots have generated a higher volume of tweet statuses ($Mdn = 18,127$) than non-bot accounts ($Mdn = 7,996.5$), $U = 64,550, p < .01$. Our results have also indicated the difference of favourite-statuses ratios between bots ($Mdn = .38$) and non-bots ($Mdn = .91$), $U = 55691, p < .01$ [18]. It is noteworthy that without considering the popularity of the account, bots in our sample are younger in age ($Mdn = 1,785.5$) than non-bots ($Mdn = 2,378$), $U = 60,770, p < .01$. 13.25% of the selected bot accounts were born in 2020, out of which 18 accounts were dedicated to aggregate or share updates and related publications about COVID-19 according to their user profiles. Examples include "a bot sharing info from the CDC about #COVID19", "automatically post papers about the coronavirus...", "a bot tweeting people's #mentalhealth during #COVID", etc. In contrast, only 4.75% of non-bots were created in 2020. However, it is interesting to observe that bots have a higher ratio of followers to friends ($Mdn = .85$) than non-bots ($Mdn = .69$), $U = 74,055, p < .05$. This implicates the possibility of bots being influential in Twitter scholarly communication, serving the function of information dissemination.

As shown in Fig. 2, it is evident that bots tweeted academic articles more often than non-bots. This is consistent with the observations in existing scholarship [8]. First, bots

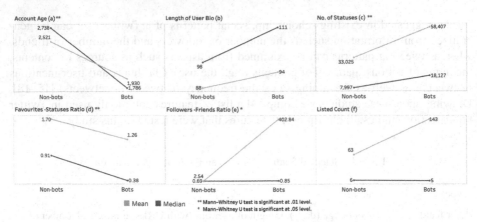

Fig. 1. Users feature: bots vs. non-bots

generated a larger tweet volume mentioning COVID-19 publications ($Mdn = 4$) than non-bots ($Mdn = 1$), $U = 35{,}594.5$, $p < .01$. The number of tweets generated by the sampled bot accounts can be high as 193, while the maximum among non-bots was 21. Moreover, bots tended to mention the same article more ($Mdn = 1.33$) than non-bots ($Mdn = 1.00$, $U = 42016.5$, $p < .01$. Users' average responding time to the newly published articles has reflected the inaccuracy of articles' date of availability as negative values were observed. To tackle this, for each article, we assigned dense rank to each user based on the time when they first reacted to the article and compared their average ranking. As a result, we found that non-bots have been responding to the articles faster than bots on average as they were ranked higher ($Mdn = 3$) than bots ($Mdn = 4$), $U = 64{,}980.5$, $p < .01$. Possible reasons include 1) bots are running on predefined schedules and not all of them were designed to catch up with the published articles promptly.

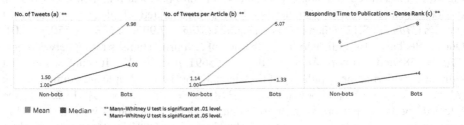

Fig. 2. Tweets mentioning COVID-19 publications

Regarding the patterns of tweets shown in Fig. 3, bot accounts seemed to have used more hashtags ($Mdn = 0$) *than non-bots* ($Mdn = 0$), $U = 69{,}010$, $p < .01$. Similarly, more @mentions were added in a tweet among bots ($Mdn = 1$) than non-bots ($Mdn = 1$), $U = 72{,}056$, $p < .01$. This corresponds to a finding in existing studies that spam tweets may use slightly higher number of mentions and hashtags [19]. The top 10 hashtags most commonly used by bot-generated tweets incudes #COVID19, #SARSCoV2, #coronavirus, #covid19, #hydoxychloroquine, #COVID-19, #chloroquine, #COVID, #Covid19, and

#Covid_19. Similarly, the top 10 hashtags used among non-bot accounts were also variants of COVID-19 and related medication, including #COVID19, #SARSCoV2, #covid19, #coronavirus, #Ritonavir, #Covid19, #Lopinavir, #Kaletra, #Hospitalized, and #Coronavirus.

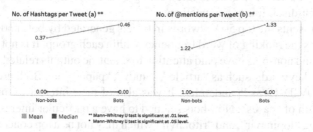

Fig. 3. Tweet features (1): bots vs. non-bots

As shown in Fig. 4, when comparing the tweeting patterns among selected accounts who posted more than 1 tweet in our sample ($N_{non-bots} = 89$, $N_{bots} = 271$), significant difference was observed in the average number of tweets per day and the retweet-tweet ratio. A bot is likely to generate more tweets ($Mdn = 1.75$) than a non-bot ($Mdn = 1.20$) on a single day, $U = 2,610.5$, $p < .01$. Surprisingly, bot accounts have a lower retweet-tweet ratio ($Mdn = .15$) than non-bots in our sample ($Mdn = .75$), $U = 2,500.5$, $p < .01$. This might be different from a Twitter bot that aggressively retweets in a generic context [14].

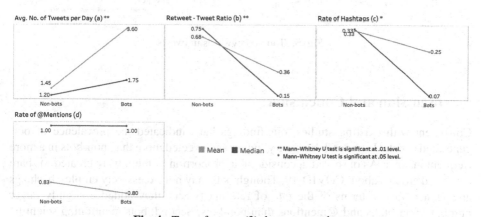

Fig. 4. Tweet features (2): bots vs. non-bots

Bots and non-bots may have different preferences when tweeting academic articles as well. For instance, bots were more likely to mention open access (OA) articles than non-bots with 96.6% and 95% of tweets mentioning OA articles respectively, $x^2 = 4.92$, $p < .05$. Though statistical significance was observed in the chi-square test when comparing the tweet distribution between bots and non-bots by SJR Quartiles, $x^2 = 11.11$, $p < .05$, they both have strongly preferred articles from high impacts journals.

On average, non-bots have over 92.5% tweets mentioning articles from Q1 journals, while this percentage among bots was also high as 90.8%. Regarding the discipline of articles tweeted, as COVID-19 is considered as a health crisis, both groups have paid great attention to articles in medical and health sciences, though non-bots have shown a higher variety of interest in articles interpreting COVID-19 from social science, public health, and multidisciplinary perspectives.

Figure 5 presents the top 50 keywords in tweets generated by bots and non-bots. The text size reflects the ranking of word frequency within each group. It is not difficult to tell that both bots and non-bots have paid attention to scientific outputs related to COIVD-19, represented by keywords, such as "article", "study", "paper", etc. Both groups may have interpreted COVID-19 as "pandemic". It was also of their interest to monitor updates about the growth of "cases". Non-bots seemed to have a particular interest in the related meditation, e.g., "lopinavir", and "ritonavir" which may not be a top concern among bots. There may also exist political bots that mention scientific articles as "trump" seems to be frequently mentioned by bot accounts in our sample.

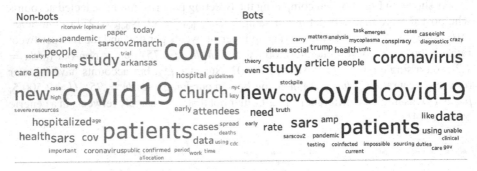

Fig. 5. Top 50 keywords in tweets

5   Discussion and Conclusion

Consistent with existing studies, our findings have indicated the prevalence of bot-generated tweets. In general, bots are younger and tweeted more than non-bots in a more frequent manner. As observed, a considerable proportion of them were created to share news and articles about COVID-19. Though bots may not excessively employ hashtags and @mentions in terms of the rate of relevant tweets, they added a slightly larger number of hashtags and @mentions than non-bots. Second, bots mentioning scientific publications tweeted differently from non-bots and bots in a generic context. For instance, bots in our sample retweeted less than non-bots and have a relatively higher followers-friends ratio. In addition, bots and non-bots seem not to share common content selection criteria though they both prefer articles from high impact journals.

To summarize, the potentials of bots in affecting the validity of Twitter metrics in assessing research should be recognized. Sharing similar features of spambots [19], bots in our sample were found to generate excessive Twitter activities mentioning academic works. Moreover, with a relatively higher followers-friends ratio and efforts in employing hashtags and @mentions, bots may have the power to affect the process of communication. Additionally, automated algorithms to select articles based on specific criteria, e.g., specific research disciplines of source titles and journal impact factors, may result in bias of Twitter metrics. However, it is encouraging to observe original tweets, likely sourcing from external platforms [9], among automated bots. In other words, bots may serve as idea starters and positively contribute to scholarly communication on the social web.

A major limitation of this study is that we did not have a manually labeled dataset, and the dataset that we used for analysis was relatively small. Other than that, without in-depth text analysis and more granular account classification, we cannot tell whether the implications of automated accounts are positive or negative. Also, as we focused on publications related to COVID-19, a trending topic on Twitter, our findings may not be applicable to publications on other topics. However, from this study, we do see the potential, as well as the necessity, of bot-related studies in the context of online scholarly communication. With data on a larger scale and more sophisticated bot detection techniques, we will be able to present more rigorous findings regarding the implications of automated bots. Attaining a comprehensive understanding of the role of bots in the process of scholarly communication will be beneficial for us to further assess Twitter metrics, and figure out possible solutions to enhance their validity as research impact indicators.

References

1. Sugimoto, C.R., Work, S., Larivière, V., Haustein, S.: Scholarly use of social media and altmetrics: a review of the literature. J. Assoc. Inf. Sci. Technol. **68**, 2037–2062 (2017). https://doi.org/10.1002/asi.23833
2. Robinson-Garcia, N., van Leeuwen, T.N., Rafols, I.: Using altmetrics for contextualised mapping of societal impact: from hits to networks. Sci. Public Policy **45**, 815–826 (2018). https://doi.org/10.1093/scipol/scy024
3. Van Noorden, R.: Online collaboration: scientists and the social network. Nature **512**, 126–129 (2014). https://doi.org/10.1038/512126a
4. Hassan, S.-U., Imran, M., Gillani, U., Aljohani, N.R., Bowman, T.D., Didegah, F.: Measuring social media activity of scientific literature: an exhaustive comparison of scopus and novel altmetrics big data. Scientometrics **113**(2), 1037–1057 (2017). https://doi.org/10.1007/s11192-017-2512-x
5. Darling, E., Shiffman, D., Côté, I., Drew, J.: The role of Twitter in the life cycle of a scientific publication. Ideas Ecol. Evol. **6** (2013). https://doi.org/10.4033/iee.2013.6.6.f
6. Robinson-Garcia, N., Costas, R., Isett, K., Melkers, J., Hicks, D.: The unbearable emptiness of tweeting—about journal articles. PLoS ONE **12**, e0183551 (2017). https://doi.org/10.1371/journal.pone.0183551
7. Robinson-Garcia, N., Arroyo-Machado, W., Torres-Salinas, D.: Mapping social media attention in Microbiology: identifying main topics and actors. FEMS Microbiol. Lett. **366** (2019). https://doi.org/10.1093/femsle/fnz075
8. Haustein, S.: Scholarly Twitter metrics. In: Glänzel, W., Moed, H.F., Schmoch, U., Thelwall, M. (eds.) Handbook of Quantitative Science and Technology Research (2018). https://arxiv.org/abs/1806.02201

9. Haustein, S., Bowman, T.D., Holmberg, K., Tsou, A., Sugimoto, C.R., Larivière, V.: Tweets as impact indicators: examining the implications of automated "bot" accounts on Twitter. J. Assoc. Inf. Sci. Technol. (2016). https://doi.org/10.1002/asi.23456

10. Yu, H.: Context of altmetrics data matters: an investigation of count type and user category. Scientometrics **111**, 267–283 (2017). https://doi.org/10.1007/s11192-017-2251-z

11. Haustein, S., Toupin, R., Alperin, J.P.: "Not sure if scientist or just Twitter bot" Or: who tweets about scholarly papers (2018). https://www.altmetric.com/blog/not-sure-if-scientist-or-just-twitter-bot-or-who-tweets-about-scholarly-papers/

12. Aljohani, N.R., Fayoumi, A., Hassan, S.-U.: Bot prediction on social networks of Twitter in altmetrics using deep graph convolutional networks. Soft. Comput. **24**(15), 11109–11120 (2020). https://doi.org/10.1007/s00500-020-04689-y

13. Kousha, K., Thelwall, M.: COVID-19 publications: database coverage, citations, readers, tweets, news, Facebook walls, Reddit posts. Quant. Sci. Stud. 1–24 (2020). https://doi.org/10.1162/qss_a_00066

14. Chu, Z., Gianvecchio, S., Wang, H., Jajodia, S.: Detecting automation of twitter accounts: are you a human, bot, or cyborg? IEEE Trans. Dependable Secur. Comput. **9**, 811–824 (2012). https://doi.org/10.1109/TDSC.2012.75

15. Kantepe, M., Ganiz, M.C.: Preprocessing framework for Twitter bot detection. In: 2017 International Conference on Computer Science and Engineering (UBMK), pp. 630–634. IEEE (2017). https://doi.org/10.1109/UBMK.2017.8093483

16. Oentaryo, R.J., Murdopo, A., Prasetyo, P.K., Lim, E.-P.: On profiling bots in social media. In: Spiro, E., Ahn, Y.-Y. (eds.) SocInfo 2016. LNCS, vol. 10046, pp. 92–109. Springer, Cham (2016). https://doi.org/10.1007/978-3-319-47880-7_6

17. Kudugunta, S., Ferrara, E.: Deep neural networks for bot detection. Inf. Sci. **467**, 312–322 (2018). https://doi.org/10.1016/j.ins.2018.08.019

18. Gilani, Z., Kochmar, E., Crowcroft, J.: Classification of Twitter accounts into automated agents and human users. In: Proceedings of the 2017 IEEE/ACM International Conference on Advances in Social Networks Analysis and Mining 2017, pp. 489-496 (2017). https://doi.org/10.1145/3110025.3110091

19. Sedhai, S., Sun, A.: HSpam14: a collection of 14 million tweets for hashtag-oriented spam research. In: Proceedings of the 38th International ACM SIGIR Conference on Research and Development in Information Retrieval, pp. 223–232 (2015). https://doi.org/10.1145/2766462.2767701

Uncovering Topics Related to COVID-19 Pandemic on Twitter

Han Zheng$^{(\boxtimes)}$, Dion Hoe-Lian Goh, Edmund Wei Jian Lee, Chei Sian Lee, and Yin-Leng Theng

Nanyang Technological University, Singapore, Singapore
{han019,ashlgoh,edmundlee,leecs,tyltheng}@ntu.edu.sg

Abstract. The World Health Organization declared COVID-19 as a pandemic on 11 March 2020 due to its rapid spread worldwide. This work-in-progress paper aims to uncover topics related to COVID-19 discussed on Twitter. Using topic modelling, we analyzed two weeks of tweets (11 March–25 March 2020) in English and found 17 latent topics, covering a broad range of issues such as health and economic impact, political and legislative responses, prevention measures, as well as disruption to individuals' daily lives. The results of this preliminary study show a helpful step to understand public communications about the virus and thus inform health practitioners to propose effective safety measures against COVID-19.

Keywords: COVID-19 · Tweets · Topic modelling

1 Introduction

The World Health Organization (WHO) declared COVID-19 as a pandemic on 11 March 2020, due to its rapid spread in many countries of the world [1]. At the time of this writing, the COVID-19 pandemic has become a major global threat to public health. It has affected more than 15 million infections and 640,000 deaths worldwide [2]. The emerging, rapidly evolving situation has already exposed multiple serious issues. For example, cities were in lockdowns and people were advised to stay at home [3]. These issues resulted in economic and social disruption. Consequently, the situation caused uncertainty and anxiety among people as they pondered on the virus and how it would affect their lives in the future.

During the COVID-19 pandemic, virus-related information also spread fast on social media. Twitter is a natural platform for the public to share information related to COVID-19, particularly in English-speaking countries. Analyzing discussions on Twitter may provide some helpful insights on how the public responds to the COVID-19 pandemic [4]. Such information might help government agencies and health professionals to target different groups and to propose effective preventive measures. Therefore, this work-in-progress paper analyses two weeks of tweets, from 11 March to 25 March 2020, in English about COVID-19 to uncover popular topics discussed among social media users.

© Springer Nature Switzerland AG 2020
E. Ishita et al. (Eds.): ICADL 2020, LNCS 12504, pp. 307–312, 2020.
https://doi.org/10.1007/978-3-030-64452-9_28

2 Method

The data used in this study were from a public Twitter dataset, which actively collected novel coronavirus-related tweets from 28 January 2020, using a list of keywords (e.g., coronavirus, Covid-19, corona, etc.) [5]. The dataset is available on GitHub and only the Tweet IDs of the collected tweets were released. We therefore used the software Hydrator to extract the detailed tweets for analysis [6]. Since we were interested in the topics emerged on Twitter when the pandemic was officially declared by the WHO, we collected two-week tweets from 11 March 2020 to 25 March 2020. There were a total of more than 15 million tweets during this period. Due to the enormous volume of data, we randomly selected 315,136 tweets (around 2% of the whole dataset) for analysis.

Data were analyzed using Jupyter Notebook for Python 3.6. First, we removed duplicate and non-English tweets in the dataset, leaving 101,181 tweets for further analysis. Next, we preprocessed the corpus of tweets by eliminating contents including usernames, "RT" (retweet) text, URL links, numbers and punctuations. We then tokenized each tweet into single words with lower case. Further, we excluded a list of commonly used words (e.g., "and," "the," "but," etc.) as well as some additional words that frequently appeared in the tweets ("coronavirus," "covid-19," "virus," etc.). We identified some n-grams in the tweets as well. An n-gram refers to a sequence of words that can form compounds to generate new meaning (e.g., "tested_positive" in our study). Finally, we lemmatized the corpus in order to reduce the inflected words into their dictionary forms.

LDA topic modelling via MALLET, a Java-based package for implementation of Gibbs sampling algorithm was employed to identify the topics discussed in the corpus [7]. This method can automatically generate topics from documents (i.e., tweets in our study) and categorizes similar documents to one or more of these topics based on the distribution of words. First, we iteratively trained a variety of topic models, ranging from 2 to 20, in order to select the optimal number of topics that can best describe the corpus. In this process, the topic coherence score was computed to measure the semantic similarity between high scoring words in each topic [8]. A higher value of coherence score indicates a better validity of the identified topics. As shown in Fig. 1, the coherence score was the highest for the model with 17 topics (0.3798). Additionally, we manually assessed the words in each topic and found that the 17-topic model was the most semantically meaningful and each topic could be reasonably interpreted. Last but not least, we labelled each of the 17 topics to reflect its focus.

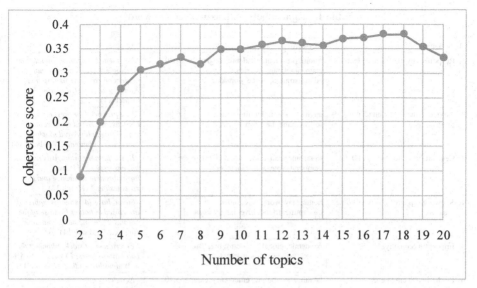

Fig. 1. Distribution of topic coherence score.

3   Results

Table 1 shows the topic names with their associated keywords, topic rate in the corpus, and examples of this topic. To label the topics, we first read the keywords generated by the topic modelling and assigned an initial name to each topic. Next, we explored the use of the keywords within the tweets to ensure correct interpretation of the topics. For example, the keywords in topic 5 were "pandemic," "global," and "economy." We labelled this topic as "impact on economy" to indicate how the COVID-19 pandemic influenced the global economy. We further checked some representative tweets that had a high probability belonging to this topic. For instance, one tweet on March 11 wrote that *"Entertainment stocks plummet on coronavirus fears; LYV down 16.5% in Wednesday trading."* Likewise, another tweet, on March 25, also wrote that *"There's a global recession/depression looming, unemployment is about to surge, while GDP collapses."* These tweets helped us to further understand the meaning of this topic and to confirm our label. In this way, we labelled all the 17 topics as shown in Table 1.

While one tweet could contain multiple topics, typically it had one predominant topic. We found that the most common predominant topic in our corpus was responses by the US president (8.79%), followed by showing support for stay-at-home measures (7.23%) and advice to the public on COVID-19 prevention (6.96%). The least common topics included news sharing about COVID-19 (4.79%), non-government support for fighting against COVID-19 (4.62%), and government support to stop COVID-19 spread (4.22%).

Table 1. Topic labels with associated keywords.

Topic name	Keywords	Rate (%)	Example
1. Responses by the US president	trump, president, pandemic, response, team, american, america, administration, office, donald	8.79	*"President Trump gives update on meeting w/GOP congressional leaders on coronavirus response & getting tested himself."* (March 11)
2. Advice to the public on COVID-19 prevention	advice, good, thing, time, read, follow, hand, face, wait, hear	6.96	*"Best practices for preventing coronavirus: Avoid close contact with sick people; Avoid touching eyes, nose and mouth..."* (March 11)
3. Legislation related to COVID-19	time, american, back, bill, real, house, democrat, vote, act, remember	6.49	*"House passes coronavirus response bill ensuring paid leave, unemployment insurance and free virus testing."* (March 14)
4. Showing support for stay-at-home measures	home, stay, work, safe, order, quarantine, friend, love, family, issue	7.23	*"Siena, Italy. My street is empty. All are closed in homes because of the corona. Then one neighbour starts singing..."* (March 14)
5. Impact on economy	pandemic, global, economy, big, bad, tweet, deal, question, panic, fear	6.10	*"Entertainment stocks plummet on coronavirus fears; LYV down 16.5% in Wednesday trading."* (March 11)
6. Public health emergency	health, state, public, emergency, care, official, test_positive, person, govt, national	5.70	*"Newsletter on #coronavirus, a serious and urgent public health issue."* (March 12)
7. Reports on lockdowns	lockdown, day, country, close, school, shut, travel, open, city, announce	5.83	*"Lockdown is needed now. They closed schools earlier, mandatory lockdown."* (March 21)
8. Impact on international relations	china, call, world, chinese, lie, medium, start, blame, wuhan, control	6.61	*"Trump's national security adviser accuses China of a two-month cover-up which stopped the world getting to grips with corona..."* (March 12)
9. Shopping for groceries and essentials	make, man, find, happen, run, guy, long, food, buy, feel	5.68	*"The grocery store has a line wrapped around the building & they only letting 5 people in at a time & most the shelves EMPTY..."* (March 17)
10. Impact on personal lives	put, life, worker, give, pay, job, risk, sick, lose, money	4.98	*"Up to 74% of all workers in America are living paycheck-to-paycheck. And almost 3/10 have no emergency savings."* (March 16)
11. Cancellation of activities and events	week, due, year, cancel, outbreak, break, student, move, march, suspend	5.46	*"Malaysians who intend to take trip within the country and visit tourist spots are advised to cancel such vacation plans..."* (March 17)
12. Mortality of COVID-19	people, die, india, kill, pm, lock, understand, dear, young, war	4.98	*"But mortality from 1957 outbreak in the USA was U-shaped, as most pandemics are, killing the very young and very old."* (March 15)
13. News sharing about COVID-19	today, news, show, watch, great, live, video, talk, end, full	4.79	*"I was sent this video from Bergamo, Italy. The military has been asked to transport dead bodies and coffins because..."* (March 19)
14. Reports of confirmed cases/statistics	case, death, Italy, report, update, number, confirm, break, day, total	5.65	*"Spain has 1,646 confirmed cases of Covid-19. 782 of these are in the Madrid region..."* (March 11)

(continued)

Table 1. (*continued*)

Topic name	Keywords	Rate (%)	Example
15. Government support to stop COVID-19 spread	spread, government, stop, outbreak, plan, continue, place, part, measure, epidemic	4.22	*"Following the spread of #COVID19, each government has been forced to take urgent measures by declaring…"* (March 20)
16. Non-government support for fighting against COVID-19	support, time, free, important, business, share, fight, give, check, provide	4.62	*"A total of 1.8 million face masks and 100,000 #coronavirus test kits donated by Jack Ma Foundation and Alibaba Foundation."* (March 12)
17. Medical resources for COVID-19	symptom, medical, patient, test, hospital, doctor, testing, mask, positive, disease	5.92	*"TRs 15,000 crore allotted for #Coronavirus testing facilities, PPEs, ICUs, Ventilators and training medical workers…"* (March 24)

4 Discussion

In this study, we present a first step in understanding topics related to COVID-19 on Twitter. Using LDA topic modelling, we uncovered seventeen diverse topics. Our results revealed what had been discussed in the public since the declaration of COVID-19 as a pandemic.

We found that several topics reflected the impact of COVIID-19 on various aspects, such as economy, international relations, and personal lives. These topics demonstrated that people concerned much about the negative consequences of coronavirus and they tended to obtain and disseminate such information on social media. For example, there were multiple discussions on the origin of coronavirus. On 17 March 2020, the US president labelled the pandemic as a "Chinese virus." The tensions between the US and Chinese officials further deteriorated, which triggered racial prejudice on social media. In fact, we found that a large portion of tweets related to the topic "impact on international relations" described the criticism on Chinese people. For example, one tweet on March 11 said that *"The virus is literally from Wuhan. China lied about it…"* Thus, global health emergency such as COVID-19 pandemic is also a manifestation of a societal illness. The content on Twitter might trigger racist or discriminating behavior towards Chinese or Asian citizens who live in America [9]. As such, government agencies need to take necessary measures to prevent such racism during this period.

Also, we found some topics (e.g., topic 2, 15, and 16) were related to how the public combated the virus. These topics suggest that a portion of tweets were intended to disseminate knowledge such as preventive measures in the public. For example, since the outbreak of COVID-19, the WHO posted a large number of tweets to educate the public about this novel virus [10]. It indicates that Twitter played a powerful role in public health education during a pandemic.

From a public health perspective, understanding the topics discussed on Twitter during the pandemic can help to identify individuals' information needs. Governmental organizations and medical professionals can target segments of the population based on types of communication on social media. For example, they could devise autonomous tools that identify users who are negatively affected by COVID-19 and connect them with relevant agencies so that follow-up actions to check on the well-being can be conducted.

Tailoring automatic responses based on topics of tweets would redirect the discussion to useful and reliable information [11].

This study has some limitations. First, due to the large size of dataset, we only selected a small sample of two-week tweets in our analysis, which may introduce some selection bias. Future studies may analyze more tweets to identify if there are additional emergent topics as the COVID-19 pandemic progresses over time. Second, we only analyzed English tweets in this study. Results of this study could not reflect the comprehensive picture of discussions on Twitter. Future research would benefit from taking tweets in other languages into account in the analysis.

In our future work, we plan to investigate how the topics identified by LDA topic modelling could predict individuals' information sharing behavior on Twitter. In addition, we are also planning to examine how other factors such as the richness of tweet content, tweet sentiment, and influence of Twitter users can contribute to tweets sharing behavior. Specifically, negative binomial regression will be employed to identify the potential predictors of information sharing on Twitter during the pandemic.

References

1. World Health Organization: Rolling updates on a coronavirus disease (COVID-19) (2020). https://www.who.int/%0Demergencies/diseases/novel-coronavirus-2019/events-as-they-happen. Accessed 27 July 2020
2. World Health Organization: WHO Coronavirus Disease (COVID-19) Dashboard (2020). https://covid19.who.int/?gclid=CjwKCAjw9vn4BRBaEiwAh0muDM7M4UppMHY1C6C 8Vnu_UW5EeNLPBRlgKwU3IAbK3Dp4OY3gaaN_QhoC4JAQAvD_BwE. Accessed 27 July 2020
3. Anderson, M., Vogels, E.A.: Americans turn to technology during COVID-19 outbreak, say an outage would be a problem. Pew Research Center (2020). https://www.pewresearch.org/fact-tank/2020/03/31/americans-turn-to-technology-during-covid-19-outbreak-say-an-out age-would-be-a-problem/
4. Thelwall, M., Thelwall, S.: Covid-19 tweeting in English: Gender differences. arXiv Preprint arXiv:2003.11090 (2020)
5. Chen, E., Lerman, K., Ferrara, E.: Tracking social media discourse about the COVID-19 pandemic: development of a public coronavirus Twitter data set. JMIR Public Heal. Surveill. 6(2), e19273 (2020)
6. Summers, E.: DocNow hydrator for tweets. GitHub Repository (2017). https://github.com/DocNow/hydrator. Accessed 24 July 2020
7. McCallum, A.K.: MALLET: A Machine Learning for Language Toolkit (2002)
8. Newman, D., Noh, Y., Talley, E., Karimi, S., Baldwin, T.: Evaluating topic models for digital libraries. In: Proceedings of the 10th Annual Joint Conference on Digital Libraries, pp. 215–224 (2010)
9. Rich, M.: As Coronavirus Spreads, So Does Anti-Chinese Sentiment. New York Times (2020). https://www.nytimes.com/2020/01/30/world/asia/coronavirus-chinese-racism.html. Accessed 24 July 2020
10. World Health Organization: World Health Organization Twitter Account (2020). https://twitter.com/WHO?ref_src=twsrc%5Egoogle%7Ctwcamp%5Eserp%7Ctwgr%5Eauthor. Accessed 24 July 2020
11. Medford, R.J., Saleh, S.N., Sumarsono, A., Perl, T.M., Lehmann, C.U.: An 'Infodemic': leveraging high-volume Twitter data to understand early public sentiment for the COVID-19 outbreak. In Open Forum Infectious Diseases (2020)

Classification in the LdoD Archive: A Crowdsourcing and Gamification Approach

Gonçalo Montalvão Marques[1], António Rito Silva[1(✉)] (iD),
and Manuel Portela[2] (iD)

[1] ESW - INESC-ID, Instituto Superior Técnico, University of Lisbon,
Lisbon, Portugal
{goncalo.m.marques,rito.silva}@tecnico.ulisboa.pt
[2] CLP-Centre for Portuguese Literature, University of Coimbra, Coimbra, Portugal
mportela@fl.uc.pt

Abstract. This article presents a solution developed on top of the *LdoD Archive* for the classification of fragments in the context of a virtual edition, through the use of a serious game strategy. Participants select a classification for a fragment after following a series of steps that require them to propose tags for fragments and then vote on other participants' tags. The goal of the game is twofold: it can be used as a crowdsourced tool to classify texts from the *Book of Disquiet*, in the context of a virtual edition, and it functions as a collaborative learning tool for the reading and analysis of texts from the *Book of Disquiet*.

Keywords. Digital humanities · Gamification · Crowdsourcing · Digital Archive

1 Introduction

The emergence of Web platforms and sites resulted in the surge of crowdsourcing [6], making it both a business alternative as well as useful option in Galleries, Libraries, Archives and Museums (GLAM's) industry [2]. Geiger and Shader [3] describe four archetypes of crowdsourcing systems: (1) crowdprocessing, where contributions are homogeneous and the value results from each individual contribution, for instance, in the classification of galaxies; (2) crowdrating, in which homogeneous contributions are used to generate a value resulting from the combination of the contributions, for instance, collective assessment of restaurants; (3) crowdsolving, where heterogeneous contributions are individually valued, for instance, suggesting ideas of solutions for a problem; and (4) crowdcreation, where heterogeneous contributions are integrated to provide a solution, for instance, *Wikipedia*. These concepts are important for the conceptualization of our game.

Besides the surge of crowdsourcing, another concept which has received increased attention is gamification, which is the use of game design features

© Springer Nature Switzerland AG 2020
E. Ishita et al. (Eds.): ICADL 2020, LNCS 12504, pp. 313–319, 2020.
https://doi.org/10.1007/978-3-030-64452-9_29

to motivate the participation of people in no-game activities. Despite the fact that the term was introduced in the 2000s, it is only after 2010 [5] that we see a significant growth in the use of the concept. Furthermore, gamification techniques have been applied to crowdsourcing projects to foster the participation of volunteers [8]. To foster the participation in the crowdsourcing systems, projects sometimes resort to gamification techniques. Gamification can then be defined as the use of game design elements in non-game contexts [1]. According to a recent literature review [8] on gamified crowdsourcing systems for homogeneous activities, it is generally recommended that crowdprocessing and crowdrating use simple game elements, such as scoring and leaderboards, since rich game designs can be redundant in such contexts.

Some interesting examples of the application of gamification techniques in Digital Humanities can be found in the gamification of libraries [7] where, for instance, users gain points and badges by engaging with the library such as visiting, checking a book and other interactions.

Inspired by previous work on gamified crowdsourcing for classification [4, 11], in this article we describe the design of a crowdsourcing activity integrated with gamification techniques within the context of a Digital Humanities project, applied to Fernando Pessoa's *Book of Disquiet*, which is implemented as a digital archive [9,10]. The tool is build on top of the *LdoD Archive* for the classification of fragments from the *Book of Disquiet*.

In the next Section we describe the game mechanisms and their rationale. Section 3 presents and discusses the results, concluding the paper.

2   The LdoD Classification Game

The *LdoD Classification Game* is a game that aims to use the *Archive*'s virtual editions, and its ability to classify and categorize fragments, as a means to create crowdsourced tagged virtual editions in a fun and entertaining way. An *LdoD Classification Game* is an online, real-time and synchronous environment, where several users collaborate with the goal of categorizing a fragment of a virtual edition, resulting in the enrichment of the virtual edition with new community categories, made in a collaborative and interactive way.

The game follows a mix of two different crowdsourcing processes. It consists of a crowdcreating process whose goal is to create artifacts based on a diversity of heterogeneous contributions, and in a crowdrating process in which the wisdom of crowds is harnessed to filter the artefacts into one, such that a synthesis can be obtained. How do those two processes relate to the game itself? The game consists of three different rounds: one in which each user individually suggests tags for a fragment's paragraph (crowdcreating); another round in which the player sees the suggestions of the other participants for that paragraph and can choose between maintaining his or her own suggestion or changing the tag by choosing another suggestion (crowdrating); and, finally, a more collaborative round, in which all users see winner tags for each one of the paragraphs and, as group, vote on the best tag for the fragment as a whole (crowdrating).

A game can also be created in two different ways: it can be created by the *LdoD Archive* administrators or it can be custom-created by registered users. The former is a game created by the *LdoD Archive* and abstracts all of the configurations necessary to create games. Currently, there is a new game available every 15 min in which any registered *LdoD Archive* user can participate in the classification of a fragment randomly selected from the set of fragments of a virtual edition. Every day a new set of 96 games are generated to be played in the following day.

On the other hand, a custom game consists of a personalized environment that can be directly related to a teacher-student scenario or some other group interaction, for instance. It allows the registered user to define a set of configuration parameters: (a) choose the virtual edition within which the game will be played; (b) decide which fragment will be classified in the game; (c) define who are the possible game participants, whether any registered user can participate or only the virtual edition editors, and (d) define the day and time the game is going to take place. Note that in the current version of the game the classification is based on a taxonomy with an open vocabulary, which means that the participants are not restricted to a set of categories to use when tagging the paragraphs.

2.1 Game Mechanics

The game is initiated in a new console, which is opened from the main site, accessible only to the registered users of the *LdoD Archive*. As expected the users will have to log in on the game website in order to participate. The game platform has an *About* section where users will have the opportunity to read about the game rules, objectives and additional information about the game.

As mentioned above, the game is split into three rounds: the first (crowd-creating) and second (crowdrating) rounds are applied to each paragraph of the fragment, and the third (crowdrating) round is applied to the fragment as a whole.

The fragment used in the game is split into paragraphs and the time available for each tagging round depends on the paragraph's size, determined when the game switches to the next paragraph. Finally, in the third round, which begins after the final paragraph is tagged, the participants are invited to vote on a tag for the whole fragment.

Round One: Individually Submitting Tags. In this round, the participants' goal is to submit a tag for each paragraph of the fragment. The user will see a paragraph of the fragment placed at the centre of the screen and, immediately below, a category submission area. In the bottom area of the webpage, the user can see a progress bar showing visually how many paragraphs are still missing. At the top of the screen, in the centre, the user has a steps interface showing their current round and which round follows next. Above that, and still in the centre area, they can see the amount of time remaining in the current round (note that the time varies according to the size of the text). At the top left, users can see the number of people participating online. Summarizing, the player must, in the given time, read the text carefully, think about it, and submit one tag they believe is appropriate. The allowed input is equal to the input available in the *LdoD Archive* for a taxonomy category, which is any string above one character. The time and game context in which a tag is suggested also has impact on the calculation of scores. Let us consider that player A suggests a particular tag and, in the same round, a player B submits ten seconds later this same tag. Player A is considered the author of the tag and player B is a co-author or voter of the tag submitted by player A. This is important for the players' scoring, because player A will get more points than player B, as is described next.

Round Two: Choosing a Tag. In round two, the interface is very similar, showing again the same paragraph of the fragment, but now below. The interface will contain the categories that have been suggested by all participants in round one. The goal in this round is to decide on a winner category, and the user has the ability to choose from a range of options. This means that the user can now vote only in one category, which she believes is the most suitable for the paragraph that was analyzed. Note that the user can even choose the category that he/she submitted. At this point the game becomes more interesting because the players now must simultaneously find a category they consider fit while also trying to think which category will be chosen by the other participants. For round two the time is independent of the size of the paragraph, since the players had earlier read and analyzed the text. For this round the timer is set at 30 s.

Round Three: Reviewing and Deciding. After round one and two finish for all paragraphs, the challenge reaches the reviewing and deciding round. The interface changes: the complete fragment is now presented at the bottom part of the screen while at the top part there is a voting area containing the categories that won each of the previous voting rounds (round two). Additionally, we also have a timer, and the indication that the game is in its final round. This round is the final crowdrating process, since the players must now vote on one of the tags in order to elect a tag that best captures the classification of the fragment. The most voted tag will be included in the virtual edition as part of its user-generated taxonomy. However, this stage is more dynamic and iterative due to the fact that users now can switch their vote while the timer does not expire, whereas in the second round, once voted, they could not change their vote. Note that, to foster the selection of a representative tag, all players can see the points received by each tag, the current top tag in real time, and the points changing as players vote and change votes. This allows users to change their opinion depending on the feedback they get from the current classification. This presents the challenge of trying to simultaneously chose the best available tag whilst trying to predict the winner tag.

The score of a participant follows the formula for each paragraph in rounds one and two:

$$score(p) = s + v_{rwt} + s_{rwt}$$

where: s: submit on round one a tag (1 point); v_{rwt}: choose on round two the winning tag (2 points); s_{rwt}: submit on round two the winning tag (5 points).

This formula intends to foster participation: submitting a tag during round one corresponds to 1 point, which promotes participation; 5 points are given for the paragraph winner, thus motivating the players to carefully read the paragraphs in order to accurately submit the best tags; the voting on the winner tag provides 2 points in round two, thus motivating the players to not stick to their own submissions if they consider that another player submission is better.

And the participant score for the third round, the classification of the whole text, is given by the formula:

$$score(t) = v_{gwt} + s_{gwt} - c$$

where: v_{gwt}: vote on the round three the winning tag (5 points); s_{gwt}: submit on round three the winning tag (10 points); c: total of vote changes during round three.

As happens with the paragraph scoring, this formula intends to foster participation and accuracy, and, additionally – since in round three the participants can see which is the tag that has more votes, and can change their vote to try to find the best synthesis of proposed tags –, the scoring system hinders the constant change of vote to avoid that the final tag is the result of an opportunistic change of vote. Every time a player changes his final vote he may increase the chances of winning 5 points but he loses one point.

The final points of a player in the game are given by the sum of her paragraph scores plus the final text score. Note that, in order to have a single winner associated with a tag, submitting a classification earlier is key, since it allows for him or her to be considered the author of a tag, which introduces another timing pressure in the game. The player that suggested the winning tag will have their name credited as the author of the tagging of the fragment in the virtual edition.

3   Results and Discussion

As the fundamental objective of the created application is to be a text-based game, we asked colleagues, family members, existing users of the *LdoD Archive* to test the prototype, in order to better understand its positives and negatives.

After testing the game prototype, participants were requested to fill in a questionnaire that assesses and profiles the user. Part one of the questionnaire focuses on group age, gender, acquaintance with the work of Fernando Pessoa, and gaming habits. The second part targeted characterization of the game itself, such as its ease of understanding, rules and entertainment. The questionnaire had sixteen responses.

Regarding the profile of the respondents we can say that nine of the survey respondents are men and seven are women; the majority of the participants have an age between 19 and 24, and all of the inquired have a higher education degree (the majority, 10, a graduation). When questioned about the *Book of Disquiet* only two said that they had not heard of its existence. Furthermore, half of the people had read at least part of the book, and also half selected *I am a normal reader of* Fernando Pessoa *knowing only mandatory works* as the option that best described them. Five considered themselves as an above average reader and three as experts. Finally, only one person never plays games and a significant group (five people) plays games daily.

The next section of the questionnaire focused on finding about the game experience the players had. In a scale from 1 to 5 (*very easy, easy, normal, hard, very hard*) users had to rate the game regarding the difficulty of understanding it (objectives and rules). The results were: seven chose rating *very easy*, two chose rating *easy*, three *normal*, three *hard* and one found it *very hard*. Regarding the entertainment that the game provided to the participants, from 1 (*not fun*) to 5 (*very fun*), two people found it *not fun* while a majority (8) found it *fun* and six others found it *normal*. The majority (eleven people) would consider playing again and would recommend the game to another person. Two people said they would not play again and five responded as maybe regarding recommending the game.

The question asking if the game made it interesting to read and learn more about the *Book of Disquiet* and Fernando Pessoa, was very split with seven people saying *yes, a lot*, other four *not at all* and the rest in between with *a bit*.

So, from this, we can say that, for now, the game seems to be easy to follow. Although it has not reached a high level of entertainment, it has the potential to entice players to play again and could also attract other users to join.

After this, the questions were of open format and not mandatory. The questions were what did the user like the most and the least, which aspects did the user consider that could be improved, and any other suggestions.

The most relevant points brought up for each of these questions were: most liked were the ability to compare what other participants wrote, originality, and reading and knowing fragments of the book in a fun manner; least liked: time pressure; improvements: interface related changes (text size, formatting and UI in general), weekly rankings, increase time, and at the end of the game present the tags other players in other games had chosen for that same fragment; general suggestions: ranks and social achievements, increase times, provide suggestions of classifications in round 1, explain the game better (for a general audience, particularly how a game must be created and what are its rules).

In conclusion, the game has potential, but the users disliked the time pressure associated with the rounds, what suggests that it may have an additional potential as a learning tool, used in the context of a class to analyze texts from this book, where time pressure is not relevant and the ability to see each others' tags may trigger interesting discussions.

The source code is publicly available in a GitHub repository[1] and the game can be accessed at the game homepage[2].

---

[1] https://github.com/socialsoftware/edition.
[2] https://ldod.uc.pt/classification-game.

Acknowledgement. This work was supported by national funds through Fundação para a Ciência e Tecnologia (FCT) with reference UIDB/50021/2020.

References

1. Deterding, S., Dixon, D., Khaled, R., Nacke, L.: From game design elements to gamefulness: defining "gamification". In: Proceedings of the 15th International Academic MindTrek Conference: Envisioning Future Media Environments, MindTrek 2011, pp. 9–15. Association for Computing Machinery, New York (2011)
2. Doan, A., Ramakrishnan, R., Halevy, A.Y.: Crowdsourcing systems on the worldwide web. Commun. ACM **54**(4), 86–96 (2011)
3. Geiger, D., Schader, M.: Personalized task recommendation in crowdsourcing information systems - current state of the art. Decis. Support Syst. **65**(C), 3–16 (2014)
4. Goncalves, J., Hosio, S., Ferreira, D., Kostakos, V.: Game of words: tagging places through crowdsourcing on public displays. In: Proceedings of the 2014 Conference on Designing Interactive Systems, DIS 2014, pp. 705–714. Association for Computing Machinery, New York (2014)
5. Groh, F.: Gamification: state of the art definition and utilization. In: Research Trends in Media Informatics, pp. 39–46 (2012)
6. Howe, J.: The rise of crowdsourcing. Wired Mag. **14**(06), 1–5 (2006)
7. Kim, B.: Understanding gamification. Libr. Technol. Rep. **51**(2) (2015)
8. Morschheuser, B., Hamari, J., Koivisto, J., Maedche, A.: Gamified crowdsourcing: conceptualization, literature review, and future agenda. Int. J. Hum Comput Stud. **106**, 26–43 (2017)
9. Portela, M., Rito Silva, A.: A model for a virtual LdoD. Digit. Sch. Humanit. **30**(3), 354–370 (2014)
10. Rito Silva, A., Portela, M.: TEI4LdoD: textual encoding and social editing in web 2.0 environment. J. Text Encoding Initiat. 8 (2014)
11. von Ahn, L., Dabbish, L.: Labeling images with a computer game. In: Proceedings of the SIGCHI Conference on Human Factors in Computing Systems, CHI 2004, pp. 319–326. Association for Computing Machinery, New York (2004)

Metadata and Infrastructure

SchenQL: Evaluation of a Query Language for Bibliographic Metadata

Christin Katharina Kreutz(✉)(iD), Michael Wolz(iD), Benjamin Weyers(iD),
and Ralf Schenkel(iD)

Trier University, 54286 Trier, Germany
{kreutzch,weyers,schenkel}@uni-trier.de

Abstract. Information access needs to be uncomplicated, as users may
not benefit from complex and potentially richer data that may be
less easy to obtain. A user's demand for answering more sophisticated
research questions including aggregations could be fulfilled by the usage
of SQL. However, this comes with the cost of high complexity, which
requires for a high level of expertise even for trained programmers. A
domain-specific query language could provide a straightforward solution
to this problem. Although less generic, it is desirable that users not familiar with query construction are supported in the formulation of complex
information needs.

In this paper, we extend and evaluate SchenQL, a simple and applicable query language that is accompanied by a prototypical GUI. SchenQL
focuses on querying bibliographic metadata while using the vocabulary
of domain-experts. The easy-to-learn domain-specific query language is
suitable for domain-experts as well as casual users while still providing
the possibility to answer complicated queries. Query construction and
information exploration is supported by the prototypical GUI. Eventually, the complete system is evaluated: interviews with domain-experts
and a bipartite quantitative user study demonstrate SchenQL's suitability and high level of users' acceptance.

Keywords: Domain-specific query language · Bibliographic
metadata · Digital libraries · Graphical user interface

1 Introduction

Scientific writing almost always starts with a thorough bibliographic research
on relevant publications, authors, conferences, journals and institutions. While
web search is excellent for question answering and intuitively performed, not
all retrieved information is correct, unbiased and categorized [11]. The arising
problem is people's tendency of rather using poor information sources that are
easy to query than more reliable sources which might be harder to access [12].
This introduces the need for more formal and structured information sources
such as digital libraries specialised in the underlying data, that at the same time

© Springer Nature Switzerland AG 2020
E. Ishita et al. (Eds.): ICADL 2020, LNCS 12504, pp. 323–339, 2020.
https://doi.org/10.1007/978-3-030-64452-9_30

need to be easy to query. Existing interfaces of digital libraries often provide keyword search on metadata or to query attributes [1,3,6,22,30]. However, in many cases, these interfaces do not allow to directly express advanced queries such as *"Which are the five most cited articles written by person P about topic T after year Y?"*, but require complex interaction. Popular examples of such limited systems are dblp [30] or Semantic Scholar [6]. More complex tools such as GrapAL [2,15] are capable of answering said complex queries, but require specific and uncommon programming skills. Another option is to use structured query languages such as SQL, a widespread language for querying databases, which unfortunately tends to be difficult to master [39]. This is critical as in most cases domain-experts are familiar with the schema of the data but are not experienced in using all-purpose query languages such as SQL [9,31]. This is even worse for casual users of digital libraries who neither have knowledge of the structure of the data nor of SQL.

To close this gap, we presented the SchenQL Query Language for the domain of bibliographic metadata [28]. SchenQL is designed to be easily utilised by domain-experts as well as casual users as it uses the vocabulary of digital libraries in its syntax. While domain-specific query languages (DSLs) provide a multitude of advantages [17], the most important aspect in the conception of SchenQL was that no programming skills or database schema knowledge is required to use it. For SchenQL to be widely applicable, we introduce a prototypical graphical user interface (the SchenQL GUI) which supports the construction of queries, offers visualisations of query results and an additional dimension of retrieving information by exploring data and its relations through clicking. As an example of SchenQL, the aforementioned question can be formulated as follows: MOST CITED (ARTICLES WRITTEN BY "P" ABOUT "T" AFTER Y) LIMIT 5.

The major contribution of this paper is the empirical evaluation of SchenQL as domain-specific query language on bibliographic metadata including the investigation of a prototypical GUI that is designed to assist users in creating queries. SchenQL is evaluated two-fold: 1) interviews with domain-experts were conducted to identify applications as well as options for further development and 2) a quantitative user study consisting of two parts measured effectiveness, efficiency and users' satisfaction with our whole system: we first evaluated usage of command line SchenQL against SQL, followed by a study which compared usage of the SchenQL GUI to the previous results. Here, the User Experience Questionnaire [36] was conducted for assessment of user experience.

The remainder of this paper is structured as follows: Sect. 2 discusses related work. Section 3 introduces the structure and syntax of SchenQL including the presentation of the SchenQL GUI, which is evaluated in two parts in the following Sect. 4. The last Sect. 5 describes possible future research.

2   Related Work

Areas adjacent to the one we are tackling are *search on digital libraries, search interfaces on bibliographic metadata* and *domain-specific query languages.*

For *search on digital libraries*, the MARC format is a standard for information exchange [11]. While it is useful for known-item search, topical search might be problematic as contents of the corresponding fields can only be interpreted by domain-experts [11]. Most interfaces on digital libraries provide field-based Boolean search [35] which can lead to difficulties in formulating queries that require the definition and concatenation of multiple attributes. This might cause a substantial cognitive workload on the user [14]. In contrast, withholding or restriction of faceted search on these engines fails to answer complex search tasks [13]. Thus, we focus on a search of topical information that even casual users can utilise while also offering the possibility to clearly define search terms for numerous attributes in a single query.

Several *search interfaces on bibliographic metadata* exist such as dblp [26,30], Bibsonomy [22], Google Scholar [1], ResearchGate [3] or Semantic Scholar [6]. All of those systems allow for systematic refinement of result sets by application of filter options via facets to varying extends. Only dblp and Semantic Scholar (on a small scale) support search on venues. The formulation of complex queries with aggregations is not targeted by any of them. In contrast, SchenQL supported by a GUI specialises on these functionalities. GrapAL [2,15] actually provides all functions of SchenQL but is a complex tool utilising the Cypher [20] query language (QL).

Domain-specific query languages come in various shapes. They can be SQL-like [29], visual QLs [9,18] or use domain-specific vocabulary [38] but are typically specialised on a certain area. They also come in different complexities: for example MathQL [21] is a query language in markup style on RDF repositories but a user needs to be mathematician to be able to operate it. The DSL proposed by Madaan [31] stems from the medical domain and is designed to be used by inexperienced patients as well as medical staff. Some DSLs are domain-unspecific such as the aforementioned Cypher [20], BiQL [19] or SnQL [32] and depend on complicated SQL-like syntax. With SchenQL, we provide a QL which uses vocabulary from the domain of bibliographic metadata while being useful for experts as well as casual users and avoiding complicated syntax.

3   SchenQL: QL and GUI

For simplicity, we refer to SchenQL including its GUI as the *SchenQL system*. SchenQL was developed to access bibliographic metadata textually, which resembles natural language for casual as well as expert users of digital libraries [27]. The fundamental idea is to hide complex syntax behind plain domain-specific vocabulary. This enables usage from anyone versed in the vocabulary of the domain without experience in sophisticated query languages such as SQL. The prototypical GUI supports SchenQL: it helps in query formulation with auto-completion and keyword suggestion. Additionally, it provides visual exploration of query results supporting two standard visualisations: Ego Graph [34] and BowTie [25].

For our data model we assume bibliographic metadata consists of persons and publications they authored or edited. These persons can be affiliated with

Table 1. SchenQL base concepts `Publications` (PU), `persons` (PE), `conferences` (C), `journals` (J) and `institutions` (I) with their respective literals (L), specialisations (S), filters (F) and standard return values (V, relevant for the CLI).

	PUBLICATION	PERSON	CONFERENCE	JOURNAL	INSTITUTION
L	key, title	key, primary name, orcid	key, acronym	key, acronym	
S	MASTERTHESIS, BOOK, CHAPTER, PHDTHESIS, ARTICLE	AUTHOR, EDITOR			
F	PUBLISHED BY (I), ABOUT (keywords), WRITTEN BY (PE), EDITED BY (PE), APPEARED IN (C|J), BEFORE year, IN YEAR year, AFTER year, TITLED title, REFERENCES (PU), CITED BY (PU)	PUBLISHED IN (C|J), PUBLISHED WITH (I), WORKS FOR (I), NAMED name, ORCID orcid, AUTHORED (PU), REFERENCES (PU), CITED BY (PU)	ACRONYM acronym, ABOUT (keywords), BEFORE year, IN YEAR year, AFTER year	NAMED name, ACRONYM acronym, ABOUT (keywords), BEFORE year, IN YEAR year, VOLUME volume	NAMED name, CITY city, COUNTRY country, MEMBERS (PE)
V	title	primary name	acronym	acronym	primary name + location

certain institutions. Publications can be of multiple types and may be published in conferences or journals. Publications can reference previously published papers and might be cited themselves by more recent work building upon them.

3.1   Building Blocks

Base concepts are the basic return objects of SchenQL. A base concept is connected to an entity of the dataset and has multiple attributes. Those base concepts are **publications**, **persons**, **conferences**, **journals** and **institutions**. Upon these concepts, queries can be constructed. Base concepts can be specialised. For example **publications** can be refined by specialisations **books**, **chapters**, **articles**, **master** or **PhD theses**. A specialisation can be used instead of a base concept in a query.

Filters can restrict base concepts by extracting a subset of the data. Literals can be used as identifiers for objects from base concepts, they can be utilised to query for specific data. Attributes of base concepts can be queried, for a list of attributes see Kreutz et al. [28]. Table 1 gives an overview of literals, specialisations, filters and the standard return value for every base concept.

Functions are used to aggregate data or offer domain-specific operations. Right now, four functions are implemented in SchenQL: MOST CITED, COUNT, KEYWORDS OF and COAUTHORS OF. The function MOST CITED (PUBLICATION) can be applied on publications. It returns titles as well as numbers of citations of papers in the following set. By default, the top five results are returned. COUNT returns the number of objects contained in the following sub-query. KEYWORDS OF (PUBLICATION | CONFERENCE | JOURNAL) returns the keywords associated with the following base concept. COAUTHORS OF (PERSON) returns the coauthors of an author. The LIMIT x operator with $x \in \mathbb{N}$ can be appended at the end of any query to change the number of displayed results to at most x.

3.2 Syntax and Implementation

The syntax of SchenQL follows simple rules resulting in queries similar to natural language which are aiming at simple construction. Sub-queries have to be surrounded by parentheses. It is possible to write singular or plural when using base concepts or specialisations (e.g. JOURNAL or JOURNALS). Filters following base concepts or their specialisations can be in arbitrary order and get connected via conjunction if not specified otherwise (OR and NOT are also possible). Most filters expect a base concept as parameter (e.g. WRITTEN BY (PERSONS)), however some filters anticipate a string as parameter (e.g. COUNTRY "de"). Specialisations can be used in place of base concepts. Instead of a query PERSON NAMED "Ralf Schenkel" a specialisation like AUTHOR NAMED "Ralf Schenkel" would be possible. If a filter requires a base concept, parentheses are needed except for the case of using literals for identifying objects of the base concept. For example PUBLICATIONS WRITTEN BY "Ralf Schenkel" is semantically equivalent to PUBLICATIONS WRITTEN BY (PERSONS NAMED "Ralf Schenkel"). Attributes of base concepts can be accessed by putting the queried for attribute(s) in front of a base concept and connecting both parts with an OF (e.g. "name", "acronym" OF CONFERENCES ABOUT KEYWORDS ["DL", "QLs"]).

For implementation, lexer and parser of the compiler for SchenQL were built using ANTLR with Java as target language. The compiler translates queries from SchenQL to SQL and runs them against a MySQL 8.0.16 database holding the data. Data on references and citations is contained in a single table. SchenQL can be used in a terminal client similar to the MySQL shell.

3.3 GUI

The GUI is inspired by results from the qualitative study described in Sect. 4.2. It provides access to information by supporting the construction of queries including the interactive navigation with the GUI. It also offers auto-completion of SchenQL query keywords and suggestions for the formulation of queries. Results of queries can be sorted for every column of the result table. In Fig. 1b query formulation with suggested keywords and result representation in the SchenQL GUI is depicted. If a search result is selected by clicking on it, detail views open (see Fig. 1a) which offer all information available for the respective element of a base concept. Furthermore we incorporated two already established visualisations: *Ego Graph* [34] and *BowTie* [25]. The *Ego Graph* for persons (see Fig. 1a top) supports the analysis of persons' most important co-authorships. The *BowTie* visualisation can be used for easy estimation of a person's, publication's or venue's influence in terms of gained citations and its actuality (see Fig. 1c).

Person

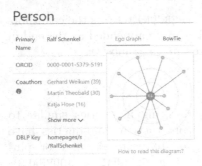

Primary Name	Ralf Schenkel	Ego Graph	BowTie
ORCID	0000-0001-5379-5191		
Coauthors	Gerhard Weikum (39)		
	Martin Theobald (30)		
	Katja Hose (16)		
	Show more ⌄		
DBLP Key	homepages/s /RalfSchenkel		

How to read this diagram?

Publications

Title ▲▼	Year ▲▼	Type ▲▼
SchenQL - A Domain-Specific Query Language...	2019	article ▶...
Analyzing online schema extraction approache...	2019	inpr... ▶...

(a) Person detail view with Ego Graph. Nodes symbolise authors, the further an author is from the middle, the less publications he shares with the person in focus.

PUBLICATIONS WRITTEN BY "Ralf Schenkel" IN YEAR 2018

WRITTEN BY | EDITED BY | PUBLISHED BY | ABOUT KEYWORD | ABOUT | AFTER | BEFORE | IN YEAR | APPEARED IN | CITED BY | REFERENCES | TITLED | AND | OR | NOT

Title ▲▼	Year ▲▼	Type ▲▼
ReCAP - Information Retrieval and Case-Based Reasoning for Robust Deli...	2018	inprocee... ▶...
Prioritizing and Scheduling Conferences for Metadata Harvesting in dblp...	2018	article ▶...

(b) SchenQL GUI for a search with suggested language components and search result.

Year: 2006 - Citations: 46

(c) BowTie view of referenced and citing papers of a person with numbers of referenced(bows left of knot)/citing(bows right of knot) papers per year in single slices. The higher the number of citations or references, the longer the bow.

Fig. 1. SchenQL GUI (top right), detail view of a person with Ego Graph (left) and BowTie view (bottom right).

4   Evaluation

Our evaluation of the SchenQL system consists of a qualitative and a quantitative investigation. In a first qualitative study, we examine domain experts' use-cases and desired functionality of a DSL such as SchenQL as well as an accompanied GUI. The major goal of this first investigation was to check SchenQL for completeness and suitability for the addressed use cases. In a subsequent step, we conducted a quantitative study in which we first compared SchenQL with SQL, both used through a command line interface (CLI) to ensure comparability. The goal was to measure the effectiveness, efficiency and users' satisfaction with SchenQL as query language. As a follow-up, we evaluated the web-based GUI of the SchenQL system using the same queries and compared the results with those received from usage of the SchenQL CLI. We additionally investigated the SchenQL system's user experience using the User Experience Questionnaire (UEQ) [36].

Considering the overall goals for SchenQL, we derived the following three hypotheses to be investigated:

H_1. Utilisation of the SchenQL CLI achieves better results in terms of higher correctness, lower perceived difficulty of query construction as well as lower required time for query formulation than usage of SQL.

H_2. SchenQL is suitable for domain-experts as well as non-experts.

H_3. The SchenQL system provides high suitability and user experience (indicated by values $>.8$ for all six quality dimensions assessed with the UEQ [7]) for users not familiar with structured queries.

For the studies, we used a dataset from the area of computer science: our structures were filled with data from dblp [30] mapped on data from Semantic Scholar [6] and enriched with information about institutions from Wikidata [8].

4.1 Qualitative Study: Interviews

To get a comprehensive picture of SchenQL's completeness and suitability, we conducted semi-structured one-on-one interviews with four employees of the dblp team to discover realistic use-cases as well as desirable functionalities and potential extensions. Leading questions were which queries they would like to answer with the data and which functions or visualisations they envisioned in a GUI. The participants do work daily on digital libraries and are thus considered highly experienced in the area. They were only aware of the domain of interest and the underlying dataset but did not know anything about SchenQL.

The interviews showed that the dblp staff wished to formulate queries to compute keywords of other publications that were published in the same journal as a given publication, the determination of the most productive or cited authors, as well as the most cited authors with few co-authors. Furthermore, a GUI should support numerous visualisations: colour coded topics of publications or co-author-groups were explicitly asked for. Another participant requested intermateable components for the visualisation of graphs to display co-publications, co-institutions or connections between venues. Other desired functionalities were a fault-tolerant person name search and sophisticated ranking methods.

As expected, the experts' suggestions were quite specific and strongly shaped by their daily work with dblp, which may not fit classic non-expert use of digital libraries. SchenQL is able to formulate several of the desired questions, however it needs to be evaluated by non-power-users as we have done in the quantitative evaluation described below to ensure usability for casual users as well. Comments on visualisation drove the design of the GUI's visual analysis components.

4.2 Quantitative Study: SchenQL CLI Vs. SQL, GUI and UEQ

Our quantitative study consists of two parts: the SchenQL CLI is compared to SQL, then the usability of the GUI and thus the SchenQL system as a whole is assessed. For the first part, it is not feasible to compare a specialised system such as the SchenQL CLI to a commercial search engine, differences between the compared systems should be minor [24]. Additionally, as stated above, search interfaces in this domain [1,3,6,22,30] do not provide as many functionalities as SchenQL. We also refrained from evaluating the CLI against other DSLs such as Cypher [20] as test users would have been required to learn two new query languages. Comparing our CLI against SPARQL would have required the definition of classes, properties and labels for the dataset and was therefore also disregarded in favour of the comparison against SQL.

Users participated voluntarily in the study, they were aware of being able to quit any time without negative consequences. They actively agreed on their data being collected anonymously and their screens being captured. We assume gender does not influence the measured values so it is not seen as additional factor in the evaluation [24]. We assume domain-experts are versed in the vocabulary and connections between bibliographic objects, non-experts might have their first encounter with bibliographic metadata.

For significance tests, we used an independent two-sample t-test in case data is normally distributed (checked with Shapiro-Wilk test) and variances are homogeneous (checked with Levene's test). Otherwise and if we do not specify differently we applied Mann-Whitney U tests. We consider a p-value of .05 as significance level.

Queries. In both parts of the study, we asked the participants to find answers to the queries given in Table 2 using either SchenQL CLI/SQL (part I) or the GUI (part II). The used queries are inspired by everyday search tasks of users of digital libraries [16,33]. We formulated four different types of queries targeting core concepts found in the domain. Variables were switched between query languages to prevent learning effects based on query results. Q_1, Q_3 and Q_4 are publication searches while Q_2 targets person search. Q_1 and Q_2 can be answered by using dblp [30] alone. Except for Q_3, Semantic Scholar [6] could technically be used to find answers for the queries. The following formulation of Q_3 in SQL intends to show the complexity of those queries:

```
SELECT DISTINCT title
FROM publication p, publication_references pr
WHERE p.publicationKey = pr.pub2Key AND pr.pub1Key IN (
  SELECT publicationKey
  FROM person_authored_publication NATURAL JOIN person_names
    NATURAL JOIN publication
  WHERE person_names.name = "A" AND year = Y);
```

In SchenQL, the query could be formulated as follows (for all queries see [27]):

```
PUBLICATIONS CITED BY (PUBLICATIONS WRITTEN BY "A" IN YEAR Y);
```

We refrained from evaluating more complex queries to keep the construction time for SQL queries feasible.

Table 2. Templates of all queries used in the qualitative evaluations. A are different authors, C is a conference and Y is a year.

Q_1	What are the titles of publications written by author A?
Q_2	What are the names of authors which published at conference C?
Q_3	What are the titles of the publications referenced by author A in year Y?
Q_4	What are the titles of the five most cited publications written by author A?

Table 3. Correctness (CORR) in percent, assessed average difficulty (DIFF) and average time in minutes for the four queries for SQL and the SchenQL CLI.

	SQL			SchenQL CLI		
	CORR	DIFF	Time	CORR	DIFF	Time
Q_1	90.48	2.86	4:57	90.48	1.57	2:57
Q_2	90.48	3	4:35	100	2.1	3:11
Q_3	23.81	4.86	8:55	47.62	2.71	3:33
Q_4	23.81	5.91	10:36	95.24	1.71	1:53

Table 4. Correctness (CORR) in percent, assessed average difficulty (DIFF) and average time in minutes for the four queries for the GUI.

	SchenQL GUI		
	CORR	DIFF	Time
Q_1	90	1.3	1:05
Q_2	90	2.2	1:41
Q_3	40	3.6	2:56
Q_4	90	2.4	2:18

Part I: SchenQL CLI vs. SQL

With this first part of the quantitative study, we assess the usability, suitability as well as user satisfaction of usage of the SchenQL CLI compared to SQL for queries typically answered with an information retrieval system operating on bibliographic metadata. Additionally, the need for a DSL in the domain of bibliographic metadata is analysed as we try to verify or falsify hypotheses H_1 and H_2. Participants of this evaluation needed to be familiar with SQL.

Setting. We defined the evaluation process of our archetypical interactive information retrieval study [24] as follows: every user performed the evaluation alone in presence of a passive investigator on a computer with two monitors. The screens were captured in order to measure times used to formulate the queries. A query language was assigned with which a user was going to start the evaluation to compensate for learning effects. Users were permitted to use the internet at any stage of the evaluation. A SchenQL cheat sheet, the ER diagram and examples for the database schema provided to test subjects can be found in Kreutz et al. [27].

At first, a video tutorial [4] for the introduction and usage of SQL and the SchenQL CLI was shown, afterwards subjects were permitted to formulate queries using the system they were starting to work with. Following this optional step, users were asked to answer a first online questionnaire to assess their familiarity with the domain of bibliographic metadata. Participants were asked to submit the queries in SQL and SchenQL respectively. This part of the first quantitative evaluation was concluded with a second online questionnaire regarding the overall impression of SchenQL, the rating of SchenQL and SQL for the formulation of queries as well as several open questions targeting possible advantages and improvements of SchenQL. We evaluated 21 participants from the area of computer science with SQL knowledge. In total, ten subjects started by using SQL, eleven participants began the evaluation using SchenQL.

Analysis of H_1. To assess validity of hypothesis H_1 of SchenQL leading to better results than using SQL, we observe the *number of correctly formulated queries*, the *rated difficulty* and the *required time* for the formulation of queries with the SchenQL CLI and SQL. For each of these values, we first conducted significance tests on all four queries together, here the two languages SchenQL and SQL were regarded as groups, afterwards we performed significance tests on each of the four queries. Table 3 gives an overview of correctness, average rated difficulty and average time for all four queries for both languages. Difficulty was rated on a scale from 1 (very easy) to 7 (very difficult) to allow neutral ratings.

Correctness. 57.14% of queries were correctly formulated using SQL whereas 83.33% of queries were correctly formulated using SchenQL. This result clearly shows the significantly superior effectiveness of SchenQL compared to SQL in terms of overall correctness. While Q_1 and Q_2 were answered correctly by most participants, the number of correctly formulated queries for Q_3 and Q_4 highly depends on the system. Q_4 was correctly answered by a quarter of subjects using SQL while more than 95% of users were able to formulate the query in SchenQL, this difference is significant. These observations support the partial verification of H_1 in terms of higher number of correctly formulated queries with the SchenQL CLI compared to SQL.

Rated Difficulty. The mean rating of difficulty of the formulation of queries with SQL was 4.16 ($\sigma = 1.94$), with SchenQL the mean rating was significantly lower (2.02, $\sigma = 1.11$). On average, query construction using SQL is rated more difficult for every query. The averaged highest rated difficulty for a query in SchenQL is still lower than the averaged lowest rated difficulty of a query in SQL. We found significantly lower ratings of difficulties of queries for all four queries (for Q_3 t-test) when using SchenQL compared to utilisation of SQL. These observations support the partial verification of H_1 in terms lower perceived difficulty in query formulation with the SchenQL CLI compared to SQL.

Time. Average construction of queries in SQL took 7:15 min ($\sigma = 4:47$ min), with the CLI the construction was significantly quicker and took 2:52 min ($\sigma = 1:51$ min) on average. This documents the efficiency of SchenQL. We found significantly lower required times for query formulation all four queries (for Q_1 t-test) when using SchenQL compared to utilisation of SQL. These observations support the partial verification of H_1 in terms of lower required time for query formulation with the SchenQL CLI compared to SQL.

General Results. The queries Q_3 and Q_4 in SQL are assumed to be complex which is supported by the low percentage of correct formulations using SQL. They are also much longer than the respective SchenQL ones so the time required to write them down is higher and there is more opportunity to make mistakes which causes query reformulation [35]. The overall rating of suitability of SchenQL for constructing the queries resulted in an average of 6.43 ($\sigma = .6$) while the rating was significantly lower (3.14, $\sigma = 1.2$) for SQL on a scale from 1 (very bad) to 7 (very good). While SQL was rated below mediocre, SchenQL was evaluated as excellent which shows users' satisfaction with it. These results lead to the conclusion of SchenQL being highly suitable for solving the given tasks which represent everyday queries of users of digital libraries and a high user acceptance of SchenQL.

In summary, utilisation of SchenQL achieves higher correctness of queries, lower perceived difficulty and requires less time than using SQL, which together verifies hypothesis H_1.

Analysis of H_2. To assess validity of hypothesis H_2 of SchenQL being suitable for experts and non-experts, we conduct significance tests on all queries independent by system, all queries dependent on system and each separate query for the three aforementioned values (correctness, rated difficulty and required time). The 21 participants from before form the two user groups: nine participants are non-experts and twelve participants are familiar with bibliographic metadata.

Correctness. In general, 75% of queries were correctly formulated by domain-experts whereas non-experts achieved only 63.89% in both QLs. (Non-)Experts were able to solve 65.58% (47.22%) of queries in SQL and 85.42% (80.56%) in SchenQL. Tian et al. [38] stated that for a domain-expert, it would be easier to write queries in a DSL than in SQL. We found no significant differences between the two groups for correctness (separated by system, by query and in general).

Rated Difficulty. We found no significant differences between the two groups for rated difficulty (separated by system, by query and in general).

Time. We found no significant differences between the two groups for required time (separated by system and in general). We found significant differences for times needed to complete Q_3 and Q_4 with SQL when applying t-tests for the two user groups. With Q_3 the twelve participants versed in the domain were much slower to complete the task (inexperienced: 6:04 min, $\sigma = 2:51$ min; experienced: 11:02 min, $\sigma = 5:41$ min) while with Q_4 users with experience in bibliographic metadata were faster (inexperienced: 13:26 min, $\sigma = 6.17$ min; experienced: 8:28 min, $\sigma = 4:27$ min). We observed that domain-experts tend to review the result of their query online and therefore need more time to answer Q_3 than non-experts. Another explanation could be that since they are experienced with the principle of citations they were more confused with the one needed table as it contains publications and their references instead of two tables for papers, one which holds its citations and one which holds its references. Domain-experts are faster in formulating Q_4 as the query might be familiar and they already took more time to understand the database layout of references and citations while solving Q_3 which had to be tackled beforehand.

Result. No user group is consistently better than the other, the SchenQL CLI is suitable for domain-experts as well as non-experts, thus, H_2 is verified.

Open Questions and Discussion. In the open questions, the short, easy and intuitive SchenQL queries were complimented by many participants. Users noted the comprehensible syntax was suitable for non-computer scientists as it resembles natural language. Some noted their initial confusion due to the syntax and their incomprehension of usage of literals or limitations. Others asked for auto-completion, syntax highlighting, a documentation and more functions such as most cited with variable return values. No participant wished for visualisations which could be caused by design fixation [23] or generally lower requirements for such a system compared to the experts from the qualitative study.

The average overall impression of SchenQL was rated by the subjects as 5.05 ($\sigma = .74$) on a scale from 1 (very bad) to 6 (very good), enforcing a non-neutral rating. Assessed difficulty and required times to formulate the four queries were significantly lower when utilising SchenQL compared to SQL, the overall correctness of all queries was significantly higher for SchenQL as well. This verified hypothesis H_1 of the CLI leading to generally better results than SQL. Our hypothesis H_2 of the SchenQL system being suitable for domain-experts as well as casual users is also verified. No user group was found to be consistently significantly better than the other one.

This evaluation lead to the construction of the prototypical GUI with its syntax suggestion as well as auto-completion features. Additionally, although they were not mentioned by participants in this evaluation, some visualisations were included following suggestions from the qualitative evaluation.

Part II: SchenQL GUI vs. CLI and User Experience Questionnaire

This second part of the quantitative study focused on evaluating the GUI and, thus, the SchenQL system as a whole. We assessed how usage of the web interface compared to users' impressions and performance when utilising the SchenQL CLI. Beside a part where test users answered queries with the GUI, we conducted the User Experience Questionnaire [36] to measure user experience with the SchenQL system. To resemble our target audience we did not pose the precondition of users being familiar with SQL or formulation of structured queries. Here, we intend to assess the hypothesis H_3.

Setting. This evaluation is performed analogous to the previous part: every user performed the evaluation alone but in presence of a passive investigator on a computer with two monitors. We measured times used to find answers by capturing screens. The same SchenQL cheat sheet as in the first part was provided to the test subjects. At first, a video tutorial [5] introduced the usage of the SchenQL GUI. The next part was the formulation or the navigation towards solutions of the four queries introduced in Table 2 using the GUI. Afterwards, the subjects completed the User Experience Questionnaire [36] followed by questions regarding the overall impression of the GUI as well as possible improvements.

We evaluated ten participants from the area of computer science and adjacent fields which did not yet take part in a previous evaluation of the SchenQL system.

Partial Analysis of H_3: Users Unfamiliar with Query Formulation.
To assess partial validity of hypothesis H_3 in terms of the GUI's suitability for users unfamiliar with query formulation, we conduct significance tests on all queries together and each separate query for correctness, rated difficulty and

required time. We observe the results from usage of the SchenQL CLI from the previous evaluation and participants' results from utilisation of the GUI as the two groups. Table 4 gives an overview of correctness, average rated difficulty and average required time for all four queries when using the SchenQL system.

Correctness. Except for Q_3, participants mostly solved the queries correctly, resulting in an overall correctness of 77.5% (-10.83% compared to CLI, difference not significant). We found no significant differences between the two groups for correctness in any of the four queries.

Rated Difficulty. Users rated the difficulty of queries as 2.38 ($+.35$ compared to CLI, difference not significant) on average. We found no significant differences between the two groups for rated difficulty in any of the four queries.

Time. Users took about 2:15 min for retrieval of the solution ($-0:37$ min compared to CLI, difference is significant) on average. We found significant differences in times required to solve queries Q_1 and Q_2. Times required for formulating the queries with the GUI were significantly lower than those resulting from using the CLI. As these queries were relatively simple, we assume the auto-completion and suggestion-feature of the GUI is especially helpful in the fast construction of straightforward queries or the GUI offering other suitable ways of quickly obtaining simple bibliographic information. Usage of the GUI might be more intuitive compared to writing simple queries in the SchenQL CLI.

General Results. We want to point out that participants from the first part of the quantitative study who were familiar with query formulation, but were not offered help in the construction, did not significantly differ in rating of difficulty and correctness from users of this user study. In case of the GUI, subjects were supported in the formulation of queries but were not necessarily familiar with this kind of task. Hence, we assume the system's suggestion and auto-completion feature is useful for redemption of unequal prior knowledge in this case.

Correctness and rating of difficulty did not differ significantly between usage of CLI and GUI, but users were significantly faster in finding answers for simple queries with the GUI which underlines the suitability of the interface for everyday usage. Participants from this study resemble SchenQL's target audience, which additionally emphasizes its usefulness and partly verifies hypothesis H_3 in terms of the GUI being suitable for users not versed with structured query formulation.

Partial Analysis of H_3: UEQ. Attractiveness, perspicuity, efficiency, dependability, simulation and novelty of interactive products can be measured with the UEQ [36] even at small sample sizes. Here, we want to conclude the assessment of validity of hypothesis H_3 in terms of rating of user experience.

Participants of this study answered the 26 questions of the UEQ regarding usage of the SchenQL system. Ratings on pairs of contrasting stances (-3 to 3) such as *complicated-easy* or *boring-exciting* were then grouped to the six dimensions mentioned before. Values above .8 are generally considered as positively evaluated equalling high user experience, values above 2 are rarely encountered [7].

In general, users seem to enjoy using the SchenQL system (attractiveness = 2.07, σ = .25). The handling of our system is extremely easy learned (perspicuity = 2.3, σ = .19). Tasks can be solved without unnecessary effort (efficiency = 2.03, σ = .49) and users feel in control of the system (dependability = 1.83, σ = .63). They seem exited to use the SchenQL system (stimulation = 1.73, σ = .33) and rate the system as innovative and interesting (novelty = 1.58, σ = .68).

As all six quality dimensions achieved ratings well over .8, the system is positively evaluated which equals high user experience and partially verifies H_3.

Open Questions and Discussion. In the open questions, participants praised the intuitive usability, the auto-completion and the suggestion feature. For future development, suggestions for literals were requested and two participants wished for a voice input. Remarkably, not a single user mentioned the need for more or other visualisations, this is possibly attributed to design fixation [23] but might also stem from the advanced needs of power users from the expert interviews.

Users were significantly faster in solving simple queries when using the GUI compared to the CLI. As we found no significant impairments from usage of the GUI, we assume its usefulness and usability for query formulation. Participants from this study were less familiar with construction of structured queries compared to those of the previous study but seemed to be adequately supported by the GUI in retrieval of information. Together with the UEQ which showed users' high ratings ($>$.8) for all six quality dimensions (which proves high user experience [7]), hypothesis H_3 could be partially verified.

5   Conclusion and Future Work

We evaluated SchenQL, a domain-specific query language operating on bibliographic metadata from the area of computer science with accompanying GUI supporting query formulation. Our thorough evaluation against SQL showed the need for such a DSL. Test subjects' satisfaction with the SchenQL system was assessed with application of the UEQ. The introduction of a GUI and its evaluation with users resembling our target audience did not significantly change the correctness of answers or the users' rating of difficulty of the queries compared to the CLI but instead the time needed to formulate simple queries was reduced significantly. Missing prior knowledge with structured query formulation seems to be compensated by using a GUI with a suggestions and auto-completion feature. As the CLI and the GUI proved to be viable tools for information retrieval on bibliographic metadata, users' preferences should decide which one to use.

Using SchenQL lead to generally better results compared to utilisation of SQL (H_1). The system is suitable for domain-experts and non-experts (H_2). Our GUI has high usability for users not familiar with structured query formulation (H_3).

Enhancements of functionalities could include more visualisations such as color-coded topics or graph visualisation as the experts from the qualitative study requested. Furthermore, more specific query options such as a filter for papers with few co-authors or most cited with variable return values could be included. As visualisations were not relevant for users in our quantitative evaluation, future efforts could focus on supporting more advanced query options: algorithms for social network analysis as PageRank, computation of mutual neighbours, hubs and authorities or connected components [37] would fit. Centrality of authors, the length of a shortest path between two authors and the introduction of aliases for finding co-citations [19] would also be useful query building blocks. Incorporation of social relevance in the search and result representation process as shown in [10] could also be an extension. User profiles could store papers and keywords, which in terms influence results of search and exploration.

References

1. Google Scholar. https://scholar.google.com/
2. GrapAL. https://grapal.allenai.org/
3. ResearchGate. https://www.researchgate.net
4. SchenQL Evaluation CLI vs. SQL - Tutorial. https://youtu.be/g7J64wzbE5I
5. SchenQL Evaluation GUI - Tutorial. https://youtu.be/56-23zyUDPQ
6. Semantic Scholar. https://www.semanticscholar.org
7. User Experience Questionnaire Handbook. https://www.ueq-online.org/Material/Handbook.pdf
8. Wikdata. https://www.wikidata.org/wiki/Wikidata:Main_Page
9. Amaral, V., Helmer, S., Moerkotte, G.: A visual query language for HEP analysis. In: IEEE NSS 2003, vol. 2, pp. 829–833. IEEE Computer Society (2003)
10. Amer-Yahia, S., Lakshmanan, L.V.S., Yu, C.: SocialScope: enabling information discovery on social content sites. In: CIDR 2009 (2009). http://www.cidrdb.org
11. Baeza-Yates, R., Ribeiro-Neto, B.A.: Modern Information Retrieval - The Concepts and Technology Behind Search, 2nd edn. Pearson Education Ltd., Harlow (2011)
12. Bates, M.: Task Force Recommendation 2.3 Research and Design Review: Improving User Access to Library Catalog and Portal Information: Final Report (version 3) (2003)
13. Beall, J.: The weaknesses of full-text searching. J. Acad. Librariansh. 34(5), 438–444 (2008)
14. Berget, G., Sandnes, F.E.: Why textual search interfaces fail: a study of cognitive skills needed to construct successful queries. Inf. Res. 24(1) (2019)
15. Betts, C., Power, J., Ammar, W.: GrapAL: connecting the dots in scientific literature. In: ACL 2019, pp. 147–152. ACL (2019)
16. Bloehdorn, S., et al.: Ontology-based question answering for digital libraries. In: Kovács, L., Fuhr, N., Meghini, C. (eds.) ECDL 2007. LNCS, vol. 4675, pp. 14–25. Springer, Heidelberg (2007). https://doi.org/10.1007/978-3-540-74851-9_2
17. Borodin, A., Kiselev, Y., Mirvoda, S., Porshnev, S.: On design of domain-specific query language for the metallurgical industry. In: Kozielski, S., Mrozek, D., Kasprowski, P., Małysiak-Mrozek, B., Kostrzewa, D. (eds.) BDAS 2015. CCIS, vol. 521, pp. 505–515. Springer, Cham (2015). https://doi.org/10.1007/978-3-319-18422-7_45

18. Collberg, C.S.: A fuzzy visual query language for a domain-specific web search engine. In: Hegarty, M., Meyer, B., Narayanan, N.H. (eds.) Diagrams 2002. LNCS (LNAI), vol. 2317, pp. 176–190. Springer, Heidelberg (2002). https://doi.org/10.1007/3-540-46037-3_20

19. Dries, A., Nijssen, S., De Raedt, L.: BiQL: a query language for analyzing information networks. In: Berthold, M.R. (ed.) Bisociative Knowledge Discovery. LNCS (LNAI), vol. 7250, pp. 147–165. Springer, Heidelberg (2012). https://doi.org/10.1007/978-3-642-31830-6_11

20. Francis, N., et al.: Cypher: an evolving query language for property graphs. In: SIGMOD 2018, pp. 1433–1445. ACM (2018)

21. Guidi, F., Schena, I.: A query language for a metadata framework about mathematical resources. In: Asperti, A., Buchberger, B., Davenport, J.H. (eds.) MKM 2003. LNCS, vol. 2594, pp. 105–118. Springer, Heidelberg (2003). https://doi.org/10.1007/3-540-36469-2_9

22. Hotho, A., et al.: Social bookmarking am Beispiel BibSonomy. In: Blumauer, A., Pellegrini, T. (eds.) Social Semantic Web 2009, pp. 363–391. Springer, Heidelberg (2009). https://doi.org/10.1007/978-3-540-72216-8_18

23. Jansson, D.G., Smith, S.M.: Design fixation. Design Stud. 12(1), 3–11 (1991)

24. Kelly, D.: Methods for evaluating interactive information retrieval systems with users. Found. Trends Inf. Ret. 3(1–2), 1–224 (2009)

25. Khazaei, T., Hoeber, O.: Supporting academic search tasks through citation visualization and exploration. Int. J. Digit. Libr. 18(1), 59–72 (2017)

26. Klink, S., Ley, M., Rabbidge, E., Reuther, P., Walter, B., Weber, A.: Browsing and visualizing digital bibliographic data. In: VisSym 2004, pp. 237–242. Eurographics Association (2004)

27. Kreutz, C.K., Wolz, M., Schenkel, R.: SchenQL - A Domain-Specific Query Language on Bibliographic Metadata. CoRR abs/1906.06132 (2019)

28. Kreutz, C.K., Wolz, M., Schenkel, R.: SchenQL: a concept of a domain-specific query language on bibliographic metadata. In: Jatowt, A., Maeda, A., Syn, S.Y. (eds.) ICADL 2019. LNCS, vol. 11853, pp. 239–246. Springer, Cham (2019). https://doi.org/10.1007/978-3-030-34058-2_22

29. Leser, U.: A query language for biological networks. In: ECCB/JBI 2005, p. 39 (2005)

30. Ley, M.: DBLP - some lessons learned. PVLDB 2(2), 1493–1500 (2009)

31. Madaan, A.: Domain specific multi-stage query language for medical document repositories. PVLDB 6(12), 1410–1415 (2013)

32. Martín, M.S., Gutiérrez, C., Wood, P.T.: SNQL: a social networks query and transformation language. In: AMW 2011, vol. 749 (2011). CEUR-WS.org

33. Pirolli, P.: Powers of 10: modeling complex information-seeking systems at multiple scales. IEEE Comput. 42(3), 33–40 (2009)

34. Reitz, F.: A framework for an ego-centered and time-aware visualization of relations in arbitrary data repositories. CoRR abs/1009.5183 (2010)

35. Schaefer, A., Jordan, M., Klas, C., Fuhr, N.: Active support for query formulation in virtual digital libraries: a case study with DAFFODIL. In: ECDL 2005 (2005)

36. Schrepp, M., Hinderks, A., Thomaschewski, J.: Applying the user experience questionnaire (UEQ) in different evaluation scenarios. In: Marcus, A. (ed.) DUXU 2014. LNCS, vol. 8517, pp. 383–392. Springer, Cham (2014). https://doi.org/10.1007/978-3-319-07668-3_37

37. Seo, J., Guo, S., Lam, M.S.: SociaLite: an efficient graph query language based on datalog. IEEE Trans. Knowl. Data Eng. 27(7), 1824–1837 (2015)

38. Tian, H., Sunderraman, R., Calin-Jageman, R., Yang, H., Zhu, Y., Katz, P.S.: NeuroQL: a domain-specific query language for neuroscience data. In: Grust, T., et al. (eds.) EDBT 2006. LNCS, vol. 4254, pp. 613–624. Springer, Heidelberg (2006). https://doi.org/10.1007/11896548_46
39. Xu, B., et al.: NADAQ: natural language database querying based on deep learning. IEEE Access **7**, 35012–35017 (2019)

Domain-Focused Linked Data Crawling Driven by a Semantically Defined Frontier
A Cultural Heritage Case Study in Europeana

Nuno Freire[1]([✉]) [iD] and Mário J. Silva[1,2]

[1] INESC-ID, Lisbon, Portugal
{nuno.freire,mario.gaspar.silva}@tecnico.ulisboa.pt
[2] Universidade de Lisboa, Lisbon, Portugal

Abstract. We propose a method for focused crawling of linked data with a frontier based on the semantic data elements in use within a knowledge domain. This method addresses the challenges of crawling large volumes of heterogeneous linked data, aiming to achieve improvements in crawling efficiency and accuracy. We present the results obtained by our method in a case study on the cultural heritage domain, more specifically on Europeana, the European Union digital platform for cultural heritage. We have evaluated the crawling method in two Europeana data providers that are publishing linked metadata with Schema.org elements. We conclude that the proposed focused crawling method worked well in the case study, but it may need to be complemented with complementary frontier delimiting strategies when applied to other domains.

Keywords: Linked data · Focused crawling · Crawling frontier · Semantics · Cultural heritage

1 Introduction

A large volume of linked data is globally accessible nowadays. Although the semantics that linked data provides allows for much automated processing, the data volume and variety demand significant computing resource to acquire and process it. Systems for using linked data apply several software components for specific sub-problems of using linked data. This paper addresses the first of the sub-problems – linked data acquisition.

Some applications based on linked data use specific datasets for their purposes, and obtain the datasets via file-based distributions. This kind of distribution, however, does not address the needs of all applications because they use linked data without being confined to a limited set of datasets, or use only small parts of several datasets. In such cases, applications rely on crawling approaches that are initialized with a set of URIs (i.e., crawling seeds) to start the crawling process and continue to follow links to other resources found in the crawled data, until their criteria for the crawling frontier is met.

We present a method of crawling frontier definition for linked data. It defines the frontier based on the semantic data elements in use within a domain. Our method involves two main tasks. First, we represent in machine readable form, the domain's knowledge

© Springer Nature Switzerland AG 2020
E. Ishita et al. (Eds.): ICADL 2020, LNCS 12504, pp. 340–348, 2020.
https://doi.org/10.1007/978-3-030-64452-9_31

about semantic data elements, and import it into a knowledge base. Secondly, a linked data crawler uses the knowledge base to make decisions on which RDF statements and resources to continue crawling and which ones to ignore. This allows for focusing the crawler on the data that the domain will be able to interpret.

We studied this task on the domain of cultural heritage by conducting a case study in the network of Europeana, which is formed by cultural heritage institutions, data aggregators, and Europeana Foundation, the central aggregator. In this study, we defined the semantics-based frontier for this domain, and applied our method to crawl the URIs of 10,667 cultural heritage objects from 4 datasets of 2 data providers.

We have analyzed the resulting data from the crawling process, and calculated statistics about how the semantics-based frontier contributed for driving the crawling process. The evaluation results provide relevant information for understanding the contribution of semantics for the efficiency of crawling linked data.

We follow with related work on linked data crawling and the cultural domain. Section 3 presents our proposed method and Sect. 4 describes the case study for evaluating it. Section 5 presents the evaluation and our analysis. Section 6 highlights the conclusions of the study and describes future work.

2 Related Work

Crawling linked data is a similar process to crawling the Web of Documents. While WWW crawlers follow (mostly) HTML hyperlinks, linked data crawlers follow URIs present in RDF statements. Bing (2012, chapter 8) describes the underlaying concepts of web crawling and a categorization of different crawling methods [1]. According to the terminology used by Bing (2012), our crawling method falls in the type of preferential crawlers, which drive the crawling process by applying different forms of selective criteria toward some pages or hyperlinks (e.g., most "relevant"/topical, closest to seeds, popularity, the rate and amount of change, etc.). The method we propose mostly has characteristics from focused crawling, since it applies a heuristic to drive the crawling, however, it may also be considered a form of topic crawling, since the frontier of crawling is defined with criteria regarding data semantics. Some solid references in preferential crawling are the works of Chakrabarti et al. (1999) and Menczer et al. (2004), although unlike in our case, they have addressed the crawling of the Web of Documents and not the Web of Data [2, 3].

Software for linked data crawling has been researched and stable implementations are available [4]. Such software provides a typical crawling parametrization based on URI seeds and maximum crawling depth, as well as detailed configuration of the subtasks of crawling, allowing for programmatic control of the whole crawling task.

Regarding research on focused linked data crawling, Bai et al. (2015) uses context graphs to delimit the crawling to similar RDF resources, applying machine learning classifiers [5]. Another case is the work from Emamdadi et al. (2014) that focuses on crawling RDF embedded, or referenced, in HTML documents [6]. It crawls both HTML hyperlinks and RDF URIs, and guides the crawling task by calculating probabilities of a link not having any RDF data available. The most similar work to ours are those crawlers that use semantics of the crawled data [7, 8] but, although based on semantics, these address a different use case to ours. Bedi et al. (2012) tries to crawl related data for acquiring further data on a topic [8]. Do Vale et al. (2014) proposes a searching method in ontologies to make recommendations of related semantic data elements to support the work of data model experts [7].

Regarding data models in use within cultural heritage, the Europeana Data Model (EDM) [9] is used in Europeana and also in other networks using similar approaches for data aggregation. One example is the Digital Public Library of America (DPLA), which operates within the United States of America and uses a model based on EDM for the aggregation process of its network [10]. EDM has been a collaborative, community-based effort from the very start, involving representatives from all the domains represented in Europeana: libraries, museums, archives, and galleries. It is under continuous improvement since its creation, with the coordination and maintenance of the Europeana Foundation.

Our work also involves the Schema.org vocabulary, which aims to encourage the publication and consumption of structured data in the Internet. Its main application is to include structured data in web pages so that the data can be processed by search engines and other applications that use this structured data, in addition to text and links from the HTML body. Although developed with web pages in mind, Schema.org is also widely applied in linked data. Our experience within cultural heritage indicates that these institutions are increasingly adopting Schema.org as a means to improve the discovery of their holdings via Internet search engines.

Europeana is developing its capacities for handling cultural heritage data when represented with Schema.org. Europeana has published its research results in aligning EDM with Schema.org and also recommendations for cultural heritage institutions willing to represent their holdings using Schema.org [11]. Europeana has also researched the alignment of the two data models in the opposite direction [12]. It investigated the suitability of the Schema.org vocabulary to represent cultural heritage resources, and the conversion of Schema.org data into EDM.

3   The Crawling Method

Our work aims for an efficient crawling method, based on the definition of the crawling frontier by the semantics of data elements. In many domains, the high variety of linked data, mainly in terms of data models and vocabularies, makes it unfeasible to scan all the available data. In such cases, focusing the crawling on data with known semantic elements may reduce effort and demand for computing resources.

The typical crawling parameterization includes the configuration of crawling frontiers with parameters that are agnostic of any semantics. Among the most typical parameters are: a maximum limit of crawling depth; a maximum number of resources; and lists of domain names or IP addresses. With the rough frontier definition caused by the application of this type of parameters, crawling will in some cases require extensive network communication resources, and also high computation in post-crawl data analysis to find the actual data fitting the domain's purposes. In the end, the high demand for computational resources may make linked data crawling an unviable solution for smaller organizations.

Our crawling method improves the following aspects:

- Resource Usage Efficiency: unnecessary resources are skipped, leading to smaller volumes of the collected datasets and less network communication.
- Crawled Dataset Accuracy: by limiting the scope of a crawl by standard semantic metadata elements, we expect that our crawler will seek deeper within the crawled information sources, with no negative impact on computational resources usage efficiency.

Our method operates in two phases. First, we represent the domain's knowledge in terms of semantic data elements in the crawler's knowledge base. In the cultural heritage domain, this could be obtained through generating a semantic mapping of EDM to Schema.org to import the domain knowledge into the crawler's knowledge base. Secondly, a linked data crawler uses the knowledge base to make decisions on which RDF statements and resources to continue crawling and which ones to ignore.

To represent the domain's knowledge, we defined an RDF model with the following information:

- The RDF classes that are known to the domain.
- For each class, the RDF properties that can be applied to the class and are known by the domain.
- For each property, how their values are supported by the domain: as an RDF resource, or as an URI (when a property is applied by the domain for referring to resources only).

The above representation enables the crawler to make crawling decisions about which triples should be crawled, and about which crawling behaviour should be applied to each one. This allows for focusing the crawler on the data that the domain will be able to interpret. The representation enables the crawler to infer the following:

- The class instances that should be crawled or ignored.
- The properties that should be crawled or ignored.
- The crawled properties that, when referring to an RDF resource, should be collected but without further crawling to the referred resource.

With this information, it is possible for the crawler to avoid some of the limitations of the parameters applied in the general linked data crawling.

The crawler applies an algorithm that, guided by the knowledge base, dynamically redefines the crawling frontier as the crawling proceeds. The crawler invokes the frontier algorithm after an RDF resource has been collected (either one of the initial seeds or a subsequently crawled resource).

The algorithm, receives as input a set S of all RDF statements about the crawled resource, and three sets of URIs (of Schema.org data elements) derived from the knowledge base of the domain:

- The set S of all RDF statements about the resource.
- Three sets derived from the knowledge base of the semantics in the domain:

- Set C of classes known in the domain.
- Set P of properties known in the domain.
- Set R of properties used in the domain as references only, such that $R \subseteq P$.

The output of the algorithm consists of two sets:

- The subset of statements from S that can be interpreted by the domain (variable T in the algorithm below).
- The set of URIs found in interpretable statements of S, which the crawler should continue to crawl (variable V in the algorithm below).

The algorithm is executed as described in Fig. 1.

```
K ← ∅          ◄ a set of URIs to check for interpretable types
T ← ∅          ◄ a set of RDF statements (those interpretable)
V ← ∅          ◄ a set of URIs to be crawled
for each statement s of S
   if (predicate(s)=rdf:type) ∧ (object(s) ∉ C)
      K ← K ∪ object(s)
if K = ∅
   return ∅, ∅
for each statement s of S
   if predicate(s) ∈ P
      T ← T ∪ s
      if predicate(s) ∉ R ∧ IsURI(object(s)
         V ← V ∪ object(s)
   Return T, V
```

Fig. 1. Pseudo-code of the algorithm that computes the semantic crawling frontier.

For the implementation of the linked data crawler, we have adapted the software that we used in past research on linked data crawling [13]. We have instrumented the crawler with detailed logging on its intermediate execution stages, so that we could evaluate how the knowledge base guides a crawling process. In addition to the functionality of typical Web crawlers, our crawler also has built-in knowledge about the RDF(S) underlying concepts, allowing it to make crawl decisions by reasoning on the semantics of the crawled data.

4   Case Study

The case study aimed to evaluate our method, in a real scenario by analysing its crawling behaviour and the resulting crawled data. We used the cultural heritage domain and the network of organizations formed by Europeana and its data providers.

An overview of the process of the study is shown in Fig. 2. We applied our domain-focused linked data crawler as if it were used by Europeana. As a data aggregator, Europeana crawls the linked datasets from its data providers to obtain data on instances of the main entity of its data model - the cultural heritage object[1] More specifically, we used the case study to evaluate the extent to which our approach is able to define the frontiers for the linked data graph that concerns a singular cultural heritage object, or a set of such objects.

We have defined the knowledge base for the crawler's semantic frontier by aligning Schema.org and Europeana's EDM[2]. We then used the obtained Schema.org knowledge base for crawling the published linked data available from two Europeana data providers, the National Libraries of Finland and The Netherlands.

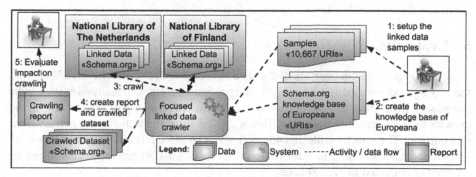

Fig. 2. An overview of the case study on Schema.org in Europeana.

Table 1. Data providers, datasets and number of URI seeds used for the evaluation. The dataset from Finland has more seeds than the three from the Netherlands combined.

Data provider	Name of dataset	URI seeds
National Library of The Netherlands	Children's books	340
	Alba amicorum	2,155
	Centsprenten	1,255
National Library of Finland	Fennica	6,917
Total		**10,667**

Regarding the mapping of the Europeana knowledge base to Schema.org, we identified 18 classes defined by Schema.org that are mapped to EDM classes. Within these 18 classes, 408 properties are being used by Europeana, with most of them used in more than one class (54 distinct properties of the 408). The listings of these classes and properties may be consulted in [14].

---

[1] Defined by EDM as "This class includes the Cultural Heritage objects that Europeana collects descriptions about" [9].

[2] We defined the knowledge base using the earlier work on alignment between EDM and Schema.org in both directions [11, 12] and also consulted the internal documentation of Europeana which contained additional updated information that is not yet publicly published.

The crawler was initialized with 3,750 URI seeds provided by the National Library of The Netherlands and 6,917 URI seeds provided by the National Library of Finland. The URI seeds from The Netherlands included the totality of the available data, while the URI seeds from Finland were just a portion of the complete dataset. We had three datasets from The Netherlands and one from Finland available for the evaluation. All datasets from The Netherlands were used because each one describes cultural objects of different types, each using different classes and properties of Schema.org. By using all datasets, we intended to obtain a more heterogeneous sample covering a wider range of Schema.org vocabulary elements. The distribution of URI seeds by collection in the sample is shown in Table 1.

5   Evaluation

This section presents an analysis of the data collected with the crawler initialised with the 10,667 seeds obtained as described in the previous section. Our analysis of the results focuses on measuring the extent to which the knowledge base was able to inform the crawler to make crawling decisions. Tables 2 and 3 show the statistics we extracted for this purpose. The crawler collected 45,236 interpretable RDF resources. The Europeana knowledge base was able to inform the crawler when a URI reference should not be crawled or collected in 72,309 cases.

Table 3 shows additional details about the different kinds of stop signals provided by the knowledge base. The most frequent signals were statements with predicates not interpretable by Europeana (57% of the stop signals), followed by signals resulting from RDF resources that did not contain any rdf:type that Europeana could interpret (36%). The third kind were statements with predicates that Europeana uses only with references to URI's and does not process the actual resources (7%).

Table 2. Statistics about how the crawling process was guided by the knowledge base in deciding when to continue crawling.

Data provider	URI seeds	RDF resources collected	Deeper crawling stopped	Maximum depth of 10 reached
National Library of The Netherlands	3,750	5,937	5,773	0
National Library of Finland	6,917	39,299	66,536	0
Total	10,667	45,236	72,309	0

The rightmost column of Table 2 indicates that the maximum depth was never reached in neither of the datasets (the crawling parameters were set for a maximum depth of 10). This implies that the semantically-defined frontier was capable to stop the crawler from requesting excessive, and unnecessary, data for the domain. Never reaching the maximum depth also implies that all relevant data crawled – the crawler always stopped crawling based on data with unknown semantics for the domain.

Table 3. Statistics about the different kinds of stop signals provided by the knowledge base.

Data provider	URI references collected	Predicates not interpretable	Types not interpretable
National Library of The Netherlands	5,046	696	31
National Library of Finland	0	40,282	26,254
Total	**5,046 (7%)**	**40,978 (57%)**	**26,285 (36%)**

Table 4 presents statistics of the data collected by the crawler. The initial 10,667 seeds resulted in a dataset containing 45,236 RDF resources and 138,857 statements all of which are interpretable by the cultural heritage domain.

Table 4. Statistics about the RDF dataset resulting from the crawling process.

Data provider	RDF resources collected	Statements collected
National Library of The Netherlands	5,937	74,093
National Library of Finland	39,299	64,764
Total	45,236	138,857

6 Conclusion and Future Work

Our study showed how limiting the focused crawling of linked data using semantic data elements, can lead to significant improvements in efficiency of crawling linked data. We delimited the frontiers for crawling based on the knowledge that the Europeana domain holds about the semantics of RDF(S) and Schema.org, and analysed its effect on the crawling process.

In the study, a large number of stop signals was triggered by the semantically-defined frontier, supporting that it can provide improvements in crawling efficiency. The crawler was parametrized with a maximum crawling depth of 10, and that depth was never reached in the tested datasets. This implies that this method for defining the frontier was capable of signalling to the crawler of the presence of data unnecessary data for the domain. Never reaching maximum depth, also implies that the crawler always stopped crawling based on data with unknown semantics for the domain.

Although our study shows that applying a semantically-defined frontier will generally improve the efficiency of crawling linked data, extrapolation of the results obtained in this study to other application domains, must be considered with care. Linked data is characteristically varied at large. For example, in a domain with extensive semantics, the interpretable linked data graph may become much larger and inter-connected, preventing a semantically-defined frontier from triggering sufficient stop signals. In such cases, it is likely that the crawler will need to be complemented with other crawling frontier strategies.

Regarding future work, we expect to conduct further research in investigating the usage of other vocabularies within Europeana's specifications and evaluate the results of extending the crawling method to these vocabularies.

Acknowledgments. This work was partly supported by Portuguese national funds through Fundação para a Ciência e a Tecnologia (FCT) with reference UIDB/50021/2020.

References

1. Liu, B.: Web Data Mining: Exploring Hyperlinks, Contents, and Usage Data, 2nd edn. Springer, Heidelberg (2011)
2. Chakrabarti, S., Van Den, M., Dom, B.E.: Focused crawling: a new approach to topic-specific Web resource discovery. Comput. Netw. Int. J. Comput. Telecommun. Netw. **31**, 1623–1640. (1999)
3. Menczer, F., Pant, G., Srinivasan, P.: Topical Web Crawl. Evaluating Adaptive Algorithms. ACM Trans. Internet Technol. (TOIT) **4**, 378-419 (2004)
4. Isele, R., Umbrich, J., Bizer, C., Harth, A.: LDSpider: an open-source crawling framework for the Web of linked data. In: Proceedings of the 9th International Semantic Web Conference Posters and Demos (ISWC 2010). CEUR-WS.org. (2010)
5. Bai, S., Hussain, S., Khoja, S.: A framework for focused linked data crawler using context graphs. In: 2015 International Conference on Information and Communication Technologies (ICICT). IEEE (2015)
6. Emamdadi, R., Kahani, M., Zarrinkalam, F.: A focused linked data crawler based on HTML link analysis. In: The 4th International Conference on Computer and Knowledge Engineering (ICCKE). IEEE (2014)
7. do Vale, A.G.R., Casanova, M.A., Lopes, G.R., Paes Leme, L.A.P.: CRAWLER-LD: a multilevel metadata focused crawler framework for linked data. In: Cordeiro, J., Hammoudi, S., Maciaszek, L., Camp, O., Filipe, J. (eds.) ICEIS 2014. LNBIP, vol. 227, pp. 302–319. Springer, Cham (2015). https://doi.org/10.1007/978-3-319-22348-3_17
8. Bedi, P., Thukral, A., Banati, H., Behl, A., Mendiratta, V.A.: Multi-threaded semantic focused crawler. J. Comput. Sci. Technol. **27**(6), 1233–1242 (2012)
9. Europeana Foundation: Definition of the Europeana Data Model v5.2.8. (2017). http://pro.europeana.eu/edm-documentation
10. Digital Public Library of America: Metadata Application Profile, version 4.0. (2015). https://dp.la/info/wp-content/uploads/2015/03/MAPv4.pdf
11. Wallis, R., Isaac, A., Charles, V., Manguinhas, H.: Recommendations for the application of Schema.org to aggregated cultural heritage metadata to increase relevance and visibility to search engines: the case of Europeana. Code4Lib J. **36** (2017)
12. Freire, N., Charles, V., Isaac, A.: Evaluation of Schema.org for aggregation of cultural heritage metadata. In: Gangemi, A., et al. (eds.) ESWC 2018. LNCS, vol. 10843, pp. 225–239. Springer, Cham (2018). https://doi.org/10.1007/978-3-319-93417-4_15
13. Freire, N., Meijers, E., Voorburg, R., Cornelissen, R., Isaac, A., de Valk, S.: Aggregation of linked data: a case study in the cultural heritage domain. In: Information, MPDI, vol. 10, no. 8 (2019)
14. Freire, N.: Domain-focused linked data crawling driven by a semantically defined frontier a cultural heritage case study in Europeana [Data set]. Zenodo. http://doi.org/10.5281/zenodo.4037857

The Intellectual Property Risks of Integrating Public Digital Cultural Resources in China

Yi Chen[1](✉) and Si Li[2](✉)

[1] Wuhan University, Wuhan 430072, Hubei, China
chenyi@whu.edu.cn
[2] Peking University, Peking 100871, China
pkulisi@pku.edu.cn

Abstract. To integrate public digital cultural resources is to cluster, integrate, and reorganize the scattered and relatively independent digital resources from libraries, museums, art galleries, cultural museums, and other public cultural institutions, to form an orderly joined digital resource system. However, there are intellectual property risks in the integration process. This paper discusses the intellectual property risks of integrating public digital cultural resources from three aspects: the change of the subject, object, and content. Moreover, some management measures are put forward, including easing restrictions on the integration of public digital cultural resources, establishing a copyright collective agency system, publishing necessary copyright statements, and protecting independent intellectual property.

Keywords: Public digital cultural resources · Integration · Intellectual property · Risks

1 Introduction

The integration of public digital cultural resources refers to the process of clustering, merging, and reorganizing scattered, disordered, and relatively independent digital objects from libraries, museums, art galleries, cultural museums, and other public cultural institutions [1]. Relying on modern digital network technology, the integration of public digital cultural resources has the potential to improve the efficiency of public cultural services.

In the process of integration of public digital cultural resources, the original interest of various copyright subjects and objects may be broken or reorganized, which inevitably involves many intellectual property issues. Ministry of Culture and Tourism of the People's republic of China has released a document to "strengthen the protection of intellectual property of public digital cultural resources [2]." Therefore, it is worth examining possible intellectual property risks during the process of integrating public digital cultural resources.

© Springer Nature Switzerland AG 2020
E. Ishita et al. (Eds.): ICADL 2020, LNCS 12504, pp. 349–354, 2020.
https://doi.org/10.1007/978-3-030-64452-9_32

2 Intellectual Property Risks in the Integration of Public Digital Cultural Resources

2.1 Change of Subject

The subject of copyright could be a natural person, a legal person, an unincorporated organization, or even a state. According to the different ways of acquiring rights, it can be divided into original subjects and successor subjects. The integration of public digital cultural resources may lead to the change of the subject of intellectual property rights. The ownership of the collection copyright in museums and art galleries is more complicated than that in libraries. It is worth noting that the property ownership of the collection as tangible property and the copyright of the collection are two completely different concepts. Museums and art galleries have property rights to the original collection, but it does not mean that they have copyright.

The complex nature of collections of different cultural institutions determines the complexity of their resource digitization. Institutions must obtain the authorization of copyright owners when digitizing their own proprietary collections. Although public cultural institutions such as libraries have a certain degree of "immunity" in resource reproduction, this is only limited to "the need for display or preservation of versions." Cultural resources integration, which requires large-scale digitization of resources, obviously does not belong to this scope. The digitized works may be either works of duty or works commissioned by others. One organization's own collection and the copyright of digital resources are both complex, which leads to a complicated copyright relationship in the process of resource integration where a lack of timely authorization and unclear contract agreement will bring new copyright risks.

The integration of public cultural digital resources requires that the digital resources originally distributed in various institutions should be integrated into a unified platform, and the subject of rights will be changed. If the agreement signed by the collection copyright owner and the cultural institution does not stipulate whether the digitalized resources can be used outside the institution, the institution's unauthorized integration of digital resources might violate the legitimate rights and interests of the copyright owner. Although Article 22 of the Copyright law of the People's Republic of China [3] and Article 7 of the Regulations on the Protection of the Right of Information Network Communication [4] have made special provisions on the issue of "reasonable use," they also emphasize that the importance of "providing services to the service objects in the library premises." After integrating digital resources, its communication far exceeds the scope of "the library premises."

The integration of digital cultural resources is for cultural popularization; whether it is reasonable use, both the direct purpose of using works and associated potential market influence should be considered. The change of subject contributes to the uncertainty of this factor. The resources have changed from being open only to their own users to being integrated into a unified platform to serve users of the whole network. Reasonable use must not be commercial use, but non-profit use may not be reasonable use.

2.2 Change of Object

With the development of science and technology, many new types of protected objects emerge, which makes the intellectual property problem more complex. All kinds of resources must be ordered and repackaged before they can be presented on the platform, such as the contrast of light and shade, color adjustment of images, which makes them have certain originality. Such copied works should be protected by copyright law due to their originality. The research results and derivative products obtained in the process of digital resource construction can also become the object of copyright because they meet the requirements of originality, perceptibility, and reproducibility. However, it is necessary to clarify the relationship between derivative works and original works. Derivative works that meet the original standards should be protected.

To integrate public cultural digital resources is mainly to establish a large number of databases with different characteristics through the digitalization of resources. A large number of large-scale and distinctive information databases are important to resource integration and information sharing. The database is a common way of organizing digital resources. If the selection or arrangement of the database is original, it will meet the standards of copyright protection in China. Since the 1990s, database protection has gradually adopted the standard of "selection or arrangement." According to the World Intellectual Property Organization Copyright Treaty [5], Directive 96/9/EC of the European Parliament and of the Council [6] and the Copyright law of China, compilations of data or other material, in any form, which by reason of the selection or arrangement of their contents constitute intellectual creations, are protected as such.

2.3 Change of Content

The integration of digital cultural resources is accompanied by new forms of information organization, new means of communication, and technical means, which may bring many unexpected situations. There will be new content of rights, including the rights of authors such as the right of information network communication, the right of reproduction, the right of distribution, and the rights of disseminators such as the right of publishers. Moreover, with the development of the Internet, the conflict between the privacy of copyright and public access and knowledge sharing is increasingly prominent. According to the traditional rules of copyright protection, it seems impossible to obtain authorization for massive information on the Internet, which will affect the efficiency of information dissemination negatively. Will the production of new copyright content affect the space of reasonable use and legal license? These problems have brought new challenges to intellectual property problems.

3 Intellectual Property Management Strategy for Integrating Public Digital Culture Resources

In the digital age, copyright protection is a means instead of an end. The ultimate purpose of copyright protection is to realize the reasonable dissemination of information and cultivate the market consisting of related industries, so as to promote the development of related industries.

LIBER, Europe's largest network of research libraries, has set out its position on European copyright reform through a statement prioritizing three high-level principles: ① Copyright should foster, not hinder, innovation and competitiveness; ② Access to and use of publicly funded research should not be unduly restricted by copyright; ③ Preservation of, and access to, cultural heritage must be supported by copyright exceptions. International Federation of Library Associations and Institutions (IFLA) issued Lyon Declaration on Access to Information and Development [7] on August 18, 2014, and The Declaration called upon United Nations Member States to make an international commitment through the UN 2030 Agenda for Sustainable Development to ensure that everyone has access to, and is able to understand, use and share the information that is necessary to promote sustainable development and democratic societies. LIBER issued The Hague Declaration on Knowledge Discovery in the Digital Age (Price, 2015) on May 6, 2015. The Declaration asserts that copyright was never designed to regulate the sharing of facts, data, and ideas – nor should it. The right to receive and impart information and ideas is guaranteed by the Universal Declaration of Human Rights but the modern application of IP law often limits this right, even when these most simple building blocks of knowledge are used [8]. Apparently, promoting the coordination of copyright and public access is the consistent position of IFLA and LIBER, which is also an international trend.

3.1 Easing Restrictions on the Integration of Public Digital Culture Resources

Although the Regulations on the Protection of the Right of Information Network Communication promulgated by the Chinese government lists exceptions for the digitization of resources in public institutions such as libraries, museums, memorials, and art galleries, there are strict restrictions on their use that do not apply to the integration of public digital cultural resources.

Integrating public digital cultural resources is for the public interest. This paper suggests that we should appropriately ease restrictions on the rights of libraries, museums, cultural centers, and other cultural institutions in the integration of digital cultural resources. The digitization and resource dissemination for resource integration should be included in the scope of reasonable use, so as to effectively avoid the risk of infringement caused by the change of subject or the issue of prior rights. Copyright amendment (digital agenda) act 2000 [9] in Australia allows libraries to reproduce and disseminate works to other libraries using digital technology for statutory interlibrary lending purposes. Considering the current situation of the integration of public digital cultural resources in China, this paper suggests that resource dissemination for user research or learning purposes, production and dissemination for Interlibrary borrowing and document transmission, and non-profit lectures for knowledge dissemination to the public and online broadcasting should all be in the scope of reasonable use. Extending the scope of reasonable use, the way of using works will be more flexible, thus reducing the risk of infringement.

3.2 Establishing the Collective Agency System of Copyright to Avoid the Conflict of Interest

The integration of public digital cultural resources mainly focuses on reproduction, compilation, and information network dissemination. Due to a large number of works involved and of related authors, it is almost impossible to obtain authorization from authors one by one. The traditional way for individuals to implement their rights has encountered great obstacles. Therefore, many countries choose Collective Management of Copyright and Related Rights [10] to deal with such authorization. The copyright collective management organization designated by the state or established by the industry association shall carry out agency authorization, collect royalties uniformly, and collect the objections of the obligee. The integration platform of public digital cultural resources can entrust this organization to sign copyright licensing agreements with various information resource owners to realize centralized authorization and management, so as to ensure the widespread dissemination of works without violating the authors' will.

3.3 Releasing Copyright Statements to Reduce the Risk of Resource Integration Infringement

It is an effective way to issue the necessary copyright statement on the homepage of public digital cultural resources integration platform to avoid infringement and protect their legitimate rights and interests. The copyright statement should achieve the following goals: first, it indicates the position of intellectual property protection of the system; second, it declares the intellectual property rights; third, it guides the user's use behavior; fourth, it informs the obligee of the measures to be taken; fifth, it meets the requirements of Chinese Copyright Law on the reasonable duty of care. Chineses National Digital Culture Network [11] published a statement on its website, and the National Digital Library of China also issued a copyright statement. However, almost all websites put the copyright statement at the bottom of the page, and few users actively click it. It is recommended that copyright statements should be placed in a prominent position on the webpage to minimize the risk of infringement.

3.4 Protect the Independent Intellectual Property Rights of the Integrated Platform

The integration of public digital cultural resources is the collection, organization, and compilation of various types of public cultural resources. As a whole and original data set, it has independent intellectual property rights. First, the protection of domain names. As a systematic naming mechanism, the domain name has become the code or logo of the owner of the web page. It has the characteristics of identity, uniqueness, and exclusiveness, and has an independent legal value. Secondly, the intellectual property rights of the original database built by the platform should be protected. Besides, the system security of the platform itself should always be maintained. Platform technicians should regularly maintain and update the system, repair system vulnerabilities, and constantly strengthen the system's security protection to prevent websites from collapse and malicious attacks.

4 Conclusion

Intellectual property problems may arise at all stages of the integration of public digital cultural resources. Intellectual property emphasizes the monopolization or monopoly of intellectual products by the obligee, while resource integration values the convenient access of resources by the public. Undoubtedly, there is a certain conflict between them. However, both share the essential purpose to promote cultural development and technological progress. To ensure the orderly dissemination of works and promote the progress of social science and culture, we should start from the actual needs of the social development, give full play to the vitality of resource innovation within the framework of legal permission, and maintain an appropriate balance between the interests of the obligee and the public.

References

1. Xiao, X.M., WanYan, D.D.: Research on ontology-based semantic interoperability of public digital cultural resources integration. J. Nat. Libr. China **3**, 43–48,49 (2015)
2. Ministry of Culture and Tourism of the People's republic of China. The construction plan of public digital culture during the 13th five-year plan of the Ministry of culture. http://zwgk.mct.gov.cn/auto255/201708/t20170801_688980.html?keywords=. Accessed 25 May 2020
3. Copyright law of the People's Republic of China. http://www.npc.gov.cn/npc/c2200/fls yywd_list.shtml
4. Regulations on the Protection of the Right of Information Network Communication. http://www.china.com.cn/policy/zhuanti/wlsq/2006-05/29/content_8126515_2.htm
5. WIPO Copyright Treaty. https://www.wipo.int/edocs/lexdocs/treaties/en/wct/trt_wct_001en.pdf. Accessed 25 May 2020
6. European Commission. https://ec.europa.eu/digital-single-market/en/protection-databases. Accessed 30 May 2020
7. IFLA, The Lyon Declaration. https://www.ifla.org/publications/node/11146. Accessed 30 May 2020
8. Library Journal. https://www.infodocket.com/2015/05/06/the-hague-declaration-on-knowle dge-discovery-in-the-digital-age-launches/. Accessed 02 June 2020
9. Australian Government. Copyright Amendment (Digital Agenda) Act 2000. https://www.leg islation.gov.au/Details/C2004C01235. Accessed 02 June 2020
10. WIPO. https://www.wipo.int/copyright/en/management/. Accessed 02 June 2020
11. Chineses National Digital Culture Network, http://www.ndcnc.gov.cn/. Accessed 02 June 2020

Metadata Interoperability for Institutional Repositories: A Case Study in Malang City Academic Libraries

Gani Nur Pramudyo[1]([✉]) [ID] and Muhammad Rosyihan Hendrawan[2]

[1] Department of Library and Information Science, Universitas Indonesia,
Jakarta 16424, Indonesia
gani_nurp@yahoo.com
[2] Department of Library and Information Science, Universitas Brawijaya,
Malang 65145, Indonesia
mrhendrawan@ub.ac.id

Abstract. The aim of this study is to understand, describe, and analyze metadata interoperability in Universitas Brawijaya Library that used Brawijaya Knowledge Garden (BKG) and Eprints software, University of Muhammadiyah Malang Library that used Ganesha Digital Library (GDL) and Eprints software, and Malang State Library that used Muatan Lokal (Mulok) software. This study also discussed supporting and inhibiting factors for interoperability metadata. This study employed a case study-qualitative approach. The finding indicates that the metadata interoperability can be performed by using metadata crosswalks. Implementation metadata crosswalks by mapping BKG fields and GDL Fields to the Dublin Core Metadata Element Set (DCMES). The results in the mapping of appropriate metadata schemes without removing the existing metadata scheme element and demonstrating technical specifications for standard metadata. Open Archives Initiative Protocol for Metadata Harvesting (OAI-PMH) features can use for metadata interoperability in the union catalog that have been being developed by the National Library of Indonesia, called Indonesia OneSearch. The supporting factors in metadata interoperability are standard metadata and a standard protocol for interoperability; whereas, the inhibiting factor is the minimum human resources having metadata capability and the open access policy that has not applied to each academic libraries. All of those academic libraries need to make an effort to external interoperability to union catalogs to improve visibility digital content and applied open access policies.

Keywords: Metadata crosswalks · Metadata interoperability · Institutional repositories

1 Introduction

Digital library development has encouraging academic libraries to adapt this situation. Digital library development in academic libraries, also known as an

E. Ishita et al. (Eds.): ICADL 2020, LNCS 12504, pp. 355–363, 2020.
https://doi.org/10.1007/978-3-030-64452-9_33

institutional repository, can facilitate information governance. The institutional repository is a set of services provided by the university for their community in digital resources management and dissemination [1]. To supporting digital resources management and dissemination, the library needs institutional repository software. The library can choose open-source software such as Dspace and Eprints, or develop their institutional repository software such as BKG and Mulok [2].

In Indonesia, there are 487 universities and 80 institutional repositories indexed by Webometrics. They revealed a lack of Indonesia repository developments [3]. Currently, 2.694 universities [4] and 116 institutional repositories in Indonesia [5] are indexed by Webometrics. They show a slight increase in Indonesia's repository developments. Furthermore, 137 Indonesia repositories registered in OpenDOAR. Eprints are the most popular software used by the institution (78%), followed by DSpace (9%), Bepress (1%), Omeka (1%), Weko (1%), and other (10%) [6]. In addition, one of the initiators Indonesia OneSearch (2018), recommend: "Eprints are easy to manage, process, maintain, backup, and use the Dublin Core Metadata Element Set (DCMES) and Open Archives Initiative Protocol for Metadata Harvesting (OAI-PMH)". Eprints can use as alternative software to develop institutional repositories in academic library.

Implementation of institutional repository software deals with resource description, metadata schema, and various other data. Metadata is structured information about information resources from multiple media types or formats [7]. Metadata has many purposes, such as resource identification and description, information retrieval, managing information resources, managing intellectual property rights, interoperability, and information governance [8]. Several metadata examples are used by institution such as DCMES, MARC, MODS, and EAD [9].

In Malang City academic libraries, diversity of software and metadata schemes occur at Universitas Brawijaya Library, University of Muhammadiyah Malang Library, and Malang State University Library. Universitas Brawijaya Library makes data migration from BKG to Eprints, and University of Muhammadiyah Malang Library makes data migration from GDL to Eprints. BKG and GDL have no metadata standard, difficult to indexing, have no support developing, whereas Eprints has support for developing, popular, Dublin Core, support indexing, and support for the webometric repository. In contrast, Malang State University Library was used and developed Mulok by creating attribute Dublin Core and OAI-PMH.

Differences between software and metadata schema can impact the library for the exchange and data sharing. Thus, the library needs to achieve metadata interoperability. Nevertheless, in their implementation, uniform for software and metadata schema is challenging to achieve and for instance, using MARC and DCMES that have different purposes. The library needs to adapt the method for the implementation of metadata interoperability [10].

The effort of achieving metadata interoperability can employ metadata frameworks, crosswalks, application profiles, and metadata registries [11].

Metadata crosswalks is a popular method for achieving metadata interoperability in different metadata scheme. Metadata crosswalks used to describe the implementation of metadata scheme in institutional repository software, to compare different metadata schema, to show interoperability between different software and metadata schema for exchange and sharing of data [10]. Metadata crosswalks are intellectual activity to compare and analyze two metadata schema and crosswalks as the visual product of mapping [12].

However, a few researchers who tried to examine metadata interoperability used metadata crosswalks [10,13,14]. Several issues have no discussed in metadata interoperability, such as the implementation of metadata interoperability in institutional software when exchange and sharing of data, also inhibiting and supporting factors. The aim of this study is to understand, describe, and analyze metadata interoperability in institutional repository software; Universitas Brawijaya Library, University of Muhammadiyah Malang Library, and Malang State University Library. This study also discusses inhibiting and supporting factors to perform metadata interoperability in institutional repository software.

2   Related Works

Several studies discussed metadata interoperability. First, Metadata interoperability performs in repository and metadata projects. This study employs descriptive qualitative approach. Metadata interoperability is divided into three levels such as scheme, record, and repository level. Metadata interoperability on scheme level comprise derivation, application profiles, crosswalks, switching-across, framework, and registry [10]. Second, Metadata interoperability on scheme level using metadata crosswalks for EAD and MODS. Its study employs a descriptive qualitative approach. The result describes semantic metadata interoperability that analyzes metadata mapping from EAD to MODS [13]. Third, metadata interoperability on scheme level using metadata crosswalks for ONIX Version 3.0 and MARC 21. It study employ a descriptive qualitative approach. Implementation of metadata crosswalks is mapping metadata elements of ONIX to MARC 21. This study revealed the capability metadata scheme to exchange and sharing of data [14].

This study is using metadata crosswalks to achieve metadata interoperability on the scheme level. Metadata crosswalks facilitate mapping source metadata schemes to target metadata schemes discussed in this study. This study also examined supporting and inhibiting factors in achieving metadata interoperability at Universitas Brawijaya Library, University of Muhammadiyah Malang Library, and Malang State University Library.

3   Research Method

The study employ a case study qualitative approach. This study employs four types of data collection techniques such as observation, interview, document, and audio-video material. The researcher performs direct observation in repository

Universitas Brawijaya Library, University of Muhammadiyah Malang Library, and Malang State University Library. To collect primary sources, a structured interview was used. The study involved interviewing 16 informants, there are library manager, expert staff, Coordinator and IT Staff, librarian, and users. The technique for selecting the informants is sampling purposeful. The sampling purposeful is selected individuals and places to study due to they provide understanding of the research problem and the phenomena in the study [15]. The supporting document are library guide, regulation of institutional repository, Standard Operational Procedure (SOP). In addition, photo and interview recordings are collected as Audio-video material to support this research. The study perform data collection from 1 February to 30 April 2018.

The result of data capture was processed and analyzed using Creswell data analysis. The data analysis in this study are following: 1) Organize and prepare the data for analysis; 2) Read or look at all the data 3) Start coding all of the data 4) Generate a description and themes 5) Generate a description and themes 6) Write Interpretation of data [16]. The validity of the data used the triangulation of information data sources, conducting a question and answer with fellow researchers, and inviting an auditor to review the entire research project. Reliability procedure used checking results of the transcription, ensuring there are no floating definitions and meanings of the codes during the coding process, and cross-checking the codes developed by other researchers by comparing the results obtained independently [16].

4   Results and Discussion

4.1   Metadata Interoperability

Universitas Brawijaya Library performs internal metadata interoperability when migration BKG to Eprints by IT staff. IT staff is understanding database structure of Eprints and BKG, searching for similar fields, and implementing a mapping scheme. When mapping scheme, there are different fields such as contributor, bibliographic citation, language, extend, date accepted, and year submitted have to discarded because not be needed. On the other side, abstract with Indonesia language and English added in Eprints.

In University of Muhammadiyah Malang Library, internal metadata interoperability has no perform when migration GDL to Eprints. Librarian uploads manually for each file one by one to Eprints. GDL and Eprints still used in University of Muhammadiyah Malang Library because there is no decision about using one repository software.

In contrast, Malang State University Library still used Mulok software to support library needs. Metadata interoperability problems do not exist in the library. Malang State University Library does not follow other libraries that used open-source repository software such as Eprints or DSpace and prefer to develop Mulok as institutional development repository software.

Furthermore, Universitas Brawijaya Library, University of Muhammadiyah Malang Library, and Malang State University Library were implementing external metadata interoperability. Each library was joining Indonesia OneSearch. Indonesia OneSearch is the Indonesia union catalog that integrated online catalog, institutional repository, and e-resources from the library, archive, museum, other documentation institution in Indonesia on a centralized database. Indonesia OneSearch harvest metadata for each institution. University of Muhammadiyah Malang Library also joins in Open DOAR and ROARMAP. Open DOAR is a union catalog that contains repository in the world level, and ROARMAP is a registry search that contains policies and open access privilege.

4.2   Metadata Crosswalks

Metadata interoperability issues occur due to various software and metadata schemes. These issues emerge to achieve metadata interoperability for institutional repositories. The differences between institutional repository software and metadata schemes can be searched, exchanged, transferred, used, and understood by institutions for different purposes by implementing interoperability such a metadata crosswalks [11]. In this research, example of metadata crosswalks refers to metadata interoperability in Malang City academic libraries. There are four institutional repository software and three metadata schemes, see Table 1.

Table 1. Metadata and repository software in Malang City academic libraries.

No	Institution	Software	Metadata
1	Universitas Brawijaya Library	BKG version 2.0	BKG Fields
		Eprints version 3.3	DCMES
2	University of Muhammadiyah Malang Library	GDL version 4.2	GDL Fields
		Eprints version 3.3	DCMES
3	Malang State University Library	Mulok	DCMES
	Total	4	3

Metadata crosswalks is a table or chart, shows the relationship and equality between two or more metadata formats. Metadata crosswalks are used to compare metadata elements from one scheme or more to others [17]. The study perform mapping scheme from BKG fields and GDL fields (source metadata scheme) to DCMES (target metadata scheme). The mapping scheme used relative crosswalking approach. Relative crosswalking is used to map all elements of source schema to at least one target schema element, regardless of whether two elements are semantic or unequal [10].

Metadata crosswalks perform by identifying attributes of BKG fields and GDL fields, identifying attributes of DCMES, and mapping metadata elements from BKG and GDL fields to DCMES. For instance, mapping title elements on BKG fields and GDL fields to DCMES. The title is the name given to the

resource. Typically, the title will be a name whose resources are formally known
[7]. Each attribute identified to ensure that the element is consistent.

Table 2. Example of metadata crosswalks mapping.

No	Attribute	DCMES	BKG Fields	GDL Fields
1	Title	dc.title	dl_detil_ct100_label11	Title
2	Creator	dc.creator	dl_detil_ct100_label16	Creator
3	Subject	dc.subject	dl_detil_ct100_label13	Subject
4	Description	dc.description	dl_detil_ct100_label19	Description
5	Type	dc.type	dl_detil_ctl00_Label3	Type

Refer to Table 2, BKG fields and GDL fields can map to DCMES. Metadata
crosswalks are used as the first step to the interoperability of institutional repository software. Metadata crosswalks can keep and maintain metadata elements
when performing metadata interoperability. Metadata crosswalks are also used
to analyze metadata schemes, compare metadata schemes, and bridge different
metadata schemes. Institutions that have a different metadata scheme can share
and exchange data. Theese findings are appropriate with Woodley [12], different
metadata content basically can be exchanged and shared; the use of uniform
metadata standards is challenging to create by institutions because they have
different needs. Metadata crosswalks [10] shows that different metadata schemes
can be exchanged and shared.

Metadata crosswalks are not implementing in Universitas Brawijaya Library
when migrating BKG fields into Eprints. Several elements were lost when migrating data such as contributors, bibliographic citation, languages, extend, date
accepted, and date submitted. In University of Muhammadiyah Malang Library,
metadata cross-walks not implemented too, as they upload data manually. It
requires a long process, as they have many digital contents. In Malang State
University Library, metadata crosswalks is useful for analyzing metadata scheme
and metadata interoperability capabilities.

4.3   Implementation of Metadata Crosswalks

The primary use of metadata crosswalks is to serve as base specifications for
physically converting records from one metadata scheme to another for record
exchange, contribution to union catalogs, or metadata harvesting (Caplan, 2003).
Metadata crosswalks can be used to analyze metadata schemes and exchange
data repository in union catalog

Metadata interoperability can be performed in union catalog, for instance:
integrating repository into Indonesia OneSearch. The first, Academic library
has to register and add a repository in Indonesia OneSearch that can access
http://onesearch.id. Hereafter, academic library creates a new account and fill

required data. Adding repository is selecting with add repository menu and filling out the repository form. The repository form contains repository information to add institutional repositories, journal information to add journals, system information containing software characteristics and metadata used, technical contact, repository groups, and subject area information can fill as needed, see Fig. 1.

Fig. 1. Repository form in Indonesia OneSearch

Eprints and Mulok that has DCMES and OAI-PMH features can be joining and integrating their data into Indonesia OneSearch. While BKC and CDL have no metadata standard and OAI-PMH features, as they not available to join and integrate data into Indonesia OneSearch. After joining and integrating data into Indonesia OneSearch, registered repository will automatically harvested metadata within every day, week, or month. The harvest metadata was in a centralized database and each institution in it will be integrated. For instance, when user is searching for a collection, Indonesia OneSearch will automatically integrate the collected metadata and show result of digital resources or institutions catalogs that joined it.

4.4 Supporting and Inhibit Factor on Metadata Interoperability

Supporting Factor. All of those Malang City academic libraries' institutional repository use DCMES that makes it easy to describe sources and retrieve information objects in a web search system. DCMES [7] is a general-purpose scheme for resource description originally intended to facilitate discovery of information objects on the Web. DCMES used to descriptions of source and retrieval in the web search system. DCMES also used as a standard minimum to metadata interoperability using OAI-PMH. BKG and GDL can adapt DCMES in repository like Mulok that formerly has no metadata standard.

OAI-PMH provides an application-independent interoperability framework based on harvesting metadata. Metadata from various sources can be collected in central database, and their services can be provided based on centralized data [18]. All of those Malang City academic libraries' institutional repository have OAI-PMH features that can use for metadata interoperability in Indonesia OneSearch. OAI-PMH features can be added in BKG and GDL by accessing http://wiki.onesearch.id/doku.php?id=oai-pmh-sample. This site provides an OAI-PMH source code that can add to BKG and GDL.

Inhibit Factors. Without qualified human resources, library aims were not working effectively. Qualified human resources such a system librarian has an important role in developing software [19]. The software and hardware will not be able to operate without system librarians that operate it. The human resources in all of those Malang City academic libraries have an important role to achieve metadata crosswalks. Metadata crosswalks require in depth knowledge and specialized expertise in related metadata standards. A common mistake in applying metadata crosswalks such as metadata standard is often used independently and determined using particular terminology, methods, and processes [20]. The difference in label naming, definition, and usage of metadata elements in BKG fields, GDL fields, and DCMES must be considered.

Open access refers to a variety of digital literature that is available online, free of charge, and free from all bound or copyright or licensing restrictions. The provider puts various files, and each file provided to anyone who can access [21]. Metadata crosswalks can be performed by integrating repository into Indonesia OneSearch. However, each library has no enact an open access policy, thus users only see abstract and bibliographic descriptions in their institutional repositories.

5   Conclusion

Metadata interoperability of BKG, Eprints, GDL, and Mulok software can perform using metadata crosswalks. Metadata crosswalks used as the first step of interoperability that produced a mapping scheme. Metadata crosswalks show each institutional repository software has interoperability capability, standardized and non-standard metadata, and makes it easier to arrange institutional repository software before migration. Metadata crosswalks use to understand, analyze, and describe repository software that supports the exchange and sharing of data in union catalogs, for in-stance, Indonesia OneSearch. All of those Malang City academic libraries' institutional repository have DCMES and OAI-PMH features that support interoperability in Indonesia OneSearch. Otherwise, BKG and GDL has no standard metadata and OAI-PMH features.

As a suggestion, to improve interoperability and the visibility of digital content at the world level, libraries need to join the OCLC WorldCat, ROARMAP, and Open DOAR. Furthermore, the open access policy in institutional repositories needs to enact in academic libraries.

References

1. Lynch, C.A.: Institutional repositories: essential infrastructure for scholarship in the digital age. Portal Libr. Acad. **3**(2), 327–36 (2003)
2. Pramudyo, G.N., Hendrawan, M.R.: Pemilihan Perangkat Lunak Repositori Institusi Perpustakaan Perguruan Tinggi Di Kota Malang (Studi Kasus Di Perpustakaan Universitas Brawijaya, Perpustakaan Universitas Negeri Malang, dan Perpustakaan Universitas Muhammadiyah Malang). Baca J. Dokumentasi Dan Inf. **39**, 161–177 (2018)
3. Prasetyawan, Y.Y.: Perkembangan Open Access dan Kontribusinya bagi Komunikasi Ilmiah di Indonesia. Anuva J. Kaji. Budaya, Perpustakaan, dan Inf. **1**, 93–100 (2017)
4. Webometrics.info: Indonesia—Ranking Web of Universities: Webometrics ranks 30000 institutions. https://www.webometrics.info/en/asia/indonesia. Accessed 19 Sept 2020
5. Webometrics.info: TRANSPARENT RANKING: Institutional Repositories by Google Scholar (April 2020)—Ranking Web of Repositories. https://repositories.webometrics.info/en/institutional. Accessed 19 Sept 2020
6. OpenDOAR: Open DOAR Browse by Country and Region
7. Caplan, P.: Metadata fundamentals for all librarians. American Library Association (ALA), USA (2003)
8. Haynes, D.: Metadata for Information Management and Retrieval: Understanding Metadata and its Use. Facet Publishing, London (2018)
9. NISO: Understanding Metadata: What is Metadata, and What is it For?: A Primer (2017)
10. Chan, L.M., Zeng, M.L.: Metadata interoperability and standardization - a study of methodology part I. D Lib. Mag. **12**, 1–18 (2006). https://doi.org/10.1045/june2006-zeng
11. Hodge, G.: Metadata for electronic information resources: from variety to interoperability. Inf. Serv. Use. **25**, 35–45 (2005)
12. Baca, M.: Introduction to Metadata. Getty Publications, Los Angeles (2016)
13. Bountouri, L., Gergatsoulis, M.: Interoperability between archival and bibliographic metadata: an EAD to MODS crosswalk. J. Libr. Metadata **9**, 98–133 (2009). https://doi.org/10.1080/19386380903095107
14. Godby, C.J.: A Crosswalk from ONIX Version 3.0 for Books to MARC 21. OCLC Research, Dublin (2012)
15. Creswell, J.: Penelitian kualitatif dan desain Riset: Memilih di antara lima pendekatan. Pustaka Pelajar, Yogyakarta (2015)
16. Creswell, J.: Research Design: Pendekatan metode kualitatif, kuantitatif, dan campuran. Pustaka Pelajar, Yogyakarta (2016)
17. Baca, M.: Introduction to Metadata. Getty Publications, Los Angeles (2008)
18. Open Archive: The Open Archives Initiative Protocol for Metadata Harvesting (2015). https://www.openarchives.org/pmh/
19. Pendit, P.L.: Perpustakaan Digital: Perspektif Perpustakaan Perguruan Tinggi. Sagung Seto, Jakarta (2007)
20. St. Pierre, M., LaPlant, W.P.: Issues in crosswalking content metadata standards. Inf. Stand. Q. (1999)
21. Pendit, P.L.: Perpustakaan Digital dari A sampai Z. Citra Karyakarsa Mandiri, Jakarta (2008)

MetaProfiles - A Mechanism to Express Metadata Schema, Privacy, Rights and Provenance for Data Interoperability

Nishad Thalhath[1]([⊠])[iD], Mitsuharu Nagamori[2][iD], and Tetsuo Sakaguchi[2][iD]

[1] Graduate School of Library, Information and Media Studies, Tsukuba, Japan
nishad@slis.tsukuba.ac.jp
[2] Faculty of Library, Information and Media Studies, University of Tsukuba,
Tsukuba, Japan
{nagamori,saka}@slis.tsukuba.ac.jp
https://www.slis.tsukuba.ac.jp

Abstract. Documenting datasets in an actionable way is an essential approach to ensure data interoperability. Guidelines like FAIR (Findability, Accessibility, Interoperability, and Reusability) ensures better use-cases for the data. Proposals like metadata applications profiles provide mechanisms to express constraints and metadata schema of the datasets. In order to provide Ethical, Legal, and Social Aspects/Implications (ELSA/ELSI), datasets require more than the application profiles. Along with the schema, expressing privacy aspects of the data and constraints on rights and licenses also ensures proper ELSI. A good dataset profile needs validation rules provided in actionable formats and with human-readable documentation. A sample data will help the consumers to streamline the process of adapting the datasets. Different solutions exist to express these various components required to represent the datasets, such as DCAT to express the datasets, ShEx, and SHACL to provide validation for datasets, Datapackage for providing the schema for tabular data, DCAP for creating metadata application profiles, vocabularies like DPV to provide privacy constraints and ORDL to express rights of datasets. However, there is no simplified mechanism to interlink and distinguish these various elements in an actionable format. This research is intended to devise a mechanism to express a complete profile package for datasets, as 'MetaProfile.' MetaProfile is intended to cover a dataset's profile with privacy, rights, and other essential components to ensure ELSI and interoperability of datasets. This research's expected outcome is to provide a format and vocabulary to fill in the gaps of existing solutions for interlinking and notating different components of a profile.

Keywords: Metadata · Data publishing · Datasets · FAIR · ELSI · Data privacy · Semantic Web

E. Ishita et al. (Eds.): ICADL 2020, LNCS 12504, pp. 364–370, 2020.
https://doi.org/10.1007/978-3-030-64452-9_34

1   Introduction

1.1   Significance of FAIR and ELSI

One of the underlying guidelines for data management that ensures data find-ability is the FAIR principle [11]: —Findability, Accessibility, Interoperability, and Reusability formulated by FORCE11 - The Future of Research Communications and e- Scholarship. FAIR principles are not protocols or standards but are underlying guidelines that relies on data/metadata standards to allow for data to be reused by machines and humans.

Publishing findable datasets that ensures data reuse allows data stakehold-ers to verify inferences, reanalyze or merge new datasets. For example, data journalism that relies on open data to bring in transparency, accountability and increased citizen awareness in governance polices relies on the availability of open data that are easily accessible, linkable and findable [7]. At the same time data publishers needs to express the constraints on privacy, rights and licenses of the datasets.

Since the Ethical, Legal, and Social Aspect/Implication (ELSA/ELSI) is con-ceptual, it can only be inferred from existing practical elements, such as privacy, legal, and licensing constraints or documentation. To ensure ELSI/ELSA of the datasets and their acceptance by any automated systems or human consumers, clear privacy and rights expression – both machine-actionable formats and doc-umentation of the data – are required.

1.2   Existing Standards in Expressing Datasets

Some of the standards and vocabularies for defining data/metadata that ensure data longevity and stewardship based on FAIR principles include: Dublin Core, Data Catalog Vocabulary (DCAT), VOID -Vocabulary for Interlinked Data [3], schema.org, etc. W3C's DCAT is an resource description file (RDF) vocabulary designed to facilitate interoperability between data catalogs published on the Web. Dublin Core[TM] Metadata Initiative (DCMI) brought forward the Dublin Core[TM] Metadata Element (Dublin Core) and additional vocabularies referred to as "DCMI metadata terms" for use in RDF vocabularies for making data linkable. DCAT addresses the heterogeneity of metadata standards required across different dataset maintenance combining the Dublin Core vocabularies and SKOS vocabularies. VOID uses RDF based schema for describing metadata and is complementary to the DCAT model. Schema.org provides framework to provide supporting information descriptions of data which makes data discov-ery easier through services like Google Dataset Search engine. Data Privacy Vocabulary (DPV)[1] provides an complete set of vocabularies to express privacy constraints.

---

[1] https://www.w3.org/ns/dpv.

1.3   State of the Art in Explaining the Data and Profiles

Metadata Application Profiles. Metadata application profiles (MAP) provides a means to structure and customise the metadata instance by documenting the elements, policies, guidelines, and vocabularies for that particular implementation along with the schemas, and applicable constraints [4]. MAP gives the specific syntax guidelines and data format, description set profiles (DSP), domain consensus and alignment [1,5]. DSP format is obtained from the DCMI guidelines, expressed through XML or RDF. With the emergence of Semantic Web concept, application profiles are expressed using JSON-LD and OWL with increasing use cases using validation tools like ShEx or SHACL. MAP authoring formats like YAMA [10] uses YAML for authoring MAP.

Data Profiles. Data profiles are profiles generally intended to express the structure and organization of the data of data sources like CSV and JSON. Data packages may not necessarily express the metadata of the data elements or express the properties of the elements. On the other hand, data packages provide validation schemas and related tooling ecosystems to verify, reuse, and convert the data. Well established data profiles like Frictionless data DataPackage[2] provides JSON schemas to describe the data resources and express constraints, mostly on tabular data. Data profile specifications also explain mechanisms to notate RDF friendly metadata by expressing URIs as rich types[3]. A minimal subset of CSVW can be used in expressing data profiles of tabular data [9]. However, generally, CSVW is more suitable in explaining linkable data from tabular data resources.

The Profiles Vocabulary. Profiles vocabulary [2] is an RDF vocabulary which allows to semantically link datasets with the machine-readable description of the profiles. The idea of Profiles Vocabulary (PROF) was triggered by the appearance of multiple profiles of the DCAT and examples of profile description and implementation guidance systems such as the guidelines for DCAP and the OpenGeospatial Consortium's standard for modular specifications. Profile resources may be human-readable documents (PDFs, textual documents), vocabularies, schemas or ontologies (XSD, RDF), constraint language resources used by specific validation tools (SHACL, ShEx, Schematron), or any other files or profile resources with each profile resource assigned to roles that define its functions within the profile.

1.4   Limitations of Existing Solutions

The FAIR principle is a set of recommendations, and these recommendations should be implemented using existing standards. FAIR does not provide a practical framework or guidelines for satisfying these recommendations in data publishing. In order to make FAIR concepts acceptable for all levels of expertise,

---

[2] https://specs.frictionlessdata.io/data-package/.

[3] https://specs.frictionlessdata.io/table-schema/#rich-types.

there should be some robust framework and guidelines. Also, FAIR cannot be achieved with a single standard. Different existing standards are needed to be combined to incorporate maximum FAIR concepts in the datasets. Combining these standards requires higher skills and resources. FAIR alone is not sufficient enough in expressing the ethical, legal, and social implications of datasets. Hence, the implementation of FAIR concepts expressing datasets should also include mechanisms to express ELSI elements as well.

To support data interoperability as per FAIR principles, there should be different components to express the metadata, data validation, and human-readable documentation. Existing solutions lack a detailed mechanism for organizing these components and expressing and pointing to individual resources satisfying these requirements in a distinguishable, accessible, and actionable way. A detailed comparison matrix of major existing standards – Data Catalog Vocabulary (DCAT), Dataset Publishing Language (DSPL)[4], schema.org Dataset[5], Open Digital Rights Language (ODRL) [6], Profiles Vocabulary (PROF), DublinCore Application Profile (DCAP)[6], Metadata Vocabulary for Tabular Data (CSVW), Data Cube [8], Data Privacy Vocabulary (DPV), Data Package, Vocabulary of Interlinked Datasets (VoID) – is provided in Table 1. It is evidential that to achieve a higher level of FAIR with ELSI, these standards should be combined and organized.

Table 1. Comparison matrix of existing approaches

	Vocabulary	RDF	Non-RDF	Privacy	Rights	Profile	Expressed in
DCAT	Yes	Yes	Yes	No	Minimal	No	RDF
DSPL	No	No	Yes	No	Minimal	Yes	Custom
schema.org	Yes	Yes	Yes	No	Minimal	No	Independent
ORDL	Yes	Yes	Yes	No	Yes	No	RDF, JSON-LD
PROF	Yes	Yes	Yes	No	Minimal	Yes	RDF
DCAP	Yes	Yes	Yes	No	No	Yes	Custom
CSVW	Yes	No	Yes	No	Minimal	Yes	JSON
Data cube	Yes	Yes	No	No	No	No	RDF
DPV	Yes	Yes	Yes	Yes	No	No	RDF
Data package	No	No	Yes	No	Minimal	Yes	JSON
VoID	Yes	Yes	No	No	No	No	RDF

2   Methods

There are no significant studies on ELSA of FAIR models within a proper technical perspective. Ensuring the ethical & legal framework is also important for

[4] https://developers.google.com/public-data/overview.
[5] https://schema.org/Dataset.
[6] https://dcmi.github.io/dcap/.

ensuring the fairness of FAIR data. This research aims to devise some mechanism to express the profile of a dataset with privacy, rights, and other essential components to ensure ELSA within FAIR principles.

Major goals of this attempt are:

1. Identify and combine possible standards to express FAIR with ELSI for datasets.
2. Develop a set of vocabulary terms to combine existing standards and formats as a complete profile package.
3. Produce a set of tools to make the authoring and validation of the data profile conveniently, for non-experts as well.

2.1   MetaProfile

MetaProfile is the work in progress outcome of this investigation. MetaProfile is defined as a profile framework for datasets, supporting FAIR and ELSI for data publication. MetaProfile is not an attempt to create a new set of standards but to create a comprehensive and simplified profile framework using existing standards. MetaProfile is modular and extensible by providing coverage for diverse real-world use-cases. A schematic representation of the proposed simplified model of MetaProfile is illustrated in Fig. 1. The model of MetaProfile and its components are listed in Table 2.

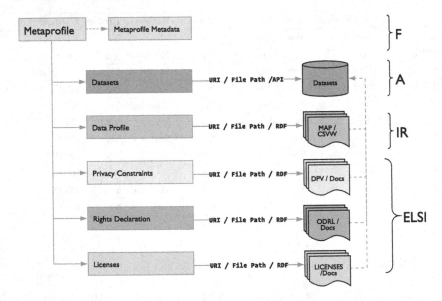

Fig. 1. MetaProfiile overview, components and corresponding FAIR+ELSI elements.

Table 2. MetaProfile components

Component	Description
MetaProfile metadata	Metadata of the profile - Version of the profile, Schema version of the profile, Identifier
Datasets	Locators for the dataset, which is expressed by this profile - URI, API/Endpoints, File Path, Data expressed as RDF within the MetaProfile
Data profiles	Explain structure of the datasets - Profiles can be actionable or documentation. Eg: Application Profiles, CSVW, Human readable documentation, Datapackage Format, RDF/OWL
Privacy constraints	A formal privacy declaration language like DPV expressed in RDF or human readable documentation, It can be a separate files, or declare within the MetaProfile
Rights declaration	Rights can be declared either as in ODRL vocabulary in RDF or as a human readable rights policy documentation.
Licenses	Licenses should be declared with its relationship to the corresponding sections of the datasets. One or many license can be declared, Licenses can be actionable, different license files or URIs

3   Progress and Validation

This investigation is progressing with identifying a complete set of terms to express minimal but essential FAIR+ELSI components, recognizing the missing elements from available vocabularies, and developing a minimal custom vocabulary to fill the gaps. Some of the anticipated outcomes are developing a set of tools and a simplified format to write/create these standard expressions. For evaluation of the proposal, the authors are intending to validate the output formats, and qualitatively evaluate the capability of these outputs in expressing FAIR+ELSI components.

4   Conclusion

There are significant studies and models to explain and adapt FAIR in data publishing. Also, there are limited but notable studies on ELSI/A of data publishing and reuse. However, there are no significant studies on ELSA of FAIR models within a proper technical perspective. Ensuring the ethical & legal framework is also important for ensuring the fairness of FAIR data. This work-in-progress research aims to devise a suitable mechanism to express the profile of a dataset with privacy, rights, and other essential components to ensure ELSA within FAIR principles by identifying and combining possible standards to express FAIR with ELSI for datasets and to develop a set of vocabulary terms to create a complete profile package for expressing datasets.

References

1. Baca, M.: Introduction to Metadata (2016). http://www.getty.edu/publications/intrometadata
2. Car, N.: The profiles vocabulary. W3C note, W3C, December 2019. https://www.w3.org/TR/2019/NOTE-dx-prof-20191218/
3. Cyganiak, R., Alexander, K., Hausenblas, M., Zhao, J.: Describing linked datasets with the VoID vocabulary. W3C note, W3C, March 2011. https://www.w3.org/TR/2011/NOTE-void-20110303/
4. Heery, R., Patel, M.: Application Profiles: Mixing and Matching Metadata Schemas. Ariadne, no. 25 (2000). http://www.ariadne.ac.uk/issue/25/app-profiles/
5. Hillmann, D.: Metadata standards and applications, Metadata Management Associates LLC (2006). http://managemetadata.com/
6. Iannella, R., Villata, S.: ODRL information model 2.2. W3C recommendation, W3C, February 2018. https://www.w3.org/TR/2018/REC-odrl-model-20180215/
7. Nichols, B.N., et al.: Linked Data in Neuroscience: Applications, Benefits, and Challenges. bioRxiv p. 053934, Cold Spring Harbor Laboratory Section: Confirmatory Results, November 2016. https://doi.org/10.1101/053934, https://www.biorxiv.org/content/10.1101/053934v2
8. Reynolds, D., Cyganiak, R.: The RDF data cube vocabulary. W3C recommendation, W3C, January 2014. https://www.w3.org/TR/2014/REC-vocab-data-cube-20140116/
9. Tennison, J.: CSV on the web: A primer. W3C note, W3C, February 2016. https://www.w3.org/TR/2016/NOTE-tabular-data-primer-20160225/
10. Thalhath, N., Nagamori, M., Sakaguchi, T., Sugimoto, S.: Yet another metadata application profile (YAMA): authoring, versioning and publishing of application profiles. In: International Conference on Dublin Core and Metadata Applications, vol. 0, pp. 114–125, December 2019. https://dcpapers.dublincore.org/pubs/article/view/4055
11. Wilkinson, M.D., et al.: The FAIR guiding principles for scientific data management and stewardship. Sci. Data **3**(1), 160018 (2016). Nature Publishing Group. https://doi.org/10.1038/sdata.2016.18, https://www.nature.com/articles/sdata201618

Scholarly Data Mining

Creating a Scholarly Knowledge Graph from Survey Article Tables

Allard Oelen[1,2](✉) [iD], Markus Stocker[2] [iD], and Sören Auer[1,2] [iD]

[1] L3S Research Center, Leibniz University of Hannover, Hannover, Germany
oelen@l3s.de
[2] TIB Leibniz Information Centre for Science and Technology, Hannover, Germany
{markus.stocker,auer}@tib.eu

Abstract. Due to the lack of structure, scholarly knowledge remains hardly accessible for machines. Scholarly knowledge graphs have been proposed as a solution. Creating such a knowledge graph requires manual effort and domain experts, and is therefore time-consuming and cumbersome. In this work, we present a human-in-the-loop methodology used to build a scholarly knowledge graph leveraging literature survey articles. Survey articles often contain manually curated and high-quality tabular information that summarizes findings published in the scientific literature. Consequently, survey articles are an excellent resource for generating a scholarly knowledge graph. The presented methodology consists of five steps, in which tables and references are extracted from PDF articles, tables are formatted and finally ingested into the knowledge graph. To evaluate the methodology, 92 survey articles, containing 160 survey tables, have been imported in the graph. In total, 2626 papers have been added to the knowledge graph using the presented methodology. The results demonstrate the feasibility of our approach, but also indicate that manual effort is required and thus underscore the important role of human experts.

Keywords: Scholarly communication · Scholarly knowledge graphs · Tabular data extraction

1 Introduction

Scholarly communication is mainly document-based and the communicated scholarly knowledge therefore hardly machine-actionable [21]. Scholarly knowledge graphs have the potential to solve these issues by making knowledge structured and thus more machine processable. Existing initiatives for scholarly information systems, e.g., the Microsoft Academic Graph [8] or Crossref [15] mainly focus on bibliographic metadata and not on the actual research contributions. The Open Research Knowledge Graph (ORKG) [10] aims to build a knowledge graph infrastructure that publishes the research contributions of scholarly publications rather than only the metadata. The approach is to crowdsource structured paper descriptions by including paper authors and domain

© Springer Nature Switzerland AG 2020
E. Ishita et al. (Eds.): ICADL 2020, LNCS 12504, pp. 373–389, 2020.
https://doi.org/10.1007/978-3-030-64452-9_35

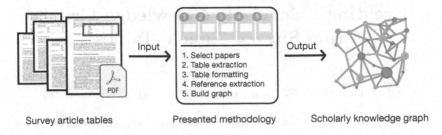

Fig. 1. Systematic workflow in which survey articles are used to build a scholarly knowledge graph. The input of our methodology is survey articles in PDF format and the output is a scholarly knowledge graph.

experts. ORKG primarily relies on synergistically combining crowdsourcing and automated extraction rather than, as other systems such as Semantic Scholar[1], exclusively on automated techniques to extract knowledge from scholarly articles. Mainly because automated extraction methods, for example Natural Language Processing (NLP), do not have sufficient accuracy to generate the high-quality knowledge graph needed to obtain suitable state-of-the-art overviews for researchers.

In this work, we present a human-in-the-loop methodology to create a scholarly knowledge graph by extracting knowledge from survey tables. We leverage survey tables from literature review papers, specifically. Tables in survey papers generally consist of high-quality research data that has been manually curated by domain experts. Conducting a literature review is a labour-intensive task and writing a review article is often more time-consuming than writing a research article [32]. Compared to natural text, tables present information in a semi-structured manner, making the creation of a structured graph from such data less complicated. Additionally, survey tables present relevant information which is why the survey was conducted and published in the first place. We present a supervised approach to firstly extract data from survey articles and afterwards build a knowledge graph from this data. Compared to sole crowdsourcing, the approach of extracting knowledge is more efficient because the review has already been conducted by the authors of the survey paper. Taking into account the previously mentioned considerations, our work addresses the following research question: *How to efficiently populate a scholarly knowledge graph with high-quality knowledge?* We propose a methodology for extracting tabular survey data. This methodology is used to create a scholarly knowledge graph from survey articles. An overview of the systematic workflow is depicted in Fig. 1.

The rest of this paper is structured as follows. Section 2 discusses the related work. Section 3 introduces the proposed five-step methodology for building the knowledge graph from survey articles. Section 4 presents the results. Section 5 discusses the present and future work. Finally, Sect. 6 concludes the presented work.

---

[1] https://www.semanticscholar.org.

2   Related Work

Survey articles provide well-structured overviews of the literature [33]. The terms "literature review" and "literature survey" are sometimes used interchangeably in the literature, but we make the following distinction. We refer to the tables within review articles as *literature surveys*. Together with a (textual) analysis and explanation, they form the *literature review*. Among other things, literature reviews are helpful in delimiting the research problem, avoiding fruitless approaches [5] and to discover new research directions [6]. Conducting a literature review is a complicated and time-consuming activity [33]. When literature reviews are not available for certain fields, its development could be weakened [32]. Because of the importance of literature surveys to scientific research, leveraging surveys to build a graph results in a high-quality and relevant scholarly knowledge graph. Some existing work with respect to semantifying literature surveys exists [4,23,29]. However, those approaches are not (semi-)automated and are therefore not scaling well to larger amounts of survey articles.

One aspect of the proposed methodology is table extraction from survey articles. Portable Document Format (PDF) is the most common format for scientific articles [12]. Extracting tables from PDF documents is a cumbersome process since the tabular structure is not stored within the file itself [11]. This means that regular PDF extraction tools are only able to extract the text within a table, but loosing the tabular structure. Tools that specifically focus on table extraction from PDF files use segmentation techniques to estimate the position of rows and columns [7]. Corrêa et al. did a literature survey on table extraction tools [3]. They concluded that Tabula[2] is the most suitable open-source tool. Based of these findings, we decided to use Tabula. Tabula is criticized because of the lack of documentation [26], but for our use case this is not considered problematic. Another aspect of the proposed methodology is reference extraction from PDFs. Since every individual article referenced within a survey table is imported, metadata from this article should be collected. This is done by parsing the references that are used within a table. For this, we use the state-of-the-art PDF extraction tool GROBID [13]. GROBID focuses specifically on extracting bibliographic data from scholarly articles [19]. Lipinski et al. [17] compared GROBID to other PDF metadata extraction tools, and found out that GROBID performed best.

Publishing data as structured or semantic data is a well researched topic among various domains. For example, challenges related to publishing semantic open government data are similar to the challenges in our research. This includes extracting data from legacy documents, often in PDF format [2,3]. Furthermore, in the literature use cases are described on publishing unstructured data as semantic data (e.g., [9,20,27]). These existing approaches differ from our approach since they generally aim to semantify a homogeneous set of documents. This enables them to create data specific ontologies. In our case, this is not feasible since we work with a highly heterogeneous set of survey tables coming from different domains and comparing different aspects of papers. Table 1 provides a

---

[2] https://tabula.technology.

Table 1. Related work compared to the method presented in our study. The full comparison is available via the ORKG. (https://www.orkg.org/orkg/comparison/R36099)

Study	Name	Method automation	Scope	Input format	Output format	KG[a] creation	Reference extraction	User interface
This study	ORKG	Semi-Automatic	Survey tables	PDF	JSON, RDF[b]	✓	✓	✓
[28]	SemAnn	Semi-Automatic	Scholarly articles	PDF	RDF[b]	✗	✗	✓
[16]	Web Tables	Automatic	Web tables	HTML	JSON	✗	✗	✗
[18]	TableSeer	Automatic	Scholarly articles	PDF	Relational database	✗	✗	✓
[25]	TEXUS	Automatic	Documents (application agnostic)	PDF	Abstract table representation	✗	✗	✗
[1]	*None*	Automatic	Web tables	HTML, Spreadsheet	Relational schema	✗	✗	✗

[a] Knowledge Graph; [b] Resource Description Framework

related work overview. In this overview, our proposed method is compared to other related approaches. To the best of our knowledge, this work is the first to build a knowledge graph at scale from survey tables.

Use Case: Open Research Knowledge Graph.
Extracted survey data can be imported in a variety of different (scholarly) knowledge graphs, such as the Microsoft Academic Graph, Wikidata [14] or ORKG. We chose ORKG as our use case for the following reasons. The ORKG provides tools that specifically focus on building paper comparisons (i.e., literature surveys), making it the most suitable infrastructure for this study. By using the extracted survey data, the ORKG automatically generates a similar tabular survey view as was originally presented in the review paper [22]. Additionally, the literature surveys within ORKG are compliant [23] with the FAIR data principles [34] thus making them Findable, Accessible, Interoperable and Reusable. The imported survey tables are FAIR in contrast to the originally presented ones in the non-FAIR PDF article. This has several benefits, among others:

- Comparisons can evolve over time, are not static and do not become stale after publication.
- Comparisons do represent a broader community consensus, since many researchers and curators can revise, discuss and annotate.

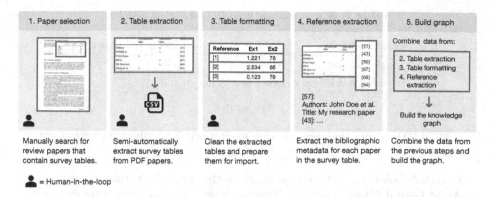

Fig. 2. Methodology for importing survey tables into the scholarly knowledge graph.

- Via the ORKG search interface it is possible to search for specific comparisons and to create dynamic custom comparison views.
- Survey data can be reused by other researchers more easily because of its machine readable export formats (e.g., export as CSV or RDF).

3 Methodology

We now present a five-step methodology for the creation of a scholarly knowledge graph from survey tables. In order to reach sufficient quality, the methodology takes a human-in-the-loop approach in which multiple steps require human interaction. Data quality improves with human evaluation and, if needed, correction of the extracted data. The methodology is displayed in Fig. 2. The scripts required to perform the steps are available online.[3]

3.1 Paper Selection

In the first step, suitable survey papers are selected based on multiple criteria. The purpose is to find survey papers from a diverse range of domains. Therefore, a protocol has been designed to determine which papers are suitable for data extraction. The structured nature of the selection process is needed to be able to make conclusions about the percentage of survey papers that present the information in such a way that extracting data is relatively straightforward.

Search Strategy. Table 2 lists the search engines used to find survey articles. Google Scholar is chosen to ensure that survey papers from various fields are searched. Additionally, ACM Digital Library has been selected because the ORKG currently focuses mainly on the Computer Science domain. The search is

---

[3] https://doi.org/10.5281/zenodo.3739427.

Table 2. Search engines used to find survey articles.

Search engine	Field	Evaluated papers
Google Scholar	All	335
ACM Digital Library	Computer Science	80

limited to 100 papers that are suitable for import. The following search criteria are used:

- Google Scholar: the article title contains the term "literature survey".
- ACM Digital Library: queries "literature review" and "literature survey".
- The survey article has been published after 2002.
- The results are sorted by relevance.

The rationale for selecting papers published after the year 2002 is because in general more recent papers are more interesting for research and should therefore have more priority in the scholarly knowledge graph. In the end, articles published before 2002 can still be part of the graph, since this criterion only applies to the survey articles themselves, and not to the papers being reviewed in those articles.

Selection Criteria. Papers that satisfy the inclusion criteria are selected for the import process. The inclusion criteria are defined as follows:

1. The article contains at least one table that lists scientific literature (i.e., the literature is presented in a semi-structured manner).
2. The article compares literature based on published results and does not solely textually summarize the content of original papers.
3. The survey table should be in markup format and not included as raster image.
4. The table structure should be suitable for import (e.g., one table row should provide information about one publication).
5. The article is written in English.

Inclusion criterion 1 ensures that a survey article does not only textually summarize the literature, but does also provide a semi-structured comparison (in tabular form). Although papers that are textually reviewing scientific literature are interesting for importing as well, it is out of scope for this work. Criterion 2 ensures only surveys that compare actual paper results are included. This excludes surveys researching, for instance, the growth of a field. Criterion 3 excludes tables in image format. This is because of the tabular extraction method we use, which is based on character extraction and does not use Optical Character Recognition (OCR) needed to support image extraction [30]. Criterion 4 only selects tables that are suitable for import. Our methodology does only support paper import when one row in a table represents one paper. Although minor changes can be made manually (e.g. merging multiple tables), in case the structure of the table deviates significantly from the required format, the table is excluded. Finally, criterion 5 ensures a homogeneous semantic integration into the currently English monolingual knowledge graph. The result of this step is a set of the selected papers in PDF format.

3.2 Table Extraction

This step focuses on extracting the tables from the PDF files collected in the previous step. Not only the text within the table should be extracted, but the tabular structure should be preserved as well. As explained in the related work section, we use Tabula to perform the table extraction. Each PDF article is uploaded via the Tabula user interface. Afterwards, the regions of the tables are manually selected within the interface. Although Tabula provides a functionality to automatically detect tables, the accuracy is not sufficient for our use case. The performance is especially low for articles with a two-column layout. Additionally, not all tables within an article have to be extracted since not all of them are listing and comparing literature. Arguably, the manual selection method is most useful in this methodology since human judgment is needed in the selection process. Part of the extraction step is quality assurance after the extraction. When needed, extraction errors are manually fixed. Tabula supports two types of extraction, namely "Stream" and "Lattice". The Stream extraction method is based on white space between columns while Lattice is based on boundary lines between columns. During the extraction it is possible to switch between the different methods, which allows for selecting the best method for a particular table. The result of this step is a set of CSV files, in which each file represents one survey table from a review article.

3.3 Table Formatting

The CSV files containing the extracted tables from the review articles should be formatted in a structure that is suitable for building a graph. Since the data from the CSV file is extracted automatically, all tables should have the same format. In this step, the formatting of the tables is changed when necessary. For some tables, a considerable amount of changes is required while for other tables only minor changes are needed. Changes could include merging, splitting, adding and removing both columns and rows. We use OpenRefine [31] to perform bulk operations on tables. A table is formatted in such a way that it adheres to the following rules:

1. The first row of the table is the header.
2. Each row represents one reviewed paper.
3. Each row has a column called: "Reference".
4. The reference cell should contain the citation key for a paper.
5. Non-literal values are prefixed with "[R]" in the column header.
6. When needed, abbreviations are replaced by the full value from the legend.

For rule 2, in some cases a multidimensional table has to be flattened. This can often be accomplished by adding additional columns to the table. Also, in some cases a table has to be transposed to ensure that each row contains one paper. Rules 3 and 4 ensure that bibliographic metadata can be fetched for each paper in the next step. Rule 5 makes a distinction between literal values and resources. The default cell type is a literal, and when [R] is prefixed to a header label, the cells are considered as resources. Finally, rule 6 makes the content of the table readable without requiring the original text from the legend. Often table legends are used to condense information to improve user readability.

3.4   Extracting References

As mentioned earlier, each table row represents one paper. For each row, there is a value that contains the reference key from the original paper. The reference key is often a numerical reference, in the form of $[n]$, where n represents the reference number. In another frequently used citation style, the author names combined with their publication year is used as a reference key. The citation key is used to automatically capture the bibliographic metadata for an article. In order to extract references from article, we use the PDF extraction tool GROBID. GROBID processes the full PDF article. In the first place to extract all citations from the paper's reference list and then to connect the citation keys used in the text to their respective citation string. In case a reference key cannot be extracted from the paper's text, a reference key is generated automatically based on the author's name and publication year.

When the citation is extracted and parsed, five additional columns are appended to the table: paper title, authors, publication month, publication year and the DOI[4]. In case a citation key could not be automatically mapped to an actual citation, a citation can be provided manually. The full citation text can be copied directly from the paper (including paper title, authors etc.) and is then parsed by GROBID to get structured bibliographic metadata. To perform the process of adding references, we created a Python script.[5] This script first tries to automatically fetch the metadata. In case the reference is not found, a command line input field is displayed to enter the citation manually.

3.5   Build Graph

The final step is to build a knowledge graph from the previously created CSV files. An example of the resulting graph for a single paper is depicted in Fig. 3. Firstly, a settings file is created which lists the table numbers, a suitable title for the table and a reference to the original survey article. The reference is required to attribute the work done by the authors of the survey article. The table title is manually created based on the original table caption. In case no suitable caption is available, a more suitable title is written.

---

[4] Digital Object Identifier.
[5] File 4_reference_extraction.py from https://doi.org/10.5281/zenodo.3739427.

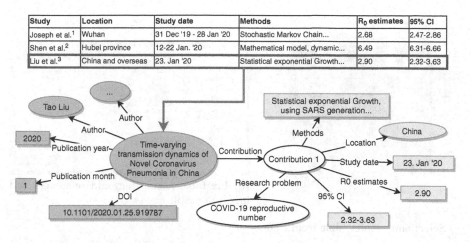

Study	Location	Study date	Methods	R₀ estimates	95% CI
Joseph et al.[1]	Wuhan	31 Dec '19 - 28 Jan '20	Stochastic Markov Chain...	2.68	2.47-2.86
Shen et al.[2]	Hubei province	12-22 Jan. '20	Mathematical model, dynamic...	6.49	6.31-6.66
Liu et al.[3]	China and overseas	23. Jan '20	Statistical exponential Growth...	2.90	2.32-3.63

Fig. 3. Example of the resulting subgraph for importing a single paper from a survey table. Metadata captured by reference extraction is displayed in blue. Data coming from the survey table is displayed in orange and ORKG specific data is displayed in white. (Color figure online)

Next, a Python script[6] is used to select all rows from the tables. For each row, a paper is added to the graph via the ORKG API. For each table, a comparison is created in ORKG. The title and reference from the previously generated settings file are attached to this comparison. The comparison can be used later in ORKG to generate the same tabular literature overview as originally presented in the survey paper.

3.6   User Interface

Based on the steps from our methodology, a web User Interface (UI) is created that integrates all steps into a single interface. The interface provides a streamlined process for importing survey tables as depicted in Fig. 4. The UI is specifically designed to make importing a table an effortless task without the need of downloading any tools or the need to be able to operate these tools. In the background, the same tools from the methodology are used to extract tables (Tabula) and extract references (GROBID). The first step is to upload a PDF file and select the survey table within this file. Afterwards, the table is extracted and the formatting can be fixed with an integrated spreadsheet editor. Then, for each row the respective paper reference is extracted. Finally, the data is ingested in the knowledge graph.

The UI is not used to import the surveys tables presented in Sect. 4. The interface is designed to import individual survey tables rather than importing large amounts of tables at once. In the UI, all steps required to import a single table should be performed consecutively. To increase efficiency when importing

---

[6] File 5_build_graph.py from https://doi.org/10.5281/zenodo.3739427.

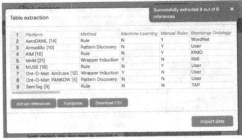

(b) Fix table formatting, add references and ingest in graph.

(a) Select and extract table from PDF.

Fig. 4. Survey table import user interface integrating all steps from the methodology.

large amounts of tables, it helps to first finish a step for all papers before moving to the next step. The UI provides a method to extend the graph beyond the extracted surveys from this work. In the future, this interface will therefore be integrated in the ORKG.

4   Results

In this section, we report the results of the import process for each step of the methodology. Table 3 summarizes the results for all steps.

4.1   Paper Selection

The dataset of the results are published online [24]. This set contains the selected papers, the ORKG comparisons and the ingested papers. The selected papers file lists IDs, paper titles, table references, sources and references. The IDs are used to record any additional information about the import process for this specific paper. IDs are missing for papers that were selected in the first place, but were excluded after revising the inclusion criteria. Additionally, table references refer to the original table references used in the survey article.

In total, 335 papers from Google Scholar were evaluated against the selection criteria described in Sect. 3.1. Out of these papers, 78 met the criteria and have therefore been selected for importing. From the ACM Digital Library 80 papers were evaluated and 14 papers have been selected. In total 22% of the evaluated review papers are suitable to be imported with the presented approach.

Table 3. Summary of the results of all steps.

Description	Amount
Paper selection	
Amount of evaluated papers	415
Amount of selected papers	92
Table extraction	
Total amount of extractions (partial tables)	265
Amount of extracted complete tables	160
Reference extraction	
Found references	2 069
Not found references	1 137
Build graph	
Individual amount of imported papers	2 626
Imported data cells (with metadata)	40 584
Imported data cells (without metadata)	21 240

4.2   Table Extraction

We extracted 160 tables from the 92 survey articles. In 22 cases, tables stretched across multiple pages, which results in a total of 265 extractions performed with Tabula. Table 4 lists the most frequently occurred issues with the extraction. Issue 1 and 2 occur mostly when no boundary lines are present between table columns. In this case, the Stream extraction method has to be used, which often results in rows that are not correctly merged (e.g., multi-line sentences are put in separate rows while in the original table they are in the same row). Also, issue

Table 4. Issues that occurred during the extraction of tables from the survey articles. Issues are counted per article.

#	Issue	Percentage %
1	Columns are not extracted correctly	26
2	Rows are not extracted correctly	14
3	Empty columns in the extracted table	14
4	Text not correctly recognized (e.g., missing letters or formulas)	12
5	Issue with table header text	12
6	Vertical text not imported correctly	4
7	Cell value not supported (e.g., use of image instead of text check marks)	3
8	Table within table not extracted correctly	3

3 is mostly present when using the Stream method. When the Lattice method can be used for the extraction, the result is generally of higher quality. When no table borders (or boundary lines) are present, this method does not work and the Stream method has to be used. Issue 4 is caused by general extraction errors, which can result in tables with wrongly extracted text. Additionally, formulas and other text styling are not supported, which compounds this issue. Issues 7 and 8 result in tables that are not, or only partially, imported. The other issues are self-explanatory.

4.3 Reference Extraction

In total, we extracted unique 2 626 papers from 3 206 rows. For each paper, the respective citation was retrieved. In 2 069 cases the citation could be extracted automatically from the row (65% of the cases). In 1 137 cases it was not possible to automatically extract the reference (35% of the cases). For those cases, the citation is manually copied from the paper. There were multiple reasons why automatic reference extraction was not successful. Most issues occurred for references that used a numeric citation key. GROBID's performance for extracting numeric references from tables was low, oftentimes numeric table references were not recognized. The amount of rows is higher than the amount of extracted papers because multiple rows could refer to the same paper. Each paper only has one graph entry and any additional data is added to the existing paper.

In case a reference is only used in a table and not somewhere else in the article, automatic reference extraction was oftentimes not possible. When an author name was used as citation key, problems occurred mostly because of the different citation styles. While some citation formats only use the last name of the first author, suffixed by *et al.*, other formats could list all author names. When a format was used that deviates from the standard implementation, automatic extraction was not possible.

4.4 Build Graph

In total, we added 2 626 papers to the knowledge graph. These papers are used in 160 different comparisons. A complete list of the generated ORKG comparisons and a list of all ingested papers is available via [24]. In total, 21 240 table cells have been imported, excluding the bibliographic metadata. Including metadata, the total is 40 584 data cells.

5   Discussion and Future Work

5.1   Time Performance

The presented methodology takes a human-in-the-loop approach as opposed to a fully automated approach. Compared to a fully manual approach, the proposed approach saves considerable time. In previous work [23], we manually imported only four survey articles. On average, this process took 4 hours per article. For each of the papers, a Python script was created specifically to import the survey table with its references and data. An example of such a script for one paper can be found online.[7] For the methodology used in this paper, the time to import one survey article was on average 15 min. Compared to the 4 h of the manual approach, this is considerably faster (i.e., 16 fold increase in speed). The minimum amount of time needed to import a relatively small table was 2 min. The table could be extracted without any issues. The maximum amount of required time was approximately 60 min. This was for a table with a complex layout, stretched across multiple pages. Also, this table did not have boundary lines. Most time was spend on fixing extraction issues. To further improve time performance, we identified two tasks that are time-consuming and can potentially be improved. The first task relates to fixing errors occurred during the table extraction by Tabula. Most errors occurred when tables did not have boundary lines between columns and rows. A potential solution, and possible future research direction, is to create an interface that supports manually drawing boundary lines between rows and columns. The second task is related to adding missing references, which have to be manually copied from the PDF article. In total, 65% of the references were extracted automatically. By applying more advanced heuristics to match reference keys with their respective reference, this percentage can be improved.

5.2 Impact of Methodology

The impact of the methodology relates to the amount of survey papers that are suitable for our approach (i.e., surveys representing information in tabular format). To order to provide insights on the impact, a structured search protocol has been employed in the paper selection step. As the results show, out of the 415 evaluated papers, 92 of them are suitable to be imported. This indicates that since 2002, 22% of the published survey papers contain comparison tables. Therefore, arguably our methodology can have considerable impact when applied more broadly. In the paper selection, non-survey papers were excluded. However, it is not uncommon for research articles to also contain tables with related work (e.g., Table 1 in this article). Thus the paper selection step could be extended to also include other articles to have a broader impact.

5.3 Semantics of Data

The extracted knowledge graph consists of structured scholarly data. The quality of the knowledge graph could be further improved by providing more semantics to the data. Currently, a primitive method is used to map existing properties and resources. This is based on a lookup by resource label, in case a result is found, the resource is mapped. If not, a new resource is created. A more advanced mapping of resources and properties to existing ontologies improves

---

[7] https://gitlab.com/TIBHannover/orkg/orkg-papers/-/blob/master/question-answering-import.py.

the machine readability of the data. Tables containing large amounts of natural text (e.g., textually describing a methodology) could be further processed using named entity recognition and linking. This results in more structured data and therefore a higher quality knowledge graph. Approaches to improve the overall quality of the graph are part of future work.

5.4 Future Research Directions

In total, we extracted 92 survey articles from a variety of domains. In the future, more survey articles will be ingested in ORKG. This will be done for multiple domains. The User Interface (UI) presented in Sect. 3.6 can be used to support users to import survey tables. The UI will be further improved to make to process more efficient. Due to the dynamic nature of the interface (especially compared to a regular spreadsheet editor), mapping properties and resources to existing concepts is better supported. In the end, we aim to import as many surveys from a specific domain as possible. There are several reasons why such an approach is useful. In the first place, ORKG can serve as a digital library for literature surveys. As discussed in the related work, the platform provides tools to better find and organize surveys. Additionally, when all existing reviews for a domain are imported, the ORKG can be used as a source to find literature surveys. In case a survey is not present in the ORKG, it means that is does not (yet) exist. This can be used as a basis to start working on new literature surveys.

6   Conclusions

Knowledge graphs are useful to make scholarly knowledge more machine action-able. Manually building such a knowledge graph is time-consuming and requires the expertise of paper authors and domain experts. In order to efficiently build a high-quality scholarly knowledge graph, we leverage survey tables from review articles. Generally, survey tables contain high-quality, relevant, semi-structured and manually curated data, and are therefore an excellent source for building a scholarly knowledge graph. We presented a methodology used to extract 2 626 papers from 92 survey articles. The methodology adopts a human-in-the-loop approach to ensure the quality and usefulness of the extracted data. Compared to manually reviewing and entering research data, or to manually importing literature surveys, the methodology is considerably more efficient. In conclu-sion, the presented methodology provides a full pipeline that can be used to extract knowledge from PDF documents and represent the extracted knowledge in a knowledge graph. The corresponding evaluation with survey articles demon-strates the effectiveness and efficiency of the proposed methodology.

Acknowledgements. This work was co-funded by the European Research Council for the project ScienceGRAPH (Grant agreement ID: 819536) and the TIB Leibniz Infor-mation Centre for Science and Technology. We want to thank our colleagues Mohamad Yaser Jaradeh and Kheir Eddine Farfar for their contributions to this work.

References

1. Adelfio, M.D., Samet, H.: Schema extraction for tabular data on the web. Proc. VLDB Endowment **6**, 421–432 (2013). https://doi.org/10.14778/2536336.2536343
2. Corrêa, A.S., Corrêa, P.L.P., Da Silva, F.S.C.: Transparency portals versus open government data. An assessment of openness in Brazilian municipalities. In: ACM International Conference Proceeding Series, pp. 178–185 (2014). https://doi.org/10.1145/2612733.2612760
3. Corrêa, A.S., Zander, P.O.: Unleashing tabular content to open data: a survey on PDF table extraction methods and tools. In: ACM International Conference Proceeding Series, pp. 54–63 (2017). https://doi.org/10.1145/3085228.3085278
4. Fathalla, S., Vahdati, S., Auer, S., Lange, C.: Towards a knowledge graph representing research findings by semantifying survey articles. In: Kamps, J., Tsakonas, G., Manolopoulos, Y., Iliadis, L., Karydis, I. (eds.) TPDL 2017. LNCS, vol. 10450, pp. 315–327. Springer, Cham (2017). https://doi.org/10.1007/978-3-319-67008-9_25
5. Gall, M.D., Borg, W.R.: Educational Research: An introduction, 6th edn. Longman Publishers USA, White Plains (1996)
6. Hart, C.: Doing a Literature Review: Releasing the Social Science Research Imagination. Sage, Thousand Oaks (1998)
7. Hassan, T., Baumgartner, R.: Table recognition and understanding from PDF files. In: Proceedings of the International Conference on Document Analysis and Recognition, ICDAR, pp. 1143–1147 (2007). https://doi.org/10.1109/ICDAR.2007.4377094
8. Herrmannova, D., Knoth, P.: An analysis of the microsoft academic graph. D-lib Mag. **22**(9/10) (2016). https://doi.org/10.1045/september2016-herrmannova
9. Hyvönen, E.: Publishing and using cultural heritage linked data on the semantic web. Synth. Lect. Semant. Web Theory Technol. **2**(1), 1–159 (2012). https://doi.org/10.2200/S00452ED1V01Y201210WBE003
10. Jaradeh, M.Y., et al.: Open research knowledge graph: Next generation infrastructure for semantic scholarly knowledge. In: K-CAP 2019 - Proceedings of the 10th International Conference on Knowledge Capture, pp. 243–246 (2019). https://doi.org/10.1145/3360901.3364435
11. Jiang, D., Yang, X.: Converting PDF to HTML approach based on text detection. In: Proceedings of the 2nd International Conference on Interaction Sciences: Information Technology, Culture and Human, vol. 403, pp. 982–985 (2009). https://doi.org/10.1145/1655925.1656103
12. Klampfl, S., Granitzer, M., Jack, K., Kern, R.: Unsupervised document structure analysis of digital scientific articles. Int. J. Digit. Libr. **14**(3), 83–99 (2014). https://doi.org/10.1007/s00799-014-0115-1
13. Körner, M., Ghavimi, B., Mayr, P., Hartmann, H., Staab, S.: Evaluating reference string extraction using line-based conditional random fields: a case study with German language publications. In: Kirikova, M., et al. (eds.) ADBIS 2017. CCIS, vol. 767, pp. 137–145. Springer, Cham (2017). https://doi.org/10.1007/978-3-319-67162-8_15
14. Krotzsch, M., Vrandecic, D.: Wikidata : a free collaborative knowledge base. Commun. ACM **57**(10), 78–85 (2014). https://doi.org/10.1145/2629489
15. Lammey, R.: CrossRef text and data mining services. Insights UKSG J. **28**(2), 62–68 (2015). https://doi.org/10.1629/uksg.233

16. Lehmberg, O., Ritze, D., Meusel, R., Bizer, C.: A large public corpus of web tables containing time and context metadata. In: Proceedings of the 25th International Conference Companion on World Wide Web - WWW 2016 Companion (2016). https://doi.org/10.1145/2872518.2889386

17. Lipinski, M., Yao, K., Breitinger, C., Beel, J., Gipp, B.: Evaluation of header metadata extraction approaches and tools for scientific PDF documents. In: Proceedings of the ACM/IEEE Joint Conference on Digital Libraries, pp. 385–386 (2013). https://doi.org/10.1145/2467696.2467753

18. Liu, Y., Bai, K., Mitra, P., Giles, C.L.: TableSeer: automatic table metadata extraction and searching in digital libraries. In: Proceedings of the 2007 Conference on Digital Libraries - JCDL 2007 (2007). https://doi.org/10.1145/1255175.1255193

19. Lopez, P.: GROBID: combining automatic bibliographic data recognition and term extraction for scholarship publications. In: Agosti, M., Borbinha, J., Kapidakis, S., Papatheodorou, C., Tsakonas, G. (eds.) ECDL 2009. LNCS, vol. 5714, pp. 473–474. Springer, Heidelberg (2009). https://doi.org/10.1007/978-3-642-04346-8_62

20. Mäkelä, E., Hyvönen, E., Ruotsalo, T.: How to deal with massively heterogeneous cultural heritage data - lessons learned in CultureSampo. Semant. Web 3(1), 85–109 (2012). https://doi.org/10.3233/sw-2012-0049

21. Mons, B., Velterop, J.: Nano-publication in the e-science era. In: Workshop on Semantic Web Applications in Scientific Discourse (SWASD 2009), pp. 14–15 (2009)

22. Oelen, A., Jaradeh, M.Y., Farfar, K.E., Stocker, M., Auer, S.: Comparing research contributions in a scholarly knowledge graph. In: Proceedings of the Third International Workshop on Capturing Scientific Knowledge (SciKnow19), pp. 21–26 (2019)

23. Oelen, A., Jaradeh, M.Y., Stocker, M., Auer, S.: Generate FAIR literature surveys with scholarly knowledge graphs. In: JCDL 2020: The 20th ACM/IEEE Joint Conference on Digital Libraries (In Press) (2020). https://doi.org/10.1145/3383583.3398520

24. Oelen, A., Stocker, M., Auer, S.: Dataset for creating a scholarly knowledge graph from survey article tables (2020). https://doi.org/10.5281/ZENODO.3735152

25. Rastan, R., Paik, H.Y., Shepherd, J.: Texus. In: Proceedings of the 2015 ACM Symposium on Document Engineering - DocEng 2015 (2015). https://doi.org/10.1145/2682571.2797069

26. Ros, G.: Analysis of tabula : a PDF-Table extraction tool (2019)

27. Skjæveland, M.G., Lian, E.H., Horrocks, I.: Publishing the norwegian petroleum directorate's FactPages as semantic web data. In: International Semantic Web Conference, vol. 8219, pp. 162–177 (2013). https://doi.org/10.1007/978-3-642-41338-4_11

28. Takis, J., Islam, A.S., Lange, C., Auer, S.: Crowdsourced semantic annotation of scientific publications and tabular data in pdf. In: SEMANTICS 2015 Proceedings of the 11th International Conference on Semantic Systems (2015). https://doi.org/10.1145/2814864.2814887

29. Vahdati, S., Fathalla, S., Auer, S., Lange, C., Vidal, M.E.: Semantic representation of scientific publications. In: International Conference on Theory and Practice of Digital Libraries, vol. 11799, pp. 375–379 (2019). https://doi.org/10.1007/978-3-030-30760-8_37

30. Vasileiadis, M., Kaklanis, N., Votis, K., Tzovaras, D.: Extraction of tabular data from document images. In: Proceedings of the 14th Web for All Conference, W4A (2017). https://doi.org/10.1145/3058555.3058581

31. Verborgh, R., De Wilde, M.: Using OpenRefine. Packt Publishing Ltd., Birmingham (2013)
32. Webster, J., Watson, R.T.: Analyzing the Past to Prepare for the Future: writing a Literature Review. MIS Q. **26**(2), xiii–xxiii (2002)
33. Wee, B.V., Banister, D.: How to Write a literature review paper? Transp. Rev. **36**(2), 278–288 (2016). https://doi.org/10.1080/01441647.2015.1065456
34. Wilkinson, M.D., et al.: Comment: the FAIR guiding principles for scientific data management and stewardship. Sci. Data **3**, 1–9 (2016). https://doi.org/10.1038/sdata.2016.18

A Novel Researcher Search System Based on Research Content Similarity and Geographic Information

Tetsuya Takahashi(✉), Koya Tango, Yuto Chikazawa, and Marie Katsurai(✉) [ORCID]

Doshisha University, 1-3 Tatara Miyakodani, Kyotanabe-shi, Kyoto, Japan
{takahashi,katsurai}@mm.doshisha.ac.jp

Abstract. Collaborative research is becoming increasingly important because it yields effective results and helps difficult research projects run smoothly. Previous studies have proposed many kinds of collaborator recommendation methods based on research features, such as specialty fields. However, few studies have constructed systems in which users can discover experts who have similar research interests using recommendation techniques. This paper proposes a novel researcher search system where users can efficiently discover potential candidates whose work locations are near theirs. Researchers are visualized on a map by our proposed system and users can use researcher's names and research keywords to narrow down the search. Specifically, given a researcher's name as a query, the system displays its relevant individuals based on either one of the following measures among researchers: research content similarity or collaborative relationship similarity. Our experiments demonstrated that recommendation results of these two similarity measures are minimally overlapped one another, indicating that our system could potentially help researchers discover collaborator candidates.

Keywords: Researcher search system · Collaborator recommendation · Researcher similarity · Academic database analysis

1 Introduction

Complex research project can be conducted effectively through collaborative research. Several studies have explored the relationship between collaboration and productivity. For example, Lee and Bozeman [11] investigated how the number of collaborators has influenced journal publication. Abramo et al. [1] analyzed the correlation among several types of collaborations, including interdisciplinary research, extramural collaborative research, industry-academia collaborative research, and their achievements, to assess the correlation between

This research was partly supported by JST ACT-I (Grant number: JPMJPR18UC), JST ACT-X (Grant number: JPMJAX1909), and JSPS KAKENHI (Grant number: 20H04484).

© Springer Nature Switzerland AG 2020
E. Ishita et al. (Eds.): ICADL 2020, LNCS 12504, pp. 390–398, 2020.
https://doi.org/10.1007/978-3-030-64452-9_36

scientific productivity and collaboration intensity. Lopes et al. [13] proposed a method for ranking research quality and found that authors of high-ranking research collaborated more. In the field of scholarly data mining, several collaborator recommendation methods have been proposed [2,3,5,9,10,12,14–16]. Most conventional methods defined the researcher similarity using bibliographic analysis, such as the closeness of existing relationships and correlation between research fields. However, few studies constructed systems in which users could discover researchers based on the existing recommendation methods.

Here, we focus on the recent work [16], which demonstrated that including the locations of researchers' affiliations improved research candidate recommender's performance. Inspired from this work, this study proposes a novel researcher search system based on research content similarity and geographic information to promote domestic collaboration opportunities. The proposed system allows users to search for potential collaborator candidates using researchers' names and research keywords. Subsequently, users can then filter results based on (i) researchers whose published works feature at least one of the keywords, (ii) existing collaborative partnerships among researchers when searching a researcher's name, and (iii) researchers whose interests or collaborative partnerships similar to the query researcher's those. In particular, in the third function, users can use the research content or existing collaborative relationships as features to calculate the similarity among researchers. Search results are displayed on a map of Japan using yellow pins. When a user clicks a pin, our system displays the researcher's information, including their specializations and past research projects. Our system enables users to discover researchers with desired specializations from their neighboring area, which helps encourage collaboration and discussion between researchers and local research institutions. We constructed the system using the Database of Grants-in-Aid for Scientific Research (KAKEN)[1]. Our experiments showed that there is little overlap between researchers found using content similarity and those in existing collaboration relationships, indicating that the proposed method can effectively help users to find potential collaborator candidates using these two different similarity measures.

2 Proposed System

2.1 System Overview

The proposed system's architecture is shown in Fig. 1. Researcher similarity is regularly analyzed on a local computer as batch processing, and the results are stored in a database on the cloud. To fulfill an API request from a client, the server cuts down a large network to extract a small network. By processing response sent from the server to the client, users can see results interactively. The client's home screen is shown in Fig. 2. When users click the search button, a search query field appears, as shown in Fig. 3. Users can use search queries appearing as candidates for the query. Clicking a yellow pin displays that

---

[1] https://kaken.nii.ac.jp/.

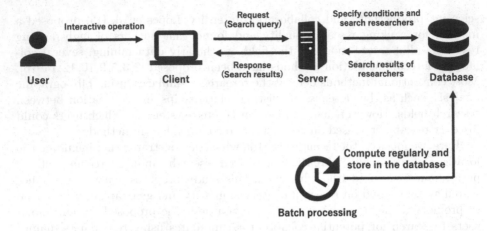

Fig. 1. The proposed system's architecture.

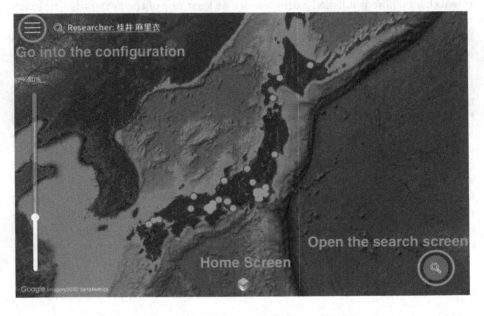

Fig. 2. The proposed system's home screen.

researcher's details (Fig. 4). Users have the option to have the pins displayed on an aerial photo (as in Fig. 4) or on a street map (as in Fig. 5). Hence, local information, such as train stations near the researcher's office, can be confirmed.

Users can filter search results by checking corresponding boxes, allowing them to tailor results based on (i) researchers whose published works feature at least one of the keywords used, (ii) existing collaborative partnerships among researchers when searching a researcher's name, and (iii) researchers whose interests or collaborative partnerships similar to the query researcher's those.

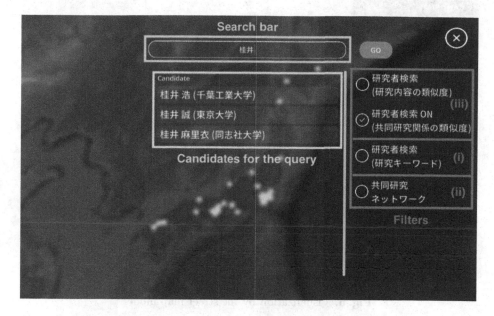

Fig. 3. The proposed system's search interface.

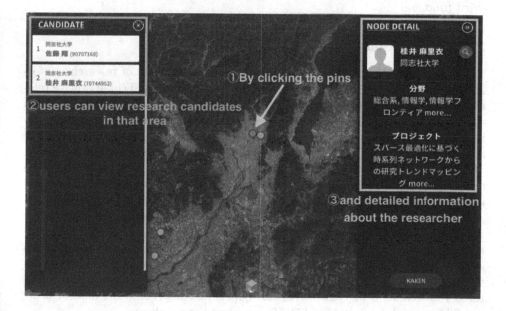

Fig. 4. Detail screen of a researcher. (Color figure online)

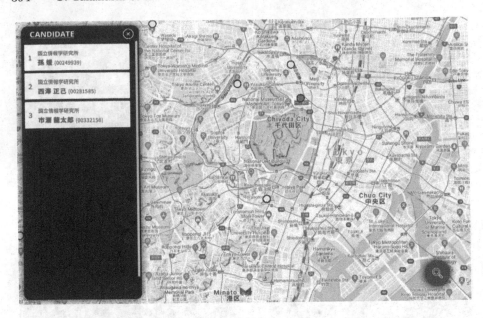

Fig. 5. Visualization by the street map mode.

Section 2.2 describes how to construct a dataset to implement the first and the second functions, while Sect. 2.3 describes two similarity measures to realize the third function.

2.2   Dataset Construction and Basic Search

This subsection describes our system's dataset that consists of researcher information (i.e., research projects, work location information, and collaborative relationships). In this study, we used KAKEN to construct the researcher search system. KAKEN is the Database of Grants-in-Aid for Scientific Research (KAKENHI) projects granted by the Ministry of Education, Culture, Sports, Science and Technology (MEXT) and the Japan Society for the Promotion of Science (JSPS). All of the database's research reports cover all research fields. Compared to other academic databases, it is better because it has a lower field deviation and all data can be searched using the same form. KAKEN covers many researchers and research projects compared with other academic databases because KAKENHI is the most representative research funding in Japan. KAKEN assigns unique numbers to researchers, which are linked to their research projects, which display project names, principal investigators, co-investigators, research institutions, research fields, research keywords, summaries, and corresponding registered researchers' achievements. In this paper, we constructed the dataset using 911,724 research projects and 259,509 registered researchers.

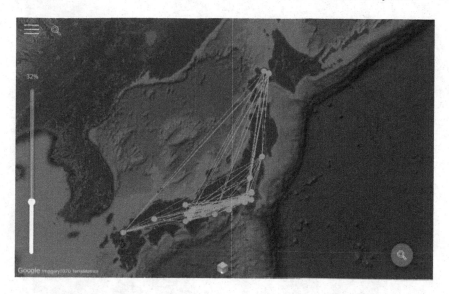

Fig. 6. A screenshot of the window for visualizing existing collaborative relationships among researchers.

Geographic Information: The proposed system displays institutions each researcher belong to using information based on latest research projects. Institution name registered in KAKEN's projects had spelling inconsistencies, which we corrected manually. Work location information (i.c., latitude and longitude) was obtained using Google Maps API[2], which is visualized on a map of Japan.

Research Keywords: In KAKEN, each researcher is assigned keywords based on the contents of their research. Users can use these keywords when performing searches. Researchers containing keywords corresponding to the search query are displayed on the map. Through this, users can find researchers who work in specific fields.

Existing Collaborative Partnerships: We constructed a network whose nodes were represented by researchers and whose edges were represented by collaborative relationships in KAKEN projects. When users search a researcher's name, the researcher's collaborative relationships are also displayed on the map. Specifically, the system obtains the network associated with a researcher ID from the server and displays the collaborative relationships, which enables users to find experts who actually work with the query researcher. Figure 6 shows an example of the relationships between researchers.

---

[2] https://cloud.google.com/maps-platform/.

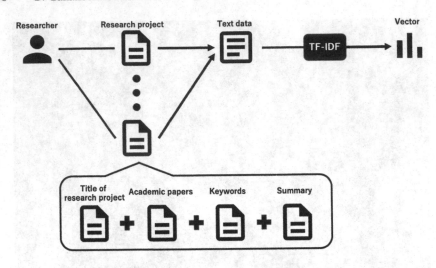

Fig. 7. The process of creating a vector that represents research content.

2.3   Computing Researcher Similarity and Displaying Potential Collaborators

To search potential collaborators, users can choose the similarity of collaborative relationships or the similarity based on the contents of researcher's projects. First, let R_{r_1}, R_{r_2} be two sets of research collaborators with each researcher r_1, r_2. Let the similarity of collaborative relationships between two researchers be represented by the Jaccard index as follows:

$$sim1(r_1, r_2) = \frac{|R_{r_1} \cap R_{r_2}|}{|R_{r_1} \cup R_{r_2}|}. \tag{1}$$

When there is no overlap between research collaborators, $sim1$ is 0.

Next, we compute the similarity between researchers based on the contents of their research. Each research project is considered to be a text data that reflects researcher's interests because each of them is influenced by each contributing researcher's achievements. Therefore, we computed the TF-IDF vector using the titles of research projects, titles of academic papers registered as achievement, research keywords, and the summary, as shown in Fig. 7.

Although the word embedding can be used to vectorize documents (as which was used in the related work [8]), we decided to use the TF-IDF vector to clearly understand coincidence of research interest in the proposed system and consider the importance of each word. How to effectively combine these different word features will be discussed in our future work. Let $vec1$ and $vec2$ be the TF-IDF vectors calculated for researchers r_1 and r_2. We calculated the similarity based on the contents of their research using the cosine similarity:

$$sim2 = cosine(vec1, vec2). \tag{2}$$

The $sim2$ of 1 means the contents of their research is exactly the same.

In general, it is not realistic to compute similarity between over 100,000 researchers in any combination because it requires much calculation cost. Therefore, we used FAISS [7], which includes the nearest-neighbor search, to perform quick computation. FAISS reduces the dimensionality of a vector through product quantization [4,6] and performs an approximate nearest-neighbor search. FAISS previously divided a set of vectors for search into Voronoï regions to improve search speed and specify search scope. In this study, there were 100 Voronoï, and the search scope was 10. Thus, 500 candidates for collaborative research were computed and saved in the database.

3   Evaluation Experiment

To show that the two methods for computing similarity described in Sect. 2.3 were useful for discovering potential collaborators, we determined the number of researchers yielded in the search results based on research contents. Specifically, we computed the overlap ratio of search results $overlap$ as follows:

$$overlap(sim1, sim2) = \frac{|S_{sim1} \cap S_{sim2}|}{|S_{sim1}|}, \tag{3}$$

where S_{sim} denotes a set of researchers based on similarity sim. The lower $overlap(sim1, sim2)$ is, the more novel researchers excluded based on similarity $sim2$ are discovered using similarity $sim1$. In this experiment, 100 researchers were chosen at random and the overlap ratio was computed for all pairs. As a result, the mean value of $overlap$(sim1, sim2) is 0.199. Because the value is small, we demonstrated that it is possible to present potential collaborators that users cannot discover through existing relationships via switching these two similarity functions.

4   Conclusions and Future Work

This paper presented a novel researcher search system based on research content similarity and geographic information. In the proposed system, users can freely search for researchers in Japan using their names and research keywords. Specifically, we implemented three filters: researchers whose published works feature at least one of the keywords used, existing collaborative partnerships among researchers when searching a researcher's name, and researchers whose work or collaborative partnerships similar to the query researcher's those. It is expected that the proposed system will facilitate research collaboration and discussion among researchers and users that work near one another. In our future work, we will qualitatively evaluate the system's usability and consider more methods to compute similarity.

398   T. Takahashi et al.

References

1. Abramo, G., D'Angelo, C.A., Di Costa, F.: Research collaboration and productivity: is there correlation? High. Educ. **57**(2), 155–171 (2009). https://doi.org/10.1007/s10734-008-9139-z
2. Araki, M., Katsurai, M., Ohmukai, I., Takeda, H.: Interdisciplinary collaborator recommendation based on research content similarity. IEICE Trans. Inf. Syst. **100**(4), 785–792 (2017)
3. Chen, H.H., Gou, L., Zhang, X., Giles, C.L.: CollabSeer: a search engine for collaboration discovery. In: Proceedings of the 11th Annual International ACM/IEEE Joint Conference on Digital Libraries, pp. 231–240. ACM (2011)
4. Ge, T., He, K., Ke, Q., Sun, J.: Optimized product quantization for approximate nearest neighbor search. In: Proceedings of the IEEE Conference on Computer Vision and Pattern Recognition, pp. 2946–2953 (2013)
5. Guo, Y., Chen, X.: Cross-domain scientific collaborations prediction with citation information. In: 2014 IEEE 38th International Computer Software and Applications Conference Workshops (COMPSACW), pp. 229–233. IEEE (2014)
6. Jegou, H., Douze, M., Schmid, C.: Product quantization for nearest neighbor search. IEEE Trans. Pattern Anal. Mach. Intell. **33**(1), 117–128 (2010)
7. Johnson, J., Douze, M., Jégou, H.: Billion-scale similarity search with GPUs. arXiv preprint arXiv:1702.08734 (2017)
8. Kawamura, T., Watanabe, K., Matsumoto, N., Egami, S.: Mapping science based on research content similarity, July 2018. https://doi.org/10.5772/intechopen.77067
9. Kong, X., Jiang, H., Wang, W., Bekele, T.M., Xu, Z., Wang, M.: Exploring dynamic research interest and academic influence for scientific collaborator recommendation. Scientometrics **113**(1), 369–385 (2017). https://doi.org/10.1007/s11192-017-2485-9
10. Lee, D.H., Brusilovsky, P., Schleyer, T.: Recommending collaborators using social features and MeSH terms. Proc. Assoc. Inf. Sci. Technol. **48**(1), 1–10 (2011)
11. Lee, S., Bozeman, B.: The Impact of research collaboration on scientific productivity. Soc. Stud. Sci. **35**(5), 673–702 (2005)
12. Li, J., Xia, F., Wang, W., Chen, Z., Asabere, N.Y., Jiang, H.: ACRec: a co-authorship based random walk model for academic collaboration recommendation. In: Proceedings of the 23rd International Conference on World Wide Web, pp. 1209–1214. ACM (2014)
13. Lopes, G., Moro, M., Silva, R., Barbosa, E., Palazzo Moreira de Oliveira, J.: Ranking strategy for graduate programs evaluation, January 2011
14. Lopes, G.R., Moro, M.M., Wives, L.K., de Oliveira, J.P.M.: Collaboration recommendation on academic social networks. In: Trujillo, J., et al. (eds.) ER 2010. LNCS, vol. 6413, pp. 190–199. Springer, Heidelberg (2010). https://doi.org/10.1007/978-3-642-16385-2_24
15. Tang, J., Wu, S., Sun, J., Su, H.: Cross-domain collaboration recommendation. In: Proceedings of the 18th ACM SIGKDD International Conference on Knowledge Discovery and Data Mining, pp. 1285–1293. ACM (2012)
16. Zhang, Q., Mao, R., Li, R.: Spatial–temporal restricted supervised learning for collaboration recommendation. Scientometrics **119**(3), 1497–1517 (2019). https://doi.org/10.1007/s11192-019-03100-4

Predicting Response Quantity from Linguistic Characteristics of Questions on Academic Social Q&A Sites

Lei Li[1], Anrunze Li[1], Xue Song[1], Xinran Li[1], Kun Huang[1(✉)], and Edwin Mouda Ye[2]

[1] Beijing Normal University, Beijing, China
{leili,lianrunze,songxue,lixinran,huangkun}@bnu.edu.cn
[2] University of South Australia, Adelaide, Australia
mouda.ye@mymail.unisa.edu.au

Abstract. Academic social Q&A websites have a lower response quantity than other types of social Q&A. To help academic social Q&A platforms implement mechanisms to improve the quantities of responses to questions that are rarely answered and to predict these quantities, this study uses 93 features representing the linguistic characteristics of academic questions, and compares several methods of prediction to determine the one that delivers the best performance. It also identifies the most useful feature set for such predictions.

Keywords: Academic questions · Response quantity prediction · Linguistic characteristics · Academic social Q&A

1 Introduction

Academic social networking sites (ASNSs) are growing in popularity, and an increasing number of scholars are using them to share and exchange academic information. ASNSs also provide a question-answering service called "academic social Q&A," where scholars exchange academic information by asking questions and getting answers. Traditionally, the most common way to obtain academic information is through academic papers or books published by scholars. However, it usually takes a while for papers and books to go from conception to publication, which hinders the quick acquisition of cutting-edge academic research. With the recent development of such services as academic social Q&A, scholars can post their questions and receive quick responses from other researchers. On academic social Q&A sites, researchers can conveniently and quickly obtain academic information, and can exchange and discuss ideas with other scholars. However, studies in the area have shown that scholars' participation in ASNSs is lower than user engagement on other types of social media [1]. Therefore, many questions on academic social Q&A sites have few or no answers.

The response quantity has been investigated in the context of a variety of social media sites, such as generic social Q&A sites (e.g., Yahoo! Answers) [2], Facebook [3], and Weibo [4]. In previous research, we noted that academic social Q&A, as a professional

© Springer Nature Switzerland AG 2020
E. Ishita et al. (Eds.): ICADL 2020, LNCS 12504, pp. 399–406, 2020.
https://doi.org/10.1007/978-3-030-64452-9_37

social media platform for scholars, is different from generic social Q&A in terms of content and user characteristics [5, 6]. It is hence expected that factors influencing the quantity of response to questions on academic social Q&A may be different from those for other types of social media. Therefore, a study on the response quantity targeting academic social Q&A websites in particular is important. In past research, features of both the questioner and the content of the question have been explored to determine whether they influence the quantity of responses to questions on academic social Q&A sites. The results have shown that the characteristics of the questioner do not significantly affect the quantity of response, and only a few characteristics of the content of the question influence it [7]. This paper proposes more characteristics of questions to examine the quantity of responses to them on academic social Q&A sites.

We predict the quantity of responses to questions published on academic social Q&A sites by using the linguistic characteristics of the questions. Inspired by Teevan et al. (2011), who noted that "the phrasing of questions posed to one's social network directly influences the online responses received" [3], this paper focuses on the linguistic characteristics of academic questions to explore the extent to which they can be used to accurately predict the quantity of response. We collected 1,969 academic questions and the numbers of responses to them from ResearchGate Q&A, the most popular ASNS. To ensure that the dataset was representative, questions in the fields of linguistics, applied psychology, mathematical physics, data science, and public health were crawled for. They represented the disciplines of the humanities, social science, natural science, formal science, and applied science, respectively. A linguistic analysis was then conducted to obtain the linguistic characteristics of the contents of the questions. We used LIWC as tool for analysis; it has been widely used in many fields [8, 9]. The LIWC yielded 93 features describing the linguistic characteristics of the contents of questions from the seven categories. These features were used to generate comprehensive descriptions of the characteristics, which were subsequently used to predict whether the questions were answered. Finally, multiple classification methods were used to predict the quantity of responses to questions on ResearchGate Q&A. This study seeks to address the following research question:

RQ1: What is the best predictive performance that can be obtained using the linguistic characteristics of the contents of questions?
Specifically, this study obtains the best predictive performance by answering the following three sub-questions:
RQ1a: Which method of prediction considered delivers the best performance?
RQ1b: What categories, or combination of categories, of linguistic characteristics can best predict the quantity of responses to questions?
RQ1c: Which method of prediction can get the best performance by using the best combination of linguistic characteristics?

To the best of our knowledge, this study is the first in the literature to predict the quantity of responses to questions on academic social Q&A services. This research will help academic social Q&A platforms identify questions that are less likely to be answered through their linguistic analysis. Accordingly, they can take measures, such as priority display or recommendations to scholars from the related fields, to prompt more answers to such questions.

2 Method

2.1 Dataset

We collected data from the social Q&A platform of the world's largest academic social network: ResearchGate. This ResearchGate Q&A builds a homepage for each question. To collect information on each question, we first needed its homepage URL. Research-Gate Q&A classifies questions into topics according to the tags assigned to them by the questioners. To ensure the comprehensiveness of the data obtained on the question, according to the hierarchy of academic discipline, questions related to a topic under each highest level of the hierarchy were selected as data collection object. The questions chosen were from linguistics in the humanities, applied psychology in the social sciences, mathematical physics in natural science, data science in formal science, and public health in applied science. These five topics were chosen because the numbers of questions for each were similar, and some of these questions were answered less. We searched the ResearchGate Q&A using each of these five topic-related words, and collected the URLs of questions that had been assigned the relevant tags.

Having obtained the URLs of the questions, a crawler program was used to obtain the following information for each: its title, description, number of answers to, and the time at which it was posted. We obtained 448 data items on the question in linguistics, 339 items for the question in applied psychology, 375 for the one in mathematical physics, 328 from the question in data science, and 478 data items for the question in public health. A total of 1,968 question items were thus obtained.

2.2 Linguistic Characteristics

LIWC2015, the latest version of the LIWC linguistic analysis tool, was used to analyze the linguistic characteristics of a combination of the title and description of each question. The LIWC was used for three reasons. First, it has been widely used in psychology, education, marketing, and other fields to analyze the linguistic characteristics of speech and writing. It has also been used to analyze the characteristics of various types of user-generated content on social media. It has proven to be an effective tool for linguistic analysis. Second, the LIWC obtains linguistic characteristics by classifying and counting words that form content by matching them with words from previously prepared dictionaries. Compared with other complex methods of natural language processing, it has no restrictions of parameter setting and application scenarios, and thus is more widely applicable. Third, compared with its previous version, LIWC2015 has a more rigorous way of constructing dictionaries to ensure that they are internally consistent.

Using LIWC2015, we obtained 93 linguistic characteristics for each question in seven categories. They consisted of four summary language variables (analytical thinking, clout, authenticity, and emotional tone), four general descriptor categories (number of words, words per sentence, percentage of target words captured by the dictionary, and percentage of words in the text longer than six letters), 21 standard linguistic dimensions (e.g., percentage of words in the text that are pronouns, and articles), 40 word categories representing psychological constructs (e.g., affect, cognition, and biological processes), six personal concern categories (e.g., work, home, and leisure activities), six informal language markers (such as assents, fillers, and swear words), and 12 punctuation categories (periods, commas, etc.). For a complete list and a detailed explanation of these 93 linguistic characteristics, the interested reader can view the official documentation [10]. These linguistic characteristics were used as features to predict the rates of responses to the questions.

2.3 Response Quantity

According to the number of responses received, we divided the quantity of response into two levels. To ensure that the quantity of response calculated was based on the number of answers responded over the same duration, to avoid the impact of different durations of exposure on the response quantity, we calculated the average number of answers received in a month during the question capture time and question asking time, where the 21 questions that had been posted for less than a month were deleted. Then, we noticed that there were still questions with zero responses among the questions published more than one month. Since we cannot confirm whether and how many responses can be obtained for these questions in the future, these questions with zero responses have also been deleted. Eventually, the dataset was reduced to include 1858 question items.

By conducting a normality test on the number of responses to the questions, we got that the p value of the Kolmogorov-Smirnov test is .000, which means that the number of responses did not conform to the normal distribution. Therefore, we used the median number of answers to questions on the same topic within a month to divide the levels of response quantity. If the number of answers to a question was smaller than the median number of answers to questions on the same topic, this was defined as a "low" response rate. If the number of answers to a given question was greater than the median, this was be defined as a "high" response rate. Our final dataset contained 927 questions with a high response rate, and 931 questions with a low response rate.

2.4 Data Analysis

We treated predictions of the two levels of quantity of responses to the questions as a classification problem. To build a prediction model and identify the best prediction method, logistic regression, the J48 decision tree, support vector machine (SVM), and random forest were used to predict the quantity level of responses to the questions. In addition, we normalized the features because some classification algorithms, such as the SVM, require eliminating the influence of differences in scale among features to treat each feature equally. Precision, recall, F1, accuracy, and AUC scores were used to evaluate the performance of each algorithm, and 10-fold cross-validation was used to ensure the accuracy of the evaluation scores.

3   Results

Table 1 shows the results of prediction using the four classification methods. In terms of the accuracy and AUC score, random forest delivered the best performance, but its performance in terms of predicting low response quantity was worse than that of SVM, which had a lower recall and F1 than SVM. Both methods had merit, however, the other two methods were worse than random forest or SVM on each indicator.

Table 1. Results of the four prediction models

Response rate		Logistic regression	J48 decision tree	SVM	Random forest
Accuracy		56.512%	52.099%	57.589%	57.750%
AUC scores		0.59	0.52	0.58	0.61
Precision	Low	0.57	0.52	0.58	0.58
	High	0.56	0.52	0.57	0.57
Recall	Low	0.56	0.49	0.57	0.56
	High	0.57	0.55	0.58	0.60
F1	Low	0.56	0.51	0.58	0.57
	High	0.57	0.54	0.58	0.58

Further, we used random forest and SVM with the seven categories of linguistic characteristics calculated by the LIWC to predict the quantity of response respectively, and the results are shown in Table 2. It is clear that the general descriptor categories yielded the best predictive accuracy using SVM, where this was higher than the result obtained using all the linguistic characteristics shown in Table 1. However, its AUC score and the recall and F1 values of the predicted high response quantity were slightly worse than when all the characteristics shown in Table 1 were used.

To obtain the characteristics that can be combined to obtain the best predictive performance, we implemented feature selection [11] to identify the following nine: number of words, number of words matching with predefined dictionaries in LIWC, number of affective words, number of future-focused words, number of common verb words, number of commas, number of differentiations expressed words, number of second-person pronouns, and number of sadness expressed words.

Table 3 shows the performance of this best combination of characteristics with each of the four prediction methods. It is clear that logistic regression delivered the best performance in terms of the accuracy and AUC score, but its prediction of questions with low response quantity and the recall and F1 values with high response quantity was poorer than the prediction using only certain category of linguistic characteristics as shown in Table 2.

Table 2. Results of random forest and SVM prediction using seven categories of linguistic characteristics respectively

Prediction models	Categories	Accuracy	AUC scores	Precision		Recall		F1	
				Low	High	Low	High	Low	High
Random forest	1	50.75%	0.51	0.51	0.51	0.49	0.52	0.50	0.52
	2	57.70%	0.60	0.58	0.57	0.56	0.60	0.57	0.59
	3	56.24%	0.59	0.57	0.56	0.55	0.58	0.56	0.57
	4	54.58%	0.56	0.55	0.54	0.54	0.55	0.54	0.55
	5	50.59%	0.50	0.51	0.51	0.57	0.44	0.54	0.47
	6	50.92%	0.51	0.51	0.53	0.89	0.13	0.65	0.21
	7	52.91%	0.53	0.53	0.53	0.51	0.55	0.52	0.54
SVM	1	50.43%	0.50	0.51	0.50	0.48	0.53	0.49	0.52
	2	58.13%	0.58	0.58	0.58	0.61	0.56	0.59	0.57
	3	55.27%	0.55	0.56	0.55	0.54	0.57	0.55	0.56
	4	55.38%	0.55	0.56	0.55	0.54	0.57	0.55	0.56
	5	52.74%	0.53	0.53	0.52	0.46	0.60	0.49	0.56
	6	51.88%	0.52	0.60	0.51	0.12	0.92	0.20	0.66
	7	54.20%	0.54	0.54	0.54	0.54	0.55	0.54	0.55

Note: 1-Summary language variables; 2-General descriptor categories; 3-Standard linguistic dimensions; 4-Psychological constructs; 5-Personal concern categories; 6-Informal language markers; 7- Punctuation

Table 3. Results of the four prediction models using the best combination of characteristics

Response rate		Logistic regression	J48 decision tree	SVM	Random forest
Accuracy		59.36%	57.00%	58.93%	57.75%
AUC scores		0.62	0.57	0.59	0.60
Precision	Low	0.59	0.58	0.59	0.58
	High	0.59	0.56	0.59	0.58
Recall	Low	0.60	0.50	0.62	0.57
	High	0.60	0.64	0.56	0.59
F1	Low	0.60	0.54	0.60	0.58
	High	0.59	0.60	0.58	0.58

4 Discussion

No previous study has examined the predicted quantities of responses to academic questions. The relevant study has studies on whether a given question on general social media websites can receive a response. The highest predictive accuracy reported for this is 74% [4]. In comparison, the predictive performance reported in this study was not good enough. This might have obtained because the characteristics of the questions considered were not suitable or adequate for the given purposes. This study identified only the feature set that yielded the best predictive performance based on the linguistic characteristics of the contents of the questions. Although these linguistic characteristics were abundant, they were based only on the classification and number of words in the contents of the questions, and lacked a deeper-level representation of their meanings. In future research, we will use the important linguistic characteristics identified in this study as a guide to introduce detailed content-related features.

In addition, it is not comprehensive to study scholars' responses to questions only from the question content itself. Whether the scholar will respond to the question may also be affected by various factors, such as the motivation of the scholar to reply, the incentive measures of the platform, etc., so we will continue to explore the impact of other factors on the response quantity of questions on the academic social Q&A platform.

5   Conclusion

This pilot study compared several methods to predict the quantities of responses to questions on an academic social Q&A platform using a variety of features representing the contents of the questions, and determined the best one. Although the results of prediction were not ideal, we were able to identify the combination of features that can best predict the quantities of responses to academic questions.

Acknowledgments. This work was supported by National Social Science Fund Project (No. 19CTQ032).

References

1. Muscanell, N., Utz, S.: Social networking for scientists: an analysis on how and why academics use ResearchGate. Online Inf. Rev. **41**(5), 744–759 (2017)
2. Choi, E., Kitzie, V., Shah, C.: A machine learning-based approach to predicting success of questions on social question-answering. In: IConference (2013)
3. Teevan, J., Morris, M., Panovich, K.: Factors affecting response quantity, quality, and speed for questions asked via social network status messages. In: Proceedings of the ICWSM (2011)
4. Liu, Z., Jansen, B.J.: Questioner or question: predicting the response rate in social question and answering on Sina Weibo. Inf. Process. Manage. **54**, 159–174 (2018)
5. Li, L., He, D., Jeng, W., Goodwin, S., Zhang, C.: Answer quality characteristics and prediction on an academic Q&A site: a case study on ResearchGate. In: WWW, pp. 1453–1458 (2015)
6. Li, L., He, D., Zhang, C., Geng, L., Zhang, K.: Characterizing peer-judged answer quality on academic Q&A sites: a cross-disciplinary case study on ResearchGate. Aslib J. Inf. Manage. **70**(3), 269–287 (2018)
7. Li, L., Huang, K., Ye, E.M., Zhang, C.: Questions or questioners: factors affect-ing response quantity on academic social Q&A sites. Proc. Assoc. Inf. Sci. Technol. **56**(1), 709–711 (2019)
8. Schwartz, H.A., et al.: Personality, gender, and age in the language of social media: The open-vocabulary approach. PLoS ONE **8**, e73791 (2013)

9. Warner, E.L., Ellington, L., Kirchhoff, A.C., Cloyes, K.G.: Acquisition of social support and linguistic characteristics of social media posts about young adult cancer. J. Adolesc. Young Adult Oncol. **7**, 196–203 (2018)

10. Pennebaker, J.W., Boyd, R.L., Jordan, K., Blackburn, K.: The development and psychometric properties of LIWC2015. University of Texas at Austin, Austin, TX (2015)

11. Hall, M.A.: Correlation-based feature subset selection for machine learning. Hamilton, New Zealand (1998)

An Empirical Study of Importance of Different Sections in Research Articles Towards Ascertaining Their Appropriateness to a Journal

Tirthankar Ghosal[✉], Rajeev Verma, Asif Ekbal, Sriparna Saha,
and Pushpak Bhattacharyya

Indian Institute of Technology Patna, Bihta, Patna 801106, Bihar, India
{tirthankar.pcs16,rajeev.ee15,asif,sriparna,pb}@iitp.ac.in

Abstract. Deciding the appropriateness of a manuscript to the aims and scope of a journal is very important in the first stage of peer review. Editors should be confident about the article's suitability to the intended journal to further channel its progress through the steps in the review process. However, not all sections in a research article are equally contributory or essential to determine its aptness to the journal under consideration. Here in this work, we investigate which sections in a manuscript are more significant to decide on its belongingness to the intended journal's scope. Our empirical studies on two Computer Science journals suggest that the meta information from bibliography and author profiles can reach a competitive benchmark to full-text performance. The features we develop in this study display the potential to evolve as a decision support system for the journal editors to identify *out-of-scope* submissions.

Keywords: Scope of a journal · Domain of a manuscript · Venue recommendation

1 Introduction

Peer review is at the heart of scholarly communication. The first stage in the academic peer review process is usually the initial screening at the editor's desk. Here, the editors, who are generally domain experts, primarily look into the suitability of the submitted article to the journal's aims, scope, and standards [5]. Along with they also consider certain other factors like plagiarism [8], template inconsistencies, language, grammar, etc. [6] for the initial screening, which is better known as the *editorial review*. More or less, with these factors, editors decide whether to forward the article to expert reviewers for meticulous evaluation or to reject the paper outright from the desk. Despite having merit, editors reject around 25–30% [11] of submitted manuscripts because they do not conform to the journal guidelines or do not possess enough content to cater to the

© Springer Nature Switzerland AG 2020
E. Ishita et al. (Eds.): ICADL 2020, LNCS 12504, pp. 407–415, 2020.
https://doi.org/10.1007/978-3-030-64452-9_38

journal's audience. Reputed journal publishers usually have their own recommender system, which suggests a ranked list of publisher-specific journals to the authors where they may consider to submit their article. These systems typically take the *Title* and the *Abstract* of the prospective manuscript as input and then generates a ranked list of candidate journals. Here we are intrigued with: *Are Title and Abstract, good indicators of the scope or domain of a manuscript? How do the other sections in the paper contribute to determining its relevance to the journal in concern?* We base the current study on our earlier work [4], where we investigate useful features to determine whether a manuscript is within the scope of the intended journal. However, this work's primary objective is to discover domain knowledge from different sections of a scientific article and thereby investigate the significance of those sections to the problem under concern (*scope detection*). Here, we assume a limited definition of scope: *the domain or the range of topics the given journal caters.* Although the investigation may seem obvious (as we incorporate more information from other parts, we get a clearer view of the scope of the manuscript), our experiments provide an empirical basis for the observations. Our feature engineering effort can instigate the development of an automated system to identify *out-of-scope* submissions [3].

2   Data Description

We perform our experiments with two Computer Science journals, *Artificial Intelligence* (ARTINT) and *Computer Networks* (COMNET). We consider the accepted (ACC) and published articles as the benchmark of reference for the *domain of operation* of these two journals (*heuristics: past is a good indicator of future*). We reserve a portion of the published papers to create the various reference lists (Sect. 3) and another portion for training/testing our machine learning (ML) model. The later is our positive data and is purposefully temporally forward (published later) than those we use to generate the domain reference lists. The reason being we intend to use past data to form our reference knowledge about the venue. We procure our negative data (papers which are Desk-Rejected (DR) for being *Out-Of-Scope* (OOS)) from the actual publisher. However, rejected papers are publisher-sensitive and were not adequate to meet our supervised ML needs. Hence we consider accepted papers of distantly related journals as a portion of our negative data (for example, ARTINT accepted papers as DR-OOS for COMNET). Table 1 shows the data (papers) we use in our experiments.

Table 1. Data statistics for the two journals

Data statistics	ARTINT	COMNET
Total accepted papers	3743	3878
Accepted papers used for lists generation	2743	2878
Accepted papers used in experiment	1000	1000
Rejected papers used in experiment	1000	1000
Actual DR-OOS papers	627	633

3   Data Preparation

We use GROBID [7] to parse our articles in PDF. We create the following domain lists from the ACC articles of these two journals.

- **L1: Keyword List (Author Given)** For each journal, we create lists of the author provided keywords from the accepted articles and record their frequency. Upon sorting, we found that the representative domain-specific terms appear at the top.
- **L2: Keyword List (Abstract+Title)** We create a frequency list by extracting keywords words from the *Title* and *Abstract*. From the *Title*, we remove the stop words. From the *Abstract*, we extract keywords using the RAKE [10] keyword extraction algorithm.
- **L3: Keyword List (Body)** We generate the keyword frequency list from the paper full-text.
- **L4, L5: Keyword List (Bibliography-Title/Venue)** From the *bibliography* section we generate two separate lists for referred *Paper Titles* and *Publication Venues*. *Paper Titles* and *Venues* are the entities that consist domain information. From paper titles, we remove the stop words and take the content words. From venue information, we automatically remove publisher, edition, place, date, pages, and some commonly occurring words like *Proceedings, Journal, Conference, National, International, etc.* and take only the domain-specific content words.
- **L6: Title List (Bibliography)** We create a separate list of all paper titles that the Bibliography refers to. Along with we record their in-text citation frequency and occurrence across all the accepted articles. Thus, we calculate the value for an article title (T_i) in the exhaustive list as:

$$Value \quad V(T_i) = \sum_{j=1}^{n} f_j(T_i) \tag{1}$$

where $f_j(T_i)$ corresponds to the number of times article j cites title T_i, and n is the number of accepted articles.

- **L7: Venue List (Bibliography)** We create a frequency list of venues in which articles referenced by the accepted papers of the corresponding journal are published. Thus the value for a venue (X_i) in the exhaustive list is calculated as :

$$Value \quad V(X_i) = \sum_{j=1}^{n} f_j(X_i) \tag{2}$$

where $f_j(C_i)$ corresponds to the number of times conference C_i appears in the reference section of an article j and n is the number of accepted articles under consideration.

For L6 and L7, we consider the occurrence of elements across all accepted papers and their in-text citations. We term this in-text citation count as the *Citation Effect*. Citation Effect corresponds to :

- the number of in-citations of X_i within the body of a candidate article j, if X_i is a paper title.
- the number of occurrences of X_i within the bibliography section of article j, if X_i is a venue (conference/journal/symposium/workshop/book, etc.).

The intuitions behind such lists are :

- Articles that are highly in-cited by accepted articles of a particular journal have higher relevance to that journal's scope.
- Similarly, venues that are more common in the bibliography section of ACC articles of a particular journal could be considered to have higher relevance to that journal's scope.

Quite obvious, the relevant, popular, highly cited, domain-specific paper titles and venues have a higher frequency.

- **L8: Author List** With the intuition that the more an author publishes articles in a certain domain, the greater is the chance that her prospective next would be in the same domain, we record the publication frequency of authors in each journal. From Google Scholar, we collect the author's area(s) of interest, publication venues, and paper titles in the past five years. This information is indicative of the domain in which the author(s) are currently working. Not all authors have Google Scholar profiles, especially new authors. We can replace it with any other automatic knowledge bases (like DBLP, etc.), or the corresponding features could be turned off. However, our investigation does show that the author(s) recent activity plays a crucial role. Also, we assume that new author(s) usually write with their supervisor(s), who already have a distinct operation domain. However, *Author Name Disambiguation* is a challenge, and we intend to mitigate it in our future work. For the current experiment, we rely on our automated crawler upon Google Scholar profiles.

4   Feature Engineering: ABC Features for Scope

We divide our features into three categories: *Author (A) Profiles*, *Bibliography* (B), and *Content* (C); together we call the ABC features for article scope.

4.1   Author Profiles

1. **(F1) Author Interests**: For each paper, we take the set of author interest keywords from their Google Scholar profile. We then consider the weighted average of the keywords match with L1 (see Eq. 3).
2. **(F2) Author Venues**: The venues in which the authors have been publishing in the past is a good indicator of the domain in which the authors are working. We consider the venues in which the authors have published in the last five years from Google Scholar. We then assume the weighted overlap with L7 (Eq. 5)
3. **(F3) Author Title Keywords**: The title of the papers carry domain information. We extract keywords from all the paper titles published by the authors in the last five years. and take a weighted keyword match with L4 (Eq. 3).
4. **(F4) Author Domain Publication Frequency**: For a candidate article, we take the average of the publication frequency of its authors in the concerned journal from the author list (L8).

4.2   Content

1. **(F5) Title Keyword**: We extract keywords from the candidate paper and consider the weighted keyword match (L2, Eq. 3).
2. **(F6) Abstract Keyword**: We extract keywords from the abstract and consider the weighted keyword match with L2 (Eq. 3).
3. **(F7) Author Listed Keyword Match**: We design this feature to emphasize the containment and relative importance of the keywords in the candidate article with respect to the Keyword Dictionary. We calculate the value for this feature for a candidate article Y as:

$$KWScore_Y = \frac{|KW_Y \cap KW_D|}{|KW_Y|} \times \sum_{i=1}^{|KW_Y \cap KW_D|} f(K_i) \qquad (3)$$

   – KW_Y: is the set of author-defined keywords in the candidate article Y
   – KW_D: is the set of keywords in the Keyword Dictionary D
   – $f(K_i)$: is the frequency of keyword K_i as listed in D
   – $K_i \in \{KW_Y \cap KW_D\}$

   Frequently occurring keywords are domain-specific, hence have higher weights.
4. **(F8) Body Keywords**: We extract keywords from the body of the candidate article and then take a weighted keywords match (L3, Eq. 3).
5. **(F9) Cluster Distance**: The distance of a given research article from the set of semantic clusters formed on the accepted articles may contribute to determining its scope. Any outlier to such clusters may be considered as *out-of-scope* [4].

4.3   Bibliography

1. **(F10) Biblio-Title**: We calculate these features from the bibliography section of a candidate article Y. From the exhaustive list of paper titles as discussed in Sect. 3 we calculate the Title Score (T_Y) of a candidate article Y as:

$$T_Y = \sum_{i=1}^{m} V(T_i) \qquad (4)$$

   where m is the total number of references in Y. $V(T_i)$ is calculated using Eq. 1 from L5.
2. **(F11) Biblio-Venue**: From exhaustive lists of venues, we calculate the Venue Scope (V_Y):

$$V_Y = \sum_{k=1}^{m} V(v_k) \qquad (5)$$

   $V(v_k)$ is derived from table look-up L7.
3. **(F12) Biblio-Title-Keyword**: Not all referenced titles would be present in the exhaustive list. Thus we also take the weighted keyword match extracted from bibliographic titles with L4. We remove the stop words.

4. **(F13) Biblio-Venue-Keyword**: Similarly not all venues would be present in the exhaustive venue list. Hence we extract keywords from bibliographic venues (which are highly domain specific) and take their weighted match score with L5.

We normalize our features using *min-max* [9].

5   Experiments and Results

We take 1000 ACC and 1000 DR-OOS articles each from ARTINT and COM-NET as candidates for our cross-validation (*10-fold*) experiments (i.e., 4000 full-text articles). We tried with several classifiers, but Random Forest [1] performed the best. As a baseline, we consider only the features F5 and F6 (*Title* and *Abstract* keywords), which is the usual practice in most of the journal recommender systems.

5.1   Results

Table 2 shows the results obtained by our approach. We probe into the effect of various sections of a manuscript to determine its domain and perform appropriate ablation studies. We observe that additional features extracted from the different sections of the manuscript surpass the baseline (only *Title* and *Abstract*) by a wide margin (which is obvious). We chose ARTINT and COMNET as our experimental testbed since ARTINT caters to a wide domain of topics whereas COMNET is comparatively restrictive in topical coverage.

Table 2. Classification results for *out-of-scope* (O) and In-Scope (I), $P \rightarrow Precision$, $R \rightarrow Recall$, Random Forest as the classifier. The Accuracy (A) values (†) are statistically significant over baseline performance (two-tailed t-test, p< 0.05), $S1 \rightarrow$Baseline

Journals	Sect	Features	P(I)	R(I)	P(O)	R(O)	A
ARTINT	S1	Title+Abstract Keywords (F5+F6)	0.700	0.735	0.729	0.694	71.42
	S2	S1 + Author-listed (F7) + Body Keywords (F8)	0.872	0.887	0.888	0.873	87.98
	S3	S1 + Author (F1+F2+F3+F4)	0.820	0.839	0.840	0.821	82.97
	S4	S1 + Bibliography (F10+F11+F12+F13)	0.894	0.889	0.892	0.897	89.31
	S5	Author + Content	0.909	0.919	0.921	0.910	91.48
	S6	Author + Bibliography	0.909	0.881	0.888	0.914	89.78
	S7	All features	**0.931**	**0.927**	**0.929**	**0.933**	**92.99** †
COMNET	S1	Title+Abstract Keywords (F5+F6)	0.783	0.576	0.600	0.799	67.48
	S2	S1 + Author-listed (F7) + Body Keywords (F8)	0.833	0.862	0.819	0.783	82.71
	S3	S1 + Author (F1+F2+F3+F4)	0.843	0.877	0.837	0.794	84.04
	S4	S1 + Bibliography (F10+F11+F12+F13)	0.891	0.928	0.905	0.857	89.67
	S5	Author + Content	0.924	0.921	0.901	0.905	91.41
	S6	Author + Bibliography	0.902	0.932	0.911	0.873	90.59
	S7	All features	**0.944**	**0.952**	**0.939**	**0.928**	**94.17**†

5.2 Feature Significance

Next, we study the significance of the ABC features based on their Information Gain (IG) (see Table 3). Other content features (F7, F8, F9) prove effective than the baseline ones (F5, F6). Semantic Distance (F9) from ACC article clusters contributed highly to COMNET but not so much for ARTINT. The reason could be: since ARTINT is a wider domain journal, we could not find dense clusters; while COMNET being a comparatively restricted one, we obtain good clusters, and hence semantic distance for DR-OOS papers are quite distinct in COMNET. Quite obvious that the body section (F8) of an article would hold a good amount of domain information. Bibliographic features (F13, F12, F11) fared best for ARTINT, while both content (F9, F8) and bibliographic features (F10, F11) for COMNET. Author interests (F1) and the tendency of authors to publish in similar domain venues (F2) also came within the top 10 significant features.

Table 3. Feature ranking (top 10) based on Information Gain (IG), † signifies baseline features, $A \rightarrow$Author Features, $B \rightarrow$Bibliography Features, $C \rightarrow$Content

ARTINT			COMNET	
Rank	Feature	IG	Feature	IG
1	F13 (B)	0.4056	F9 (C)	0.5063
2	F8 (C)	0.3941	F8 (C)	0.4035
3	F12 (B)	0.3083	F10 (B)	0.4014
4	F11 (B)	0.2973	F11 (B)	0.3048
5	F1 (A)	0.2782	F7 (C)	0.226
6	F6 † (C)	0.2768	F3 (A)	0.1462
7	F7 (C)	0.1833	F1 (A)	0.1347
8	F3 (A)	0.0936	F2 (A)	0.0999
9	F2 (A)	0.0637	F6 † (C)	0.0962
10	F9 (C)	0.0469	F5†(C)	0.0777

5.3 Observations

1. We find that with baseline features F5 and F6 (which is also the usual practice in journal recommender systems), we have many False Positives and False Negatives. Only relying on Abstract and Title would not be that consistent with the objective to classify the article as *In-Scope* or *Out-Scope*.
2. We see that inclusion of author given keywords (F7) and keywords extracted from the body of the paper (F8) enhances the accuracy of classification by almost 16% in ARTINT and COMNET. This signifies that body sections like *Introduction, Related Works, Methods, Experiments, Results, and Discussions Conclusions* hold a good amount of domain information to classify an article. But again, subjecting the entire new manuscript may not be a choice of the

authors and also be computationally expensive. So we investigate the other sections that may enable us to reach a competitive benchmark as full-text.

3. Our results clearly show that the authors' recent domains of interest certainly have a positive influence on the current manuscript. We observe an 11–17% improvement in accuracy over the baseline after incorporating author profile features.

4. Other than full-text, *Bibliography* is perhaps the most significant section of the manuscript that carries a good amount of domain information. We came up with the heuristics: *if most of the citations belong to a particular domain, the citing manuscript possibly belongs to the same domain.* Thus in our feature set, we encompass the bibliographic venue information (journal/conference/workshop). In-domain venues always have a high frequency of appearance in accepted articles. We obtain a performance improvement of 18–22% over the baseline on the introduction of bibliographic features.

5. Even if we exclude the content features (S6), we achieve a comparable performance in identifying *In-Scope/Out-Scope* manuscripts.

6   Challenges to Address

1. Correctly disambiguated author profiles, and bibliography would enhance a paper-journal matching/recommender system's performance. Author disambiguation, venue abbreviation mapping/entity resolution are the challenges we would attempt next.

2. We need to test the efficacy of our approach against journals whose scope is extensive (e.g., journals accepting review papers or systems) or whose scope is closely related to the manuscript's quality irrespective of the domain (e.g.., Nature or Science). However, for journals having defined domain of operation, our approach would work well.

3. Improvement in article pre-processing, information extraction from PDFs would enhance performance.

4. Improvisations like semantic clustering of keywords, titles, venues would enable better mapping.

5. Uncited references, citations not in the proper format are some other challenges we would need to address further.

7   Conclusions

Here in this work, we present an extensive investigation of section importance towards evaluating a given manuscript's appropriateness to a target journal. With obvious exceptions, the features we explore indicate the domain characteristics of a manuscript and could be suitably applied to develop an automated article classification system for the editors to locate *out-of-scope* submissions. Our approach takes into account almost all sections of a research article. We see that if we consider the meta-information from author profiles and bibliography together with abstract and title, we could reach a performance close to full-text (which is computationally expensive). Our investigation could also improvise the existing journal recommender systems [2]; to help the author(s) find the best-fit journal for their work. With our next effort, we would look forward to addressing the challenges we identified in Sect. 6.

References

1. Breiman, L.: Random forests. Mach. Learn. **45**(1), 5–32 (2001). https://doi.org/10.1023/A:1010933404
2. Ghosal, T., Chakraborty, A., Sonam, R., Ekbal, A., Saha, S., Bhattacharyya, P.: Incorporating full text and bibliographic features to improve scholarly journal recommendation. In: Bonn, M., Wu, D., Downie, J.S., Martaus, A. (eds.) 19th ACM/IEEE Joint Conference on Digital Libraries, JCDL 2019, Champaign, IL, USA, June 2–6, 2019, pp. 374–375 (2019). IEEE. https://doi.org/10.1109/JCDL.2019.00077
3. Ghosal, T., Raj, A., Ekbal, A., Saha, S., Bhattacharyya, P.: A deep multimodal investigation to determine the appropriateness of scholarly submissions. In: Bonn, M., Wu, D., Downie, J.S., Martaus, A. (eds.) 19th ACM/IEEE Joint Conference on Digital Libraries, JCDL 2019, Champaign, IL, USA, 2–6 June 2019, pp. 227–236 (2019). IEEE. https://doi.org/10.1109/JCDL.2019.00039
4. Ghosal, T., Sonam, R., Ekbal, A., Saha, S., Bhattacharyya, P.: Is the paper within scope? Are you fishing in the right pond? In: Bonn, M., Wu, D., Downie, J.S., Martaus, A. (eds.) 19th ACM/IEEE Joint Conference on Digital Libraries, JCDL 2019, Champaign, IL, USA, 2–6 June 2019, pp. 237–240 (2019). IEEE. https://doi.org/10.1109/JCDL.2019.00040
5. Ghosal, T., Sonam, R., Saha, S., Ekbal, A., Bhattacharyya, P.: Investigating domain features for scope detection and classification of scientific articles. In: Proceedings of the Eleventh International Conference on Language Resources and Evaluation (LREC 2018), pp. 7–12 (2018)
6. Ghosal, T., Verma, R., Ekbal, A., Saha, S., Bhattacharyya, P.: Investigating impact features in editorial pre-screening of research papers. In: Proceedings of the 18th ACM/IEEE on Joint Conference on Digital Libraries, JCDL 2018, Fort Worth, TX, USA, 03–07 June 2018, pp. 333–334 (2018). https://doi.org/10.1145/3197026.3203910
7. Lopez, P.: GROBID: combining automatic bibliographic data recognition and term extraction for scholarship publications. In: Agosti, M., Borbinha, J., Kapidakis, S., Papatheodorou, C., Tsakonas, G. (eds.) ECDL 2009. LNCS, vol. 5714, pp. 473–474. Springer, Heidelberg (2009). https://doi.org/10.1007/978-3-642-04346-8_62
8. Maurer, H.A., Kappe, F., Zaka, B.: Plagiarism - A survey. J. UCS **12**(8), 1050–1084 (2006). https://doi.org/10.3217/jucs-012-08-1050
9. Patro, S., Sahu, K.K.: Normalization: A preprocessing stage. arXiv preprint arXiv:1503.06462 (2015)
10. Rose, S., Engel, D., Cramer, N., Cowley, W.: Automatic keyword extraction from individual documents. Text Min. Appl. Theory **1**, 1–20 (2010)
11. Trumbore, S., Carr, M.E., Mikaloff-Fletcher, S.: Criteria for rejection of papers without review. Global Biogeochem. Cycles **29**(8), 1123–1123 (2015)

On the Correlation Between Research Complexity and Academic Competitiveness

Jing Ren[1], Ivan Lee[2], Lei Wang[1], Xiangtai Chen[1], and Feng Xia[3]([✉])

[1] School of Software, Dalian University of Technology, Dalian 116620, China
ch.yum@outlook.com, leonard_wl@outlook.com, chenxiangtai@outlook.com
[2] STEM, University of South Australia, Adelaide, SA 5001, Australia
ivan.lee@unisa.edu.au
[3] School of Engineering, IT and Physical Sciences, Federation University Australia,
Ballarat, VIC 3353, Australia
f.xia@ieee.org

Abstract. Academic capacity is a common way to reflect the educational level of a country or district. The aim of this study is to explore the difference between the scientific research level of institutions and countries. By proposing an indicator named Citation-weighted Research Complexity Index (CRCI), we profile the academic capacity of universities and countries with respect to research complexity. The relationships between CRCI of universities and other relevant academic evaluation indicators are examined. To explore the correlation between academic capacity and economic level, the relationship between research complexity and GDP per capita is analysed. With experiments on the Microsoft Academic Graph data set, we investigate publications across 183 countries and universities from the Academic Ranking of World Universities in 19 research fields. Experimental results reveal that universities with higher research complexity have higher fitness. In addition, for developed countries, the development of economics has a positive correlation with scientific research. Furthermore, we visualize the current level of scientific research across all disciplines from a global perspective.

Keywords: Big scholarly data · Correlation analysis · Research complexity · Academic competitiveness · Scientometrics

1 Introduction

Research output assessment and analysis have always been the essential component in most academic ranking systems [6,10]. Nowadays, no matter for universities or countries, academic research is playing a significant role in improving international competitiveness. Specifically, knowledge innovation is regarded as the core element among national competitiveness [3]. High achievement in research activity can help universities apply for research funds and projects,

© Springer Nature Switzerland AG 2020
E. Ishita et al. (Eds.): ICADL 2020, LNCS 12504, pp. 416–422, 2020.
https://doi.org/10.1007/978-3-030-64452-9_39

promote academic and industrial collaborations, as well as attract talents [5]. Thus, evaluating current scientific research from diverse perspectives is crucial for both universities and countries.

Over the last couple of decades, many institutions have applied bibliometrics to evaluate the academic performance of universities [14,15]. A common approach of evaluating academic impact is university ranking. Common world university ranking systems, such as Quacquarelli Symonds World University Ranking (QS), Shanghai Jiao Tong Academic Ranking of World Universities (ARWU), and Times Higher Education World University Rankings (THE), all regard research achievement as a major impact factor in their ranking algorithms [11,12]. Therefore, the rankings of these algorithms are similar with each other every year.

In order to measure the comprehensive capacity of academic research, Research Complexity Index (RCI) was proposed to profile universities [9]. However, this indicator only takes the number of publications into consideration, while regardless of their impacts. Therefore, we propose Citation-weighted Research Complexity Index (CRCI), which imposes citation as weight to denote publications instead of the simple count of publications. Comparing with the previous studies in academic capacity analysis, this paper proposes a new indicator, from the perspective of research complexity instead of research productions, to profile universities and countries. Major contributions of this paper include:

1. Proposing an indicator Citation-weighted Research Complexity Index (CRCI) to profile the current scientific research of universities and countries from a new perspective.
2. Exploring the relationship between research complexity with fitness and opportunity value of universities, and GDP per capita of countries.
3. Comparing the research complexity difference of countries in different fields.
4. Visualizing the geographical distribution of research complexity of 64 top-ranked universities and 183 countries.

2   Revealed Symmetric Comparative Advantage

Except for research production, it is also important to consider research specialisation when profiling an institution or country. Revealed Comparative Advantage (RCA) [1] in this paper can be understood as a relative indicator to judge whether the academic capacity is above average. In this paper, multi-disciplinary papers in the data set are labeled with different fields and subfields. As for papers labeled with more than one research field, the weight is allocated to each research field equally. Let u denote university, and f denote research field. Let $Z(u, f)$ denote a set including all papers $p(u, f)$ published by university u in research field f. Considering that a paper may be cited by different number of publications, a weighting factor $n_{p(u,f)}$ is applied, denoting that paper $p(u, f)$ is cited by n publications. Therefore, the academic achievement P_{uf} of university u in research field f can be calculated as:

$$P_{uf} = \sum_{p(u,f) \in Z(u,f)} n_{p(u,f)}. \tag{1}$$

According to P_{uf}, the revealed comparative advantage $RSCA_{uf}$ [7] for university u in research field f can be calculated as

$$RSCA_{uf} = \frac{P_{uf} \sum_{u,f} P_{uf} - \sum_u P_{uf} \sum_f P_{uf}}{P_{uf} \sum_{u,f} P_{uf} + \sum_u P_{uf} \sum_f P_{uf}}. \tag{2}$$

When we calculate the corresponding variables for countries, u denoting universities in equations can be replaced by c denoting countries. All equations corresponding to universities are suitable for countries as well.

3   Citation-Weighted Research Complexity Index

In order to study the complexity and diversity of academic research, research complexity index and opportunity value [9] are adopted to analyze the research specialisation of universities in different disciplines. According to the definition in Sect. 2, the bool value of M_{uf} indicates whether university u has revealed comparative advantage in field f. Diversity of university D_u is initialized to the number of research fields having revealed comparative advantage:

$$D_u = k(u,0) = \sum_f M_{uf}. \tag{3}$$

Similarly, ubiquity of field U_f can be regarded as the number of universities who have revealed comparative advantage in field f, which is formulated as Eq. 4:

$$U_f = k(f,0) = \sum_u M_{uf}. \tag{4}$$

Considering the symmetry of the university-publication bipartite network, *Method of Reflections* [4] can be adopted to calculate $k(u,n)$ in terms of $k(f, n-1)$:

$$k(u,n) = \frac{1}{k(u,0)} \sum_f M_{uf} k(f, n-1). \tag{5}$$

Likewise, the value $k(f,n)$ can be obtained in terms of $k(u, n-1)$ as follows:

$$k(f,n) = \frac{1}{k(f,0)} \sum_u M_{uf} k(u, n-1). \tag{6}$$

The citation-weighted research complexity index of a university $CRCI(u)$, is calculated as:

$$CRCI(u) = \frac{K_u - \overline{K_u}}{\sigma(K_u)}, \tag{7}$$

where $\boldsymbol{K_u}$ denotes the eigenvector of $\widetilde{M}_{uu'}$ associated with the second largest eigenvalue [2], and $\sigma(\boldsymbol{K_u})$ denotes the standard deviation of the $\boldsymbol{K_u}$ vector. The opportunity value OV of a university u is defined as:

$$OV(u) = \sum_{f'}(1 - d(u, f'))(1 - M(u, f'))CFCI(f'). \tag{8}$$

According to the definition of opportunity value, universities with high opportunity value denotes having more research fields in close proximity, or their research fields can be complex easier than universities with low opportunity value.

4   Fitness and Complexity

The raw fitness value of a university and the raw complexity value of a field can be obtained as follows:

$$\widetilde{F}_u^{(n+1)} = \sum_f M_{uf}Q_f^{(n)}, \tag{9}$$

$$\widetilde{Q}_f^{(n+1)} = \left[\sum_u M_{uf}(F_u^{(n)})^{-1}\right]^{-1}, \tag{10}$$

where $\widetilde{F}_u^{(n+1)}$ denotes the raw fitness value of a university u, and $\widetilde{Q}_f^{(n+1)}$ denotes the raw complexity value of a field at the n+1-th iteration. $F_u^{(n)}$ and $Q_f^{(n)}$ are the normalised values of fitness and complexity respectively. They are defined as:

$$F_u^{(n)} = \frac{\widetilde{F}_u^{(n)}}{N_u^{-1}\sum_u \widetilde{F}_u^{(n)}}, \tag{11}$$

$$Q_f^{(n)} = \frac{\widetilde{Q}_f^{(n)}}{N_f^{-1}\sum_f \widetilde{Q}_f^{(n)}}, \tag{12}$$

where N_u and N_f are the total numbers of universities and research fields, respectively. The initial values of fitness $F_u^{(0)}$ and complexity $Q_f^{(0)}$ are set to 1.

According to the calculation formula mentioned above, fitness can be understood as how many complex research fields a university has revealed comparative advantage [8]. Universities possessing more complex research fields have higher fitness value than universities with less. The fitness value is also influenced by the complexity degree of research fields. In turn, Complexity of a research field depends on how many universities have revealed comparative advantage. For example, the complexity of a research field with only one university possessing revealed comparative advantage would be higher than that of two.

5   Experiments

In this section, Microsoft Academic Graph (MAG) [13] is used to analyze research output. Besides, we compare the difference of CRCI with other methods of academic capacity evaluation, and carry out several analysis and visualizations on the ranking results.

5.1   Data of Universities and Countries

During the period of 2003–2017, 64 universities that are always located in the top 100 list of (ARWU) are chosen as the experimental targets in this paper. As for the countries, all countries involved in MAG (183 totally) are used to observe the difference between their research complexity. The year of publications selected in this paper range from 1970 to 2017. The gross domestic product per capita of the country is obtained from THE WORLD BANK[1].

5.2   Experimental Results

In Fig. 1a, a strong correlation between fitness and CRCI can be observed. By fitting a curve of the second order regression, the value of fitness can well fit as a quadratic function of CRCI with R^2 equal to 0.46 approximately. The result shows that universities with higher research complexity have higher value of fitness, meaning that a university with strong comprehensive strength is more competitive. In Fig. 1b, the correlation between opportunity value and CRCI well fit as a quadratic function with the opening down, where R^2 equal to 0.58 approximately. This result shows that, as for the universities with lower research complexity, they have more opportunities to improve their research complexity by means of breaking through new research fields than others. The scatter plots of CRCI versus GDP_{pc} is shown in Fig. 1c. With R^2 equal to 0.21, GDP_{pc} fit as a first order regression of CRCI for only developed countries, indicating that the scientific research of university can impact a country's economic development.

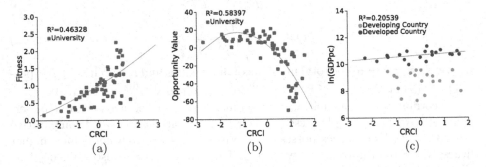

Fig. 1. (a) Scatter plot of Fitness against CRCI of universities. (b) Scatter plot of opportunity value against CRCI of universities. (c) Scatter plot of $ln(GDP_{pc})$ against CRCI of countries.

Visualization. The geographical distribution of CRCI values from 64 top universities and 183 countries is shown in Fig. 2. The colour of countries represent the value of CRCI, with red denoting high research complexity of countries.

---

[1] https://www.worldbank.org.

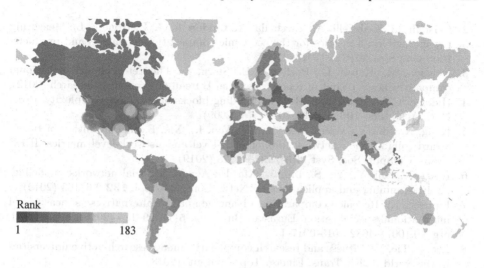

Fig. 2. The geographical distribution of 64 top-ranked universities and research complexity of 183 countries in 2015. (Color figure online)

Besides, the colorful bubbles denote different universities, with larger size representing high research complexity. It should be noted that the color of bubble just for better differentiation, without any practical meanings. The geographical longitude and latitude of the selected universities are extracted from Google. From observation, top-ranked universities mainly locate in countries with high levels of research complexity.

6   Conclusion

This paper has proposed an indicator to profile the academic capacity of universities and countries from the perspective of research complexity. By profiling the scientific research of academic entities from various perspectives, this method can empower explorers with comprehensive and valuable information that will encourage them to take on the challenge, thereby speeding up the process of academic and economic development. Through the analysis of the competitive advantage of countries in different fields, we can see clearly which field needs to be improved and extended, and which field has been studied thoroughly by many countries.

In future work, this indicator could be extended to profile other groups of universities, such as the intra-national universities. Besides, the research complexity can also be applied to offer insights to fund allocation, policy decision and brain gain.

References

1. Balassa, B.: Trade liberalisation and revealed comparative advantage 1. Manchester Sch. **33**(2), 99–123 (1965)

2. Cristelli, M., Gabrielli, A., Tacchella, A., Caldarelli, G., Pietronero, L.: Measuring the intangibles: a metrics for the economic complexity of countries and products. PloS One **8**(8), e70726 (2013)

3. Delgado, M., Ketels, C., Porter, M.E., Stern, S.: The determinants of national competitiveness. Technical report, National Bureau of Economic Research (2012)

4. Hidalgo, C.A., Hausmann, R.: The building blocks of economic complexity. Proc. Natl. Acad. Sci. **106**(26), 10570–10575 (2009)

5. Kong, X., Shi, Y., Wang, W., Ma, K., Wan, L., Xia, F.: The evolution of turing award collaboration network: bibliometric-level and network-level metrics. IEEE Trans. Comput. Soc. Syst. **6**(6), 1318–1328 (2019)

6. Kong, X., Shi, Y., Yu, S., Liu, J., Xia, F.: Academic social networks: modeling, analysis, mining and applications. J. Netw. Comput. Appl. **132**, 86–103 (2019)

7. Laursen, K.: Revealed comparative advantage and the alternatives as measures of international specialization. Eurasian Bus. Rev. **5**(1), 99–115 (2015). https://doi. org/10.1007/s40821-015-0017-1

8. Lee, I., Tie, Y.: Fitness and research complexity among research-active universities in the world. IEEE Trans. Emerg. Top. Comput. (2018)

9. Lee, I., Xia, F., Roos, G.: An observation of research complexity in top universities based on research publications. In: Proceedings of the 26th International Conference on World Wide Web Companion, pp. 1259–1265. International World Wide Web Conferences Steering Committee (2017)

10. Ren, J., et al.: API: an index for quantifying a scholar's academic potential. IEEE Access **7**, 178675–178684 (2019)

11. Robinson-Garcia, N., Torres-Salinas, D., Herrera-Viedma, E., Docampo, D.: Mining university rankings: Publication output and citation impact as their basis. arXiv preprint arXiv:1905.07141 (2019)

12. Selten, F., Neylon, C., Huang, C.K., Groth, P.: A longitudinal analysis of university rankings. arXiv preprint arXiv:1908.10632 (2019)

13. Sinha, A., et al.: An overview of microsoft academic service (MAS) and applications. In: Proceedings of the 24th International Conference on World Wide Web, pp. 243–246 (2015)

14. Xia, F., Wang, W., Bekele, T.M., Liu, H.: Big scholarly data: a survey. IEEE Trans. Big Data **3**(1), 18–35 (2017)

15. Yu, S., Liu, Y., Ren, J., Bedru, H.D., Bekele, T.M.: Mining key scholars via collapsed core and truss. In: 2019 IEEE International Conference on Cloud and Big Data Computing, pp. 305–308. IEEE (2019)

Author Index

Printed in the United States
by Baker & Taylor Publisher Services

Printed in the United States
by Baker & Taylor Publisher Services